The Teachings of Modern Protestantism
on Law, Politics, and Human Nature

The Teachings of Modern Protestantism

❖ ON LAW, POLITICS, AND HUMAN NATURE ❖

EDITED BY

John Witte Jr. and Frank S. Alexander

INTRODUCTION BY

Mark A. Noll

COLUMBIA UNIVERSITY PRESS   NEW YORK

Columbia University Press
Publishers Since 1893
New York   Chichester, West Sussex
Copyright © 2007 Columbia University Press
All rights reserved

Library of Congress Cataloging-in-Publication Data
The Teachings of modern Protestantism on law, politics, and human nature / edited by
John Witte Jr. and Frank S. Alexander ; introduction by Mark A. Noll.
p.   cm.
Includes index.
ISBN 978-0-231-14262-5 (cloth : alk. paper) — ISBN 978-0-231-14263-2 (pbk.)
1. Protestant churches—Doctrines.   2. Protestantism.   I. Witte, John, 1959–
II. Alexander, Frank S., 1952–   III. Title.
BX4811.3.T43   2007
261.8088'2804—dc22   2007002771

Columbia University Press books are printed on permanent and durable acid-free paper.
This book was printed on paper with recycled content.

Printed in the United States of America

c 10 9 8 7 6 5 4 3 2 1
p 10 9 8 7 6 5 4 3 2 1

References to Internet Web sites (URLs) were accurate at the time of writing. Neither the
volume editors nor the authors nor Columbia University Press is responsible for URLs
that may have expired or changed since the manuscript was prepared.

BUT WHAT IS government itself, but the greatest of all reflections on human nature? If men were angels, no government would be necessary. If angels were to govern men, neither external nor internal controls on government would be necessary. In framing a government which is to be administered by men over men, the great difficulty lies in this: you must first enable the government to control the governed; and in the next place oblige it to control itself. A dependence on the people is, no doubt, the primary control on the government; but experience has taught mankind the necessity of auxiliary precautions.

—*James Madison, Federalist Paper No. 51*

Contents

3. Karl Barth (1886–1968)

Commentary

4. Dietrich Bonhoeffer (1906–1945)

Commentary

5. Reinhold Niebuhr (1892–1971)

Commentary

Original Source Materials

6. Martin Luther King Jr. (1929–1968)

Commentary

Original Source Material

7. William Stringfellow (1928–1985)

Commentary

Original Source Materials

8. John Howard Yoder (1927–1997)

Commentary
DUNCAN B. FORRESTER   406

Original Source Materials

Foreword

THIS VOLUME IS part and product of a major new project on Christian Jurisprudence undertaken by our Center for the Study of Law and Religion at Emory University. We first published this work as a two-volume cloth edition designed to provide a comparative analysis of modern Catholic, Protestant, and Orthodox Christian teachings on law, politics, and human nature. One volume provided an illustrative collection of primary texts written by a score of Christian scholars and activists who led the main movements in Catholicism, Protestantism, and Orthodoxy in the later nineteenth and twentieth centuries. A second cloth volume provided a collection of fresh essays that analyzed the theology and jurisprudence of these modern Christian leaders. The introductions to these volumes and the opening and closing essays to the second volume sought to situate these Catholic, Protestant, and Orthodox Christian contributions in the broader context of law, politics, and society, and to compare and contrast them with one another and with various secular legal and political philosophies. We have been most gratified by the generous reception of the first edition, and the glowing reviews it has occasioned. The volumes seem to have struck a real nerve in Christian and non-Christian circles alike, and have opened whole new areas of teaching and research for our readers. Indeed, our project on Christian jurisprudence has commissioned two dozen new volumes to amplify some of the themes set forth therein.

This three-volume edition offers a leaner and more denominationally specific presentation of the same modern Christian teachings on law, politics, and society. Each volume now focuses specifically on Catholic, Protestant, or Orthodox teachings with a short introduction to provide broader comparative and ecumenical perspective. Each volume also couples analytical essays on the selected modern Christian scholars with those scholars' original source materials. We have presented the material in this form not because we have given up on ecumenism but because we have given thought to pedagogy. We are eager to have these volumes read and used not only by scholars and church leaders but also by students, novitiates, and catechumens in churches, colleges, graduate schools, law schools, seminaries, divinity schools, Sunday schools, and various learned societies. For most such classrooms, the cloth volumes are too wide in sweep, too weighty in tone, and too hard on the wallet. Hence this more accessible and economical edition—updated and corrected a bit for even more ready use.

We express anew our warmest thanks to our friends at Columbia University Press, notably Wendy Lochner and Christine Mortlock, for lending so generously of their time and talents. We express our profound gratitude for the generous support of our project on Christian jurisprudence by our friends at The Pew Charitable Trusts, Inc., particularly Rebecca Rimel and Susan Billington Harper; our friends at the Lilly Endowment, Inc., notably Craig Dykstra; and our friends at the Alonzo L. McDonald Family Foundation, notably Alonzo, Peter, and Suzie McDonald, and Robert Pool. Finally, we express our warmest appreciation to our colleague Linda King for her expert work on the production of this volume and its companions.

—*John Witte Jr. and Frank S. Alexander, Emory University*

Acknowledgments

THIS VOLUME AND its companions are products of a three-year project of the Center for the Study of Law and Religion at Emory University, parts of a broader effort of The Pew Charitable Trusts and the University of Notre Dame to stimulate and support new scholarship on the place of Christianity in various fields of academic specialty. Armed with a major grant from Pew, Notre Dame Provost Nathan O. Hatch and his colleagues have assembled ten groups of scholars in the fields of law, philosophy, literature, economics, and other subjects who have an interest in the scholarly place of Christianity in their particular discipline. Each group of specialists has been asked to address the general theme of "Christianity and the nature of the person" from the perspective of its particular discipline and to produce a major new study that speaks to this theme in a manner edifying both to scholars in other fields and to peers of all faiths in its own field.

We have been privileged to lead the team on law. We wish to thank the immensely talented group of contributors to this volume and to the companion volumes on the Catholic and Orthodox traditions. We give special thanks to Professor Mark A. Noll for his brilliant introduction.

On behalf of our colleagues in the Center for the Study of Law and Religion, we express our deep gratitude to our friends at The Pew Charitable Trusts for their generous support of this project, particularly Pew's President Rebecca Rimel, and Program officers Dr. Luis Lugo, Dr. Susan Billington Harper, and Dr. Diane Winston. We also express our gratitude to our friends at the University of Notre Dame, particularly then-Provost Dr. Nathan O. Hatch, who now serves as President of Wake Forest University.

We wish to thank Dr. Craig Dykstra and his colleagues at the Lilly Endowment, Inc. in Indianapolis for their generous grant in support of John Witte's project on "Law, Religion, and the Protestant Tradition," which has provided him with release time to work on this and other book projects.

We wish to recognize and thank several of our colleagues in the Center for the Study of Law and Religion for their exceptional work on the administration of this project and the production of the original two volumes. We are particularly grateful to Ms. Linda King for masterminding the administration of the project, for coordinating the three conferences that it occasioned, and for working so expertly and assiduously on the production of the resulting manuscripts. We express our gratitude to Ms. Anita Mann, Ms. Amy Wheeler, Ms. Eliza Ellison, and Ms. Janice Wiggins for sharing so generously of their administrative expertise.

Finally, we would like to thank Wendy Lochner and her colleagues at Columbia University Press for taking on these volumes and working so efficiently and effectively to ensure their timely production. And we appreciate the very helpful criticisms and suggestions of the three anonymous outside reviewers of an earlier version of this manuscript.

This volume is dedicated to the students of the Center for the Study of Law and Religion at Emory University, past, present, and future.

—*John Witte Jr. and Frank S. Alexander, Emory University*

Contributors

FRANK S. ALEXANDER, J.D. (Harvard), M.T.S. (Harvard), is professor of law; Founding Director, Center for the Study of Law and Religion, and Director of the Project on Affordable Housing and Community Development at Emory University.

MILNER BALL, J.D. (Georgia), S.T.B. (Harvard), holds the Harmon W. Caldwell Chair in Constitutional Law at the University of Georgia.

DAVISON M. DOUGLAS, J.D. (Yale), M.A.R. (Yale), Ph.D. (Yale), is the Arthur B. Hanson Professor of Law and former Director of the Institute of Bill of Rights Law at the College of William and Mary.

DUNCAN B. FORRESTER, D.PHIL. (Sussex), B.D. (Edinburgh), M.A. (St. Andrews), is professor of theology and public issues, emeritus, at New College, University of Edinburgh.

GEORGE HUNSINGER, PH.D. (Yale), B.D. (Harvard), is Hazel Thompson McCord Professor of Systematic Theology at Princeton Theological Seminary.

TIMOTHY P. JACKSON, PH.D. (Yale), M.Phil (Yale), M.A. (Yale), is professor of Christian Ethics at the Candler School of Theology, Emory University.

MARK A. NOLL, PH.D. (Vanderbilt University), is the Francis A. McAnaney Professor of History, University of Notre Dame.

MARY D. PELLAUER, PH.D. (University of Chicago), is a freelance writer in Chicago.

JOHN WITTE JR., J.D. (Harvard), is Jonas Robitscher Professor of Law and Director of the Center for the Study of Law and Religion at Emory University.

NICHOLAS P. WOLTERSTORFF, PH.D. (Harvard), M.A. (Harvard), is Noah Porter Professor Emeritus of Philosophical Theology, Yale University, and Senior Fellow, Institute for Advanced Studies in Culture, University of Virginia.

Introduction

THE CONTEXT

The better the society, the less law there will be. In Heaven there will be no law, and the lion will lie down with the lamb. . . . In Hell there will be nothing but law, and due process will be meticulously observed.

SO REMARKED THE eminent legal scholar Grant Gilmore in closing his 1974 lecture series at Yale Law School, later published as *The Ages of American Law*. Gilmore crafted this catchy couplet to capture the pessimistic view of law, politics, and society made popular by the American jurist and Supreme Court Justice Oliver Wendell Holmes Jr. (1841–1935). Contrary to the conventional portrait of Holmes as the sage and sartorial "Yankee from Olympus,"[1] Gilmore saw him as a "harsh and cruel" man, chastened and charred by the savagery of the American Civil War and the gluttony of the industrial revolution. These experiences, Gilmore argued, had made Holmes "a bitter and lifelong pessimist who saw in the course of human life nothing but a continuing struggle in which the rich and powerful impose their will on the poor and the weak."[2] The cruel excesses of the Bolshevik Revolution, World War I, and the Great Depression in the first third of the twentieth century only confirmed Holmes in his pessimism that human life was "without values."[3]

This bleak view of human nature shaped Holmes's bleak view of law, politics, and society. He regarded law principally as a barrier against human depravity—a means to check the worst instincts of the proverbial "bad man" against his worst instincts and to make him pay dearly if he yielded to temptation.[4] Holmes also regarded law as a buffer against human suffering—a means to protect the vulnerable against the worst exploitation by corporations, churches, and Congress. For him, there was no higher law in heaven to guide the law below. There was no path of legal virtue up which a man should go. The "path of the law" cut a horizontal line between human sanctity and depravity. Law served to keep society and its members from sliding into the abyss of hell, but it could do nothing to guide its members in their ascent to heaven.

Holmes was the "high priest" of a new "age of faith" in American law, Gilmore wrote with intended irony, that replaced an earlier era dominated by the church and the clergy.[5] The confession of this new age of faith was that America was a land "ruled by laws, not by men." Its catechism was the new case law method of the law school classroom. Its canon was the new concordance of legal codes, amply augmented by New Deal legislation. Its church was the common law court where the rituals of judicial formalism and due process would yield legal truth. Its church council was the Supreme Court, which now issued opinions with as much dogmatic confidence as the divines of Nicaea, Augsburg, and Trent.

This new age of faith in American law was in part the product of a new faith in the positivist theory of knowledge that swept over America in the later nineteenth and twentieth centuries, eclipsing earlier theories that gave religion and the church a more prominent place in the law. The turn to positivism proceeded in two stages. The first stage was scientific. Inspired by the successes of the early modern scientific revolution—from Copernicus to Newton—eighteenth-century European and nineteenth-century American jurists set out to create a method of law that was every bit as scientific and rigorous as that of the new mathematics and the new physics. This was not merely an exercise in professional rivalry. It was an earnest attempt to show that law had an autonomous place in the cadre of positive sciences, that it could not and should not be subsumed by theology, politics, philosophy, or economics. In testimony to this claim, jurists in this period poured forth a staggering number of new legal codes, new constitutions, new legal encyclopedias, dictionaries, textbooks, and other legal syntheses that still grace, and bow, the shelves of our law libraries.[6]

The second stage of the positivist turn in law was philosophical. A new movement—known variously as legal positivism, legal formalism, and analytical jurisprudence—sought to reduce the subject matter of law to its most essential core. If physics could be reduced to "matter in motion" and biology to "survival of the fittest," then surely law and legal study could be reduced to a core subject as well. The formula was produced in the mid-nineteenth century, most famously by John Austin in England and Christopher Columbus Langdell in America: Law is simply the concrete rules and procedures posited by the sovereign and enforced by the courts. Many other institutions and practices might be normative and important for social coherence and political concordance, but they are not law. They are the subjects of theology, ethics, economics, politics, psychology, sociology, anthropology, and other humane disciplines. They stand beyond the province of jurisprudence properly determined.[7]

This positivist theory of law, which swept over American universities from the 1890s onward, rendered legal study increasingly narrow and insular. Law was simply the sovereign's rules. Legal study was simply the analysis of those rules and their application in particular cases. Why the rules were posited, whether their positing was for good or ill, how they affected society, politics, or morality were not relevant questions for legal study. By the early twentieth century, it was rather common to read in legal textbooks that law is an autonomous science; that its doctrines, language, and methods are self-sufficient; and that its study is self-contained.[8] It was rather common to think that law has the engines of change within itself, that through its own design and dynamic, law marches teleologically through time "from trespass to case to negligence, from contract to quasi-contract to implied warranty."[9]

Holmes was an early champion of this positivist theory of law and legal development. He rebuked more traditional views with a series of famous aphorisms that are still often quoted today. Against those who insisted that the legal tradition was more than simply a product of pragmatic evolution, he wrote: "The life of the law is not logic but experience."[10] Against those who appealed to a higher natural law to guide the positive law of the state, he cracked: "There is no such brooding omnipresence in the sky."[11] Against those who argued for a more principled jurisprudence, he retorted: "General principles do not decide concrete cases."[12] Against those who insisted that law needed basic moral premises to be cogent, he mused: "I should be glad if we could get rid of the whole moral phraseology which I think has tended to distort the law. In fact even in the domain of morals I think that it would be a gain, at least for the educated, to get rid of the word and notion [of] Sin."[13]

Despite its new prominence, American legal positivism had ample detractors. Already in the 1920s and 1930s, sociologists of law argued that the nature and purpose of law and politics cannot be understood without reference to the spirit of a people and their times—a *Volksgeist und Zeitgeist,* as their German counterparts put it. The legal realist movement of the 1930s and 1940s used the new insights of psychology and anthropology to cast doubt on the immutability and ineluctability of judicial reasoning. The revived natural law movement of the 1940s and 1950s saw in the horrors of Hitler's Holocaust and Stalin's gulags the perils of constructing a legal system without transcendent checks and balances. The international human rights movement of the 1950s and 1960s pressed the law to address more directly the sources and sanctions of civil, political, social, cultural, and economic rights. Marxist, feminist, and neo-Kantian movements in the 1960s and 1970s used linguistic and structural critiques to expose the fallacies and false equalities of legal and political doctrines. Watergate and other political scandals in the 1970s and 1980s highlighted the need for a more comprehensive understanding of legal ethics and political accountability.

By the early 1970s, the confluence of these and other movements had exposed the limitations of a positivist definition of law standing alone. Leading jurists of the day—Lon Fuller, Jerome Hall, Karl Llewellyn, Harold Berman, and others—were pressing for a broader understanding and definition of law.[14] Of course, they said in concurrence with legal positivists, law consists of rules—the black letter rules of contracts, torts, property, corporations, and sundry other familiar subjects. Of course, law draws to itself a distinctive legal science, an "artificial reason," as Sir Edward Coke once put it.[15] But law is much more than the rules of the state and how we apply and analyze them. Law is also the social activity by which certain norms are formulated by legitimate authorities and actualized by people subject to those authorities. The process of legal formulation involves legislating, adjudicating, administering, and other conduct by legitimate officials. The process of legal actualization involves obeying, negotiating, litigating, and other conduct by legal subjects. Law is a set of rules, plus the social and political processes of formulating, enforcing, and responding to those rules.[16] Numerous other institutions besides the state are involved. The rules, customs, and processes of churches, colleges, corporations, clubs, charities, and other nonstate associations are just as much part of a society's legal system as those of the state. Numerous other norms besides legal rules are involved. Order and obedience, authority and liberty are exercised out of a complex blend of concerns and conditions—class, gender, persuasion, piety, charisma, clemency, courage, moderation, temperance, force, faith, and more.

Legal positivism could not, by itself, come to terms with law understood in this broader sense. In the last third of the twentieth century, American jurists thus began to (re)turn with increasing alacrity to the methods and insights of other disciplines to enhance their formulations. This was the birthing process of the modern movement of interdisciplinary legal study. The movement was born to enhance the province and purview of legal study, to refigure the roots and routes of legal analysis, and to render more holistic and realistic our appreciation of law in community, in context, in concert with politics, social sciences, and other disciplines.[17] In the 1970s, a number of interdisciplinary approaches began to enter the mainstream of American legal education—combining legal study with the study of philosophy, economics, medicine, politics, and sociology. In the 1980s and 1990s, new interdisciplinary legal approaches appeared in rapid succession—the study of law coupled with the study of anthropology, literature, environmental science, urban studies, women's studies, gay-lesbian studies, and African American studies. And, importantly for our purposes, in these last two decades, the study of law was also recombined with the study of religion, including Christianity.

THE CONTENT

In this context, it is no surprise that, until recently, modern Western Christian teachings on law, politics, and society have been largely lost on the academy.[18] To be sure, medieval and early modern Christian influences on the Western legal tradition were recognized. And the valuable contributions of a few Christian lights of the twentieth century—Reinhold Niebuhr, Jacques Maritain, and Martin Luther King Jr. especially—have long been closely studied. But the prevailing assumption of most scholars has been that, for good or ill, the historical contributions of Christianity to our understanding of law, politics, and society were gradually eclipsed in the modern period. Outside of specialty discussions of natural law and church-state relations, it has been widely assumed, modern Christianity has had little constructive or original to say.

The premise of this volume and its two companions is that modern Christianity did have a great deal to say about law, politics, and society, and its teachings can still have a salutary influence today, in the West and well beyond. Many branches of modern Christianity did become theologically anemic, ethically compromised, and jurisprudentially barren. But in each generation, we submit, strong schools of Christian legal, political, and social teaching remained, each grounded in a rich and nuanced Christian theology—including a theology of human nature or, more technically, a theological anthropology. Not surprisingly, given the prominence of legal positivism, most of the best such teaching happened outside of the legal profession—in seminaries and church councils, among philosophers and ethicists, on soapboxes and in prison cells, in intellectual isolation if not outright exile. But by word, by deed, and by declaration, modern Christians addressed the cardinal issues of law, politics, and society, drawing on a rich theology of human nature.

These three volumes sample these teachings and map their insights for the most pressing issues of our day. Such issues include topics familiar to scholars of law, politics, and society whatever their persuasion: the nature and purpose of law and authority, the mandate and limits of rule and obedience, the rights and duties of officials and subjects, the care and nurture of the needy and innocent, the rights and wrongs of war and violence, the separation and cooperation of church and state, and the sources and sanctions of legal reasoning. Such issues also include questions more specifically Christian in accent but no less important for our understanding of law, politics, and society: Are people fundamentally good or evil? Is human dignity essentially rational or relational? Is law inherently coercive or liberating? Is law a stairway to heaven or a fence against hell? Did government predate or postdate the fall into sin? Should authorities only proscribe vices or also prescribe virtues? Is the state a divine or a popular sovereign? Are social institutions fundamentally hierarchical or egalitarian in internal structure and external relations? Are they rooted in creation or custom, covenant or contract? What is justice, and what must a Christian do in its absence?

Together these volumes address the lives, writing, and thought of twenty leading modern Catholic, Protestant, and Orthodox Christians who addressed just these types of questions: modern theologians, philosophers, ethicists, jurists, statesmen, and churchmen who spoke to many issues of law, politics, and society on the strength of their theological anthropology—or spoke to one or two issues with particular acuity and originality. They are introduced by analytical essays followed by a set of illustrative selections from their main writings.

Permit us a few words about how we have selected and arranged the figures included in these volumes. First, the focus is on *modern* Christian teachings on law, politics, society, and human nature. "Modern," "modernism," and "modernity" are highly contested labels these days— not least within Christian churches, where the terms have often been associated with dangerous liberal tendencies. We are using the word "modern" nontechnically. We are focused principally on twentieth-century Christianity, reaching back into the later nineteenth century to understand movements that culminated more recently. The time period in question includes the Reconstruction era after the American Civil War, the later industrial revolution, the Bolshevik Revolution and the emergence of socialism, two world wars, the Holocaust and the Stalinist purges, the modern human rights revolution, the Great Depression and the rise of the Western welfare state, the technological revolution, and the emergence of globalization. These modern moments and movements had monumental, and sometimes devastating, effects on modern Christianity.

Many of these twentieth-century movements were continuous with earlier movements that are often also described as "modern." Among these are the Glorious Revolution of England (1689), the American Revolution (1776), and the French Revolution (1789). Important also was the scientific revolution in the seventeenth and eighteenth centuries and the later rise of what Max Weber called technical rationality and the bureaucratization of the state and society. Most important of all was the eighteenth- and nineteenth-century Enlightenment in Europe and North America, with its new secular theology of individualism, rationalism, and nationalism that often challenged core Christian beliefs. To Enlightenment exponents, the individual was no longer viewed primarily as a sinner seeking salvation in the life hereafter. Every individual was created equal in virtue and dignity, vested with inherent rights of life, liberty, and property, and capable of choosing his or her own means and measures of happiness. Reason was no longer the handmaiden of revelation, rational disputation was no longer subordinate to homiletic declaration. The rational process, conducted privately by each person and collectively in the open marketplace of ideas, was considered a sufficient source of private morality and public law. The nation-state was no longer identified with a national church or a divinely blessed covenant people. It was to be glorified in its own right. Its constitutions and laws were sacred texts reflecting the morals and mores of the collective national culture. Its officials were secular priests, representing the sovereignty and will of the people.

The introductions address some of the earlier phases of the modern age, but not all of them, and not with a depth that will satisfy specialists. It would require a set of volumes considerably heftier than these to take full account of these earlier modern movements and their impact on Christian teachings on law, politics, and society. The later modern period is less known, and it is the period with which these volumes are principally occupied.

Second, we have deliberately used the term "teachings," rather than "theories," "theologies," or other formal labels, to describe what modern Christianity has offered to law, politics, and society. In part, this is to underscore that the call to "teach" is what all Christians, despite their vast denominational differences, have in common. Christ's last words to his disciples, after all, were, "Go ye, therefore, and make disciples of all nations . . . *teaching* them to observe all that I have commanded you."[19] In part this is to recognize that "social teachings," "political teachings," "moral teachings," and "legal teachings" have become terms of art in current scholarship. Particularly in the Catholic and Protestant worlds, "social teaching" has become shorthand for a fantastic range of speculation on issues of law, politics, society, and morality.[20] And, in part, we use "teachings" to underscore that modern Christians have contributed to our understanding of law, politics, and society by word and by deed, by books and by speeches, by brilliant writings and by sacrificial acts. It would be foolish to dismiss the novel teachings of Susan B. Anthony or Dorothy Day just because they had thin resumes. It would be equally foolish not to draw lessons from the martyrdom of Mother Maria, Dietrich Bonhoeffer, or Martin Luther King Jr. just because they left their papers in disarray.

Third, we have divided the twenty figures covered in these three volumes into Catholic, Protestant, and Orthodox Christian groups, while recognizing that some were more ecumenically minded than others. We have included an introduction to each tradition to contextualize and connect the studies of the individuals that are included and have arranged the chapters more or less chronologically for each tradition, assigning varying word limits and selections for each figure in accordance with their relative importance for the themes of these volumes.

Fourth, with respect to the Catholic tradition, we have blended episcopal and lay voices from both sides of the Atlantic. Leo XIII, John XXIII, and John Paul II offered the most original and enduring contributions among modern popes, though Pope Pius XII was important as well. Leo XIII led the revival and reconstruction of the thought of the thirteenth-century sage Thomas Aquinas. He applied this "neo-Thomism," as it was called, to the formulation of several of the Catholic Church's core "social teachings," not least a theory of social institutions that would later ripen into subsidiarity doctrine, and a theory of labor that would later form the backbone of the church's stand for social, cultural, and economic rights. John XXIII was the architect of the Second Vatican Council (1962–65), with its transforming vision of religious liberty, human dignity, and democracy, and its deliberate agenda to modernize the Catholic Church's political platforms and social teachings. John Paul II, who faced the ravages of both the Nazi occupation and the Communist takeover of his native Poland, was a fierce champion of democratization and human rights in the first years of his pontificate, as well as an active sponsor of rapprochement among Catholics, Protestants, and Jews and of revitalization of the church's canon law. In his last years, he also became an equally fierce critic of the growing secularization of society, liberalization of theology, and exploitation of human nature. These latter concerns have drawn the church's leadership to new (and sometimes controversial) interpretations of its earlier "social teachings."

The French philosopher Jacques Maritain and the American theologian John Courtney Murray were among the most original and influential of the many European and American Catholic writers in the mid-twentieth century. Maritain combined neo-Thomism and French existentialism into an intricate new theory of natural law, natural rights, human dignity, equality, and fraternity, which inspired the Universal Declaration of Human Rights (1948). Murray combined neo-Thomism and American democratic theory into a powerful new argument for natural law, human dignity, religious liberty, church-state relations, and social organization. Both theories were initially controversial. Maritain was blistered by his reviewers; Murray was censored for a time by the church. But they and the many scholars they influenced laid much of the foundation for the Second Vatican Council's declaration on human dignity and religious freedom and the church's emerging global advocacy of human rights and democratization.

American political activist Dorothy Day and Latin American liberation theologian Gustavo Gutiérrez represent important new strains of social and political critique and activism within modern Catholicism. Day defied state and church authorities alike in her relentless crusade to protect the rights of workers and the poor and to protest warfare, grounding her work in a robust theology of personalism. Gutiérrez combined some of the teachings of Vatican II and Marxism into a searing critique of global capitalism and its devastating impact on the poor and on the underdeveloped world. Both Day and Gutiérrez adduced the Bible above all to press for a preferential option for the poor, the needy, and the vulnerable. Both figures have been controversial and both drew episcopal censure, but they have helped to illustrate, if not inspire, many new forms of social and political activism among Catholics worldwide.

Fifth, the Protestant tradition, with its hundreds of independent denominations that share only the Bible as their common authority, does not lend itself to easy illustration. We present Abraham Kuyper and Karl Barth as two strong and independent voices who addressed, and sometimes defined, many of the main themes of law, politics, society, and human nature that have occupied many modern Protestants. Kuyper, though not so well known today, was something like the Protestant Leo XIII of his day. He called for a return to the cardinal teachings of the sixteenth-century Protestant Reformation and developed a comprehensive Reformed theory of human nature and human knowledge. He also developed an important new "sphere sovereignty" theory of liberty, democracy, and social institutions, which would become a Protestant analogue, if not answer, to Catholic subsidiarity theory.

If Kuyper was the Leo of modern Protestantism, Barth was its Maritain. This brilliant Swiss theologian produced the most comprehensive Protestant dogmatic system of the twentieth century, centered on the Bible and on Christ. Many theories of law, politics, and society were embedded in his massive writings, not least his famous critique of theories of natural law and natural rights, the source of a strong antinaturalist and antirights tendency among many later Protestants. Most memorable was Barth's leadership in crafting the Barmen Declaration of 1934, which denounced the emerging laws and policies of Adolf Hitler and the German Nazi Party.

German theologian Dietrich Bonhoeffer knew firsthand about Nazi belligerence: he was killed in a concentration camp for conspiring to assassinate Hitler. Bonhoeffer's decision to join the plot had required a complex rethinking of his own Lutheran tradition of political ethics and Christian discipleship, and of the proper relations of the church and its members to a world that had abandoned reason and religion in pursuit of tribalism and totalitarianism. Bonhoeffer's American contemporary Reinhold Niebuhr saw some of these same lusts for power and self-interest in modern states and corporations. Building on the classic Protestant doctrine of total depravity, Niebuhr developed an applied theology of Christian realism that prized democratic government, but with strong checks and balances; that protected human rights, but informed by moral duties; and that championed racial equality and economic justice.

We have included Susan B. Anthony, a freethinking Quaker, as an early exemplar of an important tendency of modern American Protestants to counsel legal disobedience and legal reform simultaneously on selected issues. Today, these Protestant political preoccupations include abortion, same-sex marriage, faith-based initiatives, and religion in public schools. For Anthony, the cardinal issue was women's rights. Using basic biblical texts as her guide, she worked relentlessly to effect many legal reforms in Congress and the states, not least passage of the Nineteenth Amendment to the Constitution, the world's first modern constitutional guarantee of a woman's right to vote.

Martin Luther King Jr. and William Stringfellow later led comparable movements for racial and economic justice, although they grounded their advocacy more deeply in traditional biblical warrants and allied themselves more closely with the church. King was "America's Amos" who used pulpit, pamphlet, and political platform alike to lead America to greater racial justice, including passage of the Civil Rights Act of 1964. When he faced political opposition and repression, King also developed a novel theology of nonviolent resistance to authority. William Stringfellow spent much of his career representing the interests of the poor and needy in Harlem as well as those who protested America's war policy, appearing in several sensational cases. He grounded his work in a novel Protestant theory of law and gospel. The Mennonite theologian John Howard Yoder likewise pressed for social and economic justice and democratic virtues, on the strength of a classic Anabaptist biblicism and pacifism coupled with a new appreciation for natural law, human rights, and democratization.

Sixth, we have thought it imperative to devote one of these three volumes to the Eastern Orthodox tradition. Many leading Orthodox lights dealt with fundamental questions of law, politics, society, and human nature with novel insight, often giving distinct readings and renderings of the biblical, apostolic, and patristic sources. Moreover, the Orthodox Church has immense spiritual resources and experiences whose implications are only now beginning to be seen. These resources lie, in part, in Orthodox worship—the passion of the liturgy, the pathos of the icons, the power of spiritual silence. They lie, in part, in Orthodox church life—the distinct balancing of hierarchy and congregationalism through autocephaly, of uniform worship and liturgical freedom through alternative vernacular rites, of community and individuality through a trinitarian communalism, centered on the parish, the extended family, and the wise grandmother, the *babushka*. And these spiritual resources lie, in part, in the massive martyrdom of millions of Orthodox faithful in the twentieth century—whether suffered by Russian Orthodox under the Communist Party, Greek and Armenian Orthodox under Turkish and Iranian radicals, Middle Eastern Copts at the hands of religious extremists, North African Orthodox under all manner of fascist autocrats and tribal strongmen.[21]

These deep spiritual resources of the Orthodox Church have no exact parallels in modern Catholicism and Protestantism, and most of their implications for law, politics, and society have still to be drawn out. It would be wise to hear what an ancient church, newly charred and chastened by decades of oppression and martyrdom, considers essential to the regime of human rights. It would be enlightening to watch how ancient Orthodox communities, still largely centered on the parish and the family, reconstruct Christian theories of society. It would be instructive to hear how a tradition that still celebrates spiritual silence as its highest virtue recasts the meaning of freedom of speech and expression. And it would be illuminating to feel how a people that has long cherished and celebrated the role of the woman—the wizened babushka of the home, the faithful remnant in the parish pews, the living icon of the Dormition of the Mother of God—elaborates the meaning of gender equality.

To illustrate the potential of some of these resources and the rich theological anthropologies that Orthodoxy has already produced, we have selected three key Russian Orthodox scholars—Soloviev, Berdyaev, and Lossky. Each interacted with several Western Christian thinkers. Each challenged the (increasingly compromised) Russian Orthodox authorities of their day, while channeling the best theology and jurisprudence of their tradition into fundamentally new directions. Vladimir Soloviev, a philosopher, was the first modern Russian to work out an intricate Orthodox philosophy of law that grounded law and political order in morality and anchored morality directly in a Christian theology of salvation. Soloviev also challenged the traditional Orthodox theology of theocracy, which tied church, state, and nation into an organic whole and laid some of the foundations for a new theory of social pluralism. Nicholas Berdyaev, a theologian, worked out a complex new theology of human nature anchored in an ethic of creation, redemption, and law. He also crafted an original theory of human dignity and salvation that he tied to the Orthodox doctrine of theosis. Vladimir Lossky, a philosopher, drew from several earlier church fathers and mystics a brilliant new theory of human dignity, freedom, and discipline anchored in the Orthodox doctrine of the Trinity. He also challenged the politically compromised church and its socially anemic members to reclaim both their freedoms and their duties to discharge divinely appointed tasks. The Romanian theologian Dumitru Stăniloae drew from some of the same predecessors a comparable theory of the meaning of human freedom and sinfulness and the symphony of natural and supernatural sources of law and authority. Unlike Lossky, he supported Romanian ethnic nationalism and had little say to about the political compromises of the Romanian Orthodox Church during the period of Communism.

We have also included a chapter on the Russian nun and social reformer Mother Maria Skobtsova, whose thought and example evoke images of both Dorothy Day and Dietrich Bonhoeffer. Maria, who was exiled in Paris, worked tirelessly in the hostels feeding the poor and needy, while developing a rich theology of incarnational living and sacramental care and a harsh critique of some of the reclusive tendencies of many monastics. Her work during the Nazi occupation of Paris brought her to the attention of the Gestapo, which condemned her to death in a concentration camp.

The biographies of some of these figures are as edifying as their writings, and the chapters that follow spend time recounting them. Fifteen of these people served, at least for a time, as university professors of theology, philosophy, ethics, history, or law. Ten served in traditional church offices: three as popes (Leo XIII, John XXIII, and John Paul II), five as pastors (Gutiérrez, Barth, Bonhoeffer, Niebuhr, and King), two as monastics (Maria and Murray). Two served in political office—Kuyper as the prime minister of the Netherlands, Maritain as France's ambassador to the Vatican. One served as a lawyer (Stringfellow). One was active as a political advisor (Niebuhr). Eight were stirred to radical social or political activism (Gutiérrez, Day, Barth, Bonhoeffer, Niebuhr, King, Stringfellow, and Maria). Four were censured by church authorities (Anthony, Day, Murray, and Gutiérrez). Three were exiled from their homeland (Berdyaev, Lossky, and Maria). Two were removed from their professorships (Bonhoeffer and Stăniloae). Nine were indicted or imprisoned by state authorities (Anthony, Day, Bonhoeffer, King, Stringfellow, Soloviev, Berdyaev, Maria, and Stăniloae). One faced brutal and lengthy political imprisonment (Stăniloae). Two were murdered in concentration camps (Bonhoeffer and Maria). One fell to an assassin's bullet (King).

The diversity of these biographies underscores an important criterion of selection that we have used in assembling these three volumes. The twenty figures included herein are intended to be points on a large canvas, not entries on an exhaustive roll of modern Christian teachers of law, society, and politics. We present them as illustrations of different venues, vectors, and visions of what a Christian understanding of law, politics, and society entails. Some of these figures were lone voices. Others attracted huge throngs of allies and disciples, many of whom make no appearance in these pages. Moreover, we have not included some who are still alive and well today—including several authors in these volumes—whose work will likely shape Christian teachings on law, politics, and society in the twenty-first century.

Many readers will thus look in vain for some of their favorite authors. Missing from the collection are some who did or do speak to some issues of law, politics, and society with a distinctly Christian understanding of human nature: Hans Urs von Balthasar, John Finnis, Joseph Fuchs, Mary Ann Glendon, Germain Grisez, Etienne Gilson, Bernard Lonergan, Karl Rahner, Heinrich Rommen, Thomas Schaeffer, and Yves Simon, among Catholics; Emil Brunner, Herman Dooyeweerd, Johannes Heckel, Carl Henry, Karl Holl, Wolfgang Huber, Richard Niebuhr, Oliver O'Donovan, Wolfhart Pannenberg, Paul Ramsey, Walter Rauschenbusch, and Rudolph Sohm, among Protestants; John Erickson, Pavel Florensky, Georges Florovsky, John Meyendorff, and Christoph Yannaras, among Orthodox. Every reader will have a list of favorites beyond those represented here. The greatest compliment that could be made to this book is that it stimulates the production of many more and better studies of the scores of other modern Christian thinkers who deserve analysis.

THE CHALLENGE

This last point invites a few final reflections on some of the main challenges that remain—beyond the formidable task of filling in the vast canvas of modern Christian teachings on law, politics, society, and human nature.

One challenge is to trace the roots of these modern Christian teachings back to the earlier modern period of the seventeenth through early nineteenth centuries. Scholars have written a great deal about patristic, scholastic, early Protestant, and post-Tridentine Catholic contributions to law, politics, and society. But many of the best accounts stop in 1625. That was the year the father of international law, Hugo Grotius, uttered the impious hypothesis that law, politics, and society would continue even if "we should concede that which cannot be conceded without the utmost wickedness, that there is no God, or that the affairs of men are of no concern to him."[22] While many subsequent writers conceded Grotius's hypothesis and embarked on the great secular projects of the Enlightenment, many great Christian writers did not. They have been forgotten to all but specialists. Their thinking on law, politics, and society needs to be retrieved, restudied, and reconstructed for our day.

A second challenge is to make these modern Christian teachings on law, politics, and society more concrete. In centuries past, the Catholic, Protestant, and Orthodox traditions all produced massive codes of canon law and church discipline that covered many areas of private and public life. They instituted sophisticated tribunals for the equitable enforcement of these laws and produced massive works of political theology and theological jurisprudence, with ample handholds in catechisms, creeds, and confessional books, to guide the faithful. Some of that sophisticated legal and political work continues today. Modern Christian ethicists still take up some of the old questions. Some Christian jurists have contributed to the current discussion of human rights, family law, and church-state relations. But the legal structure and sophistication of the modern Christian church as a whole is a pale shadow of what went before. It needs to be restored lest the church lose its capacity for Christian self-rule and its members lose their capacity to serve as responsible Christian "prophets, priests, and kings."

A third challenge is for modern Catholic, Protestant, and Orthodox Christians to develop a rigorous ecumenical understanding of law, politics, and society. This is a daunting task. Only in the past three decades, with the collapse of Communism and the rise of globalization, have these three ancient warring sects begun to come together and to understand one another. It will take many generations to work out the great theological disputes over the nature of the Trinity or the doctrine of justification by faith. But there is more confluence than conflict in Catholic, Protestant, and Orthodox understandings of law, politics, and society, especially if they are viewed in long and responsible historical perspective. Scholars from these three great Christian traditions need to join together to work out a comprehensive new ecumenical "concordance of discordant canons" that incorporates the best of these traditions, is earnest about its ecumenism, and is honest about the greatest points of tension. Few studies would do more both to spur the great project of Christian ecumenism and to drive modern churches to get their legal houses in order.

A final, and perhaps the greatest, challenge will be to join the principally Western Christian story of law, politics, and society told in these volumes with comparable stories that are told in the rest of the Christian world. Over the past two centuries, Christianity has become very much a world religion, claiming nearly two billion souls. Strong new capitals and captains of Christianity now stand in the south and the east—in Latin America and sub-Saharan Africa, in Eastern Europe and the Russian theater, in Korea, China, the Indian subcontinent, and beyond. In some of these new zones of Christianity, the Western Christian classics, including the works of some of the figures represented here, are still being read and studied. But rich new indigenous forms and norms of law, politics, and society are emerging, premised on very different Christian understandings of theology and anthropology. It would take a special kind of cultural arrogance for Western and non-Western Christians to refuse to learn from each other.

NOTES

1. Catherine Drinker Bowen, *Yankee from Olympus: Justice Holmes and His Family* (Boston: Little, Brown, 1944).
2. Grant Gilmore, *Ages of American Law* (New Haven, Conn.: Yale University Press, 1977), 48–56, 110, 147*n*12.
3. Albert W. Alschuler, *Life Without Values: The Life, Work and Legacy of Justice Holmes* (Chicago: University of Chicago Press, 2000).
4. Oliver Wendell Holmes Jr., *Collected Legal Papers* (New York: Harcourt, Brace and Howe, 1920), 170.
5. Gilmore, *Ages of American Law*, 41–67.

6. I. Bernard Cohen, *Revolution in Science* (Cambridge, Mass.: Harvard University Press, 1985); Donald R. Kelly, *The Human Measure: Social Thought in the Western Legal Tradition* (Cambridge, Mass.: Harvard University Press, 1990).

7. See especially John Austin, *The Province of Jurisprudence Determined, Being the First of a Series of Lectures on Jurisprudence, or, The Philosophy of Positive Law*, 2nd ed., 3 vols. (London: John Murray, 1861–63); Christopher Columbus Langdell, *A Selection of Cases on the Law of Contracts*, 2nd ed. (Boston: Little, Brown, 1879), preface; Langdell, "Harvard Celebration Speeches," *Law Quarterly Review* 3 (1887): 123.

8. See, e.g., John Wigmore, "Nova Methodus Discendae Docendaeque Jurisprudentiae," *Harvard Law Review* 30 (1917): 812; Holmes, *Collected Legal Papers*, 139, 231; Robert Stevens, *Law School: Legal Education in America from the 1850s to the 1980s* (Chapel Hill: University of North Carolina Press, 1983).

9. Barbara Shapiro, "Law and Science in Seventeenth-Century England," *Stanford Law Review* 21 (1969): 724, 728.

10. Oliver Wendell Holmes Jr., *The Common Law* (Boston: Little, Brown, 1881), 1.

11. *S. Pac. Co. v. Jensen*, 244 U.S. 205, 222 (1917) (Holmes, J. dissenting); see also Michael H. Hoffheimer, *Justice Holmes and the Natural Law* (New York: Garland, 1992).

12. *Lochner v. New York*, 198 U.S. 45, 76 (1905).

13. Letter to Sir Frederick Pollock (May 30, 1927) in *Holmes-Pollock Letters: The Correspondence of Mr. Justice Holmes and Sir Frederick Pollock, 1874–1932*, ed. Mark DeWolfe Howe, 2 vols. (Cambridge, Mass.: Harvard University Press, 1941), 2:200.

14. See especially Karl Llewellyn, *Jurisprudence* (Chicago: University of Chicago Press, 1962); Lon L. Fuller, *The Morality of Law*, rev. ed. (New Haven, Conn.: Yale University Press, 1964); Jerome Hall, *Studies in Jurisprudence and Criminal Theory* (New York: Oceana Publishers, 1958); Hall, *Foundations of Jurisprudence* (Indianapolis: Bobbs-Merrill, 1973); Harold J. Berman, *The Interaction of Law and Religion* (Nashville, Tenn.: Abingdon Press, 1974).

15. Anthony Lewis, "Sir Edward Coke (1552–1633): His Theory of 'Artificial Reason' as a Context for Modern Basic Legal Theory," *Law Quarterly Review* 84 (1968): 330.

16. See Harold J. Berman, *Law and Revolution: The Formation of the Western Legal Tradition* (Cambridge, Mass.: Harvard University Press, 1983), 4–5; Jerome Hall, *Comparative Law and Social Theory* (Baton Rouge: Louisiana State University Press, 1963), 78–82.

17. See, e.g., Richard A. Posner, "The Present Situation in Legal Scholarship," *Yale Law Journal* 90 (1981): 1113; Robert C. Clark, "The Interdisciplinary Study of Legal Education," *Yale Law Journal* 90 (1981): 1238; Symposium, "American Legal Scholarship: Directions and Dilemmas," *Journal of Legal Education* 33 (1983): 403.

18. For a notable recent exception, see Michael W. McConnell, Robert F. Cochran Jr., and Angela C. Carmella, eds., *Christian Perspectives on Legal Thought* (New Haven, Conn.: Yale University Press, 2000).

19. Matthew 28:20.

20. See, e.g., Ernst Troeltsch, *The Social Teachings of the Christian Churches*, trans. Olive Wyon, 2 vols. (Chicago: University of Chicago Press, 1981), and review of later literature in John Witte Jr., *Law and Protestantism: The Legal Teachings of the Lutheran Reformation* (New York: Cambridge University Press, 2002).

21. See James H. Billington, "Orthodox Christianity and the Russian Transformation," in *Proselytism and Orthodoxy in Russia: The New War for Souls*, ed. John Witte Jr. and Michael Bourdeaux (Maryknoll, N.Y.: Orbis Books, 1999), 51; Billington, "The Case for Orthodoxy," *The New Republic* (May 30, 1994), 24.

22. Hugo Grotius, *De Iure Belli ac Pacis* (1625), Prolegomena, 11, discussed in Oliver O'Donovan and Joan Lockwood O'Donovan, *From Irenaeus to Grotius: Christian Political Thought, 100–1625* (Grand Rapids, Mich.: Eerdmans, 1999); Brian Tierney, *The Idea of Natural Rights: Studies on Natural Rights, Natural Law, and Church Law, 1150–1625* (Atlanta: Scholars Press, 1997).

Introduction to Modern Protestantism

MARK A. NOLL

It is always precarious to attempt a history of Protestants because there are so many different kinds of them, they exist in so many different places, and (at least for the purposes of this book) they have approached questions of law, politics, and society in so many different ways.[1] Today, for example, a satisfactory general account of Protestantism would have to treat long-standing differences that have divided Protestants from each other: Lutheran from the Reformed, Anglicans and Episcopalians from Mennonites, Presbyterians from Baptists or Methodists, and still other ancestral groupings from each other. It should take into account broad liberal and conservative tendencies that now run as strongly within denominations as between them. In addition, it would need to include treatment of the many new Protestant churches, especially the Pentecostals, that have sprung up in such rich profusion since the start of the twentieth century. And, at the start of the twenty-first century, it should by rights deal with the spread of Protestant movements around the globe: Baptists and Anglicans are now present in more than 160 counties, Presbyterians and the Reformed in more than 140, Lutherans and Methodists in more than 100, and other, somewhat smaller bodies are almost as widely spread.[2]

Rapid and nearly unprecedented change in the shape of world Christianity over recent decades adds special complexity to the engagement of Protestants with the law, politics, and society. In the course of the twentieth century, Protestantism precipitously declined as a culture-shaping force in Europe and some traditional European dependencies (such as Canada, Australia, and New Zealand). In the United States, where there are more Protestants than in any other single country in the world, Protestantism has been fragmented and reshaped into forms and proportions looking very different in the early twenty-first century than they did in the early twentieth. And although it is difficult to adjust to new worldwide realities, it is simply the case that there are today many more active Protestants in Nigeria than in Great Britain, many more in Brazil than in Germany, more in the Congo than in Denmark and Finland combined, about three times as many in Indonesia as in the Netherlands, more each in India and the Philippines than in any European country except perhaps Germany, nearly twice as many in each of Tanzania, Uganda, Kenya, or South Korea than in Canada—and these comparisons do not include China, where a tremendous number (though only imperfectly counted) of Protestants or Protestant-like Christians have emerged in just the last three decades.[3] Providing a succinct historical introduction as a context for specific consideration of the eight Protestant thinkers treated in this book is not, in other words, a simple task.

That task, however, does become somewhat more manageable if attention remains fixed on Europe and North America where these particular thinkers lived. Even if less than half of the world's affiliated Protestants now dwell in these two parts of the world (down from over 90 percent in 1900), the story of Protestants in these former heartlands still possesses a certain coherence because of a continuous history stretching back to the Reformation of the sixteenth century. Despite massive demographic shifts, much of worldwide Protestantism still looks to Western Europe and North America as the crucial educational centers. In only a few years it will almost certainly not be possible to treat Western Europe and North America as the Protestant keys for intellectual and theological endeavor. Rather, the sort of political-religious connections explored recently by Paul Freston for Evangelical groups outside of Western Europe and North America will almost certainly be moving to center stage.[4] Yet for the purposes of this book, a focus limited to the main Protestant movements of the West not only provides a useful introduction to treatment of important figures from the late nineteenth and twentieth centuries, but also offers an important (historical) story in itself.

STATUS QUO ANTE: PROTESTANTISM IN 1900

At the end of the nineteenth century, world Protestantism was still most easily and obviously identified with the churches of the magisterial Reformation.[5] In the German empire and in Scandinavia, Lutheran territorial churches enjoyed state support and exercised proprietary oversight over national religious life. In uneasy coexistence with the Catholic Church, they also attempted, though with diminishing success, to maintain their hereditary oversight of intellectual and social aspects of public life. A roughly similar situation obtained in Great Britain, where Anglicans in England and Presbyterians in Scotland were trying to exercise the same sort of state-sanctioned authority. Reformed, or Calvinist, churches enjoyed a similar establishmentarian status in the Netherlands and several Swiss cantons. In parts of France, Hungary, and Germany, Reformed churches enjoyed state recognition and some state support as, in effect, the second-string established churches after the Catholics or the Lutherans. Throughout Europe relatively small minorities of Free Church or dissenting Protestants were tolerated to one degree or another. Nonconformists—Independents, Wesleyans, and Baptists—were most vigorous in England and Wales (as were Presbyterians in the north of Ireland), where for more than a century they had exerted a significant influence on British economic, educational, and political history. Pockets of Mennonites and other Anabaptists descended from sixteenth-century movements lived quietly in the Netherlands, southern Germany, Switzerland, and amid the German diaspora in Eastern Europe, but faithfulness to pacifist teaching had mostly meant their withdrawal from European public life.

All of the established or quasi-established Protestant churches had been weakened in different ways by events and circumstances of the nineteenth century. Early in that century the Prussian monarch had forced most Lutheran and Reformed churches in his territory to merge into an Evangelical Union, which subsequently manifested less self-directing energy than had the original churches. Strong theological partisanship between pietistic-leaning and modern-leaning or scientific-leaning factions weakened the remaining Lutheran state churches, even as similar partisan differences divided Anglicans into high church (often Anglo-Catholic), low church (often Evangelical), and broad church (often liberal) factions. Schism among Dutch Reformed and Scottish Presbyterians testified to the feisty vigor of the splintering factions but also to a general drift among the Reformed and Presbyterian traditions in general. While Evangelical or Pietist movements had breathed new life into some dissenting churches and led to the creation of entirely new free (or nonestablished) churches, those revival movements, which also touched the established churches, were not able to overcome the increasing disengagement of working-class populations from church life. Yet well into the twentieth century, and in some cases until today, European Protestantism was most easily identified with the territorial state churches descended from the Protestant Reformation. Together they constituted a Protestant Christendom aspiring to the same establishmentarian place that European Christendom had exercised for over a millennium and that remained even more vigorous in some Catholic sections of Europe.

In North America the situation by 1900 was substantially different. Canada remained somewhat closer to European patterns, but the democratic character of the United States had affected religion as much as politics, economics, and society. Most obviously, there were no established churches. To be sure, older denominations with Old World roots still exercised some of the proprietary and civilizing functions of the European state churches. For lack of a better term, they can be called the formalist denominations. Thus, Episcopalians (or Anglicans in Canada), Congregationalists, and Presbyterians, who had enjoyed considerable prestige as established or quasi-established churches in the colonial period, continued to be major sponsors of seminaries, colleges, and social programs; they continued as well to enjoy the patronage of well-placed business and political leaders. These denominations were joined in their comprehensive cultural interests by the Lutheran churches of Pennsylvania, the Upper Midwest, and the Canadian prairies that from mid-century had been greatly strengthened by immigration from Germany and Scandinavia. Yet in the United States, these churches, which most closely resembled European established churches in their self-conception and social duties, were vastly outnumbered by what might be termed the antiformalist denominations. In 1890, against roughly 5,000 Episcopal, 5,000 Congregational, 8,500 Lutheran, and 25,000 Presbyterian churches, there were in the United States more than 40,000 Baptist churches, more than 50,000 Methodist churches, and probably another 50,000 or so churches representing an incredibly broad diversity of smaller, often sectarian denominations.[6] Moreover, a substantial portion of the churchgoing population was made up of African Americans (mostly Baptist and Methodist) whose churches shared considerable Christian doctrine with the white churches, but who were products of an oppressive social history unlike anything ever experienced in the entire history of Protestantism.[7] None of the churches had enjoyed establishmentarian status or privileges since early in the history of the American republic. In comparative terms, the United States benefited from an unusual combination: vigorous church life and a nearly complete freedom of religion (though never experienced fully by African Americans, Catholics in some predominately Protestant regions, and members of minority Christian and non-Christian groups in many parts of the country).

What Alexis de Tocqueville identified in the 1830s in his landmark book *Democracy in America* still characterized religion in the United States: "America is . . . the place in the world where the Christian religion has most preserved genuine powers over souls; and nothing shows better how useful and natural to man it is in our day, since the country in which it exercises the greatest empire is at the same time the most enlightened and most free."[8]

To be sure, American Protestants had not enjoyed an easy progress through the nineteenth century. The American Civil War (1861–65) witnessed a significant failing in theology as Bible-believing Northerners and Bible-believing Southerners found no means except war to resolve their differences over what the scriptures mandated concerning slavery.[9] The postwar adjustment to rapid industrialization and urbanization was just as disquieting, since Protestants who had mastered social and political life in rural and small-town America seemed overmastered by the realities of large-scale manufacturing, mass-market commerce, and the new media of popular culture.[10] In the face of heavy immigration by Roman Catholics, Jews, and nonbelievers, American Protestants wavered between following the universalistic claims of democratic freedom and asserting a hereditary right to act as arbiters of the public sphere. Growing deference to self-directed scientific inquiry in universities organized for largely secular purposes was also threatening what had been, in effect, a Protestant hegemony in American higher education.[11]

Still, at the end of the nineteenth century there were no organized movements of thought, voluntary organization, or civil influence that rivaled the importance of Protestant institutions in American life. The Roman Catholic population, though having become the largest of any specific Christian tradition, was more taken up with constructing its own churches, schools, and community organizations than with contending for dominance in public. The nation's most respected educational and eleemosynary institutions remained Protestant in some general sense. And there was also a strong Protestant position in publishing and the mass media. Protestants were not supported by governmental funding, as was still often the case in Europe, but precisely for that reason they probably exercised a broader cultural influence than did Protestants on the other side of the Atlantic.

In Canada, outside of French and Catholic Quebec, Protestants were in an even stronger position than in the United States.[12] The older proprietary churches, especially Anglican, Presbyterian, Methodist, and (in the Maritime Provinces) Baptist, were the most important institutions of any kind for providing education, direction for public organizations, and standards for public morality. Protestant churchgoers probably made up a higher percentage of the population in English Canada than in any other Western nation.

At the end of the nineteenth century, Protestants in North America joined their European counterparts in struggling to adjust to the exigencies of mass industrialization and mass consumer culture. Relationships with Roman Catholics remained strained in most regions. Yet Protestants were still shaping culture, and they still provided a potent vocabulary for talking about law, politics, and society. The rapid survey that follows of geopolitical history, as well as of church history and theology, reveals a rising tide of intellectual, social, and economic challenges in the twentieth century. Yet it also shows that, amid many reverses and renovations of inherited positions, Protestants of several kinds were able to contribute significantly to critical discussions about the functioning of human beings in society.

PROTESTANT GEOPOLITICS

In the course of the twentieth century, Protestant geopolitics experienced dramatic change. To put matters in starkly simplistic terms: European Christendom, including the Protestant part of Christendom, imploded. American Protestantism developed from a regional into an international force. And worldwide Protestant leadership had no sooner passed from Europe to America than the entire character of Protestantism began to be transformed by the realities of globalization.

The implosion of European Protestantism over the course of the twentieth century, and with accelerating speed in the century's last half, awaits a satisfactory general history. For the change from a situation where one-quarter to one-half, or more, of the people in Protestant regions regularly attended church to one where substantially less than one-tenth of Protestant populations now do so, there must perforce be multiple, subtle explanations. Even casual observers, however, can sense that the seventy-five years of hot and cold war that stretched from 1914 (the outbreak of World War I) to 1989 (the beginning of the end of state communism) took a grievous toll on the churches. The unprecedented destruction of World War I, the chaos of politics, economies, and ideologies that followed through much of the next two decades, the even greater death and destruction of World War II, the division of Europe into West and East that followed hard on the heels of the defeat of Nazism, the sudden collapse of Marxist regimes and the tangled course of reconstruction that has followed this collapse—all overpowered the efforts of churches to manage, or even fathom, events. Cataclysmic warfare, the brutal displacement of populations, genocide aimed at the entire Jewish people, and manifest failures of much-trumpeted ideologies do not necessarily create conditions inimical to Christian faith. The rise of Pietism after the Thirty

Years' War of the seventeenth century and, much more recently, the emergence of vigorous Christian movements in China after the surpassing destruction of Mao Zedong show the capacity of Protestant or Protestant-like forms of Christianity to advance amid great social disorder.[13] Yet in twentieth-century Europe, recession rather than advance has characterized the Protestant churches.

It is impossible to say to what extent this recession was owing directly to the wars, armed camps, and preoccupation with military security of this most bellicose European century, or whether it can be accounted for more by the exhaustion of doctrinal, liturgical, and intellectual traditions, by the success of capitalist and Marxist varieties of materialism in displacing religious loyalties, or by preoccupation with entertainment or self-fulfillment borne along by a wave of enticing mass media. It was certainly not the case that European Protestants were struck dumb by the scourges of war or class conflict. In the crises of World War II alone it is possible to find many examples of vigorous Protestant conviction: The Barmen Declaration of 1934 spoke courageously against the promotion of a "German Christianity" adapting itself to Hitlerism. Dietrich Bonhoeffer found resources in classical Christian teaching for actions of great ecclesiastical, and then great political courage. The Anglican bishop, George Bell, displayed a similar courage in chastising the Allies for indiscriminate fire bombing of German cities. The French pastor André Trocmé drew on the traditions of his historic Reformed faith to nerve his rescue of Jewish children. And Helmut Thielicke from his pulpit in a bombed-out Hamburg knew how to proclaim a message of gospel hope given shape by a revived theology of the Reformation.[14] Even when moving forward several more decades into a Europe that had become much more systemically secular, it is remarkable that the public demonstrations of 1989 leading to regime change in both East Germany and Romania began in churches (Lutheran and Hungarian Reformed, respectively) where at least some residue of Protestant teaching remained alive. In the face of Europe's vicious tribal wars and its determined flight from forms of Christian faith that had guided its life through centuries, Protestant Christianity did not simply wither away. But, objectively considered, it was much reduced in both reach and influence.

In North America, Protestant communions seemed to have adjusted better to modern culture and society. Canada, to be sure, experienced a history that eventually conformed to a European pattern.[15] Into the 1960s, church attendance and other marks of religious practice remained considerably higher than in the United States. But after that time religious observance declined to levels that, while remaining above the European average, fell considerably below the American. In the years immediately after World War II, Canadians were leaders at the United Nations and other international gatherings in defending references to God and religious belief as critical for international peace.[16] And when the British Parliament repatriated the Canadian Constitution in 1982, an action that acknowledged full Canadian control over every aspect of Canadian government, that constitution began with an assertion that "Canada is founded upon principles that recognize the supremacy of God and the rule of law."[17] Despite these indications of hereditary religious conviction, Canada since the 1960s has secularized faster and more comprehensively than its national neighbor to the south.

To be sure, the twentieth-century history of Protestantism in the United States has been anything but tranquil. Yet through a whole series of reversals, unanticipated innovations, and incursions of modernity, adherence to Protestant churches has remained strong. In the last half-century the once dominant mainline churches (Methodist, Presbyterian, Lutheran, Episcopal, and Congregational), while maintaining large and relatively well-funded denominations, have yielded public space to a multitude of more Evangelical, fundamentalist, Pentecostal, sectarian, Holiness, and independent churches. Careful empirical research suggests that mainline Protestants now make up about 15 percent of the total population, with 26 percent adhering to mostly Caucasian Evangelical or conservative Protestant churches, 9 percent to African American churches, 20 percent to the Catholic Church, 10 percent to other religious groups, and 20 percent functionally unattached.[18] For many years the Southern Baptist Convention, which since 1979 has moved decisively in a more conservative direction, has been the largest Protestant denomination in the country, and one of the largest in the world.[19] A few more details on recent American history are presented below, but from a global perspective it is important to make this point: as American society throughout the twentieth century became more affluent, more modern, and more diverse, it has not followed the European pattern in experiencing a decline in church adherence. Instead, American religion, with sectarian and theologically conservative Protestants in the lead, has adjusted to modern circumstances. The result may be a thinner form of Christianity than present in the strongly Protestant sections of the country a century ago, since it now must compete with many more alternative activities and worldviews. It is also a Christianity that tacitly accepts the fact that education, mass media, the courts, and most governments now take less guidance from the churches than ever before in American history. But by comparison with Europe, there are more people who actively practice Protestant faiths, the vitality of

Protestant churches and voluntary organizations is greater, and the influence of Protestants in public life is much more extensive.

The shift of worldwide influence from Europe to America, which arises as a consequence of contrasting national histories during the twentieth century, can be indicated by examining the ranks of overseas missionary personnel.[20] Of course, much else goes into the exertion of religious influence around the world than just missionary endeavor; in all of recorded history, imperialistic expansion through military or commercial means has regularly paved the way for an expansion of the imperialists' religion as well. But missionary statistics offer one concrete means of charting the direction of global Christian influence.

In 1903 roughly one-fourth of all Protestant missionaries serving outside their home countries were American. Britain's missionary force was probably twice that of the American. By 1972, the proportions were reversed: almost two-thirds of all Protestant missionaries serving overseas were American, and the number of American missionaries was more than five times the number of British missionaries. Significantly, as the American proportion of the worldwide Protestant missionary force increased, so also did the Evangelical proportion rise among American missionaries. Early in the century, mainline denominations contributed the overwhelming majority of all American missionaries; by 1950 the division was about half and half; by the end of the century Evangelical denominations and independent agencies sponsored about 90 percent of the American overseas personnel.

Just as important as the rise of the United States as a missionary-sending country, however, has been the more recent proliferation of missionary-sending nations. Even though the total number of American Protestant missionaries has remained relatively steady since the early 1970s, when the United States contributed about two-thirds of all the Protestants missionaries in the world, by 2001 the United States now sponsored slightly less than half. New Protestant missionaries are as likely to come from Brazil, South Korea, the Philippines, Nigeria, or India as from the United States. Overseas mission work, in other words, has been globalized in the same way that Christianity itself has been globalized. While major missionary-sending bodies like the Southern Baptist Convention, the Churches of Christ, and the Assemblies of God still draw most of their volunteers from the United States, the interdenominational and independent agencies are now much more likely to recruit from outside the United States. Thus, in 2001 less than 10 percent of Campus Crusade for Christ's more than 15,000 international workers were American, less than 20 percent of Youth with a Mission's nearly 12,000 workers, and less than 40 percent of the more than 7,000 missionaries with the Wycliffe Bible Translators.

Statistics for missionary service, as with all other statistics, must be handled cautiously. But the suggested patterns are clear. As Europe has declined as a global Protestant presence, the United States has grown, but now Western Protestantism as a whole is beginning to recede as a worldwide force due to the rapid expansion of Protestant churches in other parts of the globe.

The globalization of Christianity, including Protestant Christianity, is now being recognized as one of the great events of the twentieth century. It is reflected in many striking phenomena. The availability of the Christian scriptures in non-Western languages has burgeoned over the course of the century.[21] In China, where during the Great Proletarian Cultural Revolution of 1966–76 every one of the vast nation's churches was shuttered, the dramatic emergence of Christian groups over the last three decades has been little short of astounding, and that emergence has owed very little to direct Western influence. Indigenous forms of Pentecostal and loosely Protestant faith, which are linked lightly to Western Christianity, if at all, now spread rapidly in many parts of Africa, Latin America, and Oceania.[22]

These sudden changes have dramatically altered the shape of worldwide Protestantism. Yet they make Western Protestant reflection on law, politics, and society more, rather than less, important. Christian civilization, Christian learning, and formal Christian theology—in contrast to numbers of Christian adherents—still remain concentrated in the Western world. Protestants from all over the globe still look to the West for educational guidance. What Western Protestants think about the place of humans in society may have an even greater influence throughout the world than was imaginable when Christians dwelt primarily in the West. Protestants in other parts of the world will never simply accept Western reasoning wholesale, but the deliberations probed in this book are now available to much wider potential audiences than when they were first spoken or published. Karl Barth wrote with Germany, Switzerland, Europe, or the West in view, but he is being read today in Sao Paolo, Manila, and Seoul. John Howard Yoder produced his theology of Christian pacifism as an argument against the assumptions of Western Christendom, but he has the potential now to influence believers in Sudan, Nigeria, India, Indonesia, and other places where violence intrudes into daily life. Recent Protestant reflections on the state of human culture and law in the West have taken place against the backdrop of immense change in the configuration of the world. Because the growth of Christian adherence always brings with it a concern for Christian ethics, Christian political action, and Christian civilization, what Western figures have said on these matters now assumes worldwide significance.

CHURCH HISTORY

The church history, more narrowly conceived, of Europe and North America has always provided an important frame for Protestant reflection on law, politics, and society. What figures as disparate as Susan B. Anthony and Abraham Kuyper at the end of the nineteenth century or Martin Luther King Jr., William Stringfellow, and John Howard Yoder in the last part of the twentieth century wrote about the great issues of human destiny was always affected by the local and national faith communities where their firsthand experiences lay. Those experiences, in turn, were always connected to main developments in the broader ecclesiastical world. A sketch of some of those developments illuminates more of the terrain in which significant Protestant thinking took place on issues of law, politics, and society. In a tumultuous flood of events, people, organizations, and relationships, it is useful to think of Protestant church history in the recent past as experiencing an era of ecumenicity, an era of Catholic engagement, an era of women, an era of the Holy Spirit, and an era of dechristianization.

ECUMENICITY

The World Missionary Conference that was held at Edinburgh in June 1910 represented a landmark in Protestant ecumenical history.[23] Although earlier organizations like the Evangelical Alliance and earlier mission conferences (London 1888, New York 1900) had drawn participants from both Europe and North America, Edinburgh exceeded earlier efforts both in the number of its participants and the extent of its goals. About 1,200 delegates attended the conference, with the great majority from Britain and North America, but also substantial representation from the European continent. (Edinburgh spoke much of Christianity in the non-Western world, but it was the last such major Protestant gathering without substantial non-Western participation.) The conference organizers and those who addressed the gathering expressed the hope that the kind of Christian cooperation that marked many mission fields would catch fire in Protestant homelands as well. Besides the theme of Christian unity, the conference also directed major attention to other matters that would loom large in succeeding decades, including the relationship of churches to governments and the encounter between Christianity and non-Christian religions.

In retrospect, it is evident that the Edinburgh conference represented the high tide of Western missionary expansion. Soon the traumas of World War I would combine with vigorous Christian growth in the non-Western world to end the Western dominance of world Christianity. Yet the positive experience of the conference had a wide-ranging effect on Protestant ecumenicity. Discussions and personal connections begun at Edinburgh carried on and eventually led to the founding of the International Missionary Council (1921) and then less directly to two other significant organizations. The Universal Christian Conference on Life and Work convened for the first time at Stockholm in 1925, and the World Conference on Faith and Order held its inaugural meeting at Lausanne in 1927. The first of these explored ways in which Protestant churches might cooperate on practical social questions, the second pursued consideration of doctrine and practice more directly. These two bodies were the principal motivators leading in 1948 to the creation of the World Council of Churches. Its programs and international meetings went on to provide unprecedented opportunities for dialogue and cooperation among Protestants connected to the older, more traditional denominations, and eventually also to non-Western Protestants linked to these same denominations.

Within the various Western nations, parallel movements drew together increasing numbers for fellowship, discussion, and united action. The ecumenical process went furthest in Canada, where in 1925 a United Church was constructed by the merger of the country's Methodist, Congregational, and a majority of its Presbyterian churches.[24] In its early years the United Church of Canada combined Evangelical and Social Gospel emphases; subsequently it became a champion of liberal theology and liberal social policy. In the United States the National Council of Churches of Christ was founded in 1950 as a successor to a Federal Council of Churches that had been launched early in the century. Through its social services arm, Church World Service, the National Council has promoted development projects in many parts of the world. At home it was the primary sponsor of the Revised Standard Version, a major updating of the King James Bible that has enjoyed great currency in mainline churches. Most of the European countries have also developed cooperative church councils similar in constituency and programs to the American National Council.

Evangelicals, Fundamentalists, Pentecostals, Anabaptists, conservative Lutherans, and most Holiness denominations did not join the National

Council or the World Council, but rather sought partners for fellowship and practical action in bodies like the National Association of Evangelicals (1942) or in agencies, like the Mennonite Central Committee, defined by denominational traditions. To use terms popularized by Ernst Troeltsch at the end of the nineteenth century, "sectarian" bodies have been more reluctant than "churchly" bodies to join broad ecumenical coalitions. But the sectarians have excelled in informal fellowship. As an example, the Lausanne Conference on World Evangelization of 1974, which was sponsored by the Billy Graham Evangelistic Association, drew 2,700 delegates from more countries and more denominations than any other international Protestant meeting ever held to that time. The worldwide travels of Billy Graham, as also similar journeys by the Pentecostal evangelist Oral Roberts and the Anglican Bible expositor John R. W. Stott, have functioned as powerful devices for creating broad networks of conservative Protestant believers.[25]

In whatever shape—formal and conciliar or informal and ad hoc—Protestantism became thoroughly ecumenical over the course of the twentieth century. That process has meant that, although Christian thinkers may speak out of their own distinctive traditions, their voices are increasingly heard by audiences far from home.

CATHOLIC ENGAGEMENT

During the last four decades of the twentieth century, a special ecumenism of a hitherto unthinkable sort exerted a growing influence on world Protantism. This ecumenism concerned the Roman Catholic Church. Since the Reformation of the sixteenth century, Protestants with only a few exceptions had defined themselves over against the Catholics. Well into the twentieth century, the historical antagonism between these two streams of Western Christianity influenced much formal church life and thought in both Europe and North America. This situation began to change as a direct result of the Second Vatican Council (1962–65), which Pope John XXIII convened in order to breathe new life into worldwide Catholicism. The council's treatment of non-Catholic Christians (as well as of non-Christian religions in general) was much gentler than in previous Catholic dispensations, and this visible softening led to a series of official dialogues initiated by the Vatican. These dialogues were, however, only the most visible public signs of many Catholic–Protestant connections, ranging from shared neighborhood Bible studies to high-level theological exchange.

The high point of discussions sparked by Vatican II was the announcement by the Vatican and the Lutheran World Federation in October 1997 that a substantial measure of official agreement had been reached on the doctrine of justification by faith. This crux of the Protestant Reformation had historically been one of the great sticking points with the Catholic Church. Now, however, the joint committee declared that Catholics and Lutherans could agree on two essentials: God redeemed humans freely and only by his grace; redeemed humans properly responded to the reception of God's grace by doing good works. Not all Protestants and not all Catholics were convinced that this joint declaration overcame as much contentious history as its promoters suggested. But by comparison with only a few decades earlier, the degree of agreement (however interpreted) was astounding.

For Protestant deliberations on law, politics, and society, the increasing pace of Protestant–Catholic dialogue is unusually important. Catholic traditions of natural law reasoning, which were developed with particular ability by Thomas Aquinas in the thirteenth century and by modern neo-Thomists in the twentieth century, are now more easily exploited by Protestants. Protestants also look more self-consciously to landmark Catholic statements on society and political responsibility, like Pope Leo XIII's *Rerum Novarum* of 1891 and some of the encyclicals of Pope John Paul II, to find constructive assistance for their own deliberations. Breakthroughs in Catholic–Protestant ecumenism have probably done as much for Protestant reflection on social-political matters as any other significant development of the recent past.

WOMEN

The twentieth century also witnessed a much more comprehensive participation by women in the public life of Protestant churches than was possible during earlier centuries. Women have contributed a majority of members in almost all Christian communions in all times and places, but only in the last period of Western history have women become recognized public leaders. Even before Susan B. Anthony brought resources from her Quaker experience to bear on questions of suffrage and women's rights, women in other sectarian traditions, especially Wesleyan and Holiness churches, had begun to take a more active part in preaching, evangelizing, and organizing church programs. Missionary service enjoyed a long history as a viable platform for such work.[26] The Pentecostal movements that spread so rapidly in the early twentieth century likewise led to further participation by women who felt called by the Holy Spirit to take on public tasks.

Before too many years had passed in the twentieth century, female voices were gaining public recognition as important promoters of Christian faith and practice. As examples, in England the lay Anglican Dorothy L. Sayers (1893–1957) exploited her fame as a writer of detective novels to produce several notable Christian dramas, introduce Dante to wide audiences, and publish articulate expositions of classically Christian orthodoxy. In America, the Methodist deacon Georgia Harkness (1891–1979) became a key participant in early meetings of Life and Work and the World Council of Churches, while her older contemporary, the Baptist scholar, Helen Barrett Montgomery (1861–1934), was a notable promoter of missions as well as an accomplished translator of scripture.[27]

After mid-century, the traditional mainline denominations joined a range of Wesleyan, Holiness, and Pentecostal denominations in beginning to ordain women for the office of pastor.[28] This departure from traditional practice worried, and continues to worry, some confessional and conservative Protestants, and it provided the occasion for a noteworthy exchange between Georgia Harkness and Karl Barth at the first meeting of the World Council of Churches in 1948. But by the end of the century broader public participation by women in church activities throughout the Protestant world had become an accepted fact of religious life.

For thinking about law, politics, and society, the fuller participation of Protestant women has produced overt and subtle effects. Overtly, the range of issues now routinely canvassed has broadened considerably. Books like Jean Bethke Elshtain's *Women and War* (1987) were not unknown in earlier generations, but they became much more common as women began to study and teach in all of the theological institutions and when women were more routinely included as full participants in ecclesiastical councils. More subtly, the public agency of Protestant women has assured that questions of family, procreation, gender, domestic economy, and health care—that is, the range of issues related to practical Christian life in the world—receive attention from more angles and with broader resources of scriptural exegesis and life experience than was the case when men monopolized the public life of the churches.

HOLY SPIRIT

The rise of Pentecostalism and, then later, of charismatic movements has also worked broad and deep changes in Protestant life over the last century.[29] Formally recognized Pentecostalism is usually traced to the revival at Azusa Street in Los Angeles that began in 1906, and particularly to the manifestation there of the sign gift of speaking in tongues. But themes stressing the Holy Spirit, the immediate touch of God for healing or wisdom, and the possibilities for higher levels of consecration had influenced many Christian movements throughout the nineteenth century and earlier.

Pentecostalism remained a curiosity for several decades, with flamboyant, but appealing, preachers like Aimee Semple McPherson and her Angelus Temple in Los Angeles presenting to the public a dramatic picture of healing, spectacle, and media savvy.[30] Soon, however, the development of strong denominations like the mostly black Church of God in Christ and the mostly white Assemblies of God, along with effective mission work at home and abroad, transformed Pentecostal currents into major tributaries of modern Christianity. Pentecostal emphases caught on also in Eastern, Southern, and Western Europe, though never to the same degree as in North America. When, after World War II, Pentecostal and Pentecostal-like churches began to proliferate in the non-Western world, the movement was transformed into a genuinely global force.

In recent decades charismatic impulses within older Protestant denominations, as well as the Catholic Church, have transformed the face of much Christian worship. These impulses owe much to Pentecostalism with their stress on immediate apprehension of the Holy Spirit and a style of worship marked by exuberance, spontaneity, subjective song lyrics, and the exploitation of pop, folk, and soft rock music. Even churches that have not embraced Pentecostal or charismatic principles as such now often reflect in public worship a line of influence that began at Azusa Street.

Pentecostals have not as yet contributed a great deal to reflections on legal, political, or social issues. Yet Protestants who have taken such matters seriously sometimes function as tutors, especially to second and third generation Pentecostals, both in the West and the rest of the world, who want to add meaningful public service to personal and small-group renewal. Since charismatic themes have not loomed large in historic Protestant consideration of law and human nature, the rise of Pentecostalism may point toward an important intellectual challenge. When added to historic Protestant reflections on the work of God the Father and Christ the Son, Pentecostal emphasis on the person and work of the Holy Spirit may push Protestant reflections to a more fully Trinitarian stance on public issues, as well as for more narrowly theological concerns. That, at least, is the potential for systematic social reflection opened up by the dramatic rise of Pentecostal Christianity.

DECHRISTIANIZATION

A final feature of Protestant church history since the late nineteenth century has been the retreat of Protestantism from some parts of Europe and North America where the Protestant churches had once been a dominant cultural presence.[31] It is sobering to realize that the vigorous Protestant constituencies that nourished the thought of, for example, Abraham Kuyper in the Netherlands, Karl Barth in Switzerland, Dietrich Bonhoeffer in Germany, and Reinhold Niebuhr among the elite educational stratum of the American East Coast have all declined precipitously since those landmark thinkers did their work. The Dutch Reformed, Swiss Reformed, German Lutheran, and mainline American Protestant churches that provided the first audiences for these intellectual giants are by no means exhausted, but the commanding position they once enjoyed, and from which prescient observers surveyed the whole of Christendom, have been much reduced.

Dechristianization could come with a rush, as when the Nazis strong-armed German churches to exchange traditional Christianity for a semi-pagan Hitlerism. Much more typically it has arisen from the incremental advance of material, therapeutic, commercial, or entertainment concerns at the expense of historic Christian commitments. In whatever form it has appeared, in most of Protestant Europe and Protestant Canada and in significant sectors of American society, dechristianization poses challenges for the use of Christian thinking, as it does to every other aspect of the Christian religion.

Given this situation, there could be a temptation to treat the proposals of the authors surveyed in this book as voices from an unrecoverable past, as perhaps relevant to their worlds where Christian memories, if not always Christian practice, were firmly embedded in a broad expanse of culture, but now mostly irrelevant since the Christian cultures in and to which they spoke are rapidly passing away. This logic can, however, be met with a counterlogic. If Christian reflections on law, politics, and society were part of a social order in which a certain measure of general Christian vitality could be taken for granted, or at least remembered, then serious attention to that Christian reflection may now be more relevant rather than less. If what has been lost, or is being lost, represented a fully formed Christian civilization in which wellsprings of personal piety watered rivers of vigorous Christian tradition flowing to seas of Christian culture, then critical attention to the proper functioning of Christian cultures may offer a way to recommend personal piety and vigorous Christian tradition, as well as the broader reconsideration of Christian culture that presupposed a measure of spiritual health among persons and in churches. Dechristianization, in other words, may offer students of legal, political, and social principles an unexpected opportunity for evangelism alongside more ordinary tasks of cultural analysis.

The foregoing brief commentary on ecumenism, engagement with Roman Catholics, women, Pentecostals, and dechristianization by no means constitutes an adequate general history of modern Protestantism. What such snapshots do make possible, however, is a sense of the shifting backgrounds against which notable Protestant thinkers and actors did their work.

THEOLOGY

The story of Protestant theology since the end of the nineteenth century lacks the defining plot lines found among the Orthodox and the Catholics. Orthodoxy and Catholicism both feature much theological pluralism. In the Orthodox case, this pluralism comes from different responses to a similar question—how to preserve the practices of traditional faith and the norms of traditional worship midst the tumults of revolution, war, and immigration. In the Catholic case, it comes from differing reactions to a single series of events—what were the effects of neo-Thomist dominance and what happened after neo-Thomism was unsettled in the wake of the Second Vatican Council?

Protestant theology, by contrast, has had a nearly chaotic recent history. A pessimist might suggest that Protestant theology has simply collapsed into a series of "modernisms" defined as Christian glossing for convictions rooted substantially in some other contemporary absolutism. Modernisms on the radical left have included Christianized versions of Marxism, extreme feminism, or nature mysticism; on the more moderate left of inevitable progress and divine-right self-fulfillment; and on the right of American messianism, cantankerous antigovernmentalism, and prophetic apocalypticism. In all cases the "modernism" emerges when Christian reasoning from scripture and broad Christian tradition gives way to reasoning based on some certainty of the contemporary age. Of such "modernisms" there have been no shortage among Protestant groups, large and small, whether in Europe or North America, whether early or late. Adding sting to the pessimist's indictment is the observation that publishers regularly sell many more books promoting these modernist viewpoints than they do in marketing more sober and traditional theological efforts.

A pessimist might likewise want to make the case that the most important events in Protestant theological history since the late nineteenth century have been contentious standoffs testifying to the sterility of Protestant reasoning as a whole. Proof of this assessment would begin with attention to the persistent division between liberals and conservatives, which took one shape in Abraham Kuyper's Netherlands, with strife between confessionalists like Kuyper who rejected the sovereignty of Enlightenment reason and liberals who championed it. That division took another shape in the split between American fundamentalists who insisted on an inerrant Bible interpreted by the canons of static Baconian science versus liberals who insisted on a mythological Bible interpreted by the canons of organic Darwinian science. This indictment could go on to document implacable Protestant struggles on a range of issues related to gender, sexuality, and the family: the use of contraceptives, the ordination of women, the access to abortion, and the right to same sex marriage—all issues on which Protestants have opposed Protestants with determined conviction based on contradictory interpretations of scripture, church tradition, and personal religious experience. Spectacular individual disagreements—with the most spectacular coming in the 1930s with Barth's denial and Emil Brunner's defense of the usefulness of natural revelation for distinctly Christian purposes—could also be multiplied as an indication of the inability of Protestants to promote cohesive and compelling theology.

If this indictment were all that could be said about recent Protestant theology, it would be devastating for commentary on issues of law, politics, and society, since such commentary would be thoroughly compromised by the fragmented incoherence of theological foundations.

In fact, however, much more can be said than that Protestants have regularly battled each other over many conflicted issues and in many venues. A more comprehensive view reveals, not necessarily theological coherence, balance, or completeness, but rather vitality of several sorts and visible in many parts of the Protestant world. The compelling Protestant theologians of the recent past have not spoken with one voice, for differences among Protestant traditions and local differences in working out Protestant practices prevent such cohesion, not to speak of the absence of any universally recognized pope or patriarch who could persuade all Protestants to reason together.

Notwithstanding manifest Protestant diversity, a common approach can be identified for those Protestants who have made the type of enduring theological contribution that provides stable grounding for legal, social, and political analysis. That is, for most of the Protestant figures examined in the chapters that follow, it is possible to discern similar processes at work. These figures were, first, serious about the riches found in scripture. To be sure, their uses of the Bible differed considerably among themselves—from Reinhold Niebuhr's evocation of biblical symbols and Karl Barth's Christocentric hermeneutic to Martin Luther King Jr's tropes of liberation and William Stringfellow's call for radical biblical justice. But all of them were serious Protestant thinkers, only because they were first serious students of the Bible. They were also solidly informed by Christian tradition. Several, including Barth and Dietrich Bonhoeffer, mastered significant aspects of patristic and medieval theology, as well as materials since the Reformation. But all—for instance, Kuyper as a Dutch Calvinist, John Howard Yoder as a committed Anabaptist, King as a beneficiary of African American experiential religion—were given major impetus by a specific tradition of weighty theology. They were, third, also unusually thoughtful about the usefulness of reason and experience to complement their study of scripture and appropriation of tradition, and unlike many of their contemporaries they worked carefully to mold scripture, tradition, reason, and experience into a coherent whole. Barth was the great exemplar in this balancing act, although all of the figures were both broad in their search for theological resources and discriminating in how they put them to use. Finally, they were creative in assessing their contemporary circumstances in light of divine revelation. Kuyper, in his educational and journalistic exposure to conditions in the Netherlands, Barth in his involvement with church politics that led to the Barmen Declaration, Niebuhr through his participation in many debates over public policy, Bonhoeffer in the crises of the Nazi era, King in addressing the realities of civil discrimination, Stringfellow in his demand for justice to the poor and needy in the streets, Yoder as a theologian of peace at the height of the Cold War—all were thinkers deeply immersed in their own times, yet never simply a product of those times. In fact, their ability to do consequential theology depended on securing a standpoint grounded in religious resources from which to address the pressing issues of the day.

Susan B. Anthony presents an exception to this pattern, though Stringfellow emulates her somewhat, since she said what she wanted to say in opposition to what she perceived as the manifest errors of scripture, the ineffectiveness of traditional theological reasoning, and the relative unimportance of systematic thought. Anthony's experience-driven and action-oriented achievements, however, did open a way for other women who in the wake of Anthony's generation of feminist pioneers were able to appropriate for their own purposes the standard repertory of theological procedures that were so powerfully at work among the other notables profiled below.

Kuyper, Barth, Niebuhr, Bonhoeffer, Stringfellow, King, and Yoder were able to offer telling theological reflections about problems in society in large part because of their broader theological achievements. Kuyper skillfully blended elements from traditional Dutch Calvinism and from the populist piety he experienced as a young minister to forge a vision of Reformed faith and life that continues to win eager readers to this day. Barth became the century's most widely read academic theologian because of an even greater skill at enlivening central themes of continental Reformed tradition with his own energetic study of scripture and his own mastery of European philosophical debate. Niebuhr was less interested in the traditional *loci* of theology as such, but the dialectics with which he interpreted events (humanity as sinner and saint, subject to history and shaper of history, egotistical but able to live for others) were effective because they were rooted in classical Christian categories. The trauma of events pushed Bonhoeffer far beyond the standard categories of his inherited Lutheranism, but his theology forged in crisis continues to inspire many throughout the world, again, at least in part because it was so profoundly Lutheran. King took black preaching into the streets and by so doing altered it to suit his purposes, but the worldwide impact of that preaching is unimaginable apart from the rock of African American tradition from which it was hewn. Yoder engaged in the sort of broad-ranging ecumenical dialogue that was quite foreign to his Mennonite heritage, but it was the innovative grasp of that heritage that made Yoder's ecumenical contribution so powerful. In a word, the Protestant figures described in this book testify decisively to the ongoing vigor of Protestant theology.

If this were a comprehensive history of recent Protestantism, the signs of vitality could be multiplied. The Anglican world, despite reverses in its English homeland and a large measure of controversy over what modern Anglicanism should mean, continued to produce theologians distinguished by their immersion in Christian tradition, their sensitivity to scripture, and their responsiveness to the challenges of the hour. Archbishop William Temple (1881–1943), who combined philosophical interests with ecumenical and social advocacy, and Oliver O'Donovan (b. 1945), who has looked to the resurrection of Christ as the key to enduring ethical integrity, are only two of the many who have extended the strength of

Anglican reasoning to the present.[32] Theological vitality of a very different sort arose in the twentieth century from the proclamation of nondenominational classical Christian orthodoxy, or "mere Christianity." The Oxford and Cambridge don, C.S. Lewis (1898–1963), was the great exemplar of this kind of exposition, but there were many other imitators in several other communions.[33] A recovery of measured theology from the ranks of former fundamentalists was also notable development of the recent past. Led by the American educator and editor, Carl F.H. Henry (b. 1913), a growing number of those who had once despised formal learning have made increasingly significant contributions to the recovery of theology.[34] Similar quickening has marked the ranks of some mainline bodies, with the narrative theology of Hans Frei (1922–88) and George Lindbeck (b. 1923) among the most notable examples.[35] Thinkers out of France, Switzerland, and especially Germany made an especially notable contribution to the recovery of moral and theological balance amid the devastations of a traumatic century. Such ones include Oscar Cullmann (1902–99), with discerning biblical reflection on the "powers" in their ancient and contemporary manifestation;[36] Emil Brunner (1889–1966), with special attention to God's concern for all of life;[37] Jürgen Moltmann (b. 1926), with concern for how hope in evil days may grow from the central biblical narrative;[38] and Wolfhart Pannenberg (b. 1928), with wide-ranging arguments for the pertinence of the biblical narrative for modern science, modern historical understanding, and much else.[39]

Protestant theology has passed through many difficulties in the recent past; it is all but impossible to overstate the amount of theological negligence or the degree of theological irresponsibility manifest among Protestants since the end of the nineteenth century. But along with much dross has appeared as well much depth. That theological depth, which is represented so well by the figures in this Protestant section of the volume, has meant that when Christian thinkers turned to questions of law and human nature, they had something to say.

REFLECTIONS ON LAW, POLITICS, AND SOCIETY

The main legal, political, and social subjects of interest to significant Protestant thinkers are well explored in the chapters that follow. Reflecting the multivalent character of Protestantism itself, these subjects range widely. If they do not focus as comprehensively on issues of community or social solidarity as Catholic thinkers have done, they nonetheless offer a great deal on a wide array of critically important subjects.

The positive regard for the state, as an institution created by God and intended by God for the flourishing of all people, was a strong theme in Abraham Kuyper's groundbreaking practical labor, as well as in what he wrote. Yet Kuyper's picture of "sphere sovereignty" also provided for significant checks on the power of any state that would overstep the boundaries that were also set by God. The result was a vision of political responsibility that has encouraged many, especially Reformed Christians, in many parts of the world, to contend for a properly functioning state within God-ordained limits as a distinctly Christian good. Dietrich Bonhoeffer's reasoning about the Christian's obligation to the state took a very different course, but ended with similarly profound insights about the potential (for good and for ill) of the state.

Karl Barth and Reinhold Niebuhr are among the most important twentieth-century voices to make arguments of similar force respecting the virtues of democracy and the rule of law. Neither was blithely optimistic about the workings of a democratic polity, for they regarded democratic structures as just as susceptible to ordinary failings as any other human institution. Yet, with unusual clarity, Barth and Niebuhr were able to highlight the important advantages of democracy as, among possible political systems, preserving important elements of what God had provided for the flourishing of human society. Barth's commitment to democracy and his wariness of political abuse from unchecked power fed directly into his lifelong commitment to socialism. Niebuhr was eventually weaned from earlier socialist convictions, but never from a commitment to democracy as a gift from God.

The power of God-ordained action to reform degenerate or evil social structures may be the most widely shared product of Protestant thinking during recent decades. In this sense, at least some Protestants have retained a proclivity for the type of witness that originally brought the Protestant churches into existence. Susan B. Anthony thought that she could find in purified Christian tradition, as well as more general experience rightly apprehended, an engine for reducing the evils of patriarchy and offering liberation for women. Kuyper felt that living Calvinism, rightly understood, could rectify injustices of Dutch education and society. The basis of Niebuhr's realism was the use of Christian resources, rightly interpreted, to encourage a measured, incremental, but determined push for justice. Stringfellow took the basic biblical themes of the incarnation, crucifixion, and resurrection, and classic Protestant doctrines of worship, vocation, and law-gospel directly into his efforts to reform the laws of the state, particularly on subjects of war, poverty, and social justice. Yoder thought he possessed in wisdom from the marginalized communities of the Anabaptists exactly the tonic that the violence-ravaged world needed as an alternative to tearing itself apart. Supremely, King knew how to combine basic Christian principles with the professed ideals of the United States in order to stimulate a long-overdue attention to civil rights, first for African Americans but soon by extension for many others in the world as well. Much Protestant effort has always gone into protecting the status quo of rights, privileges, and property of Protestants themselves. But at their most attractive, Protestant insights have also provided a great impetus for altruistic reform.

The Protestant appeal for reform draws attention to one major Protestant figure who is not profiled in this book. Walter Rauschenbusch (1861–1918) was a German American who served for eleven years as a pastor during an age of uncontrolled industrialization in one of the most squalid sections of New York City.[40] That experience drove him to rethink the theology he had been taught in the United States and Germany, to study the scriptures afresh, and to cultivate contacts with others who worried about the degradation left behind by runaway laissez-faire industrial capitalism. The result was a landmark book from 1907, *Christianity and the Social Crisis*, as well as a number of other significant publications in the years that followed. Drawing inspiration from the biblical concept of the Kingdom of God, Rauschenbusch appealed for progressive, democratic reform guided by the spirit of Christ. The start of World War I sobered Rauschenbusch and led him to place greater stress on the reality of sin and the need for an active divine presence in the world. But in both early and later periods of his life, Rauschenbusch's understanding of the "Social Gospel" represented a powerful Protestant response to the rapidly changing conditions of urban modernity. The significance of his work is indicated by the fact that it has inspired many later thinkers and reformers, including Reinhold Niebuhr and Martin Luther King Jr.

The theological resources that these Protestant thinkers brought to their tasks were drawn from the standard array of classical Christian tradition, but with a few particular emphases. As explained in greater detail in the chapter by Davison Douglas below, Niebuhr found in Augustine's depictions of sin and human nature a subtle, complex, and conflicted understanding of humanity that matched the subtle, complex, and conflicted circumstances of modern society. Barth and Bonhoeffer in their different ways were, if anything, more fundamentally shaped by the assertions of the Chalcedonian definition about Jesus as fully God and fully human in one perfectly integrated person. Yoder made equal capital from the Anabaptist conviction that the New Testament presented the church as an alternative community standing over against the world in judgment and love.

The use of such theological resources for social and political analysis was never harmonious. Barth and Yoder, for example, were much less sanguine about the prospect of finding universal natural law in scripture and general human experience than was, for example, Kuyper with his considerable confidence in what God had generously bestowed on all peoples by "common grace." Yet those with patience to examine such differences over how best to use the resources of Christian tradition receive the greatest heuristic benefit from studying these thinkers with care.

At the start of the twenty-first century, religion is more obviously alive as a public force—in the West, as well as the rest of the world—than it has ever been in living memory. International politics is once again fixated on conflicts involving Christians, Muslims, and Jews. The European Union, itself to all appearances the product of strictly secular developments, has paused to deliberate at some length on whether to include mention of God in its new constitution. In several European countries authorities are shaken by the sudden appearance of large Christian congregations made up of Caribbean and African believers. In more European countries, there is even more consternation resulting from the rising tide of Muslim citizens and immigrants. In the United States, controversy swirls around the display of the Ten Commandments in public space, the phrase "under God" in the Pledge of Allegiance, and the use of governmental funding for social services operated by religious organizations. In Canada, federal proposals to legitimate same-sex marriage on the same basis as male-female marriage have elicited the kind of religiously inspired tumult that Canadians have long prided themselves as avoiding.

In the midst of such unusual attention to religion and public life the great need for both religious communities and the public at large is for solidly grounded argument that might be as persuasive in its claims as it is humane in its purposes. The chapters that follow offer by no means the only sources for such argument. But their accounts of serious Protestant wrestling with momentous issues concerning persons, societies, law, and politics deserve to be taken seriously indeed. Among many other things, they are a timely Protestant gift from the past to the present.

NOTES

1. A good general survey from an earlier generation is Martin E. Marty, *Protestantism: Its Churches and Cultures, Rituals and Doctrines, Yesterday and Today* (New York: Holt, Rinehart and Winston, 1972).

2. David Barrett et al., *World Christian Encyclopedia*, 2d ed., 2 vols. (New York: Oxford University Press, 2001), 1:16.

3. Ibid., 836–837.

4. Paul Freston, *Evangelicals and Politics in Asia, Africa and Latin America* (New York: Cambridge University Press, 2001).

5. Outstanding overviews are found in Hugh McLeod, ed., *European Religion in the Age of Great Cities, 1830–1930* (London: Routledge, 1995), and *Secularization in Western Europe, 1848–1914* (New York: St. Martin's, 2000).

6. Edwin Scott Gaustad and Philip L. Barlow, *New Historical Atlas of Religion in America* (New York: Oxford University Press, 2001), 401.

7. For the continuing effects of this singular situation, see Michael O. Emerson and Christian Smith, *Divided by Race: Evangelical Religion and the Problem of Race in America* (New York: Oxford University Press, 2000).

8. Alexis de Tocqueville, *Democracy in America*, ed. Harvey Claflin Mansfield and Delba Winthrop (Chicago: University of Chicago Press, 2000), 278.

9. See Mark A. Noll, *America's God, from Jonathan Edwards to Abraham Lincoln* (New York: Oxford University Press, 2002), 367–437.

10. See Henry F. May, *Protestant Churches and Industrial America* (New York: Harper, 1949); Paul Carter, *The Spiritual Crisis of the Gilded Age* (DeKalb: Northern Illinois University Press, 1971).

11. A solid survey is Robert Handy, *Undermined Establishment: Church-State Relations in America, 1880–1920* (Princeton, N.J.: Princeton University Press, 1991).

12. Outstanding are John Webster Grant, *A Profusion of Spires: Religion in Nineteenth-Century Ontario* (Toronto: University of Toronto Press, 1988), and *The Church in the Canadian Era*, 2d ed. (Burlington, Ontario: Welch, 1988).

13. Daniel H. Bays, "Chinese Protestant Christianity Today," *China Quarterly* 174 (June 2003): 489–504.

14. See R.C.D. Jasper, *George Bell, Bishop of Chichester* (New York: Oxford University Press, 1967); Philip Paul Hallie, *Lest Innocent Blood Be Shed: The Story of the Village of Le Chambon, and How Goodness Happened There* (New York: Harper & Row, 1979); and Helmut Thielicke, *Notes from a Wayfarer: The Autobiography of Helmut Thielicke* (New York: Paragon House, 1995).

15. Expert guidance is provided in a series of books by Reginald W. Bibby, including *Fragmented Gods: The Poverty and Potential of Religion in Canada* (Toronto: Irwin, 1987) and *Restless Gods: The Renaissance of Religion in Canada* (Toronto: Stoddard, 2002).

16. George Egerton, "Entering the Age of Human Rights: Religion, Politics, and Canadian Liberalism, 1945–1950," paper delivered at the Anglo-American Conference of Historians, University of London, 2000.

17. "The Constitution Act, 1982," in *Canada and the New Constitution*, ed. S.M. Beck and I. Bernier, 2 vols. (Montreal: Institute for Research on Public Policy, 1982), 2:253.

18. A summary may be found in Mark A. Noll, *The Old Religion in a New World: The History of North American Christianity* (Grand Rapids, Mich.: Eerdmans, 2002), 288–290, which draws heavily on the work of political scientists John Green, James Guth, Lyman Kellstedt, and Corwin Smidt.

19. On the leaders who engineered the conservative change, see Barry Hankins, *Uneasy in Babylon: Southern Baptist Conservatives and American Culture* (Tuscaloosa: University of Alabama Press, 2002).

20. The following comparisons are drawn from information provided in Harlan P. Beach and Charles H. Fahs, *World Missionary Atlas* (New York: Institute of Social and Religious Research, 1925), 76; Joel A. Carpenter, "Appendix: The Evangelical Missionary Force in the 1930s," in *Earthen Vessels: American Evangelicals and Foreign Missions, 1880–1980*, ed. Joel A. Carpenter and Wilbert R. Shenk (Grand Rapids, Mich.: Eerdmans, 1990), 335–342; Edward R. Dayton, ed., *Mission Handbook 1973* (Monrovia, Calif.: MARC, 1973); A. Scott Moreau, "Putting the Survey in Perspective," in *Mission Handbook 2001–2003*, ed. John A. Siewert and Dotsey Wellner, 18th ed. (Wheaton, Ill.: EMIS, 2001), 33–79; and Patrick Johnstone and Jason Mandryk, *Operation World* (Carlisle, England: Paternoster, 2001).

21. Lamin Sanneh, *Translating the Message* (Maryknoll, N.Y.: Orbis Books, 1989).

22. For implications, see Andrew Walls, *The Missionary Movement in Christian History* (Maryknoll, N.Y.: Orbis Books, 1996); Walls, *The Cross-Cultural Process in Christian History* (Maryknoll, N.Y.: Orbis Books, 2002); and David Martin, *Pentecostalism: The World Their Parish* (Oxford: Blackwell, 2002).

23. For orientation, see Brian Stanley, "Twentieth-Century World Christianity: A Perspective from the History of Missions," in *Christianity Reborn: The Global Expansion of Evangelicalism in the Twentieth Century*, ed. Donald M. Lewis, (Grand Rapids, Mich.: Eerdmans, 1998), 52–83.

24. An outstanding study is N. Keith Clifford, *The Resistance to Church Union in Canada, 1904–1939* (Vancouver: University of British Columbia Press, 1985).

25. Works stressing these worldwide connections include David Edwin Harrell, *Oral Roberts: An American Life* (Bloomington: Indiana University Press, 1985); Billy Graham, *Just As I Am: The Autobiography of Billy Graham* (San Francisco: HarperCollins, 1997); and Timothy Dudley-Smith, *John Stott*, 2 vols. (Leicester, England: Inter-Varsity Press, 1999–2001).

26. Dana Robert, *American Women in Mission* (Macon, Ga.: Mercer University Press, 1996).

27. Barbara Reynolds, *Dorothy L. Sayers: Her Life and Soul* (New York: St. Martin's, 1993); Georgia Harkness, *Grace Abounding* (Nashville, Tenn.: Abingdon Press, 1969); H. B. Montgomery, *Helen Barrett Montgomery: From Campus to World Citizenship* (New York: Revell, 1940).

28. Mark Chaves, *Ordaining Women: Culture and Conflict in Religious Organizations* (Cambridge, Mass.: Harvard University Press, 1997).

29. Grant Wacker, *Heaven Below: Early Pentecostals and American Culture* (Cambridge, Mass.: Harvard University Press, 2001); Vinson Synan, *The Century of the Holy Spirit* (Nashville, Tenn.: Thomas Nelson, 2001).

30. Edith Blumhofer, *Aimee Semple McPherson: Everybody's Sister* (Grand Rapids, Mich.: Eerdmans, 1993).

31. Hugh McLeod, *Religion and the People of Western Europe, 1789–1989*, 2d ed. (New York: Oxford University Press, 1997); Grace Davie, *Religion in Britain Since 1945: Believing Without Belonging* (Oxford: Blackwell, 1994).

32. See, e.g., William Temple, *Nature, Man and God* (London: Macmillan, 1934); Oliver O'Donovan, *Resurrection and Moral Order* (Grand Rapids, Mich.: Eerdmans, 1986).

33. C. S. Lewis, *Mere Christianity: The Case for Christianity, Christian Behavior, and Beyond Personality* (New York: Macmillan, 1952).

34. Carl F. H. Henry, *Confessions of a Theologian: An Autobiography* (Waco, Tex.: Word, 1986).

35. Hans W. Frei, *The Eclipse of Biblical Narrative* (New Haven, Conn.: Yale University Press, 1974); George A. Lindbeck, *The Nature of Doctrine* (Philadelphia: Westminster, 1984).

36. Oscar Cullmann, *Christ and Time* (London: SCM, 1951).

37. Emil Brunner, *Christianity and Civilisation* (London: Nisbet, 1948).

38. Jürgen Moltmann, *Theology of Hope: On the Ground and the Implications of a Christian Theology*, trans. James W. Leitch (New York: Harper & Row, 1967); Moltmann, *The Crucified God: The Cross as the Foundation and Criticism of Christian Theology*, trans. R. A. Wilson and John Bowden (New York: Harper & Row, 1974).

39. Wolfhart Pannenberg, *Systematic Theology*, trans. Geoffrey W. Bromiley, 3 vols. (Grand Rapids, Mich.: Eerdmans, 1991–98).

40. See Paul M. Minus, *Walter Rauschenbusch, American Reformer* (New York: Macmillan, 1988); and Robert T. Handy, ed., *The Social Gospel in America, 1870–1920* (New York: Oxford University Press, 1966).

[CHAPTER 1]

Abraham Kuyper (1837–1920)

COMMENTARY

NICHOLAS P. WOLTERSTORFF

Abraham Kuyper was born in Maassluis, near Rotterdam, in 1837 to a Dutch Reformed minister and a former schoolteacher; he died at The Hague in 1920. He was an astonishing polymath and an organizational genius. He was originally an ordained minister in the Dutch Reformed Church; in 1892, he became one of the founders of a new denomination, the Gereformeerde Kerken in Nederland. He was the founder of a nationwide society to promote the formation and funding of Calvinist day schools (1878), the founder of the Free University of Amsterdam (1880), a professor of theology in the Free University for some twenty years (1880–1901), and rector of the university on several occasions. He was the chief editor for almost fifty years of the daily newspaper *De Standaard* and of its weekly supplement, *De Heraut*. He was the founder (1879) and acknowledged leader until his death of the first mass political party in the Netherlands, the Anti-Revolutionary Party. He twice served as a member of the Dutch Parliament and was prime minister of the Netherlands from 1901 to 1905. In addition to all this he was, throughout his adult life, a writer of devotional literature, of theological treatises, of social and cultural analyses, and of an astonishing number of "tracts for the occasion," as well as being an extraordinarily gifted and busy platform speaker and lecturer.

He was a polymath, but by no means a dilettante. In all that he did, diverse though it was, Kuyper was a religious leader, albeit of an unusual sort. In the course of his theological studies at the University of Leiden (1855–63), Kuyper studied the classics of the Reformed (Calvinist) tradition and wrote a dissertation on Calvin and the Polish reformer John à Lasco. Simultaneously, he became enamored with the theological modernism of some of his professors. That got him into trouble during his first pastorate, in the small country village of Beesd in the southern part of the Netherlands. A number of devout parishioners refused to attend services because his modernism offended their orthodox Calvinist theological convictions. Rather than simply ignore these "malcontents," Kuyper called on them and listened to their complaints. He was fascinated. Here "was more than mere routine. Here was conviction. Here the topics of conversation went beyond the nice weather and who happened to be ill and who had dismissed his workman. Here was interest in spiritual matters." The eventual effect was that Kuyper was jolted out of his theological modernism and moved to embrace the same Calvinist tradition that inspired his orthodox parishioners.[1]

His embrace was an embrace with a difference, however. Here already, at the beginning of his career, was manifested what would become an endemic habit of mind—the habit, namely, of digging beneath the surface of whatever religious, social, cultural, or intellectual development he was dealing with to discover its fundamental principles. Thus, he committed himself not to the particular form of theologically conservative Calvinism that he found among his critics in Beesd, but to the "essence" of the Calvinist tradition, to the "Reformed ground-principles," as he would later call them.

At this point, Kuyper made an imaginative and fateful move. Though doctrine, piety, and familiarity with the Bible seem to have been prominent in the minds of his discontented parishioners in Beesd, the young Kuyper concluded that the essence of the authentic Calvinist tradition was not so much a body of theological doctrine as a certain *Weltanschauung*, a world-and-life view—in Dutch, a *wereldbeschouwing*. Calvinism is a world-and-life view in competition with other such views. Throughout his career Kuyper would be opposed by theological conservatives who disputed this worldview-construal of the Calvinist tradition.[2]

In 1867, when Kuyper left his pastorate in Beesd, his religious identity was firmly formed and would not change to any significant degree thereafter. Already upon arriving in Beesd, he said: "I longed with all my soul for a sanctified Church wherein my soul and those of my loved ones can enjoy the quiet refreshment of peace, far from all confusion, under its firm, lasting, and authoritative guidance."[3] His experience with the "malcontents" in Beesd gave form to this longing; it was for the orthodox Calvinist tradition and understanding of the church that he now labored. He embraced with all his heart what he understood to be the world-and-life view of historic Calvinism. He sang its praises whenever the occasion arose and attributed all manner of good things to its influence, and he committed himself passionately to its revivification in the Netherlands.

He soon came to believe that this *Weltanschauung* remained alive in a good many of the laypeople of the Reformed churches in the Netherlands—the "small people," *kleine luyden*, as he called them.[4] Or, if it was not actually alive, Kuyper believed that it could be stirred to life. He also soon came to believe, however, that in all sorts of ways those with power in church and state made it difficult if not impossible for these traditionally Calvinist laypeople to live out their Calvinist world-and-life view in the modern world. They were inhibited and oppressed. It was these convictions that gave specific form to Kuyper's religious leadership.

Because it has become a shopworn phrase, one hesitates to call the movement Kuyper initiated and led a "liberation movement." Yet, undeniably, that is what it was.[5] It was a movement to secure for these Calvinist laypeople the social, political, and ecclesiastical space necessary for the free exercise of their religion. Given Kuyper's understanding of the character of their religion—not just theological convictions but a "comprehensive perspective," to use John Rawls's phrase—what was required was not just the relatively narrow space necessary for freedom of conscience and worship, but the much broader space necessary for them to live out their world-and-life view.[6] Hence it was that Kuyper's religious leadership required action on such a dizzying variety of fronts.

Not just action was required, but theory—descriptive and normative analysis. Kuyper did not regard the infringement by the power elite of church and state on the religious free exercise of the traditionally Calvinist laypeople of the Netherlands as a matter of mere happenstance. Nor did he regard it as the consequence merely of ill will on the part of the elite, although he both discerned, and by his often aggressive polemics and determined organizational activities provoked, a great deal of it. He thought the oppression was ultimately the consequence of mistaken understandings of society, religion, and religion's place in society. If his liberation program was to succeed, he had to develop a critique of those mistaken understandings and to articulate alternatives.[7]

It was for this reason that he developed his theories of sphere sovereignty and of the pluralist society, which we will examine to discover his theological account of human nature and the legal theories that, he argued, were not his own invention but simply the articulation of strands of thought deep in the Calvinist world-and-life view.

It was not in the serenity of the scholar's study that Kuyper developed the analyses that we shall be considering, but in the hurly-burly of leading a liberation movement. An implication is that Kuyper's articulation of his views rather often fails to measure up to the standards of development and rigor of the present-day academy. Kuyper was an intuitive genius given to a passionate and flowery baroque sort of rhetoric; he had neither time nor inclination for careful, rigorous, detailed, methodical articulation. Nor indeed was that what the occasion called for. So when interpreting him, one often has to look around and past the details of exposition so as to discern what he was getting at, rather than engaging in close exegesis.

The sociopolitical vision that Kuyper developed has proven to be the most influential appropriation and elaboration of the sociopolitical dimension of the Calvinist tradition in the past two centuries. Kuyper's closest competitor for such influence is probably Karl Barth, but Barth's influence has mainly been among academics. Partly because Kuyper was not just a theorist but an activist who tried to implement his theories, partly because he wrote regularly in the popular press and spoke regularly in the public arena, partly because he offered concrete analyses of modern society and its dynamics, and partly because his views often have obvious and direct implications for social and political action, Kuyper's influence has proven far more widespread than Barth's. It has gripped the imagination of readers of many sorts in many different places on the globe.

HISTORICAL CONTEXT AND CAREER

Already, in my attempt to describe what sort of religious leader Kuyper was, some of the details of his life and circumstances have come to light. But more must be said on both counts if we are fully to understand his thought.

The French Revolution represented for Kuyper—and for many others, of course—a watershed in European history.[8] Kuyper's horror at the Revolution constituted an ever-present background to his thought. Though the name of the political party that he founded, the Anti-Revolutionary Party, was no doubt meant to express opposition to revolution in general, for him and his followers the paradigmatic example of the sort of revolution to which they were opposed was the French Revolution.

The French Revolution represented at least four great evils for Kuyper. First and foremost, it represented aggressive atheism. Kuyper believed with all his heart that we must expect something like the French Revolution to happen when political power falls into the hands of militant atheists, hostile to religion, who believe that there is no transcendent source of authority by which our actions are to be measured. Second, it represented rampant individualism. Instead of seeing individuals as inescapably members of social formations that in good measure determine their identity and provide the conditions for their flourishing, the revolutionaries tended to see society as composed of individuals whose equal freedom to act as they see fit is of paramount importance. In this view, social formations are created by compact among sovereign individuals for utilitarian considerations. Third, the French Revolution represented the destruction of civil society; the totalitarian regime of the state replaced society's multiple, dispersed loci of authority and claimed that all authority belongs ultimately to the state. Lastly, it represented for Kuyper the triumph of abstract reason. Rather than honor the organic unfolding of society, the leaders of the French Revolution reasoned their way to what they thought would be a better social order and then set about implementing their plans.

The abstract/organic contrast captures the last of these four aspects of what, in Kuyper's view, went wrong with the French Revolution. In fact, one regularly finds him using the contrast to characterize each of the last three aspects. A descriptive and normative understanding of society as organic in its structure and functioning will recognize that individuals are at least as much shaped by social formations as such formations are formed by them, and that that is how it must be. Such an understanding will recognize that a healthy social order requires a thick and rich civil society whose diverse loci of authority are not derived from the state but instead require the state's protection; and it will be suspicious of all rational centralized planning, especially of centralized planning that does not take due account of the actualities of how a society has developed. The great evil of the French Revolution, apart from its aggressive atheism, was that it thought abstractly rather than organically about society, thus failing to recognize society as the organic entity that it is and refusing to allow it to be the organic entity that it should be.[9]

It has often been charged that Kuyper's own reform program was itself highly rational and ideological. Though adamantly opposed to revolution, nonetheless Kuyper himself, so it is said, rode roughshod over the traditional Dutch way of doing things in favor of a rationally determined better way. It is true that Kuyper did not share the social conservatism characteristic of many Romantics; Kuyper was not a Dutch Edmund Burke. Nonetheless, Kuyper would have insisted that he was not promoting some rational plan for Dutch society. Rather, convinced as he was that the organic development of life in the Netherlands, especially the religious life of the *kleine luyden* of whom he was the leader, was stifled and inhibited by rules and laws laid down without the consent of the people by the elite of state and church, he, Kuyper, was struggling for the elimination of those inhibiting rules and laws. Kuyper had the better of this argument.

Kuyper's liberation movement took several directions. By the beginning of the nineteenth century, the glorious days of the Dutch Republic of the seventeenth century were but a distant memory. Poverty was widespread. And though Napoleon was gone, replaced for the first time in the history of the Lowlands by a king (William I, r. 1813–40), whatever hopes there might have been of restored political glory were dashed by the loss in 1830 of what became Belgium. Religious unrest was widespread. In 1816, William reorganized the governance of the Dutch Reformed Church (Nederlandse Hervormde Kerk) so as to bring church affairs under the direct regulation of the state. This action by itself created unrest. When the state later imposed new liturgical regulations while at the same time doing nothing to halt the spread of theological liberalism in pulpits and theological faculties, the unrest increased until there was a rupture (*Afscheiding*) in 1834, and a separate free church was formed.

Under the leadership of Johan R. Thorbecke, a constitution was put in place in 1848 whereby the government became a constitutional monarchy, sovereignty being divided between the monarch and a newly formed parliament, divided into one chamber representing the provinces and another directly elected by the people. The Constitution evoked protests from some conservatives, but nothing like those that arose when Thorbecke succeeded in severely limiting the scope of the franchise by the device of imposing a tax on voters, and when, in April 1853, he proposed allowing the reintroduction of the Catholic hierarchy into the Netherlands. The Protestant populace exploded in protest against this last move—ineffective protest, as it turned out, since the archbishop did return to Utrecht.

The decade of the 1860s, when Kuyper concluded his university training and entered the pastorate, was, on the account of some historians, "the most decisive of modern Dutch history."[10] In his edition of Kuyper's selected writings, James Bratt observes,

> Politically, "the half-way solutions, the policy of adaptation, evasion, and delay practised by the 'higher classes,' the blurring of issues by the moderates, these were no longer acceptable." Internationally, colonial questions regarding the Netherlands Indies spelled trouble at a distance; the unification of Germany and Italy raised threats nearby. Industrialization would finally begin at the end of the decade and with it a rapid process of differentiation that multiplied the number of interest groups and voluntary associations in society. Custom and local hierarchy broke down as the orbit of life and mode of control, inviting new grids to replace them. . . . In 1867 regulations for church elections were altered so that consistories

(congregational boards) would no longer be self-perpetuating but subject to congregational vote. In 1868 the long-standing parliamentary coalition between Liberals and Catholics broke up, the latter's gratitude for 1853 no longer compensating for the former's secular agenda. In 1869 the first Radical-Liberal was elected to the Second Chamber and the Conservative caucus entered its years of dissolution. If things were pliable in church and state, the reduction of statutory and economic restrictions on voluntary associations and the popular press supplied new tools for the right sculptor.[11]

Kuyper correctly discerned that the new church law represented an opportunity to break the control of the ecclesiastical elite. He began his public career with an 1867 pamphlet urging laypeople to use the new law to get orthodox Calvinists elected to church office. That same year he left Beesd for a pastorate in Utrecht. Here he spoke and wrote forcefully in favor of retaining the traditional creeds of the Dutch Reformed Church, thereby stirring up the opposition of a number of leading theologians and ministers. He also entered the fray concerning the school system by arguing that state schooling could not possibly be neutral and that, accordingly, Christians should have the freedom to establish confessionally based schools independent of the state system. He was severely disappointed by the fact that, though he saw himself as fighting for Calvinist orthodoxy, the conservative clergy in Utrecht refused to support him. Thus when a call came in 1870 to a pastorate in Amsterdam, he accepted.

His farewell sermon in Utrecht was a blast against a pattern of thought he called "killing conservatism." Authentic Christianity cannot "refrain from raging against a false conservatism which seeks to dam up the stream of life, swears by the status quo, and resists the surgery needed to save the sick."[12] The conservatives want to repristinate, but "*repristination* is an undertaking that is self-condemned."[13] If you wish to honor your forebears, as you should, "first seek to have for yourself the life your fathers had and then hold fast what you have. Then articulate that life in your own language as they did in theirs. Struggle as they did to pump that life into the arteries of the life of our church and society."[14] "It is our calling to hold fast what we have in Christ *in our own time*, not in theirs, and so it is from our own time that we must take the material with which to prepare that form today."[15]

A year after arriving in Amsterdam, Kuyper, in order to advance the cause that he now saw lying before him, became chief editor of the weekly religious periodical *De Heraut*. The next year, in 1871, he founded and became chief editor of the daily newspaper *De Standaard*. (*De Heraut* soon became a weekly supplement of *De Standaard*.) In these papers he published hundreds of articles on a wide variety of religious, social, political, cultural, and educational issues.

In 1874 he presented himself as a candidate in a by-election for the lower house of Parliament and was elected by a comfortable majority. As required by law, he resigned from clerical orders. By no means did he see that resignation as meaning that he was choosing no longer to be a religious leader; rather, he would now be giving that leadership from a different location.

He used his first full parliamentary address to pick up the school cause that he had joined in Utrecht. He argued that though it was the responsibility of the federal government to set general standards for lower school education, that education itself should not be a function of the state but of independent boards and societies, and that all parents should have the right to send their children to schools where the education offered was in accord with their own worldview. The speech stirred up a vigorous defense of the state monopoly in education, to which Kuyper replied with charges of "state absolutism" and "liberalistic despotism." In 1877 he resigned his seat in Parliament to concentrate on his editorship of *De Standaard*, which he had interrupted for about a year on account of a nervous breakdown.

In 1878 the school question broke out once again when the prime minister (from the Liberal caucus) introduced a bill that required a wide range of educational reforms and stipulated that whereas the federal government would pay for the cost of these reforms in the state schools, independent schools would have to pay for the cost on their own. In the interim between the time that Parliament passed the bill and the king (Willem III) was to sign it, Kuyper, along with Catholic leaders, organized a huge petition-signing campaign urging the king to reject the bill; altogether some 469,000 signatures were collected (at a time when only 122,000 people enjoyed the franchise). The petition was presented to the king in August 1878. The king had made it clear that Kuyper would not be welcome in the delegation; two weeks later the king signed the bill.

In January 1879, building on the enthusiasm evoked by the petition-signing campaign, Kuyper and his followers established a national organization to promote the formation and funding of independent Christian schools; and in April of that same year, they established the Anti-Revolutionary Party, which, as mentioned earlier, was the first mass political party in the Netherlands. Previously there had been little more than caucuses and factions.

Action was simultaneously taking place on the front of university education. In 1876 Parliament had passed a bill, at the instigation of a conservative member of Parliament, reaffirming the principle of educational freedom stipulated in the 1848 Constitution and making it somewhat easier for nonstate institutions of higher education to be formed. Kuyper seized the opportunity offered. In 1878 he was instrumental in establishing the Society for Higher Education on the Basis of Reformed Principles. In June 1879 the Society elected directors and a board of trustees; in September they appointed Kuyper and F. L. Rutgers to chairs in theology; and in October 1880 the Free University of Amsterdam officially opened with a ceremony in the venerable New Church in Amsterdam. Kuyper, as the new university's first Rector Magnificus, gave as his inaugural address the now-famous "Sovereignty Within Its Own Sphere" ("Souvereiniteit in Eigen Kring").

Kuyper retained his positions as leader of the Anti-Revolutionary Party and chief editor of *De Standaard* and *De Heraut* while serving as professor of theology. In his position as party leader, he argued vigorously that the ARP should cooperate in Parliament with the Catholic caucus, a position that many of his followers found hard to swallow given their long-standing antipapalism. Nonetheless, Kuyper's position became official ARP policy at its convention in 1887; and in the general election of 1888, the Anti-Revolutionary Party and the Catholics together won a majority of seats in Parliament, enabling them to form a coalition cabinet. A bill on primary education was shortly introduced and passed, making possible for the first time the partial subsidy of nonstate schools, whether religiously oriented or not. (In 1917 full subsidy was finally granted, thereby laying to rest "the school question" that had so long agitated Dutch politics.)

Two other aspects of Kuyper's political thought and action should be mentioned before we conclude this background and biographical sketch. As might be expected, Kuyper was vigorously in favor of extending the franchise beyond those few well-to-do males who, on Thorbecke's proposal, could afford to vote. Kuyper's struggle to break the power of the political and ecclesiastical elites and to liberate and empower the Reformed little people (*kleine luyden*) to live out their Calvinistic worldview in the various spheres (*kringen*) of society naturally required that they be allowed to choose their own political leaders. It was Kuyper's view that the same should be the case for the other members of Dutch society—Catholics, Lutherans, secular socialists, libertarians, whomever. As we shall see in some detail later, it was an important plank in Kuyper's Calvinistic-Christian view of society that Christians are not to have special political privileges; for example, religious qualifications are not to be attached to the franchise.

On the other hand, Kuyper was also opposed to a one person, one vote extension of the franchise; that smacked to him of the individualism born of the Enlightenment and come to maturity in the calamity of the French Revolution. The proper unit of the franchise is not the individual person but the household. If there is a male head of the household, then that person should cast the vote; if the head of the household is a woman—a widow, say—then she would cast the vote. When in 1893 a Liberal member of Parliament introduced a bill proposing universal male suffrage, Kuyper, against strong opposition within his own party, came out in favor of the bill on the ground that it came relatively close to the Anti-Revolutionary ideal of universal household suffrage.

A second aspect of Kuyper's struggle to liberate and empower the little people was his concern over the impoverishment of the working class in the late-nineteenth-century Netherlands. At the First Christian Social Congress in the Netherlands, held in November 1891, Kuyper gave a speech titled "The Social Question and the Christian Religion."[16] Whole paragraphs read as if they had been written by a late-twentieth-century liberation theologian. This, for example: "When rich and poor stand opposed to each other, [Jesus] never takes His place with the wealthier, but always stands with the poorer. He is born in a stable; and while foxes have holes and birds have nests, the Son of Man has nowhere to lay His head. . . . Both the Christ and also just as much His apostles after Him as the prophets before Him, invariably took sides *against* those who were powerful and living in luxury, and *for* the suffering and oppressed."[17] And this:

> God has not willed that one should drudge hard and yet have *no bread* for himself and for his family. And still less has God willed that any man with hands to work and a will to work should suffer hunger or be reduced to the beggar's staff just *because* there is no work. If we have "food and clothing" then it is true the holy apostle demands that we should be therewith content. But it neither can nor may ever be excused in us that, while our Father in heaven wills with divine kindness that an abundance of food comes forth from the ground, through *our* guilt this rich bounty should be divided so *unequally* that while one is surfeited with bread, another goes with empty stomach to his pallet, and sometimes must even go without a pallet.[18]

Kuyper attributed the social misery that he was witnessing in the Netherlands, of which poverty was but the most tragic manifestation, to a laissez-faire political system arising from the Enlightenment coupled with an economic system motivated by profit-seeking. The result was a class struggle. Kuyper's analysis becomes strikingly similar to Marx's:

> On the side of the *bourgeoisie*, there was experience and insight, ability and association, available money and available influence. On the other side was the rural population and the working class, bereft of all means of help, and forced to accept any condition, no matter how unjust, through the constant necessity for food. Even without prophetic gifts, the result of this struggle could readily be foreseen. It could not end otherwise than in the absorption of all calculable value by the larger and smaller capitalists, leaving for the lower strata of society only as much as appeared strictly necessary to maintain these instruments for nourishing capital—for in this system, that is all the workers are held to be.[19]

Only if we once again see society not as a heap of souls on a piece of ground but as a God-willed community, a living human organism, can there be a cure for the misery of poverty. And that, says Kuyper, is "the socialist path." He adds, "I do not shrink from the word," provided one not identify socialism with the program of the Social Democrats.[20] A program, though, is indeed necessary—a program of social reform. Piety and charity are not sufficient, for it is a *social* question we are dealing with, not a devotional or philanthropic question.

> This one thing is necessary if a social question is to exist for you: that you realize the *untenability* of the present situation, and that you realize this untenability to be one not of incidental causes, but one involving the very *basis* of our social association. For one who does *not* acknowledge this and who thinks that the evil can be exorcised through an increase in piety, through friendlier treatment or kindlier charity, there exists possibly a religious question and possibly a philanthropic question, but not a *social* question. This does not exist for you until you exercise an *architectonic* critique of human society itself and hence desire and think possible a different arrangement of the social structure.[21]

The years from 1880 to 1900 were Kuyper's most productive as a thinker and writer. He delivered four rectoral addresses (1881, 1888, 1892, and 1899) in addition to his initial "Sovereignty Within Its Own Sphere," and composed a three-volume theological treatise with the title, quaint to our present-day ears, *Encyclopedia of Sacred Theology*. He published a large number of pamphlets on a wide variety of topics, most of them the texts of lectures or speeches that he had given or a collection of newspaper articles that he had written on some topic. In 1907 a five-volume treatise on systematic theology appeared, derived from notes made by students of his lectures. He published large, multivolume books on the Holy Spirit, on the Heidelberg Catechism, on the doctrine of common grace, and on the Reformed liturgy, all of these being assembled from his weekly columns in *De Heraut*, as was a multivolume book of meditations. The capstone of his career as social, political, and cultural theorist was the six Stone Lectures that he gave at Princeton Theological Seminary in 1898 under the title *Calvinism*; here he put it all together. It is these lectures on Calvinism that will be most useful to us in our analysis of his views on human nature and the law, along with some passages from his *Encyclopedia of Sacred Theology*[22] and the excellent selection of shorter writings assembled by James Bratt on the centennial of Kuyper's Stone Lectures in *Abraham Kuyper: A Centennial Reader*.

HUMAN NATURE AND THEORETICAL KNOWLEDGE

Dutch society in the latter half of the nineteenth century and the early decades of the twentieth had become religiously pluralistic. Kuyper thought that any attempt to get rid of that pluralism by force would be not only futile but also a violation of the right to liberty of conscience; there could be no going back to the religious unanimity of earlier days. Furthermore, Kuyper believed that the right of his followers for which he was fighting, the right to exercise their religious worldview in church, society, and polity, was the right of all other Dutch citizens as well. Accordingly, as with John Locke in the late seventeenth century and John Rawls in the late twentieth, one of the fundamental questions around which Kuyper's thought about law and the state revolved was this: how can people of diverse worldviews, religious and otherwise, live together in peace and justice within the same polity?

Unlike Locke and Rawls, Kuyper's answer to this question did not involve trying to find some body of principles that as a totality is ample for settling at least the basic political issues that confront us, and that individually are such that we can fairly ask everybody to appeal to them when debating and deciding basic political issues. Kuyper broke at this point with classic liberal theory. Let it be said that the sort of society Kuyper was arguing and struggling for was a liberal democratic society. He was in favor of all the basic rights definitive of such a society—freedom of speech, freedom of assembly, the right to choose one's representatives, and so forth. Indeed, when it came to such issues as the scope of the franchise,

Kuyper was more democratic in his thinking than were most of his opponents. His disagreement was not with liberal democratic society but with classic liberal theory.

I remarked that, as with Locke and Rawls, Kuyper's thought about law and the state was in good measure shaped by the question of how people of diverse worldviews can live together in peace and justice within the same polity. What is distinctive of Kuyper is that this particular angle of approach to law and the state was set within the context of reflections on social practices and institutions generally; and that always the same question guided his reflections. No matter what shared social institution or practice he was discussing—the state, the university, schooling in general, whatever—each time we find him asking how, given our religious diversity, we can work together in peace and justice within those common practices and institutions. We would miss the full import of Kuyper's reflections on law and the state if we did not set them within this larger context. That then will be our project for the next several sections.

It was in good measure Kuyper's anthropology that led him to take a different tack from Locke and Rawls; and what was especially decisive here was his view concerning the workings of human thought and the nature of religion. Kuyper's most careful reflections on these matters are to be found in his discussions of how a person's practice of theoretical learning is shaped by his or her worldview.[23] So, let us look at what he has to say on that matter, keeping in mind that his views were the same concerning the bearing of a person's worldview on his or her social or political thought. The essential point is that a person's religious or nonreligious worldview is not something added on to other convictions; a person's worldview pervades and comprehends his or her thought in general.

Theoretical learning, Kuyper insisted, is not something done individually by this person here and individually by that person there; it is a shared social practice into which individuals are inducted and within which they participate. "The subject of science cannot be this man or that," he says.[24] If you insist on specifying a subject for it, it is best to say that its subject is "man*kind* at large, or, if you please, *the* human consciousness."[25]

The goal of this social practice is, of course, to engage reality in such a way that the theoretical disciplines, the *wetenschapen*, are built up. The main point Kuyper wanted to make about this engagement was that a particular person's participation in theoretical learning does not and cannot consist simply of allowing episodes of outer or inner experience to activate one's innate belief-forming faculties of perception and introspection. It is true, of course, that at the bottom of the whole enterprise there has to be the activation of these faculties; reality has to act on us. But that, Kuyper insisted, is not sufficient for the construction of theoretical learning.

Kuyper emphasized that in the theoretical disciplines, our goal is not just to collect individual facts but also to arrive at an account of their interconnections. Accordingly, since "science means that our human consciousness shall take up into itself what exists as an organic whole, it goes without saying that she makes no progress whatever by the simple presentation of the elements; and that she can achieve her purpose only when, in addition to a fairly complete presentation of the *elements*, she also comes to a fairly complete study of their *relations*."[26] For the most part, however, these interconnections are not part of what is "given" us. Accordingly, when we move beyond elementary reporting, counting, weighing, measuring, and the like to developing an account of interconnections, we must ourselves make a contribution to the engagement.

Theorizing emerges from engagement with an organically interconnected reality by a complex body of thought developed so as to capture those interconnections. Our faculties of perception and introspection only put us in touch with, as it were, the periphery of that organically interconnected reality. In its totality, theoretical learning is not so much report as construction. At the point where theoretical learning goes beyond the "given" to constructing a comprehensive account of interconnections, it unavoidably incorporates a subjective element: "That a science should be free from the influence of the subjective factor is inconceivable."[27]

This thesis is true, as Kuyper saw it, for the natural sciences; it is even truer for the human sciences, where human consciousness is itself a component of the subject matter. Kuyper concluded a discussion of empiricism in the human sciences with a brief and dismissive comment: "Your own subjective-psychical life is ever shown to be your starting-point [in the human sciences], and empiricism leaves you in the lurch. This is most forcibly illustrated by Philosophy in the narrower sense, which, just because it tries logically to interpret, if not the cosmos itself, at least the image received of it by us, ever bears a strongly subjective character, and with its [leaders], least of all, is able to escape this individual stamp."[28] With the downfall of empiricism over the past thirty or forty years, the perspective that Kuyper expressed has become widely accepted; Kuyper was making the point more than a hundred years ago.

The entrance into the academy in recent years of forthrightly particularized perspectival learning, in the form of feminist perspectives, African American perspectives, and the like, has made Kuyper's next point similarly familiar:

The subjective character which is inseparable from all spiritual science, in itself would have nothing objectionable in it, if . . . the subjectivity of A would merely be a variation of the subjectivity in B. In virtue of the organic affinity between the two, their subjectivity would not be mutually antagonistic, and the sense of one would harmoniously support and confirm the sense of the other. . . . But, alas, such is not the case in the domain of science. It is all too often evident, that in this domain the natural harmony of subjective expression is hopelessly broken; and for the feeding of scepticism this want of harmony has no equal. By an investigation of self and of the cosmos you have obtained a well-founded scientific conviction, but when you state it, it meets with no response from those who, in their way, have investigated with equally painstaking efforts; and not only is the unity of science broken, but you are shaken in the assurance of your conviction. For when you spoke your conviction, you did not mean simply to give expression to the insight of your own *ego*, but to the universal human insight; which, indeed, it ought to be, if it were wholly accurate. But of necessity we must accept this hard reality, and in every theory of knowledge which is not to deceive itself, the fact of sin must henceforth claim a more serious consideration.[29]

"The fact of sin." The fact that when we move beyond the elementary recording of data to offer an account of the connections and significance of it all, we regularly get into near-intractable disagreements with each other, is, so Kuyper said, on account of sin. I think he was in error on that point. Better if he had said "fallenness," or, to use his own word, "disturbance." For though some of our near-intractable disagreements are the manifestation or consequence of culpable action or inaction on the part of one or the other of us, not all are, nor did Kuyper think they are. I doubt that all are due even to our fallenness; some are due to our finitude. I readily concede to Kuyper, however, that many of them are due to sin or fallenness.

So fundamental is the phenomenon of disagreement that is resistant to resolution within our social practice of theoretical learning, Kuyper said, that it would not be an exaggeration to say that "the entire interpretation of science, applied to the cosmos as it presents itself to us now, and is studied by the subject 'man' as he now exists, is in an absolute sense governed by the question whether or no[t] a disturbance has been brought about by sin either in the object or in the subject of science."[30] That is to say: in accounting for this phenomenon of near-intractable disagreements within our shared social practice of theoretical learning, can we avoid acknowledging the presence of a "disturbance . . . brought about by sin"? Kuyper's answer was that we cannot. To put flesh on the bones of this theological claim, he then embarked on an extensive discussion of the ways in which our fallenness affects our work in the academy;[31] he structured his discussion by developing a typology and then offering examples of the various types. The whole discussion is extraordinarily insightful and suggestive. So as to give the flavor of it, let me cite three of the types, along with a few examples of each.

One source of near-intractable theoretical disagreement "is the influence of the sin-disorganized *relationships of life*—an influence which makes itself especially felt with the pedagogic and the social sciences."[32] For example: "He who has had his bringing-up in the midst of want and neglect will entertain entirely different views of jural relationships and social regulations from him who from his youth has been bathed in prosperity. Thus, also, your view of civil rights would be altogether different, if you had grown up under a despotism, than if you had spent the years of early manhood under the excesses of anarchism."[33]

Another source of near-intractable disagreement is our distorted and parochial "personal interests." For example: "An Englishman will look upon the history of the Dutch naval battles with the British fleet very differently from a Netherlandish historian; not because each purposely desires to falsify the truth, but because both are unconsciously governed by national interests. . . . A Roman Catholic has an entirely different idea of the history of the Reformation from a Protestant's, not because he purposely violates the truth, but simply because without his knowing it his church interests lead him away from the right path."[34]

And third, our dislikes and hatreds are often at the root of our disagreements, as are our conflicting loves. Where "love, the sympathy of existence," is active,

> you understand much better and more accurately than where this sympathy is wanting. A friend of children understands the child and the child life. A lover of animals understands the life of the animal. In order to study nature in its material operations, you must love her. . . . Sin is the opposite of love. . . . Our mind feels itself isolated; the object lies outside of it, and the bond of love is wanting by which to enter into and learn to understand it. . . . What once existed organically, exists now consequently as foreign to each other, and this *estrangement* from the object of our knowledge is the greatest obstacle in the way to our knowledge of it.[35]

Kuyper clearly found these three types of disturbance in human existence crucially important for understanding our near-intractable disagreements in theoretical learning; however, for him none of them has anywhere near the importance of our diverse worldviews, be they religious or not, in accounting for those disagreements. Of course it was this, all along, that he wanted to get to.

In *Principles of Sacred Theology*, Kuyper's argument took a somewhat unexpected turn at this point, one more explicitly biblical and theological. He did not just argue that many if not most of us operate with what amounts to a worldview, and that there is a distinctly Christian worldview, or perhaps *range* of worldviews. Instead, without actually referring to Augustine, Kuyper rung a change on Augustine's doctrine of the two cities, the city of God and the city of the world, created by two loves, love of God and love of what is other than God. Kuyper appealed to St. Paul's teaching that the Christian is one who has been born again of the Spirit; and then he argued that this second birth inevitably "exercises . . . an influence upon his *consciousness*"—that is, upon his or her way of thinking.[36] In agreement with Augustine, Kuyper argued that there is a change in the object of love deeper than this change in thinking: at the spiritual center of the Christian's existence is the sense and reality of living before the face of God in love and adoration. Nonetheless, Kuyper was adamant in his opposition to all purely spiritualistic or moralistic understandings of Christian existence. Speaking of "a religion," but clearly meaning Christianity, and writing in exuberantly Romantic language, he said:

> A religion confined to feeling or will is . . . unthinkable to the Calvinist. The sacred anointing of the priest of creation must reach down to his beard and to the hem of his garment. His whole being, including all his abilities and powers, must be pervaded by the *sensus divinitatis*, and how then could he exclude his rational consciousness,—the *logos* which is in him,—the light of thought which comes from God Himself to irradiate him? To possess his God for the underground world of his feelings, and in the outworks of the exertion of his will, but not in his inner self, in the very centre of his consciousness, and his thought; . . . all of this [is] the very denying of the Eternal Logos."[37]

A question that ineluctably comes to mind at this point is whether we must just resign ourselves to the perpetuation in the academy of disagreements rooted in the sort of phenomena to which Kuyper has called attention, and in particular, to those rooted in distinct religious or nonreligious worldviews. The same question, of course, is faced by each of that considerable number of thinkers who nowadays join with Kuyper in defending a particularist perspectival account of theoretical learning. The problem is more acute in Kuyper's case, however, since his defense of particularist perspectivalism seems to have plunged his overall account of learning into internal contradiction.

I began this part of our discussion by citing Kuyper's point that theoretical learning is a shared human social practice. Rather than something that we each do individually, theoretical learning is larger than any of us, something within which we participate; what is required for participation is merely competence, not any particular religion, philosophy, social orientation, or whatever. I then presented Kuyper's claim that the particular mode of engagement with the world that constitutes theoretical learning is necessarily a blend of subjectivity with receptivity—or to use Kantian language, of spontaneity with receptivity. And from there I moved on to present Kuyper's way of accounting for the fact that the contribution of subjectivity, rather than being shared by all alike, is riddled with near-intractable disagreements. But does not this last point conflict with the first? In what way is theoretical learning still a shared human practice if the subjective contribution, rather than being shared, is broken into fragments?

The true genius of Kuyper's position lies in his answer to this question—a question often put to him in his own lifetime. Those who expound and defend a particularist perspectival view of learning today often combine that view, tacitly or explicitly, with a doctrine of incommensurability: learning shaped by one perspective is incommensurable with learning shaped by another. In Kuyper's own day, the "Lockean" picture of the academy, as we may call the opposing viewpoint, was much more common: when engaging in the practice of theoretical learning, we are to put in cold storage all that we have come to believe from our life in the everyday and make use only of our generically human belief-forming faculties. Kuyper steered a path between these two positions. De facto what we find in theoretical learning is a plurality of particularistic perspectives; but we are not to rest content with this fractured actuality. The actuality is a science of this type of person and a science of that type of person; but our goal is a shared science, humanity's science. Bodies of learning shaped by different worldviews are not incommensurable on account of being so shaped.

Throughout this section I have spoken not of intractable, but of "near-intractable," disagreements, not of disagreements impossible of resolution but of disagreements "resistant" to resolution. It is true that the ideal will never be reached; we pursue it nonetheless. Not, however, by the Lockean strategy of trying to shed all one's particularities upon entering the academy so as to function as a generic human being; that is impossible. We engage in learning as who we are, with whatever our particularities; and then, as part of that engagement, we engage each other in dialogue, each trying to show the other where he or she has gone wrong and listening to the other as he or she tries to show where we have gone wrong. Engaged pluralism, one might call it.

Kuyper put it this way in one passage: "In the domain of the sciences, . . . experience shows that, after much resistance and trial, the man of stronger and purer thought prevails at length over the men of weaker and less pure thought, convinces them, and compels them to think as he thinks, or at least to yield to the result of his thinking. Many convictions are now the common property of the universal human consciousness, which once were only entertained by individual thinkers."[38]

A fascinating feature of the passage is the almost inadvertent recognition of the role of power in the academy. But let that pass, so as to take note of the caveat that Kuyper immediately added. Yes, it often happens that the other person convinces me of my error; and sometimes, even though I am not convinced, I am silenced. But while not minimizing the point, we must also not exaggerate it; the ideal of consensus, and certainly the ideal of rationally achieved consensus, remains beyond our grasp. One of the reasons for this elusiveness, apart from those already highlighted, is that all too often what drives the scientist is not just the aim, focused on the objects, of discovering them in their relationships, but the aim, focused on his or her colleagues, of squelching their views and advancing his or her own. Once again we touch on sin and fallenness; had there been no "disturbance," there would have been no such prideful defensiveness. It is because of sin that

> where two scientific men arrive at directly opposite results, each will see the truth in his own result, and falsehood in the result of his opponent, and both will deem it their duty to fight in the defence of what seems to them the truth, and to struggle against what seems to them the lie. If this concerns a mere point of detail, it has no further results; but if this antithesis assumes a more universal and radical character, school will form itself against school, system against system, world-view against world-view, and two entirely different and mutually exclusive representations of the object, each in organic relation, will come at length to dominate whole series of subjects. From both sides it is said: "Truth is with us, and falsehood with you." And the notion that science can settle this dispute is of course entirely vain, for we speak of two all-embracing representations of the object, both of which have been obtained as the result of very serious scientific study.[39]

The "unity of science is gone. The one [person] cannot be forced [by argument] to accept what the other holds as truth, and what according to his view he has found to be truth."[40] And to suppose that there is some sort of "absolute science" available to us human beings that would settle such issues "is nothing but a criminal self-deception."[41] "There is no . . . objective certainty to compel universal homage, which can bring about a unity of settled result."[42] Sometimes dialogue is fundamentally inadequate for achieving agreement; what is needed is conversion of one sort or another.

POLITICS, LAW, AND CHURCH

All these points have their exact parallels in Kuyper's reflections on politics. A corollary of Augustine's distinction between the *civitas dei* and the *civitas terrena* is that just as the institutional church is the polity of the *civitas dei*, so the state is the polity of the *civitas terrena*. The citizens of these two polities are intermingled in this present age, so much so that a member of the *civitas dei* may occupy a position in the state, and a (hypocritical) member of the *civitas terrena* may occupy a position in the institutional church; nonetheless, so Augustine held, each of these two fellowships has its own polity, its own governance.

Earlier, in our discussion of theorizing, I mentioned an important way in which Kuyper was Augustinian in his thinking. Indispensable to understanding his thought about law, however, is the realization that he broke decisively with Augustine in his understanding of the state. When it comes to the church, Kuyper distinguished between the church as organism and the church as institution; the distinction, in all but its fine-mesh details, is the same as Augustine's between the City of God, on the one hand, and its institutional governance, on the other.[43] But for Kuyper, the state is not the governing institution of the *civitas terrena*; the *civitas terrena* has no governing institution peculiar to itself. The state is the governing institution of all of us together, Christian and non-Christian, members of the *civitas dei* and members of the *civitas terrena*. Kuyper's way of thinking of the state is analogous at this point to his way of thinking of the practice of theoretical learning; just as academic learning is a social practice of humankind generally, not just of Christians or non-Christians, so too the state is the governing institution of all the human beings who live in a certain area, Christian and non-Christian alike. Christians are not resident aliens vis-à-vis the government of Holland or the United States; they do not carry green cards. They are citizens; they carry passports. Christians have dual citizenship. They are all, in the modern world, citizens of some state and also citizens of the institutional church. In Kuyper's own words, "It is one and the same *I* who is a citizen of the country and a member of the church."[44]

What, then, is to be the basis of politics in the modern world, given that the citizenry of every state is religiously diverse? More specifically, what is to be the basis of politics in a liberal democracy? On what basis are we, the citizens, to debate political issues and make political decisions? For of course weighing and measuring, counting and polling, are no more adequate for settling political issues than for settling theoretical issues. Our convictions about political issues are shaped by all those same "subjective" factors that Kuyper highlighted when he was talking about theorizing—in particular, by our diverse world-and-life views, be they religious or otherwise.

Kuyper was not presented with John Rawls's proposal, a variant of the classic liberal theorists' attempt to find a neutral basis for politics. Rawls proposed that we obtain a neutral basis—a social foundation acceptable to all the comprehensive perspectives represented in the society—by articulating the core idea of a liberal democratic society into principles of justice.[45] There can be no doubt what Kuyper's response to this proposal would have been. We must expect that our diverse comprehensive perspectives will yield both different views as to the acceptability of this proposal and different articulations of the idea of a liberal democratic society. Neutrality is as much a will-o'-the-wisp in politics as in the academy.

There is a vigorous debate currently taking place on these matters between "inclusionists" and "exclusionists." The inclusionists hold that the ethos of a citizen of a liberal democratic society allows a citizen to use his or her particular comprehensive perspective, religious or otherwise, to debate and decide political issues. The exclusionists disagree. Though citizens may offer and use such reasons if they wish, the decisive considerations must always be drawn from shared "public reason." Religious reasons are never to be anything more than dispensable add-ons. One knows where Kuyper would come down: firmly on the side of the inclusionists. Kuyper's own decisive reasons for the political positions he adopted were usually explicitly biblical and theological; reasons drawn from "public reason" were for him the dispensable add-ons.

No exclusionist proposes making it illegal to give decisive weight to religious reasons in political debate and decision. Persuade people that it is against the ethos of a citizen of a liberal democracy; but do not make it illegal. Accordingly, this aspect of Kuyper's views on how people of diverse worldviews are to live together within a single liberal democratic state, though exceedingly important as part of the whole picture and influential in many quarters, does not speak directly to the issue of legal structure. Quite the contrary for another aspect.

Every religious community has some sort of institutional basis for its religious life. The most obvious of such bases are those institutions whose purpose is (or includes) the conduct of communal worship. Only slightly less obvious are the educational and journalistic institutions that many religious communities establish: Catholic and Muslim day schools, Presbyterian and

Jewish weeklies, and so forth. Of course, religious communities differ from each other a great deal with respect to the scope and diversity of such institutional bases. Presbyterians in the United States, unlike Catholics and Lutherans, have seldom established Presbyterian day schools; they have established Presbyterian colleges. Quakers, unlike Catholics, have rarely if ever established Quaker hospitals; they have established Quaker relief organizations. One of the reasons Kuyper stirred up so much enthusiasm among some, and so much hostility among others, was that he not only saw the need for new and strengthened institutional bases for religious communities, but he also set about forming those institutions for his followers: a political party, a university, a denomination, day schools, a labor union, daily newspapers, weekly journals—the list goes on and on. University professors are easily ignored. But a religiously based political party, labor union, broadcasting organization, newspaper, university: these are in your face!

Because the lives of religious communities have these institutional bases, the existence of a diversity of comprehensive perspectives within the citizenry of a single liberal democratic state confronts us with a new issue. We have already considered the question of the basis upon which political issues are to be debated and decided; but the institutional bases of religion confront us with the following issue as well: how is the state to be related to the religiously oriented institutions present within society? In the United States this issue is often discussed under the rubric of church and state. But if one means by "church" the institutional church—what Kuyper called "the church as institute"—then the question is obviously much broader than the question of how the state is to be related to the various ecclesiastical institutions present in society. It includes, for example, what the Dutch called "the school question"—a question which, as we saw earlier, agitated Dutch politics for a good many decades and in which Kuyper participated passionately.[46]

Beginning during World War II and until recently, the United States Supreme Court has quite consistently interpreted the First Amendment to the Constitution as mandating a no-support/neutrality policy on the part of the federal and state governments. That is to say, the Court has interpreted the First Amendment as mandating that the primary purpose of a piece of legislation shall never be to give financial support to some religiously oriented institution, and conversely, that the institutions the government does operate or support shall be neutral in their orientation vis-à-vis each and all of the religions present in American society. It is clear from Kuyper's answer to "the school question" that his position was not one of no-support/neutrality, but instead that the government should follow what might be called an impartiality policy: In its operation and support of institutions, the government is to treat the religious and irreligious present in society impartially. For example, if the government decides to fund *any* schools, it should impartially fund *all* schools regardless of their orientation, religious or otherwise, provided only that they meet certain formal educational requirements.

Kuyper's argument was twofold. He thought that there could not be such a thing as a religiously neutral program of day school education, for a reason that will now be familiar to the reader: day school education necessarily goes beyond the weighing and measuring, the counting and recording, that we can all pretty much agree on. Like theorizing and politics, day school education is shaped by our diverse "subjectivities," and by our diverse worldviews in particular. Second, given this fact about education, it is a violation of both equity and the right to free exercise of one's religion if the state funds schools of one orientation and not those of another. On this latter point, perhaps it is worth reminding the reader that, in Kuyper's understanding, a religion, whatever else it may be, incorporates a certain *Weltanschauung*. That worldview will come to expression in how the community that embraces the particular religion worships. But the worldview will also come to expression in how it wants its children to be educated, in what it thinks the policy of the state should be on such matters as welfare, abortion, and international law, in what it thinks about art and business, and so forth. The right to free exercise of one's religion is thus far more comprehensive than the right to worship freely.

It need scarcely be said that a legal structure determined by an impartiality policy on the part of the government will be considerably different from a legal structure determined by a no-support/neutrality policy. It is a matter of debate as to which is more equitable; but the legal structure of a society can be of either sort in a liberal democracy. It would be implausible to hold that the Netherlands, on account of having a legal structure shaped in good measure by the impartiality policy, is not a liberal democracy. It would likewise be implausible to hold that the United States, on account of having a legal structure shaped in good measure by the no-support/ neutrality policy, is not a liberal democracy.

COMMON GRACE AND HUMAN PROGRESS

Kuyper is particularly famous for his doctrine of common grace. It is common practice among theologians to debate whether the doctrine of creation plays an adequate role in this or that theologian's thought—or whether, perhaps, it plays an inflated role. The doctrine plays an exceedingly important role in Kuyper's thought, though often it functions as ancillary to his doctrine of common grace.

A persistent theme in Kuyper is opposition to all versions of Christianity that give priority to the salvation of individual souls. The error of people who embrace such constructions of Christianity lies, he says, in that they "focus on *their own salvation* instead of on the *glory of God*."[47] What Kuyper had in mind by this reference to the glory of God is eloquently conveyed in a passage from his argument concerning the image of God. Kuyper is here arguing that the image referred to in Genesis must be understood socially rather than individualistically; only humankind as a whole can adequately image God, and then only in the culmination of its historical development. With his rhetorical powers in full flower, Kuyper wrote:

> The social side of man's creation in God's image has nothing to do with salvation nor in any way with each person's state before God. This social element tells us only that in creating human beings in his likeness God deposited an infinite number of nuclei for high human development in our nature and that these nuclei cannot develop except *through the social bond between people*. From this viewpoint the highly ramified development of humanity acquires a significance of its own, an independent goal, a reason for being aside from the issue of salvation. If it has pleased God to mirror the richness of his image in the social multiplicity and fullness of our human race, and if he himself has deposited the nuclei of that development in human nature, *then* the brilliance of his image *has to* appear. Then that richness *may not* remain concealed, those nuclei *may not* dry up and wither, and humanity will *have* to remain on earth for as long as it takes to unfold as fully and richly as necessary those nuclei of human potential. Then will have occurred that full development of humanity in which all the glory of God's image can mirror itself.[48]

Kuyper does not dispute that the "salvation of souls" also bespeaks God's glory; but the truly grand work of God with respect to human beings, that for the sake of which God created humankind and guides its history, is the full development of the potentials "deposited" in our species. "A finished world will glorify God as Builder and supreme Craftsman. What Paradise was in bud will then be in full bloom."[49]

And what of sin? Sin disturbs and disrupts this grand march of humankind toward fulfillment. But God responds to sin with a grace, a favor, a generosity that can be thought of as re-creative. This re-creative grace takes two forms. It takes the form of "a *temporal restraining* grace, which holds back and blocks the effect of sin" so that humankind's full flowering, for which God created us, is not frustrated; and it takes the form of "a *saving grace*, which in the end abolishes sin and completely undoes its consequences."[50] The latter is particular in scope; only some are destined for God's New Creation. This is Kuyper's orthodox Calvinist doctrine of election. The former is universal in scope; that mode of divine generosity whereby God restrains the effects of sin is dispensed to all humankind. This is common grace. "To every rational creature, grace is the air he breathes."[51]

God's common grace is to be seen at work in the inward life of humankind wherever "civic virtue, a sense of domesticity, natural love, the practice of human virtue, the improvement of the public conscience, integrity, mutual loyalty among people, and a feeling for piety leaven life." It is to be seen at work in the outward existence of humankind "when human power over nature increases, when invention upon invention enriches life, when international communication is improved, the arts flourish, the sciences increase our understanding, the conveniences and joys of life multiply, all expressions of life become more vital and radiant, forms become more refined, and the general image of life becomes more winsome."[52]

This doctrine of common grace proved to be, in Kuyper's hand, an extraordinarily rich mine for argumentation. In particular, it provided him with an argument for action by Christians in political, social, and cultural affairs, against all those forms of Christianity that concentrate on the salvation of souls and their own "dear, devout fellowships."[53] Since there is "*grace* operating outside the church," since "there is *grace* even where it does not lead to eternal salvation," we are "duty-bound to honor [this] operation of divine grace in human civic life by which the curse of sin, and sin itself, is restrained even though the link with salvation is lacking."[54] To focus all one's attention on the church is to deny, tacitly or explicitly, the existence of grace outside the church.[55] Kuyper thought that those on the opposite end of the spectrum from the sectarians, those who promote a national church of which all citizens are members, likewise operate with the assumption that "all that lies outside and cannot be absorbed in the church remains bereft of grace and so helplessly in bondage to the curse."[56] Rather than distinguish common from special grace and affirming the existence of both, proponents of a national church absorb the special into the common, blending church into civil society; thereby they deprive the church of any distinct voice within society and culture.

The church, if it remains true to itself, recognizing and living by special grace in distinction from common grace and not becoming merely the place where the nation expresses its religiosity, has something distinct to say—that is, something distinct to say about society and culture. The "lamp of the Christian religion" burns within the walls of the church as institute. But the light of that lamp "shines out through its windows to areas far beyond, illumining all the sectors and associations that appear across the wide range of human life and activity. Justice, law, the home and family, business, vocation, public opinion and literature, art and science, and so much more are all illuminated by that light, and that illumination will be stronger and more penetrating as the lamp of the gospel is allowed to shine more brightly and clearly in the church institute."[57]

The goal of Christian social and cultural action is not to confessionalize society. "What we want," Kuyper insisted, "is a strong confessional church but *not* a confessional civil society *nor* a confessional state," adding that the "secularization of state and society is one of the most basic ideas of Calvinism."[58] "The Christian character of society . . . cannot be secured by the baptism of the whole citizenry but is to be found in the influence that the church of Christ exerts upon the whole organization of national life. By its influence on the state and civil society the church of Christ aims only at a *moral triumph,* not at the imposition of confessional bonds nor at the exercise of authoritarian control."[59]

> Terms such as "a Christian nation," "a Christian country," "a Christian society," "Christian art," and the like, do not mean that such a nation consists mainly of regenerate Christian persons or that such a society has already been transposed into the kingdom of heaven. . . . No, it means that in such a country special grace in the church and among believers exerted so strong a formative influence on common grace that common grace thereby attained its highest development. The adjective "Christian" therefore says nothing about the spiritual state of the inhabitants of such a country but only witnesses to the fact that public opinion, the general mind-set, the ruling ideas, the moral norms, the laws and customs there clearly betoken the influence of the Christian faith. Though this is attributable to special grace, it is manifested on the terrain of common grace, i.e., in ordinary civil life. This influence leads to the abolition of slavery in the laws and life of a country, to the improved position of women, to the maintenance of public virtue, respect for the Sabbath, compassion for the poor, consistent regard for the ideal over the material, and—even in manners—the elevation of all that is human from its sunken state to a higher standpoint.[60]

It will now be clearer than it was before why Kuyper was opposed to conservatism. Orthodoxy, yes; conservatism in church and society, no.

"The tendency in devout circles to oppose. . . . progress and perpetual development of human life" is "misguided. . . . Those who are in Christ must not oppose such development and progress, must not even distance themselves from it. Their calling. . . . is rather to be in the vanguard. . . . The ongoing development of humanity is *contained in the plan of God*. It follows that the history of our race resulting from this development is not from Satan nor from man *but from God* and that all those who reject and fail to appreciate this development deny the work of God in history. Scripture speaks of the 'consummation of the ages.'"[61]

SPHERE SOVEREIGNTY AND ORGANIC DEVELOPMENT

The main topic that remains to be considered, so as to have the structure of Kuyper's reflections on law fully before us, is his doctrine of sphere sovereignty. It was for this doctrine, along with that of common grace, that Kuyper became most famous. The doctrine, at its core, is a normative understanding of civil society and its relation to the state. This normative understanding is, once again, a striking departure from classic liberal theory while remaining, nonetheless, a defense of the liberal democratic society.

The doctrine of sphere sovereignty sits at the intersection of a number of different lines of thought in Kuyper. Let us begin by picking up where we have just left off. When regarded in its totality, the story of humankind on earth is not the story of the same old things happening over and over again but the story of progress. And the story of progress is the story of the progressive actualization, by human beings, of "the powers, which, by virtue of the ordinances of creation, are innate in nature itself." Theoretical learning is "the application to the cosmos of the powers of investigation and thought created within us." Art is "the natural productivity of the potencies of our imagination."[62] And so forth. The picture one gets from Kuyper is that of human existence, seen in its totality, filled with teeming life. Over and over he employs his organic metaphor at this point. The "expressions of life" in theoretical learning, art, business, and so forth, "all together. . . . form the life of creation, in accord with the ordinances of creation, and therefore are *organically* developed."[63] "The development is spontaneous, just as that of the stem and the branches of a plant."[64]

A crucial point about Kuyper's understanding of this organic development is that, as it progresses, distinct social spheres of activity emerge. Kuyper does not give theoretical articulation to this concept of a sphere;

he does not, for example, give criteria for the identity and diversity of spheres. For this omission he has been much criticized. One of Kuyper's followers in the twentieth century, the Dutch philosopher Herman Dooyeweerd, tried to repair what he saw as Kuyper's deficiency on this point.[65]

But Kuyper's concept of a sphere was not a technical one; had it been that, he would indeed have owed us a careful explanation. It was a concept borrowed by Kuyper from ordinary language. You and I, more than a century later, still employ the concept. Consider, for example, the following passage in Kuyper: "Just as we speak of a 'moral world,' a 'scientific world,' a 'business world,' the 'world of art,' so we can more properly speak of a 'sphere' of morality, of the family, of social life, each with its own *domain*."[66] You and I still speak familiarly of "the art world," "the business world," "the world of politics"; in so doing, we are employing the same concept of a sphere, a *kring*, that Kuyper employed. Let it be added that this was also the concept employed by Max Weber when he developed his theory of differentiation as the hallmark of a modernized society: a modernized society is one in which human activity is differentiated into distinct social spheres. Weber goes somewhat beyond Kuyper in claiming that what differentiates one sphere from another is that a different ultimate value is pursued: the governing value in the art world is different from the governing value in the business world. But if one reads just a bit between the lines, I think it is clear that Kuyper assumes this without ever quite saying it.[67]

Should Kuyper be faulted for not having developed a theoretical ontological articulation of this ordinary concept of a social sphere? That would have been a worthwhile contribution to theory. But his failure to do so does not represent a fatal gap in his social thought, any more than Weber's failure to do so represents a fatal gap in his thought, or the failure, say, of writers on philosophy of art to do so when speaking of "the art world" represents a fatal gap in their thought.

A second crucial point that Kuyper makes about the organic development of human life on earth is that authority, dominion, sovereignty—he uses the words interchangeably—naturally and spontaneously emerge in the course of this development. This "organic social authority"[68] comes in two significantly different forms. One such form is that of "personal sovereignty," or "the sovereignty of genius." Kuyper's thought is that in any field (sphere, sector, world), certain individuals come to have a dominating formative impact on how that field develops. Take, for example, the "dominion of men like Aristotle and Plato, Lombard and Aqinas, Luther and Calvin, Kant and Darwin." The "dominion" of each of these figures extends "over a field of ages. Genius is a *sovereign* power; it forms schools; it lays hold on the spirits of men, with irresistible might; and it exercises an immeasurable influence on the whole condition of human life. This sovereignty of genius is a gift of God."[69]

Though this sovereignty of genius is important for Kuyper, its importance is overshadowed by that of the other kind of sovereignty that spontaneously emerges from the organic development of life. Social institutions and their authority structures emerge—authority in this case being the right to issue directives to others that place those others under the (prima facie) obligation to obey. Life could not flourish, and many if not most modes of life could not even exist, without the emergence of institutional bases for such life along with their authority structures. And when the life of humankind is differentiated into distinct spheres, institutions and authority structures specific to those spheres emerge. Theoretical learning could scarcely exist, and certainly could not flourish, without such institutional bases as universities, colleges, research institutes, and the like, each with its head or governing body.

Kuyper placed governmental authority within this grand picture of directive authority as pervading our human existence. Governmental authority is but one species of a vast genus. We will misunderstand both its nature and its proper scope if we do not place our thinking about it within that context.

What, then, is sphere sovereignty? Two ideas come together here. One is the idea that authority structures always have a limited scope: they have the right to issue directives only to certain people and only on certain matters; God alone has the right to issue directives to all human beings on all matters. Second, and rather obviously, for an authority structure, to be sovereign within its own sphere is to have the right to issue directives on matters that fall within that sphere (sector, world). "The University exercises scientific dominion; the Academy of fine arts is possessed of art-power; the guild exercised a technical dominion; the trades-union rules over labour; and each of these spheres or corporations is conscious of the power of exclusive independent judgment and authoritative action, within its proper sphere of operation."[70]

Of course, the fact that a certain authority structure has the right to issue directives within its sphere does not imply that it has the right to issue directives for the totality of life within that sphere; the president of Yale has no right to issue directives to the students and staff of Harvard University. Thus Kuyper says that "the social life of cities and villages forms a sphere of existence, which arises from the very necessities of life, and which therefore must be autonomous;"[71] and thus he mentions the "lower magistrates" in France of Calvin's time as an example of a distinct sphere.

Obviously, he was here using "sphere" in a somewhat different sense from how he customarily used it.

Now for the crucial questions: What grounds the right of authority structures to issue directives within their spheres? And what determines the rightness or wrongness of their directives—assuming that those directives can be right or wrong?

Start with the former: Kuyper was almost fierce in his insistence that no human being (or institution) just comes with the right to issue authoritative directives to another. All authority to issue directives to one's fellow human beings is grounded, ultimately, in God's authority to issue directives to human beings.[72] What Kuyper says in the context of his discussion of governmental authority is clearly meant to apply to authority in general: "Authority over men cannot arise from men. . . . When God says to me, 'obey,' then I humbly bow my head, without compromising in the least my personal dignity, as a man. For in like proportion as you degrade yourself, by bowing low to a child of man, whose breath is in his nostrils; so, on the other hand do you raise yourself, if you submit to the authority of the Lord of heaven and earth."[73]

Human authority, in all its forms, is in one way or another to be understood, at bottom, as divinely delegated authority. God, our "supreme Sovereign," "delegates his authority to human beings, so that on earth one never directly encounters God Himself in visible things but always sees his sovereign authority exercised in *human* office."[74] What this implies, naturally, is that the criterion for right and wrong directives is God's will for life in that sphere, at that time and place; right directives are those that conform to God's "ordinances," wrong directives, those that do not conform. All humanity "must exist for [God's] glory and consequently after his ordinances, in order that in their well-being, when they walk after His ordinances, His divine wisdom may shine forth."[75]

The epistemological question now rears its head: how do we know God's ordinances? Which is to say: how do we know what will promote the proper development and authentic flourishing of humankind? Kuyper's answer was always twofold. On one hand, humankind is created with the capacity to discover the answer to this question; and though sin threatened to undo this capacity, the doctrine of common grace implies that it was only impaired, not destroyed. On the other hand, the light of the gospel illuminates what promotes our authentic flourishing; hence the imperative for Christians to be active in social and cultural matters.

To say that the gospel illuminates God's will for our social and cultural development is not to say that authority structures within the various spheres of life are to take instructions from the church. What Kuyper says concerning government applies to all: "The government has to judge and to decide independently. Not as an appendix to the Church, nor as its pupil. The sphere of State stands itself under the majesty of the Lord. In that sphere therefore an independent responsibility is to be maintained. The sphere of the State is not profane. But both Church and State must, each in their own sphere, obey God and serve His honor. And to that end in either sphere *God's Word* must rule, but in the sphere of the State only through the conscience of the persons invested with authority."[76]

THE MECHANICAL SOVEREIGNTY OF THE STATE

The question that remains for our discussion to be complete is how the directive authority of the state is to be related to all the other authority structures present within society. Before we get to that, though, a word must be said about the nature of governmental authority.

Kuyper wanted us to see directive authority as pervading our social existence, and he presented governmental authority as one species of the genus. He nonetheless held that the authority of the state is a very distinct species. To highlight one aspect of what makes it distinct, Kuyper often called its authority mechanical as distinct from organic: "The sovereignty of God, in its descent upon men, separates itself into two spheres. On the one hand the mechanical sphere of *State-authority*, and on the other hand the organic sphere of the authority of the *Social circles*. [In both spheres] the inherent authority is sovereign, that is to say, it has above itself nothing but God."[77]

What does he mean in calling the authority of the state "mechanical"? Well, the actualization of humankind's in-created potentials gives rise not only to institutional bases for theoretical learning, economic activity, and the like, along with their authority structures, but also to states, or more generally, governments. The "impulse to form states arises from man's social nature," says Kuyper, adding that this thought "was expressed already by Aristotle when he called man a ['political animal']."[78] In that respect, the state is as much an organic development as universities, the academy of fine arts, and so forth.

In this fallen world of ours, however, the dominant task of the state has become to restrain sin. As such, the state is a primary instrument of God's common grace.[79] Kuyper speculates that had there been no sin, political life "would have evolved itself, after a patriarchal fashion, from the life of the family."[80] There would have been no magistrates, no police, no army. In fact, however, every state is a "means of compelling order and of guaranteeing a safe course of life." As such, it is "mechanical," "always something unnatural," "something against which the deeper aspirations of our nature rebel."[81] *God has instituted the magistrates, by reason of sin*"; they "rule mechanically, and do not harmonize with our nature."[82]

Not only is the magistrates' relation to human development "mechanical" in this way rather than "organic," but the magistrates are also themselves fallen. They are constantly seeking to expand their authority beyond its proper scope in one direction, and allowing it to be unduly restricted or influenced in another. Hence there is always a duality in the Christian attitude toward the state. On one hand, we "gratefully . . . receive, from the hand of God, the institution of the State with its magistrates, as a means of preservation, now indeed indispensable." On the other hand, "we must ever watch against the danger, which lurks, for our personal liberty, in the power of the State."[83]

So much for the nature of state authority and how it differs from other modes of directive authority; now for how state authority ought to be related to those other authority structures. The overarching point is that authority structures ought to have authority only within their own spheres. In particular, the authority structures of civil society and of family life ought not to be divisions of state or church; all attempts at state and church aggrandizement must be vigorously resisted. The authority structures within a given sector of society are directly responsible to God for their exercise of authority, not indirectly responsible through the mediation of state or church—nor indeed, of any other authority structure outside their own sphere. "The family, the business, science, art and so forth are all social spheres, which do not owe their existence to the State, and which do not derive the law of their life from the superiority of the state, but obey a high authority within their own bosom; an authority which rules, by the grace of God, just as the sovereignty of the State does. . . . These different developments of social life *have nothing above themselves but God.*" Kuyper added: "As you feel at once, this is the deeply interesting question of our *civil liberties.*"[84] A large component in Kuyper's lifelong opposition to the French Revolution was that he saw in it the attempt by the state to get as much directive authority into its own hands as possible. "The State may never become an octopus, which stifles the whole of life."[85]

This understanding of the role of the state, so far, is negative. What is the positive role of the state? Strictly speaking, there is no sphere within society of which the state is sovereign; in that way, too, it is unlike other authority structures. It is, as it were, "the *sphere of spheres*, which encircles the whole extent of human life."[86] So what then is its role?

"Neither the life of science nor of art, nor of agriculture, nor of industry, nor of commerce, nor of navigation, nor of the family, nor of human relationship may be coerced to suit itself to the grace of government." Government "must occupy its own place, on its own root, among all the other trees of the forest, and thus it has to honour and maintain every form of life, which grows independently, in its own sacred autonomy."[87] What that amounts to, Kuyper suggested, is a "threefold right and duty" on the part of the state: "1. Whenever different spheres clash, to compel mutual regard for the boundary-lines of each; 2. To defend individuals and the weak ones, in those spheres, against the abuse of power of the rest; and 3. To coerce all together to bear *personal* and *financial* burdens for the maintenance of the natural unity of the State."[88]

So far, and no farther. "A people. . . . which abandons to State Supremacy the right of the family, or a University which abandons to it the rights of science, is just as guilty before God, as a nation which lays its hands upon the rights of the magistrates. And thus the struggle for liberty is not only declared permissible, but is made a duty for each individual in his own sphere."[89] The best protection against state aggrandizement is a vital civil society and a vigorous defense thereof.

Kuyper's words about the importance of a vital civil society for the defense of freedom have proved prescient of developments in the twentieth century. Ultimately "it depends on the life-spheres themselves whether they will flourish in freedom or groan under State coercion. With moral tensile strength they cannot be pushed in, they will not permit themselves to be cramped. But servility, once it's become shackled, has lost even the right to complain."[90]

And, last, what is the overarching goal of the state in its interventions? Justice and the common good: "The highest duty of the government remains therefore unchangeably that of *justice*, and in the second place it has to care for the people as a unit, partly *at home*, in order that its unity may grow ever deeper and may not be disturbed, and partly *abroad*, lest the national existence suffer harm."[91]

The entire picture is compellingly summarized in the following lengthy but vivid passage from that address on sphere sovereignty that Kuyper gave at the founding of the Free University:

The cogwheels of all these spheres engage each other, and precisely through that interaction emerges the rich, multifaceted multiformity of human life. Hence also rises the danger that one sphere in life may encroach on its neighbor like a sticky wheel that shears off one cog after another until the whole operation is disrupted. Hence also the raison d'être for the special sphere of authority that emerged in the State. It must provide for sound mutual interaction among the various spheres, insofar as they are externally manifest, and keep them within just limits. Furthermore, since personal life can be suppressed by the group in which one lives, the state must protect the individual from the tyranny of his own circle. This Sovereign, as Scripture tersely puts it, "gives stability to the land by justice" [Prov. 29:4], for *without* justice it destroys itself and falls. Thus the sovereignty of the State, as the power that protects the individual and defines the mutual relationships among the visible spheres, rises high *above* them by its right to command and compel. But *within* these spheres that does not obtain. There another authority rules, an authority that descends directly from God apart from the State. This authority the State does not *confer* but *acknowledges.* Even in defining laws for the mutual relationships among the spheres, the State may not set its own will as the standard but is *bound* by the choice of a Higher will, as expressed in the nature and purpose of these spheres. The State must see that the wheels operate as intended. Not to suppress life nor to shackle freedom but to make possible the free movement of life in and for every sphere: does not this ideal beckon every nobler head of state?[92]

CONCLUSIONS AND LEGACY

Abraham Kuyper's theological reflections on law, politics, society, and human nature are now before us. What remains is only to highlight a few points in conclusion. Several times I have remarked that while Kuyper defended a liberal democratic polity,[93] he departed in significant ways from classic liberal theory. Two points of difference especially stand out. First, Kuyper defended what I have called an impartiality policy of the state with respect to the religiously (and antireligiously) oriented institutions in society, rather than a no-support/neutrality policy. Second, in his rights-based defense against the aggrandizement of the state, Kuyper combined a defense of the rights of individuals with an even more emphatic and articulate defense of the rights of social institutions. It is evident that these differences will yield a quite different legal structure for liberal democracy from that favored by such classic liberals as John Locke and John Rawls. Some of the differences jump out; others require the sort of detailed analysis and speculation characteristic of legal theorists to be brought to light. And no doubt others will turn up only when jurists are confronted with cases that no one had anticipated.

As to Kuyper's view of the ontology and epistemology of law: right law is law that conforms to God's will for the development of humankind.

When such law emerges, that emergence should be seen as "a jewel coming down to us from God himself" rather than the product of "a functionally developing organ of nature."[94] And though our in-created capacity to discern right law has been damaged by sin, by virtue of common grace it has by no means been destroyed. Accordingly, when considering issues of law, all of us together, each from our own worldview, are to reflect on what it is that serves justice and human flourishing; for it is justice and flourishing that God desires for humankind. On the other hand, Holy Scripture provides a special source of light on justice and the common good; it is the calling of those who recognize that light to cast it on the public debate rather than keeping it hidden within the institutional church.

What of Kuyper's legacy? From its small beginnings in 1880, the Free University of Amsterdam has expanded until today it is one of the major comprehensive universities within the Dutch university system. Not only its size but also its religious orientation would make it unrecognizable to Kuyper. Though it announces itself as a Protestant Christian university, and though it (along with the Catholic University of Nijmegen) has the status within Dutch educational law of being a confessional university, what it is to be a Protestant Christian confessional university is for it today a topic of perennial discussion rather than of settled conviction. For decades now it has declined to affirm Kuyper's goal of a university whose education and research are based on Reformed principles. And the legacy of Kuyper's Anti-Revolutionary Party, which no longer exists, has been dispersed into a number of different confessionally oriented parties, the largest of which currently is the Christian Democratic Appeal, a union of Calvinist and Catholic parties. What remains striking to an American is the degree to which there remain Dutch social and political institutions organized along confessional lines, this, in good measure, being Kuyper's legacy. What would strike Kuyper himself is how little distinctive institutional expression there remains of his own beloved version of the Calvinist tradition. My examples of this change-within-continuity have been the university and the party that Kuyper founded; the same point could be made for his institution-founding efforts in lower school education, in journalism, and so forth.

In the first sixty or so years of the twentieth century, a substantial number of Dutch people inspired by Kuyper's vision emigrated to the United States and Canada, where their institution-building impulses have gone mainly, though not exclusively, into the formation of educational institutions, both a system of elementary and secondary schools (Christian Schools International, headquartered in Grand Rapids, Michigan), and a number of institutions of higher education, the oldest and largest of which is Calvin College, also in Grand Rapids. There can be no doubt that

Kuyper's religious and intellectual legacy is reflected more faithfully in these American and Canadian educational institutions than it is in the educational institutions that Kuyper founded in the Netherlands.

A sizable number of thinkers, especially in the Netherlands and North America, have employed Kuyper's idea of sphere sovereignty, and his alternative theory of the liberal democratic society that I sketched out above, in writing on political and legal affairs. Of these, the one who articulated Kuyper's political and legal thought most elaborately is Herman Dooyeweerd (1894–1977), longtime professor of jurisprudence at the Free University of Amsterdam. Dooyeweerd developed an ontology of the state, a topic that seems to have been of no interest to Kuyper himself, gave theoretical articulation to Kuyper's concept of a sphere, and discussed in far more detail than Kuyper ever did the proper goals and limits of state activity. Dooyeweerd's major work, already referred to, was *The New Critique of Theoretical Thought*; his major legal work was a multivolume *Encyclopedia of Legal Science*. A good deal of Kuyper's influence on legal and political thought has been transmitted through Dooyeweerd. John Witte Jr., one of the editors of this anthology, is a prominent example of a jurist who uses some of Kuyper's and Dooyeweerd's teachings on law, politics, and society.

It has to be said, however, that though Kuyper's legacy in political and legal thought has been substantial, both in Dooyeweerdian and non-Dooyeweerdian forms, it has not entered the mainstream of discussion in North America. Perhaps that will change as thinkers cast about for alternatives to the increasingly discredited Lockean-Rawlsian account of liberal democracy.

NOTES

1. Kuyper himself tells the story in *Confidentially*, excerpted in *Abraham Kuyper: A Centennial Reader*, ed. James D. Bratt (Grand Rapids, Mich.: Eerdmans, 1998), 46–61. The quotation here is found at page 55. "Of course I did my best," adds Kuyper, "to maintain my ministerial honor but despite myself I felt more inclined to listen than to speak during these encounters." Ibid., 56.

2. More than thirty years later, introducing the third of his Stone Lectures, on Calvinism and politics, Kuyper would say that in the lecture he would be combating "the unhistorical suggestion, that Calvinism represents an exclusively ecclesiastical and dogmatic movement." Abraham Kuyper, *Calvinism: Six Lectures Delivered in the Theological Seminary at Princeton* (New York: Revell, 1899), 98.

3. Kuyper, *Confidentially*, 55.

4. Kuyper writes that in the "malcontents" of Beesd he found, in addition to piety, Bible knowledge, and orthodox Calvinist doctrine, "a well-ordered worldview, be it of the old Reformed type." Ibid.

5. It is striking, for example, how often the word "free" and its linguistic variants occur already in the final sermon of Kuyper's pastorate in Utrecht. See "Conservatism and Orthodoxy: False and True Preservation," in *Abraham Kuyper: A Centennial Reader*, 66–85.

6. While struggling against the power elite of church and state for this multifaceted freedom, Kuyper also never ceased to remind his followers of the comprehensive character of true religion. Here is just one of very many passages: "The Christian spirit is not an oil that floats on the surface of the water but a caustic fluid that has to permeate every drop of your stream of life. . . . Almost all of us have families; we are all members of a society and the sons and daughters of a nation. Those connections too are indispensable and must be bound to the reality of the eternal to keep that eternal life. Christ does not tolerate our living a double life: our lives must be one, controlled by one principle, wherever it may express itself. Life forms in all its rich ramifications one high and holy temple in which the fragrance of the eternal must rise" Kuyper, "Conservatism and Orthodoxy," 82–83.

7. "A confessing Christian who lives amid this world cannot be satisfied with a profession of faith but, like anyone, needs a firm understanding of the world in which he lives. Without the guidance of Christian scholarship, he cannot help but absorb the conclusions of unbelievers. Doing so, he will live with a world-and-life view that does not fit but comes into conflict with his confession on any number of points. His thinking will divide into two." Abraham Kuyper, *Common Grace in Scholarship and Art*, in *Abraham Kuyper: A Centennial Reader*, 474.

8. Kuyper calls 1789 "the birth year of modern life" in *Uniformity: The Curse of Modern Life*, in *Abraham Kuyper: A Centennial Reader*, 24.

9. The *locus classicus* for Kuyper's celebration of organic life as opposed to the rationally planned is his *Uniformity: The Curse of Modern Life*. It is, in fact, the most witty and eloquent attack on the pressures toward uniformity of the modern world that I know of. Here is a sample: Everything must "become uniform, level, flat, homogeneous, monotonous. No longer should each baby drink warm milk from the breast of its own mother; we should have some tepid mixture prepared for all babies collectively." Ibid, 32.

10. E. H. Kossman, *The Low Countries, 1780–1940* (Oxford: Clarendon Press, 1978), 283.

11. James D. Bratt, "Abraham Kuyper: His Work and Work," in *Abraham Kuyper: A Centennial Reader*, 9–10.

12. Kuyper, "Conservatism and Orthodoxy," 71.

13. Ibid., 73. In this chapter, all emphases within quotes are from the original.

14. Ibid., 74.

15. Ibid., 82.

16. Two years earlier, Kuyper published a series of articles on the issue in *De Standaard*; these were collected in a pamphlet called *Manual Labor*. See *Abraham Kuyper: A Centennial Reader*, 231–254.

17. Abraham Kuyper, *Christianity and the Class Struggle*, trans. Dirk Jellema (Grand Rapids, Mich.: Piet Hein Press, 1950), 27–28, 50.

18. Ibid., 48–49.

19. Ibid., 35–36.

20. Ibid., 40.

21. Ibid.

22. Abraham Kuyper, *Encyclopedia of Sacred Theology: Its Principles*, trans. J. Hendrick De Vries (New York: Charles Scribner's Sons, 1898).

23. "Theoretical learning" is the translation that I prefer for the Dutch *wetenschap*, cognate with the German *Wissenschaft*. Both the Dutch and German words are often translated as "science"; they are so translated in passages that I will be quoting. But our English word "science" has come to have a considerably narrower scope of application than the Dutch and German words. Philosophy is one of the *wetenschapen*, one of the *Wissenschaften*. Nobody would think to call it a *science*!

24. Kuyper, *Principles of Sacred Theology*, 63. *Principles of Sacred Theology* is made of up translated selections from Kuyper's three-volume *Encyclopedia of Theology*.

25. Ibid.

26. Ibid., 75.

27. Ibid., 169. Elsewhere Kuyper writes, "I readily grant that if our *natural sciences* strictly limited themselves to weighing and measuring, the wedge of principle would not be at the door. But who would do that? What natural scientist operates without a hypothesis? Does not everyone who practices science as a *man* and not as a *measuring stick* view things through a subjective lens and always fill in the unseen part of the circle according to subjective opinion?" *Abraham Kuyper: A Centennial Reader*, 487–488.

28. Kuyper, *Principles of Sacred Theology*, 103–104.

29. Ibid., 106–107.

30. Ibid., 92.

31. Ibid., 106–114.

32. Ibid., 109.

33. Ibid.

34. Ibid., 110.

35. Ibid., 111.

36. Ibid., 152. Here is the central passage: the Christian religion "speaks of a regeneration (*palingenesis*), of a 'being begotten anew' (*anagenesis*), followed by an enlightening (*photismos*), which changes man in his very being; and that indeed by a change or transformation which is effected by a supernatural cause. . . . This 'regeneration' breaks humanity in two, and repeals the unity of the human consciousness. If this fact of 'being begotten anew,' coming in from without, establishes a radical change in *the being* of man, be it only potentially, and if this change exercises at the same time an influence upon his *consciousness*, then as far as it has or has not undergone this transformation,

there is an abyss in the universal human consciousness across which no bridge can be laid." Ibid.

37. Kuyper, *Calvinism*, 62.
38. Kuyper, *Principles of Sacred Theology*, 151.
39. Ibid., 117–118.
40. Ibid., 119.
41. Ibid., 118.
42. Ibid., 116.
43. For Kuyper's elaboration of the distinction, see *Abraham Kuyper: A Centennial Reader*, 187–188.
44. Ibid., 185.
45. See John Rawls, *Political Liberalism* (New York: Columbia University Press, 1993).
46. It is worth noting that "the school question" is also now agitating American politics and litigation and has done so for a long time, though never with the intensity of its agitation of Dutch politics late in the nineteenth century and early in the twentieth.
47. Ibid., 169.
48. Ibid., 178.
49. Ibid., 181.
50. Ibid., 168.
51. Ibid., 167.
52. Ibid., 181. Common grace "opens a history, unlocks an enormous space of time, triggers a vast and long-lasting stream of events, in a word, precipitates a series of successive centuries. If that series of centuries is not directed toward an endless, unvarying repetition of the same things, then over the course of those centuries there has to be constant change, modification, transformation in human life. Though it pass through periods of deepening darkness, this change has to ignite ever more light, consistently enrich human life, and so bear the character of perpetual development from less to more, a progressively fuller unfolding of life." Ibid., 174.
53. The quoted phrase can be found at ibid., 192. Speaking to the sectarian Christian who denies common grace, Kuyper says, "You run the danger of isolating Christ for your soul and you view life in and for the world as something that exists *alongside* your Christian religion, not controlled by it. Then the word 'Christian' seems appropriate to you only when it concerns certain matters of faith or things directly connected with the faith—your church, your school, missions and the like—but all the remaining spheres of life fall for you *outside the Christ*. In the world you conduct yourselves as others do; that is less holy, almost unholy, territory that must somehow take care of itself. . . . [You] concentrated all sanctity in the human soul and dug a deep chasm between this inward-looking spirituality and life all around. Then scholarship becomes unholy; the development of art, trade, and business becomes unholy, unholy also the functions of government; in short, all that is not directly spiritual and aimed at

the soul. This way of thinking results in your living in two distinct circles of thought: in the very circumscribed circle of your soul's salvation on the one hand, and in the spacious, life-encompassing sphere of the world on the other. Your Christ is at home in the former but not in the latter." Ibid., 172.

54. Ibid., 193.

55. The "doctrine of common grace proceeds directly from the Sovereignty of the Lord which is ever the root conviction of all Reformed thinking. If God is sovereign, then his Lordship *must* remain over *all* life and cannot be closed up within church walls or Christian circles. The extra-Christian world has not been given over to Satan or to fallen humanity or to chance. God's Sovereignty is great and all-ruling also in unbaptized realms, and therefore neither Christ's work in the world nor that of God's child can be pulled back out of life. If his God works in the world, then there he must put his hand to the plow so that there too the Name of the Lord is glorified." Abraham Kuyper, "Voorwoord," in *De Gemeene Gratie*, 3 vols. (Amsterdam: Höveker & Wormser, 1902–4), quoted in *Abraham Kuyper: A Centennial Reader*, 166.

56. Kuyper, *Common Grace*, 192.

57. Ibid., 194.

58. Ibid., 197.

59. Ibid.

60. Ibid., 198–199.

61. Ibid., 175.

62. Kuyper, *Calvinism*, 118.

63. Ibid.

64. Ibid., 117.

65. Dooyeweerd's major work is *A New Critique of Theoretical Thought*, 4 vols., trans. D. H. Freeman and W. S. Young (Philadelphia: Presbyterian and Reformed Publishing Co., 1953–58).

66. Kuyper, "Sphere Sovereignty," 467.

67. A good access to Weber's thought on these matters is the collection of his writings translated and edited by H. H. Gerth and C. Wright Mills, *From Max Weber: Essays in Sociology* (New York: Oxford University Press, 1977).

68. Kuyper, *Calvinism*, 121.

69. Ibid., 122.

70. Ibid., 123.

71. Ibid.

72. Thus Kuyper opposes both the theory of popular sovereignty and the theory of state-sovereignty, which holds that states possess sovereignty inherently. See ibid., 108–113.

73. Ibid., 104. "No one on earth can claim authority over his fellow-men, unless it be laid upon him '*by the grace of God*'; and therefore, the ultimate duty of obedience, is imposed upon us not by man, but by God Himself." Ibid., 106. "God only—and never any creature—is possessed of sovereign rights, in the destiny of nations, because God alone created them, maintains them by His Almighty

power, and rules them, by His ordinances. . . . Man never possesses power over his fellow-man, in any other way than by an authority which descends upon him from the majesty of God." Ibid., 108.

74. Kuyper, "Sphere Sovereignty," 466.

75. Kuyper, *Calvinism*, 103.

76. Ibid., 134–135. "Every magistrate is in duty bound to investigate the rights of God, both in the natural life and in His Word. Not to subject himself to the decision of any church, but in order that he himself may catch the light which he needs for the knowledge of the Divine will." Ibid., 133–134.

77. Ibid., 121.

78. Ibid., 100.

79. "The magistrate is an instrument of 'common grace,' to thwart all license and outrage and to shield the good against the evil. . . . He is instituted by God as *His Servant*, in order that he may preserve the glorious work of God, in the creation of humanity, from total destruction." Ibid., 104–105.

80. Ibid., 101.

81. Ibid.

82. Ibid., 102. "It is . . . of the highest importance sharply to keep in mind the difference in grade between the *organic* life of society and the *mechanical* character of the government. Whatever among men originates directly from creation, is possessed of all the data for its development, in human nature as such . . . The development is spontaneous, just as that of the stem and the branches of a plant." Ibid., 116–117. The state, as we know it in this fallen world, is for the most part not "a natural head, which organically grew from the body of the people, but a *mechanical* head, which from without has been placed upon the trunk of the nation. A mere remedy therefore, for a wrong condition supervening. A stick placed beside the plant to hold it up, since without it, by reason of its inherent weakness, it would fall to the ground." Ibid., 119.

83. Ibid., 102–103.

84. Ibid., 116.

85. Ibid., 124.

86. Kuyper, "Sphere Sovereignty," 472.

87. Kuyper, *Calvinism*, 124.

88. Ibid., 124–125.

89. Ibid., 127.

90. Kuyper, "Sphere Sovereignty," 473.

91. Kuyper, *Calvinism*, 120.

92. Kuyper, "Sphere Sovereignty," 467–468.

93. My attention here has focused entirely on the *liberal* aspect of the polity that Kuyper defends, not the *democratic*; but in fact a good deal, for example, of the Stone Lectures devoted to Calvinism and politics is a defense of democracy. See Kuyper, *Calvinism*, chap. 3.

94. Kuyper, "Sphere Sovereignty," 487.

ORIGINAL SOURCE MATERIALS

CONFIDENTIALLY (CONFIDENTIE)

I was entrusted with a congregation to which I came not primarily to give out of what I possessed but with the quiet prayer that my empty heart would be quickened and fed by the life of the church. For many days that hope was disappointed. The circles in which I moved were (with some exceptions) characterized by a rigid conservatism, orthodox in appearance but without the genuine glow. . . . Everybody was content with the way things went. . . . I heard that there was a small group of malcontents in the flock, but the rumors about these know-it-alls were more for ill than good. They were a bunch of cantankerous, proud eccentrics who "make life miserable for every minister." Besides, most of them were of such low social status that it was deemed best not to worry about them but to ignore them, just as previous ministers had done.

But I found it impossible to do so. Thus, with a trembling heart that befits a young minister who has to face such fires, I knocked in the course of my visitations on the doors of these "fanatics" too. The reception that awaited me was far from cordial. . . . Nonetheless, these simple, if somewhat irritated, souls did not repel me. For here, I realized, was more than mere routine. Here was conviction. Here the topics of conversation went beyond the nice weather and who happened to be ill and who had dismissed his workman. Here was interest in spiritual matters. Moreover, here was knowledge. With the meager Bible knowledge I had picked up at the university I could not measure up to these simple folk. And not just knowledge of the Bible but also of a well-ordered worldview, be it of the old Reformed type. . . . All this made me come back, and that in turn won their welcome. And so the debate began.

It was soon over. Of course I did my best to maintain my ministerial honor but despite myself I felt more inclined to listen than to speak during these encounters. And somehow I noticed that, after such a meeting, the preaching on Sunday went better. Yet it annoyed me that these people were so inflexible. Having shown so much sensitivity myself, I felt I could rightfully claim a more flexible response. But no, never even a hint of budging. I observed that they were not intent on winning my sympathy but on the triumph of their cause. They knew of no compromise or concession, and more and more I found myself confronted with a painful choice: either sharply resist them or unconditionally join them in a principled recognition of "full sovereign grace"—as they called it. . . . Well, dear brother, I did not oppose them and I still thank God that I made that choice. Their unremitting perseverance has become the blessing of my heart, the rise of the morning star for my life. . . .

Yet, you can see, they didn't give me enough. . . . Their world of thought was literally still rooted in the days immediately following the Reformation. Where could I find help?[1]

LECTURES ON CALVINISM

Calvinism as a Life System

Clearness of presentation demands that in this first lecture I begin by fixing the *conception* of Calvinism *historically*. [After dismissing a few conceptions as too narrow, Kuyper continues.] Historically, the name of Calvinism indicates the channel in which the Reformation moved, so far as it was neither Lutheran, nor Anabaptist nor Socinian. . . . Thus understood, Calvinism is rooted in a form of religion which was peculiarly its own, and from this specific religious consciousness there was developed first a peculiar theology, then a special church-order, and then a given form for political and social life, for the interpretation of the moral world-order, for the relation between nature and grace, between Christianity and the world, between church and state, and finally for art and science; and amid all these life-utterances it remained always the self-same Calvinism, in so far as simultaneously and spontaneously all these developments sprang from its deepest life-principle. Hence to this extent it stands in line with those other great *complexes* of human life, known as Paganism, Islamism and Romanism. . . .[2]

The supreme interest here at stake, however, forbids our accepting without more positive proof the fact that Calvinism really provides us with such an unity of life-system. . . . Hence we must first ask what are the required conditions for such general systems of life, as Paganism, Islamism, Romanism and Modernism, and then show that Calvinism really fulfils these conditions.

These conditions demand in the first place, that from a special principle a peculiar insight be obtained into the three fundamental relations of all human life, viz, 1. our relation *to God*, 2. our relation *to man*, and 3. our relation *to the world*.

Calvinism . . . does not seek God *in* the creature, as Paganism, it does not *isolate* God *from* the creature, as Islamism; it posits no *mediate communion* between God and the creature, as does Romanism; but proclaims the exalted thought that, although standing in high majesty above the creature, God enters *into immediate fellowship with the creature*, as God the Holy Spirit. . . .

This brings us of itself to the second condition, with which, for the sake of creating a life system every profound movement has to comply: viz., a fundamental interpretation of its own touching *the relation of man to man*. . . . There is no uniformity among men, but endless multiformity. In creation itself the difference has been established between woman and man. Physical and spiritual gifts and talents cause one person to differ from the other. Past generations and our own personal life create distinctions. The social position of the rich and poor differs widely. Now, these differences are in a special way *weakened* or *accentuated* by every consistent life system. . . .

Modernism, which denies and abolishes every difference, cannot rest until it has made woman man and man woman, and, putting every distinction on a common level, kills life by placing it under the ban of uniformity. . . . In the same way Calvinism has derived from *its* fundamental relation to God a peculiar interpretation of man's relation to man. . . . If Calvinism places our entire human life immediately before God, then it follows that all men or women, rich or poor, weak or strong, dull or talented, as creatures of God, and as lost sinners, have no claim whatsoever to lord over one another, and that we stand as equals before God, and consequently equal as man to man. Hence we cannot recognize any distinction among men, save such as has been imposed by God Himself, in that He gave one authority over the other, or enriched one with more talents than the other, in order that the man of more talents should serve the man with less, and in him serve his God. Hence Calvinism condemns not merely all open slavery and systems of caste, but also all covert slavery of woman and of the poor; it is opposed to all hierarchy among men; it tolerates no aristocracy save such as is able, either in person or in family, by the grace of God, to exhibit superiority of character or talent, and to show that it does not claim this superiority for self-aggrandizement or ambitious pride, but for the sake of spending it in the service of God. So Calvinism was bound to find its utterance in the democratic interpretation of life; to proclaim the liberty of nations; and not to rest until both politically and socially every man, simply because he is man, should be recognized, respected and dealt with as a creature created after the Divine likeness. . . .

The third fundamental relation which decides the interpretation of life is the relation which you bear *to the world*. . . . Of Paganism it can be said in general, that it places *too high* an estimate upon the world, and therefore to some extent it both stands in fear of, and loses itself in it. On the other hand Islamism places *too low* an estimate upon the world, makes sport of it and triumphs over it in reaching after the visionary world of a sensual paradise.... Under the hierarchy of Rome the Church and the World were placed over against each other, the one as being sanctified and the other as being still under the curse. Everything outside the Church was under the influence of demons, and exorcism banished this demoniacal power from everything that came under the protection, influence and inspiration of the Church. Hence in a Christian country the entire social life was to be covered by the wings of the Church.... This was a gigantic effort to claim the entire world for Christ but one which of necessity brought with it the severest judgment upon every life-tendency which either as heretical or as demoniacal withdrew itself from the blessing of the Church....

Thus making its appearance in a dualistic social state Calvinism has wrought an entire change in the world of thoughts and conceptions. In this also, placing itself before the face of God, it has not only honored *man* for the sake of his likeness to the Divine image, but also *the world* as a Divine creation, and has at once placed to the front the great principle that there is a *particular grace* which works Salvation, and also a *common grace* by which God, maintaining the life of the world, relaxes the curse which rests upon it, arrests its process of corruption, and thus allows the untrammeled development of our life in which to glorify Himself as Creator. Thus the Church receded in order to be neither more nor less than the congregation of believers, and in every department the life of the world was not emancipated from God, but from the dominion of the Church.... Henceforth the curse should no longer rest upon the *world* itself, but upon that which is *sinful* in it, and instead of monastic flight *from* the world the duty is now emphasized of serving God in the world, in every position in life....

Thus it is shown that Calvinism has a sharply-defined starting-point of its own for the three fundamental relations of all human existence: viz., our relation to *God*, to *man* and to the *world*.... This justifies us fully in our statement that Calvinism duly answers the three above named conditions, and thus is incontestably entitled to take its stand by the side of Paganism, Islamism, Romanism and Modernism, and to claim for itself the glory of possessing a well-defined principle and an all-embracing life-system.[3]

Calvinism and Religion

Of course, religion, as such produces *also* a blessing for man, but it does not exist for the sake of man. It is not God who exists for the sake of His creation;—the creation exists for the sake of God. For, as the Scripture says, He has created all things for Himself....

Just as the entire creation reaches its culminating point in man, so also religion finds its clear expression only in man who is made in the image of God, and this not because man seeks it, but because God Himself implanted in man's nature the real essential religious expression, by means of the "seed of religion" (*semen religionis*) as Calvin defines it, sown in our human heart.

God Himself *makes* man religious by means of the *sensus divinitatis*, i.e., the sense of the Divine, which He causes to strike the chords on the harp of his soul. A sound of need interrupts the pure harmony of this divine melody, but only in consequence of sin. In its original form, in its natural condition, religion is exclusively a sentiment of *admiration* and *adoration*, which elevates and unites, not a feeling of dependence which severs and depresses. . . . The starting-point of every motive in religion is God and not Man. Man is the instrument and means, God alone is here the goal, the point of departure and the point of arrival, the fountain from which the waters flow, and at the same time, the ocean into which they finally return. . . .

This leads me naturally, to the . . . question: Is religion *partial*, or it is all-subduing, and comprehensive,—*universal* in the strict sense of the word? Now if the aim of religion be found in man himself and if its realization be made dependent on clerical mediators, religion cannot be but *partial*. In that case it follows logically that every man confines his religion to those occurrences of his life by which his religious needs are stirred, and to those cases in which he finds human intervention at his disposal. The partial character of this sort of religion shows itself in three particulars: in the religious *organ* through which, in the *sphere* in which, and in the *group of persons* among which, religion has to thrive and flourish.

Recent controversy affords a pertinent illustration of the first limitation. The wise men of our generation maintain that religion has to retire from the precinct of the human intellect. It must seek to express itself either by means of the mystical feelings, or else by means of the practical will. Mystical and ethical inclinations are hailed with enthusiasm, in the domain of religion, but in that same domain the intellect, as leading to metaphysical hallucinations, must be muzzled. Metaphysics and Dogmatics are increasingly tabooed. . . .

[Thus] religion is excluded from science, and its authority from the domain of public life; henceforth the inner chamber, the cell for prayer, and the secrecy of the heart should be its exclusive dwelling place. . . . And the result is that, in many different ways, religion, once the central force of human life, is now placed alongside of it. . . .

This brings us naturally to the third characteristic note of this partial view of religion;—religion as pertaining not to all, but only to *the group of pious people* among our generation. Thus the limitation of the *organ* of religion brings about the limitation of its *sphere*, and the limitation of its sphere consequently brings about the limitation of its group or *circle* among men. . . . It so happens that the great bulk of the people are almost devoid of mystical feeling, and energetic strength of will. . . .

Now this whole view of the matter is squarely antagonized by Calvinism, which vindicates for religion its full universal character, and its complete universal application. If everything that is, exists for the sake of God, then it follows that the whole creation must give glory to God. The sun, moon, and stars in the firmament, the birds of the air, the whole of Nature around us, but, above all, man himself, who, priestlike, must consecrate to God the whole of creation, and all life thriving in it. And although sin has deadened a large part of creation to the glory of God, the demand,—the ideal, remains unchangeable, that *every* creature must be immersed in the stream of religion, and end by lying as a religious offering on the altar of the Almighty. A religion confined to feeling or will is therefore unthinkable to the Calvinist. The sacred anointing of the priest of creation must reach down to his beard and to the hem of his garment. His whole being, including all his abilities and powers, must be pervaded by the *sensus divinitatis*, and how then could he exclude his rational consciousness, —the *logos which* is in him, —the light of thought which comes from God Himself to irradiate him?. . . .

The same character of universality was claimed by the Calvinist for the *sphere* of religion and its *circle* of influence among men. Everything that has been created was, in its creation, furnished by God with an unchangeable law of its existence. And because God has fully ordained such laws and ordinances for all life, therefore the Calvinist demands that all life be consecrated to His service, in strict obedience. A religion confined to the closet, the cell, or the church, therefore, Calvin abhors. . . . No sphere of human life is conceivable in which religion does not maintain its demands that God shall be praised, that God's ordinances shall be observed, and that every *labora* shall be permeated with its *ora* in fervent and ceaseless prayer. . . . Consequently, it is impossible for a Calvinist to confine religion to a single group, or to some circles among men. Religion concerns the whole of our human race. . . . To be sure there is a concentration of religious light and life in the Church, but then in the walls of this church, there are wide open windows, and through these spacious windows the light of the Eternal has to radiate over the whole world. Here is a city, set upon a hill, which every man can see afar off. . . . And even he who does not yet imbibe the higher light, or maybe shuts his eyes to it, is nevertheless admonished, with equal emphasis, and in all things, to give glory to the name of the Lord. . . . [4]

This brings us, without any further transition, to our fourth main question, *viz.*, Must religion be *normal* or abnormal, i.e., *soteriological*? The distinction which I have in mind here is concerned with the question, whether in the matter of religion we must reckon *de facto* with man in his present condition as *normal* or as having fallen into sin, and having therefore become *abnormal*. In the latter case religion must necessarily assume a soteriological character. Now the prevailing idea, at present, favors the view that religion has to start from man as being *normal*. Not of course as though our race as a whole should conform already to the highest religious norm. This nobody affirms. . . . As a matter of fact, we meet with much irreligiousness, and imperfect religious development continues to be the rule. But precisely in this slow and gradual progress from the lowest forms to the highest ideals, the development demanded by this normal view of religion contends that it has found confirmation. . . .

Now, this whole theory is opposed by that other and entirely different theory, which, without denying the preformation of so much that is human, in the animal . . . nevertheless maintains that the first man was created in perfect relation to his God, *i.e.*, as imbued by a pure and genuine religion, and consequently explains the many low, imperfect and absurd forms of religion found in Paganism, not as the result of his creation but as the outcome of his Fall. These low and imperfect forms of religion are not to be understood as a process that leads from a lower to a higher, but as a lamentable degeneration. . . . Now in the choice between these two theories Calvinism allows no hesitation. . . . Every attempt to explain sin, as an incomplete stage on the road to perfection, aroused his wrath, as an insult to the majesty of God.

What now does the Calvinist mean by his faith in the ordinances of God?[5] Nothing less than the firmly rooted conviction that all life has first been in the *thoughts* of God, before it came to be realized in *Creation*. Hence all created life necessarily bears in itself a law for its existence, instituted by God Himself. There is no life outside us in Nature, without such divine ordinances,—ordinances which are called the laws of Nature; —a term which we are willing to accept, provided we understand thereby, not laws originating *from* Nature, but laws imposed *upon* Nature. So, there are ordinances of God for the firmament above, and ordinances for the earth below. . . . These ordinances are the servants of God. Consequently there are ordinances of God for our bodies. . . . And even so are there ordinances of God, in Logic, to regulate our thoughts; ordinances of God for our imagination, in the domain of aesthetics; and so, also, strict ordinances of God for the whole of human life in the *domain of morals*. . . . And those ordinances of God, ruling both the mightiest problems and the smallest trifles, are urged upon us, not like the statutes of a law-book, not like rules which may be read from paper, not like a codification of life, which could even for a single moment, exercise any authority of itself, —but they are urged upon us as the constant will of the Omnipresent and Almighty God. . . .

Thence it follows that the true Calvinist adjusts himself to these ordinances not by force, as though they were a yoke of which he would like to rid himself, but with the same readiness with which we follow a guide through the desert, recognizing that *we* are ignorant of the path, which the guide knows, and therefore acknowledging that there is no safety but in closely following in his footsteps. When our respiration is disturbed, we try irresistibly and immediately to remove the disturbance. . . . Just so, in every disturbance of the moral life the believer has to strive as speedily as possible to restore his spiritual respiration, according to the moral commands of his God, because only after this restoration can the inward life again thrive freely in his soul, and renewed energetic action become possible. Therefore every distinction between general moral ordinances, and more special *Christian* commandments is unknown to him. Can we imagine that at one time God willed to rule things in a certain moral order, but that now, in Christ, He wills to rule it otherwise? . . . Verily Christ has swept away the dust with which man's sinful limitations had covered up this world-order, and has made it glitter again in its original brilliancy. Verily Christ and He alone has disclosed to us the eternal love of God, which was, from the beginning, the moving principle of this world order. Above all, Christ has strengthened in us the ability to walk in this world-order with a firm, unfaltering step. But the world-order itself remains just what it was from the beginning. It lays full claim, not only to the believer (as though less were required from the unbeliever), but to every human being and to all human relationships. . . .[6]

ENCYCLOPEDIA OF SACRED THEOLOGY: ITS PRINCIPLES

Subject and Object

In the conception of science the root-idea of *to know* must be sharply maintained. And the question arises: Who is the *subject* of this knowledge, and what is the *object*? Each of us knows innumerable things which lie entirely outside of the realm of science. . . . Science is not the sum-total of what A knows, neither is it the aggregate of what A, B and C know.

The subject of science cannot be this man or that, but must be mankind at large, or, if you please, *the* human consciousness. And the content of knowledge already known by this human consciousness is so immeasurably great, that the most learned and the most richly endowed mind can never know but a very small part of it. Consequently you cannot attain unto a conception of "science" in the higher sense, until you take humanity as an organic whole. Science does not operate atomistically. . . . No, science works organically, i.e. in the sense that the thirst for knowledge lies in human nature; that within certain bounds human nature can obtain knowledge; that the impulse to devote oneself to this task, together with the gifts which enable one to work at it, become apparent of themselves; and that in the realm of intellectual pursuits these coryphaei of our race, without perceiving it and almost unconsciously, go to work according to a plan by which humanity at large advances. . . .

If the subject of science, i.e. the subject that wants to know and that acquires knowledge, lies in the consciousness of humanity, the *object* of science must be *all existing things*, as far as they have discovered their existence to our human consciousness, and will hereafter discover it or leave it to be inferred. . . . This object, as such, could never constitute the material of science for man, if it existed purely atomistically, or if it could only be atomistically known. . . . For the idea of science implies, that from the manifold things I know a *connected* knowledge is born, which would not be possible if there were no relation among the several parts of the object. The necessity of organic inter-relations, which was found to be indispensable in the subject, repeats itself in the object. . . . As long as something is merely *discovered*, it is taken up into our knowledge but not into our science. Only when the inference and the subsequent insight that the parts of the object are organically related prove themselves correct, is that distinction born between the special and the general which learns to recognize in the general the uniting factor of the special. . . .

Even yet enough has not been said. It is not sufficient that the subject of science, i.e. the human consciousness, lives organically in thinking individuals, and that the *object*, about which thinking man wants to know everything he can, exists organically in its parts; but there must also be an organic relation between this subject and this object. This follows already from what was said above, viz. that the subject itself, as well as the thinking of the subject, become objects of science. If there were no organic relation between everything that exists outside of us and ourselves, our consciousness included, the relation in the object would be wanting. But this organic relation between our person and the object of science is much more necessary, in order to render the *science* of the object possible for us. . . .

Thus for all science a threefold organic relation between subject and object is necessary. There must be an organic relation between that object and our *nature*, between that object and our *consciousness*, and between that object and our *world of thought*. . . .

By saying that our *consciousness* stands in the desired organic relation to the object of our science, we simply affirm that it is possible for man to have an apprehension, a perception, and an impression of the existence and of the method of existence of the object. . . . Perception and observation are simply impossible when all organic relation is wanting between any object and our consciousness. . . .

By this, however, this object has not yet been introduced into the world of our *thought*, and without further aid it would still lie outside of our "science. . . ."

[For] there are qualities belonging to the object which lie beyond the reach of the organs of sense, and therefore refuse all representation of themselves. . . . If science means that our human consciousness shall take up into itself what exists as an organic whole, it goes without saying that she makes no progress whatever by the simple presentation of the elements; and that she can achieve her purpose only when, in addition to a fairly complete presentation of the *elements*, she also comes to a fairly complete study of their *relations*. . . . That these relations can be grasped by thought alone and not by presentation lies in their nature. . . .

Thus understood, *science* presents itself to us *as a necessary and ever-continued impulse in the human mind to reflect within itself the cosmos, plastically as to its elements, and to think it through logically as to its relations; always with the understanding that the human mind is capable of this by reason of its organic affinity to its object. . . .* [7]

Suppose that no disturbance by sin had taken place in the subject or object, we should arrive by way of recapitulation at the following conclusion: The *subject* of science is the universal ego in the universal human consciousness; the *object* is the cosmos. This subject and object each exists *organically*, and an organic *relation* exists between the two. Because the *ego* exists dichotomically, i.e. psychically as well as somatically, our consciousness has two fundamental forms, which lead to *representations* and to *conceptions*; while in the object we find the corresponding distinction between *elements* and *relations*. And it is in virtue of this correspondence that science leads to an understanding of the cosmos, both as to its elements and relations. . . .

In this state of things, the *universality* and *necessity*, which are the indispensable characteristics of our knowledge of the cosmos if it is to bear the scientific stamp, would *not* have clashed with our subjectivism. Though it is inconceivable that in a sin*less* development of our race all individuals would have been uniform repetitions of the self-same model; . . . yet in the absence of a disturbance, this multiformity would have been as *harmonious*, as now it works *unharmoniously*. With mutual supplementation there would have been no conflict. And there would have been no desire on the part of one individual subject to push other subjects aside, or to transform the object after itself. . . .

Science and Sin

If there were no sin, nor any of its results, the subjectivity of A would merely be a variation of the subjectivity in B. In virtue of the organic affinity between the two, their subjectivity would not be mutually antagonistic, and the sense of one would harmoniously support and confirm the sense of the other. . . . But, alas, such is not the case in the domain of science. It is all too often evident, that in this domain the natural harmony of subjective expression is hopelessly broken; and for the feeding of skepticism this want of harmony has no equal. By an investigation of self and of the cosmos you have obtained a well-founded scientific conviction, but when you state it, it meets with no response from those who, in their way, have investigated with equally painstaking efforts; and not only is the unity of science broken, but you are shaken in the assurance of your conviction. For when you spoke your conviction, you did not mean simply to give expression to the insight of your own *ego*, but to the universal human insight; which, indeed, it ought to be, if it were wholly accurate.

But of necessity we must accept this hard reality, and in every theory of knowledge which is not to deceive itself, the fact of sin must henceforth claim a more serious consideration. . . .

 It by no means follows, that you should skeptically doubt all science, but simply that it will not do to omit the fact of sin from your theory of knowledge. This would not be warranted if sin were only a thelematic conception and therefore purely ethic; how much less, now, since immediately as well as mediately, sin modifies so largely all those data with which you have to deal in the intellectual domain and in the building-up of your *science*. Ignorance wrought by sin is the most difficult obstacle in the way of all true science.[8]

CALVINISM AND POLITICS

In order that the influence of Calvinism on our political development may be felt, it must be shown, for what fundamental political conceptions

Calvinism has opened the door, and how these political conceptions sprang from its root principle.

This dominating principle was not, soteriologically, justification by faith, but, in the widest sense cosmologically, *the Sovereignty of the Triune God over the whole Cosmos*, in all its spheres and kingdoms, visible and invisible. A *primordial* Sovereignty which eradiates in mankind in a threefold deduced supremacy, *viz.* 1. The Sovereignty in the *State*; 2. The Sovereignty in *Society*; and 3. The Sovereignty in the *Church*. . . .

First then a deduced Sovereignty in that political sphere, which is defined as *the State*. . . . The impulse to form states arises from man's social nature, which was expressed already by Aristotle, when he called man a *zoon politikon*. . . . Man is created from man, and by virtue of his birth he is organically united with the whole race. Together we form *one humanity*. . . . The conception of *States*, however, which subdivide the earth into continents, and each continent into morsels, does not harmonize with this idea. Then only would the organic unity of our race be realized politically, if *one State* could embrace all the world, and if the whole of humanity were associated in one world-empire. Had sin not intervened, no doubt, this would actually have been so. . . . The mistake of the Alexanders, and of the Augusti, and of the Napoleons was not, that they were charmed with the thought of the *One World-empire*, but it was this—that they endeavored to realize this idea notwithstanding that the force of sin had dissolved our unity. . . .

For indeed without sin there would have been neither magistrate nor state-order; but political life, in its entirety, would have evolved itself, after a patriarchal fashion, from the life of the family. Neither bar of justice, nor police nor army, nor navy is conceivable in a world without sin; and thus every rule and ordinance and law would drop away, even as all control and assertion of the power of the magistrate would disappear, were life to develop itself, normally and without hindrance, from its own organic impulse. Who binds up, where nothing is broken? Who uses crutches, where the limbs are sound?

Every State formation, every assertion of the power of the magistrate, every mechanical means of compelling order and of guaranteeing a safe course of life is therefore always something unnatural; something, against which the deeper aspirations of our nature rebel; and which, on this very account, may become the source both of a dreadful abuse of power, on the part of those who exercise it, and of a contumacious revolt on the part the multitude. . . . And thus all true conception of the nature of the State and of the assumption of authority by the magistrate, and on the other hand all true conception of the right and duty of the people to defend liberty, depend on what Calvinism has here placed in the foreground, as the primordial truth—*that God has instituted the magistrates, by reason of sin.*

In this one thought are hidden both the *light-side* and the *shady-side* of the life of the State. . . . These magistrates rule mechanically and do not harmonize with our nature. And this authority of government is exercised by sinful *men*, and is therefore subject to all manner of despotic ambitions. But the *light-side* also, for a sinful humanity, without division in states, without law and government, and without ruling authority, would be a veritable hell on earth. . . . Calvinism has therefore, by its deep conception of sin, laid bare the true root of state-life, and has taught us two things: First—that we have gratefully to receive, from the hand of God, the institution of the State with its magistrates, as a means of preservation, now indeed indispensable. And on the other hand also that, by virtue of our natural impulse, we must ever watch against the danger, which lurks, for our personal liberty, in the power of the State. . . .

No man has the right to rule over another man, otherwise such a right necessarily, and immediately becomes, *the right of the strongest.* . . .

Nor can a group of men, by contract, from their own right, compel you to obey a fellow-man. What binding force is there for me in the allegation, that ages ago one of my progenitors made a "Contract Social," with other men of that time? As man I stand, free and bold, over against the most powerful of my fellow-men.

I do not speak of the family, for here organic, natural ties rule; but in the sphere of the State I do not yield or bow down to anyone, who is man, as I am.

Authority over men cannot arise from men. . . . And thus to the first Calvinistic thesis that *sin alone has necessitated the institution of governments*, this second and no less momentous thesis is added that: *all authority of governments on earth, originates from the Sovereignty of God alone.* When God says to me, "obey," then I humbly bow my head, without compromising in the least my personal dignity, as a man. For, in like proportion as you degrade yourself, by bowing low to a child of man, whose breath is in his nostrils; so, on the other hand do you raise yourself, if you submit to the authority of the Lord of heaven and earth.

Thus the word of Scripture stands: "By Me kings reign," or as the apostle has elsewhere declared: "The powers, that be, are ordained of God. Therefore he that resisteth the power, withstandeth the ordinance of God." The magistrate is an instrument of "common grace," to thwart all license and outrage and to shield the good against the evil. But he is more. Besides all this he is instituted by God as *His* Servant, in order that he may preserve the glorious work of God, in the creation of humanity, from total destruction. Sin attacks God's handiwork, God's plan, God's justice, God's honor, as the supreme Artificer and Builder. Thus God, ordaining the powers that be, in order that, through their instrumentality, He might maintain *His* justice against the strivings of sin, has given to the magistrate the terrible right of life and death. Therefore all the powers that be, whether in empires or in republics, in cities or in states, rule *"by the grace of God."* For the same reason justice bears a holy character. And from the same motive every citizen is bound to obey, not only from dread of punishment, but for the sake of conscience. . . .

Therefore in opposition both to the atheistic popular-sovereignty of the Encyclopedians, and the pantheistic state-sovereignty of German philosophers, the Calvinist maintains the sovereignty of God, as the source of all authority among men. . . . [Calvinism] teaches us to look upward from the existing law to the source of the eternal Right in God, and it creates in us the indomitable courage incessantly to protest against the unrighteousness of the law in the name of this highest Right. . . .

So much for the sovereignty of the State. We now come to *sovereignty in the sphere of Society.*[9]

In a Calvinistic sense we understand hereby, that the family, the business, science, art and so forth are all social spheres, which do not owe their existence to the State, and which do not derive the law of their life from the superiority of the state, but obey a high authority within their own bosom; an authority which rules, by the grace of God, just as the sovereignty of the State does. . . .

In this independent character a special *higher authority* is of necessity involved and this highest authority we intentionally call—*sovereignty in the individual social spheres*, in order that it may be sharply and decidedly expressed that these different developments of social life have *nothing above themselves but God*, and that the State cannot intrude here, and has nothing to command in their domain. As you feel at once, this is the deeply interesting question of our *civil liberties.*

It is here of the highest importance sharply to keep in mind the difference in grade between the *organic* life of society and the *mechanical* character of the government. Whatever among men originates directly from creation, is possessed of all the data for its development, in human nature as such. You see this at once in the family and in the connection of blood relations and other ties . . . which dominate the whole of family-life. In all this there is nothing mechanical. The development is spontaneous, just as that of the stem and the branches of a plant. True, sin here also has exerted its disturbing influence and has distorted much which was intended for a blessing, into a curse. But this fatal efficiency of sin has been stopped by common grace. . . .

The same may be said of the other spheres of life.

Nature about us may have lost the glory of paradise . . . [yet] the chief aim of all human effort remains, what it was by virtue of our creation and before the fall—namely *dominion over nature.* And this dominion cannot be acquired, except by the exercise of the powers, which, by virtue of the ordinances of creation, are innate in nature itself. Accordingly all Science is only the application to the cosmos of the powers of investigation and thought, created within us; and Art is nothing but the natural productivity of the potencies of our imagination. When we admit therefore that sin, though arrested by "common grace," has caused many modifications of these several expressions of life . . . we still maintain that the fundamental character of these expressions remains as it was originally. All together they form the life of creation, in accord with the ordinances of creation, and therefore are *organically* developed.

But the case is wholly different with the assertion of the powers of government. For though it be admitted that even without sin the need would have asserted itself of combining the many families, in a higher unity; this unity would have *internally* been bound up in the Kingship of God, which would have ruled regularly; directly and harmoniously in the hearts of all men, and which would *externally* have incorporated itself in a patriarchal hierarchy. Thus no States would have existed, but only one organic world-empire, with God as its King; exactly what is prophesied for the future which awaits us, when all sin shall have disappeared.

But it is exactly this, which sin has now eliminated from our human life. This unity does no longer exist. . . . Thus peoples and nations originated. These peoples formed States. And over these States God appointed *governments.* And thus, if I may be allowed the expression, it is not a natural head, which organically grew from the body of the people, but a *mechanical* head, which from without has been placed upon the trunk of the nation. A mere remedy therefore, for a wrong condition supervening. A stick placed beside the plant to hold it up, since without it, by reason of its inherent weakness, it would fall to the ground. . . .

According to the apostolic testimony the magistrate bears the sword, and this sword has a threefold meaning. It is the sword of *justice*, to mete out corporeal punishment to the criminal. It is the sword of *war* to defend the honor and the rights and the interests of the State against its enemies. And it is the sword of *order*, to thwart at home all forcible rebellion. . . .

The highest duty of the government remains therefore unchangeably that of *justice*, and in the second place it has to care for the people as an unit, partly *at home*, in order that its unity may grow ever deeper and may not be disturbed, and partly *abroad*, lest the national existence suffer harm. The consequence of all this is that on the one hand, in a people, all sorts of *organic* phenomena of life arise, from its *social* spheres, but that, high above all these, the *mechanical* unifying force of the government is observable. From this arises all friction and clashing. For the government is always inclined, with its *mechanical* authority, to invade social life, to subject it and mechanically to arrange it. But on the other hand social life always endeavors to shake off the authority of the government. . . . It will be admitted that all healthy life of people or state has ever been the historical consequence of the struggle between these two powers. It was the so-called "'constitutional government," which endeavored more firmly to regulate the mutual relation of these two. And in this struggle Calvinism was the first to take its stand. For just in proportion as it honored the authority of the magistrate, instituted by God, did it lift up that *second sovereignty*, which had been implanted by God in the social spheres, in accordance with the ordinances of creation.

It demanded for both independence in their own sphere and regulation of the relation between both, not by the executive, but *under the law*. And by this stern demand, Calvinism may be said to have generated constitutional public law, from its own fundamental idea. . . .

The idea is here fundamental therefore that the sovereignty of God, in its descent upon men, separates itself into two spheres. On the one hand the mechanical sphere of *State-authority*, and on the other hand the organic sphere of the authority of the *Social circles*. And in both these spheres the inherent authority is sovereign, that is to say, it has above itself nothing but God.

Now for the mechanically coercing authority of the government any further explanation is superfluous, not so, however, for the organic social authority.

Nowhere is the dominating character of this organic social authority more plainly discernable than in the sphere of Science. . . . The dominion of men like Aristotle and Plato, Lombard and Thomas, Luther and Calvin, Kant and Darwin, extends, for each of them, over a field of ages. Genius is a *sovereign* power; it forms schools; it lays hold on the spirits of men, with irresistible might; and it exercises an immeasurable influence on the whole condition of human life. This sovereignty of genius is a gift of God, possessed only by His grace. It is subject to no one and is responsible to Him alone Who has granted it this ascendancy. . . .

In relation herewith, and on entirely the same ground of organic superiority, there exists, side by side with this personal sovereignty, the sovereignty of *the sphere*. The University exercises scientific dominion; the Academy of fine arts is possessed of art-power; the guild exercised a technical dominion; the trades-union rules over labor; —and each of these spheres or corporations is conscious of the power of exclusive independent judgment and authoritative action, within its proper sphere of operation. Behind these organic spheres, with intellectual, aesthetical and technical sovereignty, the sphere of the family opens itself, with its right of marriage, domestic peace, education and possession; and in this sphere also the natural head is conscious of exercising an inherent authority, —not because the government allows it, but because God has imposed it. . . .

In all these [various] spheres the State-government cannot impose its laws, but must reverence the innate law of life. God rules in these spheres, just as supremely and sovereignly through his chosen *virtuosi*, as He exercises dominion in the sphere of the State itself, through his chosen *magistrates*.

Bound by its own mandate therefore the government may neither ignore nor modify nor disrupt the divine mandate, under which these social spheres stand. The sovereignty, by the grace of God, of the government is here set aside and limited, for God's sake, by another sovereignty, which is equally divine in origin. Neither the life of science nor of art, nor of agriculture, nor of industry, nor of commerce, nor of navigation, nor of the family, nor of human relationship may be coerced to suit itself to the grace of the government. The State may never become an octopus, which stifles the whole of life. It must occupy its own place, on its own root, among all the other trees of the forest, and thus it has to honor and maintain every form of life, which grows independently, in its own sacred autonomy.

Does this mean that the government has no right *whatever* of interference in these autonomous spheres of life? Not at all.

It possesses the threefold right and duty: 1. Whenever different spheres clash, to compel mutual regard for the boundary-lines of each; 2. To defend individuals and the weak ones, in those spheres, against the abuse of power of the rest; and 3. To coerce all together to bear *personal* and *financial* burdens for the maintenance of the natural unity of the State. The decision cannot, however, in these cases, *unilaterally* rest with the magistrate. The Law here has to indicate the rights of each, and the rights of the citizens over their own purses must remain the invincible bulwark against the abuse of power on the part of the government. . . .

Calvinism is to be praised for having built a dam across [state absolutism] not by appealing to popular force, nor to the hallucination of human greatness, but by deducing those rights and liberties of social life from the

same source, from which the high authority of the government flows—
even the *absolute sovereignty of God*. From this *one* source, in God, *sovereignty in the individual sphere*, in the family and in every social circle, is just as directly derived as the *supremacy of State-authority*. These two must therefore come to an understanding, and both have the same sacred obligation to maintain their God-given sovereign authority and to make it subservient to the majesty of God.

A people therefore which abandons to State Supremacy the right of the family, or a University which abandons to it the rights of science, is just as guilty before God, as a nation which lays its hands upon the rights of the magistrates. And thus the struggle for liberty is not only declared permissible, but is made a duty for each individual in his own sphere. . . .

Now let us put the theory itself to the test and look successively at the duty of the magistrate in things spiritual: 1. towards *God*, 2. towards the *Church*, and 3. towards *individuals*. As regards the first point, the magistrates are and remain—"God's servants." They have to recognize God as Supreme Ruler, from Whom they derive their power. They have to serve God, by ruling the people according to *His* ordinances. They have to restrain blasphemy, where it directly assumes the character of an affront to the Divine Majesty. And God's supremacy is to be recognized, by confessing His name in the Constitution as the Source of all political power, by maintaining the Sabbath, by proclaiming days of prayer and thanksgiving, and by invoking His Divine blessing.

Therefore in order that they may govern, according to His holy ordinances, every magistrate is in duty bound to investigate the rights of God, both in the natural life and in His Word. Not to subject himself to the decision of any church, but in order that he himself may catch the light which he needs for the knowledge of the Divine will. And as regards blasphemy, the *right* of the magistrate to restrain it rests in the God-consciousness innate in every man; and the *duty* to exercise this right flows from the fact that God is the Supreme and Sovereign Ruler over every State and over every Nation. But for this very reason the fact of blasphemy is only then to be deemed established, when the intention is apparent contumaciously to affront this majesty of God *as Supreme Ruler of the State*. What is then punished is not the religious offence, nor the impious sentiment, but the attack upon the foundation of public law, upon which both the State and its government are resting.

Meanwhile there is in this respect a noteworthy difference between States which are absolutely governed by a monarch and States which are governed constitutionally; or in a republic, in a still wider range, by an extensive assembly. . . .

But whether you are dealing with the will of a single individual, or with the will of many men, in a decision arrived at by a vote, the principal thing remains that the government has to judge and to decide independently. Not as an appendix to the Church, nor as its pupil. The sphere of State stands itself under the majesty of the Lord. In that sphere therefore an independent responsibility to God is to be maintained. The sphere of the State is not profane. But both Church and State must, each in their own sphere, obey God and serve His honor. And to that end in either sphere *God's Word* must rule, but in the sphere of the State only through the conscience of the persons invested with authority. The first thing of course is, and remains, that all nations shall be governed in a Christian way; that is to say, in accordance with the principle which, for all statecraft, flow from the Christ. But this can never be realized except through the subjective convictions of those in authority, according to their personal views of the demands of that Christian principle, as regards the public service.

Of an entirely different nature is the second question, what ought to be the relation between the government and the *visible Church. . . .* Nearly all nations begin with unity of religion. But it is equally natural that this unity is split up, where the individual life, in the process of development, gains in strength, and where multiformity asserts itself, as the undeniable demand of a richer development of life. And thus we are confronted with the fact that the visible church has been split up, and that in no country whatever the absolute unity of the visible church can be any longer maintained.

What then is the duty of the government?

Must it—for the question may be reduced to this—must it now form an individual judgment, as to which of those many churches is the true one? And must it maintain this one over against the others? Or is it the duty of the government to suspend its own judgment and to consider the multiform complex of all these denominations, as the totality of the manifestation of the Church of Christ on earth?

From a Calvinistic standpoint we must decide in favor of the latter suggestion. Not from a false idea of neutrality, nor as if Calvinism could ever be indifferent to what is true and what false, *but because the government lacks the data of judgment,* and because every magisterial judgment here infringes the *sovereignty of the Church. . . .*

Hence it is that the Calvinists have always struggled so proudly and courageously for the liberty, that is to say for the sovereignty, of the Church, within her own sphere, in distinction from the Lutheran theologians. In Christ, they contended, the Church has her own King. Her position in the

State is not assigned her by the permission of the Government, but *jure divino*. She has her own organization. She possesses her own office-bearers. And in a similar way she has her own gifts to distinguish truth from the lie. It is therefore her privilege, and not that of the State, to determine her own characteristics as the true Church, and to proclaim her own confession, as the confession of the truth. . . .

But this can in no regard break the fundamental rule that the government must honor the complex of Christian churches, as the multiform manifestation of the Church of Christ on earth. That the magistrate has to respect the liberty, *i.e.*, the sovereignty of the Church of Christ in the individual sphere of these churches. That churches flourish most richly, when the government allows them to live from their own strength on the voluntary principle. . . . Only the system of a free Church, in a free State, may be honored from a Calvinistic standpoint. . . .

Of an entirely different nature, on the contrary, is the last question, to which I referred, namely the duty of the government, as regards the *sovereignty of the individual person.*

In the second part of this lecture I have already indicated that the developed man also possesses an individual sphere of life, with sovereignty in his own circle. . . .

(In some respect every man is a sovereign, for everybody must have and has, a sphere of life of his own, in which he has no one above him, but God alone.) I do not point to this to over-estimate the importance of conscience, for whosoever wishes to liberate conscience, where God and His Word are concerned, I meet as an opponent, not as an ally. This however does not prevent my maintaining the sovereignty of conscience, as the palladium of all personal liberty, in this sense—that conscience is never subject to man but always and ever to God Almighty.

This need of the personal liberty of conscience, however, does not immediately assert itself. It does not express itself with emphasis in the child, but only in the mature man; and in the same way it mostly slumbers among undeveloped peoples, and is irresistible only among highly developed nations. A man of ripe and rich development will rather become a voluntary exile, will rather suffer imprisonment, nay even sacrifice life itself, than tolerate constraint in the forum of his conscience. And the deeply rooted repugnance against the Inquisition, which for three long centuries would not be assuaged, grew up from the conviction that its practices violated and assaulted human life in man. This imposes on the government a twofold obligation. In the first place, it must cause this liberty of conscience to be respected by the Church; and in the second place, it must give way itself to the sovereign conscience.

As regards the first, the sovereignty of the Church find its natural limitation in the sovereignty of the free personality. Sovereign within her own domain, she has no power over those who live outside of that sphere. And wherever, in violation of this principle, transgression of power may occur, the government has to respect the claims on protection of every citizen. The Church may not be forced to tolerate as a member one whom she feels obliged to expel from her circle; but on the other hand no citizen of the State must be compelled to remain in a church which his conscience forces him to leave.

Meantime what the government in this respect demands of the churches, it must practice itself, by allowing to each and every citizen liberty of conscience, as the primordial and inalienable right of all men.

It has cost a heroic struggle to wrest this greatest of all human liberties from the grasp of despotism; and streams of human blood have been poured out before the object was attained. But for this very reason every son of the Reformation tramples upon the honor of the fathers, who does not assiduously and without retrenching, defend this palladium of our liberties. In order that it may be able to rule *men*, the government must respect this deepest ethical power of our human existence. A nation, consisting of citizens whose consciences are bruised, is itself broken in its national strength. . . .

In the French Revolution a civil liberty for every·Christian *to agree with the unbelieving majority*; in Calvinism, a liberty of conscience, which enables every man to serve God, *according to his own conviction and the dictates of his own heart*.[10]

COMMON GRACE

There is neither doubt nor uncertainty about the situation that followed the fall. On the one hand, Scripture vividly pictures it to us; on the other, it continues in part to this day and can therefore be read from what we see and hear all around us. We have noted before that this newly inaugurated situation did not correspond to what had been predicted as the consequence of sin. Death, in its full effect, did not set in on that day, and Reformed theologians have consistently pointed out how in this non-arrival of what was prophesied for ill we see the emergence of a saving and long-suffering grace. Nor was this the first manifestation of grace, for human life in Paradise was inconceivable without an environing and invasive grace. To every rational creature grace is the air he breathes. But now for the first time this divine grace assumes its character as saving grace in which, inasmuch as we are sinners, we first and most naturally recognize the grace of God. . . .

This manifestation of grace served ultimately not to save us but to bring out the glory of the Divine Being, and only in the second place, as the consequence of this end, to snatch us from our self-sought ruin. This manifestation of grace consisted in restraining, blocking, or redirecting the consequences that would otherwise have resulted from sin. It intercepts the natural outworking of the poison of sin and either diverts and alters it or opposes and destroys it. For that reason we must distinguish two dimensions in this manifestation of grace: 1. a *saving* grace, which in the end abolishes sin and completely undoes its consequences; and 2. a *temporal restraining* grace, which holds back and blocks the effect of sin. The former, that is saving grace, is in the nature of the case *special* and restricted to God's elect. The second, *common* grace, is extended to the whole of our human life. The question then arises whether these two forms of grace, this *special* and this *common* grace, exist independently side-by-side or operate in connection with each other, and if so, how. . . . The connection is . . . undeniable, but how are we to construe it? . . .

Certainly; there is nothing wrong in saying that everything happens for Christ's sake, that therefore the *body of Christ* is the all-controlling and central element in history, and that on this basis the church of Christ is the pivot on which the life of humanity hinges. Those who overlook or deny this reality will never find any unity in the course of history. For them century follows century, and in the process development follows decline and regression progression, but the stream of life as a whole is not going anywhere, has no goal. This life lacks a center, a pivot on which it turns. . . . The Reformed confession—which maintains that all things, also in this world, aim at the Christ, that his Body is the key component, and that in this sense one can say the church of Christ forms the center of world history— offers a basis for a view of history far superior to the common one. So we will think twice before we will detract in any way from this confession. Not *common* grace but the order of *special grace* prevails.

But this thesis leads to a purer confession only if you respect the *order*. All things exist *for the sake of Christ* and only as a corollary for his *Body* and the *Church*—hence not for *you* and then for the *Church* and so also for the *Body* of Christ and finally for the *Christ*. No: Christ, by whom all things exist including ourselves, is before all things. He is the reflection of God's glory and bears the very stamp of his nature. We confess that all things are created by him—whether visible or invisible, in heaven and on earth—in whom all things now hold together. That is the Christ around whom all things revolve, since in him the fullness of God dwells bodily and before him every knee shall bow and every tongue confess that Christ is *Lord* to the glory of God the Father (Col. 1:16–19, Phil. 2: 10–11). Certainly the *Body* also shares in that honor. Something of his radiance is reflected by his church on earth, and every *elect* person catches some part of it. But surely that is very different from starting with myself as an elect person, putting myself in the foreground, and only from there ending up with Christ. In the only true system everything else is second, Christ is at the head and is made central not insofar as he became our brother but because he is the Son of God the Father, and because the Father loves the Son and glorifies him with everlasting honor. . . .

We have no right to conceptualize the image of the Mediator in ways other than Scripture presents it. People fall into one-sidedness. . . . if, reflecting on the Christ, they think exclusively of the blood shed in atonement and refuse to take account of the significance of Christ for the body, for the visible world, and for the outcome of world history. Consider carefully: by taking this tack you run the danger of isolating Christ for your soul and you view life in and for the world as something that exists *alongside* your Christian religion, not controlled by it. Then the word "Christian" seems appropriate to you only when it concerns certain matters of faith or things directly connected with the faith—your church, your school, missions and the like—but all the remaining spheres of life fall for you *outside the Christ*. In the world you conduct yourself as others do; that is less holy, almost unholy, territory which must somehow take care of itself. You only have to take a small step more before landing in the Anabaptist position which concentrated all sanctity in the human soul and dug a deep chasm between this inward-looking spirituality and life all around. Then scholarship becomes unholy; the development of art, trade, and business becomes unholy; unholy also the functions of government; in short, all that is not directly spiritual and aimed at the soul. This way of thinking results in your living in two distinct circles of thought: in the very circumscribed circle of your soul's salvation on the one hand, and in the spacious, life-encompassing sphere of the world on the other. Your Christ is at home in the former but not in the latter. . . .

. . . Scripture continually points out that the *Savior* of the world is also the *Creator* of the world, indeed that he could become its Savior only *because* he already was its *Creator*. . . .

Common grace opens a history, unlocks an enormous space of time, triggers a vast and long-lasting stream of events, in a word, precipitates a series of successive centuries. If that series of centuries is not directed toward an endless, unvarying repetition of the same things, then over the course of those centuries there has to be constant change, modification, transformation in human life. Though it pass through periods of deepening darkness, this change has to ignite ever more light, consistently enrich human life, and so bear the character of perpetual development from less to more, a progressively fuller unfolding of life. If one pictures the distance that exists even now between the life of a Hottentot in his kraal and the life of a highly refined family in European society, one can measure that progress in the blink of an eye. And though people imagine at the end of every century that its progress has been so astonishing that further progress can hardly be imagined, every century nevertheless teaches us that the new things added each time surpass all that has been imagined before. How has the nineteenth century not changed and enriched our human life and blessed it with new conveniences!

The tendency in devout circles to oppose that progress and perpetual development of human life was therefore quite misguided. It must undoubtedly be acknowledged that Christians, by refusing to participate in that development, were the reason why morally and religiously that development often took a wrong turn. Those who are in Christ must not oppose such development and progress, must not even distance themselves from it. Their calling also in this cultural realm is rather to be in the vanguard. . . .

Therefore, we must emphatically state that the interval of centuries that have passed since the fall is not a blank space in the plan of God. The ages lying behind us, by God's decree, must have a purpose and goal, and that purpose can be understood only if we understand that the ongoing development of humanity is *contained in the plan of God*. It follows that the history of our race resulting from this development is not from Satan nor from man *but from God* and that all those who reject and fail to appreciate this development deny the work of God in history. Scripture speaks of the "consummation of the ages" (Matt. 13:39–40), a term that does not mean the centuries will terminate at some point but that they are directed toward a final goal and that everything contained in those centuries is linked to that final goal. . . .

So then, we arrive at this clear insight. The ages must continue not solely for the sake of the elect, nor solely for God to disclose means to us in our struggle against suffering, but in the interest of developing the world itself to its consummation—for as long as is needed to take the world from its beginning and the earliest germination of our human life to the point where the whole process is complete and God has truly reached the final goal he had in mind for it. Thus not a half century, not even a quarter century, will be wasted. There is neither vacuity nor stagnation here. The things that do not yet grow above ground already grow underground in the germination of the seed or the strengthening of the root-system. Not a year, not a day, not an hour can be spared. For all those centuries God has restlessly continued his work in our human race, in the totality of the life of this world. Nothing in it is purposeless or redundant. Things had to go as they did, there was no other way, and the sign of the Son of man will appear in the clouds only when the whole magnificent work of God is complete and the consummation of the world has been inaugurated.

Therefore every view that would confine God's work to the small sector we might label "church life" must be set aside. There is beside the great work of God in *special* grace also that totally other work of God in the realm of *common* grace. That work encompasses the whole life of the world. . . . All of it was an indispensable part of the great work that God is doing to consummate the world's development. And though a great deal in all this *we* cannot connect with the Kingdom or the content of our faith, nevertheless it all has meaning. None of it can be spared because it pleases God, despite Satan's devices and human sin, to actualize everything he had put into this world at the time of creation, to insist on its realization, to develop it so completely that the full sum of its vital energies may enter the light of day at the consummation of the world.

The national church[11] preaches the principle that an entire people, an entire nation, must be incorporated into the church by baptism. . . . even though everybody knows that the real believers comprise no more than a painfully small number among the large masses of people. . . . Directly opposed to it is the system of the *church as organism.* . . . It maintains that the blessing of Christianity can only be truly effective in the wider circle [of human life] if the institutional church organizes itself in accordance with the demand of Scripture, if Baptism as an ecclesiastical sacrament is administered only to believers and their offspring, and if church discipline is consistently exercised to purify the church. Accordingly, they distinguish between the church as *organism* and the church as *institute* in order that *both* may come into their own: both the sanctity of the covenant among those who confess Christ *and* the influence that should impinge upon the world outside this circle.

This is impossible from the national-church standpoint, which recognizes only one circle, the circle of the church as institute. . . . But we believe there are two circles. First the circle of confessors, the objective church, the circle of the covenant. According to the Heidelberg Catechism, Baptism is extended solely to this first circle—that baptized children may be "*distinguished from the children of unbelievers*" (Q/A 74). The Lord's Supper is administered only within that circle, and solely within that circle can a "gathering of believers" be honored. Only the church that coincides with this circle can therefore possess the marks of the "true church" which are "the pure preaching of the gospel, the pure administration of the sacraments, and the exercise of church discipline both as to confession and the conduct of life" (Belgic Confession, art. XXIX).

But we cannot stop here. This institute does not cover everything that is Christian. Though the lamp of the Christian religion only burns within that institute's walls, its light shines out through its windows to areas far beyond, illumining all the sectors and associations that appear across the wide range of human life and activity. Justice, law, the home and family, business, vocation, public opinion and literature, art and science, and so much more are all illuminated by that light, and that illumination will be stronger and more penetrating as the lamp of the gospel is allowed to shine more brightly and clearly in the church institute.

Aside from this first circle of the institute and in necessary connection with it, we thus recognize another circle whose circumference is determined by the length of the ray that shines out from the church institute over the life of people and nation. Since this second circle is not attached to particular persons, is not circumscribed by a certain number of people listed in church directories, and does not have its own office-bearers but is interwoven with the very fabric of national life, this extra-institutional influence at work in society points us to the *church as organism.* That church, after all, exists before the institute; it lies behind the institute; it alone gives substance and value to that institute. The church as organism has its center in heaven, in Christ; it encompasses all ages from the beginning of the world to the end so as to fulfill all the ages coming after us. The church as organism may even manifest itself where all personal faith is missing but where nevertheless some of the golden glow of eternal life is reflected on the ordinary facades of the great edifice of human life. . . .

Precisely because the church, in Jesus' words, is a city set on a hill, its light must extend over a wide area. To put it in plain prose, a sanctifying and purifying influence must proceed from the church of the Lord to impact the whole society amid which it operates. That influence must begin by arousing a certain admiration for the heroic courage with which it has borne persecution and oppression. Next it must inspire respect for the earnestness and purity of life lived in church circles. It must further excite feelings of sympathy by the warm glow of love and compassion in the community of faith. And finally, as a result of all this, it must purify and ennoble the ideas in general circulation, elevate public opinion, introduce more solid principles, and so raise the view of life prevailing in state, society, and the family. In fact this has historically been the case. The church of Christ has almost nowhere established a lasting presence without also modifying the general outlook on life beyond its institutional walls. . . .

We can exert power for good, therefore, only if we are prepared to drum it into our heads that the church of Christ can never exert influence on civil society directly, only indirectly. Therefore its goal must remain (1) to assure the church full freedom of action and full authority to maintain its own unique character; (2) to avert any attempt to introduce pagan concepts and ideas into the country's laws, public institutions, and public opinion in place of Christian ones; and (3) to continually expand the dominance of nobler and purer ideas in civil society by the courageous action of its members in every area of life. In a nutshell: what we want is a strong confessional church but not a confessional civil society nor a confessional state.

This secularization of state and society is one of the most basic ideas of Calvinism, though it did not succeed in immediately and completely working out this idea in pure form. . . . Calvinism from its own roots produced the conviction that the church of Christ cannot be a national church because it had to be rigorously confessional and maintain Christian discipline, and that the Christian character of society therefore cannot be secured by the baptism of the whole citizenry but is to be found in the influence that the church of Christ exerts upon the whole organization of national life. By its influence on the state and civil society the church of Christ aims only at a *moral triumph*, not at the imposition of confessional bonds nor at the exercise of authoritarian control. The example of the United States of America, accordingly, demonstrates how the various divisions of the Christian church, the moment they unitedly adopt this position, not only give up fighting among themselves in order to contend together peacefully in matters of faith, but also that precisely these good mutual relations enable them to exert a much greater influence on civil and national conditions than the most powerful national church ever could. . . .

Terms such as "a Christian nation," "a Christian country," "a Christian society," "Christian art," and the like, do not mean that such a nation consists mainly of regenerate Christian persons or that such a society has already been transposed into the kingdom of heaven. This was never the case anywhere. Even in Israel the great majority was always apostate and idolatrous and the "faithful" always a rather small minority. No, it means that in such a country special grace in the church and among believers exerted so strong a formative influence on common grace that common grace thereby attained its highest development. The adjective "Christian" therefore says nothing about the spiritual state of the inhabitants of such a country but only witnesses to the fact that public opinion, the general mind-set, the ruling ideas, the moral norms, the laws and customs there clearly betoken the influence of the Christian faith. Though this is attributable to special grace, it is manifested on the terrain of common grace, i. e., in ordinary civil life. This influence leads to the abolition of slavery in the laws and life of a country, to the improved position of women, to the maintenance of public virtue, respect for the Sabbath, compassion for the poor, consistent regard for the ideal over the material, and—even in manners—the elevation of all that is human from its sunken state to a higher standpoint.[12]

NOTES

1. [Abraham Kuyper, "Confidentially," in *Abraham Kuyper: A Centennial Anthology*, ed. James D. Bratt (Grand Rapids, Mich.: Wm B. Eerdmans, 1988), 55–56. In 1863, having just received his doctorate in theology from the University of Leiden, where currents of theological liberalism were running strong, Kuyper took his first pastorate in the tiny village of Beesd in the southern part of the Netherlands (in the Brabant). His experience there with certain of his conservative parishioners proved formative for the rest of his life. He wrote about his experience in a small treatise that he published a few years later (1873), "Confidentially" ("Confidentie" in Dutch).]

2. [Kuyper then explains why he does not simply cite Christianity as the coordinate of paganism and Islam, but instead divides Christianity into Catholicism and Calvinism.]

3. [Abraham Kuyper, *Calvinism: Six Lectures Delivered in the Theological Seminary at Princeton* (New York: F. H. Revell, 1899), 5, 7, 12–13, 16, 18, 25–27, 29–33.]

4. [Kuyper moves on from this point to raise the question whether our condition as a whole, and religion along with it, should be seen as normal or abnormal. The terminology never became popular, but the meaning is clear enough.]

5. [Having argued that ours is the abnormal condition of creatures who have fallen from their state of religious and moral well-functioning, rather than normal creatures who are advancing to that state, Kuyper asks what is to guide us in this "abnormal" situation. His answer is: the ordinances of God. In his articulation of what he means by this, it becomes clear that he adheres to a version of natural law theory. This was of prime importance for his theory of politics in a pluralist society.]

6. [Kuyper, *Calvinism*, 52–53, 58–66. In the preceding discussion of paganism, Catholicism, Islam, modernism, and Calvinism, Kuyper was assuming that, unless they are in some way deformed, such religions, and others like them, orient a person's life in general. In this essay, the second of his Stone Lectures, Kuyper argues the case for this understanding of properly formed religion after first suggesting that religion is not an invention of human beings but the outcome of an impulse planted by God in all humankind, to the end that God's glory will be acknowledged and displayed.]

7. [Kuyper now goes on to argue that sin has introduced a "disturbance" into this picture: the human ego, which is the subject of science, has been broken up, especially at that third point of those worlds of thought whereby we try to grasp the relationships among elements; and the result of this, in turn, is that our diverse worlds of thought often obstruct rather than enable access to reality in its organic interrelationships.]

8. [Abraham Kuyper, *Encyclopedia of Sacred Theology: Its Principles*, trans. J. Hendrik De Vries (New York: Charles Scribner's Sons, 1898), 63–70, 72, 74–76, 83, 89–90, 106–107. In the preceding selections, Kuyper has argued that Calvinism in particular, and well-formed religion in general, incorporates not only a moral and an emotional component but an intellectual component as well. It comes as no surprise, then, to find him arguing that in a religiously pluralistic society, we must expect a pluralized academy as well, with some of the pluralism, though by no means all, grounded in religious disagreement. The point has its obvious analogue for politics. The Dutch word translated here as "science" is *wetenschap*, a synonym of the German *Wissenschaft*. A better translation would probably be "academic learning."]

9. [Having presented his account of state sovereignty, Kuyper now turns to his famous theory of "sphere sovereignty," without which one cannot fully understand his account of state sovereignty. Throughout his career Kuyper appealed to his theory of sphere sovereignty, most famously in his address at the opening of the Free University in 1880, titled "Sovereignty in its own Sphere" ("Souvereiniteit in eigen kring"). Probably the best statement of the theory, however, is the one that occurs here in the third of his Stone Lectures.]

10. [Kuyper, *Calvinism: Six Lectures*, 92–105, 115–127, 133–142.]

11. [Among the many uses Kuyper makes of his doctrine of common grace, prominent was his use of the doctrine to articulate his opposition to a national church.]

12. [Abraham Kuyper, "Common Grace," in *Abraham Kuyper: A Centennial Anthology*, 167–170, 172–176, 193–195, 197–199. One of the theological underpinnings of the account of human nature, law, justice, authority, civil society, and the state outlined in the preceding readings, was Kuyper's doctrine of common grace. He developed his thoughts on the matter in a long series of articles in the weekly paper he edited, *De Heraut*; these were later collected into a three-volume publication titled *Common Grace* (*De Gemeene Gratie*).]

[CHAPTER 2]

Susan B. Anthony (1820–1906)

COMMENTARY

MARY D. PELLAUER

A century after her death, Susan B. Anthony is the most familiar name of the American women's suffrage movement. Beyond her name, however, we are less well aware of what she believed and did. Anthony's religious position, which had few parallels in her time and has few even in ours, is especially unfamiliar. Yet Anthony's themes resonate, especially with those who have learned from liberation theology.

Unlike other figures analyzed in this volume, Anthony was not a professional theologian; indeed, theological education opened up for women only during the decades of her struggle. An activist's religious perspective is perhaps inevitably different from that of seminary professors, church people, or clergy. But it may be no less instructive; indeed, it may be more so. Religious disputes were routine in the suffragist movement. St. Paul's exhortations to women to "be silent in the churches" (1 Cor. 14:34–35), for instance, had to be countered, whether by suffragists or by women in the antislavery movement. Since earlier women, such as Lucretia Mott and the Grimke sisters, had pioneered in answering such claims, Anthony took it for granted that she could be a public activist against slavery and for women's rights.

A BIOGRAPHICAL SKETCH

Susan B. Anthony was born in 1820 and brought up by an unconventional Quaker family in upstate New York.[1] Her parents belonged to the abolition and suffrage causes before she did. They attended the first women's rights convention and signed its Declaration of Sentiments.

The Anthony family encouraged, supported, and often financed their daughter Susan's work throughout her life. For fifteen years, Anthony earned her living as a schoolteacher, leaving that career only for full-time devotion to struggling for justice, initially in the temperance movement and then for antislavery and women's rights.

At a temperance convention in 1853, Anthony met Elizabeth Cady Stanton, the daughter of a judge, who had been heartbroken in her youth when told that girls could not become lawyers. She was steeped in the American democratic tradition and adept at explicating legal precedents. Her husband, Henry Stanton, was a lawyer active in a less radical wing of the antislavery struggle than the one that held Anthony's allegiance. Stanton and Anthony became lifelong friends and collaborators, often working together to write speeches that one of them would deliver. Both agreed that they complemented each other's strengths.

The two women wrote and campaigned together often, especially after Stanton's children were older. They collaborated, developed tactics and strategy, comforted, and provoked each other. After Stanton's death, decades after the two women began working together, Anthony was asked what period of their lives she had enjoyed the most. She replied:

> The days when the struggle was the hardest and the fight the thickest; when the whole world was against us and we had to stand the closer to each other; when I would go to her home and help with the children and the housekeeping through the day and then we would sit up far into the night preparing our ammunition and getting ready to move on the enemy. The years since the rewards began to come have brought no enjoyment like that.[2]

In 1854, Anthony began her career as a full-time activist by systematizing a New York organization to work for women's property and custody rights. During the late 1850s, she was the general agent for the New York State Anti-Slavery Society, and, along with many speakers whose campaigns she scheduled and assisted, met her trials by mob. To Anthony, the parallels between the struggles against slavery and for women's rights were vivid. In these antislavery days she absorbed principles such as "no union with slave-holders," "no compromise," "of two evils, choose neither," "do right and leave the consequences to God," and "resistance to tyranny is obedience to God." Grassroots defiance of the Fugitive Slave Law was especially important and formative for her. In later years, she often prefaced a comment with, "I was on the old Garrison platform."[3]

After the Civil War ended in 1865, the women's rights movement split, painfully, into two wings. One group argued that "this is the Negro's hour," and therefore advocated that women should lay aside their claims so as not to detract from measures for the newly emancipated. This group became the nucleus of the Boston wing, the American Woman Suffrage Association (AWSA). A second group argued variously that all the disfranchised should stand together, or sometimes, more disastrously, that the most educated should be enfranchised first. This group became the National Woman Suffrage Association (NWSA), and it was led by Stanton and Anthony. It was more fiery and confrontational than AWSA, and focused on national rather than on state-by-state action. NWSA's conventions often featured resolutions against patriarchal religion, many of them from Stanton's pen. These resolutions claimed, for instance, that women's suffering stems from religion, whether Christianity or any other. At AWSA meetings, in contrast, with many clergy in attendance, the members voted that Christianity had done more for women's status than any other single force. The split in the woman suffrage moment was not healed until 1890, when the NWSA and the AWSA became the NAWSA, an event largely attributable to Anthony's work with younger women in the Boston group.

In the late 1860s, Anthony published the stormy paper *The Revolution*, with its slogan, "men, their rights and nothing more; women, their rights and nothing less." Stanton and Parker Pillsbury, a controversial "come-outer" from the antislavery ranks, wrote most of the copy for the paper. *The Revolution* did not hesitate to take sides on Victorian scandals, thus causing outrage among its readers and others. The paper's eventual failure committed Anthony to six years' work to repay its $10,000 debt.

In addition to her publishing work, Anthony attempted to create a working-women's association, a move that sparked friction with male unionists. She also took to the lecture circuit and tramped the country from end to end as she agitated for women's rights from a variety of angles. She spoke, for instance, on "the true woman," "homes of single women," "bread and the ballot," and "social purity." Her diary for 1871 sums up the year's efforts: "6 months of constant travel, full 8,000 miles, 108 lectures. The year's full work 13,000 miles travel, 170 meetings."[4]

The next year, 1872, was another turning point for women's rights activists. Several people had argued that the Reconstruction amendments to the Constitution, passed in the aftermath of the Civil War, already enfranchised women. Women turned out around the country to test this proposition by casting their ballots, and Anthony was one of the voters. She was the only one indicted and brought to trial for it, however, placing her in a long line of American activists who hoped the judicial system would solve the issues of their particular movements. Anthony's impassioned extempore response to this behavior is a fine example of the kind of political rhetoric that was dear to her heart.

For the next thirty years, Anthony dedicated herself to convincing the Congress to pass a constitutional amendment enfranchising women. The amendment became so identified with her that through its successive numerical designations (from XVI to XX), it was called "the Anthony Amendment."

In her sixties, Anthony—still very active in political work—turned her attention also to chronicling the movement of which she was a part. In the 1880s, Stanton and Anthony realized that no one else would write the history that they and their friends had made. The two women passed hundreds of hours with old letters and documents from women's rights conventions all over the country and by 1886 produced three large volumes (nine hundred or so pages each) of *The History of Woman Suffrage*. Anthony hated this time of enforced inactivity. "I love to make history but hate to write it," she commented in a letter to a friend.[5]

During the 1890s, while Anthony remained a prime mover in the NAWSA, Stanton was often in Europe or moving residence from the home of one child to that of another. Stanton had grown increasingly convinced that religion was at the heart of women's degradation. Gathering a group of like-minded women (several of them theologically trained), she set about writing vehement commentaries on the biblical texts related to women. The *Woman's Bible* was published in time for the NAWSA convention of 1896 to vote to dissociate itself from the project. The vote was a stinging rebuke to Stanton, a pioneer of the movement. Anthony publicly defended Stanton's freedom to express her religious beliefs as part of the suffragist platform, but she privately expressed her disagreements with Stanton's religious views. As Stanton put it, "like husband and wife, each has the feeling that we must have no differences in public."[6]

Anthony spent fifty-odd years of her life agitating for reform, enticing others to join her, and doing the tedious "common work" of reform movements. She engaged speakers, laid out their itineraries in statewide or national campaigns, and arranged publicity for them while herself giving innumerable lectures, frequently to hostile crowds. She recruited a whole generation of younger women to join the struggle. She was interminably busy at fundraising. She went door-to-door with petitions. She arranged and gave testimony to congressional committees, both state and national. She buttonholed congressmen and more than one American president. And she demanded a suffrage plank on the platforms of political parties of all sorts. Ever unmarried despite a series of reported proposals, she was castigated, mocked, stereotyped, and lied about by the press. Everywhere,

Anthony was the object of personal comments that Stanton's maternal status and respectable appearance did not provoke.

A contemporary gives a rare glimpse of the two women during the Kansas campaign of 1867:

> Of course it is nothing new to say that Mrs. Stanton was the object of honor and admiration everywhere. Miss Anthony looked after her interests and comfort in the most cheerful and kindly manner, occasionally complaining good naturedly of Mrs. Stanton's carelessness in leaving various articles of her wearing apparel scattered over the State, and of the trouble she had in recovering a gold watch which Mrs. Stanton had left hanging on the bed post in a little hotel in Southern Kansas. I remember one evening of the Convention in Lawrence when the hall was crowded with an eager and expectant audience. Miss Anthony was there early, looking after everything, seats, lights, ushers, doorkeepers, etc. Presently, Gov. Robinson came to her and said, "Where's Mrs. Stanton? It's time to commence." "She's at Mrs. ——'s waiting for some of you men to go for her with a carriage," was the reply. The hint was quickly acted upon and Mrs. Stanton, fresh, smiling and unfatigued, was presented to the audience.[7]

As the two women grew older, these patterns did not change much. An annual convention drew near, and Stanton claimed she was not going, that it was too much. A week before it opened, Anthony arrived at Stanton's home, started her writing the major address, packed her bags, and detrained with Stanton in tow and complaining all the while. Perhaps Stanton truly was growing weary. While she had grown used to accolades, her religious critiques brought her waves of outraged virulent criticism. Many AWSA members hated her and agreed to make her president of the new NAWSA only on the condition that she take a ship for Europe right after the first meeting. Anthony's star, on the other hand, shone ever more brightly as she aged, becoming "Aunt Susan" to hundreds of suffragists. In 1892 she was voted president for life of the NAWSA, venerated by all and sundry, until, at her death, she was hailed as a veritable incarnation of the Great Mother.

Anthony did not believe she was a good public speaker. "I know nothing and have known nothing of oratory or rhetoric,"[8] she said. She called Stanton her "sentencemaker" and "penartist."[9] Stanton recalled their collaboration as follows: "In writing we did better work together than either could alone. While she is slow and analytical in composition, I am rapid and synthetic. I am the better writer, she the better critic. She supplied the facts and statistics, I the philosophy and rhetoric, and together we have made arguments that have stood unshaken by the storms of thirty long years: arguments that no man has answered. Our speeches may be considered the united product of our two brains."[10]

This statement is probably true for most of the speeches the two women gave, especially about enfranchisement. Where religion was involved, however, Stanton overstates the case. Of Presbyterian origin, Stanton went through a Finneyite revival at school and was traumatized by depictions of original sin and hellfire. Her religious journey was to be tempestuous on the road to the *Woman's Bible*, one of the few projects not shared by her beloved Susan. Anthony, on the other hand, had been raised a Quaker. While she had quarrels with some of the Friends' doctrines, controversies around biblical issues left her unperturbed. To Anthony, "all those theological questions had been discussed and settled by the Quakers long ago."[11]

In larger terms, Stanton advocated "a more rational religion," one that emphasized women's right to think (the same right that Luther, Calvin, and John Knox had had), the sacredness of democratic principles (only sometimes conceded by her to be Christian principles, too),[12] and especially the "great immutable laws" that rule life both morally and physically.[13] She gave her allegiance to the God of Justice, Mercy, and Truth. Anthony, too, may have believed some or all of this; she did mention the great immutable laws on more than one occasion.

Both Anthony and Stanton rejected original sin and the need for a uniquely redeeming savior figure. Both believed that human nature is basically good and that real strides of progress can be made. Both certainly believed that democratic principles are sacred. But Anthony's emphases, as we shall see, were biblical and prophetic in character. According to Anthony, believers are especially commanded "to break every yoke and let the oppressed go free" (Isa. 58:6 RSV), "to love your neighbor as yourself" (Matt. 22:39 RSV), and to feed the hungry and clothe the naked in the awareness that as one performs these deeds for the least among us, one does them for Jesus himself (Matt. 25:31–46). Though Anthony called God "Father" or "All-Father," which strikes today's feminist ears badly, her God was a God who loved freedom and helped to bring it about.

WOMEN'S SERVITUDE: SEX-SLAVERY

Women's subjection to men was, for Anthony, the greatest injustice that women suffered. Sometimes she called this powerlessness, sometimes dependency, especially since married women did not control their earnings or property in this era. Her most pungent expression, however, was that the subjection of women was "sex-slavery." She drew explicit parallels between women's subjection and black slavery in the South. Since the Fifteenth Amendment outlawed disenfranchisement for "previous conditions of servitude," she enumerated the ways in which women's condition constituted a comparable servitude suffered by American slaves that needed to be outlawed.

Married women, Anthony argued, were in a condition of servitude because they did not have rights to custody and control of their persons or earnings or the right to sue. But more, "by all the great fundamental principles of our free government," *all* women were in servitude:

> Women are taxed without representation, governed without their consent, tried, convicted, and punished without a jury of their peers. And is all this tyranny any less humiliating and degrading to women under our democratic-republican government today than it was to men under their aristocratic, monarchical government one hundred years ago?[14]

She quoted Benjamin Franklin: "They who have no voice or vote in the electing of representatives do not enjoy liberty, but are absolutely enslaved to those who have votes and their representatives." And she quoted Tom Paine: To take away the right to vote "is to reduce a man to a state of slavery."

Anthony construed justice for women accordingly. If the injustice against women is servitude, then its remedy must be freedom. Women must be free to cast their own ballots. But more than that, they must be free to act for themselves, in their own cause, the cause of women's rights. "She who would be free, herself must strike the blow," Anthony insisted.[15] Too many women, however, lived a "hot-house existence," far from the struggles of the world and of politics, protected from reality. Working women needed the ballot to protect themselves against employers and so to raise their earning power. Less tangibly but no less important, women did not respect themselves or believe in themselves enough; they lacked allegiance to themselves first. The consciences of women were asleep. Just as antislavery workers had used fiery language to wake the conscience of the nation, so "agitation" was needed to wake up the women.

The Fugitive Slave Law, and its enforcement by the Supreme Court in the infamous Dred Scott case, had awakened abolitionists against the laws of slavery in the 1850s. A comparable awakening was needed to combat the laws of women's servitude. Anthony drew the parallel explicitly in this 1870 letter to a group in England:

All are lulled into the strictest propriety of expression, according to the gospel of St. Republican [the Republican Party]. And unless that saint shall enact some new and more blasphemous law against woman, which shall wake our confiding sisterhood into a sense of their befoolment, you will neither see nor hear a word from suffrage society or paper which will be in the slightest out of line with the plan and policy of the dominant party. Nothing less atrocious to woman than was the Fugitive Slave Law to the Negro, can possibly sting the women of this country into a knowledge of their real subserviency, and out of their sickening sycophancy to the republican politicians associated with them.

So while I do not pray for anybody or any party to commit outrages, still I do pray, and that earnestly and constantly, for some terrific shock to startle the women of this nation into a self-respect that will compel them to see the abject degradation of their present position; which will force them to break their yoke of bondage, and give them faith in themselves; which will make them proclaim their allegiance to woman first; which will enable them to see that man can no more feel, speak or act for woman than could the old slaveholder for his slave. The fact is, women are in chains and their servitude is all the more debasing because they do not realize it. O, to compel them to see and feel, and to give them the courage and conscience to speak and act for their own freedom, though they face the scorn and contempt of all the world for doing it.[16]

Much later, at the turn of the twentieth century, Anthony sometimes still said that "agitation is the word."[17] When the country was considering adding new territories without including women among the voters, she was furious with the younger generation's refusal to protest: "I really believe I shall explode if some of you young women don't wake up and raise your voice in protest. . . . I wonder if when I am under the sod—or cremated and floating in the air—I shall have to stir you and others up. How can you not be all on fire?"[18]

Drawing on Jesus' adage, "By their fruits, you will know them" (Matt. 7:16), Anthony's brand of practical religion put reformist action over the content of any particular doctrine or belief. Merely believing that the Bible was inspired by God meant nothing if people did not act upon their beliefs. Indeed, mere beliefs were only so much ineffective "creed and dogma" to Anthony. They were the nonessentials—what she sometimes called the "mint, anise and cumin" instead of "the weightier matters of the law, justice and mercy and faith" (Matt. 23:23). Indeed, her low opinion of "creed and dogma" or odd religious views was thoroughly connected to her this-worldly commitments.

The truth is, I can no more see through Theosophy than I can through Christian Science, Spiritualism, Calvinism, or any other of the theories, so I shall have to go on knocking away to remove the obstructions in the road of us mortals while in these bodies and on this planet; and leave Madam Besant and you all who have entered into the higher sphere, to revel in things unknown to me. . . . I will join you at Mrs. Miller's Saturday, and we'll chat over men, women and conditions—not theories, theosophies and theologies, they are all Greek to me.[19]

It is easy to see how such a position might be understood to be irreligious or secular. But to Anthony it was not. She copied a quote into the back of a diary: "Many are called impious, not for having a worse, but a *different* religion from their neighbors, and many atheistical, not for denying God but for thinking somewhat peculiarly of him."[20] Writing to another spiritualist, declining an invitation to visit, she said she would have enjoyed the chance "to chat over the world of work for our good cause. Of the before and after I know absolutely nothing, and have very little desire and less time to question or study. I know this seems very material to you, and *yet to me it is wholly spiritual,* for it is giving time and study rather to making things better in the between which is really all that we can influence; but perhaps when I can no longer enter into active practical work, I may lapse into speculations."[21]

In the earliest years of her activist career, she often spoke of "right action" in New Testament terms. "The plain practical principles of Jesus" included "love thy neighbor as thyself" (Matt. 22:39), the condemnation of mere lip service (Mark 7:6), and the denunciations of hypocrisy evident in the "Woe" speeches of Jesus (Matt. 23:13–36). For Anthony, the work of righteousness was "feeding the hungry, clothing the naked, visiting the sick and in prison (Matt. 25:31–46), undoing the bonds of the slave and letting the oppressed go free (Isa. 58:6)." From the abolitionists, too, she learned the moral worth of sympathy for the suffering, as many of them quoted the New Testament: "Remember those in bonds as though bound with them" (Heb. 13:3).[22] In later years she spoke more of "the energetic doing of noble deeds," but the point was always the same: "Idle wishes, vain repinings, loud-sounding declamations never can bring freedom to any human soul."[23]

Nor was mere prayer any more effective. In one of her earliest temperance speeches, Anthony said: "If we would have God answer our prayers, they must be accompanied by corresponding action."[24] When good church people told her that they were praying for the cause, she asked them pithily to pray "by action"[25] or to "pray with your ballots."[26] As she often put it,

"I pray every single second of my life; not on my knees, but with my work. My prayer is to lift woman to equality with man. Work and worship are one with me. I can not imagine a God of the universe made happy by my getting down on my knees and calling him 'great.'"[27]

She had learned this lesson from the antislavery movement. She told, with relish, a story from Frederick Douglass. When he was a slave, Douglass said, he had often prayed for freedom, but God answered only when he prayed with his heels—that is, when he ran away.

IGNORING ALL LAW

Frederick Douglass's escape from slavery was not an unusual example to Anthony, for the antislavery struggle was her highest ethical model. "I can but acknowledge to myself that Antislavery has made me richer and braver in spirit and that it is the school of schools for the true and full development of the nobler elements of life."[28] By 1857 Anthony had enough experience and confidence to begin making her antislavery speeches only from notes, rather than reading a full text. This excerpt is typical of the antislavery material in some of the primary texts:

> Everybody is anti-slavery, ministers and brethren. There are sympathy, talk, prayers and resolutions in ecclesiastical and political assemblies. Emerson says, "Good thoughts are no better than good dreams, unless they be executed"; so anti-slavery prayers, resolutions and speeches avail nothing without action. . . . Our mission is to deepen sympathy and convert it into right action; to show that the men and women of the North are slave-holders, those of the South slave-owners. The guilt rests on the North equally with the South, therefore our work is to rouse the sleeping consciences of the North. . . . We preach revolution; the politicians reform. We say, disobey every unjust law; the politician says obey them, and meanwhile labor constitutionally for repeal. [29]

Action over mere words, agitation to rouse the conscience, and the rule of ethics over the law: these were central themes in the course of Anthony's public career and central to her religious views.

In late 1860 came an unexpected test. Anthony was approached by a woman fleeing her prominent husband with her daughter. After hearing the tale, she agreed to help, and shepherded them to New York City the next day, searching for some friend to shelter them. During the following spring, while on the lecture platform, Anthony was harassed by the husband's agents, who threatened her with arrest for abducting his child. (Custody of the children, as well as all the earnings and property of the wife, was vested in the husband at this time.) Letters and telegrams from her allies poured in, warning of the terrible consequences sure to befall the movements she loved if she did not relent. Anthony was most pained by the remonstrances of Wendell Phillips and William Lloyd Garrison: "Only to think that in this great trial I should be hounded by the two men whom I adore and reverence above all others." She wrote to Garrison:

> I can not give you a satisfactory statement on paper, but I feel the strongest assurance that all I have done is wholly right. Had I turned my back upon her I should have scorned myself. In all those hours of aid and sympathy for that outraged woman, I remembered only that I was a human being. That I should stop to ask myself if my act would injure the reputation of any movement never crossed my mind, nor will I now allow such a fear to stifle my sympathies or tempt me to expose her to the cruel, inhuman treatment of her own household. Trust me that as I ignore all law to help the slave, so will I ignore it all to protect an enslaved woman.[30]

Later that spring, Anthony and Garrison were together at a convention in Albany. Garrison argued that Anthony was entirely in the wrong, for she was breaking the law. Anthony defended herself, pointing by analogy to the need to break the Fugitive Slave Law:

> He said, "Don't you know the law of Massachusetts gives the father the entire guardianship and control of the children?" "Yes, I know it," she replied, "and does not the law of the United States give the slaveholder the ownership of the slave? And don't you break it every time you help a slave to Canada?" "Yes, I do." "Well, the law which gives the father the sole ownership of the children is just as wicked and I'll break it just as quickly. You would die before you would deliver a slave to his master, and I will die before I will give up that child to its father."[31]

Anthony did find some support among her family and friends. Her friend Lydia Mott had been present when the fugitive wife appealed to Anthony. And her father had supported her: "Legally, you are wrong, but morally you are right, and I will stand by you," he said.[32] Being morally right was always most important to Anthony, the standard by which all else was judged.

Judging what was morally right was, for Anthony, the work of conscience. If conscience discerned a difference between "man-made laws" and the "higher law," there was no question but that one was justified in breaking the "man-made laws," come what will. In quite typical Quaker fashion, Anthony believed that God was to be found "now as of old in the 'still, small voice'" of conscience. This was the only access to "truth, that will never err, however hard its promptings may be sometimes."[33] These references to conscience almost always included this latter point, that conscience might lead one against the opinions of many. So Anthony exhorted the Women's Loyal League in 1863:

> And now, women of the North, I ask you to rise up with earnest, honest purpose, and go forward in the way of right, fearlessly, as an independent human being, responsible to God alone for the discharge of every duty, for the faithful use of every gift the good Father has given you. Forget conventionalisms; forget what the world will say, whether you are in your place or out of your place; think *your* best thoughts, speak your best words, do your best works, looking to your own conscience for approval.[34]

She counseled another suffragist that her power lay in speaking "the absolute truth, not in echoing the popular cry of the multitude. And so long as you look within for guidance in the spirit and letter of your utterances, you are safe. To speak as will please the people is always failure."[35]

Courage was necessary to bear the scorn that most likely would come from following one's conscience against the will of others. "Do right and trust the consequences to God" was an abolitionist slogan. It helped Anthony through many dark days when her agitation brought criticism.

> Cautious, careful people, always casting about to preserve their reputation and social standing, never can bring about a reform. Those who are really in earnest must be willing to be anything or nothing in the world's estimation, and publicly and privately, in season and out, avow their sympathy with despised and persecuted ideas and their advocates, and bear the consequences.[36]

Anthony had grown used to being mobbed in the late 1850s. In the tempestuous winter of 1861–62 she and a party of antislavery speakers were "mobbed and broken up in every city from Buffalo to Albany."[37] Later in the 1860s she would receive hisses from audiences when she mentioned women in sex scandals of the period. Newspapers did not hesitate to caricature her. Her policy was simply to persevere, ignoring such criticism.

Anthony not only ignored criticism, but she also ignored the law when it ran afoul of conscience. When "man-made laws" violate God's laws and perpetrate injustice, Anthony insisted, they must be disobeyed. Anthony's fullest indictment of unjust laws came during her trial in 1872 for illegally casting a vote. Convinced by a group of suffragists to try to change the male-only voting laws by judicial review, Anthony and a group of friends and family members (and several dozen women elsewhere around the country) had gone to the polls in November. "Well, I have been & gone & done it!! Positively voted the Republican ticket—straight—this a.m. at 7 o'clock & swore my vote in at that."[38] She was arrested and indicted. After her indictment, she stumped the local county to convince potential jurors of a woman's right to vote. When the venue of the trial was moved, she blanketed that county for a month as well.

The trial itself was a sham. Though her counsel ably rehearsed the arguments at great length, after closing arguments, the judge directed the verdict. He pulled from his pocket the written text of his conclusion, and directed the jury to find Anthony guilty and then simply dismissed them. Before pronouncing his sentence, the judge asked Anthony if she had anything to say for herself. Extemporaneously, she denounced the whole trial. When the judge protested that she had been tried according to established forms of law, she shot back:

> Yes, your honor, but by forms of law all made by men, interpreted by men, administered by men, in favor of men, and against women; and hence, your honor's directed verdict of guilty, against a United States citizen for the exercise of "that citizen's right to vote," simply because that citizen was a woman and not a man. But, yesterday, the same man-made forms of law declared it a crime punishable with $1,000 fine and six months' imprisonment, for you, or me, or any of us, to give a cup of cold water, a crust of bread, or a night's shelter to a panting fugitive as he was tracking his way to Canada. And every man or woman in whose veins course a drop of human sympathy violated that wicked law, reckless of consequences, and was justified in so doing. As then the slaves who got their freedom must take it over, or under, or through the unjust forms of law, precisely so now must women, to get their right to a voice in this government, take it; and I have taken mine, and mean to take it at every possible opportunity.[39]

Indeed, she said, she had been trying to educate women to do what she had done, "rebel against your man-made, unjust, unconstitutional forms of law, that tax, fine, imprison and hang women, while they deny them the right of representation in the Government."[40] She promised to continue to urge women to the "practical recognition" of the revolutionary maxim: "Resistance to tyranny is obedience to God."

The judge levied a fine as well as a prison sentence. She refused to pay the fine; the judge refused to imprison her until she did, thereby closing off an avenue for publicity and protest by her allies as well as foreclosing an appeal to a higher court. The cases against the other women were dropped; eventually, the officials who had been convicted of receiving their illegal ballots were given a presidential pardon.

If defying the law did not work, Anthony concluded, changing the law might be better. If women could not "take" their rights to vote under the Reconstruction amendments, there was only one way left to get women the right to vote—by another constitutional amendment. Amending the Constitution had helped former slaves; it could help women as well.

THE ANTHONY AMENDMENT

Working to change the law was not new to Anthony. Stanton and Anthony had campaigned in New York State for the Married Women's Property Act and for more liberal divorce laws. They had stumped Kansas in 1868 when its proposed state constitution sought to enfranchise both women and black men. They lost, the first of many state-by-state campaigns they were to lose over the coming decades.

What was new in this effort of legal reform was Anthony's single-minded focus on crafting and ratifying a constitutional amendment that guaranteed women the right to vote. It was "Anthony's first major departure from her twenty-five-year-long organizing strategy," says one of her biographers.[41] Typical was her 1875 comment to one of the women penning anticlerical resolutions to the NWSA, Matilda Joslyn Gage:

> I want it to be on the one & *sole point of women disfranchised*—separate & alone—and not mixed up with—or one of 19 *other points of protest*—each all of the 19 good & proper perchance.... However good and needed, we must keep our claim first and most important overshadowing every other. Mrs. Stanton answered me that she agrees with me—just women & her disfranchised—leaving the other 19 demands of the *Old Liberty* to wait our emancipation.[42]

When Stanton grew increasingly convinced that religion was at the root of women's subjection, Anthony refused to let her muddy the issues during a California campaign: "I shall no more thrust into the discussions the question of the Bible than the manufacture of wine. What I want is for the men to vote 'yes' on the suffrage amendment, and I don't ask whether they make wine on the ranches of California or Christ made it at the wedding feast."[43]

As this comment implied, though herself an old temperance fan and a firm supporter of the Women's Christian Temperance Union, Anthony tried to keep the WCTU away from suffragist campaigns, knowing full well that suffragists needed the votes of many men who were not "dry." She used her considerable influence to keep NAWSA regulars from endorsing any particular political party—a policy that continued into the League of Women Voters (NAWSA's heir) after 1920.

Today historians tend to regard this focus on the constitutional amendment as "narrowing the suffrage platform,"[44] but Anthony believed that the "one and sole point" of women disfranchised was not a small matter. The ballot was the "open sesame to equal rights."[45] It would place women and men on an equal footing in all dimensions of life. Indeed, for Anthony, it was virtually the cause of all causes: "The cause of nine-tenths of all the misfortunes which come to women, and to men also, lies in the subjection of women, and therefore the important thing is to lay the axe at the root."[46] Anthony put this point in a variety of pithy ways: "Men who fail to be just to their own mothers cannot be expected to be just to each other."[47] "It is idle for us to expect that the men who rob women (of their rights) will not rob each other as individuals, corporations and Governments."[48]

The more traditional work of women in charitable and benevolent institutions, which Anthony sometimes called mere "man-appointed missions," was bound to be ineffective. For this was work "without knowledge."

> It is aimed at the effects, not the cause; it is plucking the spoiled fruit; it is lopping off the poisonous branches of the deadly upas tree, which but makes the root more vigorous in sending out new shoots in every direction. . . . The tap-root of our social upas lies deep down at the very foundation of society. It is woman's dependence. It is woman's subjection. Hence the first and only efficient work must be to emancipate woman from her enslavement.[49]

"Any and every reform work is sure to lead women to the ballot-box," Anthony believed. Without the vote, nothing women could do would be effective. "Suffrage was the key to unlock every door."[50] "It has always been clear to me that woman suffrage is the one great principle underlying all reforms. With the ballot in her hand woman becomes a vital force—declaring her will for herself, instead of praying and beseeching men to declare it for her."[51]

Anthony again adverted to the metaphor of the Fugitive Slave Law, this time not to press people to defy the unjust man-made laws, but to illustrate going to the root of the evils around them:

> Ordinary benevolence will ever minister to individual suffering—even the Hard-Shell Democratic Fugitive Slave Law man in the olden time would hide the fleeing bondman from the chase of his master, and give him $10 to pass him on to Canada. But . . . . this Woman Suffrage movement goes to the root of the evil—demands the ballot—the right, the power, in woman's hands to help herself.[52]

These instrumentalist arguments, however, usually paled for Anthony beside the one most fundamental claim for women's right to vote: that it was just. "To prevail with the rank and file of voters, you must appeal to their sense of justice," she insisted.[53]

After Stanton's death in 1902, Anthony was asked to reflect on the changes they had seen and accomplished. After sketching a history of the suffrage cause up to the present, she noted that women's "enlarged opportunities in every direction" have almost regenerated the roles of women.

> The capability they have shown in the realm of higher education, their achievements in the business world, their capacity for organization, their executive power, have been a revelation. . . . In no department of the world's activities are the higher qualities so painfully lacking as in politics. . . . Does not logic also justify the opinion that, as they have been admitted into every other channel, the political gateways must inevitably be opened?[54]

Despite the five decades of struggle she had been through, she was still hopeful:

> The common remark that "all has been gained for women except the suffrage" is by no means true. In not one of the several departments above named do women possess perfect equality of rights, but in each so much has been granted as to make it logically sure that the rest will eventually follow. . . . The future contains more than hope—it shines in the clear light of certainty.[55]

Perhaps these many changes in American society, which she had witnessed, are why these last years brought something of a qualification to her claims about justice—not that suffrage for women would not be just, but that it was only a small bit of justice: "Such a little simple thing we have been asking for a quarter of a century. For over forty years, longer than the children of Israel wandered through the wilderness, we have been begging and praying and pleading for this act of justice."[56]

According to Anna Howard Shaw, one of her closest intimates, Anthony had a similar perception in the last few days of her life: "She never complained, but once when the consciousness of approaching death seemed strongly to impress itself upon her, she said, holding up her hand and measuring a little space on one finger, 'Just think of it, I have been striving for over sixty years for a little bit of justice no bigger than that, and yet I must die without obtaining it. Oh, it seems so cruel.' "[57]

These comments perhaps resonate more deeply with us a century later than Anthony's notion that lack of women's suffrage lay at the root of all social ills. Today, we know only too well that enfranchisement has not solved all the problems of women's emancipation. The sense that the vote is a piece of justice, yes, but only the size of the tip of one's finger, speaks to us more than it could have to Anthony. We now see that the right to vote was a necessary but not a sufficient condition for justice for women. It remains unclear whether Anthony believed it to be both necessary *and* sufficient.

Unlike Anthony, Stanton maintained to the end of her career that the subjection of women called for a complete overhaul of four different elements of society—the family, society (including education), the state, and the church. As women's rights advocates, prompted by Anthony, focused more strenuously upon the vote, Stanton became more firmly convinced that religion was the most powerful strand of women's debasement, and more vehement in her condemnations.

Unlike Stanton, Anthony had among her protégées ordained women like Anna Howard Shaw. Anthony knew that more clergymen were endorsing the cause, and put the case to Stanton:

> I cannot help but feel that in this you are talking down to the most ignorant masses, whereas your rule always has been to speak to the highest, knowing there would be a few who would comprehend and would in turn give of their best to those on the next lower round of the ladder. The cultivated men and women of today are above the need of your book. Even the liberalized orthodox ministers are coming to our aid and their conventions are passing resolutions in favor of woman's equality, and I feel that these men and women who are just born into the kingdom of liberty can better reach the minds of their followers than can any of us out-and-out radicals. But while I do not consider it my duty to tear to tatters the lingering skeletons of the old superstitions and bigotries, yet I rejoice to see them crumbling on every side.[58]

Anthony chided her old friend Stanton for "singling out the church and declaring it to be especially slow in accepting the doctrine of equality to women. I tried to make her see that it had advanced as rapidly as the other departments but I did not succeed, and it is right that she should express her own ideas, not mine."[59]

Stanton wrote many of her critiques of male-dominated religion for the *Index*, the magazine of the Free Religious Association, a left-wing group of Unitarians, whose circulation was tiny. After she and Anthony had finished their history of the women's suffrage movement, Stanton was determined to have a go at the Bible and to publish her conclusions as a book to reach a wider audience. Stanton tried to get Anthony to be part of the project; Anthony refused, arguing that this would confuse her "one and sole" point with another: "No—I don't want my name on that Bible Committee—You fight that battle—and leave me to fight the secular—the political fellows. . . . I simply don't want the enemy to be diverted from my practical ballot fight—to that of scoring me for belief one way or the other about the Bible."[60]

Anthony disagreed with her old friend, however, not only for political reasons, but because in principle she thought Stanton's antireligious approach to be wrongheaded:

> You say, "women must be emancipated from their superstitions before enfranchisement will be of any benefit," and I say just the reverse, that women must be enfranchised before they can be emancipated from their superstitions. Women would be no more superstitious today than men, if they had been men's political and business equals and gone outside the four walls of home and the other four of the church and come in contact with and discussed men and measures on the plane of this mundane sphere, instead of living in the air with Jesus and the angels. So you will have to keep pegging away, saying "Get rid of religious bigotry and then get political rights"; while I shall keep pegging away, saying, "Get political rights first and religious bigotry will melt like dew before the morning sun"; and each will continue still to believe in and defend the other.[61]

Volume 1 of Stanton's *Woman's Bible* was published in 1896, just before that year's convention of the NAWSA. A resolution on the subject came before that body: "This association is non-sectarian, being composed of persons of all shades of religious opinion, and has no official connection with the so-called 'Woman's Bible' or any theological publication."[62]

Anthony left the chair in order to speak against this resolution at some length. Her arguments were deeply influenced by William Lloyd Garrison's policies of free speech and agitation in the antislavery struggle. She opened by claiming that "the one distinct feature of our association has been the right of individual opinion for every member."[63] There had often been contention "on account of religious theories," but they had not made resolutions about them. "To pass this one is to set back the hands on the dial of reform. . . . What you should say to outsiders is that a Christian has neither more nor less rights in our association than an atheist. When our platform becomes too narrow for people of all creeds and no creeds, I myself cannot stand upon it."[64]

The policy of agitation of the old antislavery radicals was "that as public opinion was educated, they must take even more advanced positions," as one historian put it.[65] So Anthony reminded them of old examples: When Stanton had first demanded the right to vote, at Seneca Falls in 1848, some had thought she had damaged the cause. When, in 1860, Stanton made a case for divorce on the grounds of drunkenness, other friends believed she had killed the cause. Who could tell if these Bible commentaries might not prove a great help to women's emancipation in the future? It would be "narrow and illiberal" of the delegates to vote for this resolution. And the movement needed to "inspire in women a broad and catholic spirit," since suffragists were claiming that women would be a power for better government. Indeed, "ten women educated into the practice of liberal principles would be a stronger force than 10,000 organized on a platform of intolerance and bigotry."[66]

But the woman suffrage movement was no longer radical. It was respectable. The motion passed 53–41.

ANTHONY'S RELIGIOUS ACTIVISM

On public platforms, Anthony's policy of free speech meant that she was careful to be noncommittal about religious opinions stated by others. One time, however, she was drawn away from this discrete stance to offer a sort of "amen" to a speaker. The 1888 International Council of Women included a session on religion. After lengthy and very diverse speeches, a woman named Ednah Cheney said, "This has seemed to me to be a most religious meeting all through the week. . . . It has been a holy week to those who are not wont to think that religion depends on times and seasons, but on consecration to right purposes and great philanthropic and human enterprises."[67]

As chair, Anthony could only hint at her agreement. (Perhaps she also wanted to say "amen" because Cheney called them away from "the subtleties of metaphysics and theology" and back "into works.") She reminded the audience of Lucretia Mott's slogan, "Truth for Authority, not Authority for Truth," and drew their attention to a poem in a pamphlet on sale near the door:

> Thou, from on high, perceivest it were better
> All men and women should be on earth be free;
> Laws that enslave and tyrannies that enfetter
> Snap and evanish at the touch of thee.[68]

To Anthony, it was liberation from the slavery of the laws and any other kinds of bondage that was the heart of her religious view. That had been occurring, as Cheney said, "all through the week."

Away from the public platform, however, Anthony sometimes stated the focus of her faith more fully though simply. Our duty, she said, is to "make things better in the between," to put things right, or to do what we can here, because that is all we can really influence. For Anthony, the task was to follow the "plain practical principles of Jesus," the Golden Rule to "do unto others, as you would have done unto you" (Matt. 7:12). Sometimes it might be even more simply, "to help" in the way that people helped fugitive slaves to achieve their freedom. It was the consistent practice of one's beliefs, and not merely their repetition in words, that proved one's faith. Anthony did not write a treatise about any of this. She lived it.

The simple clarity of her thought was echoed in her language. If you disagreed with her, you knew it at once. There was no jargon, no highly technical language, no obfuscation, no circumlocution. She and Stanton both abhorred the circumlocution encouraged in ladies. You knew were you stood with Anthony; there were no hidden agendas.

Sympathy for others was what Anthony aimed for in her audiences— pity, sometimes, or indignation even, but perhaps more classically the "feeling-together-with" of the word's roots. "Empathy" is perhaps a more precise term: Imagine that you are a slave, or one of your loved ones. Put yourself in the other's shoes. "Make the slave's case our own," was the title of one of Anthony's antislavery speeches. "Remember those in bonds as though bound with them" (Heb. 13:3) was an old antislavery Bible verse that taught this same lesson. As Anthony said: "We are knit together for weal or woe." Her point, however, was not merely to feel with those who were oppressed; it was to deepen the sympathy, yes, and then "convert it to action," as she said in her first temperance speech.

Anthony's earliest speech in support of women's suffrage claimed that a religion that ruled one's life every day except Election Day "was not worthy of possession." It was clear to her that faith was to move into the ballot box. Her later slogans, "prayer by action" or "pray with your ballots," were developments in this line. Her analysis of the social injustices she faced led her toward the causes, not merely the symptoms, of the problems she saw in the lives of women. Simply to put bandages over the wounds was "inefficient," indeed "unphilosophical." Enfranchising women aimed to change the system, to be a radical work. Anthony did not have adequate theological or sociological language to conceptualize this, in comparison to the extended languages we now have at our disposal. But her religious activism was no less effective, or cogent.

Anthony liked to quote Isaiah 58:6: "to break the yoke and let the oppressed go free."[69] For her this was a call to religious activism. Once, when she was in the company of a famous spiritualist, she "could not conceal her disapproval" of the woman's otherworldliness. Anthony asked her, "Why don't you make that aura of yours do its gallivanting in this world, looking up the needs of the oppressed, and investigating the causes of present wrongs? Then you could reveal to us workers just what we should do to put things right, and we could be about it."[70]

Anthony's version of religious activism was a liberation theology without Marxism, born out of America's struggles against slavery and for women's rights. It was extremely difficult for her contemporaries, and even for many of her successors, to recognize this dimension of her religious life.[71] I believe this misunderstanding came because there was no religious tradition there to receive her insights. Her tradition flowered only in the last half of the twentieth century, when the civil rights struggle and the women's liberation movement gave birth to black theology and feminist theology. Black theologians have remained oriented toward tangible changes in the social order. Some feminist theologians have aimed at subtler changes, like images of God or versions of sin that do not betray androcentric bias; others have chosen political engagement. I cannot imagine that Anthony would care much for the word "praxis" so typical today in liberation theology, since she was too plainspoken for what can become a technical locution. But the notion of "praxis" is consistent with her emphasis on practical righteousness. I believe she would have rejoiced to hear that "resistance is the holy ground wherein divine presence is known and experienced."[72] She would have appreciated the insights of the German theologian Dorothee Soelle that "God has no other hands than ours,"[73] or "God's action without us is a misunderstanding."[74]

Since so few people know of Anthony's activist faith, it is hard to trace its influence on anyone in particular. Her impulses to disobedience for the sake of conscience have entered the broad stream of anti-authoritarianism in left-wing and liberal religion. (When she met Queen Victoria, Anthony shook her hand instead of curtseying, which stunned her compatriots as much as it did the English.) It is important to recognize how strange and unique this aspect of the American religious heritage may appear to others. When Soelle arrived at Union Theological Seminary in the 1970s to teach, she was startled:

> I did not know that there were people who burned their draft cards with na-palm and blocked trains that would transport weapons to Vietnam. To hear this, to meet people who almost casually tell me that they spent time in jail because of some religious and political activities made me more aware of the alternative (to obedience) than before. It made me fall in love with this non-obedient tradition in the United States. It gave me hope, it renewed my trust in the better parts of the religious tradition.[75]

That Anthony's name might be unknown in this tradition would not have bothered her, I think. On birthdays in her later years, she always seemed surprised that people were gathering to honor her. She tried to send the honors back, rehearsing the history of the suffragist movement whenever she could, starting a session of the annual conventions with the "pioneers" recounting what they did. Just as Garrison had said, "where there is a sin, there must be a sinner," she was always naming the names of those who had helped the movement. Her biographer became annoyed at this:

> And then the contest over the *names* that should be mentioned. In vain the writer begged, expostulated and protested that the book would be swamped with them. "It is all the return I can offer for the friendship, the hospitality, the loyalty of those who have made it possible for me to do my work all these years," was the unvarying reply, and not one could be smuggled out from un-der that watchful eye.[76]

In Anthony's view, it was the followers, as much as the leaders, who made the women's rights movement possible. "The life-long privates in the war for equal rights" were the ones who "enable us at the front to stand strong and steady."[77]

NOTES

1. See generally Ida Husted Harper, *The Life and Work of Susan B. Anthony*, 3 vols. (Indianapolis: Hollenbeck Press, 1898–1908), and further sources listed in Mary D. Pellauer, *Toward a Tradition of Feminist Theology: The Religious*

Social Thought of Elizabeth Cady Stanton, Susan B. Anthony, and Anna Howard Shaw (Brooklyn, N.Y.: Carlson, 1991).

2. Harper, *Life and Work*, 2:596.
3. The best brief introduction to Garrison and his conflicts is Aileen S. Kraditor, *Means and Ends in American Abolitionism: Garrison and His Critics on Strategy and Tactics, 1834–1850* (New York: Vintage Books, 1970), esp. chap. 3, "The Woman Question," and chap. 4, "Religion and the Good Society."
4. Susan B. Anthony, *Diary* (December 30–31, 1871) (unpublished ms. in Susan B. Anthony Papers, Library of Congress).
5. Harper, *Life and Work*, 2:913.
6. Elizabeth Cady Stanton et al., eds., *The History of Woman Suffrage*, 6 vols. (New York: Arno Press, 1969), 1:459.
7. Ibid., 2:254.
8. Harper, *Life and Work*, 1:507.
9. Ibid., 1:187.
10. Stanton et al., *History of Woman Suffrage*, 1:459.
11. Harper, *Life and Work*, 2:648.
12. Stanton et al., *History of Woman Suffrage*, 2:644.
13. For more on Stanton's religious perspective, see Pellauer, *Toward a Tradition of Feminist Theology*, chaps. 2–3.
14. Stanton et al., *History of Woman Suffrage*, 2:644.
15. Susan B. Anthony, "Working Man's National Congress," *The Revolution* (September 17, 1868).
16. Harper, *Life and Work*, 1:366.
17. Ibid., 2:972.
18. Alma Lutz, *Susan B. Anthony: Rebel, Crusader, Humanitarian* (Boston: Beacon Press, 1959), 283.
19. Harper, *Life and Work*, 2:918.
20. Anthony, *Diary*, 1853–55.
21. Harper, *Life and Work*, 2:899 (emphasis added).
22. Ibid., 1:389.
23. Ibid., 169.
24. Anthony, Speech on Temperance, 1852, Folder 22, Schlesinger Library, Anthony Family Collection, 21–22.
25. Harper, *Life and Work*, 2:709.
26. Ibid., 1:457.
27. Ibid., 2:289.
28. Lutz, *Susan B. Anthony*, 62.
29. Harper, *Life and Work*, 1:153.
30. Ibid., 203–204.
31. Ibid., 204.
32. Kathleen Barry, *Susan B. Anthony: A Biography* (New York: New York University Press, 1988), 144.
33. Harper, *Life and Work*, 1:215.

34. Stanton et al., *History of Woman Suffrage*, 2:58.
35. Katherine Anthony, *Susan B. Anthony: Her Personal History and Her Era* (Garden City, N.Y.: Doubleday, 1954), 182.
36. Harper, *Life and Work*, 1:158.
37. Ibid., 1:208.
38. Quoted in Barry, *Susan B. Anthony*, 249.
39. Stanton et al., *History of Woman Suffrage*, 2:688.
40. Ibid., 2:689.
41. Barry, *Susan B. Anthony*, 265.
42. Ibid., 264.
43. Harper, *Life and Work*, 2:857.
44. See, e.g., Aileen Kraditor, *The Ideas of the Woman Suffrage Movement 1890–1920* (Garden City, N.Y.: Doubleday, 1971).
45. Harper, *Life and Work*, 1:385.
46. Ibid., 2:920.
47. Ibid., 3:1386–1387.
48. Ibid., 1199–1200.
49. Ibid., 2:1011.
50. Susan B. Anthony, "Working Women's Association," *The Revolution* (September 9, 1869).
51. Harper, *Life and Work*, 2:898.
52. Anthony, "Woman's Suffrage Meeting."
53. Harper, *Life and Work*, 2:923.
54. Ibid., 3:1265–1266.
55. Ibid., 1266.
56. Stanton et al., *History of Woman Suffrage*, 4:223.
57. Harper, *Life and Work*, 3:1420.
58. Ibid., 2:856–857.
59. Ibid., 847.
60. Kraditor, *The Ideas of the Woman Suffrage Movement*, 66.
61. Harper, *Life and Work*, 2:857.
62. Stanton et al., *History of Woman Suffrage*, 4:263.
63. Ibid.
64. Ibid., 4:264.
65. Aileen S. Kraditor, *Means and Ends in American Abolitionism: Garrison and His Critics on Strategy and Tactics, 1834–1850* (New York: Vintage Books, 1967), 30.
66. Stanton et al., *History of Woman Suffrage*, 4:264.
67. *Report of the International Council of Women* (Washington, D.C.: National Woman Suffrage Association, 1888), 421.
68. Ibid, 422.
69. Harper, *Life and Work*, 2:708.
70. Anna Howard Shaw with Elizabeth Jordan, *The Story of a Pioneer* (New York: Harper, 1915), 214.

71. Even in our time, Anthony is sometimes called "secular." A recent biographer has misunderstood her as a transcendentalist owing to her occasional appreciation of nature. See Barry, *Susan B. Anthony*, 242, 293.

72. Wendy Farley, *Tragic Vision and Divine Compassion* (Louisville, Ky.: Westminster John Knox Press, 1990), 127.

73. Dorothee Soelle, *Suffering* (Philadelphia: Fortress Press, 1975), 149.

74. Dorothee Soelle, *Thinking About God: An Introduction to Theology* (Philadelphia: Trinity Press International, 1990), 85.

75. Dorothee Soelle, *Beyond Mere Obedience* (New York: Pilgrim Press, 1982), xxi.

76. Harper, *Life and Work*, 3:1116.

77. Ibid., 3:1201.

ORIGINAL SOURCE MATERIALS

A TEMPERANCE SPEECH: THE CHURCH AND
THE LIQUOR TRAFFIC (1852)

I propose this evening, to speak to you upon the connection of the Church with the Liquor Traffic. In attempting this, I am aware that I shall tread upon what the world deems "Holy Ground," and that I thereby expose myself to the anathema of Infidel, which is so universally bestowed upon all who dare enter the sacred portals of that hoary institution, the Church, and openly and fearlessly point out wherein it fails to live that blessed injunction, "Love thy neighbor as thyself," —that command on which hang all the law and the Prophets (Mt 22: 39–40).

The ravages of intemperance are so fearful and wide spread, it needs no argument to prove that the sale of rum is a violation of the Golden Rule, "Do unto others as you would that others should do unto you" (Lk 6:31). Since, according to the laws of God and man, he who is accessory to a crime is equally guilty with the perpetrator, the man or institution that sanctions or sustains the License System of our State. . . .

Now if the Church retain in its membership men who habitually use intoxicating Liquors, those who traffic in them, and those who aid in elevating to the various offices of our government, Brandy drinking men who license the sale of Liquor, does it not by so doing wink at the hideous crimes of the Distiller, Rum Seller, and Drunkard? Does it not sanction the Liquor Traffic?

Let us make enquiries into the week day occupations of the communicants of any of our large, wealthy and popular Churches, and I might safely add, most of our Churches, whether rich or poor, large or small, in country or in city, and see if we do not find many of them, in some way connected with the Liquor Traffic—see if we do not find a Deacon Distiller—a Church Member rum seller or rum drinker—a Church Member who owns a tavern stand or grocery which he rents to a Rum Seller—a Church Member who continues a business partnership with a man whom he and the world know to be engaged in the Liquor Traffic—a Church Member who will manufacture Cider and sell it to grocers, whom he knows will sell it as a beverage—a Church Member who will sell the contents of his granary, his corn, rye, oats, wheat, and barley to the brewer and distiller—a Church Member, who if elevated to the office of Justice of the Peace or Supervisor, Mayor or Alderman, will sign petitions to license the sale of Rum—a church member Senator or Assemblyman who is in favor of the continuance of the present License System—or a Church Member, who from year to year deposits his vote for men to fill these various offices, whom he knows will sign petitions for license and do all in their power to defeat the efforts of the friends of Temperance, the lovers of God and man, to annihilate the Liquor Traffic.

I believe the discipline of no Church, no associated religious bodies except the Methodist, Free Will Baptist, Old Scotch Covenanters, prohibits its members from engaging in the Liquor Traffic. And none others that requires a man to pledge himself to total Abstention from drink that can intoxicate before accepting him as a member, acknowledging him as a follower of the meek and lowly Jesus. And even in those Churches we not infrequently find men who are guilty of one if not all of the serious connections with rum. It was not long ago that I visited a college in one of our western counties where there was a Methodist Distiller, who, not satisfied with the ill-gotten gains of six days of labor, kept his Still in operation the Seventh day also. This placing of a law upon the Statute Books, when there is not a public sentiment that will enforce it, is of no avail. So with a Church Discipline, be its restrictions ever so close, it affects nothing unless the moral sentiments of its members are sufficiently strong to require (enforcement). . . .

Is it not hypocrisy for Church members, Deacon and Clergymen, to pray from day to day and from week to week through each successive year, that God will bless the Temperance Cause—that he will banish drunkenness from our land—that he will protect and comfort the wretched wife and children of the drunkard—that he will be a Father to the fatherless, and the widow's God—and then, on election day, after these long and oft repeated prayers, for those same Church members, Deacons and Clergymen, to go to the Ballot Box and deposit their votes for Brandy drinking Presidents and Congressmen, Rum drinking, Rum selling Governors, Senators and Assemblymen, Mayors and Aldermen, Justices of the Peace and Supervisors, whom they know to be in favor of the License System?

. . . The Church in the present undeveloped state of the race, is the educator of the religious element in man—if then, the church gives its sanction to either national or individual sins, it becomes the great sustainer of those evils. While the Church, retaining its present power to influence public sentiment, fails to take a decided stand on the side of Total Abstinence from Rum making, vending, drinking and voting, difficult indeed will be the efforts of the temperance reformer to persuade the masses that to be in any way connected with the Liquor Traffic, is Unchristian. . . .

. . . While the Rum sellers' petition for license is signed by Church Members, Mayors and Justices of the Peace, Deacons, Alderman and Supervisors, vain are all our arguments to prove that the rum seller possesses no moral right to sell rum to his neighbor. While the Church Member farmer annually carries his abundant harvests of grain to the brewer and distiller, to be distorted into deadly poisons, it is in vain that the apostles of the Gospel of Temperance preach to these Brewers and Distillers. They hide themselves behind their refuge of lies, the Church. While the lady Church Member annually manufactures her gooseberry and currant wines, while she partakes freely of them herself, and serves them at her social parties, it is extremely difficult to persuade the lady of fashion to abandon the use of imported wines. . . .

The time may have been, but is not now, when a Church Member, Deacon and Clergyman who voted for Brandy drinking, Rum licensing men to fill the various offices of government, might have thought themselves Christians, might have thought that a man's religion was not to go with him to the ballot box.

The time may have been, but is not now, when a Church that fellowshipped rum drinking, rum selling, rum making and rum voting members, might have thought itself the Church of God—might have imagined itself the "light of the world, the city set on a hill" (Mt 5:14). Our present type of Christianity indeed is lamentably low, and be it woman's glory, now to accept her Heaven appointed mission to preach a risen Savior, to raise high the standards of Christianity. To fully take and live the great and immutable truth taught by Jesus, that a "good tree cannot bring forth evil fruit" (Mt 7:18). The only unmistakable evidence of a man's belief in the doctrines taught by Christ, is to be found in the every day acts of his life.

The simple act of voting involves a man's love of truth and right. A man's vote is the embodiment and exponent of his principles on all questions pertaining to the good of the race—and thus the ballot box is the medium, through which he gives effectual expression to those principles. The Liquor Traffic is a creation of law and can only be revoked through the legislation of the country. Moral suasion has done its work, those who still persist in trafficking in intoxicating liquors, are possessed of stony hearts, that can be touched only by the cold fingers of the law.

. . . Inasmuch as the All-Wise acts by great immutable laws, prayers unsustained by action rise no higher than the efforts of the soul that utters them. The act that decides whether God will answer a man's prayer, that intemperance may be banished from our midst, is the dropping of a slip of paper into the ballot box on election day. If that slip of paper have on it the name of a Distiller, Rum seller, Rum drinker, or one who is not an open and avowed friend of Total Abstinence, and the Maine Law, vain worse than vain are all his long prayers.

There is an instructive moral to be drawn from the following anecdote. . . . On the morning of a cold winter day, surrounded as usual by his wife and children, the pious man prayed God to "feed the hungry and clothe the naked." As they arose from their devotion, a gentle tap was heard at the door. The stranger was bade to walk in, and there stood before them a little barefooted girl, shivering and pale, clad in the habiliments of extreme poverty, and holding in one of her shrivelled hands a basket. She timidly raised her eyes, and said to the man, "Please, Sir, will you let my mother have a half bushel of potatoes. I have no money to pay you now, Sir, but my mother is doing some sewing for Mr. Blank, and just so soon as she gets the job done, she will get the money and send it to you. We are all very hungry." The answer of that man fresh from communion with the God he worshipped was, "No! I can't let you have any, I can sell my potatoes for cash down and don't choose to let them go on trust." Thus did that praying man send away the sorrow stricken little one to her home with an empty basket. The little son went up to his father and with tears in his eyes said, "Father, I have been thinking, why you couldn't answer the prayer you made this morning yourself, and not wait for God to do it?"

Yes, friends, we ourselves are the instruments by means of which God answers our prayers. Unphilosophical indeed are they who ask God to banish from our land the three great national scourges of war, slavery and intemperance, while they from year to year aid in elevating to the various offices of government, wicked men, who know no love, either to God or man, whose highest aim is to attain to a position, that will secure to them the means of gratifying their own individual lusts after wealth, fame, power and sensual enjoyments. . . .

My friends, the religion that cannot stand the test of an election day, that dwells in the heart and governs the actions of men during 364 days of the year and then forsakes them, as they rise from the bended knee on the morning of the 365th day to repair to the polls, is not worth the possession. Hollow hearted and hypocritical are all professions of sympathy for suffering, downtrodden humanity, unless they are sustained by the man's giving his influence and his vote to elevate those only to the various governmental offices who will ever bear in mind that it is the duty of the righteous legislator, to cast his vote on the side of right, of justice, of mercy, of humanity. Is not the Christianity that sanctions the distiller, the rum seller, the rum drinker, and the man who votes for the continuance of this abomination of desolation, the Liquor Traffic—that allows the buying and selling as chattels, human beings, and thereby licenses every sort of iniquity under heaven, worse that the heathenism of the Sandwich Islands—worse than the Hindu paganism, that compels the mother to throw her loved child into the Ganges, and the widow to cast herself on the burning funeral pile of her husband. . . .

The term infidel has come to be an everyday "bugbear," which clergy thrust into the face of every one who ventures to give to the world a new view or new idea, which may chance to conflict with long established theories or practices. Its signification in the popular vocabulary is so vague that I shall not hazard any refutation in any attempt to define its exact meaning. Suffice it to say that very many of the truly great and good men and women of our day, who are loudly denounced as infidels are found doing the work of righteousness—feeding the hungry, clothing the naked, visiting the sick and in prison (Mt 25: 31–46), undoing the bonds of the slave and letting the oppressed go free (Is 58: 6), omitting the weightier matters of the Law, judgment, mercy and faith. What though they with their lips (Mk 7:6) declare the Bible a mere human production? Do not their every day acts, "the fruits by which we are to know them" (Mt 7:16), show that they believe the great and immutable truths contained therein to have emanated from none other than a Divine Source? On the other hand, do not the every day acts of very many of those who profess to believe the Bible, the "Word of God," the only infallible rule of faith and practice, plainly show disbelief. If these professors really felt every Bible declaration to be of God's revealing, think you they would knowingly fellowship in Church Communion those whom they know to be guilty of sins, upon which that Bible pronounces a woe? "No drunkard shall inherit the Kingdom of Heaven." "Woe unto him that putteth the cup to his neighbor's lips and maketh him drugged." "Woe unto those that devour widow's houses and for a pretense make long prayers" (Mt 23:14). Think you he who read the above denunciations and believe them to be of God's own handwriting will fail to cry out against the Liquor Traffickers?

If he really feels that no drunkard can inherit the kingdom of heaven, think you he can forget the mercy that God requires at his hands, the removing the temptations out of the way of his brothers? If he really believes that God's woe is upon those who devour widow's houses, will he not come out and be separate from those who make sell or vote for rum? Will he not see that his long prayers, his psalm singing, his observance of holy days, his rearing of gorgeous temples, are but the tithing of mint, anise and cumin (Mt 23:23)? "It is not all that cry Lord, Lord, but they that do work meet for repentance that shall be accepted of God" (Mt 7:21).

"A certain man had two sons, and he came to the first and said, "Son go work in my vineyard." He answered and said, 'I will not,' but afterward he repented and went. And he likewise said to the second, and he answered and said, 'I go' and went not. Whether of the twain did the will of his Father? His disciples said unto him, 'the first' " (Mt 21:28–31). Friends, the time has fully come for us to cease to waste all our precious hours in discussing questions of mystical theology and speculative faith, and adopt the plain practical principles taught by Jesus of Nazareth, the Divine founder. . . . [1]

TWO ANTISLAVERY SPEECHES

What is American Slavery? (1861)

The question of all questions that is now agitating our entire country: the one vexed question that intrudes itself upon our every thought—that is spoken of in all our news papers and magazines, that gives fertile theme to the moralist and novelist—that startles, nay, appalls, the Political Economist—that is discussed at the family fireside, at the public dinner, on the railroad car, at the corners of the streets, and wherever men and women most do congregate: What is American Slavery: the one disturbing question, that thrusts itself into every gathering of the people, that is the "apple of discord" in all our literary, political and religious organizations, that causes angry divisions and subdivisions in our churches, general assemblies, general conferences and associations, that has turned our American Congress into one great national debating club, and all our State Legislatures into schools, where declamations, both pro and con, are always in order.

What is this question of American slavery, that has thus the power to shake this mighty nation from center to circumference, and from circumference back to center again: The one blot on our nation's escutcheon, that shames the face of every true American, and astonishes the whole civilized world—the one "pet institution," that makes our professedly Christian, Democratic, Republican America, a lie—a hissing and a by-word in the mouth of all Europe, and an offense in the sight of High Heaven.

What is American slavery? It is the legalized systematized robbery of the bodies and souls of nearly four millions of men, women and children. It is the legalized traffic in God's image (Gen 1:27–28). It is the buying and selling Jesus Christ himself on the auction block as merchandise, as chattel property, in the person of the outraged slave. For the Divine Jesus said, "inasmuch as ye do it unto one of the least of these, my brethren, ye do it unto me" (Mt 25:40).

What is American slavery? It is the depriving four millions of native born citizens of these United States, of their inalienable right to life, liberty and the pursuit of happiness. It is the robbing of every sixth man, woman and child, of this glorious republic, of their God-given right to the ownership and control of their own persons, to the earnings of their own hands and brains, to the exercise of their own consciences and wills, to the possession and enjoyment of their own homes. It is the sundering of what God has joined together (Mt 19:06), the divorcing husbands and wives, parent and children, brothers and sisters. It is the robbery of every comfort, and every possession, sacred to a child of earth, and an heir of Heaven.

American slavery: It is a wholesale system of wrong and outrage perpetrated on the bodies and souls of these millions of God's children. It is the legalized prostitution of nearly two millions of the daughters of this proud republic. It is the blotting out from the soul of womanhood, the divine spark of purity, the god of her inheritance. It is the abomination of desolation spoken of by the Prophet Daniel (Dan 11:31), engrafted into the very heart of the American government. It is all and every villainy in crimes long back category, consolidated into one. It is theft, robbery, piracy, murder. It is avarice, covetousness, lust, licentiousness, concubinage, polygamy. It is atheism, blasphemy, sin against the Holy Ghost (Mt 12:31–32).

Make the Slave's Case Our Own

We are assembled here this evening for the purpose of discussing the question of American Slavery. The startling fact that there are in these United States, under the sanction of this professedly Christian, Republican government, nearly four millions of human beings now clanking the chains of slavery. Four millions of men and women and children, who are owned like horses and cattle, and bought and sold in the market. Four millions of thinking, acting, conscious beings, like ourselves, driven to unpaid toil, from the rising to the setting of the sun, through the weary days and years of their wretched life times.

Let us, my friends, for the passing hour, make the slave's case our own. As much as in us lies, let us feel that it is ourselves, and our kith and our kin who are despoiled of our inalienable rights to life, liberty and the pursuit of happiness, that it is our own backs that are bared to the slave driver's lash. That it is our own flesh that is lacerated and torn. That it is our own life blood that is poured out.

Let us feel that it is our own children, that are ruthlessly torn from our yearning mother hearts, and driven in the "coffle gang," through burning suns, and drenching rains, to be sold on the auction block to the highest bidder, and worked up, body and soul, on the cotton, sugar and rice plantations of the more remote south.

That it is our own loved sister and daughter, who are shamelessly exposed to the public market, and whose beauty of face, delicacy of complexion, symmetry of form, and grace of motion, do but enhance their monied value, and the more surely victimize them to the unbridled passions and lusts of their proud purchasers.

Could we, my friends, but make the slave's case our own—could we but feel for the slave, as bound with him (Heb 13:3)—could we but make the slave our neighbor, and "love him as ourself" (Mt 22:39), and do unto him as we would that he should do unto us (Lk 6:31)—how very easy would be the task of converting us all to Abolitionism.

If, by some magic power, the color of our skins could be instantly changed and the slave's fate made really our own, then would there by no farther need of argument or persuasion, or rhetoric or eloquence. Then would we, every one, with heart and soul, and tone and action, respond to the truth and the justice of the glorious doctrine of "immediate and unconditional emancipation," as the right of the slave and the duty of the master. Were we, ourselves, the victims of this vilest oppression the sun ever shone upon—no appeal to Bible or Constitution, no regard for peace and harmony in our religious or political associations, no blind reverence for "Union" either in church or state, could for a moment quiet our consciences, silence our voices, or stay our action. Priests, Presidents, Bishops and Statesmen, laymen and voters, synods, general assemblies and conferences, congresses, supreme courts and legislatures, if standing between us and liberty, would all be swept away, without one thought or care of consequences. What to us would then be the venerated Books, idolized parchments, time worn creeds and musty statutes of the Fathers? All, all of them would sink into utter insignificance: Freedom, God's priceless boon to man, outweighs them all. "Liberty or Death" is now our watchword.

But we are wont to contemplate this question of slavery from quite another, and an opposite, standpoint. We look upon the slave, as a being all unlike ourselves. The sallow hue of his skin, the curl of his hair, the flattened features of his face, together with the fact that he has for so many generations been the victim of the white man, seem conclusive evidence to the masses, that a condition that would be torture worse than death to us, is quite endurable, nay, congenial to him.

Then, too, we quiet our consciences with the thought that these poor creatures, however wronged and outraged their condition here, are yet, infinitely better off than they would be in their African homes across the Atlantic. Their Fathers were wild beasts living in tents, on the hills of Congo, the arid plains of Soudan, or the coasts of Guinea. And there, in their own native land, were they hunted like beasts of prey, and made to drag out their lives in a hopeless bondage to their more powerful, warlike and treacherous neighbors.

Though slaves here, subject to the will of a master, with no hope of freedom but in death, their condition is still far better than it could be in their father land, where reigns the night of heathenism were all, all is shrouded in the thick gloom of ignorance, superstition. Here, the slave is surrounded by the elevating, refining influences of civilization. Here the blessed privileges of Christianity are extended to him. Here the Gospel of Jesus Christ is preached to him.

And here, though his life, on earth, shall be one of utter wretchedness, disgust and loathing, he may take to his crushed and bleeding spirit the Christian hope of eternal rest, of unfading glory—the Christian faith, that the white winged messenger of Death will but usher him into the immediate presence of the Father of all, where there will be no clanking of chains, no torturing "cat o nine tails," no red hot branding irons, where the wicked cease from troubling and the weary are at rest.

Just think of it, my friends, a civilization elevating and refining, that makes slaves and chattels of one sixth portion of its own children, and with iron heel, crushes out their every spark of manhood. A civilization that, by statute law, denies to every sixth man, woman and child, all its educational, industrial, social and political rights and privileges! Such is our boasted American civilization, that prates of elevating and refining the very victims it tramples in the dust. Heaven defend the benighted children of Africa from such a civilization!

Here, too, the slave enjoys the blessed privileges of Christianity. Think of it: A Christianity that traffics in human beings, that barters God's image for filthy lucre. And here is the Gospel of Jesus Christ preached to the poor slave. Think of it! A Gospel that transforms every sixth child of God into chattel. A Gospel that sells Jesus Christ himself in the person of the slave on the auction block. What a profanation. What blasphemy! Such a Gospel can be none other than that of the bottomless pit. And sooner will the true Christ take to his bosom the children of heathendom's midnight darkness than allow one of these slave-holding [illegible word in original text] to slip into the light of his presence.

Again, it is argued that we of the North are not responsible for the crime of slave holding, that the guilty ones dwell in the South and lord it over the rice swamps of Georgia, the tobacco fields of Virginia, and the sugar and cotton plantations of Louisiana and the Carolinas. Thus, do we put the slave's case far away from us, forgetting that he is a human being like ourselves, forgetting that we ourselves are bound up with the slave-holder, in his guilt, forgetting that we of the North stand pledged to the support of the Federal Government, the tenure of whose existence is vested in the one idea of protection to the slave-holder, in his slave-property, forgetting that by the terms of the unholy agreement of the Fathers of our union, the only property represented on the floor of Congress, is the slave-holders property in man, forgetting that every loyal citizen of the North, himself or through his representatives, swears to support the United States Constitution, by whose special provision, the slave holder is not only secured the right to own slaves, and give them a three-fifths representation in the legislation of the nation, but every such loyal citizen is solemnly bound to return fugitive slaves to their masters, to buckle on his armor and go down to Kentucky, Tennessee or any of the fifteen slave states and aid in putting down insurrections and in shooting down men and women, for no other crime save that of hating slavery and loving liberty. Nay! More than all, forgetting that we of the North, welcome slave-holding priests to our pulpits, and slave-holding laymen to our church conferences. Think of it, professing Christians—members of any and all of our popular churches here at the North—you talk about not being responsible for the crime of slave holding, while religiously you shake hands with the southern slave-holders, the perpetrators of every vile deed in crime's black category.

The Scotch Covenanters or Reformed Presbyterians is the only evangelical church in all the nominally free states of the North that can consistently claim freedom from all sanction of, or compromise with slavery, "the sum of all villainies." The Old Scotch Covenanters refuse church fellowship not only to slave-holders, but to churches that fellowship slave-holders. They also refuse to take the oath of allegiance to the United States Government, and thus are theoretically and practically Abolitionists and thus are the doers of the commands of Jesus: "Remember them in bonds, as bound with them" (Heb 13:3). "Break every yoke and let the oppressed go free" (Isa 58:6).

But as a nation, we do deny the manhood of the slave, both politically and religiously. And it is this failure to recognize the slave's humanity that keeps him in his chains.

From the very hour of the foundation of this government has slavery been considered a national curse. Able statesmen and shrewd politicians have denounced it in the halls of legislation and labored to defeat its merciless purpose. Pious divines have hurled at its monster head the thunderbolts of God's wrath, and prayed their Avenger to drive it from the land.

And yet after seventy years of such labors and such prayers, what do we see? Why, the number of slaves increased from a half a million to nearly four millions, the number of slave states from six to fifteen, one thousand millions of dollars pours out of the public treasury for the purchase and conquest of new slave territory—all the United States territories, at first, consecrated to freedom, then thrown open, every foot of them, to the desecrating tread of the slave-holders—the nominally free states, by the late decision of the Supreme Court, made the home of the slave-holder and his slave-property. And an entire nation, which at the beginning could but blush and hang its head that it held within its wide embrace so foul a thing as slavery, now glorying in its shame, crying "great is Diana of the Ephesians"[2] (Acts 19:28, 34).[3]

ANTHONY'S SPEECH AT HER TRIAL FOR VOTING (1873)

The Court: The prisoner will stand up. Has the prisoner anything to say why sentence shall not be pronounced?

Miss ANTHONY: Yes, your honor, I have many things to say; for in your ordered verdict of guilty, you have trampled underfoot every vital principle of our government. My natural rights, my civil rights, my political rights, are all alike ignored. Robbed of the fundamental privilege of citizenship, I am degraded from the status of a citizen to that of a subject; and not only myself individually, but all of my sex, are, by your honor's verdict, doomed to political subjection under this so-called Republican government.

Judge HUNT: The Court can not listen to a rehearsal of arguments the prisoner's counsel has already consumed three hours in presenting.

Miss ANTHONY: May it please your honor, I am not arguing the question, but simply stating the reasons why sentence can not, in justice, be pronounced against me. Your denial of my citizen's right to vote is the denial of my right of consent as one of the governed, the denial of my right of representation as one of the taxed, the denial of my right to a trial by a jury of my peers as an offender against law, therefore, the denial of my sacred rights to life, liberty, property, and—

Judge HUNT: The Court can not allow the prisoner to go on.

Miss ANTHONY: But your honor will not deny me this one and only poor privilege of protest against this high-handed outrage upon my citizen's rights. May it please the Court to remember that since the day of my arrest last November, this is the first time that either myself or any person of my disfranchised class has been allowed a word of defense before judge or jury.

Judge HUNT: The prisoner must sit down; the Court can not allow it.

Miss ANTHONY: All my prosecutors, from the 8th Ward corner grocery politician, who entered the complaint, to the United States Marshal,

Commissioner, District Attorney, District Judge, your honor on the bench, not one is my peer, but each and all are my political sovereigns; and had your honor submitted my case to the jury, as was clearly your duty, even then I should have had just cause of protest, for not one of those men was my peer; but, native or foreign, white or black, rich or poor, educated or ignorant, awake or asleep, sober or drunk, each and every man of them was my political superior; hence, in no sense, my peer. Even, under such circumstances, a commoner of England, tried before a jury of lords, would have far less cause to complain than should I, a woman, tried before a jury of men. Even my counsel, the Hon. Henry R Selden, who has argued my cause so ably, so earnestly, so unanswerably before your honor, is my political sovereign. Precisely as no disfranchised person is entitled to sit upon a jury, and no woman is entitled to the franchise, so, none but a regularly admitted lawyer is allowed to practice in the courts, and no woman can gain admission to the bar—hence, jury, judge, counsel, must all be of the superior class.

Judge HUNT: The Court must insist—the prisoner has been tried according to the established forms of law.

Miss ANTHONY: Yes, your honor, but by forms of law all made by men, interpreted by men, administered by men, in favor of men, and against women; and hence, your honor's directed verdict of guilty, against a United States citizen for the exercise of "that citizen's right to vote," simply because that citizen was a woman and not a man. But, yesterday, the same man-made forms of law declared it a crime punishable with $1,000 fine and six months' imprisonment, for you, or me, or any of us, to give a cup of cold water, a crust of bread, or a night's shelter to a panting fugitive as he was tracking his way to Canada. And every man or woman in whose veins course a drop of human sympathy violated that wicked law, reckless of consequences, and was justified in so doing. As then the slaves who got their freedom must take it over, osr under, or through the unjust forms of law, precisely so now much women, to get their right to a voice in this government, take it; and I have taken mine, and mean to take it at every possible opportunity.

Judge HUNT: The Court orders the prisoner to sit down. It will not allow another word.

Miss ANTHONY: When I was brought before your honor for trial, I hoped for a broad and liberal interpretation of the Constitution and its recent amendments, that should declare all United States citizens under its protecting aegis—that should declare equality of rights the national guarantee to all persons born or naturalized in the United States. But failing to get this justice—failing, even, to get a trial by a jury *not* of my peers—I ask not leniency at your hands—but rather the full rigors of the law.

Judge HUNT: The Court must insist—(Here the prisoner sat down.)

Judge HUNT: The prisoner will stand up. (Here Miss Anthony arose again.) The sentence of the Court is that you pay a fine of one hundred dollars and the costs of the prosecution.

Miss ANTHONY: May it please your honor, I shall never pay a dollar of your unjust penalty. All the stock in trade I possess is a $10,000 debt, incurred by publishing my paper—*The Revolution*—four years ago, the sole object of which was to educate all women to do precisely as I have done, rebel against your man-made, unjust, unconstitutional forms of law, that tax, fine, imprison, and hang women, while they deny them the right of representation in the Government; and I shall work on with might and main to pay every dollar of that honest debt, but not a penny shall go to this unjust claim. And I shall earnestly and persistently continue to urge all women to the practical recognition of the old revolutionary maxim, that "Resistance to tyranny is obedience to God."

Judge HUNT: Madam, the Court will not order you committed until the fine is paid.[4]

THE BREAD OF DEPENDENCE

My purpose tonight is to demonstrate the great historical fact that disfranchisement is not only political degradation, but also moral, social, educational and industrial degradation; and that it does not matter whether the disfranchised class live under a monarchial or a republican form of government, or whether it be white workingmen of England, negroes on our southern plantations, serfs of Russia, Chinamen on our Pacific coast, or native born, tax-paying women of this republic. Wherever, on the face of the globe or on the page of history, you show me a disfranchised class, I will show you a degraded class of labor. Disfranchisement means inability to make, shape or control one's own circumstances. The disfranchised must always do the work, accept the wages, occupy the position the enfranchised assign to them. The disfranchised are in the position of the pauper. You remember the old adage, "Beggars must not be choosers"; they must take what they can get or nothing! That is exactly the position of women in the world of work today; they can not choose. If they could, do you for a moment believe they would take the subordinate places and the inferior pay? Nor is it a "new thing under the sun" for the disfranchised, the inferior classes weighed down with wrongs, to declare they "do not want to vote." The rank and file are not philosophers, they are not educated to think for themselves, but simply to accept, unquestioned, whatever comes.

Years ago in England when the workingmen, starving in the mines and factories, gathered in mobs and took bread wherever they could get it, their friends tried to educate them into a knowledge of the causes of their poverty and degradation. At one of these "monster bread meetings," held in Manchester, John Bright said to them, "Workingmen, what you need to bring to you cheap bread and plenty of it, is the franchise;" but those ignorant men shouted back to Mr. Bright, precisely as the women of America do to us today, "It is not the vote we want, it is bread"; and they broke up the meeting, refusing to allow him, their best friend, to explain to them the powers of the franchise. The condition of those workingmen was very little above that of slavery. . . .

Sad as is the condition of the workingmen of England today, it is infinitely better than it was twenty years ago. . . . This is the way in which the ballot in the hands of the masses of wage-earners, even under a monarchial form of government, makes of them a tremendous balance of power whose wants and wishes the instinct of self-interest compels the political leaders to study and obey.

The great distinctive advantage possessed by the workingmen of this republic is that the son of the humblest citizen, black or white, has equal chances with the son of the richest in the land if he take advantage of the public schools, the colleges and the many opportunities freely offered. It is this equality of rights which makes our nation a home for the oppressed of all the monarchies of the old world.

And yet, notwithstanding the declaration of our Revolutionary fathers, "all men created equal," "governments derive their just powers from the consent of the governed," "taxation and representation inseparable"— notwithstanding all these grand enunciations, our government was founded upon the blood and bones of half a million human beings, bought and sold as chattels in the market. Nearly all the original thirteen states had property qualifications which disfranchised poor white men as well as women and negroes. Thomas Jefferson, at the head of the old Democratic party, took the lead in advocating the removal of all property qualifications, as so many violations of the fundamental principle of our government "the right of consent." In New York the qualification was $250. Martin Van Buren, the chief of the Democracy, was a member of the Constitutional Convention held in Buffalo in 1821, which wiped out that qualification so far as white men were concerned. He declared, "The poor man has as good a right to a voice in the government as the rich man, and a vastly greater need to possess it as a means of protection to himself and his family." It was because the Democracy enfranchised poor white men, both native and foreign, that that strong old party held absolute sway in this country for almost forty years, with only now and then a one-term Whig administration.

... The vast numbers of wage-earning men coming from Europe to this country, where manhood suffrage prevails with no limitations, find themselves invested at once with immense political power. They organize their trades unions, but not being able to use the franchise intelligently, they continue to strike and to fight their battles with the capitalists just as they did in the old countries. Neither press nor politicians dare to condemn these strikes or to demand their suppression because the workingmen hold the balance of power, and can use it for the success or defeat of either party.

(Miss Anthony here related various timely instances of strikes where force was used to prevent non-union men from taking the places of the strikers, and neither the newspapers nor political leaders ventured to sustain the officials in the necessary steps to preserve law and order, or if they did they were defeated at the next election.)

It is said women do not need the ballot for their protection because they are supported by men. Statistics show that there are 3,000,000 women in this nation supporting themselves. In the crowded cities of the East they are compelled to work in shops, stores and factories for the merest pittance. In New York alone, there are over 50,000 of these women receiving less than fifty cents a day. Women wage-earners in different occupations have organized themselves into trades unions, from time to time, and made their strikes to get justice at the hands of their employers just as men have done, but I have yet to learn of a successful strike of any body of women. The best organized one I ever knew was that of the collar laundry women of the city of Troy, N.Y., the great emporium for the manufacture of shirts, collars and cuffs. They formed a trades union of several hundred members and demanded an increase of wages. It was refused. So one May morning in 1867, each woman threw down her scissors and her needle, her starch-pan and flat-iron, and for three long months not one returned to the factories. At the end of that time they were literally starved out, and the majority of them were compelled to go back, but not at their old wages, for their employers cut them down to even a lower figure. . . .

The question with you, as men, is not whether you want your wives and daughters to vote, nor with you, as women, whether you yourselves want to vote; but whether you will help to put this power of the ballot into the hands of the 3,000,000 wage-earning women, so that they may be able to compel politicians to legislate in their favor and employers to grant them justice.

The law of capital is to extort the greatest amount of work for the least amount of money; the rule of labor is to do the smallest amount of work for the largest amount of money. Hence there is, and in the nature of things must continue to be, antagonism between the two classes; therefore, neither should be left wholly at the mercy of the other.

It was cruel, under the old regime, to give rich men the right to rule poor men. It was wicked to allow white men absolute power over black men. It is vastly more cruel, more wicked to give to all men—rich and poor, white and black, native and foreign, educated and ignorant, virtuous and vicious—this absolute control over women. Men talk of the injustice of monopolies. There never was, there never can be, a monopoly so fraught with injustice, tyranny and degradation as this monopoly of sex, of all men over all women. Therefore I not only agree with Abraham Lincoln that, "No man is good enough to govern another man without his consent;" but I say also that no man is good enough to govern a woman without her consent, and still further, that all men combined in government are not good enough to govern all women without their consent. There might have been some plausible excuse for the rich governing the poor, the educated governing the ignorant, the Saxon governing the African; but there can be none for making the husband the ruler of the wife, the brother of the sister, the man of the woman, his peer in birth, in education, in social position, in all that stands for the best and highest in humanity.

I believe that by nature men are no more unjust than women. If from the beginning women had maintained the right to rule not only themselves but men also, the latter today doubtless would be occupying the subordinate places with inferior pay in the world of work; women would be holding the higher positions with the big salaries; widowers would be doomed to a "life interest of one-third of the family estate;" husbands would "owe service" to their wives, so that every one of you men would be begging your good wives, "Please be so kind as to 'give me' ten cents for a cigar." The principle of self-government can not be violated with impunity. The individual's right to it is sacred—regardless of class, caste, race, color, sex or any other accident or incident of birth. What we ask is that you shall cease to imagine that women are outside this law, and that you shall come into the knowledge that disfranchisement means the same degradation to your daughters as to your sons.

Governments can not afford to ignore the rights of those holding the ballot, who make and unmake every law and law-maker. It is not because the members of Congress are tyrants that women receive only half pay and are admitted only to inferior positions in the departments. It is simply in obedience to a law of political economy which makes it impossible for a government to do as much for the disfranchised as for the enfranchised. Women are no exception to the general rule. As disfranchisement always has degraded men, socially, morally and industrially, so today it is disfranchisement that degrades women in the same spheres.

Again men say it is not votes, but the law of supply and demand which regulates wages. The law of gravity is that water shall run down hill, but when men build a dam across the stream, the force of gravity is stopped and the water held back. The law of supply and demand regulates free and enfranchised labor, but disfranchisement estops its operation. What we ask is the removal of the dam, that women, like men, may reap the benefit of the law. Did the law of supply and demand regulate work and wages in the olden days of slavery? This law can no more reach the disfranchised than it did the enslaved. There is scarcely a place where a woman can earn a single dollar without a man's consent.

There are many women equally well qualified with men for principals and superintendents of schools, and yet, while three-fourths of the teachers are women, nearly all of them are relegated to subordinate positions on half or at most two-thirds the salaries paid to men. The law of supply and demand is ignored, and that of sex alone settles the question. If a business man should advertise for a bookkeeper and ten young men, equally well qualified, should present themselves and, after looking them over, he should say, "To you who have red hair, we will pay full wages, while to you with black hair we will pay half the regular price;" that would not be a more flagrant violation of the law of supply and demand than is that now perpetrated upon women because of their sex.

And then again you say, "Capital, not the vote, regulates labor." Granted, for the sake of the argument, that capital does control the labor of women, Chinamen and slaves; but no one with eyes to see and ears to hear, will concede for a moment that capital absolutely dominates the work and wages of the free and enfranchised men of this republic. It is in order to lift the millions of our wage-earning women into a position of as much power over their own labor as men possess that they should be invested with the franchise. This ought to be done not only for the sake of justice to the women, but to the men with whom they compete; for, just so long as there is a degraded class of labor in the market, it always will be used by the capitalists to checkmate and undermine the superior classes.

Now that as a result of the agitation for equality of chances, and through the invention of machinery, there has come a great revolution in the world of economics, so that wherever a man may go to earn an honest dollar a woman may go also, there is no escape from the conclusion that she must be clothed with equal power to protect herself. That power is the ballot, the symbol of freedom and equality, without which no citizen is sure of keeping even that which he hath, much less of getting that which he hath not. Women are today the peers of men in education, in the arts and sciences, in the industries and professions, and there is no escape from the conclusion that the next step must be to make them the peers of men in the government—city, State and national—to give them an equal voice in the framing, interpreting and administering of the codes and constitutions.

We recognize that the ballot is a two-edged, nay, a many-edged sword, which may be made to cut in every direction. If wily politicians and sordid capitalists may wield it for mere party and personal greed; if oppressed wage-earners may invoke it to wring justice from legislators and extort material advantages from employers; if the lowest and most degraded classes of men may use it to open wide the sluice-ways of vice and crime; if it may be the instrumentality by which the narrow, selfish, corrupt and corrupting men and measures rule—it is quite as true that noble-minded statesmen, philanthropists and reformers may make it the weapon with which to reverse the above order of things, as soon as they can have added to their now small numbers the immensely larger ratio of what men so love to call "the better half of the people." When women vote, they will make a new balance of power that must be weighed and measured and calculated in its effect upon every social and moral question which goes to the arbitrament of the ballot box. Who can doubt that when the representative women of thought and culture, who are today the moral backbone of our nation, sit in counsel with the best men of the country, higher conditions will be the result?

Insurrectionary and revolutionary methods of righting wrongs, imaginary or real, are pardonable only in the enslaved and disfranchised. The moment any class of men possess the ballot, it is their weapon and their shield. Men with a vote have no valid excuse for resorting to the use of illegal means to fight their battles. When the masses of wage-earning men are educated into a knowledge of their own rights and of their duties to others, so that they are able to vote intelligently, they can carry their measures through the ballot-box and will have no need to resort to force. But so long as they remain in ignorance and are manipulated by the political bosses they will continue to vote against their own interests and turn again to violence to right their wrongs.

If men possessing the power of the ballot are driven to desperate means to gain their ends, what shall be done by disfranchised women? There are grave questions of moral, as well as of material interest in which women are most deeply concerned. Denied the ballot, the legitimate means with which to exert their influence, and, as a rule being lovers of peace, they have recourse to prayers and tears, those potent weapons of women and children, and, when they fail, must tamely submit to wrong or rise in rebellion against the powers that be. Women's crusades against saloons, brothels and gambling dens, emptying kegs and bottles into the streets, breaking doors and windows and burning houses, all go to prove that disfranchisement, the denial of lawful means to gain desired ends, may drive even women to violations of law and order. Hence to secure both national and "domestic tranquility," to "establish justice," to carry out the spirit of our Constitution, put into the hands of all women, as you have into those of all men, the ballot, that symbol of perfect equality, that right protective of all other rights.[5]

SOCIAL PURITY

Though women, as a class, are much less addicted to drunkenness and licentiousness than men, it is universally conceded that they are by far the greater sufferers from these evils. Compelled by their position in society to depend on men for subsistence, for food, clothes, shelter, for every chance even to earn a dollar, they have no way of escape from the besotted victims of appetite and passion with whom their lot is cast. They must endure, if not endorse, these twin vices, embodied, as they so often are, in the person of father, brother, husband, son, employer. No one can doubt that the sufferings of the sober, virtuous woman, in legal subjection to the mastership of a drunken, immoral husband and father over herself and children, not only from physical abuse, but from spiritual shame and humiliation, must be such as the man himself can not possibly comprehend.

It is not my purpose to harrow your feelings by any attempt at depicting the horrible agonies of mind and body that grow out of these monster social evils. They are already but too well known. Scarce a family throughout our broad land but has had its peace and happiness marred by one or the other, or both. That these evils exist, we all know; that something must be done, we as well know; that the old methods have failed, that man, alone, has proved himself incompetent to eradicate, or even regulate them, is equally evident. It shall be my endeavor, therefore, to prove to you that we must now adopt new measures and bring to our aid new forces to accomplish the desired end. . . .

The roots of the giant evil, intemperance, are not merely moral and social; they extend deep and wide into the financial and political structure of the government; and whenever women, or men, shall intelligently and seriously set themselves about the work of uprooting the liquor traffic, they will find something more than tears and prayers needful to the task. Financial and political power must be combined with moral and social influence, all bound together in one earnest, energetic, persistent force.

(Statistics given of pauperism, lunacy, idiocy and crime growing out of intemperance.)

The prosecutions in our courts for breach of promise, divorce, adultery, bigamy, seduction, rape; the newspaper reports every day of every year of scandals and outrages, of wife murders and paramour shootings, of abortions and infanticides, are perpetual reminders of men's incapacity to cope successfully with this monster evil of society.

The statistics of New York show the number of professional prostitutes in that city to be over twenty thousand. Add to these the thousands and tens of thousands of Boston, Philadelphia, Washington, New Orleans, St. Louis, Chicago, San Francisco, and all our cities, great and small, from ocean to ocean, and what a holocaust of the womanhood of this nation is sacrificed to the insatiate Moloch of lust. And yet more: those myriads of wretched women, publicly known as prostitutes, constitute but a small portion of the numbers who actually tread the paths of vice and crime. For, as the oft broken ranks of the vast army of common drunkards are steadily filled by the boasted moderate drinkers, so are the ranks of professional prostitution continually replenished by discouraged, seduced, deserted unfortunates, who can no longer hide the terrible secret of their lives.

The Albany Law Journal, of December, 1876, says: "The laws of infanticide must be a dead letter in the District of Columbia. According to the reports of the local officials, the dead bodies of infants, still-born and murdered, which have been found during the past year, scattered over parks and vacant lots in the city of Washington, are to be numbered by hundreds."

In 1869 the Catholics established a Foundling Hospital in New York City. At the close of the first six months Sister Irene reported thirteen hundred little waifs laid in the basket at her door. That meant thirteen hundred of the daughters of New York, with trembling hands and breaking hearts, trying to bury their sorrow and their shame from the world's cruel gaze. That meant thirteen hundred mothers' hopes blighted and blasted. Thirteen hundred Rachels weeping for their children because they were not!

Nor is it womanhood alone that is thus fearfully sacrificed. For every betrayed woman, there is always the betrayer, man. For every abandoned woman, there is always *one* abandoned man and oftener many more. It is estimated that there are 50,000 professional prostitutes in London, and Dr. Ryan calculates that there are 400,000 men in that city directly or indirectly connected with them, and that this vice causes the city an annual expenditure of $40,000,000.

All attempts to describe the loathsome and contagious disease which it engenders defy human language. The Rev. Wm. G. Eliot, of St. Louis, says of it: "Few know of the terrible nature of the disease in question and its fearful ravages, not only among the guilty, but the innocent. Since its first recognized appearance in Europe in the fifteenth century, it has been a desolation and a scourge. In its worst forms it is so subtle, that its course can with difficulty be traced. It poisons the constitution, and may be imparted to others by those who have no outward or distinguishable marks of it themselves. It may be propagated months and years after it seems to have been cured. The purity of womanhood and the helplessness of infancy afford no certainty of escape.

(Medical testimony given from cities in Europe.)

Man's legislative attempts to set back this fearful tide of social corruption have proved even more futile and disastrous than have those for the suppression of intemperance—as witness the Contagious Diseases Acts of England and the St. Louis experiment. And yet efforts to establish similar laws are constantly made in our large cities, New York and Washington barely escaping last winter.

To license certain persons to keep brothels and saloons is but to throw around them and their traffic the shield of law, and thereby to blunt the edge of all moral and social efforts against them. Nevertheless, in every large city, brothels are virtually licensed. When "Maggie Smith" is made to appear before the police court at the close of each quarter, to pay her fine of $10, $25 or $100, as an inmate or a keeper of a brothel, and allowed to continue her vocation, so long as she pays her fine, *that is license*. When a grand jury fails to find cause for indictment against a well-known keeper of a house of ill-fame, that, too, is *permission* for her and all of her class to follow their trade, against the statute laws of the State, and that with impunity.

The work of woman is not to lessen the severity or the certainty of the penalty for the violation of the moral law, but to prevent this violation by the removal of the causes which lead to it. These causes are said to be wholly different with the sexes. The acknowledged incentive to this vice on the part of man is his own abnormal passion; while on the part of woman, in the great majority of cases, it is conceded to be destitution— absolute want of the necessaries of life. Lecky, the famous historian of European morals, says: "The statistics of prostitution show that a great proportion of those women who have fallen into it have been impelled by the most extreme poverty, in many instances verging on starvation." All other conscientious students of this terrible problem, on both continents, agree with Mr. Lecky. Hence, there is no escape from the conclusion that, while woman's want of bread induces her to pursue this vice, man's love of the vice itself leads him into it and holds him there. While statistics show no lessening of the passional demand on the part of man, they reveal a most frightful increase of the temptations, the necessities, on the part of woman.

In the olden times, when the daughters of the family, as well as the wife, were occupied with useful and profitable work in the household, getting the meals and washing the dishes three times in every day of every year, doing the baking, the brewing, the washing and the ironing, the white-washing, the butter and cheese and soap making, the mending and the making of clothes for the entire family, the carding, spinning and weaving of the cloth—when everything to eat, to drink and to wear was manufac-tured in the home, almost no young women "went out to work." But now, when nearly all these handicrafts are turned over to men and to machin-ery, tens of thousands, nay, millions, of the women of both hemispheres are thrust into the world's outer market of work to earn their own subsis-tence. Society, ever slow to change its conditions, presents to these mil-lions but few and meager chances. Only the barest necessaries, and oftentimes not even those, can be purchased with the proceeds of the most excessive and exhausting labor.

Hence, the reward of virtue for the homeless, friendless, penniless woman is ever a scanty larder, a pinched, patched, faded wardrobe, a dank basement or rickety garret, with the colder, shabbier scorn and neglect of the more fortunate of her sex. Nightly, as weary and worn from her day's toil she wends her way through the dark alleys toward her still darker abode, where only cold and hunger await her, she sees on every side and at every turn the gilded hand of vice and crime outstretched, beckoning her to food and clothes and shelter; hears the whisper in softest accents, "Come with me and I will give you all the comforts, pleasures and luxuries that love and wealth can bestow." Since the vast multitudes of human be-ings, women like men, are not born to the courage or conscience of the martyr, can we wonder that so many poor girls fall, that so many accept material ease and comfort at the expense of spiritual purity and peace? Should we not wonder, rather, that so many escape the sad fate?

Clearly, then, the first step toward solving this problem is to lift this vast army of poverty-stricken women who now crowd our cities, above the temptation, the necessity, to sell themselves, in marriage or out, for bread and shelter. To do that, girls, like boys, must be educated to some lucrative employment; women, like men, must have equal chances to earn a living. If the plea that poverty is the cause of woman's prostitution be not true, perfect equality of chances to earn honest bread will demonstrate the falsehood by removing that pretext and placing her on the same plane with man. Then, if she is found in the ranks of vice and crime, she will be there for the same reason that man is and, from an object of pity, she, like him, will become a fit, subject of contempt. From being the party sinned against, she will become an equal sinner, if not the greater of the two. Women, like men, must not only have "fair play" in the world of work and self-support, but, like men, must be eligible to all the honors and emoluments of society and government. Marriage, to women as to men, must be a luxury, not a necessity; an incident of life, not all of it. And the only possible way to accomplish this great change is to accord to women equal power in the making, shaping and controlling of the circumstances of life. That equality of rights and privileges is vested in the ballot, the symbol of power in a republic. Hence, our first and most urgent demand-that women shall be protected in the exercise of their inherent, personal, citizen's right to a voice in the government, municipal, state, national.

Alexander Hamilton said one hundred years ago, "Give to a man the right over my subsistence, and he has power over my whole moral being." No one doubts the truth of this assertion as between man and man; while, as between man and woman, not only does almost no one believe it, but the masses of people deny it. And yet it is the fact of man's possession of this right over woman's subsistence which gives to him the power to dictate to her a moral code vastly higher and purer than the one he chooses for himself. Not less true is it, that the fact of woman's dependence on man for her subsistence renders her utterly powerless to exact from him the same high moral code she chooses for herself.

Of the 8,000,000 women over twenty-one years of age in the United States, 800,000, one out of every ten, are unmarried, and fully one-half of the entire number, or 4,000,000, support themselves wholly or in part by the industry of their own hands and brains. All of these, married or single, have to ask man, as an individual, a corporation, or a government, to grant to them even the privilege of hard work and small pay. The tens of thousands of poor but respectable working girls soliciting copying, clerkships, shop work, teaching, must ask of men, and not seldom receive in response, "Why work for a living? There are other ways!"

Whoever controls work and wages, controls morals. Therefore, we must have women employers, superintendents, committees, legislators; wherever girls go to seek the means of subsistence, there must be some woman.

Nay, more; we must have women preachers, lawyers, doctors—that—wherever women go to seek counsel—spiritual, legal, physical—there, too, they will be sure to find the best and noblest of their own sex to minister to them.

Independence is happiness. "No man should depend upon another; not even upon his own father. By depend I mean, obey without examination-yield to the will of any one whomsoever." This is the conclusion to which Pierre, the hero of Madame Sand's "Monsieur Sylvestre," arrives, after running away from the uncle who had determined to marry him to a woman he did not choose to wed. In freedom he discovers that, though deprived of all the luxuries to which he had been accustomed, he is happy, and writes his friend that "without having realized it, he had been unhappy all his life; had suffered from his dependent condition; that nothing in his life, his pleasures, his occupations, had been of his own choice." And is not this the precise condition of what men call the "better half" of the human family?...

In a western city the wives conspired to burn down a house of ill-fame in which their husbands had placed a half-dozen of the demi-monde. Would it not have shown much more womanly wisdom and virtue for those legal wives to have refused to recognize their husbands, instead of wreaking their vengeance on the heads of those wretched women? But how could they without finding themselves, as a result, penniless and homeless? The person, the services, the children, the subsistence, of each and every one of those women belonged by law, not to herself, but to her unfaithful husband.

Now, why is it that man can hold woman to this high code of morals, like Caesar's wife-not only pure but above suspicion-and so surely and severely punish her for every departure, while she is so helpless, so powerless to check him in his license, or to extricate herself from his presence and control? His power grows out of his right over her subsistence. Her lack of power grows out of her dependence on him for her food, her clothes, her shelter.

Marriage never will cease to be a wholly unequal partnership until the law recognizes the equal ownership in the joint earnings and possessions. The true relation of the sexes never can be attained until woman is free and equal with man. Neither in the making nor executing of the laws regulating these relations has woman ever had the slightest voice. The statutes for marriage and divorce, for adultery, breach of promise, seduction, rape, bigamy, abortion, infanticide—all were made by men. They, alone, decide who are guilty of violating these laws and what shall be their punishment, with judge, jury and advocate all men, with no woman's voice heard in our courts, save as accused or witness, and in many cases the married woman is denied the poor privilege of testifying as to her own guilt or innocence of the crime charged against her. . . .

It is worse than folly, it is madness, for women to delude themselves with the idea that their children will escape the terrible penalty of the law. The taint of their birth will surely follow them. For pure women to continue to devote themselves to their man-appointed mission of visiting the dark purlieus of society and struggling to reclaim the myriads of badly-born human beings swarming there, is as hopeless as would be an attempt to ladle the ocean with a teaspoon; as unphilosophical as was the undertaking of the old American Colonization Society, which, with great labor and pains and money, redeemed from slavery and transported to Liberia annually 400 negroes; or the Fugitive Slave Societies, which succeeded in running off to Canada, on their "under-ground railroads," some 40,000 in a whole quarter of a century. While those good men were thus toiling to rescue the 400 or the 40,000 individual victims of slavery, each day saw hundreds and each year thousands of human beings born into the terrible condition of chattelism. All see and admit now what none but the Abolitionists saw then, that the only effectual work was the entire overthrow of the system of slavery; the abrogation of the law which sanctioned the right of property in man. . . .

Thus, wherever you go, you find the best women, in and out of the churches, all absorbed in establishing or maintaining benevolent or reform institutions; charitable societies, soup-houses, ragged schools, industrial schools, mite societies, mission schools—at home and abroad—homes and hospitals for the sick, the aged, the friendless, the foundling, the fallen; asylums for the orphans, the blind, the deaf and dumb, the insane, the inebriate, the idiot. The women of this century are neither idle nor indifferent. They are working with might and main to mitigate the evils which stare them in the face on every side, but much of their work is without knowledge. It is aimed at the effects, not the cause; it is plucking the spoiled fruit; it is lopping off the poisonous branches of the deadly upas tree, which but makes the root more vigorous in sending out new shoots in every direction. A right understanding of physiological law teaches us that the cause must be removed; the tree must be girdled; the tap-root must be severed.

The tap-root of our social upas lies deep down at the very foundations of society. It is woman's dependence. It is woman's subjection. Hence, the first and only efficient work must be to emancipate woman from her enslavement. The wife must no longer echo the poet Milton's ideal Eve, when she adoringly said to Adam, "God, thy law; thou, mine!" She must feel herself accountable to God alone for every act, fearing and obeying no man, save where his will is in line with her own highest idea of divine law. . . .

If the divine law visits the sins of the fathers upon the children, equally so does it transmit to them their virtues. Therefore, if it is through woman's ignorant subjection to the tyranny of man's appetites and passions that the life current of the race is corrupted, then must it be through her intelligent emancipation that the race shall be redeemed from the curse, and her children and children's children rise up to call her blessed. When the mother of Christ shall be made the true model of womanhood and motherhood, when the office of maternity shall be held sacred and the mother shall consecrate herself, as did Mary, to the one idea of bringing forth the Christ-child, then, and not till then, will this earth see a new order of men and women, prone to good rather than evil.

I am a full and firm believer in the revelation that it is through woman that the race is to be redeemed. And it is because of this faith that I ask for her immediate and unconditional emancipation from all political, industrial, social and religious subjection. . . .

A minister of Chicago sums up the infamies of that great metropolis of the West as follows: 3,000 licensed dram-shops and myriad patrons; 300 gambling houses and countless frequenters, many of them young men from the best families of the city; 79 obscene theatres, with their thousands of degraded men and boys nightly in attendance; 500 brothels, with their thousands of poor girls, bodies and souls sacrificed to the 20,000 or 30,000 depraved men—young and old, married and single—who visit them. While all the participants in all these forms of iniquity, victims and victimizers alike—the women excepted-may go to the polls on every election day and vote for the mayor and members of the common council, who will either continue to license these places, or fail to enforce the laws which would practically close them—not a single woman in that city may record her vote against those wretched blots on civilization. The profane, tobacco-chewing, whiskey-drinking, gambling libertines may vote, but not their virtuous, intelligent, sober, law-abiding wives and mothers!. . . .

As the fountain can rise no higher than the spring that feeds it, so a legislative body will enact or enforce no law above the average sentiment of the people who created it. Any and every reform work is sure to lead women to the ballot-box. It is idle for them to hope to battle successfully against the monster evils of society until they shall be armed with weapons equal to those of the enemy—votes and money. Archimedes said, "Give to me a fulcrum on which to plant my lever, and I will move the world." And I say, give to woman the ballot, the political fulcrum, on which to plant her moral lever, and she will lift the world into a nobler and purer atmosphere.

Two great necessities forced this nation to extend justice and equality to the negro:

First, Military necessity, which compelled the abolition of the crime and curse of slavery, before the rebellion could be overcome.

Second, Political necessity, which required the enfranchisement of the newly-freed men, before the work of reconstruction could begin.

The third is now pressing, Moral necessity—to emancipate woman, before Social Purity, the nation's safeguard, ever can be established.[6]

ANTHONY AND THE SPIRITUALISTS (1890S)

After the Berlin meeting Miss Anthony and I were invited to spend a week-end at the home of Mrs. Jacob Bright, that "Aunt Susan" might renew her acquaintance with Annie Besant. . . . Now she could not conceal her disapproval of the "other-worldliness" of Mrs. Besant, Mrs. Bright, and her daughter. . . .

"Annie," demanded Aunt Susan, "why don't you make that aura of yours do its gallivanting in this world, looking up the needs of the oppressed, and investigating the causes of present wrongs? Then you could reveal to us workers just what we should do to put things right, and we could be about it."

Mrs. Besant sighed and said that life was short and aeons were long, and that while every one would be perfected some time, it was useless to deal with individuals here.

"But, Annie!" exclaimed Miss Anthony, pathetically, "We *are* here! Our business is here! It's our duty to do what we can here."

Mrs. Besant seemed not to hear her. She was in a trance, gazing into the aeons. . . . It was plain that she could not bring herself back from the other world, so Miss Anthony, perforce, accompanied her to it.

"When your aura goes visiting in the other world," she asked, curiously, "does it ever meet your old friend Charles Bradlaugh?"

. . . Mrs. Besant heaved a deeper sigh. "I am very much discouraged over Mr. Bradlaugh," she admitted, wanly. "He is hovering too near this world. He cannot seem to get away from his mundane interests. He is as much concerned with parliamentary affairs now as when he was on this plane."

"Humph!" said Miss Anthony; "that's the most sensible thing I've heard yet about the other world. It encourages me. I've always felt sure that if I entered the other life before women were enfranchised nothing in the glories of heaven would interest me so much as the work for women's freedom on earth."[7]

SPEECH IN THE WOMAN'S BIBLE CONTROVERSY (1896)

The one distinct feature of our association has been the right of individual opinion for every member. We have been beset at each step with the cry that somebody was injuring the cause by the expression of sentiments which differed from those held by the majority. The religious persecution of the ages has been carried on under what was claimed to be the command of God. I distrust those people who know so well what God wants them to do, because I notice it always coincides with their own desires. All the way along the history of our movement there has been this same contest on account of religious theories. Forty years ago one of our noblest men said to me, "You would better never hold another convention than allow Ernestine L. Rose on your platform"; because that eloquent woman, who ever stood for justice and freedom, did not believe in the plenary inspiration of the Bible. Did we banish Mrs. Rose? No, indeed!

Every new generation of converts threshes over the same old straw. The point is whether you will sit in judgment on one who questions the divine inspiration of certain passages in the Bible derogatory to women. If Mrs. Stanton had written approvingly of these passages you would not have brought in this resolution for fear the case might be injured among the *liberals* in religion. In other words, if she had written *your* views, you would not have considered a resolution necessary. To pass this one is to set back the hands on the dial of reform.

What you should say to outsiders is that a Christian has neither more nor less rights in our association than an atheist. When our platform becomes too narrow for people of all creeds and of no creeds, I myself can not stand upon it. Many things have been said and done by our *orthodox* friends which I have felt to be extremely harmful to our case; but I should no more consent to a resolution denouncing them than I shall consent to this. Who is to draw the line? Who can tell now whether these commentaries may not prove a great help to woman's emancipation from old superstitions which have barred its way?

Lucretia Mott at first thought Mrs. Stanton had injured the cause of all woman's other rights by insisting upon the demand for suffrage, but she had sense enough not to bring in a resolution against it. In 1860 when Mrs. Stanton made a speech before the New York Legislature in favor of a bill making drunkenness a ground for divorce, there was a general cry among the friends that she had killed the woman's cause. I shall be pained beyond expression if the delegates here are so narrow and illiberal as to adopt this resolution. You would better not begin resolving against individual action or you will find no limit. This year it is Mrs. Stanton; next year it may be I or one of yourselves, who will be the victim.

If we do not inspire in women a broad and catholic spirit, they will fail, when enfranchised, to constitute that power for better government which we have always claimed for them. Ten women educated into the practice of liberal principles would be a stronger force than 10,000 organized on a platform of intolerance and bigotry. I pray you vote for religious liberty, without censorship or inquisition. This resolution adopted will be a vote of censure upon a woman who is without a peer in intellectual and statesmanlike ability; one who has stood for half a century the acknowledged leader of progressive thought and demand in regard to all matters pertaining to the absolute freedom of women.[8]

NOTES

1. [This is the first known speech by Susan B. Anthony, published for the first time here, I believe. Its major point—that any church member who supports any aspect of the liquor trade is guilty of its sins—is reminiscent of arguments of the antislavery people that the North, too, was implicated in the guilt of slavery, or the refusal of Quaker abolitionists to wear clothing made of cotton, since cotton was grown by slaveholders. It is studded with biblical quotations, and I have added chapter and verse for those who may not be aware of this material.]

2. [This was the cry from a crowd that believed its profit from the sale of statues of Diana was threatened by the preaching of Christians.]

3. [These unpublished speeches are from the Library of Congress; there is no date on the manuscript of the second, but it is most likely from roughly the same time as the first. The manuscript may also be missing some pages, since it simply ends in the middle of a thought. Anthony's commitment to antislavery was deep and long. After the Civil War she was incensed that abolitionists had given up agitation, since racism in the North was still strong.]

4. [Elizabeth Cady Stanton, Susan B. Anthony, et al., eds., *The History of Woman Suffrage*, 6 vols., repr. ed. (New York: Arno Press, 1969), 2:687–689. After sitting through days with lawyers expounding at the judge and jury without being able to say a word on her own behalf, Anthony was probably simmering when the judge pulled his written verdict from his pocket, instructed to jurors to find her guilty without deliberating, and then dismissed them.]

5. [Ida Husted Harper, *The Life and Work of Susan B. Anthony*, 3 vols. (Indianapolis: Hollenbeck Press, 1898–1908), 2:996–1003. In the 1870s, Anthony put her thoughts together into a speech she delivered regularly. This version was

assembled and edited by Ida Husted Harper from newspaper accounts. (In complete contradistinction to its contents, the published version called it "woman wants bread, not the ballot.")]

6. [Harper, *The Life and Work of Susan B. Anthony*, 2:1004-1012. For its time, it was relatively fearless, mentioning prostitution, infanticide, and venereal disease (though the last earned a euphemism). Its major point, that enfranchisement was necessary to regulate these evils, may seem quaint and outdated to those of us who have been through both a so-called sexual revolution and the movement to end violence against women and children. But it was important for her attempt to talk about a systemic issue that required a systemic solution.]

7. [Anna Howard Shaw with Elizabeth Jordan, *The Story of a Pioneer* (New York: Harper, 1915), 214–216. Many suffragists were involved with the spiritualist movement of the late nineteenth century, including Elizabeth Stanton. Though many of them sought to win Anthony over, she had little patience with them, as we can see in this excerpt.]

8. [*The History of Woman Suffrage*, 4:263–264. After the publication of the first volume of *The Woman's Bible*, more religiously conservative members of the NAWSA were offended. They proposed a resolution at the annual convention disavowing any connection to that work. Anthony, who had begged off from being a part of this project of Stanton's, nonetheless was distressed when the rank and file of the suffrage organization in effect disowned her old friend. She left the chair to deliver this exhortation.]

[CHAPTER 3]

Karl Barth (1886–1968)

COMMENTARY

GEORGE HUNSINGER

Pope Pius XII once described Karl Barth, the Swiss Reformed professor and pastor, as "the most important theologian since Thomas Aquinas."[1] Barth's enormous contribution to theology, church, and culture will take generations to assimilate and assess. As the principal author of the Barmen Declaration of 1934, he was the intellectual leader of the German "Confessing Church," the Protestant congregations that resisted Adolf Hitler. Among Barth's many books, sermons, and essays, the great, multivolume *Church Dogmatics*—a closely reasoned, eloquently stated argument in nearly ten thousand pages—stands out as his crowning achievement. Of this work Thomas F. Torrance has written, "Most people regard Volume IV as the high point of the *Church Dogmatics.* . . . [It] surely constitutes the most powerful work on the doctrine of atoning reconciliation ever written."[2]

Barth's ecumenical importance has been widely recognized. "We have in Barth," writes Hans Urs von Balthasar, "two crucial features: the most thorough and penetrating display of the Protestant view and the closest rapprochement with the Catholic." According to von Balthasar's assessment of Barth, "in him Protestantism has found *for the first time* its most completely consistent representative."[3] During the last decade of his life, Barth was increasingly hopeful about the "astonishing renewal" in the Catholic Church initiated by the Second Vatican Council (1962–65).[4] "I often sense in Catholicism," he once said, "a stronger Christian life than in the Protestant churches."[5] After reading Hans Küng's book *Justification* (1957), the thesis of which is that the teachings of Barth and Catholicism are compatible, Barth stated: "It occurs to me as something worth pondering that it could suddenly take place that the first will be last and the last first, that suddenly from Rome the doctrine of justification by faith alone will be proclaimed more purely than in most Protestant churches."[6]

Karl Barth was born in Basel, Switzerland, on May 10, 1886. Inspired by his father, a professor of New Testament at Bern, Barth resolved to study theology. He matriculated at the University of Bern and studied Reformed theology as well as the thought of the philosopher Immanuel Kant and theologian Friedrich Schleiermacher, who left a deep impression on him. He also studied at the University of Berlin with the great church historian Adolf von Harnack and at the University of Marburg with the neo-Kantian theologian Wilhelm Hermann. After his ordination in Geneva, he took a pastorate in Safenwil, Switzerland.

It was during this first pastorate that Barth came to an acute rethinking of his theology, as well as his views of law, politics, and society. As his biographer James B. Torrance puts it, "On the one hand, when World War I broke out, he was deeply disturbed by the 'Manifesto of the Intellectuals,' 'the black day,' as he called it, when ninety-three scholars and artists, including his own teachers Harnack and Hermann, supported the war policy of Kaiser Wilhelm II, which seemed to him to call into question his colleagues' understanding of the Bible, history, and dogmatics. Was this where the synthesis of (German) culture and religion was leading the Christian church? On the other hand, in his industrial parish, he became acutely aware of the issues of social justice, poor wages, factory legislation, and true union affairs."[7]

Never having studied for a doctorate, Barth did more than anyone to revitalize theology in the twentieth century. His massive *Church Dogmatics* remained unfinished—like the cathedral in Strasbourg, he once quipped, with its missing tower. Thoroughly modern, he rejected modernism in theology. Deeply traditional, he left no stone of tradition unturned. Without deterring easy classifications from critics, he has defied easy classification. Not since Luther and Calvin has there been a Protestant theologian so prodigious in written output and so active in worldly affairs, both ecclesiastical and political. Though Barth was reputed for sharp polemic, his infectious childlike joy, his self-deprecating humor, his love of Mozart, and his profound understanding of Holy Scripture have endeared him to many whose lives he has immeasurably enriched.

Dietrich Bonhoeffer once suggested that in Barth we find the same *hilaritas* that we do in Mozart. The good cheer that knows how to incorporate all that is negative within itself without losing its basic gladness was surely one of Barth's most appealing characteristics. It was a *hilaritas* that was informed by *gravitas* but never succumbed to it. For all his greatness, or perhaps just because of it, Barth did not take himself too seriously.

Along with *hilaritas* and *gravitas*, an element of *humilitas* pervaded his work. Barth had no higher aspiration than to place his intellect in the service of God's grace. Grace inspires the cheerfulness, gravity, and humility he saw as proper to the theologian's task.

THEOLOGY AND POLITICS

Late in life, Barth captured the thrust of his political views in a single line. In a letter of 1967 to Eberhard Bethge, he wrote of "the outlook which I presupposed without so many words and emphasized merely in passing, namely ethics, co-humanity (*Mitmenschlichkeit*), a servant Church, discipleship, Socialism, movements for peace—and throughout all these, politics."[8] Political matters, while never minor for Barth, were constantly overshadowed, as he admitted, by his chief concern, which was "to give a new interpretation of the Reformation."[9] Nevertheless, Barth's political writings make up a significant portion of his corpus. It is only because his dogmatic output looms so large that his political output seems diminutive by comparison.

Whereas Barth's work in theology was detailed and sustained, his political essays were more or less ad hoc. He always saw an integral connection between the two, with theology holding the center while politics was assigned to the periphery. He believed that they could not possibly be separated, especially when it came to grave social evils. "It is not enough," he once remarked, "only to say, 'Jesus is risen,' but then to remain silent about the Vietnam War."[10] Ethics without doctrine is nothing, he believed, but doctrine without ethics is worse than nothing. He therefore reconceived ethics as internal to the dogmatic task. In modern Protestant theology, he felt, neither the left nor the right could adequately set forth the gospel. Neither knew how to uphold doctrinal substance simultaneously with contemporary, political relevance. The left wanted relevance without substance even as the right wanted substance without relevance—the very impasse Barth discerned in the nineteenth century. "These two extremes," he stated, "are for me a thing of the past. On both sides one must go forward instead of always moving backwards."[11]

In politics as well as in theology, we might say that Barth understood himself as a "postliberal" theologian. That is, he understood himself as breaking with the thought forms of modern academic theology as well as with "economic liberalism" (modern capitalism). He usually associated the beginning of his break with theological liberalism with his turn to the left. In about 1916, during his Safenwil pastorate, he became a Swiss religious socialist. Because of his trade-union activities on behalf of the workers in his village, he was known as the Red Pastor. Looking back on that period, he once said in an interview, "I decided for theology, because I felt I needed to find a better basis for my social action."[12]

Barth's political views can be surveyed under three broad headings: church and state, democratic socialism, and international peace. Since these themes are not easy to disentangle, their separation cannot always be neat. Moreover, in a manner that could be exasperating for his critics, to say nothing of his supporters, Barth would sometimes seem to operate more intuitively in arriving at political decisions than on the basis of explicit argumentation. What he regarded as the flexibility and freedom necessary to being a Christian, others have dismissed as arbitrary. While that charge would not be impossible, it could be made to stick only after careful consideration (not always evident in his critics). It is generally true, however, that Barth's political views manifested a double aspect. A fixed side, for Barth, was always made to coexist with an open-ended side. While he wanted the fixed side to allow for stability while avoiding the pitfalls of legalism, he wanted the open-ended side to permit a fresh response to new actualities, under the sovereign leading of God.

CHURCH AND STATE

Church-state relations reached a crisis for Barth during the rise of Hitler and the Third Reich. A stance had to be taken in the 1934 Barmen Declaration[13]—one strong enough to be meaningful, yet broad enough to gain as much support from the churches as possible. The Barmen Declaration, with Barth as its principal author, served as the manifesto of the German confessing church, which resisted Hitler.

The positive thesis of Barmen Article I was this: "Jesus Christ, as he is attested for us in Holy Scripture, is the one Word of God which we have to hear and which we have to trust and obey in life and in death."[14] This thesis means that in matters of faith and practice, Jesus Christ, as attested by scripture, is both necessary and sufficient. His is the only voice that the church may trust in life and in death, and the only one that it must obey. No other person or principle can carry this authority, for no other is the Word of God.

Each positive thesis in Barmen was followed by a negative one. For Article I, the negative thesis can be paraphrased as saying that nothing apart from or alongside the authentic, scriptural voice of Jesus Christ can properly become a source of authority for the church in its own proclamation and teaching. Here Barmen famously rejected natural theology, and this rejection has implications for the question of natural law, to be discussed later. But two points about Barmen and natural theology may be noted here.

First, the Barmen Declaration rejected natural theology primarily in the form of culture-religion. The "natural" is essentially understood as something that is culturally mediated and historically conditioned. No nonmediated "nature" is accessible as such. This point pertains to how Barmen understood the centrality of Jesus Christ. Since Christ is seen as the Lord, his centrality cannot be separated from his exclusive sovereignty (in line with the First Commandment, "You shall have no other gods beside me" [Ex. 20:2; Deut. 5:7]). Where Jesus Christ "no longer speaks the first and last word, but only at best an additional word," wrote Barth, an "assimilated and domesticated theology" will be the inevitable result.[15] Even in forms that may seem benign and congenial, natural theology in its independence of revelation is always a rival claimant. Here is the place to remember, Barth urged, that the church cannot serve two masters; it will either hate the one and love the other, or be devoted to the one and despise the other (Matt. 6:24). Either Christ relativizes natural theology, or natural theology relativizes Christ.

When relativized by natural theology, Jesus Christ no longer functions as the one Lord who is necessary, sufficient, and supreme. While some forms of relativization are more blatant than others, the more subtle and sophisticated forms can serve to pave the way for versions that are cruder and even barbaric. The Christ of natural theology is always, for Barth, the relativized Christ of culture. The trajectory of natural theology leads, in effect, from the Christ who is not supreme, to the Christ who is not sufficient, and finally to the Christ who is not necessary. Culture-religion, relativization, and domestication or assimilation indicate that the Lordship of Christ is no longer acknowledged or understood. By rejecting all independent or second authorities, Barmen reaffirmed the unabridged Lordship of Jesus Christ against the modern inroads of cultural (and in Germany, finally Nazi) self-assertion in the church.

Second, it is important to realize that Barmen's rejection of natural theology was broadly cognitive in force. It did not imply that nothing good, beautiful, true, or worthwhile can be found outside of scripture and the church. "God may speak to us," wrote Barth, "through Russian communism or a flute concerto, a blossoming shrub or a dead dog. We shall do well to listen to Him if He really does so."[16] No such source can serve as an authority or norm for the church's preaching, however, for it has no independent revelatory or epistemic status. Only by criteria derived from the gospel can it be determined whether God might be speaking through those other sources or not. The question of natural theology, for Barth, is thus a question about the justification of belief.

The political implications of Barmen's first article were spelled out, in various ways, by the rest of the Declaration. Only a sketch can be given here. Article II, which asserted that no area of life falls outside the lordship of Christ, implies that faith cannot be disconnected from politics or from political judgments. Article III, which saw the church as exclusively the possession of Jesus Christ, carried the reverse implication that faith may not be reduced or made subordinate to political programs and pursuits. In other words, whereas Article II implied that faith and politics cannot be separated, Article III implied that they must not be blurred or confused. Article IV rejected the imposition on the church of an alien polity and thus suggested a measure of autonomy and nonconformity in the church's relation to the world. Article V then interpreted the traditional two-kingdoms doctrine in a Christ-centered way, so that the church's order of loyalties is clear and only conditional loyalty to the state is permitted. Finally, Article VI, which rejected any "arbitrarily chosen desires, purposes and plans,"[17] while affirming service to the message of the gospel, implied that all political activity engaged in by the church assumes the status of a witness to grace. Of these themes, two are perhaps especially important: Barmen's interpretation of the two-kingdoms doctrine and the proposal that faith and politics are related by a pattern of order, unity, and distinction.

It can be argued that in the history of the church, two competing views of governmental authority have contended with one another. One view, dominant in German Protestant theology right down to the confessing church (as well as elsewhere), understood scripture to teach that the state, because it was instituted by God, can command unconditional authority within its own sphere of competence. The secular authority is a bulwark against anarchy. No matter how repressive, it is to be resisted only if it seeks to meddle in ecclesiastical beliefs and affairs. This view is associated (perhaps more rightly than wrongly) with Augustine and Luther.

The alternate view agreed about the state's limited sphere of competence, as well as about the legitimacy of resistance if the state oversteps its boundaries relative to the church. Unlike the first view, however, this second view believed that scripture does not teach a requirement of unconditional obedience to the secular authority, no matter how repressive it might be (as long as it respects ecclesiastical boundaries). Instead, this view understood scripture to mean that the state, because it was instituted by God, has obligations to fulfill, such as rewarding good and punishing evil. If these obligations are violated so as to establish a pattern of serious malfeasance, the state forfeits its legitimacy as well as its divine mandate. This view is associated, in turn, with Aquinas and Calvin.

A salient difference between the two views is clear. The one held that to obey the state, even the radically unjust state, is to render obedience to God. The other held that times may come when obedience to God requires political disobedience and resistance to the state.

The fifth article of the Barmen Declaration, though circumspect, was so formulated as to remain open to the second view. It is a novel version of that view to the extent that the question of obligation(s) is stated, implicitly, in terms of a graduated schedule of loyalties culminating in the church's loyalty to Jesus Christ. The state is seen as divinely appointed to the task of "providing for justice and peace,"[18] and to this end it is allotted the means of coercion. The justice and peace that the state can provide will never be more than rough, however, since we live in "the as yet unredeemed world."[19] Nevertheless, if the state should grievously violate its defining purpose, then Article V implied that the church must then obey "the power of the Word of God by which God upholds all things."[20] As 1 Peter 2:17, cited at the beginning of Barmen V, suggests, although the emperor is certainly to be honored, God alone is to be feared. While the wording of Article V was not quite the open appeal for resistance that Barth would later issue in his own name, it seemed to be as close as he could come at that time for the confessing church.

During the Nazi period, especially after 1935, Barth constantly appealed to these ideas to encourage the confessing church to resistance. For, as was clear to him, the National Socialist state was increasingly implicated (to use a later terminology) in crimes against humanity and peace. Neither Article V nor Barmen as a whole was free from ambiguity, however. They did not rule out the possibility that the Barmen Declaration could be read as compatible with the very deep-seated view that requires unconditional obedience to the secular authority, no matter what. Although Barmen V set forth the state's basic obligations, it did not indicate what the church should do if they are breached. Resistance was at best a possible implication of Barmen V; although not ruled out, neither was it clearly ruled in. Barmen established a graduated schedule of loyalties, but it remained silent about what to do in cases where they come into conflict.

Barth lamented that the confessing church too often took the path of "inner immigration" rather than outward resistance. In 1943 he wrote about the Protestant churches in Europe for the American journal *Foreign Affairs*.[21] He believed that the churches in Holland, Norway, and Britain stood in contrast with the confessing church in Germany. The former were politically progressive yet theologically lacking, because while they opposed Nazism, they failed to attack culture-bound theology. The German situation was much the reverse. Theological assimilation was opposed, yet resistance to Nazism was lacking. The confessing church displayed "a kind of schizophrenia" in adopting "totally divergent yardsticks . . . for the inner and the external life."[22] The disconnection of faith and politics that Barmen rejects was overruled by the traditional two-kingdoms doctrine.

Barth often illustrated the inseparability he saw between faith and politics with the metaphor of a circle comprised of a center and a periphery. "No matter how far [the confessing church] may have progressed in other directions," he wrote, "they will have to learn from the other churches that there are a Christian center and a Christian periphery, that the Christian substance and its political application are indeed two different things, but that there is only one truth and one righteousness—and no [one] can serve two masters."[23] The center of the circle is the gospel, while political decision constitutes the periphery. Together they form an organic whole within which the two remain distinct.

The pattern of order, unity, and distinction became the hallmark of how Barth saw the relationship between faith and politics. His view of the gospel's epistemic status could be described as "nonfoundationalist." The gospel does not rest on anything other than itself, or, to put it another way, on anything other than the miracle and mystery of divine grace. Because faith in the gospel takes precedence, with politics as a secondary and dependent application, their ordering is asymmetrical. Within that asymmetry, however, the two form a unity-in-distinction. Faith and politics, the center and the periphery, are related, in effect, by the Chalcedonian pattern. They exist "without separation or division," on one hand, yet "without confusion or change," on the other. In the church, as Barth saw it, politics is a function of the gospel, but the gospel is essentially independent of politics. Politics is not central, the gospel is not peripheral, but neither can be had without the other.[24]

Between the late 1930s and the 1940s, Barth wrote several seminal essays in which he explored these matters further.[25] In particular he expanded the metaphor of a circle, with its center and periphery, so that it now included the idea of concentric circles. If we place Christ at the center, he proposed, we could then think of two concentric circles, the inner one representing the church ("the Christian community"), and the outer one the state ("the civil community"). Although a more complex pattern results from unity-in-distinction, certain aspects remain the same. By setting up the relations in this way, Barth avoided setting church and state over against one another in a fundamental opposition or dichotomy. On the contrary, each exists in its own way under the one lordship of Christ.

The overall conception that Barth proposed with his image of concentric circles can be summarized in thesis form. Christ, church, and state (center, inner circle, and outer circle) are related in these essays as follows:[26]

1 The state belongs to the redeemed creation. It involves more than the need for order under the destabilized conditions of the fall.

1.1 The state is a part of the created order (*status integritatis*), because like all of creation, it exists in its own way as a theater for the glory of God.

1.1.1 As a part of the creation, the state finds its origin and limit in God.

1.1.2 Because of its origin and limit in God, the state's tendency to deify itself, under the conditions of the fall, is illegitimate. It must not be taken seriously, but inwardly and outwardly opposed.

1.2 The state belongs to the redeemed order of creation, moreover, because all power on heaven and on earth has been given to the risen Lord, Jesus Christ.

1.2.1 Because all power (not just some) has been given to the Lord Jesus Christ, the state finds its positive goals and limits with reference to the kingdom of God.

1.2.2 Since its goals and their limits are set by its relation to God's kingdom, the state must beware not only of attempting too much, but also of attempting too little.

1.2.3 Utopian schemes, for example, would mean attempting too much while merely preventing anarchy would, in general, mean attempting too little.

1.2.4 The state has the positive task, divinely appointed, not only of preventing the worst, but also of promoting the common good, so far as possible, by securing justice, freedom, and peace.

1.2.5 The means of coercion at the state's disposal are meant to be used for the sake of justice, freedom, and peace. As far as possible, these coercive means should be subject to constitutional checks and balances and democratic controls.

2 The church is that part of creation whose special task is to bear witness to redemption.

2.1 Since the church, like the state, is a part of the good creation, its relationship to the state cannot be essentially negative.

2.1.1 Because the church's relation to the state is essentially positive, the church can never place itself in fundamental opposition to the state, no matter how corrupt, nor can it withdraw from participating in the responsibilities of the state, even when they may include the use of coercion.

2.2 Since the church knows, unlike the state, that the creation has been redeemed, the church knows the state's origins, limits, and goals better than the state does itself.

2.2.1 Knowing these origins, limits, and goals, the church has a special responsibility to work and pray that the state might conform to them.

3 The tasks of the state are, so to speak, strictly horizontal; the tasks of the church are both vertical and horizontal. The state exists for the humanization of creation; the church exists for the Christianization of human beings.

3.1 The state's tasks are horizontal because they concern relations among human beings, which pertain to the material creation.

3.1.1 The state exists for the sake of humanizing creation, because at the secular level the grace of creation involves making and keeping human life human.

3.1.2 Insofar as the state humanizes the creation as redeemed by Jesus Christ, it anticipates the kingdom of God.

3.2 The church's tasks are both vertical and horizontal because they concern the relationships of God for human beings and human beings for God, and therefore of human beings for one another.

3.2.1 The church exists for the sake of Christianizing human beings, because at the spiritual level the grace of redemption involves their conversion from themselves to Christ.

3.2.2 By Christianizing human beings as redeemed by Jesus Christ, the church anticipates the kingdom of God.

3.3 Therefore, both church and state anticipate the kingdom of God and the redemption of creation, but they do so in fundamentally different ways. Members of the church are obligated to participate in the tasks of the state, but only by working towards humanization, while members of the state (of the civil community) are obligated to participate in the tasks of the church, but only by becoming Christians.

4 The state cannot become a church, and the church cannot become a state.

4.1 The state cannot become a church, because the horizontal tasks allotted to it are relative, provisional, and external.

4.1.1 Since its tasks are horizontal, the state can have no direct concern with the relationship of God to human beings or of human beings to God.

4.1.2 Because the state's aims are relative, they can never usher in the kingdom of God or be of ultimate importance. Most importantly, they can never be made absolute. However, because they are provisional, they can and must point to God's kingdom, at least parabolically. Finally, because they are merely external, they can never make an ultimate claim on the inner, spiritual life of citizens of the state.

4.2 The church cannot become a state, because its vertical and horizontal tasks, while relative and provisional, are not only external, but also, so to speak, internal or spiritual. As such the church does not use means of coercion—and if it does, it enters into self-contradiction.

4.2.1 Since its tasks are vertical as well as horizontal, the church is properly concerned with the relationship of God to human beings and of human beings to God, as well as of human beings to one another, including their political relationships.

4.2.2 Since the church's tasks, like those of the state, are both relative and provisional, they cannot usher in God's kingdom; but they can and must point to it parabolically. Yet because the church's tasks, unlike those of the state, are internal or spiritual as well as external, they make an ultimate claim on both the inner and outer lives of its members.

4.3 Since the state cannot become a church, it has no right to establish a civil religion; and since the church cannot become a state, it has no right to establish "Christian" political organizations, such as labor unions or political parties.

4.4 Neither church nor state will exist in the kingdom of God, but God will be all in all.

5 The state needs the church, and the church needs the state.

5.1 The church needs the state to establish the orderly preconditions for the church's proclamation and witness, and the state needs the church to remind the state of its divinely appointed origins, limits, and goals.

5.2 Therefore, the state best serves the church by remaining the state, and the church best serves the state by remaining the church.

These theses reflect Barth's distinctive understanding of creation from the standpoint of redemption. This standpoint allowed Barth to establish a strong relationship between the tasks of the state and the kingdom of God. At the same time, it allowed for an essentially positive relationship between the tasks of the church and those of the state, which, though distinct, are nonetheless complementary.

If we consider these theses in light of the Barmen Declaration, we can see that they elaborate Barth's ideas along the lines Barmen sets forth. The same basic pattern of order, unity, and distinction is evident in each case. After Barmen, Barth refined and developed, but did not fundamentally change, his viewpoint. The image of concentric circles—perhaps the root metaphor of all Barth's thinking about church and society—was used to explain how, since Christ is the center, the church is then the first circle out, followed next by the larger society. The two concentric circles are each governed in distinctive ways by that single center, which establishes their unity-in-distinction. The inner circle of the church can even function, at best, as a role model for a properly ordered human society. The power of a good example, Barth believed, would do more to influence the surrounding world than would any political action in which the church might engage. Moreover, a church that is disordered within—by racism, for example, or social inequality, or chauvinism—can scarcely expect to be taken seriously if it undertakes political advocacy in the civil society for justice, freedom, and peace.

In society, Barth maintained, the church should stand for social values consistent with the gospel. The church should stand for placing the needs of concrete human beings over abstract causes, for the rule of law and constitutionality in government, for giving priority to those who are socially and economically vulnerable, for freedom of conscience and political judgment, for the political responsibility of all adult citizens regardless of race, creed, sex, or class, for the separation of powers (legislative, executive, judicial), for freedom of speech, for political power in the form of service, for the larger social good over narrow, parochial interests, and for making war and political violence legitimate only as a last resort. Barth's attempt to derive and support these positions with analogies drawn from the gospel was, as is generally recognized, only partially successful, at best. Nevertheless, it has not always been noticed that Barth explicitly presented his analogies as being suggestive rather than definitive. While his argumentation by analogy seems deficient, perhaps the task of evangelical social ethics after Barth would be not to reject his analogical procedure wholesale (as some have done), but rather to find better analogies where necessary, and to present them less impressionistically, and more carefully and extensively.

RESISTANCE TO TYRANNY

If we look back from these summary theses on church and state to Barth's earlier social ideas, some interesting developments stand out. Among them, the right to resist tyranny calls for special comment. This right was explicit in Barth's 1928–29 "Theses on Church and State," which he formulated in his course lectures on *Ethics* (published only posthumously in 1978).[27] Barth maintained that because the secular authority rests on force, persons faced with tyranny or oppression cannot rule out, as a last resort, "violent revolution on the part of the rest of the citizens."[28] Nothing even close to this idea was inserted into the Barmen Declaration, presumably not because of Barth, but because he perceived that in 1934 the German church was simply not ready for it. In his circular letters and other communications with the confessing church throughout the Nazi period, Barth repeatedly had to contend with the prevailing fear that greater resistance would be unpatriotic.

In his 1937–38 Gifford Lectures, published as *The Knowledge of God and the Service of God*, Barth took up the question of political resistance in more detail. Perhaps one reason he chose to comment on "The Scots Confession" of 1560 as the basis for his lectures was that it allowed him to address this very theme.[29] The Confession itself states that it is the Christian's duty to "repress tyranny" and "defend the oppressed." John Knox and his friends provided "unambiguous commentary," Barth observed, with "their words and deeds."[30]

Sometimes, Barth acknowledged, the abuse of political power must be endured. Under certain conditions, however, according to the Scots Confession, "there may be a *resistance* to the political power, which is not merely allowed but enjoined by God."[31] The Scots Confession drew a very clear distinction between lawful and unlawful authority. It spoke concretely on the basis of what the secular authority in question wills and does. Barth explained: "Does the political power—this king or that magistrate—do what it is its business to do? Does it abide by God's commandments? Does it remain within the bounds of justice and within the bounds of its task? Does it therefore, by showing this attitude, possess legitimate 'authoritie'? That is the question. Is it not one which can and must be raised constantly in connection with every political power? This question is certainly asked by God."[32]

The secular authority ceases to be legitimate when it violates the freedom it ought to safeguard and destroys justice and peace. Barth commented: "Just because there is no alteration in the Divine appointment of the political order, it is now manifestly true that 'God Himself does . . . judge even the judges themselves' and that the sword they wield is turned against themselves."[33] Therefore, Barth concluded, there are times when endurance is not enough, and when even passive resistance must be left behind. "It could well be," he stated, "that we had to do with a Government of liars, murderers, and incendiaries, with a Government which wished to usurp the place of God, to fetter the conscience, to suppress the church and become itself the Church of Antichrist."[34] In such cases "active resistance as such cannot and may not be excluded."[35]

It is worth noting that Barth's argument here, as elsewhere, was based solely on scripture—and on the Scots Confession that interpreted it. Barth did not move to scriptural interpretation only after having engaged in more general considerations, such as those based on "natural law." On the contrary, as was characteristic of him, he moved only from the particular to the general. Here the particularity of scripture and its witness to divine revelation were taken as sufficient (as well as necessary).

When Barth discussed resistance to tyranny, he also addressed the theme of desacralization. Whether political power is being exercised legitimately does not depend, Barth noted dryly, on whether rulers profess to be Christians: "When this is the case, one can rejoice at it for their sakes, and perhaps for the sake of the church also. But that in itself does not make clear the significance of the political order as service of God."[36] The service that the state owes to God "does not become clear by rulers professing the Christian faith and indeed being known as men who personally are sincerely pious."[37] Piety, of course, can be used to obscure injustice. Similarly, the secularism of a non-Christian ruler can make clear—and sometimes "clearer in fact than where the State seems to have a very Christian appearance"[38]—that living up to the state's divinely appointed obligations is independent of the religiosity (or lack thereof) of those who hold political office.

Earlier in his career, Barth had made much the same point with respect to political resistance. In the first edition of his commentary on Romans (1919), he wrote, "That Christians have nothing to do with monarchy, capitalism, militarism, patriotism, free-thinking, is so self-evident that I do not even need to mention it."[39] He then went on to exhort "desacralization" as a basic Christian duty: "Thou shalt starve the state of religion. Thou shalt deny it the elevation, the seriousness, and significance of the divine. Thou shalt not have your heart in your politics. Your souls are and remain alien to the ideals of the state."[40] Barth then enjoined this attitude on those engaged in active resistance: Let there be "strike, general strike, and street fighting, if need be, but no religious justification or glorification of it . . . military service as soldier or officer, if need be, but on *no* condition as military chaplain . . . social democratic but not religious socialist!"[41] Over the years Barth's political views continued to develop and became more nuanced, but the desacralizing, deflationary imperative remained a constant, as he saw it, in how the church should relate the gospel to the state.

DEMOCRATIC SOCIALISM

Parliamentary democracy, Barth believed, does not work very well without economic democracy. Economic liberalism (or capitalism) is a system that inevitably concentrates wealth and power into the hands of a small minority. By contrast, economic democracy (or democratic socialism) is a system that promises to distribute political power more equitably precisely by eliminating extreme inequalities and concentrations of wealth. Without economic democracy, parliamentary democracy is hobbled. Concentrated power in the hands of the few means that parliamentary means are twisted for elitist ends. Necessities are denied to the many while luxuries are delivered to the few. Antisocial phenomena such as huge armaments industries, imperialist adventures abroad, and nationalist diversions at home are less often the exception than the rule. Capitalism goes hand in hand with the thwarting of democratic change and with large quotients of social misery. Throughout his life Barth favored "practical," nonauthoritarian socialism, essentially because he believed in democracy.

Unlike some of his adherents, Barth was always a "public intellectual" embroiled in political controversy, a situation that persisted until the end of his life. When friends gathered for the celebration of his eightieth birthday, he reminded them of his origins:

> The reader of the *Church Dogmatics* certainly needs to know that I come from religious socialism. And I originally pursued something other than "church dogmatics"—namely, lectures on bringing factories to justice and on trade union problems—and I also became a member of the Swiss Socialist Party. And when I took part in these activities, it somehow hung together with a particular discovery—namely, that the children of this world are often wiser than the children of light.[42]

Elsewhere he reminisced further about his early pastorate: "The socialists were among the most avid listeners to my sermons, not because I preached socialism, but because they knew I was the same man who was also attempting to help them."[43]

A milestone in Barth's view of theology and socialism was his 1911 essay "Jesus Christ and the Movement for Social Justice." It was a talk he presented to the Safenwil workers during his early pastorate. Although both his theology and his socialism would change significantly as time went on, elements of continuity would remain.

Barth criticized his socialist listeners for their tactics, but not for their goals. "I have said that Jesus wanted what you want, that he wanted to help those who are least, that he wanted to establish the kingdom of God upon this earth, that he wanted to abolish self-seeking property, that he wanted to make persons into comrades. Your concerns are in line with the concerns of Jesus. *Real* socialism is real Christianity in our time."[44] Socialism fights against the capitalist system, he explained to a critic, "because the net profits which become part of the private wealth of the entrepreneur are by no means equivalent to his contribution to the common production."[45] Underlying this social analysis was a modern liberal christology. It values Jesus less for his once-for-all saving work than for the power of his saving influence: "The best and greatest thing that I can bring to you as a pastor will always be Jesus Christ and a portion of the powers which have gone out from his person into history and life."[46]

The later Barth would no longer flatly identify Jesus with a human project as he did in Safenwil; "Jesus *is* the movement for social justice," he told the workers, "and the movement for social justice *is* Jesus in the present."[47] He would distinguish more thoughtfully between two different plights: that of the victim and that of the sinner. Sin by definition is a plight, he came more clearly to see, that sinners cannot overcome by their own efforts. They need a Savior who bears their judgment for them and bears it away even as they also need one who can confer upon them the righteousness they completely lack, and so make them capable of eternal life in communion with God. Not only is the terrible plight of sin beyond human remedy, but it is also universal in scope, because no human being is excluded from it. The significance of the Savior is correspondingly universal in scope. Barth broke with the liberal view of Jesus (that saw him essentially as a source of empowerment) when he realized that Jesus is unique in kind—a unique person who came to do a unique work. Barth then embraced more fully the ecumenical faith that no one else other than Jesus would ever be God incarnate, that no one else would die for the sins of the world, and that no one else would ever be in himself or herself the mediator of righteousness and life.

For the later Barth, the plight of the sinner does not abolish the plight of the victim; but it does relocate the victim within a larger soteriological scheme. While the sinner's plight is beyond human remedy, universal in scope, and a matter of hostility and estrangement toward God, the victim's plight is essentially different. It is not beyond all human remedy, not universal in scope (since if there are victims, there are also perpetrators and bystanders), and the hostility and estrangement at stake exists primarily among human beings. Being a victim of injustice is a social disorder rooted in the deeper disorder of sin toward God; however, the God who became incarnate in order to deal with our deepest need is by no means indifferent to our lesser needs. Since God's very being is mercy, Barth argued, God takes all our distress into God's heart, participating in it by sympathy and doing what is necessary to remove it.[48] God makes the suffering of the world God's own, and abolishes it in God's own self for the good of all. Although a hierarchy of needs exists, with sin at its very root, God's compassion reaches out to every level of our misery and guilt.

The Old Testament constantly bears witness, the later Barth observed, to God's vindication of the right of all those who are vulnerable and downtrodden: the oppressed, the poor, the widows, the orphans, and the aliens in the land. "God always stands on this and only on this side, always against the exalted and for the lowly, always against those who already have rights and for those from whom they are robbed and taken away."[49] In this divine care for the downtrodden, Christians will discern a parable of how God has acted toward themselves in their plight as sinners: "There follows from this character of faith a political attitude, decisively determined by the fact that man is made responsible to all those who are poor and wretched in his eyes, that he is summoned on his part to espouse the cause of those who suffer wrong. Why? Because in them it is manifested to him what he himself is in the sight of God."[50] By any other political attitude, stated Barth, we reject the very mercy we receive from God. On these grounds, Barth concluded that the "Church must stand for social justice in the political sphere."[51] Standing for social justice is at once an end in itself and yet also an act of witness to something beyond itself.

The church is witness of the fact that the Son of Man came to seek and to save the lost. And this implies—casting all false impartiality aside—that the church must concentrate first on the lower and lowest levels of human society. The poor, the socially and economically weak and threatened, will always be the object of the church's primary and particular concern, and it will always insist on the state's special responsibility for these weaker members of society.[52]

The church must remain vigilant, for example, that "equality before the law" does not become a smokescreen behind which the weak are exploited by the strong, the poor by the rich, the dependent by the independent, the employees by the employers. To Barth this concern meant that the church must stand on the political left. That was the fixed side that then allowed, in practice, for a measure of open-endedness: "And in choosing between the various socialistic possibilities (social-liberalism? co-operativism?

syndicalism? free trade? moderate or radical Marxism?), it will always choose the movement from which it can expect the greatest measure of social justice (leaving all other considerations to one side)."[53]

Barth's argument was thus constructed from a sequence of analogies derived from the gospel. First, he established a hierarchy of needs in which the deepest misery, that of sin, stands in analogy to social misery, which, though lesser by comparison, is not trivial. The church's response to social misery, in turn, must reflect God's compassionate response to human sin as known and attested by the church. Compassion in its political form will be discerned in movements that give priority to the neediest sectors of society. For Barth, this compassion meant some form of democratic socialism—that socialism which is as wholly committed to the freedoms of parliamentary democracy and civil liberties as it is to the struggle implicit in economic democracy against the abuses that always accrue from vast concentrations of wealth and power in the hands of the privileged few. While Barth's argument was not exhaustive and left a fuller case to be made, prima facie, it seems fair to say that it was not implausible.

The high point in Barth's espousal of democratic socialism came in *Church Dogmatics*, when he discussed the ethics of work in modern society. Among the standards that Barth established for assessing work, three are especially noteworthy: the criteria of objectivity, worthy aims, and sociality. The first concerns a wholehearted engagement in the practices necessary for achieving excellence in one's field of endeavor; the second, the worthwhileness of the ends being pursued; and the third, "the humanity of human work," that is, the degree to which it promotes humane coexistence and social cooperation.[54] It was the second and third criteria, above all, that Barth brought to bear against capitalism. Work as it is now organized in Western capitalist society, he suggested, conforms poorly to the criteria of worthy aims and humane sociality.

Capitalism, Barth believed, exacerbates some of the worst propensities of human nature. It fosters a revolution of empty and inordinate desires. It promotes "lust for a superabundance," "lust for possessions," and "lust for an artificially extended area of power over [human beings] and things."[55] It generates enormous disparities in wealth and power, thus concentrating life-and-death decisions "in the hands of the relatively few, who pull all the strings . . . in a way wholly outside the control of the vast majority."[56] A system that heightens self-seeking, debases culture, and, not least, obscures its own injustices, it is "almost unequivocally demonic."[57] In these and other ways, it violates the dignity of work. Work that possesses human dignity, Barth observes, would look very different:

What are we to think of all the work which is thought worthwhile, and which is therefore done by those involved, only because they can definitely count on the stupidity and superficiality, the vanity and bad taste, the errors and vices of numerous other people? What are we to think of all the work to which people are drawn only because there are others who are prepared to ruin themselves either physically or morally? What are we to think of the work which flourishes in one place only because [human beings] elsewhere are afflicted with unemployment and therefore with want? What are we to think, as we must ask in relation to the problem of war, of direct or indirect participation in the work of an armaments factory, the achievements of which in so-called peace have often proved to be one of the most potent causes of war? Finally, what are we to think of work which, while it is intrinsically neither useful nor harmful, presents so unworthy an aspect just because it is directed neither to good nor evil, nor indeed to [human beings] at all, but past them to a purely illusory yet dynamic and in its conjunction of the two, almost unequivocally demonic process which consists in the amassing and multiplying of possessions expressed in financial calculations (or miscalculations), i.e., the "capital" which in the hands of the relatively few, who pull all the strings, may equally well, in a way wholly outside the control of the vast majority and therefore quite arbitrarily or accidentally, be a source of salvation or perdition for whole nations or generations?[58]

The Christian community, Barth urged, must not allow itself to "participate in the great self-deception" of capitalism.[59] It must not regard its supposed benefits, necessity, or even legitimacy as something that conforms to what is commanded by God. It must not accept the proposition, for example, that although the wealth under capitalism is inequitably distributed, each person's income reflects how hard or how valuably that person has worked. For "the only choice which employees often have is between starvation and doing work which either does not benefit the cause of [humanity], is detrimental to it, or is completely alien, being performed in the service of a sinister and heartless and perpetually ambiguous idol"—namely, mammon in the guise of "capital."[60] Because capitalism forces people to work for "meaningless ends and therefore dishonestly," Barth wondered whether it was not almost inevitable that communism would triumph over it. "Is it not almost inevitable," he asked, "that the Marxist tyranny should finally overwhelm us, with its new and very different injustices and calamities, to teach us *mores*, true ethics, in this respect?"[61] If we substitute the term "Islamist" for the term "Marxist" in this quotation, Barth's concerns might not seem irrelevant today.

The command of God, Barth wrote, "is self-evidently and in all circumstances a call for countermovements on behalf of humanity and against its denial in any form, and therefore a call for the championing of the weak against every kind of encroachment on the part of the strong."[62] Since the Christian community has been slow to recognize what God's command means in a capitalist society, Barth felt that it was scarcely in a position to point the finger at injustices elsewhere. Instead, he urged the Christian community to concentrate on "the disorder in the decisive form still current in the West, to remember and to assert the command of God in the face of this form, and to keep to the 'Left' in opposition to its champions, i.e., to confess that it [the Christian community] is fundamentally on the side of the victims of this disorder and to espouse their cause."[63]

INTERNATIONAL PEACE

It should not be forgotten that Barth first became a theologian in opposition to a "preemptive" war. More precisely, he felt compelled to reexamine everything he had learned from his revered teachers because of his fierce opposition to what he called their "war theology"—a theology that turned the gospel to sacralize a war of aggression.

> And then the First World War broke out and brought something which for me was almost even worse than the violation of Belgian neutrality—the horrible manifesto of the ninety-three German intellectuals who identified themselves before all the world with the war policy of Kaiser Wilhelm II and Chancellor Bethmann-Hollweg. And to my dismay, among the signatories I discovered the names of almost all my German teachers (with the honorable exception of Martin Rade). An entire world of theological exegesis, ethics, dogmatics, and preaching, which up to that point I had accepted as basically credible, was thereby shaken to the foundations, and with it everything which flowed at that time from the pens of the German theologians.[64]

Not long afterward, in a step that would lead to the rebirth of twentieth-century theology, Barth sat down under an apple tree and "began, with all the tools at my disposal, to apply myself to the Epistle to the Romans."[65]

After the outbreak of the war, things did not go smoothly for Barth even with his teacher Martin Rade, a man of pacifist leanings. Barth had once served as an assistant editor at *Die Christliche Welt*, where Rade was the longtime editor. Barth responded to Rade's first three wartime issues with a letter of protest and told him that the journal had ceased to be Christian and had simply gone over to the world. While Barth could see only a debased power struggle and a racist bid for superiority, Rade had been investing the war with a halo of piety. From a Christian standpoint, "the only possibility at the present moment," wrote Barth, "would be unconditional protest against war as such and against the human failures that brought it about."[66] If no other form of protest were possible, even silence would be better than what Rade had been putting out, because even silence would be a form of protest. But Rade was permitting Christians to support the war with a good conscience. "How are people to make progress," asked Barth, "if now, in this terrible explosion of human guilt, their actions are rewarded with the consolation of a good conscience? At the present moment, unless one prefers to keep wholly silent, can anything be said other than 'Repent'?"[67] Barth's own 1914 sermons bristled with protests against "war theology."[68]

If we consider his whole career, Barth's stance on the problem of war is not easy to characterize. He seems to have hovered somewhere between what might be called "relative pacifism" and "chastened nonpacifism." Yet in some sense he never wavered from his early Safenwil convictions: "War is always terrible, and we know that we must find a way even for our own country to extricate itself from its entanglements in militarism and armaments. Let us not be deceived by the pagan wisdom that 'whoever wants peace must prepare for war.' On the contrary, whoever wants peace must prepare for peace."[69] Or again, "God however is love and his kingdom is not of this world. God has nothing to do with violence. Love wants to dismantle injustice, to renounce the advantages of status or property. . . . There are two orders that we need to keep straight so that we don't confuse them: the one that arises from self-seeking and leads to violence; the other that aims to be based on God's love. . . . Where violence reigns, there is simply no just peace and no lasting blessing to be expected—not in the family, not in business, not in our country."[70] The gospel, according to Barth, established a self-evident presumption against war.

A presumption, however, was not, to Barth's mind, an absolute proscription. Here, too, the fixed side requires dialectical balance by an open-ended side. What God might require of us in any particular situation has to remain open. The burden of proof is always heavily on Christians who think they can participate in war, or in preparations for war, with a good conscience. Nevertheless, borderline situations cannot be ruled out in advance. Barth did not ask the abstract question: Is war intrinsically right or wrong? Nor did he ask the casuistic question: Under what general circumstances is war right or wrong? He always asked the situational question: Is this particular war actually demanded of us, in spite of everything, by God?

The upshot of Barth's complex, dialectical stance seemed to be a kind of informed intuitionism. One responds to the contingencies of the moment on the basis of discernment formed by a conscientious immersion in the ethos of the Christian community. One listens, in light of the gospel, for what God is commanding here and now through the language of the facts. One then acts on one's own responsibility (though not without consultation with others) in fear and trembling. On this basis, during World War II, Barth could give the Czech soldiers who defended their homeland a good conscience while denying it to the Germans who invaded it. He could stand for peace in 1914 and call for war in 1939. He could endorse Swiss armed neutrality against the Germans, even donning the uniform himself, but then oppose nuclear armament in Europe after the war.

We might say that Barth was a "just-war pacifist," except that his relation to the just-war tradition was idiosyncratic. He strongly upheld the *ius ad bellum* principles of last resort (into which he subsumed the principle of right intention) and acting only in self-defense. Yet he argued that war should sometimes be fought even without a reasonable chance of success, and he presupposed the principle of legitimate authority. Even more strangely, he said next to nothing about *ius in bello* principles such as noncombatant immunity and proportionality, perhaps because he took them for granted (though even that would be odd, given the brutality of twentieth-century warfare).[71]

Nevertheless, what Barth wrote about war in the *Church Dogmatics* not only reflected his peculiar dialectics of responsible, situational discernment, but also moved much closer to the pacifism of his early career than to the chastened nonpacifism of his anti-Nazi period. "It is not exaggerating," writes John Howard Yoder, "to say that in the pages devoted to the question of war Barth offers a criticism of the belligerent tradition of official Christianity which is unprecedented and unparalleled from the pen of the occupant of any official European chair of theology."[72] Barth wrote, for example, "Does not war demand that almost everything God has forbidden be done on a broad front? . . . Can it and should it nevertheless be defended and ventured? . . . [Almost] all affirmative answers to this [latter] question are wrong if they do not start with the assumption that the inflexible negative of pacifism has almost infinite arguments in its favor and is almost overpoweringly strong."[73] The mass slaughter of modern war, Barth averred, is difficult to distinguish from mass murder.[74] Peace is therefore "the real emergency,"[75] and no peace can be made secure without real social justice. As long as "interest-bearing capital" reigns supreme, the mechanism for war is already set going. It must be replaced, for the sake of peace, by democracy and social democracy in its stead.[76]

Barth's final word on the subject in the *Church Dogmatics* reflected his generally anti-ideological and situational outlook:

> The direction of Jesus must have embedded itself particularly deeply in the disciples. . . . They were neither to fear force nor to exercise it. . . . What the disciples are enjoined is that they should love their enemies (Matt. 5:44). This destroys the whole friend-foe relationship, for when we love our enemy he ceases to be our enemy. It thus abolishes the whole exercise of force, which presupposes this relationship, and has no meaning apart from it. . . . There is a concrete and incontestable direction which has to be carried out exactly as it is given. According to the sense [*Sinn*] of the New Testament we cannot be pacifists in principle, only in practice. But we have to consider very closely whether, if we are called to discipleship, we can avoid being practical pacifists, or fail to be so.[77]

Like the orientation Barth discerned in scripture toward justice for the oppressed, his presumption in favor of pacifism was patterned on the prior activity of God. Nonviolence is the pattern manifested in Christ's passion as it led him to the cross. It is therefore the pattern to which Christian obedience is called to conform.

BARTH AND NATURAL LAW

> *If the term "ethics" is taken to mean a system of ideal values purporting to be applicable to the conduct of men everywhere and in all times, then the discussion of it has no place in this book. To me there are no such things as abstract and universally applicable rules of ethics. . . . In large part, of course, what most of us would regard as ethically commendable values and virtues are culturally and sometimes religiously conditioned—culturally, even by those who are scarcely conscious of their own cultural inheritance; and religiously, even by those who would scoff at the mere suggestion that religion had anything to do with their reactions.*
>
> —GEORGE F. KENNAN, *AROUND THE CRAGGED HILL* (1993)

George F. Kennan's words are not far, in spirit, from Barth's doubts about "natural law." Much like Kennan, Barth rejected the idea of an unmediated and unconditioned moral law to which human beings have universal access, even in their fallen state. What is regarded as "natural law" is always at bottom a cultural construct. From the standpoint of Christian ethics, it can offer no reliable basis for knowing what is right, nor can it offer any firm and clear basis for making ethical decisions. Natural law theory posits an autonomous ground of ethical reflection completely separate from divine revelation. Christian ethics cannot build on this basis, Barth argued, because no such basis exists on which to build.

Like Calvin, Barth believed that God is present to us *in continuo actu*. God is not an aloof deity, passively waiting for us to discover God and the moral law. If Barth had a "moral ontology," it might best be described as "an ontology of active relations." The God whose being is in action is constantly present to us as the Lord at every moment of our lives. When we know this God by faith through the witness of the church, we enter into active fellowship with God. The Lord God does not leave us to our own devices, but rather reconfigures us into moral agents and slays us daily to make us alive, through word and sacrament, through scriptural meditation and prayer, through all that bears down upon us, all that we undergo and undertake, so that what God wills for us and commands of us emerges concretely in the texture of our lives. "For in every moment and act of human activity the point at issue is a concrete and specific human choice and decision, in which the inner intention and external action are not to be separated from each other, but make up a whole."[78] The context of decision is established by an ongoing encounter with the command of God: "And this whole of human activity is undoubtedly confronted every time by a command of God which is also concrete and specific."[79]

What would a principled imagination that was shaped by Barth's moral ontology look like? It seems that narratives are better than "cases" for conveying a thick sense of what Barth meant when he spoke of concrete existential encounters with the command of God. While he restricted himself primarily to biblical narratives, other more modern examples might also facilitate an appreciation of his argument. The following can at least be mentioned: *Lest Innocent Blood Be Shed* by Philip Hallie (Christian decision making in action); *Jane Eyre* by Charlotte Bronte (a classic not always recognized as a theological novel); *The Lost Child* by Marietta Jaeger (a true and excruciating story of sanctification); *Adam Bede* by George Eliot (Dinah's speech to Hetty); *The Hiding Place* by Corrie ten Boom (more Christian decision making); and *The Warden* by Anthony Trollope (Christian decency confronts moral ambiguity). At the risk of being cryptic, each of these narratives contains theological content that is arguably susceptible, in various ways, to a more or less Barthian ethical interpretation.

Apart from the possible difficulty of imagining how Barth's moral ontology might apply to our lives, another difficulty also commonly arises.
In trying to grasp what Barth's rejection of "natural law" implies, it is not
always appreciated that Barth actually gave back with one hand much of
what he took away with the other. Although no way exists from natural
law to the revelation of God's command in Christ, he argued, a way does
exist from this revelation to "natural law." Barth did not think about "natural law" from the general standpoint that "grace does not destroy but
takes up and perfects nature."[80] On the contrary, he thought that grace relates itself to nature according to a very different pattern: the death-and-
resurrection pattern of *Aufhebung*. Barth did not argue that the good
required of a person cannot be known in any sense outside the church; he
argued that it cannot be known in any sense "without grace."[81] Grace is
operative incognito and, so to speak, in irregular ways outside the walls of
the church (*extra muros ecclesiae*). What natural law theory would ascribe to nature, Barth critically relocated in a context of grace.[82]

Apart from an explicit reliance on grace, Barth argued, moral perceptions are always profoundly ambiguous. Taken as a whole, they lack a
proper center in Christ, and therefore in one sense are completely inadequate. Nevertheless, not every perception within the whole will be equally
dubious, and elements of validity will coexist with much that is incompatible with the gospel. Insofar as elements of validity are present, they are to
be ascribed to the secret workings of grace. What those elements may be
cannot be determined apart from the gospel—in other words, not by the
light of unaided reason. But, even outside the church, human incapacity is
constantly being overruled by the sovereignty of grace, and faith will
properly be on the alert for signs of the occurrence of that overruling. Because of grace, it may even be that the children of this world are often
wiser than the children of light; but that is no reason to set up "nature" as
a source of moral knowledge that exists independently of and alongside
grace. On the contrary, "natural" perceptions of moral law, as culturally
conditioned and historically mediated, and sometimes even influenced by
the gospel itself, must always be negated and reconstituted on the higher
plane of grace (*Aufhebung*) if they are to be properly appreciated and assessed. The Christian community cannot base its political responsibility
on natural law, nor can it appeal to natural law as an unproblematic given
in its proposals to the civil community. But the Christian community can
appeal to whatever seems valid in the cultural moral perceptions of the
time, and make arguments in and for the civil community on that basis.
And the Christian community can remain alert to "the power which God
has to make good come of evil, as He is in fact always doing in the political

order."[83] This is the light in which to set Barth's conclusion: "The tasks and problems which the Christian community is called to share, in fulfillment of its political responsibility, are 'natural,' secular, profane tasks and problems. But the norm by which it should be guided is anything but natural: it is the only norm which it can believe in and accept as a spiritual norm, and is derived from the clear law of its own faith, not from the obscure workings of a system outside itself; it is from knowledge of this norm that it will make its decisions in the political sphere."[84]

CONCLUSIONS

If we are asked to identify Barth's main disciples and schools of thought that have emerged around the legal and political topics that he addressed, then perhaps the following outlines can be sketched.

Within a few years after Barth's death in 1968, a division started to appear among his followers on matters of faith and politics. Not unlike what had happened after Hegel, "right-wing" and "left-wing" Barthians emerged on the theological scene. In the first group, probably the most prominent representative was Eberhard Jüngel of Tübingen. Jüngel, who had grown up under Communism in East Germany, argued for an essentially apolitical and nonsocialist Barth. He contended that Barth's political views were not essential to his theology. In later years Jüngel also endorsed a "mission to the Jews"—something Barth always insisted was a terrible mistake.

Meanwhile, a non-Barthian group emerged in Munich advancing the line that Barth's theology had been essentially antidemocratic and that it had contributed to the rise of fascism. Arguably, however, this interpretation was little more than special pleading on the part of regrouped liberals who were still smarting under Barth's criticism of modern academic theology. Among the representatives of this tendency were Trutz Rendtdorff and Falk Wagner.

"Left-wing" Barthianism first came to prominence with Friedrich Wilhelm Marquardt's *Theologie und Sozialismus.*[85] A student of Helmut Gollwitzer's, Marquardt generated much controversy but failed fully to persuade because of the reductionist way in which he seemed to turn Barth's theology into a mere instrument of his political commitments. Gollwitzer, whom Barth had wanted as his successor, and who was rejected because of his radical politics, remained more judicious than Marquardt. Although he was probably the quintessential "left-wing" Barthian, Gollwitzer did not like to think of himself in that way. He was simply a

Barthian, and like most European Barthians, he took strong progressive stands for justice and peace, not only in theology but also in practice.

Other Barthians distinguished themselves in the post-Holocaust era with a concern for Jewish-Christian relations. Marquardt and Gollwitzer were prominent also on this front, and they received the honor of special commendations from Jewish organizations. Eberhard Busch, Barth's great biographer, produced a massive volume on Barth's active solidarity with the Jews during the Nazi reign of terror. Perhaps even more significantly, Berthold Klappert took up the direction that Barth had laid down, developing it in creative ways that have yet to be appreciated in English-language circles.

Barth's stance toward the Jews has been subjected to admirably incisive analysis, both critical and sympathetic, by the American Jewish theologian Michael Wyschogrod. Katherine Sonderegger of Virginia Theological Seminary has also been an important American voice in this discussion. Less well known, though at once exemplary and profound, is Ulrich Simon's *A Theology of Auschwitz*,[86] written by a Barth-influenced theologian who lost close family members, including his father, in the Nazi death camps.

An anthology I edited, *Karl Barth and Radical Politics*, mediated the Marquardt thesis into American discussion. Until that time, American perceptions of Barth's political views were dominated by the interpretations of Reinhold Niebuhr and Will Herberg, who had portrayed Barth as politically irrelevant. Although the anthology seems to have had its greatest impact in South Africa and South Korea (where Reformed churches found themselves in revolutionary situations), it did change the American reception of Barth on this question.

Most recently, Barth's way of combining traditional faith with progressive politics has received a powerful boost from Jeffrey Stout, who argues that Barth shows us how to avoid the "sectarianism" of a Hauerwas and the "authoritarianism" of a Milbank, through a strong confessionalist stance that respects democratic pluralism while working passionately for justice, freedom, and peace.[87]

NOTES

1. James B. Torrance, "Barth, Karl," in *The Encyclopedia of Religion*, ed. Mircea Eliade, 16 vols. (New York: Macmillan, 1987), 2:68.
2. Thomas F. Torrance, "My Interaction with Karl Barth," in *How Karl Barth Changed My Mind*, ed. Donald K. McKim (Grand Rapids, Mich.: Eerdmans, 1986), 61–62.

3. Hans Urs von Balthasar, *The Theology of Karl Barth: Exposition and Interpretation*, trans. Edward T. Oakes (San Francisco: Ignatius Press, 1992), 22–23.

4. Karl Barth, *Gespräche 1964–1968*, ed. Eberhard Busch (Zürich: Theologischer Verlag, 1997), 324.

5. Ibid., 199.

6. Ibid., 100.

7. Torrance, "Barth," 69. See also Eberhard Busch, *Karl Barth: His Life from Letters and Autobiographical Texts*, trans. John Bowden (Philadelphia: Fortress Press, 1976).

8. Karl Barth, *Fragments Grave and Gay*, ed. Martin Rumscheidt, trans. Eric Mosbacher (London: Collins, 1971), 120–121.

9. Ibid., 120.

10. Barth, *Gespräche*, 408.

11. Ibid., 213.

12. Quoted from manuscript notes of an interview between Karl Barth and Margareta Deschner, April 26, 1956, in John Deschner, "Karl Barth as Political Activist," *Union Seminary Quarterly Review* 28 (1972): 56.

13. "The Theological Declaration of Barmen," in Arthur C. Cochrane, *Reformed Confessions of the 16th Century* (Philadelphia: Westminster Press, 1966), 334–336.

14. Ibid., 334.

15. Karl Barth, *Church Dogmatics*, 4 vols. (Edinburgh: T & T Clark, 1936–61), 2:163.

16. Ibid., 1:60.

17. "Theological Declaration of Barmen," 336.

18. Ibid.

19. Ibid., 335.

20. Ibid., 336.

21. Karl Barth, "The Protestant Churches in Europe," *Foreign Affairs* 21 (1943): 260–275.

22. Karl Barth, *The Church and the War*, trans. Antonia H. Froendt (New York: Macmillan, 1944), 12.

23. Ibid.

24. An earlier version of this analysis of Barmen appeared in George Hunsinger, "Barth, Barmen and the Confessing Church Today," *Katallagete* 9, no. 2 (1985): 14–27.

25. Karl Barth, *Community, State and Church: Three Essays* (Garden City, N.Y.: Doubleday, 1960). The essays are "Gospel and Law," "Church and State," and "The Christian Community and the Civil Community."

26. An earlier version of these theses appeared in George Hunsinger, "Karl Barth and Radical Politics: Some Further Considerations," *Studies in Religion/Sciences Religieuses* 7, no. 1 (1978): 167–191.

27. Karl Barth, *Ethics*, ed. Dietrich Braun, trans. Geoffrey W. Bromiley (New York: Seabury, 1981), 517–521.

28. Ibid., 520.
29. Karl Barth, *The Knowledge of God and the Service of God* (New York: Charles Scribner's Sons, 1939).
30. Ibid., 229.
31. Ibid.
32. Ibid., 224.
33. Ibid., 225.
34. Ibid., 230.
35. Ibid., 231.
36. Ibid., 223.
37. Ibid.
38. Ibid., 224.
39. Karl Barth, *Der Römerbrief* (Bern: G. A. Bäschlin, 1919), 381.
40. Ibid., 388.
41. Ibid., 390.
42. Barth, *Gespräche*, 401.
43. Ibid., 506.
44. Karl Barth, "Jesus Christ and the Movement for Social Justice," in *Karl Barth and Radical Politics*, ed. and trans. George Hunsinger (Philadelphia: Westminster Press, 1976), 36.
45. Ibid., 44.
46. Ibid., 19.
47. Ibid.
48. Barth, *Church Dogmatics*, 2:369.
49. Ibid., 386 (translation revised).
50. Ibid., 387.
51. Barth, *Community, State and Church*, 173.
52. Ibid.
53. Ibid.
54. Barth, *Church Dogmatics*, 3:535.
55. Ibid., 538.
56. Ibid., 532.
57. Ibid., 531.
58. Ibid., 531–532.
59. Ibid., 541.
60. Ibid., 532.
61. Ibid.
62. Ibid., 544.
63. Ibid.
64. Karl Barth, "Concluding Unscientific Postscript on Schleiermacher," in *The Theology of Schleiermacher* (Grand Rapids, Mich.: Eerdmans, 1982), 263–264.
65. Ibid., 264.
66. Karl Barth, "Letter to Martin Rade," in *Neue Wege: Blätter für religiöse Arbeit* 8 (1914): 430, quoted in Walter Bense, "The Pacifism of Karl Barth: Some Ques-

tions for John H. Yoder," in *The American Society of Christian Ethics, 1977, Selected Papers*, ed. Max L. Stackhouse (Waterloo, Ontario: Council on the Study of Religion, 1977), 63.

67. Barth, "Letter to Martin Rade," 431, quoted in Bense, "Pacifism," 63.

68. Karl Barth, *Predigten 1914*, ed. Ursula and Jochen Fähler (Zürich: Theologischer Verlag, 1974).

69. Karl Barth, *Konfirmandenunterricht, 1909–1921*, ed. Jürgen Fangmeier (Zürich: Theologischer Verlag, 1987), 174.

70. Ibid., 179–180.

71. But see Barth, *Church Dogmatics*, 3:453.

72. John Howard Yoder, *The Pacifism of Karl Barth* (Washington, D.C.: Church Peace Mission, 1964), 16.

73. Barth, *Church Dogmatics*, 3:454–455.

74. Ibid., 456.

75. Ibid., 459.

76. Ibid.

77. Barth, *Church Dogmatics*, 4:549–550.

78. Ibid., 8.

79. Ibid.

80. Ibid., 2:529.

81. Ibid., 530.

82. On this whole question, see Friedrich Lohmann, "Barths Stellung zum Naturrecht," in *Zwischen Naturrecht und Partikularismus: Grundlegung christlicher Ethik mit Blick auf die Debatte um eine universale Begründbarkeit der Menschenrechte* (Berlin: de Gruyter, 2002), 74–80.

83. Barth, "The Christian Community and the Civil Community," 165.

84. Ibid.

85. Friedrich Wilhelm Marquardt, *Theologie und Sozialismus* (Munich: Christian Kaiser Verlag, 1972, rev. 1985).

86. Ulrich Simon, *A Theology of Auschwitz* (Richmond, Va.: John Knox Press, 1979).

87. Jeffrey Stout, *Democracy and Tradition* (Princeton, N.J.: Princeton University Press, 2003).

ORIGINAL SOURCE MATERIALS

JESUS CHRIST AND THE MOVEMENT FOR SOCIAL JUSTICE

I am happy to be able to speak to you about *Jesus*, especially because the initiative for it has come from your side. The best and greatest thing that I can bring to you as a pastor will always be Jesus Christ and a portion of the powers which have gone out from his person into history and life. I take it as a sign of the mutual understanding between us that you for your part have come to me with a request for this best and greatest thing. I can say to you, however, that the other half of our theme lies just as much on my heart: *the movement for social justice*. A well-known theologian and author has recently argued that these two ought not to be joined together as they are in our topic: "Jesus Christ *and* the movement for social justice," for that makes it sound as if they are really two different realities which must first be connected more or less artificially. Both are seen as one and the same: Jesus *is* the movement for social justice, and the movement for social justice *is* Jesus in the present. I can adopt this view in good conscience if I reserve the right to show more precisely in what sense I do so. The real contents of the person of Jesus can in fact be summed up by the words: "movement for social justice."

And now, in conclusion, allow me a few personal words which I would like to say to you as a pastor of this community.

First, to those friends present who up to now have related themselves to socialism in an indifferent, reserved, or *hostile* way: At this moment you are perhaps feeling somewhat disappointed and upset, so that it would not be inconceivable that one or another might go out from here and report: "He said that the socialists are right." I would be sorry if anyone said that. I repeat once again: I have spoken about what socialists *want*, not about the manner in which they *act* to attain it. *About what they want, I say*: *That is what Jesus wanted, too.* About the manner in which they *act* to attain it, I could not say the same thing. It would be easy for me to come up with a broad critique about the manner in which the socialists act to attain it. But I fail to see what good such an easy exercise would accomplish. Therefore, I have not said that the socialists are right! Nonetheless, I do not want to say that you nonsocialists should now go home comforted and reassured. If you feel upset, then that is good. If you have the feeling that "Oh, no, Christianity is a hard and dangerous matter if one gets to the roots of it," then you have rightly understood me—or, rather, not me, but *Jesus*. For I did not want to tell you my view, but the view of Jesus as I have found it in the Gospels. Consider, then, whether as followers of Jesus you ought not to bring more understanding, more goodwill, more *participation* in the movement for social justice in our time than you have up to now.

And now to my *socialist* friends who are present: I have said that Jesus wanted what you want, that he wanted to help those who are least, that he wanted to establish the kingdom of God upon this earth, that he wanted to abolish self-seeking property, that he wanted to make persons into comrades. Your concerns are in line with the concerns of Jesus. *Real* socialism is real Christianity in our time. That may fill you with pride and satisfaction about your concerns. But I hope you have also heard the rebuke implied in the distinction I have made between Jesus and yourselves! He wanted what you want—as you *act* to attain it. There you have the difference between Jesus and yourselves. He wanted what you want, but he *acted* in the way you have heard. That is generally the difference between Jesus and the rest of us, that among us the greatest part is program, whereas for Jesus program and performance were one. Therefore, Jesus says to you quite simply that you should carry out your program, that you should *enact* what you *want*. Then you will be Christians and true human beings. Leave the superficiality and the hatred, the spirit of mammon and the self-seeking, which also exists among your ranks, behind: They do *not* belong to your concerns. Let the faithfulness and energy, the sense of community and the courage for sacrifice found in Jesus be effective among you, in your whole life; then you will be true socialists.

However, the unrest and the sharpening of conscience which Jesus in this hour has hopefully brought to us all should not be the last word in this beautiful Christmas season. I think we all have the impression that Jesus was someone quite different than we are. His image stands strangely great and high above us all, socialists and nonsocialists. Precisely for that reason he has something to say to us. Precisely for that reason he can be something for us. Precisely for that reason we touch the living God himself when we touch the hem of his garment. And if we now let our gaze rest upon him, as he goes from century to century in ever-new revelations of his glory, then something is fulfilled in us of the ancient word of promise which could also be written of the movement for social justice in our day: "*The people who walked in darkness have seen a great light.*"[1]

COMMENTARY ON ROM. 13.1

Let every man be in subjection to the existing ruling power. Though subjection may assume from time to time many various concrete forms, as an ethical conception it is here pure negative. It means to withdraw and make way; it means to have no resentment, and not to overthrow. Why, then, does not the rebel turn back and become no more a rebel? Simply because the conflict in which he is immersed cannot be represented as a conflict between him and the *existing ruling powers*; it is, rather a conflict of evil with evil. Even the most radical revolution can do no more than set what *exists* against what *exists*. Even the most radical revolution—and this is so even when it is called a "spiritual" or "peaceful" revolution—can be no more than a revolt; that is to say, it is in itself simply a justification and confirmation of what already exists. For the whole relative right of what exists is established only by the relative wrong of revolution in its victory; whereas the relative right of revolution in its victory is in no way established by the relative wrong of the existing order. Similarly also, the power of resistance in the existing order is in no way broken by the victorious attack of revolution; it is merely driven backwards, embarrassed, and compelled to adopt different forms, and thus rendered the more dangerous; whereas the energy of revolution is dissipated and rendered innocuous—simply by its victory. And so the whole conduct of the rebel in no way constitutes a judgement upon the existing order, however much his act of revolution may do so. The rebel has thoughtlessly undertaken the conflict between God's Order and the existing order. Should he allow himself to appeal directly to the ordinance of God, "should he boldly and confidently storm the heavens and bring down thence his own eternal rights which hang aloft inalienable, unbroken as the stars themselves" (Schiller), he betrays thereby perception of the true "limit to the tyrant's power," but his bold storming of the heavens in no way brings about this limitation. He may be justified at the bar of history; but he is not justified before the judgement-seat of God. The sequel shows "the return of the old natural order where men oppose their fellow men." When men undertake to substitute themselves for God, the problem of God, His mind and His judgement, still remain, but they are rendered ineffective. And so, in his rebellion, the rebel stands on the side of the existing order.

Let the existing order—State, Church, Law, Society, &c., &c.—in their totality be:

$$(a\ b\ c\ d)$$

Let their dissolution by the Primal Order of God, by which their totality is contradicted, be expressed by a minus sign outside the bracket:

$$-(+a+b+c+d)$$

It is then clear that no revolution, however radical, which takes place within the realm of history, can ever be identical with the divine minus sign outside the bracket, by which the totality of human ordinances is dissolved. Revolution can do no more than change the plus sign within the bracket—the plus, that is to say, which existing ordinances possess within the bracket because they exist—into a minus sign. The result of a successful revolution is therefore:

$$-(-a-b-c-d)$$

And now we see that for the first time the great divine minus sign outside the bracket has transformed the anticipatory, revolutionary minus sign into a genuine plus sign. Revolution has, therefore, the effect of restoring the old after its downfall in a new and more powerful form. (Equally false, however, is the reckoning of the legitimists: false, because they consciously and as a matter of principle—in their consciousness and in their appeal to principle lies the arrogant and titanic element in Legitimism—add a positive sign to the terms within the bracket. But the divine minus sign outside the bracket means that all human consciousness, all human principles and axioms and orthodoxies and—isms, all *principality and power and dominion*, are AS SUCH subjected to the destructive judgement of God. *Let every man be in subjection* means, therefore, that every man should consider the falsity of all human reckoning as such. We are not competent to place the decisive minus sign before the bracket; we are only competent to perceive how completely it damages our plus and our minus. Accordingly, the subjection here recommended must not be allowed to develop into a new and subtle manner of reckoning, whereby we reintroduce once more an absolute right. It is evident that there can be no more devastating undermining of the existing order than the recognition of it which is here recommended, a recognition rid of all illusion and devoid of all the joy of triumph. State, Church, Society, Positive Right, Family, Organized Research, &c, &c, live of the credulity of those who have been nurtured upon vigorous sermons-delivered-on-the-field-of-battle and upon other suchlike solemn humbug. Deprive them of their PATHOS, and they will be starved out; but stir up revolution against them, and their PATHOS is provided with fresh fodder. No-revolution is the best preparation for the true Revolution; but even no-revolution is no safe recipe. *To be in subjection* is, when it is rightly understood, an action void of purpose, an action, that is to say, which can spring only from obedience to God. Its meaning is that men have encountered God, and are thereby compelled to leave the judgement to Him. The actual occurrence of this judgement cannot be identified with the purpose or with the secret reckoning of the man of this world.)[2]

ETHICS

Theses on Church and State

I. Church

1. The humility required of us, as repentance before God, means concretely that our action takes place in the order of the church and confirms the order of the church. The correlation between repentance and the church rests on the incarnation of the Christ who summons us to repentance; in this the church has its basis.

2. The church is not an order of creation. It is an order of grace relating to sin. It is not to be confused with the "barest, purest, and simplest religion" (Luther, EA, o.e. 1.1, 133) of the lost state of innocence. Nor, according to Revelation 21:22, will there any longer be a church in the consummation.

3. The church is the order, sanctified by the actual presence of the Word and Spirit of God, in which, by the grace of God, the message of man's reconciliation with God through Christ is proclaimed, where, by the grace of God, the right answer is given to this by man, i.e., the act of repentance, and where, again by the grace of God, the fellowship of men takes place in this hearing and answering, the only possible and real fellowship.

4. In virtue of the actual presence of God and to his glory, the church is the one order, holy and infallible, which is binding on all men, outside which there is no salvation, and which is the legitimate bearer and recipient of the prophetic and apostolic witness. But this actual presence of God as the ontic and noetic ground of these qualities has to be continually given to it, and therefore believed in it and acknowledged as grace in the act of repentance before God.

5. As a human work, and therefore in all its reality apart from the grace of God, the church has a share in the folly and wickedness of man, whose sin has been forgiven but has not ceased to be sin. It cannot ignore, then, the improper nature of that which is actively or passively done by men in it. It will not be led astray by the opposition of the rest of the world to its task and promise, but it will also be constantly reminded by this of its own worldliness and therefore of its starting-point, allowing itself to be referred back to the grace of God. It cannot abandon its fundamental and concrete attitude of humility before the World and Spirit of God that constitute it, in favor of a disposable plenitude of truth and power inherent either in its offices or in the whole community. Even as the bride of Christ,

it cannot for a single moment or in any respect cease to be his handmaid. It knows that it can only be *led* into all truth [cf. John 16:13].

6. The human work of the church is thus the service of God in the broadest sense, because it can never act effectively except under the proviso of the grace of God. It is the setting up of the symbol of proclamation and repentance whose reality is God's work alone. The symbol of this symbol is divine service in the narrower sense of the word (worship). This is the characteristic function of the church as such (in distinction from other human orders and societies which are not intrinsically the church).

7. The decisive elements of divine service in the narrower sense are as follows:

a. personal, commissioned, and responsible transmission of the biblical witness to Christ in preaching and the administration of the sacraments as necessary recollection of the givenness of this witness which is not tied to human speech and hearing.

b. all the other cultic possibilities which have their inner and outer criterion in whether or not they are commanded and responsible as expressions of repentance before God and to that extent as means of edification.

8. With the task of divine service in the broader and narrower senses the following special tasks are assigned to the church:

a. individual pastoral care, which is not possible without energetic physical care of every type;

b. the acts of individual members of the church as such, as these are characterized by repentance before God, namely, their participation and cooperation in the word of preaching oriented to the biblical witness;

c. Christian education of youth, whose Christian nature can be basically only a human question and a divine answer;

d. evangelization and missions as a necessary expression of the church's life and its responsible proclamation to the rest of the world, which is alien to it but with which it must reckon in humility before God;

e. theology, i.e., the never unnecessary critical self-reflection of the church on its origin, on the promises and warnings of its history, on its nature, and on its central and also its peripheral task.

9. The task and promise of this human work is fundamentally given to the church as such, i.e., to all its members. The holders of its special offices (the offices of pastor, deacon, theologian, and administrator) are no less servants of Christ, if God gives them grace, because they are also and as such separated servants of the community. The exalting of a special episcopal office

above that of the pastor, being a disruption of the created balance of leadership and equality, is a poor symbol of the fact that in the community, as all serve the sovereign God, so each can only serve the other.

II. The State

1. As service of the neighbor the humility required of us means concretely that our action takes place in the order of the state and confirms the order of the state. The correlation between service and the state also rests on the incarnation of Christ, which is the basis of the possibility of people being for one another—not merely living with one another before God, but also living for one another among one another. This living for one another among one another is the purpose of the state.

2. The state, too, is not an order of creation. Even more palpably than the church, it is an order of grace relating to sin. It is particularly an order of the patience of God which finds its limit and end in the eternal consummation. It is "a necessary remedy for corrupt nature" [Luther, EA, o.e. 1.1, 130].

3. The state, too, is the order, sanctified by the actual presence of the Word and Spirit of God, in which, by the grace of God, the rules are set up and upheld for common life, all being also made responsible for each and each for all, i.e., placed in mutual service. Thus the final and true purpose of the state can only be the Christian one, that on the basis of mutual forgiveness we should be not only with one another but also for one another.

4. Insofar as the state, too, is established and upheld by the actual presence of God, it is in every possible form a minister in God's place [cf. Rom. 13:4], and it is Christian obedience to render to Caesar what is Caesar's [cf. Matt. 22:21]. The divine dignity of the state, too, is ultimately a matter of revelation and faith, so that in the age of the Reformation it was rightly made an object of church confession. This means, of course, that where the actual presence of God in the reality of the state cannot possibly be believed, i.e., where it is not at all visible, God is to be obeyed rather than men [cf. Acts 5:29] to the extent that even the service of others, which is the purpose of its reality, can sometimes be turned into its opposite.

5. As a human work, and therefore in all its reality, the state too, and even more palpably than the church, has a share in the corruption in which man, far from forgiving sin, with cunning and force pursues his own ends in the struggle for existence. The dignity of the individual state, and the respect that is owed and paid it, can for the following reasons be called service of the neighbor only in an improper sense:

a. because each individual state (contrary to its true nature) orders the common life of man and man on the assumption that the right of each must be protected and on the other hand each must be charged with his sins;

b. because the decisive means of existence of each individual state in relation to its members (contrary to its true nature) is brute force;

c. because each individual state (contrary to its true nature) is only one among others in relation to which it relies more or less on the right of might to maintain its existence. All this shows that the existing order of the state, more palpably than that of the church, is a relative order whose establishment and maintenance is service of the neighbor only insofar as it takes place in repentance before God, i.e., in the belief that God will make good what we cannot help but do badly.

6. The human work of the state is thus service of the neighbor because it, too, can act effectively only under the proviso of the grace of God. It is the setting up of the symbol of fellowship whose reality is God's work alone. The symbol of this symbol is the setting up and upholding of this rule of law in an ethnographically and geographically defined territory by which a particular state is distinguished from other states and from other entities (economic, cultural, and ecclesiastical) in and outside its sphere of sovereignty.

7. The decisive functions of the state are:

a. legislation, whose fundamental purpose is the creation of fundamentally equal rights in all questions of social life;

b. government, i.e., provision for the sure, complete, impartial, and objective observance of all existing laws;

c. justice as a system of applying the laws fairly in cases of dispute.

8. The tasks of legislation and government always include:

a. a concern to provide and protect national labor;

b. protection of all who temporarily or permanently have a part in the organization of labor;

c. promotion of free learning;

d. concern for popular education and culture;

e. concern for the freedom of action and expression of individuals, groups, and parties to the extent that this can be understood as an affirmation of the purpose of the state;

f. public acknowledgement and support of the church in particular as the society in which recollection of the ultimate purpose of the state particularly resides.

9. The task and promise of this work are fundamentally for all, and in particular they are fundamentally for men and women equally. Christians especially realize that they are personally responsible for the life of the state and its activity. Here, too, leadership and office have to be, and can only be, a commission and ministry and not an intrinsic distinction of individuals or of certain families, ranks, or classes. Insofar as office is held

by fallible people on the basis of fallible laws, it is open to criticism, and insofar as its exercise rests on force, one cannot rule out, as a last resort, in opposition to it, violent revolution on the part of the rest of the citizens.

III. Church and State

1. As Boniface VIII (bull *Unam Sanctam*, 1302) rightly presupposed, church and state, as two expressions of one and the same temporally though not eternally valid divine order, are the two swords of the one power of Jesus Christ. The dualism of this order is conditioned and demanded by the dualism of man reconciled to God as a sinner saved by grace. Christian humility will in the same way recognize the relativity of the distinction and the necessity of the relative distinction. It will not reckon, then, either with an absolutizing of the distinction (the metaphysical differentiation of a religious and a secular sphere of life) or a one-sided removal of it (caesaropapism or "theocracy").

2. There is no equality of rank between church and state but a superiority in favor of the church. "The one sword then should be subject to the other, and temporal authority subject to spiritual" (Boniface VIII). The temple is prior to the home and above it (Luther EA o.c. 1.1, 130). State and church coinhere. Yet the church is not first in the state, but the state in the church, for repentance before God establishes but does not presuppose service of the neighbor, whereas service of the neighbor presupposes but does not establish repentance before God. In all circumstances, then, the Christian is first of all a member of the church and only then and as such a citizen.

3. If the responsible representatives of the church are not to lose their humility, the church can assert its principial superiority to the state only to the glory of God as Lord of both church and state, and not to its own glory, and it can do so only with the means that have been given to it, the proclamation of the Word and repentance, and not, with Boniface VIII, by the direct or indirect uniting of the two swords in its hands, or by the exercise of quasi-political authority in competition with that of the state.

4. The church, to the extent that it acts as such, renounces not only the appeal to the individual instinct of self-preservation and the assertion of the distinction between right and wrong, and not only the use of external compulsion within or force without, but fundamentally also the setting up and upholding of any rigid rule of law. Canons and dogmas are not legal but spiritual norms, and are to be applied only as such. Church law in the strict sense can be only the church-recognized law of the state that exists even in the church. As an inevitable change into another genre the formation of special church law can be understood only as an incidental

and doubly improper function of the church, and it comes under the rule: "The less of it, the better!"

5. As one society among others, the church in practice adjusts and subordinates itself to the state as the guardian of the rule of law. In relation to the national differentiation of states, things being as they are the church will accept as nonessential its necessary distinction and characterization over against other parts of the church. The freedom and superiority which it maintains precisely in so doing are not tied to the amount of independence of leadership and organization in relation to the state, nor to the presence of a visible supernational church unity, but to the measure of certainty with which, as a fellowship of the proclamation of the Word and repentance, it maintains itself over against the justifiable and unjustifiable claims of the state as the bearer of its materially transcendent, and in fact united and therefore international, task. A state church that knows and is true to its cause, and to the unity of this cause, is to be preferred to even the freest of churches as a symbol of the ultimate unity of church and state.

6. The church acknowledges and promotes the state insofar as service of the neighbor, which is the purpose of the state, is necessarily included in its own message of reconciliation and is thus its own concern. In relation to the activity of the state, it will adopt a restrained attitude to the extent that the state diverges from this purpose or that it cannot accept co-responsibility for it as the church. Finally, with the means at its disposal, it will move on to protest against the state if the latter's activity becomes a denial of its purpose and it is no longer visible or credible as the order of God. Either way it will always confess positively the purpose of the state and therefore the national state itself.

7. If the representatives of the state are not to lose their humility, the state can assert its practical superiority over the church only to the glory of God as Lord of both church and state and not to its own glory—and it can do so only in its own field as the guardian of the rule of law, not as the herald of a philosophy or morality conformable to its own *raison d'etre*, nor with the desire for a special civil Christianity. It gives the church freedom to fashion its own worship, dogma, and constitution and to practice its own preaching and theology.

8. The state for its part cannot be tied in principle to any specific form of the church. It recognizes and supports the church insofar as its own purpose is grounded and included in that of the church. Thus far it is neither nonreligious nor nonconfessional. But it is supraconfessional insofar as it is tolerant in face of the confessional division of the church, in principle assuring the same freedom to all church bodies within the framework of law.

9. In practice, however, without intolerance to others, and as an expression of the specificity with which it is conscious of its own purpose, the state may address and claim a specific form of the church in a special way as *the* form of the church in accordance with the recognition of the specific national state which the church does not withhold. As a symbol of the ultimate unity of church and state, the qualified recognition and support of the church is, even from the state's point of view, more appropriate than the system of a real organizational separation of church and state.[3]

THE KNOWLEDGE OF GOD AND THE SERVICE OF GOD

There is a particular passage in Article 14 of the Confession, in its exposition of the sixth Commandment, to which we must now return and which compels us to go one step further in this connection. It is explicitly stated there that to the fulfillment of the commandment "Thou shalt not kill" belongs also the command "to represse tyrannie" and not to allow the shedding of innocent blood when we can prevent it. What does this mean? It means that, according to the Scottish Confession, under certain conditions there may be a *resistance* to the political power, which is not merely allowed but enjoined by God. John Knox and his friends have supplied the unambiguous commentary to this by their words and deeds. This may be not only a passive resistance but an *active* one, a resistance which can in certain circumstances be a matter of opposing *force* by force, as did occur in Scotland in the sixteenth century. It may be that the repressing of tyranny and the prevention of the shedding of innocent blood can be carried out in no other way.

What are we to say to this? I think, all things being considered, we must agree with the Confession here. We certainly cannot escape obedience to God and to the political order. Nor can we evade praying in accordance with I Timothy 2:1–4 for those who administer that order, whoever they may be and however they may do it. This prayer and this obedience may not cease, no matter whether the significance of the political order be clear or obscure. But in certain circumstances the form which this obedience and prayer take as regards the actual administrators and representatives of the political power, may be not that of the active or passive position mentioned above but a third alternative. Obedience not to the political order, but to its actual representatives can become impossible for us, if we wish at the same time to hold fast to faith and love. It could well be that we could obey specific rulers only by being disobedient to God, and by being thus in fact disobedient to the political order ordained of God as well. It could well be that we had to do with a Government of liars, murderers and incendiaries, with a Government which wished to usurp the place of God, to fetter the conscience, to suppress the church and become itself the Church of Antichrist. It would be clear in such a case that we could only choose either to obey this Government by disobeying God or to obey God by disobeying this Government. In such a case must not God be obeyed rather than men? Must it not be forbidden us then to desire merely to endure? In such a case must not faith in Jesus Christ active in love necessitate our active resistance in just the same way as it necessitates passive resistance or our positive cooperation, when we are not faced with this choice? Must it not necessitate this in precisely the same way as in corresponding circumstances it necessitates reformation and therefore a breach in the church, the breach between the true and the false church? Must not the prayer for this Government, without ceasing to be intercession for them personally before God, for their conversion and their eternal salvation become quite plainly the prayer that as political rulers they may be set aside? And in such a case would we not have to act in accordance with our prayer? Against this it may be asked, can we and have we the right as Christians to take part in the use of force in certain circumstances? This question recalls once again the position with which we began the whole subject in this chapter. We are here as we deal with church and State, so to speak, on the edge of the church in the sphere of the world not yet redeemed. To live in this world and to obey God in it is to take part in the use of force directly or indirectly. It is not first of all in connection with this last case of active resistance to definite powers that the question of force arises.

Let us be quite clear; by obeying the political order in accordance with God's command, we have in any case directly or indirectly a share in the exercise of force. We have a share in this even when we feel it is our duty to choose that middle way of passive participation. And whether the repressing of tyranny will be a matter of forcible resistance or not, is not something which can be decided in advance. But active resistance as such cannot and may not be excluded out of fear of the ultima ratio of forcible resistance. And the possible consequence of forcible resistance may certainly not be excluded in advance.

We may and should pray to be spared that choice, or, if that be not possible, at least to be spared the ultima ratio of forcible resistance. And we should and must examine our responsibilities here, indeed, if possible, even more carefully than in the decisions previously mentioned. But there is one thing which must not happen. We may neither pray nor wish to be spared obedience to God in this worldly sphere either, to be spared the political service of God as such. And since we now have been claimed for it we may not take flight from any of its consequences demanded of us. The world needs men and it would be sad if it were just the Christians who did not wish to be men.[4]

CHURCH DOGMATICS

The Mercy and Righteousness of God

The people to whom God in His righteousness turns as helper and Savior is everywhere in the Old Testament harassed and oppressed people of Israel, which, powerless in itself, has no rights, and is delivered over to the superior force of its enemies; and in Israel it is especially the poor, the widows and orphans, the weak and defenseless. The branch out of the root of Jesse "will have his delight in the fear of the Lord. He shall not judge after the sight of his eyes, neither reprove after the hearing of his ears," which means obviously that he will not vindicate him who in the common opinion is already in the right, "but with righteousness he shall judge the poor, and reprove with equity for the meek of the earth: and he shall smite the earth with the rod of his mouth, and with the breath of his life shall he slay the wicked." And so "righteousness shall be the girdle of his loins and faithfulness the girdle of his reins" (Is. 11 3f). For this reason the human righteousness required by God and established in obedience—the righteousness which according to Amos 5:24 should pour down as a mighty stream—has necessarily the character of a vindication of right in favour of the threatened innocent, the oppressed poor, widows, orphans and aliens. For this reason, in the relations and events in the life of His people, God always takes His stand unconditionally and passionately on this side and on this side alone: against the lofty and on behalf of the lowly; against those who already enjoy right and privilege and on behalf of those who are denied it and deprived of it. What does all this mean? It is not really to be explained by talking *in abstracto* of the political tendency and especially the forensic character of the Old Testament and the biblical message generally. It does in fact have this character and we cannot hear it and believe it without feeling a sense of responsibility in the direction indicated.

As a matter of fact, from the belief in God's righteousness there follows logically a very definite political problem and task. But seen and understood *in abstracto*, the latter—i.e., the connexion between justification and law in all its relevance for that between Church and state—cannot really be evident and necessary of itself. It becomes so when we appreciate the fact that God's righteousness, the faithfulness in which He is true to

Himself, is disclosed as help and salvation, as a saving divine intervention for man directly only to the poor, the wretched and the helpless as such, while with the rich and the full and the secure as such, according to His very nature He can have nothing to do. God's righteousness triumphs when man has no means of triumphing. It is light when man in himself lies in darkness, and life when man walks in the shadow of death. When we encounter divine righteousness we are all like the people of Israel, menaced and altogether lost according to its own strength. We are all widows and orphans who cannot procure right for themselves. It is obviously in the light of this confrontation that we have all those sayings in the Psalms about God's righteousness and the believer and his righteousness before God. The connexion between God's righteousness and mercy now becomes clear. The righteousness of the believer consists in the fact that God acts for him—utterly, because he cannot plead his own case and no one else can represent him. Faith grasps this full intervention on the part of God and it is therefore *eo ipso* faith in God's mercy, the faith of those who are poor and wretched before God. According to the Gospel of Luke and the Epistle of James, as also according to the message of the prophets, there follows from this character of faith a political attitude, decisively determined by the fact that man is made responsible to all those who are poor and wretched in his eyes, that he is summoned on his part to espouse the cause of those who suffer wrong. Why? Because in them it is manifested to him what he himself is in the sight of God; because the living, gracious, merciful action of God towards him consists in the fact that God Himself in His own righteousness procures right for him, the poor and wretched; because he and all men stand in the presence of God as those for whom right can be procured only by God Himself. The man who lives by the faith that this is true stands under a political responsibility. He knows that the right, that every real claim which one man has against another or others, enjoys the special protection of the God of grace. As surely as he himself lives by the grace of God he cannot evade this claim. He cannot avoid the question of human rights. He can only will and affirm a state which is based on justice. By any other political attitude he rejects the divine justification.[5]

THE CHRISTIAN COMMUNITY AND THE CIVIL COMMUNITY

The direction of Christian judgments, purposes and ideals in political affairs is based on the analogical capacities and needs of political organization.

A simple and absolute heterogeneity between State and Church on the one hand and State and Kingdom of God on the other is therefore just as much out of the question as a simple and absolute equating. The only possibility that remains—and it suggests itself compellingly—is to regard the existence of the State as an allegory, as a correspondence and an analogue to the Kingdom of God which the Church preaches and believes in. Since the State forms the outer circle, within which the Church, with the mystery of its faith and gospel, is the inner circle, since it shares a common centre with the Church, it is inevitable that, although its presuppositions and its tasks are its own and different, it is nevertheless capable of reflecting indirectly the truth and reality which constitute the Christian community.

Among the political possibilities open at any particular moment it will choose those which most suggest a correspondence to, an analogy and a reflection of, the content of its own faith and gospel.

In the decisions of the State the Church will always support the side which clarifies rather than obscures the Lordship of Jesus Christ over the whole, which includes this political sphere outside the Church. The Church desires that the shape and reality of the State in this fleeting world should point towards the Kingdom of God, not away from it. Its desire is not that human politics should cross the politics of God, but that they should proceed, however distantly, on parallel lines.

Even its political activity is therefore a profession of its Christian faith. By its political activity it calls the State from neutrality, ignorance and paganism into co-responsibility before God, thereby remaining faithful to its own particular mission. It sets in motion the historical process whose aim and content is the moulding of the State into the likeness of the Kingdom of God and hence the fulfillment of the State's own righteous purposes.

The Church is witness of the divine justification, that is, of the act in which God in Jesus Christ established and confirmed His original claim to man and hence man's claim against sin and death. The future for which the Church waits is the definitive revelation of this divine justification. This means that the Church will always be found where the order of the State is based on a commonly acknowledged law, from submission to which no one is exempt, and which also provides equal protection for all. The Church will be found where all political activity is in all circumstances regulated by this law. The Church always stands for the constitutional State, for the maximum validity and application of that twofold rule (no exemption from and full protection by the law), and therefore it will always be against any degeneration of the constitutional State into tyranny or anarchy. The Church will never be found on the side of anarchy or tyranny. In its politics it will always be urging the civil community to treat this fundamental purpose of its existence with the utmost seriousness: the limiting and the preserving of man by the quest for and the establishment of law.

The Church is witness of the fact that the Son of man came to seek and to save the lost. And this implies that—casting all false impartiality aside—the Church most concentrate first on the lower and lowest levels of human society. The poor, the socially and economically weak and threatened, will always be the object of its primary and particular concern, and it will always insist on the State's special responsibility for these weaker members of society. That it will bestow its love on them—within the framework of its own task (as part of its service), is one thing and the most important thing; but it must not concentrate on this and neglect the other thing to which it is committed by its political responsibility: the effort to achieve such a fashioning of the law as will make it impossible for "equality before the law" to become a cloak under which strong and weak, independent and dependent, rich and poor, employers and employees, in fact receive different treatment at its hands: the weak being unduly restricted, the strong unduly protected. The Church must stand for social justice in the political sphere. And in choosing between the various socialistic possibilities (social–liberalism? co-operativism? syndicalism? free trade? moderate or radical Marxism?) it will always choose the movement from which it can expect the greatest measure of social justice (leaving all other considerations on one side).[6]

CHURCH DOGMATICS

The Protection of Life

A first essential is that war should not on any account be recognized as a normal, fixed and in some sense necessary part of what on the Christian view constitutes the just state, or the political order demanded by God. Certainly the state as such possesses power and must be able to exercise it. But it does this in any case, and it is no primary concern of Christian ethics to say that it should do so, or to maintain that the exercise of power constitutes the essence of the state, i.e., its *opus proprium*, or even a part of it. What Christian ethics must insist is that it is an *opus alienum* for the state to have to exercise power. It cannot assure the state that in the exercise of power either the state or its organs may do gaily and confidently whatever they think is right. In such cases it must always confront them with the question whether there is really any necessity for this exercise.

Especially the state must not be given *carte blanche* to grasp the *ultima ratio* of organizing mass slaughter in its dealings with other states. Christian ethics cannot insist too loudly that such mass slaughter might well be mass murder, and therefore that this final possibility should not be seized like any other, but only at the very last hour in the darkest of days. The Church and theology have first and supremely to make this detached and delaying movement. If they do not first and for a long time make this the burden of their message, if they do not throw in their weight decisively on this side of the scales, they have become savourless salt, and must not be surprised if they are freely trampled underfoot on every side. It is also to be noted that, if the Church and theology think otherwise, if they do not say this first, if they do not throw in their weight on this side, if they speak tediously and tritely of war as a political *opus proprium*, then at the striking of the last hour in the darkest of days they will be in no position to say authentically and authoritatively what they may say at such a time. That is to say, they will be in no position authentically and authoritatively to issue a call to arms, to the political *opus alienum*. For they can do this only if they have previously held aloof, calling for peace right up the very last moment.

What Christian ethics has to emphasize is that neither inwardly nor outwardly does the normal task of the state, which is at issue even in time of war, consist in a process of annihilating rather than maintaining and fostering life. Nor should it be rashly maintained that annihilating life is also part of the process of maintaining and fostering it. Biological wisdom of this kind cannot serve as the norm or rule in ethics. The state which Christian ethics can and must affirm, which it has to proclaim as the political order willed and established by God, is not in itself and as such the mythological beast of the jungle, the monster with the Janus head, which by its very nature is prepared at any moment to turn thousands into killers and thousands more into killed. The Church does the state no honour, nor does it help it, if in relation to it it acts on this assumption concerning its nature. According to the Christian understanding, it is no part of the normal task of the state to wage war; its normal task is to fashion peace in such a way that life is served and war kept at bay. If there is a mistake in pacifism, apart from the inadvisable ethical absolutism of its thesis, it consists in its abstract negation of war, as if war could be understood and negated in isolation and not in relation to the so-called peace which precedes it. Our attention should be directed to this relation. It is when a state does not rightly pursue its normal task that sooner or later it is compelled to take up the abnormal one of war, and therefore to inflict this abnormal task on other states. It is when the power of the state is insufficient to meet the inner needs of the country that it will seek an outer safety-valve for the consequent unrest and think it is found in war. It is when interest-bearing capital rather than man is the object whose maintenance and increase are the meaning and goal of the political order that the mechanism is already set going which one day will send men to kill and be killed. Against such a perversion of peace neither the supposed, though already undermined and no longer steadfast, love of the masses for peace, nor the well-meant and vocal declaiming of idealists against war, is of any avail. For the point is that when war does break out it is usually the masses who march, and even the clearest words spoken against war, and the most painful recollections of previous wars, are rendered stale and impotent. A peace which is no real peace can make war inevitable. Hence the first, basic and decisive point which Christian ethics must make in this matter is that the state, the totality of responsible citizens, and each individual in his own conduct should so fashion peace while there is still time that it will not lead to this explosion but make war superfluous and unnecessary instead of inevitable. Relatively speaking, it requires no great faith, insight nor courage to condemn war radically and absolutely, for no one apart from leaders of the armaments industry and a few high-ranking officers really believes that war is preferable to peace. Again, it requires no faith, insight nor courage at all to howl with the wolves that unfortunately war belongs no less to the present world order, historical life and the nature of the state than does peace, so that from the very outset we must regard it as an emergency for which preparation must be made. What does require Christian faith, insight and courage—and the Christian Church and Christian ethics are there to show them—is to tell nations and governments that peace is the real emergency to which all our time, powers and ability must be devoted from the very outset in order that men may live and live properly, so that no refuge need be sought in war, nor need there be expected from it what peace has denied. Pacifists and militarists are usually agreed in the fact that for them the fashioning of peace as the fashioning of the state for democracy, and of democracy for social democracy, is a secondary concern as compared with rearmament or disarmament. It is for this reason that Christian ethics must be opposed to both. Neither rearmament nor disarmament can be a first concern, but the restoration of an order of life which is meaningful and just. When this is so, the two slogans will not disappear. They will have their proper place. They will come up for discussion at the proper time. But they will necessarily lose their fanatical tone, since far more urgent concerns will be up for discussion. And there can always be the hope that some day both will prove to be irrelevant.

It is only against the background of this first concern, and only as the Church has a good conscience that it is doing its best for a just peace among states and nations, that it can and should plead for the preservation of peace among states and nations, for fidelity and faith in their mutual dealings as the reasonable presupposition of a true foreign policy, for solid agreements and alliances and their honest observance, for international courts and conventions, and above all, and in all nations, for openness, understanding and patience towards others and for such education of young people as will lead them to prefer peace to war. The Church and should raise its voice against the institution of standing armies in which the officers constitute *per se* a permanent danger to peace. It can and should resist all kinds of hysterical or premature war scares. It exists in this aeon. Hence it is not commissioned to proclaim that war is absolutely avoidable. But it is certainly commissioned to oppose the satanic doctrine that war is inevitable and therefore justified, that it is unavoidable and therefore right when it occurs, so that Christians have to participate in it. Even in a world in which states and nations are still in the early stages and never at the end of the long road in respect of that first concern, there is never in practice an absolute necessity of war, and the Church certainly has neither right nor obligation to affirm this necessity either in general or in detail as the occasion may arise. We do not need optimism but simply a modicum of sane intelligence to recognize that relatively if not absolutely, in practice if not in principle, war can be avoided to a very large extent. The Church must not preach pacifism, but it must see to it that this sane intelligence is voiced and heard so long as this is possible, and that the many ways of avoiding war which now exist in practice should be honestly applied until they are all exhausted. It is better in this respect that the Church should stick to it post too long and become a forlorn hope than that it should leave it too soon and then have to realize that it has become unfaithful by yielding to the general excitement, and that it is thus the accessory to an avoidable war which can only be described as mass murder. In excitement and propaganda there lurks already the mass killing which can only be mass murder. On no account, not even *in extremis*, should the Church be found among the agitators or use their language. Deliberate agitators, and those deceived by them, must always be firmly and quietly resisted, whether they like it or not. And this is what the Church can do with its word. Hence its word must never be a howling with the pack.

If only the Church had learned the two lessons *(a)* of Christian concern for the fashioning of true peace among nations to keep war at bay, and *(b)* of Christian concern for peaceful measures and solutions among states to avert war; if only these two requirements and their unconditional primacy were the assured possession of all Christian ethics, we might feel better assured both against misunderstandings and also against threatened relapses into the post-Constantinian theology of war, and we might therefore be confident to say that we cannot accept the absolutism of the pacifist thesis, and that Christian support for war and in war is not entirely beyond the bounds of possibility.

It might be argued that it is inopportune to say this today. But surely it is always most opportune to keep to the truth. And the truth in this matter surely includes this further point. Even the cogent element of truth in the pacifist position—more cogent perhaps today than ever before—will surely benefit rather than suffer if it is not presented as the exclusive and total truth, but is deliberately qualified, perhaps at the expense of logical consistency, by this further point. After all, the consistency of ethics, or at any rate of theological ethics, may for once differ from that of logic.

This further point rests on the assumption that the conduct of one state or nation can throw another into the wholly abnormal situation of emergency in which not merely its greater or lesser prosperity but its very existence and autonomy are menaced and attacked. In consequence of the attitude of this other state, a nation can find itself faced by the question whether it must surrender or assert itself as such in face of the claims of the other. Nothing less than this final question must be at issue if a war is to be just and necessary.

Perhaps a state desires to expand politically, geographically or economically, and therefore to extend its frontiers and dominion. Perhaps it thinks it necessary to rectify its internal conditions, e.g., to bring about political unity, by external adventure. Perhaps it considers that its honour and prestige are violated by the attitude of another state. Perhaps it feels that it is threatened by a shift in the balance of power among other states. Perhaps it thinks it sees in the internal conditions of another state, whether revolutionary or reactionary, a reason for displeasure or anxiety. Perhaps it believes it can and should ascribe to itself a historical mission, e.g., a call to lead and rule other nations. All this may well be so. Yet it certainly does not constitute a valid reason for setting one's own great or little war machine in motion, for sending out one's troops to the battlefield to kill and be killed. Such aims may be well worth striving for. But they are too paltry to be worth the terrible price involved in their realization by war. War for such reasons could always have been avoided. War for such reasons is an act of murder. When such reasons lie on one side of the scale, and the knowledge of war and its necessary terrors on the other, we should have to be either incorrigible romanticists or malevolent sophists even to doubt which side ought to rise and which to fall. The Christian Church has to testify unambiguously that wars waged for such reasons are not just, and therefore ought not to be undertaken.

If the state makes participation in war obligatory upon all, the individual must face the question whether as a citizen he can approve and cooperate in war, i.e., every war as such, or whether as a citizen he must resist and evade it.

The state is not God, nor can it command as He does. No compulsory duty which it imposes on the individual, nor urgency with which it presses for its fulfillment, can alter the fact that the attitude of the individual to all its decisions and measures, and therefore to this too, is limited and defined by his relationship to God, so that, although as a citizen he is committed to what is thought right and therefore resolved by the government or the majority, he is not bound by it finally or absolutely. Hence it cannot be denied that in virtue of his relationship to God the individual may sometimes find himself compelled, even with a full sense of his loyalty as a citizen, to contradict and oppose what is thought right and resolved by the government or the majority. He will be aware of the exceptional character of this action. Such insubordination cannot be ventured too easily or frequently. He will also be aware of the risk entailed. He cannot but realize that by offering resistance he renders himself liable to prosecution. He cannot deny to the government or the majority the right to take legal and constitutional proceedings against him. He must not be surprised or aggrieved if he has to bear the consequences of his resistance. He must be content in obedience to God to accept his responsibility as a citizen in this particular way. The contradiction and resistance to compulsory military service can indeed take the form of the actual refusal of individuals to submit to conscription as legally and constitutionally imposed by the government or the majority, and therefore of their refusal to participate directly either in war itself or preparation for it. Such refusal means that these individuals think they must give a negative answer to the question posed by conscription, even though it is put to them in the form of a compulsory duty calling urgently for fulfillment.[7]

PETITION OF THE BRUDERSCHAFTEN
ON NUCLEAR WEAPONS

I. The Evangelical Church confesses that in Jesus Christ she finds "joyous liberation from the Godless bonds of the world unto free, thankful service to His creatures." (Barmen Thesis 2.) This forbids to her not only any approval of or collaboration in an atomic war and its preparation, but also her tacitly letting it happen. This awareness demands that in the obedience of faith . . . here as in every issue . . . we ourselves must take the first step to hold back the threatening destruction and to trust more in the reality of the Word of God than in the "realism" of political calculation. The first step is the act of *diakonia* which we, as Christians, owe to the menaced and anxious world of today. Let the faithless hesitate . . . we as Christians may and must dare it in trust in God, who created this World and every living creature in East and West for the sake of the suffering and victorious Jesus Christ, and will preserve the same through Christ and the preaching of His Gospel until His Day.

II. If the Synod finds itself unable to assent to this confession, we must ask how the Synod can refute it on the grounds of Scripture, the Confessions, and reason.

For the sake of the men and women for whom we are responsible, and for our own sakes, we must insist upon receiving an answer to this question. We owe it to the Synod to remind it of its spiritual responsibility, since it is in the shouldering of this responsibility that it shows itself to be the legitimate authority in the Church. It is our conviction that in the face of this issue the Church finds herself in the *status confessionis*.

If the Synod agrees with us, than an unreserved *No* is demanded of Christians facing the problem of the new weapons, must she not also say promptly and clearly to the State, that the true proclamation of the Gospel, also in the Chaplaincy, includes the testimony that the Christian may not and cannot participate in the design, testing, manufacture, stocking and use of atomic weapons, nor in training with these weapons?

III. We, therefore, ask the Synod whether she can affirm together with us the following ten propositions, for the instruction of consciences concerning Christian behavior with regard to atomic weapons:

1. War is the ultimate means, but always, in every form a questionable means, of resolving political tensions between nations.

2. For various reasons, good and less good, churches in all lands and all ages have hitherto not considered the preparation and the application of this ultimate means to be impossible.

3. The prospect of a future war to be waged with the use of modern means of annihilation has created a new situation, in the face of which the Church *cannot* remain *neutral*.

4. War, in the form of *atomic war*, means the mutual annihilation of the participating peoples as well as of countless human beings of other peoples, which are not involved in the combat between the two adversaries.

5. War, in the form of atomic war, is therefore seen to be an *instrument incapable of being used* for the resolution of political conflicts, because it destroys every presupposition of political resolution.

6. Therefore, the Church and the individual Christian can say nothing but an *a priori No* to a war with atomic weapons.

7. Even preparation for such a war is under all circumstances *sin against God and the neighbor,* for which no Church and no Christian can accept responsibility.

8. We therefore demand in the Name of the Gospel that an *immediate end be made* to preparations for such a war within our land and nation regardless of all other considerations.

9. We challenge all those who seriously want to be Christians to *renounce,* without reserve and under all circumstances, any participation in preparations for atomic war.

10. In the face of this question, the opposing point of view, or neutrality, *cannot be advocated* Christianly. Both mean the denial of all three articles of the Christian faith.[8]

THE CHRISTIAN LIFE

Fiat Iustita

. . . Christians are claimed for action in the effort and struggle for human righteousness. At issue is human, not divine righteousness. That the latter should come, intervene, assert itself, reign, and triumph can never be the affair of any human action. Those who know the reality of the kingdom, Christians, can never have anything to do with the arrogant and foolhardy enterprise of trying to bring in and build up by human hands a religious, cultic, moral, or political kingdom of God on earth. God's righteousness is the affair of God's own act, which has already been accomplished and is still awaited. God's righteousness took place in the history of Jesus Christ, and it will take place again, comprehensively and definitively, in his final manifestation. The time between that beginning and that end, our time as the time of the presence of Jesus Christ in the Holy Spirit, is for Christians the space for gratitude, hope, and prayer, and also the time of responsibility for the occurrence of human righteousness. They have to be concerned about the doing of this righteousness. On no pretext can they escape responsibility for it: not on that of the gratitude and hope with which they look to God and wait for his action; not on that of their prayer for the coming of his kingdom. For if they are really grateful and really hope, if their prayer is a brave prayer, then they are claimed for a corresponding inner and outer action which is also brave. If they draw back here, or even want to, then there is serious reason to ask whether and how far their gratitude, hope, and prayer are to be taken seriously.

Human righteousness! We shall not develop at length here the self-evident point that, measured by God's righteousness and in unconquerable distinction from it, this will always be, even at best, an imperfect, fragile and highly problematical righteousness. Others may deceive themselves in this regard, but to those who have the prayer for the kingdom in their hearts and on their lips it is indeed self-evident. Nevertheless, it is not so important that they can refrain from doing what they have to do in this relativity. We Protestants have always had a certain inclination to find it too important. We should break free from this. Those who pray that prayer start off with the thesis that the perfect righteousness of God's kingdom is not their own doing, that they can only seek it (Mt. 6:33), as is appropriate, in gratitude for its reality, in hope of its manifestation, in prayer that it may come. This means, however, that any concern for the imperfection of all human action, their own included, is taken from them as idle and pointless. They are also forbidden the lazy excuse of all lazy servants that since all they can do will always be imperfect anyway it is not worth exerting themselves and growing weary in the causes of petty human righteousness. No, precisely because perfect righteousness stands before them as God's work, precisely because they are duly forbidden to attempt the impossible, precisely because all experiments in this direction are prevented and prohibited, they are with great strictness required and with great kindness freed and empowered to do what they can do in the sphere of the relative possibilities assigned to them, to do it very imperfectly yet heartily, quietly, and cheerfully. They are absolved from wasting time and energy sighing over the impassable limits of their sphere of action and thus missing the opportunities that present themselves in this sphere. They may and can and should rise up and accept responsibility to the utmost of their power for the doing of the little righteousness. The only concern should be their awareness of how far they fall short in this sphere of what is not only commanded but also possible for them. But they can quickly rid themselves of this concern by setting to work to snatch the available possibilities of doing what is commanded and thus catching up in God's name where they are in arrears. A little righteousness and holiness of works—there will certainly never be a great deal!—does not have to be an illusion or a danger here. The only danger arising out of the (ill-founded) anxiety that one might become too righteous and too holy, a man of works, is the temptation to remain passive where what is required, with a full sense of one's limitations, is to become active.

It is not self-evident, of course, that in the sphere of human activity, alongside and far below divine righteousness, there should be in all seriousness a human righteousness which Christians are freed to do and for whose occurrence they are made responsible. It is not self-evident that the same lofty concept of righteousness, denoting on the one hand perfect divine action and on the other most imperfect human action, should be appropriate or necessary in this context. In relation to human action as such and in general, the analogy is in truth an impossible one. Here, however, we are referring to the obedience of the action of those whom God has freed and summoned to call upon him for the coming of his kingdom and the doing of righteousness. In relation to the action of these people, it cannot be denied that in all its imperfection this action stands related to the kingdom of God, and therefore to the perfect righteousness of God, inasmuch as it derives from the event of the kingdom in Jesus Christ and hastens toward its manifestation in Jesus Christ. Obviously, this whence and whither mean that it cannot be alien to it but is given a determination which it does not have in itself and cannot give itself but which it acquires, which it cannot escape as it takes place in that relation, and which cannot be denied to it. The determination that it acquires and has in that relation is that it can take place only in correspondence with its whence and whither and therefore with God's kingdom and righteousness. If it never can or will be like this, and should not try to aim at equality with it, neither can it be or remain totally unlike it. There is a third possibility. The action of those who pray for the coming of God's kingdom and therefore for the taking place of his righteousness will be *kingdom-like*, and therefore on a lower level and within its impassable limits it will be *righteous* action. Certainly we should not say too much here, yet we should not say too little either. Done in that relation, under that determination, and therefore in that correspondence, the action of Christians may in its own way and within the limits of its own sphere be called and be a righteous action. This is the one talent that is entrusted to Christians, who are neither angels nor archangels but only people, and they must not wrap it in a cloth or bury it anywhere, as did the stupid fellow in Luke 19:20 and Matthew 25:25. Following their prayer, their action can and should be kingdom-like, righteous in its own place and manner. There is not the shadow of a serious reason to contest this.[9]

NOTES

1. [Karl Barth, "Jesus Christ and the Movement for Social Justice," in *Karl Barth and Radical Politics*, ed. George Hunsinger (Philadelphia: Westminster Press, 1976), 19, 36–37.]

2. [Commentary on Romans 13:1 in *The Epistle to the Romans*, trans. Edwyn C. Hoskyns (London: Oxford University Press, 1957), 481–484.]

3. [Karl Barth, "Theses on Church and State," appendix to *Ethics*, ed. Dietrich Braun, trans. Geoffrey W. Bromiley (New York: Seabury Press, 1981), 517–521.]

4. [Karl Barth, "The State's Service of God," in *The Knowledge of God and the Service of God* (New York: Charles Scribner's Sons, 1939), 229–232.]

5. [Karl Barth, "The Mercy and Righteousness of God," in *Church Dogmatics*, 4 vols. (Edinburgh: T & T Clark, 1936–1961), vol. 2, part 1, 386–387.]

6. [Karl Barth, "The Christian Community and the Civil Community," in *Against the Stream: Shorter Post-War Writings, 1946–1952*, ed. Ronald Gregor Smith (New York: Philosophical Library, 1954), 32–36.]

7. [Karl Barth, "The Protection of Life," in *Church Dogmatics*, vol. 3, part 4, 456–467.]

8. [Karl Barth, "The Continuing Church Struggle" (petition of the Bruderschaften on nuclear weapons, addressed to the Synod of the Evangelical Church in Germany in March, 1958), in John H. Yoder, *Karl Barth and the Problem of War* (Nashville, Tenn.: Abingdon Press, 1970), 134–136.]

9. [Karl Barth, "The Struggle for Human Righteousness," in *The Christian Life: Church Dogmatics IV, 4: Lecture Fragments*, trans. Geoffrey Bromiley (Grand Rapids, Mich.: Eerdmans, 1981), 264–267.]

{ CHAPTER 4 }

Dietrich Bonhoeffer (1906–1945)

COMMENTARY

MILNER BALL

In an exceptional act in an exceptional time, Dietrich Bonhoeffer, a German Lutheran theologian and pastor, joined the conspiracy against Adolf Hitler. The Nazis imprisoned and then executed him shortly before the end of World War II.

During his final months, he developed a daring theological interpretation of his life that his closest friend and biographer, Eberhard Bethge, describes as "the relinquishment of a special Christian life and as the acceptance . . . of an incognito existence." With this theology, he achieved a breakthrough that reveals "the future normality: 'being for others' as sharing in the suffering of Jesus." His life and work lose their exceptional character and become, as Bethge says, "an example of being Christian today."[1]

A statue of Bonhoeffer is one of ten in Westminster Abbey honoring Christian martyrs of the twentieth century. But the greater living tribute lies in the challenging influence of his example beyond Europe, in places as far flung as America, Latin America, South Africa, and Korea—especially among the embattled and those led by Christ to make responsible use of power on their behalf.

Such influence has been unexpected. It could scarcely have been foreseen from the experimental, incomplete nature of Bonhoeffer's late theology and the need to piece it together from the tantalizing fragments that survived the war and his imprisonment. Nor could it have been predicted from his prior life. He was one of eight children of a privileged German family. He was an accomplished pianist, an elegant dancer, and a theologian with the promise of a brilliant career in the academy. He appeared to be far removed from the suffering of outcasts and the dark politics of military conspiracy when he entered upon his academic career in Berlin in 1931 just after a first visit to the United States. Two events intervened to change the person and the career: Bonhoeffer became a practicing believer who would no longer be merely a theologian, and Germany sank into the furious pathology of the nation-state.

Bonhoeffer was no stranger to war. Although he was too young to fight in World War I—he was born in 1906—he lost a brother in that conflict and lived with the deprivations that followed it. Even so, he could not know from that experience what the next war would bring. As he began to teach and to serve as a pastor, Germany moved toward combat and the Holocaust, and the church in Germany moved toward turmoil and division.

He would soon play a leading role in and be much influenced by the church struggle, the difficult fight for the faithfulness and integrity of the Protestant church in Germany during the Third Reich. A clear line was drawn between the majority German Christians and the minority Confessing Church when the latter adopted the Barmen Declaration in 1934, a decisive confession of faith drafted by Karl Barth. Over against the German Christians and their commitment to Hitler, the Barmen Declaration centrally affirmed that Jesus Christ "is the one Word of God whom we are to hear, whom we are to trust and obey" and that there are no "areas of our life in which we belong not to Jesus Christ but another lord."[2]

The Barmen Declaration was adopted in May 1934. The previous year had been critical for the German Evangelical Church, a federal union of twenty-eight Protestant regional churches of the Lutheran and Reformed traditions. Adolf Hitler took control of the German government in January 1933. In April of that year, anti-Semitism became official German policy with the passage of the Aryan Clause excluding Jews from civil service. Because the German Evangelical Church was a state church, its pastors, including some of Jewish descent, were considered civil servants. Church elections were held in July, and, by an overwhelming majority, German Christians assumed positions of power. A synod held in Prussia that September became known as the Brown Synod because many of the delegates appeared in brown Nazi uniforms.

These developments did not go unchallenged. A Young Reformation movement sprung up in various informal theological circles around the country, including one of Bonhoeffer's to which he delivered a controversial but prescient paper arguing that the Jewish Question was critical for the church. He and others then drafted the Bethel Confession, which was so watered down in the process of circulation and adoption that he refused to sign the final version. But shortly afterward, in response to the Brown Synod, Bonhoeffer and pastor Martin Niemöller wrote a protest to the Aryan Clause that, surprisingly, drew the signatures of two thousand pastors and gave birth to the Pastors' Emergency League. The League soon elected for its leadership a Council of Brethren that would persevere to the end of the Nazi period.

Bonhoeffer assumed pastorates in London in October 1933 and did not take part in the following year's Barmen Synod, which produced the Barmen Declaration and the formation of the Confessing Church. However, throughout his time in London, Bonhoeffer kept in close contact with the Confessing Church through correspondence, telephone calls, and visits home. His London congregations aligned themselves with the Confessing Church, and he represented that body's cause in ecumenical circles, an activity that led to his important friendship with the Anglican bishop of Chichester, George K. A. Bell.

In Germany, insistence on Aryan purity and adherence to the party line increasingly would be accompanied by regulations and intimidation and by the arrest and eventually the torture and murder of resisters. Already in 1934, nonconforming seminaries were forced to close, and the Confessing Church set about establishing its own, illegal preachers' seminaries. Bonhoeffer returned from London in 1935 to become the founding director of one of these seminaries, which eventually settled out of the way in Finkenwalde, in what was then northern Germany and is now Poland. It attracted an initial class of twenty-three students and an assistant director, Wilhelm Rott.

As Bonhoeffer developed it, Finkenwalde had the Bible at the center of its learning and living, and it featured monastic intensity, a common life, service, meditation, debate, and evangelism. Bonhoeffer was thoroughly devoted to his responsibilities and to his students. He wrote his book *Discipleship* during his years there, and his subsequent *Life Together* has the Finkenwalde discipline as its subject. The Gestapo closed the Finkenwalde seminary in 1937. Bonhoeffer carried on the work as best he could by various means in one remote place after another until the police again closed it down, and he was again forced to move. When war and persecution took over, Bonhoeffer visited, wrote, and supported his former students as long as he was able, even after military conscription became the rule and his students were sent to the front (80 of the 150 alumni would die in action).

Persecution from the outside, erosion from the inside, nationalism, war fever, and the war exacted a heavy toll on the Confessing Church and its will to resist. Already in 1938 many Confessing pastors took an oath of faith in and obedience to Hitler. Eberhard Bethge, a Finkenwalde alumnus, said it was during this year that "Bonhoeffer began to distance himself from the rearguard actions of the Confessing Church's defeated remnants."[3] War broke out shortly after he returned from a hasty second trip to the United States in 1939.

Bonhoeffer had undertaken that trip to the United States to lecture and teach for a year. After a few agonizing weeks, however, he cut the visit short and returned home. He wrote a letter of explanation to Reinhold Niebuhr, who had sponsored the visit together with Paul Lehmann, Bonhoeffer's best American friend:

> I have come to the conclusion that I have made a mistake in coming to America. I must live through this difficult period of our national history with the Christian people of Germany. I will have no right to participate in the reconstruction of Christian life in Germany after the war if I do not share the trials of this time with my people. . . . Christians in Germany will face the terrible alternative of either willing the defeat of their nation in order that Christian civilization may survive, or willing the victory of their nation and thereby destroying our civilization. I know which of these alternatives I must choose; but I cannot make that choice in security. . . . [4]

Back in Germany in 1939, Bonhoeffer soon found himself led into relationships that were well beyond the limits of anything he had been prepared for by his community and the Lutheran tradition. He joined the active conspiracy against Hitler and became a double agent in the employ of the Abwehr, the Nazi military's counterintelligence agency. The use of his ecumenical, international church connections became part of his contribution to the resistance and, at the same time, served as cover in explaining his travels to Nazi authorities.

"The year 1932 had placed Bonhoeffer in a world where things were comparatively clear-cut, where it was a matter of confessing and denying," Eberhard Bethge observed. "In 1939 he entered the difficult world of assessing what was expedient—of success and failure, tactics and camouflage."[5] Then he arrived at the "last stage: active conspiracy. For members of the Lutheran tradition this was the most difficult, since their tradition allowed for nothing of this kind. In this final stage the church offered no protection and no prior justification for something that fell outside all normal contingencies."[6]

In an affirmation of hope for the future, Bonhoeffer became engaged to Maria von Wedemeyer in January 1943. In April of that year he was arrested and jailed. He would not be released. The extent of his involvement in the conspiracy came to light after an attempt to assassinate Hitler failed on July 20, 1944.[7] Bonhoeffer was convicted of treason. On Hitler's orders he was hanged on April 9, 1945. The nation-state's butchering apparatus that had slaughtered so many people ground on through the chaos of the last days of World War II destroying many more, including not only Dietrich but also another of his brothers and two brothers-in-law. Hitler killed himself on April 30, 1945, and Germany surrendered on May 7.

Bonhoeffer did not arrive readily at his conspiratorial action or its accompanying theology. His first theological heritage was that of the typical, nineteenth-century liberal theology of the German Lutheran tradition, represented by Adolf von Harnack and Reinhold Seeberg, his teachers at Berlin University, where he had transferred after a year of study at the University of Tübingen. He soon found his thinking reoriented by Swiss theologian Karl Barth. Bonhoeffer read Barth long before he met him, a delay in personal contact that he sorely regretted. Although he was deeply indebted to Barth, and Barth praised Bonhoeffer's work, these two great Protestant theologians had their differences. In a letter from prison, Bonhoeffer made the stinging, undeserved remark that Barth's theology was "a positivism of revelation."[8]

Bonhoeffer also learned from American theologians. His initial trip to America in 1930–31 brought him to Union Theological Seminary in New York. There he studied with Reinhold Niebuhr and met Paul Lehmann. Bonhoeffer detected in Niebuhr "a lack of foundational strength in Christology," but he certainly took to heart the admonition Niebuhr wrote on one of Bonhoeffer's papers: "Obedience to God's will may be a religious experience but is not an ethical one until it issues in actions that can be socially valued."[9] Lehmann, too, gave him a thorough grounding in the political theology that figured in Bonhoeffer's own later turn to politics. Lehmann[10] and the lawyer William Stringfellow are good American representatives of those essential commitments and qualities that they had in common with Bonhoeffer. (Stringfellow had no direct connection with him.)

While he was a student in New York, Bonhoeffer was a regular participant at the Abyssinian Baptist Church, whose minister was Adam Clayton Powell. That experience gave him a deep, abiding appreciation of the black church and of the struggle of African Americans against racist oppression.

The postwar American reception of Bonhoeffer's theology was like that elsewhere. His letters and papers from prison were first published in German in the winter of 1951–52 and were greeted with surprise. A few studies of them became available in English beginning in the late 1950s. The

1960s brought some enthusiastic misinterpretation, like that of William Hamilton, who claimed that Bonhoeffer was the "father of the God-is-Dead theology."[11] Bishop John A. T. Robinson's 1963 book *Honest to God* dramatically popularized Bonhoeffer's work,[12] and Harvey Cox's widely read *The Secular City* (1965) was a theologically sound response to and development of Bonhoeffer's insights in the American context.[13]

The subject of most attention has been Bonhoeffer's post-1939 life and writings, the pieces that compose his never-completed *Ethics* and the *Letters and Papers from Prison*. Two earlier works, *Discipleship* (1937) and *Life Together* (1938), have proven equally important both for their independent contributions and for the revealing counterweight they provide to the later material.[14] His doctoral thesis, *The Communion of Saints* (1927), and the dissertation (*Habilitationschrift*) required for professorships, *Act and Being* (1931), are necessary to a thorough understanding of Bonhoeffer, and they made major contributions to theology.[15]

Eberhard Bethge was first Bonhoeffer's student, then his friend and colleague, and last his correspondent. His *Dietrich Bonhoeffer* is a remarkable achievement in its own right and is indispensable to an understanding of the life and work of its subject.

Bonhoeffer's thinking and acting have less to teach about legal theory or law and politics in the abstract than they do about using the power of law and politics, about God's use of this power and ours. Readers of Bonhoeffer's writings must be prepared both for the fragmentary, incomplete quality of the later material and for what appears to be its indulgence in contradiction. Enough does remain of his late work to provide a reliable path into the abiding challenge of his thinking, and its unfinished exploration of new territory may be taken as an invitation to carry the journey forward in our own way in our own generation. The seeming contradictions are in fact the dialectics—the simultaneous "yes" and "no"—made necessary by his venture in theology. Bonhoeffer spoke of a religionless Christianity in a world come of age, a secret discipline that enables public action, God's power as powerlessness in the world, the worldliness of believers, Christ as reality embracing all things human, and God's commandment as freeing. Bonhoeffer was developing a language for the future, and, as we have entered further into that future, it is likely that our capacity for dialectics and our need of them have increased. For us, too, there is cause both to embrace the contemporary world's vast, humanizing capacities and to reject its dehumanizing tendency.

Whatever the changes and developments that took place in Bonhoeffer's thinking and living, and however incomplete, fragmentary, or novel his later writing may be, Christ was perennially at the center. Bonhoeffer concluded his academic life with a series of lectures at the University of Berlin in the turbulent summer of 1933, not long after Hitler had become chancellor and a series of actions against Jews followed. The lectures were devoted to an exploration of christology. Although Christ was presently hidden and humiliated, Bonhoeffer declared, Christ "is the center of human existence, the center of history, and. . . . the center of nature. . . . The human who I am, Jesus has also been. Of him only is it valid to say that nothing human was alien to him. Of him, we say: 'This is God for us.'"[16] Kelly and Nelson observe that in these lectures Bonhoeffer's "life and his theology appeared to converge. . . . Christ in all the robustness of the prophetic Sermon on the Mount now stood at the very center of Bonhoeffer's vocation as a minister."[17]

CRITIQUE OF RELIGION

Bonhoeffer was familiar with Ludwig Feuerbach's critique of religion and his questions about the veracity of religion's assertions and about its concurrence with real life, questions that the liberal theology of the nineteenth century had not answered.[18] It was not Feuerbach, however, but Karl Barth whose work chiefly animated Bonhoeffer's approach. Barth's *The Word of God and the Word of Man* and his commentary on the epistle to the Romans introduced theological critique to the twentieth century. Barth said that religion is "a misfortune which takes fatal hold upon some men, and is by them passed on to others. . . . It is the misfortune . . . which laid upon Calvin's face that look which he bore at the end of his life."[19] In Barth's estimation, religion is humans' constricting, fruitless effort to justify themselves before a capricious picture of a highest being of their own imagining.[20]

Bonhoeffer agreed and believed that bringing in "against religion the God of Jesus Christ . . . remains [Barth's] greatest service."[21] But Bonhoeffer also judged that Barth's thinking about religionless Christianity was incomplete. Thus, late in his short life, Bonhoeffer undertook his own, more daring exploration of the subject. As it turned out, his thinking, too, would be incomplete. He had no chance, for example, to spell out exactly what he meant by "religion." And, as Eberhard Bethge warned, although Bonhoeffer "certainly went beyond Barth . . . he had not sufficiently considered how disturbing all this was."[22] Certainly when Bonhoeffer first became popular in America, and when little was known about the full scope of his work, the available experimental material was vulnerable to superficial interpretation.

Readers today are far less likely to be disturbed by Bonhoeffer's views on religion than they are to be initially puzzled and then challenged by his distinction between the biblical faith and religion. For Bonhoeffer, the priority and centrality of Christ lead to worldliness. A late letter from prison stated his central concern: "What is bothering me incessantly is the question what Christianity really is, or who Christ really is, for us today. . . . We are moving towards a completely religionless time."[23] The issue for Bonhoeffer is not Christ's absence but how to discern, state, and be faithful to Christ's presence in an increasingly secular world whose secularity is to be justly celebrated.

Bonhoeffer opposed the diversionary power of religion. Jesus calls a person, he believed, "not to a new religion, but to life."[24] Religion directs people away from life, away from reality. It directs us to a God beyond the boundaries of human experience and away from the God at work in the world. As human knowledge and strength push the boundaries further out, the God of religion becomes more and more distant. Religion then struggles to preserve itself. It must save a domain for its God. To contend with God's increasing distance, it summons God from outside human boundaries as a *deus ex machina*. It summons God "either for the apparent solution of insoluble problems, or as a strength in human weakness."[25] But this approach requires selling people the idea that they have the problems for which this God is the solution. It addresses and exploits peoples' weakness rather than speaking to their strength, and it makes God dependent on our needs and limits.

The companion strategy is to attempt to secure an inner domain for God in the individual's private sphere.[26] This move assumes both that individuals "can be addressed as sinners only after their weaknesses and meannesses have been spied out" and that their "essential nature consists of their inmost and most intimate background" rather than their public lives and relationships, as though "Goethe and Napoleon [were] sinners because they weren't faithful husbands."[27] This strategy, too, is demeaning and divisive. It emphasizes the sins of weakness when it is the sins of strength that matter, and, contrary to the biblical witness that takes people as wholes, it divides the inner life from the outer life and privileges the former. It tries to save space for God in personal, secret places.

Bonhoeffer thought that Christianity was perhaps the truest form of religion. He therefore tried to imagine what the consequences would be if religion proved to be a historically conditioned, transient phenomenon and not, as Barth thought, a continuing characteristic of believers. What would it mean if humans, Christians especially, were to become religionless? Bonhoeffer did not ask what a secular world would be like without Christ; he asked who Christ is in such a secular world.

This question precipitated others: "If our final judgment must be that the western form of Christianity, too, was only a preliminary stage to a complete absence of religion, what kind of situation emerges for us, for the church? How can Christ become the Lord of the religionless as well?" "What is a religionless Christianity?" "How do we speak of God—without religion?" "In what way are we 'religionless-secular' Christians?" In this latter case, "Christ is no longer an object of religion, but something quite different, really the Lord of the world. But what does that mean? What is the place of worship and prayer in religionless situation?"[28]

Bonhoeffer only started to answer these questions. As he put it:

> I . . . want to start from the premise that God shouldn't be smuggled into some last secret place, but that we should frankly recognize that the world, and people, have come of age, that we shouldn't run people down in their worldliness, but confront them with God at their strongest point, that we should give up all of our clerical tricks, and not regard psychotherapy and existentialist philosophy as God's pioneers. . . . The Word of God is far removed from this revolt of mistrust. . . . On the contrary, it reigns.[29]

THE WORLD COME OF AGE

Bonhoeffer saw signs that the world was in process of becoming religionless, of outgrowing its ward-guardian relationship with the God of religion. He described what he saw variously as a "world come of age," a "world that has come of age," and a "world coming of age."[30] Bonhoeffer seems to have been developing a realistic, theological language and way of thinking about the relation of God to the world. He thought it possible that doing away with a religious, "false conception of God, opens up a way of seeing the God of the Bible."[31] He thought that a world come of age would perhaps be closer to God exactly because it is "more godless."[32] In a 1944 message from prison, he indicated that, in a godless world, people "will once more be called so to utter the word of God that the world will be changed and renewed by it. It will be a new language, perhaps quite nonreligious, but liberating and redeeming—as was Jesus' language; it will shock people and yet overcome them by its power."[33]

Bonhoeffer intended nothing shallow by his talk of religionlessness, nothing like the "banal this-worldliness of the enlightened, the busy, the comfortable or the lascivious." Instead, he intended "the profound this-worldliness characterized by discipline and the constant knowledge of death and resur-rection."[34] Living in the belly of Nazi Germany did not allow him the luxury of dreaming that a world come of age would be a romantic idyll. This was to be a religionless world, not a sinless one. It was to be a world in which ma-ture people accept responsibility. Bethge helpfully points out that Bonhoef-fer had been using the term "autonomy" until it was replaced in his writing by the notion of "coming of age" and that this change of terms indicated his engagement with Kant's proposal that "the Enlightenment is the emergence of humanity from self-imposed immaturity. Immaturity is the incapacity to use one's own intelligence without the guidance of another person."[35] In a world come of age, humanity develops its own resources for taking respon-sibility. Christ has freed us for politics, for science, and for the liberal arts.[36]

In Bonhoeffer's thinking, this was a profound theological issue. The secularization of the world requires that we live in it without the working hypothesis of God, "that we have to live in the world *etsi deus non daretur.* And this is just what we do recognize—before God! God compels us to recognize it. So our coming of age leads us to a true recognition of our sit-uation before God. God would have us know that we must live as people who manage their lives without him."[37]

The church is thereby placed in a radically different role. Instead of ad-dressing us in our weakness, which the religious message exploits, she confronts us in our strength and responsibility and encourages and nur-tures them. The church can no longer, as Bethge puts it, "demonize world-liness, instead of helping human beings realize their true humanity."[38] And the church can no longer be a religious sanctuary to which people flee from the world. The church and the Christian, like Jesus, must enter the world fully and responsibly.

But, also like Jesus, the Christian's commitment to the world must have no share in triumphalism. Humans' realization of their true hu-manity, their taking responsibility, is given expression in the crucifixion. Because Christ is the person for others, his is the form that will mark us and our acting. Religiosity makes us look in our distress "to the power of God in the world: God is the *deus ex machina.* The Bible directs humans to God's powerlessness and suffering; only the suffering God can help."[39]

Because God is in the midst of the world in the form of the crucified Je-sus, our relation to God is not a religious, falsely transcendent relation to a highest, most powerful, supreme being. Instead "our relation to God is a new life in 'existence for others,' through participation in the being of Je-sus. The transcendental is not infinite and unattainable tasks, but the neighbor who is within reach in any given situation."[40] And our relation to our neighbors is correspondingly liberated from any need to trick or dominate them.

THE ARCANE DISCIPLINE

For persons to be set free for others, to become secular or worldly in this way, did not mean that they must abandon the worship that was critical to their understanding, action, and identity. To the contrary, their thinking and life must exhibit the ongoing interaction between discipleship and secularity.

Bonhoeffer had begun to reach this understanding already early in his life. His friends detected a change in him after his 1930–31 stay in the United States. He was in process of becoming a fully committed believer and not merely a theologian. He adopted a daily discipline of prayer, meditation, and reflective study of the Bible that he maintained for the rest of his life. (In 1942 he expressed amazement that, in the complexities of his theological and conspiratorial work, he could live for days without reading the Bible. He also found that reopening its pages was always accompanied by fresh wonder.)[41]

He came to speak of the *arcanum* of the Christian, the "arcane" or "secret discipline." The term originally referred to the early church's practice of admitting only baptized members to the celebration of the sacrament of the Lord's Supper. Such withdrawal of the community into a secret place appears to be the very kind of separation and retreat from the world that Bonhoeffer criticized as a fault of religion. There is no simple way to resolve the contradiction.

Prayer, worship, and the Bible nourished his exploration of worldliness and nonreligious Christianity. He maintained an incognito existence in the resistance movement in full solidarity with the other conspirators and at the same time practiced the arcane discipline of the Christian. His life was a performance of what he meant by the arcane and the worldly and their interdependence.

In Bonhoeffer's view, the church is not to be the world. It is to maintain its independent identity. The Confessing Church in Germany was, after all, *confessional*. It had a creed and made its confession of faith in the Barmen Declaration. It broke with other German Christians because the latter abandoned their creedal identity and surrendered to the world. The hard core of specific, theological, creedal commitment had been a focus of Bonhoeffer's from the start. He thought that the liberal theology of his German teachers wrongly allowed the world to set the church's agenda. And one of his concerns about the church in America was its self-conception as primarily denominational rather than as a church, as constituted not so much by creed as by culture, liturgy, community life, and organization.[42] In Germany, the creedal commitment of the Confessing Church required it to resist and strengthened it to do so.

Bonhoeffer did not think that religionlessness required abandonment of such distinguishing, creedal commitment. When the church is led into worldliness in a world come of age and is given a new language for addressing that world, it will still be identified as the church. Until then, the church maintains the traditional discipline in the traditional terms within the *arcanum* and is silent about it outside.

One function of the silence outside is what Bethge refers to as protection of "the world . . . from violation by religion."[43] Bonhoeffer's experience in prison provides an example of the point. In the midst of a bombing raid a fellow prisoner lay on the floor, exclaiming, "O God, O God!" Bonhoeffer offered no religious comfort: "All I did was to look at my watch and say, 'It won't last more than ten minutes now.' . . . I felt that it was wrong to force religion down his throat just then."[44]

Silence outside the *arcanum* also serves to cultivate solidarity with others. In the confusion in Germany as the war was ending, prisoners were haphazardly shuffled from one sometimes makeshift prison to another. Bonhoeffer was thrown together with a Russian, Kokorin, the nephew of the Communist leader Molotov. The day before Bonhoeffer would be executed was the Sunday after Easter. A fellow prisoner asked that he conduct worship. Reportedly he was reluctant to do so. Kokorin was an atheist, and as Bethge reports, Bonhoeffer "didn't want to ambush him with a worship service."[45] But at the request of other prisoners and with Kokorin's approval, he led the service.

In the meantime, awaiting an adequate language for addressing a world come of age, the traditional arcane discipline will continue to nourish believers in a way that "cannot be propagated or demonstrated externally."[46] This is a further and critical reason for silence outside the *arcanum*: the preservation of the integrity of the biblical story and the identity of the church. The mysteries of the faith must be defended against cheap and misleading public distribution.

The danger here is that protective secrecy creates exclusiveness and privilege. The hope is that the action of the discipline itself does not tolerate them: "In the *arcanum*," Bethge points out, "Christ takes everyone who really encounters him by the shoulder, turning them around to face their fellow human beings and the world."[47] Preservation of the mysteries paradoxically dismantles barriers. "In other words," he says, "the 'ultimate' is praised with the initiates gathered together, so that in the 'penultimate' stage there can be a share in godlessness. Christ prays a cultic psalm and dies a profane death."[48]

The interplay of "arcane discipline" and "worldliness" presented in Bonhoeffer's writings was climactically enacted in the last two days of his life. On Sunday, he led the worship that included an atheist. On Monday, he prayed before he was profanely hanged. His final recorded words, a message sent to a friend through a fellow prisoner: "This is the end—for me the beginning of life."[49]

ACTION

Bonhoeffer said that confession of faith is not to be confused with professing a religion. He thought the latter turned confession into propagandistic ammunition against the godless. Confession belongs in the *arcanum*. Outside of that context, the "primary confession of the Christian before the world is the deed which interprets itself. . . . The deed alone is our confession of faith before the world."[50] If neighbors are hungry, feed them. Neither evangelistic propaganda nor explanation accompanies the deed. To turn an act into a religious pitch, "running after people, proselytizing, every attempt to accomplish something in another person by our own power is vain and dangerous."[51]

It would certainly have been futile and dangerous for Bonhoeffer to attempt to explain his conspiracy against Hitler, or even to disclose his involvement in it to anyone other than a fellow conspirator. He could only act in the circumstance without interpreting the deed. Although in this "'inner exile' where he could no longer justify his actions before his church and fellow pastors,"[52] Bonhoeffer could nonetheless offer his fellow conspirators an encouraging, supportive interpretation of their actions. He did so in the form of an essay, "After Ten Years," done as a Christmas gift for them in 1942.[53]

When action requires the use of power, then "power enters the service of responsibility."[54] Bethge observes that, after the failure of a first coup attempt against Hitler, it became clear to the pacifist Bonhoeffer that "any opposition serious about stopping Hitler had to ensure that it held the instruments of power; only this could restrain him."[55] The necessary power was that of the army, and a military plot would be necessary to deploy it.

This was an extreme situation requiring extreme measures, but Bonhoeffer had no interest in a heroic ethics. He made it clear that action and the use of various forms of power belong to ordinary people in ordinary times. Wherever one person meets another, he said, "there arises genuine responsibility."[56] All the regular, diverse encounters that take place in our callings as parents, citizens, and laborers are occasions for responsible use of power.

God is fully and particularly in the world and engaged in its events. Hearing the call of Christ within our callings and acting in response to it in any given situation begins sensibly with an assessment of the facts, "a serious weighing up of the vocational duty which is directly given, of the dangers of interference in the responsibility of others, and finally the totality of the question which is involved."[57] This factual analysis is to be distinguished from the continuous hand-wringing of moralists who "assume that a person must continuously be doing something decisive, fulfilling some higher purpose."[58] It is instead "to recognize the significant in the factual."[59]

Bonhoeffer's unfinished essay on telling the truth, written during a period when he was under intense prison interrogation, is a good example of what factual assessment of a situation amounts to. "The more complex the actual situations of a person, the more responsible and more difficult will be the task of 'telling the truth,'" he wrote. "Telling the truth is, therefore, something which must be learnt."[60] It is no simple matter. Another example is Bonhoeffer's change of approach to the details of resistance. Early on, he had urged pastors and others to demonstrate their opposition publicly. But, as more members of the opposition were discharged from their positions, there was greater need for "people of character" to "remain at the controls at all costs and not let themselves be pushed out. That meant that things which had been issues of character now became mere bagatelles—greeting with the Hitler salute, for instance. Even if it meant giving up a 'clean slate,' they had to try to get into key positions. The use of camouflage became a moral duty."[61]

The process of weighing and judging the facts in a situation might well bar some courses of action and open others. It is a necessary start but will seldom yield a determinative answer of what to do—what to say to speak the truth, whether to give the Hitler salute, and the like. Rules, regulations, and principles provide no answer, and there is no guidebook. Nor is conscience a guide. Bonhoeffer discovered that "people whose only support is their conscience can never realize that a bad conscience may be stronger and more wholesome than a deluded one."[62] The use of camouflage as a moral duty is a recipe for a bad if healthy conscience.

After assessing the facts and possibilities of a given situation, Bonhoeffer said, "I shall be guided in the one direction or the other by a free responsibility towards the call of Jesus Christ."[63] The "I shall be guided" engages the whole person and the full range of apperception, intuition, and sensibility. It is not mysterious to people nourished by the arcane discipline. It is a function of the interaction of responsibility and freedom: the responsibility that is "the freedom of humans . . . given only in the obligation to God and our neighbor."[64] Even conscience is set free; it is free "to enter into the guilt of another person for the other person's sake."[65]

Assessment of facts and the guidance that comes with it lack mystery, but they do not lack ambiguity. Ambiguity remains because our decisions are not made for us. Our binding to God and our neighbor really does free us to take responsibility. Given ambiguity, we nonetheless take action. "Responsible action is a free venture; it is not justified by any law; it is performed without any claim to a valid self-justification, and therefore also without any claim to an ultimate valid knowledge of good and evil."[66] Succumbing to the temptation to know good and evil was the originating sin. Because we have been freed to act for others in response to the call of Christ and because we are free to accept responsibility where ambiguity accompanies the need for action, we are also free to accept guilt.

Free responsibility "depends on a God who demands responsible action in a bold venture of faith, and who promises forgiveness and consolation to the person who becomes a sinner in that venture."[67] So we seek forgiveness in place of self-justification. And although forgiveness is not cheaply given, it is freely given, thus making public action possible. As Jean Bethke Elshtain puts it: One "acts in full knowledge of guilt. One knows one cannot expiate the wrong one has committed. But one embraces forgiveness—what Hannah Arendt calls Christianity's greatest contribution to politics."[68]

Our relation to God is not religious. It is "a new life in 'existence for others,' through participation in the being of Jesus."[69] We are not to apply Christ's teachings directly to the world, and we are certainly not to apply "Christian principles." Rather, nurtured by the arcane discipline, we take freely responsible action when we are "drawn in into the form of Jesus Christ . . . when the form of Jesus Christ itself works upon us in such a manner that it molds our form in its own likeness."[70]

No deus ex machina appeared in Hitler's Germany. Bonhoeffer had to act. He did not shrink from using power and taking responsibility for it. He assumed the guilt of conspiracy and died a profane death. No deus ex machina appeared, but God was there, in the thick of the action.

> The God who lets us live in the world without the working hypothesis of God is the God before whom we stand continually. Before God and with God we live without God. God lets himself be pushed out of the world on to the

cross. He is weak and powerless in the world, and that is precisely the way, the only way, in which he is with us and helps us.[71]

THE NATURAL

Imprisonment sharpened Bonhoeffer's appreciation of the natural world. In a letter to his parents he recorded the intense pleasure he took from permitted walks in the prison yard with its nesting tomtits, anthill, and bees. But he also told them that the prisoner "may react too strongly to anything sentimental that affects him personally," and he should take "a cold shower of common sense and humor, to avoid losing his sense of proportion." He added, "I believe it is just here that Christianity, rightly understood, can help particularly."[72]

His unsentimental appreciation of the natural arose out of an understanding of nature as penultimate, the thing before the last, the preparation for the coming of Christ. "With respect to its origin," he wrote, the natural world "is called creation." "With respect to its goal it is called the 'kingdom of God.'"[73] By deriving his understanding of nature from the priority of Christ, Bonhoeffer joined Barth in recovering the category of the natural from a stern Protestant theology that had made nature the antithesis of grace. In Bonhoeffer's view, the natural is opposed to the unnatural and not to grace. It enjoys a positive relation to grace. Bonhoeffer also joined Barth in opposing the Roman Catholic regard for nature based on an analogy of being between the natural world and God. He believed that respect for nature is grounded in christology: "The natural is that which, after the Fall, is directed toward the coming of Christ."[74]

Because it is penultimate, nature cannot rule us in any of its forms, including that of natural law. But, because it is penultimate, nature is an end as well as a means and is to be cherished rather than exploited. As "the outer covering of the ultimate," nature has its own time and place supplied by Christ the ultimate.[75]

Nature prepares the way for the coming of the kingdom of God, and since that kingdom is always near at hand, natural life is an expectant political one. It is lived in a nexus of responsibility for others: "To provide the hungry person with bread is to prepare the way for the coming of grace."[76] Bonhoeffer was very careful in his expression of the obligations the natural entails. He said that "natural life must be lived within the framework of certain definite rights and certain definite duties." The order in his formula is critical. It constitutes a rejection of the order proposed by Kant who spoke first of duties and only later of rights. Bonhoeffer insisted on the biblical witness in which what is given to life comes first. What is demanded comes after. "God gives before he demands."[77]

REALITY

The worldly life, the arcane life, the responsibly active life, the natural life—these are all ways of talking about the human life that life in Christ is.[78] "To be Christian does not mean to be religious in a particular way, to make something of oneself . . . on the basis of some method or other, but to be human—not a type of human, but the human that Christ creates in us."[79] The human so created is authentically human. This is who we truly are and who we are meant to be. In this way, "the irreconcilable conflict between what is and what should be is reconciled in Christ, that is to say, in the ultimate reality."[80]

Bonhoeffer cautioned that in order to think about reality and the really human, it "is necessary to free oneself from the way of thinking which sets out from human problems and which asks for solutions on this basis." We must abandon the religious way of thinking that allows the penultimate to set the agenda for the ultimate and restrict discussion to what we think our needs to be. "The way of Jesus Christ, and therefore the way to all Christian thinking, leads not from the world to God but from God to the world."[81] We begin with the reality of God. And since the reality of God "has become manifest in Christ in the reality of the world," we cannot partake of one apart from the other anymore than we can divide the divinity of Christ from his humanity.[82] There is not a godly sphere separate from a worldly sphere. There is the one reality of Christ.

What we know of God, we know from Jesus. He is the reality of God in the world.

Jesus is also the reality of the human in the world. "Theologically expressed, human beings only know who they are from the perspective of God."[83] In Jesus we see the human from the perspective of God. We see who we authentically are. And to be conformed with him, Bonhoeffer says, "that is to be a real person."[84]

The human reality of Christ in the world is always social.[85] Christ takes form in the church. "So the Church is not a religious community of worshipers of Christ but is Christ himself who has taken form among people."[86] One can never become a new person, one conformed with Christ, as a solitary individual. One becomes a member of the body of Christ. "The new person is not the individual believer who has been justified and sanctified, but the Church, the Body of Christ, Christ himself."[87] The church, Bonhoeffer concludes, is "nothing but a section of humanity in which Christ has really taken form."[88] As the form of Christ, the church cannot separate itself from the world. It summons "the world into the fellowship of this body of Christ, to which in truth [the world] already belongs." Its sole difference from the world is the fact that it affirms in faith "God's acceptance of [all humanity] which is the property of the whole world."[89]

THE COMMANDMENT OF GOD

In his 1937 book *Discipleship*, Bonhoeffer said that following Jesus liberates people "from the hard yoke of their own laws" and allows them to submit "to the kindly yoke of Jesus Christ"—but only by single-mindedly following his command to absolute discipleship.[90] Grace is costly because it requires submission to Christ; it is grace because the burden is light.[91] Paul Lehmann detected a certain scorn of the world, an ultra-Lutheranism, just below the surface of this book.[92]

In a 1944 letter to Eberhard Bethge, Bonhoeffer said he could now see that *Discipleship* had marked the end of a long period during which he had sought to "acquire faith by trying to live a holy life" and that he had subsequently learned how it is "only by living completely in this world that one learns to have faith."[93] He said he could see dangers in the book even though he still stood by it.

Lehmann suggested that the difference between *Discipleship* and the later, unfinished writings was Bonhoeffer's steady preoccupation with "the dialectic between faith and worldliness." He proposed that Bonhoeffer had increasingly moved from "response to the Lordship of Christ in the church to response to the Lordship of Christ in and over the world."[94] In Bonhoeffer's late work, the command of God together with what he called "mandates" become references for Christ's worldly lordship and the worldliness of his disciples.

This movement is reflected in Bonhoeffer's reflections on the church's uses of the law.[95] In the Lutheran tradition, there are three uses of this law in Christian preaching: (1) believers' accomplishment of external works; (2) their recognition of their opposition to the law and their just condemnation; and (3) "as a rule of conduct for converts and as a punishment for the flesh."[96] The first use of the law, Bonhoeffer said, demonstrates that the church "does not leave the world to its own devices."[97] It is directed to secular institutions rather than to Christians in secular institutions, and "is not concerned with the christianizing of the secular institutions or with subordinating them to the Church, that is to say, with abolishing their relative autonomy; it is concerned rather with their true worldliness or 'naturalness' in obedience to God's word."[98]

The commandment of God is not a negation of the world but an affirmation of Christ's dominion in and over it. Besides forbidding and commanding, God's law joins the gospel in freeing us for action in the world. It is different "from all human laws in that it commands freedom"; it frees the person to live in the world as a person before God—as a person rather than "as a taker of ethical decisions or as a student of ethics."[99] We need not play Hercules at the crossroads, always striving to make the right decision, for the commandment frees us from the anxiety of decision making.[100] It sets us free by binding us.

Marriage is an example of Bonhoeffer's point.[101] With the binding of one person to another in marriage, understood as an institution mandated by God, "there comes an inner freedom . . . of life and action." The divine prohibition of adultery removes that subject as a preoccupying issue, and in the process the command becomes the liberating "permission to live in marriage in freedom and certainty."[102]

Psalm 119 is an artfully wrought, long poem on the law. Bonhoeffer had hoped to write on it but was able to complete meditations on only some of its verses, including verse 19: "I am a sojourner on earth; hide not thy commandments from me!" A comment he makes in response to this poem captures his understanding of God's commandment as freeing us for worldly life:

> The earth that nourishes me has a right to my work and my strength. It is not fitting that I should despise the earth on which I have my life; I owe it faithfulness and gratitude. I must not dream away my earthly life with thoughts of heaven and thereby evade my lot—that I must be a sojourner and a stranger—and with it God's call into the world of strangers. There is a very godless homesickness for the other world, and it will certainly not produce any homecoming. I am to be a sojourner, with everything that entails. I should not close my heart indifferently to earth's problems, sorrows and joys; and I am to wait patiently for the redemption of the divine promise— really wait, and not rob myself of it in advance by wishing and dreaming.[103]

MANDATES

God's commandment is "clear, definite and concrete to the last detail," Bonhoeffer said, and it comes to us in one form as "mandates."[104] There are principally four mandates understood from the Bible and history to be the will of God: family, labor, government, and church.[105] They allow us to live in the world with security and quietude in the regular flow of daily life without necessarily being always aware of the commandment.

The bearers of the mandates are deputies of God, and we owe them the duty of obedience.[106] Nevertheless, in fulfilling our mandated duties, we are to remember that it is not the duties themselves or the bearer of the mandate but Christ who calls us. And Christ's call "is never a sanctioning of worldly institutions as such; its 'yes' to them always includes at the same time an extremely emphatic 'no,' an extremely sharp protest against the world."[107] Accordingly, where a particular instance of labor, marriage, government or church "persistently and arbitrarily violates the assigned task, then the divine mandate lapses" in that instance.[108]

THE MANDATE OF GOVERNMENT

According to Bonhoeffer, the concept of the state is pagan in origin, and the New Testament replaces it with the concept of "government." The latter implies no particular form of state. Government, he says, is "the power which creates and maintains order," and is the "divinely ordained authority to exercise worldly dominion by divine right. Government is deputyship for God on earth."[109]

Bonhoeffer thereby abandoned traditional stances of both Roman Catholic and Reformation theology. Roman Catholic theology viewed the state as derived from creation and human nature. The Reformation tradition thought it to originate in response to sin. Bonhoeffer held that "the true basis of government is . . . Jesus Christ Himself"—Christ, rather than natural law.[110]

Although government "cannot itself produce or engender life" and "is not creative," it is preservative.[111] Government serves Christ's dominion on earth "in maintaining by the power of the sword an outward justice in which life is preserved and is thus held open for Christ." For Christ's sake, government is to be obeyed, and the "demand for obedience is unconditional and qualitatively total."[112]

Obedience for Christ's sake is required quite apart from the way any particular form of government comes into being. Government is an institution of God no matter if the human path to governmental office "repeatedly passes through guilt, no matter if almost every crown is stained with guilt (cf. Shakespeare's histories)."[113] And the citizen-believer enjoys no luxury of ethical isolation from a share in the guilt. "There is no glory in standing amid the ruins of one's native town in the consciousness that at least one has not oneself incurred any guilt."[114]

This is a very strong argument for involved obedience in the ordinary circumstances of life, but Bonhoeffer qualified it. The obligation to obey is not binding if government forfeits its claim by openly denying its commission and compelling offense against the divine commandment.[115] Should that happen, disobedience must be considered. Bonhoeffer was very careful to say that disobedience is "a venture undertaken on one's own responsibility."[116] No higher or greater claim can be made for it. His participation in the conspiracy against Hitler became the interpretive demonstration of what he meant the venture of disobedience to be.

THE MANDATE OF CHURCH

The church fulfills its divine mandate when she proclaims the lordship of Christ. Because this proclamation enables the Word to be realized in the world, the church acts as deputy for the world and exists for its sake.[117] Its announcement that its Lord is also the lord of the world carries with it no authority to claim that secular institutions are to be subservient to the church and no authority to attempt to Christianize the state or its ministers. Its commissioned message is the message of the world's liberation and not of its subordination to the church. "The purpose and aim of the dominion of Christ is not to make the worldly order godly or to subordinate it to the Church but to set it free for true worldliness."[118] The office of the church is to free the world to be the world.

CHURCH AND STATE

Just as the mandate of government implies no particular form of the state, it also implies no single form of church-state relations. Whatever the form, Bonhoeffer argued, always essential to it is the church's responsibility to proclaim the dominion of Jesus Christ over the state as well as the church. Its aim in doing so "is not that government should pursue a Christian policy ... but that it should be true government" in obedience to Christ.[119] Bonhoeffer clearly did not think in terms of two, separate realms for church and state.

The emancipation of the state to be the state takes place in its encounter with the proclamation and life of the church. The state, therefore, serves its own best interest when it supports this encounter by making room for the church. Bonhoeffer's notion of "making room" for the church should not be misread. In his visits to America he had heard much talk of religious freedom, where "freedom" meant "the possibility of unhindered activity given by the world to the church." Bonhoeffer was critical of such talk. He understood the freedom of the church not as the possibility but as the power of the gospel to make "room for itself on earth." This freedom "is not the gift of the world to the church, but the freedom of the Word of God itself to gain a hearing." Bonhoeffer thought that the American churches' praise of freedom can stem from a pact with the world "in which the true freedom of the Word of God is surrendered."[120] If the state makes room for the church, any gift it bestows is a gift to itself: the possibility of its own liberation in encounter with the proclamation of the Word. Bonhoeffer had in mind a coexistence of church and state characterized by mutual limitation and tension.[121]

The church should continually remind the state of government's divine commission and draw attention to its shortcomings when it is derelict. Although no particular form of state is necessary, Bonhoeffer did think that there are some types relatively better than others in fulfilling government's commission. A state is relatively better when it makes the divine origin of government evident. It is relatively better when it sustains its power by doing justice, specifically by protecting the rights of family and labor and by protecting the proclamation of the gospel. And it is relatively better when it attaches itself to its subjects by just action and truthful speech.[122] These characteristics of the better state could be read as possible general subjects of the church's exhortation to the state.

The church does not fulfill its responsibility of proclamation to the state by offering "dogmatically correct delivery" or "general ethical principles." "What is needed is concrete instruction in the concrete situation."[123] There is no Christian solution for the world's problems, and instruction cannot be based on some rational or natural law knowledge that the church shares with the world.[124] Rather, instruction "follows solely from the preaching of Christ." Then "by the authority of the word of God," the church will necessarily declare wrong such things as "economic attitudes or forms . . . which obviously obstruct belief in Jesus Christ." Additionally, "not by the authority of God but merely on the authority of the responsible advice of Christian specialists and experts, she will be able to make her contribution towards the establishment of a new order."[125]

If government abandons its commission, it acts on its own without divine mandate, and the church's responsibility may take different shape. Bonhoeffer had to confront the subject in April 1933, when the German government adopted the Aryan Clause excluding Jews from civil service and cultural life, including church office for those who had converted to Christianity. He wrote *The Church and the Jewish Question* for a church group assembled to take action.[126] In this tract, Bonhoeffer proposed that the church is compelled to question the state about the legitimacy of its action when it provides either too much or too little law and order. It provides "too little" law and order, "if any group of subjects [is] deprived of their rights, too much where the state [intervenes] in the character of the church and its proclamation, e.g. in the forced exclusion of baptized Jews from . . . Christian congregations." In the latter case, the church must reject the encroachment because of the church's "better knowledge of the state and the limitations of its action." Such confrontation of the state is the first possibility for church action. The church can also then aid the victims as part of its "unconditional obligation to the victims of any ordering society, even if they do not belong to the Christian community." And, finally, it can not only "bandage the victims under the wheel, but . . . put a spoke in the wheel itself."[127]

Bonhoeffer was the first pastor to identify Nazi treatment of Jews as critical and central, and his proposal was remarkable in its time and place. That the church should "put a spoke in the wheel" of the state was a singular statement for a Lutheran to make to Lutherans.

SOLIDARITY WITH THE OPPRESSED: BONHOEFFER'S LEGACY

Geffrey Kelly and Burton Nelson, the editors of *A Testament to Freedom*, a highly acclaimed presentation of selected Bonhoeffer writings, chose as the title for their introduction "Solidarity with the Oppressed" because they believed that it states the animating heart of his conspiratorial life and late theology.[128] Bonhoeffer had written, perhaps to his fellow conspirators, "We have for once learnt to see the great events of world history from below, from the perspective of the outcast, the suspects, the maltreated, the powerless, the oppressed, the reviled—in short, from the perspective of those who suffer." He added that justice must be done "from a higher satisfaction, whose foundation is beyond any talk of 'from below' or 'from above.'"[129]

Paul Lehmann suggested that this perspective accounts for the shift in Bonhoeffer's expression of his central question. In a letter of June 30, 1944, two months after he asked "who Christ really is for us today," Bonhoeffer wrote, "Let me just summarize briefly what I am concerned about—how to claim for Jesus Christ a world that has come of age."[130] Lehmann proposed that the difference in formulation was "a sign of Bonhoeffer's own move from the implicit to the explicit in the obedience of faith, from the perspective of the powerful upon the story to the story from the perspective of those who suffer."[131] Bonhoeffer had now learned to see events from the perspective of the outcast because he had been cast out. His solidarity with the oppressed is his response to the question about how to claim for Jesus Christ a world come of age.

Bonhoeffer's proposal that the church—and not just the individual Christian—must "put a spoke in the wheel" of a state bent on oppressing Jews was unique. Nonetheless, it was still burdened with statements indicating that Bonhoeffer was not yet free of the anti-Semitism of his culture and his religious tradition. "We were against Hitler's church policy," Bethge repentantly said years after the war, "but at the same time we were anti- Semites."[132] Bethge had grown in self-critical understanding, and it is likely that Bonhoeffer, too, would have done so or had done so in fact. By the time he was writing his *Ethics*, he had come to see that "an expulsion of the Jews from the West must necessarily bring with it the expulsion of Christ. For Jesus Christ was a Jew."[133] And he declared that the church was "guilty of the deaths of the weakest and most defenseless brothers and sisters of Christ."[134]

The German treatment of Jews was central and critical for Bonhoeffer's thinking in later life. But Bonhoeffer had likely already learned something of the meaning of "solidarity with the oppressed" earlier during his time in New York, where he witnessed the American treatment of African Americans. The Abyssinian Baptist Church in New York, where he was a regular participant, would have given him early instruction on this theme. Josiah Young wagers "that Bonhoeffer's ongoing commitment to obey Christ concretely . . . was related to the 'visible emotion' of the black worship that he experienced."[135] Bonhoeffer's thought and life would later make a return gift, for young African American ministers, "desperate to understand the racial injustice that surrounded them . . . looked to Bonhoeffer for theological insight."[136] It was the ministers of The Sanctified Church, the Soul Saving Station, who introduced Young to Bonhoeffer's work.[137] They found in Bonhoeffer's witness a strengthening "denunciation of the racism that threatens to sabotage the possibilities for life together."[138]

The fruits of Bonhoeffer's solidarity with the oppressed and his theological interpretation of it have also nourished liberation theology. "Most of us, South of the Rio Grande, experience an overwhelming, incomprehensible nightmare," Otto Maduro writes. "This may be why, of all the modern, liberal Christian theologians, Dietrich Bonhoeffer is the closest to our hearts."[139] Clarke Chapman explains that liberation theologians particularly welcome Bonhoeffer's "vision of ultimate reality, a vision that undermines oppression."[140] But he adds that the reception has not been uncritical, and he offers the example of Gustavo Gutierrez's criticism that economic and social analysis are missing from Bonhoeffer's theology.

When Bonhoeffer "speaks of a world come of age he never refers to the underside of this world."[141]

The Seventh International Bonhoeffer Congress was held in 1996 in Cape Town, South Africa. Bonhoeffer has been the subject of academic study in South Africa, but also and more significantly, John de Gruchy reports, participants in the struggle for justice and liberation "discovered fragments of his theology which have helped them remain faithful and hopeful."[142] De Gruchy says that Bonhoeffer has been a particular challenge to members of the white elite and has helped liberate them to be of some use in seeking solidarity with the victims and enemies of apartheid.[143]

Chung Hyun Kyung, a theologian from South Korea, invited to address the Bonhoeffer Congress in South Africa, said she had "stopped reading dead white European men's theologies and memoirs" after completing her doctorate but reacquainted herself with Bonhoeffer in preparation for the Congress.[144] She had been introduced to his life and thought by her participation in the persecuted Korean Christian Student movement, for which Bonhoeffer was the "major theological mentor."[145] The Western orientation of his theology led Koreans to lose interest in him, she said, but young pastors returned to Bonhoeffer in the late 1980s in their search for identity during the period of Korea's rapid secularization.

Kyung tested Bonhoeffer's designation of Jesus as the exemplary "man for others." She found that it did not work as "women for others" because of its oppressive patriarchal overtones: Women are already compelled to be for others and now need to be for themselves first.[146] For similar reasons she questioned Bonhoeffer's emphasis on suffering and death. She thought it ill suited for Asian women: "We ask not what we can die for, because our children's lives are dependent on us. We ask rather what we can live for?"[147] The present need "is to find the way to invigorate Life in our midst."[148]

Chung Hyun Kyung's presentation was cast as an imagined letter to Bonhoeffer. One can imagine a reply in which Bonhoeffer eagerly encourages further correspondence and questioning. He begins by repeating a statement he had made earlier in another context: "I [too] should like to speak of God . . . not in weakness but in strength; and therefore not in death and guilt but in human life and goodness."[149] Women have rights, he says, and a rightful need to embrace themselves even as God embraces them. And he asks about discoveries for ways to invigorate Life that she and other Asian women have made. His question springs from a keenly felt hope.

For years, Bonhoeffer sought to travel to Asia. Not long after he took up a pastorate in London in 1933, he wrote his brother Karl-Friedrich that, since he was "becoming more convinced each day that Christianity is approaching its end in the West—at least in its previous form and its previous interpretation—I should like to go to the Far East."[150] To Barth's great puzzlement, Bonhoeffer laid plans for a trip to India, where he would stay with Gandhi. He wanted to learn from Asian spirituality and political action. He would not be shopping for religions. Nor would he abandon or dilute the arcane discipline. He suspected he would be led to possibilities for the arcane discipline's new forms and new interpretation. He would celebrate God's love of all things human.

It was not to be. As Bethge put it, Bonhoeffer had "presented the path of liberation of the [W]estern spirit, law, philosophy, and secular life."[151] He would be denied firsthand exposure to the path of liberation of Eastern spirituality, thought, and political action presented by people like Gandhi and, now, Chung Hyun Kyung.

NOTES

1. Eberhard Bethge, *Dietrich Bonhoeffer: A Biography*, ed. Victoria Barnett (Minneapolis: Fortress, 2000), 886.
2. John Leith, ed., *Creeds of the Churches* (Garden City, N.Y.: Anchor Books, 1963), 520.
3. Bethge, *Dietrich Bonhoeffer*, 607.
4. Dietrich Bonhoeffer, *A Testament to Freedom: The Essential Writings of Dietrich Bonhoeffer*, ed. Geffrey B. Kelly and F. Burton Nelson (San Francisco: HarperCollins, 1990), 504.
5. Bethge, *Dietrich Bonhoeffer*, 678.
6. Ibid., 792.
7. Other members of Bonhoeffer's family were also involved. Bonhoeffer's assignments included such tasks as passing on information to Allied sources and seeking information on possible peace terms and aims. The lasting merit of his participation may lie in what Bethge says is his "effective witness" from inside the conspiracy as "a Christian theologian of the resistance." Ibid., 796; see also ibid., 626–702.
8. Dietrich Bonhoeffer, *Letters and Papers from Prison*, ed. Eberhard Bethge, trans. Reginald Fuller (New York: Simon & Schuster, 1997), 328. Stanley Hauerwas says that Bonhoeffer's offhand remark betrays the deep continuity between the two theologians. Hauerwas, *With the Grain of the Universe* (Grand Rapids, Mich.: Brazos Press, 2001), 190 n. 37.
9. Quoted in the introduction to Bonhoeffer, *A Testament to Freedom*, 10.
10. Paul Lehmann, *Ethics in a Christian Context* (New York: Harper & Row, 1963), *The Transformation of Politics* (New York: Harper & Row, 1975), and *The Decalogue and a Human Future* (Grand Rapids, Mich.: Eerdmans, 1995).
11. William Hamilton, "A Secular Theology for a World Come of Age," *Theology Today* 18 (1962): 440; quoted in Ralf Wüstenberg, "Bonhoeffer's Christianity:

Dietrich Bonhoeffer's Tegel Theology," in *Bonhoeffer for a New Day*, ed. John W. de Gruchy (Grand Rapids, Mich.: Eerdmans, 1996), 58.

12. John A. T. Robinson, *Honest to God* (London: SCM, 1963).

13. Harvey Cox, *The Secular City* (New York: Macmillan, 1965).

14. Dietrich Bonhoeffer, *Discipleship*, trans. Martin Kaske and Ilse Tödt, *Dietrich Bonhoeffer Works* (Minneapolis: Fortress Press, 1996), vol. 6; Dietrich Bonhoeffer, *Life Together*, trans. John Doberstein (New York: Harper & Row, 1954).

15. Dietrich Bonhoeffer, *The Communion of Saints*, trans. Ronald Gregor Smith et al. (New York: Harper & Row, 1963); and *Act and Being*, trans. Bernard Noble (New York: Harper & Row, 1962). All of his works have been assembled and published in German in the seventeen volumes of the *Dietrich Bonhoeffer Werke*, now being translated into English as *Dietrich Bonhoeffer Works*. The International Bonhoeffer Society maintains a web site at http://www.dbonhoeffer.org that provides information about Bonhoeffer studies, as well as the society's activities.

16. Bonhoeffer, *A Testament to Freedom*, 127.

17. Ibid., 118.

18. Ralf Wüstenberg, *A Theology of Life* (Grand Rapids, Mich.: Eerdmans, 1998), 51.

19. Karl Barth, *The Epistle to the Romans*, trans. Edwyn C. Hoskyns, 3d ed. (London: Oxford University Press, 1953), 258–259.

20. Karl Barth, *Church Dogmatics*, 4 vols. (Edinburgh: T & T Clark, 1936–61), 1:280–361.

21. Bonhoeffer, *Letters and Papers*, 328.

22. Bethge, *Dietrich Bonhoeffer*, 872.

23. Bonhoeffer, *Letters and Papers*, 279.

24. Ibid., 362.

25. Ibid., 281–282.

26. Ibid., 341.

27. Ibid., 345.

28. Ibid., 280–281.

29. Ibid., 346.

30. Bonhoeffer's thinking about autonomy and maturity—a world come of age—drew upon Wilhelm Dilthey's philosophy of life. See generally Wüstenberg, *A Theology of Life*.

31. Bonhoeffer, *Letters and Papers*, 361–362.

32. Ibid., 362.

33. Ibid., 300.

34. Ibid., 369.

35. Quoted in Bethge, *Dietrich Bonhoeffer*, 867.

36. W. H. Auden expresses it this way:

Because in Him the Flesh is united to the Word without magical transformation, Imagination is redeemed from promiscuous fornication with her own images. . . .

Because in Him all passions find a logical In-Order-That, by Him is the
perpetual recurrence of Art assured. . . .
Because in Him the Word is united to the Flesh without loss of perfection,
Reason is redeemed from incestuous fixation on her own logic. . . .
Because in Him abstraction finds a passionate For-The-Sake-Of, by Him is
the continuous development of Science assured.

W. H. Auden, "For the Time Being," in *The Collected Poetry of W. H. Auden*
(New York: Random House, 1945), 405.

37. Bonhoeffer, *Letters and Papers*, 360.
38. Bethge, *Dietrich Bonhoeffer*, 869.
39. Bonhoeffer, *Letters and Papers*, 361.
40. Bonhoeffer, *A Testament to Freedom*, 536.
41. Bethge, *Dietrich Bonhoeffer*, 721–722.
42. Dietrich Bonhoeffer, *No Rusty Swords*, ed. Edwin H. Robertson, trans. Edwin
    H. Robertson and John Bowden (London: Collins, 1965), 100–101.
43. Bethge, *Dietrich Bonhoeffer*, 882–883.
44. Bonhoeffer, *Letters and Papers*, 199.
45. Bethge, *Dietrich Bonhoeffer*, 926.
46. Ibid., 882.
47. Ibid., 883.
48. Ibid., 884.
49. Quoted ibid., 927. The message was sent through the English officer Payne
    Best to Bonhoeffer's friend in England, the Bishop of Chichester. Ibid., 927,
    1022 n. 54.
50. Bonhoeffer, *A Testament to Freedom*, 91. See also the formulation, "our being
    Christian today will be limited to two things: prayer and righteous action
    among people." Bonhoeffer, *Letters and Papers*, 300.
51. Bonhoeffer, *Discipleship*, 172.
52. Bonhoeffer, *A Testament to Freedom*, 506.
53. Bonhoeffer, *Letters and Papers*, 1–17.
54. Dietrich Bonhoeffer, *Ethik*, in *Dietrich Bonhoeffer Werke*, 6:244.
55. Bethge, *Dietrich Bonhoeffer*, 627.
56. Dietrich Bonhoeffer, *Ethics*, trans. Neville Horton Smith (New York: Simon &
    Schuster, 1995), 247.
57. Ibid., 245.
58. Ibid., 260.
59. Ibid., 71.
60. Ibid., 359.
61. Bethge, *Dietrich Bonhoeffer*, 628.
62. Bonhoeffer, *Letters and Papers*, 4.
63. Bonhoeffer, *Ethics*, 254.
64. Ibid., 244.

65. Ibid., 240.

66. Ibid., 245.

67. Bonhoeffer, *Letters and Papers*, 6.

68. Jean Bethke Elshtain, "Freedom and Responsibility in a World Come of Age," in *Theology and the Practice of Responsibility: Essays on Dietrich Bonhoeffer*, ed. Wayne Whitson Floyd, Jr. and Charles Marsh (Valley Forge, Pa.: Trinity Press International, 1994), 277. There was a Bonhoeffer-like quality to William Stringfellow's practice of law. He found that any practice of law is an engagement in politics, power, and violence and that religion had nothing positive to do with such things. He was totally reliant on the grace of God that freed him for an exuberant practice of law. See chapter 7, this volume.

69. Bonhoeffer, *Letters and Papers*, 210.

70. Bonhoeffer, *Ethics*, 81–82.

71. Bonhoeffer, *Letters and Papers*, 360.

72. Ibid., 71.

73. Bonhoeffer, *Ethics*, 191.

74. Ibid., 143. In his lectures on christology, Bonhoeffer had explained: "In the sacrament of the Church, the old enslaved creature is set free to its new freedom. As the center of human existence and of history, Christ was the fulfillment of the unfulfilled law, i.e., their reconciliation. But nature is creation under the curse—not guilt, for it lacks freedom. Thus nature finds in Christ as its center, not reconciliation, but redemption. Once again, this redemption, which happens in Christ, is not evident, nor can it be proved, but it is proclaimed. The word of preaching is that enslaved nature is redeemed in hope. A sign of this is given in the sacraments, where elements of the old creation are become elements of the new. In the sacraments they are set free from their dumbness and proclaim directly to the believer the new creative Word of God. They no longer need the explanation of man. Enslaved nature does not speak the Word of God to us directly. But the sacraments do. In the sacrament, Christ is the mediator between nature and God and stands for all creatures before God." Bonhoeffer, *A Testament to Freedom*, 127.

75. Bonhoeffer, *Ethics*, 131.

76. Ibid., 136.

77. Ibid., 150.

78. In prison, Bonhoeffer undertook a systematic reading of Wilhelm Dilthey, from whom he had drawn his thinking about a world come of age. Bonhoeffer's emphasis on "life" is a further reflection of his dependence on Dilthey. As opposed to metaphysics and abstraction, Dilthey's "point of departure is always human life as it is actually lived in a particular epoch." Wüstenberg, *A Theology of Life*, 104. Bonhoeffer had read William James during his time at Union Seminary in New York, and James, too, was an important influence in his thinking about life as well as his thinking about religionlessness. Ibid., 96. Bonhoeffer arrived at his own nonreligious, theological interpretation of "life": Authentically human life is life in Christ in being for others.

79. Bonhoeffer, *Letters and Papers*, 361.

80. Bonhoeffer, *Ethics*, 192–193.

81. Ibid., 351.

82. Ibid., 195.

83. Dietrich Bonhoeffer, *Who Is Christ for Us?* ed. and trans. Craig Nessan and Renate Wind (Minneapolis: Fortress Press, 2002), 34.

84. Bonhoeffer, *Ethics*, 82.

85. See Clifford Green, *Dietrich Bonhoeffer: A Theology of Sociality* (Grand Rapids, Mich.: Eerdmans, 1999).

86. Bonhoeffer, *Ethics*, 84.

87. Bethge, *Dietrich Bonhoeffer*, 455.

88. Bonhoeffer, *Ethics*, 85.

89. Ibid., 203.

90. Bonhoeffer, *Discipleship*, 39.

91. Ibid., 45.

92. Paul Lehmann, "Faith and Worldliness in Bonhoeffer's Thought," in *Bonhoeffer in a World Come of Age*, ed. Peter Vorkink (Philadelphia: Fortress Press, 1968), 37.

93. Bonhoeffer, *Letters and Papers*, 369.

94. Lehmann, "Faith and Worldliness," 38.

95. In August 1942, Bonhoeffer presented a study of the subject to a group of the Confessing Church appointed to prepare a declaration on the Commandment "Thou shalt not kill." Bethge, *Dietrich Bonhoeffer*, 709. The subject of Bonhoeffer's paper was the first use of the law, which, he said, concerns the Church's responsibility for the world. In the preaching of the law, the congregation will be reminded of the universality of its mission to the world. Otherwise "it would become a mere religious association." Bonhoeffer, *Ethics*, 311. After Bonhoeffer's imprisonment, the Confessing Church adopted a statement on the Fifth Commandment that denounced the "elimination" of Jews and called for reading a message on a day of repentance that included the statement: "Woe to us and our nation if it is held to be justified to kill people because they belong to another race." Quoted in Bethge, *Dietrich Bonhoeffer*, 709.

96. Bonhoeffer, *Ethics*, 301.

97. Ibid., 321.

98. Ibid.

99. Ibid., 277.

100. Ibid., 279, 276.

101. Ibid., 272.

102. Ibid., 276.

103. Quoted in Bethge, *Dietrich Bonhoeffer*, 620. For his Psalm 114 meditations, see Dietrich Bonhoeffer, *Meditations on the Word*, ed. and trans. David M. Gracie (Cambridge, Mass.: Cowley, 1986).

104. Bonhoeffer, *Ethics*, 273. He opposed that term to the traditional Lutheran terms "orders of creation" and "orders of preservation," which were subject to appropriation by Nazi ideology.

105. Ibid., 272–274.

106. Ibid., 282.

107. Ibid., 251.

108. Ibid., 205.

109. Ibid., 327.

110. Ibid., 332. Bonhoeffer argued that natural law "can furnish equally cogent arguments in favor of the state which is founded on force and the state which is founded on justice, for the nation-state and for imperialism, for democracy and for dictatorship. A solid basis is afforded only by the biblical derivation of government from Jesus Christ. Whether and to what extent a new natural law can be established on this foundation is a theological question which still remains open." Ibid., 334. The state will take actions that are not Christian but that do not exclude Christ if the second table of the Decalogue as a criterion has become known from the preaching of the Church. In pagan governments, there is "a providential congruity between the contents of the second table and the inherent law of historical life itself. Failure to observe the second table destroys the very life which government is charged with preserving. . . . Does this mean that the state is after all based on natural law? No; for in fact it is a matter here only of the government which does not understand itself but which now is providentially enabled to acquire the same knowledge, of crucial significance for its task, as is disclosed to the government which does understand itself in the true sense in Jesus Christ. One might, therefore, say that in this case natural law has its foundation in Jesus Christ." Ibid., 336.

111. Ibid., 339.

112. Ibid., 337.

113. Ibid., 334.

114. Ibid., 335.

115. Ibid., 337–338.

116. Ibid., 338.

117. Ibid., 208, 295–296.

118. Ibid., 324.

119. Ibid., 342.

120. Bonhoeffer, *No Rusty Swords*, 104.

121. Bonhoeffer, *A Testament to Freedom*, 97.

122. Bonhoeffer, *Ethics*, 347–348.

123. Ibid., 349.

124. Ibid., 353.

125. Ibid., 355–356.

126. Reprinted in Bonhoeffer, *No Rusty Swords*, 221–229.

127. Ibid., 224–225.

128. Introduction to Bonhoeffer, *A Testament to Freedom*, 5.

129. Bonhoeffer, *Letters and Papers*, 17.

130. Ibid., 342.

131. Paul Lehmann, "The Indian Situation as a Question of Accountability," *Church & Society* 75, no. 3 (1985): 66.

132. Quoted in Dagmar Herzog, "Theology of Betrayal," *Tikkun* 16, no. 3 (2001): 70.

133. Bonhoeffer, *Ethics*, 90–91.

134. Bonhoeffer, *A Testament to Freedom*, 373. On the issue of Bonhoeffer and Jews, see Robert Ericksen and Susannah Heschel, eds., *Betrayal: German Churches and the Holocaust* (Minneapolis: Augsburg Fortress, 1999); Eberhard Bethge, "Dietrich Bonhoeffer and the Jews," in *Ethical Responsibility: Bonhoeffer's Legacy to the Churches*, ed. John Godsey and Geffrey Kelly (Lewiston, N.Y.: Edwin Mellen Press, 1981), 43; Geffrey B. Kelly, "Bonhoeffer and the Jews: Implications for Jewish-Christian Reconciliation," in *Reflections on Bonhoeffer: Essays in Honor of F. Burton Nelson*, ed. Geffrey B. Kelly and C. John Weborg, 133–166 (Chicago: Covenant Publications, 1999).

135. Josiah Ulysses Young III, *No Difference in the Fare: Dietrich Bonhoeffer and the Problem of Racism* (Grand Rapids, Mich.: Eerdmans, 1998), 8.

136. Ibid., 6.

137. Ibid., 1.

138. Ibid., 14.

139. Otto A. Maduro, "The Modern Nightmare: A Latin American Christian Indictment," in *Theology and the Practice of Responsibility: Essays on Dietrich Bonhoeffer*, ed. Wayne Whitson Floyd Jr. and Charles Marsh (Valley Forge, Pa: Trinity Press International, 1994), 81. Geffrey B. Kelly draws a comparison between Bonhoeffer and Archbishop Romero, "defender of the poor of El Salvador," in "Bonhoeffer and Romero: Prophets of Justice for the Oppressed," in *Theology and the Practice of Responsibility*, 85.

140. G. Clarke Chapman, "Bonhoeffer, Liberation Theology, and the 1990s," in Kelly and Weborg, *Reflections on Bonhoeffer*, 301.

141. Gustavo Gutiérrez, *The Truth Shall Make You Free: Confrontations* (Maryknoll, N.Y.: Orbis, 1990), 24.

142. John W. de Gruchy, "Bonhoeffer, Apartheid and Beyond: The Reception of Bonhoeffer in South Africa," in de Gruchy, *Bonhoeffer for a New Day*, 354.

143. Ibid., 355, 359.

144. Chung Hyun Kyung, "Dear Dietrich Bonhoeffer: A Letter," in de Gruchy, *Bonhoeffer for a New Day*, 11.

145. Ibid., 10.

146. Ibid., 15.

147. Ibid., 17.

148. Ibid., 18.

149. Bonhoeffer, *Letters and Papers*, 282.

150. Quoted in Bethge, *Dietrich Bonhoeffer*, 406.

151. Ibid., 869.

ORIGINAL SOURCE MATERIALS

THE NATURE OF THE CHURCH: SUMMER 1932

Confession of faith is not be confused with professing a religion. Such profession uses the confession as propaganda and ammunition against the Godless. The confession of faith belongs rather to the "Discipline of the Secret" (*Arkanum*) in the Christian gathering of those who believe. Nowhere else is it tenable. It is, for example, untenable in the new "Confession sessions" now coming into vogue in which one dialogues with those antagonistic to faith. The primary confession of the Christian before the world is the deed that interprets itself. If this deed is to have become a force, then the world itself will long to confess the Word. This is not the same as loudly shrieking out propaganda. This Word must be preserved as the most sacred possession of the community. This is a matter between God and the community, not between the community and the world. It is the Word of recognition between friends, not a word to use against enemies. This attitude was first learned at baptism. The deed alone is our confession of faith before the world.[1]

THY KINGDOM COME: THE PRAYER OF THE CHURCH FOR THE KINGDOM OF GOD ON EARTH

We are otherworldly—ever since we hit upon the devious trick of being religious, yes even "Christian," at the expense of the earth. Otherworldliness affords a splendid environment in which to live. Whenever life begins to become oppressive and troublesome a person just leaps into the air with a bold kick and soars relieved and unencumbered into so-called eternal fields. He leaps over the present. He disdains the earth; he is better than it. After all, besides the temporal defeats he still has his eternal victories, and they are so easily achieved. Other-worldliness also makes it easy to preach and to speak words of comfort. An other-worldly church can be certain that it will in no time win over all the weaklings, all who are only too glad to be deceived and deluded, all utopianists, all disloyal sons of the earth. When an explosion seems imminent, who would not be so human as to quickly mount the chariot that comes down from the skies with the promise of taking him to a better world beyond? What church would be so merciless, so inhuman, as not to deal compassionately with this weakness of suffering humans thereby save souls for the kingdom of heaven? Humans are weak; they cannot bear having the earth so near, the earth that bears them. They cannot stand it, because the earth is stronger than they and because they want to be better than the evil earth. So people extricate themselves from it; they refuse to take it seriously. Who could blame them for that—who but the have-nots in their envy? Humans are weak, that's just the way they are; and these weaklings are open to the religion of otherworldliness. "Should it be denied them? Should the weaklings remain without help? Would that be in the spirit of Jesus Christ? No, the weak should receive help. They do in fact receive help, from Christ. However, Christ does not will or intend this weakness; instead, he makes humans strong. He does not lead them in a religious flight from this world to other worlds beyond; rather, he gives them back to the earth as its loyal children. . . .

The kingdom of God is not found in some other world beyond, but in the midst of this world. Our obedience is demanded in terms of its contradictory appearance, and then, through our obedience, the miracle, like lightning, is allowed to flash up again and again from the perfect, blessed new world of the final promise. God wants us to honor him on earth; he wants us to honor him in our fellow man and woman—and nowhere else. He sinks his kingdom down into the cursed ground. Let us open our eyes, become sober, and obey him here. "Come, O blessed of my Father, inherit the kingdom!" This the Lord will say to no other than the one to whom he says, "I was hungry and you gave me food, I was thirsty and you gave me drink. . . . As you did it to one of the least of my brethren, you did it to me" (Matt. 25:34, 35, 40).[2]

CREATION AND FALL: THE IMAGE OF GOD ON EARTH

. . . In the language of the Bible, freedom is not something persons have for themselves but something they have for others. No one enjoys freedom "in itself," that is, in a vacuum, the same way that one may be musical, intelligent, or blind as such. Freedom is not a quality of the human person. Nor is it an ability, a disposition, a kind of being that somehow deeply germinates in a person. Whoever scrutinizes the human to discover freedom will find nothing of it. Why? Because freedom is not a quality that can be discovered. It is not a possession, a presence, or an object. Nor is it a pattern for existence. Rather, it is a relationship; otherwise, it is nothing. Indeed it is a relationship between two persons. Being free means "being free for the other," because the other has bound me to himself or herself. Only in relationship with the other am I free. . . .

Those who are created are free in that they are in relationship with other creatures; the human person is free for others. And he created them a man and a woman. The man is not alone; he exists in duality and it is in this dependence on the other that his creatureliness consists. The creatureliness of humans, no more than their freedom, is neither a quality, nor a disposition to be encountered, nor is it a mode of being. It is to be defined, rather, as absolutely nothing other than the relations of human beings with one another, over against one another, in dependence on one another. The "image . . . after God's likeness" is, consequently, not an *analogia entis* (analogy of being) by which humans, in their existence in and for themselves, would in their being live in the likeness to God's being. Indeed, there is no such analogy between God and the human . . . The likeness, the analogy, of the human to God, is not *analogia entis* but *analogia relationis* (analogy of relationship).[3]

DISCIPLESHIP

When holy scripture speaks of following Jesus, it proclaims that people are free from all human rules, from everything which pressures, burdens, or causes worry and torment of conscience. In following Jesus, people are released from the hard yoke of their own laws to be under the gentle yoke of Jesus Christ. Does this disparage the seriousness of Jesus' commandments? No. Instead, only where Jesus' entire commandment and the call to unlimited discipleship remain intact are persons fully free to enter into Jesus' community. Those who follow Jesus' commandment entirely, who let Jesus' yoke rest on them without resistance, will find the burdens they must bear to be light. In the gentle pressure of this yoke they will receive the strength to walk the right path without becoming weary. . . .

Cheap grace is the deadly enemy of our Church. We are fighting today for costly grace.

Cheap grace means grace sold on the market like cheapjack's wares. The sacraments, the forgiveness of sin, and the consolations of religion are thrown away at cut prices. . . . Grace without price; grace without cost! The essence of grace, we suppose, is that the account has been paid in advance; and, because it has been paid, everything can be had for nothing. . . .

Cheap grace means grace as a doctrine, a principle, a system. It means forgiveness of sins proclaimed as a general truth; it means God's love as merely a Christian idea of God. Those who affirm it have already had their sins forgiven. . . .

Cheap grace means the justification of sin without the justification of the sinner. Because grace alone does everything, everything can stay in its old ways. . . .

Cheap grace is the preaching of forgiveness without repentance; it is baptism without the discipline of community; it is the Lord's Supper without confession of sin; it is absolution without personal confession. Cheap grace is grace without discipleship, grace without the cross, grace without the living, incarnate Jesus Christ.

Costly grace is the treasure hidden in the field; for the sake of which people go and sell with joy everything they have. It is the costly pearl, for whose price the merchant sells all that he has. . . . It is the call of Jesus Christ which causes a disciple to leave his nets and to follow him. . . .

Above all, grace is costly because it was costly to God, because it costs God the life of God's son. . . .

It comes to us as a gracious call to follow Jesus; it comes as a forgiving word to the fearful spirit and the broken heart. Grace is costly, because it forces people under the yoke of following Jesus Christ; it is grace when Jesus says: "My yoke is easy and my burden is light."[4]

TEMPTATION

Lead us not into temptation. Natural humans and moral humans cannot understand this prayer. Natural humans want to prove their strength in adventure, in struggle, in encounter with the enemy. That is life. "If you do not stake your life you will never win it." Only the life which has run the risk of death is life which has been won. That is what natural humans know. Moral humans also know that their knowledge is true and convincing only when it is tried out and proved, they know that the good can live only from evil, and that it would not be good but for evil. So moral humans call out evil, their daily prayer is—Lead us into temptation, that we may test out the power of the good in us.

If temptation were really what natural humans and moral humans understand by it, namely, testing of their own strength—whether their vital or their moral or even their Christian strength—in resistance, on the enemy, then it is true that Christ's prayer would be incomprehensible. . . . The temptation of which the whole bible speaks does not have to do with the testing of my strength—to my horror, and without my being able to do anything about it—is turned against me; really all my powers, including my good and pious powers (the strength of my faith), fall into the hands of the enemy power and are now led into the field against me. . . .

A defeat shows the physical and the moral humans that their powers have to increase before they can withstand the trial. So their defeat is never irrevocable. Christians know that in every hour of temptation all their strength will leave them. For them temptation means a dark hour which can be irrevocable. They do not seek for their strength to be proved, but they pray, "Lead us not into temptation." So the biblical meaning of temptation is not a testing of strength, but the loss of all strength, defenseless deliverance into Satan's hands. . . .

So Christians live from the times of God, and not from their own ideas of life. They do not say that they live in constant temptation and constant testing, but in the time when they are preserved from temptation they pray that God may not let the time of temptation come over them.[5]

LETTERS AND PAPERS FROM PRISON

Prologue: After Ten Years

Ten years is a long time in anyone's life. As time is the most valuable thing that we have, because it is the most irrevocable, the thought of any lost time troubles us whenever we look back. Time lost is time in which we have failed to live a full human life, gain experience, learn, create, enjoy, and suffer; it is time that has not been filled up, but left empty. These last years have certainly not been like that. Our losses have been great and immeasurable, but time has not been lost. . . . In the following pages I should like to try to give some account of what we have experienced and learnt in common during these years—not personal experiences, or anything systematically arranged, or arguments and theories, but conclusions reached more or less in common by a circle of like-minded people, and related to the business of human life, put down one after the other, the only connection between them being that of concrete experience. . . . One cannot write about these things without a constant sense of gratitude for the fellowship of spirit and community of life that have been proved and preserved throughout these years.

No Ground Under Our Feet

One may ask whether there have ever before in human history been people with so little ground under their feet—people to whom every available alternative seemed equally intolerable, repugnant, and futile, who looked beyond all these existing alternatives for the source of their strength so entirely in the past or in the future, and who yet, without being dreamers, were able to await the success of their cause so quietly and confidently. Or perhaps one should rather ask whether the responsible thinking people of any generation that stood at a turning-point in history did not feel much as we do, simply because something new was emerging that could not be seen in the existing alternatives.

Who Stands Fast?

The great masquerade of evil has played havoc with all our ethical concepts. For evil to appear disguised as light, charity, historical necessity, or social justice is quite bewildering to anyone brought up on our traditional ethical concepts, while for Christians who base their lives on the Bible it merely confirms the fundamental wickedness of evil.

The "reasonable" people's failure is obvious. With the best intentions and a naive lack of realism, they think that with a little reason they can bend back into position the framework that has got out of joint. In their lack of vision they want to do justice to all sides, and so the conflicting forces wear them down with nothing achieved. Disappointed by the work's unreasonableness, they see themselves condemned to ineffectiveness; they step aside in resignation or collapse before the stronger party.

Still more pathetic is the total collapse of moral *fanaticism*. Fanatics think that their single-minded principles qualify them to do battle with the powers of evil; but like a bull they rush at the red cloak instead of the person who is holding it; they exhaust themselves and are beaten. They get tangled in non-essentials and fall into the trap set by cleverer people.

Then there are the people with a *conscience*, who fight single-handed against heavy odds in situations that call for a decision. But the scale of the conflicts in which they have to choose—with no advice or support except from their own consciences—tears them to pieces. Evil approaches them in so many respectable and seductive disguises that their conscience becomes nervous and vacillating, till at last they content themselves with a salved instead of a clear conscience. . . .

Who stands fast? Only those whose final standard is not their reason, their principles, their conscience, their freedom, or their virtue, but who are ready to sacrifice all this when they are called to obedient and responsible action in faith and in exclusive allegiance to God—responsible people, who try to make their whole life an answer to the question and call of God. Where are these responsible people?

Civil Courage?

What lies behind the complaint about the dearth of civil courage? In recent years we have seen a great deal of bravery and self-sacrifice, but civil courage hardly anywhere, even among ourselves. To attribute this simply to personal cowardice would be too facile a psychology. . . . Civil courage, in fact, can grow only out of the free responsibility of free people. Only now are the Germans beginning to discover the meaning of free responsibility. It depends on a God who demands responsible action in a bold venture of faith, and who promises forgiveness and consolation to the person who becomes a sinner in that venture.

Of Success

Although it is certainly not true that success justifies an evil deed and shady means, it is impossible to regard success as something that is ethically quite neutral. The fact is that historical success creates a basis for the continuance of life, and it is still a moot point whether it is ethically more responsible to take the field like a Don Quixote against a new age, or to admit one's defeat, accept the new age, and agree to serve it. In the last resort success makes history; and the ruler of history repeatedly brings good out of evil over the heads of the history-makers. . . . As long as goodness is successful, we can afford the luxury of regarding it as having no ethical significance; it is when success is achieved by evil means that the problem arises. . . . We . . . must take our share of responsibility for the molding of history in every situation and at every moment, whether we are the victors or the vanquished. . . .

Contempt For Humanity?

There is a very real danger of our drifting into an attitude of contempt for humanity. We know quite well that we have no right to do so, and that it would lead us into the most sterile relation to our fellow humans. The following thoughts may keep us from such a temptation. It means that we at once fall into the worst blunders of our opponents. The people who despise others will never be able to make anything of them. Nothing that we despise in the other is entirely absent from ourselves. We often expect from others more than we are willing to do ourselves. Why have we hitherto thought so intemperately about humans and their frailty and temptability? We must learn to regard people less in the light of what they do or omit to do, and more in the light of what they suffer. The only profitable relationship to others—and especially to our weaker brothers and sisters—is one of love, and that means the will to hold fellowship with them. God himself did not despise humanity, but became human for human's sake. . . .

A Few Articles of Faith on the Sovereignty of God in History

I believe that God can and will bring good out of evil, even out of the greatest evil. For that purpose he needs people who make the best use of everything. I believe that God will give us all the strength we need to help us resist in all time of distress. But he never gives it in advance, lest we should rely on ourselves and not on him alone. A faith such as this should allay our fears for the future. I believe that even our mistakes and shortcomings are turned to good account, and that it is no harder for God to deal with them than with our supposedly good deeds. I believe that God is no timeless fate, but that he waits for and answers sincere prayers and responsible actions. . . .

Are We Still of Any Use?

We have been silent witnesses of evil deeds; we have been drenched by many storms; we have learnt the arts of equivocation and pretense; experience has made us suspicious of others and kept us from being truthful and open; intolerable conflicts have worn us down and even made us cynical. Are we still of any use? What we shall need is not geniuses, or cynics, or misanthropes, or clever tacticians, but plain, honest, straightforward people. Will our inward power of resistance be strong enough, and our honesty with ourselves remorseless enough, for us to find our way back to simplicity and straightforwardness?

The View from Below

There remains an experience of incomparable value. We have for once learnt to see the great events of world history from below, from the perspective of the outcast, the suspects, the maltreated, the powerless, the oppressed, the reviled—in short, from the perspective of those who suffer. The important thing is that neither bitterness nor envy should have gnawed at the heart during this time, that we should have come to look with new eyes at matters great and small, sorrow and joy, strength and weakness, that our perception of generosity, humanity, justice and mercy should have become clearer, freer, less corruptible. We have to learn that personal suffering is a more effective key, a more rewarding principle for exploring the world in thought and action than personal good fortune. This perspective from below must not become the partisan possession of those who are eternally dissatisfied; rather, we must do justice to life in all its dimensions from a higher satisfaction, whose foundation is beyond any talk of "from below" or "from above." This is the way in which we may affirm it. . . .[6]

LETTERS TO EBERHARD BETHGE

December 5, 1943

My thoughts and feelings seem to be getting more and more like those of the Old Testament, and in recent months I have been reading the Old

Testament much more than the New. It is only when one knows the un-
utterability of the name of God that one can utter the name of Jesus
Christ; it is only when one loves life and the earth so much that without
them everything seems to be over that one may believe in the resurrection and a new world; it is only when one submits to God's law that one
may speak of grace; and it is only when God's wrath and vengeance are
hanging as grim realities over the heads of one's enemies that something
of what it means to love and forgive them can touch our hearts. In my
opinion it is not Christian to want to take our thoughts and feelings too
quickly and too directly from the New Testament. We have already
talked about this several times, and every day confirms my opinion. One
cannot and must not speak the last word before the last but one. We live
in the last but one and believe the last, don't we? Lutherans (so-called!)
and pietists would shudder at the thought, but it is true all the same. In
The Cost of Discipleship (ch. I) I just hinted at this, but did not follow it
up; I must do so later. But the logical conclusions are far-reaching, e.g.
for the problem of Catholicism, for the concept of the ministry, for the
use of the Bible, etc., and above all for ethics. Why is it that in the Old
Testament people tell lies vigorously and often to the glory of God (I've
now collected the passages), kill, deceive, rob, divorce, and even forni-
cate (see the genealogy of Jesus), doubt, blaspheme, and curse, whereas
in the New Testament there is nothing of all this? "An earlier stage" of
religion? That is a very naive way out; it is one and the same God. But
more of this later when we meet. . . .

I've been thinking again over what I wrote to you recently about our
own fear. I think that here, under the guise of honesty, something is being passed off as "natural" that is at bottom a symptom of sin; it is really
quite analogous to talking openly about sexual matters. After all, "truth-
fulness" does not mean uncovering everything that exists. God himself
made clothes for humans; and that means that *in statu corruptionis*
many things in human life ought to remain covered, and that evil, even
though it cannot be eradicated, ought at least to be concealed. Exposure
is cynical, and although cynics pride themselves on their exceptional
honesty, or claim to want truth at all costs, they miss the crucial fact
that since the fall there must be reticence and secrecy. . . . I believe we
Germans have never properly grasped the meaning of "concealment," i.e.,
what is in the end the *status corruptionis* of the world. Kant says quite
rightly in his *Anthropologie* that anyone who misunderstands or questions the significance of outward appearance in the world is a traitor to
humanity.[7]

December 18, 1943

. . . I believe that we ought so to love and trust God in our *lives*, and in all the good things that he sends us, that when the time comes (but not before!) we may go to him with love, trust, and joy. But, to put it plainly, for a husband in his wife's arms to be hankering after the other world is, in mild terms, a piece of bad taste, and not God's will. We ought to find and love God in what he actually gives us; if it pleases him to allow us to enjoy some overwhelming earthly happiness, we mustn't try to be more pious than God himself and allow our happiness to be corrupted by presumption and arrogance, and by unbridled religious fantasy which is never satisfied with what God gives.[8]

April 30, 1944

. . . You would be surprised, and perhaps even worried, by my theological thoughts and the conclusions that they lead to; and this is where I miss you most of all, because I don't know anyone else with whom I could so well discuss them to have my thinking clarified. What is bothering me incessantly is the question what Christianity really is, or indeed who Christ really is, for us today. The time when people could be told everything by means of words, whether theological or pious, is over, and so is the time of inwardness and conscience—and that means the time of religion in general. We are moving towards a completely religionless time; people as they are now simply cannot be religious any more. Even those who honestly describe themselves as "religious" do not in the least act up to it, and so they presumably mean something quite different by "religious."

Our whole nineteen-hundred-year-old Christian preaching and theology rest on the "religious *a priori*" of humankind. "Christianity" has always been a form—perhaps the true form—of "religion." But if one day it becomes clear that this *a priori* does not exist at all, but was a historically conditioned and transient form of human self-expression, and if therefore people become radically religionless—and I think that that is already more or less the case (else how is it, for example, that this war, in contrast to all previous ones, is not calling forth any "religious" reaction?)—what does that mean for "Christianity"? It means that the foundation is taken away from the whole of what has up to now been our "Christianity," and that there remain only a few "last survivors of the age of chivalry," or a few intellectually dishonest people, on whom we can descend as "religious." Are they to be the chosen few? Is it on this dubious group of people that we are to pounce in fervour, pique, or indignation, in order to sell them our goods? Are we to fall upon a few unfortunate people in their hour of need and exercise a sort of religious compulsion on them? If we don't want to do all that, if our final judgment must be that the western form of Christianity, too, was only a preliminary stage to a complete absence of religion, what kind of situation emerges for us, for the church? How can Christ become the Lord of the religionless as well? Are there religionless Christians? If religion is only a garment of Christianity—and even this garment has looked very different at different times—then what is a religionless Christianity?

Barth, who is the only one to have started along this line of thought, did not carry it to completion, but arrived at a positivism of revelation, which in the last analysis is essentially a restoration. For the religionless working person (or any other person) nothing decisive is gained here. The questions to be answered would surely be: What do a church, a community, a sermon, a liturgy, a Christian life mean in a religionless world? How do we speak of God—without religion, i.e. without the temporally conditioned presuppositions of metaphysics, inwardness, and so on? How do we speak (or perhaps we cannot now even "speak" as we used to) in a "secular" way about "God"? In what way are we "religionless—secular" Christians, in what way are we the *ek-klesia*, those who are called forth, not regarding ourselves from a religious point of view as specially favoured, but rather as belonging wholly to the world? In that case Christ is no longer an object of religion, but something quite different, really the Lord of the world. But what does that mean? What is the place of worship and prayer in a religionless situation? Does the secret discipline, or alternatively the difference (which I have suggested to you before) between penultimate and ultimate, take on a new importance here? . . .

. . . The Pauline question whether [circumcision] is a condition of justification seems to me in present-day terms to be whether religion is a condition of salvation. Freedom from [circumcision] is also freedom from religion. I often ask myself why a "Christian instinct" often draws me more to the religionless people than to the religious, by which I don't in the least mean with any evangelizing intention, but, I might almost say, "in brotherhood." While I'm often reluctant to mention God by name to religious people—because that name somehow seems to me here not to ring true, and I feel myself to be slightly dishonest (it's particularly bad when others start to talk in religious jargon; I then dry up almost completely and feel awkward and uncomfortable)—to people with no religion I can on occasion mention him by name quite calmly and as a matter of course. Religious people speak of God when human knowledge (perhaps simply because they are too lazy to think) has come to an end, or when human resources fail—in fact it is always the *deus ex machina* that they bring on to the scene, either for the apparent solution of insoluble problems, or as strength in human failure—always, that is to say, exploiting human weakness or human boundaries. Of necessity, that can go on only till people can by their own strength push these boundaries somewhat further out, so that God becomes superfluous as a *deus ex machina*. I've come to be doubtful of talking about any human boundaries (is even death, which people now hardly fear, and is sin, which they now hardly understand, still a genuine boundary today?). It always seems to me that we are trying anxiously in this way to reserve some space for God; I should like to speak of God not on the boundaries but at the centre, not in weaknesses but in strength; and therefore not in death and guilt but in a person's life and goodness. As to the boundaries, it seems to me better to be silent and leave the insoluble unsolved. Belief in the resurrection is *not* the "solution" of the problem of death. God's "beyond" is not the beyond of our cognitive faculties. The transcendence of epistemological theory has nothing to do with the transcendence of God. God is beyond in the midst of our life. The church stands, not at the boundaries where human powers give out, but in the middle of the village. That is how it is in the Old Testament, and in this sense we still read the New Testament far too little in the light of the Old. How this religionless Christianity looks, what form it takes, is something that I'm thinking about a great deal, and I shall be writing to you again about it soon. It may be that on us in particular, midway between East and West, there will fall a heavy responsibility.[9]

May 5, 1944

. . . A few more words about "religionlessness." I expect you remember Bultmann's essay on the "demythologizing" of the New Testament? My view of it today would be, not that he went "too far," as most people thought, but that he didn't go far enough. It's not only the "mythological" concepts, such as miracle, ascension, and so on (which are not in principle separable from the concepts of God, faith, etc.), but "religious" concepts generally, which are problematic. You can't, as Bultmann supposes, separate God and miracle, but you must be able to interpret and proclaim *both* in a "non-religious" sense. Bultmann's approach is fundamentally still a liberal one (i.e. abridging the gospel), whereas I'm trying to think theologically.

What does it mean to "interpret in a religious sense"? I think it means to speak on the one hand metaphysically, and on the other hand individualistically. Neither of these is relevant to the biblical message or to the person of today. Hasn't the individualistic question about personal salvation almost completely left us all? Aren't we really under the impression that there are more important things than that question (perhaps not more important than the *matter* itself, but more important than the *question*!)? I know it sounds pretty monstrous to say that. But, fundamentally, isn't this in fact biblical? Does the question about saving one's soul appear in the Old Testament at all? Aren't righteousness and the Kingdom of God on earth the focus of everything, and isn't it true that Rom. 3.24ff. is not an individualistic doctrine of salvation, but the culmination of the view that God alone is righteous? It is not with the beyond that we are concerned, but with this world as created and preserved, subjected to laws, reconciled, and restored. What is above this world is, in the gospel, intended to exist *for* this world; I mean that, not in the anthropocentric sense of liberal, mystic pietistic, ethical theology, but in the biblical sense of the creation and of the incarnation, crucifixion, and resurrection of Jesus Christ. . . .

I'm thinking about how we can reinterpret in a "worldly" sense—in the sense of the Old Testament and of John 1.14—the concepts of repentance, faith, justification, rebirth, and sanctification. I shall be writing to you about it again. . . . [10]

THOUGHTS ON THE DAY OF THE BAPTISM OF
DIETRICH WILHELM RÜDIGER BETHGE

. . . Our church, which has been fighting in these years only for its self-preservation, as though that were an end in itself, is incapable of taking the word of reconciliation and redemption to humankind and the world. Our earlier words are therefore bound to lose their force and cease, and our being Christians today will be limited to two things: prayer and righteous action among people. All Christian thinking, speaking, and organizing must be born anew out of this prayer and action. By the time you have grown up, the church's form will have changed greatly. We are not yet out of the melting-pot, and any attempt to help the church prematurely to a new expansion of its organization will merely delay its conversion and purification. It is not for us to prophesy the day (though the day will come) when people will once more be called so to utter the word of God that the world will be changed and renewed by it. It will be a new language, perhaps quite non-religious, but liberating and redeeming—as was Jesus' language; it will shock people and yet overcome them by its power; it will be the language of a new righteousness and truth, proclaiming God's peace with humans and the coming of his kingdom. . . . [11]

FURTHER LETTERS TO EBERHARD BETHGE

May 29, 1944

Weizsäcker's book *The World-View of Physics*. . . . has again brought home to me quite clearly how wrong it is to use God as a stop-gap for the incompleteness of our knowledge. If in fact the frontiers of knowledge are being pushed further and further back (and that is bound to be the case), then God is being pushed back with them, and is therefore continually in retreat. We are to find God in what we know, not in what we don't know; God wants us to realize his presence, not in unsolved problems but in those that are solved. That is true of the relationship between God and scientific knowledge, but it is also true of the wider human problems of death, suffering, and guilt. It is now possible to find, even for these questions, human answers that take no account whatever of God. In point of fact, people deal with these questions without God (it has always been so), and it is simply not true to say that only Christianity has the answers to them. As to the idea of "solving" problems, it may be that the Christian answers are just as unconvincing—or convincing—as any others. Here again, God is no stop-gap; he must be recognized at the centre of life, not when we are at the end of our resources; it is his will to be recognized in life, and not only when death comes; in health and vigour, and not only in suffering; in our activities, and not only in sin. The ground for this lies in the revelation of God in Jesus Christ. He is the centre of life, and he certainly didn't "come" to answer our unsolved problems. From the centre of life certain questions, and their answers, are seen to be wholly irrelevant (I'm thinking of the judgment pronounced on Job's friends). In Christ there are no "Christian problems." Enough of this; I've just been disturbed again.[12]

June 8, 1944

You now ask so many important questions on the subjects that have been occupying me lately, that I should be happy if I could answer them myself. But it's all very much in the early stages; and, as usual, I'm being led on more by an instinctive feeling for questions that will arise later than by any conclusions that I've already reached about them. I'll try to define my position from the historical angle.

The movement that began about the thirteenth century (I'm not going to get involved in any argument about the exact date) towards the autonomy of humans (in which I should include the discovery of the laws by which the world lives and deals with itself in science, social and political matters, art, ethics, and religion) has in our time reached an undoubted completion. People have learned to deal with themselves in all questions of importance without recourse to the "working hypothesis" called "God." In questions of science, art, and ethics this has become an understood thing at which one now hardly dares to tilt. But for the last hundred years or so it has also become increasingly true of religious questions; it is becoming evident that everything gets along without "God"—and, in fact, just as well as before. As in the scientific field, so in human affairs generally, "God" is being pushed more and more out of life, losing more and more ground.

Roman Catholic and Protestant historians agree that it is in this development that the great defection from God, from Christ, is to be seen; and the more they claim and playoff God and Christ against it, the more the development considers itself to be anti-Christian. The world that has become conscious of itself and the laws that govern its own existence has grown self-confident in what seems to us to be an uncanny way. False developments and failures do not make the world doubt the necessity of the course that it is taking, or of its development; they are accepted with fortitude and detachment as part of the bargain, and even an event like the present war is no exception. Christian apologetic has taken the most varied forms of opposition to this self-assurance. Efforts are made to prove to a world thus come of age that it cannot live without the tutelage of "God." Even though there has been surrender on all secular problems, there still remain the so-called "ultimate questions"—death, guilt—to which only "God" can give an answer, and because of which we need God and the church and the pastor. So we live, in some degree, on these so-called ultimate questions of humanity. But what if one day they no longer exist as such, if they too can be answered "without God"? Of course, we now have the secularized offshoots of Christian theology, namely existentialist philosophy and the psychotherapists, who demonstrate to secure, contented, and happy humankind that it is really unhappy and desperate and simply unwilling to admit that it is in a predicament about which it knows nothing, and from which only they can rescue it. Wherever there is health, strength, security, simplicity, they scent luscious fruit to gnaw at or to lay their pernicious eggs in. They set themselves to drive people to inward despair, and then the game is in their hands. That is secularized methodism. And whom does it touch? A small number of intellectuals, of degenerates, of people who regard themselves as the most important thing in the world, and who therefore like to busy themselves with themselves. Ordinary people, who spend their everyday lives at work and with their families, and of course with all kinds of diversions, are not affected. They have neither the time nor the inclination to concern themselves with their existential despair, or to regard their perhaps modest share of happiness as a trial, a trouble, or a calamity.

The attack by Christian apologetic on the adulthood of the world I consider to be in the first place pointless, in the second place ignoble, and in the third place unchristian. Pointless, because it seems to me like an attempt to put grown-ups back into adolescence, i.e. to make them dependent on things on which they are, in fact, no longer dependent, and thrusting them into problems that are, in fact, no longer problems to them. Ignoble, because it amounts to an attempt to exploit people's weakness for purposes that are alien to them and to which they have not freely assented. Unchristian, because it confuses Christ with one particular stage in human's religiousness, i.e. with a human law. More about this later.

But first, a little more about the historical position. The question is: Christ and the world that has come of age. The weakness of liberal theology was that it conceded to the world the right to determine Christ's place in the world; in the conflict between the church and the world it accepted the comparatively easy terms of peace that the world dictated. Its strength was that it did not try to put the clock back, and that it genuinely accepted the battle (Troeltsch), even though this ended with its defeat.

Defeat was followed by surrender, and by an attempt to make a completely fresh start based on the fundamentals of the Bible and the Reformation. . . .

Barth was the first to realize the mistake that all these attempts (which were all, in fact, still sailing, though unintentionally, in the channel of liberal theology) were making in leaving clear a space for religion in the world or against the world. He brought in against religion the God of Jesus Christ, "*pneuma* against *sarx*." That remains his greatest service. . . . [13]

June 27, 1944

The decisive factor is said to be that in Christianity the hope of resurrection is proclaimed, and that that means the emergence of a genuine religion of redemption, the main emphasis now being on the far side of the boundary drawn by death. But it seems to me that this is just where the mistake and the danger lie. Redemption now means redemption from cares, distress, fears, and longings, from sin and death, in a better world beyond the grave. But is this really the essential character of the proclamation of Christ in the gospels and by Paul? I should say it is not. The difference between the Christian hope of resurrection and the mythological hope is that the former sends a person back to life on earth in a wholly new way which is even more sharply defined than it is in the Old Testament. Christians, unlike the devotees of the redemption myths, have no last line of escape available from earthly tasks and difficulties into the eternal, but, like Christ himself ("My God, why hast thou forsaken me?"), they must drink the earthly cup to the dregs, and only in their doing so is the crucified and risen Lord with them, and they crucified and risen with Christ. This world must not be permanently written off; in this the Old and New Testaments are at one. Redemption myths arise from human boundary-experiences, but Christ takes hold of persons at the centre of their life.[14]

June 30, 1944

Now I will try to go on with the theological reflections that I broke off not long since. I had been saying that God is being increasingly pushed out of a world that has come of age, out of the spheres of our knowledge and life, and that since Kant he has been relegated to a realm beyond the world of experience. Theology has on the one hand resisted this development with apologetics, and has taken up arms—in vain—against Darwinism, etc. On the other hand, it has accommodated itself to the development by restricting God to the so-called ultimate questions as a *deus ex machina*; that means that he becomes the answer to life's problems, and the solution of its needs and conflicts. So if people have no such difficulties, or if they refuses to go into these things, to allow others to pity them, then either they cannot be open to God; or else they must be shown that they are, in fact, deeply involved in such problems, needs, and conflicts, without admitting or knowing it. If that can be done—and existentialist philosophy and psychotherapy have worked out some quite ingenious methods in that direction—then these people can now be claimed for God, and methodism can celebrate its triumph. But if they cannot be brought to see and admit that their happiness is really an evil, their health sickness, and their vigour despair, theologians are at their wits' end. It's a case of having to do either with a hardened sinner of a particularly ugly type, or with a person of "bourgeois complacency," and the one is as far from salvation as the other.

You see, that is the attitude that I am contending against. When Jesus blessed sinners, they were real sinners, but Jesus did not make everyone a sinner first. He called them away from their sin, not into their sin. It is true that encounter with Jesus meant the reversal of all human values. So it was in the conversion of Paul, though in his case the encounter with Jesus preceded the realization of sin. It is true that Jesus cared about people on the fringe of human society, such as harlots and tax-collectors, but never about them alone, for he sought to care about the person as such.

Never did he question a person's health, vigour, or happiness, regarded in themselves, or regard them as evil fruits; else why should he heal the sick and restore strength to the weak? Jesus claims for himself and the Kingdom of God the whole of human life in all its manifestations.

Of course I have to be interrupted just now! Let me just summarize briefly what I'm concerned about—How to claim for Jesus Christ a world that has come of age.

I can't write any more today, or else the letter will be kept here another week, and I don't want that to happen. So: To be continued![15]

July 8, 1944

Now for a few more thoughts on our theme. Marshalling the biblical evidence needs more lucidity and concentration than I can command at present. Wait a few more days, till it gets cooler! I haven't forgotten, either, that I owe you something about the nonreligious interpretation of biblical concepts. But for today, here are a few preliminary remarks:

The displacement of God from the world, and from the public part of human life, led to the attempt to keep his place secure at least in the sphere of the "personal," the "inner," and the "private." And all individuals still have a private sphere somewhere, that is where they were thought to be the most vulnerable. The secrets known to a person's servant—that is, to put it crudely, the range of one's intimate life, from prayer to one's sexual life—have become the hunting-ground of modern pastoral workers. In that way they resemble (though with quite different intentions) the dirtiest gutter journalists. . . . In the one case it's social, financial, or political blackmail and in the other, religious blackmail.

Regarded theologically, the error is twofold. First, it is thought that people can be addressed as sinners only after their weaknesses and meannesses have been spied out. Secondly, it is thought that people's essential nature consists of their inmost and most intimate background; that is defined as their "inner life," and it is precisely in those secret human places that God is to have his domain!

On the first point it is to be said that humans are certainly sinners, but they are far from being mean or common on that account. To put it rather tritely, were Goethe and Napoleon sinners because they weren't always faithful husbands? It's not the sins of weakness, but the sins of strength, which matter here. It's not in the least necessary to spy out things; the Bible never does so. . . .

On the second point: the Bible does not recognize our distinction between the outward and the inward. Why should it? It is always concerned with *anthropôs teleios*, the *whole* person, even where, as in the Sermon on the Mount, the decalogue is pressed home to refer to "inward disposition." That a good "disposition" can take the place of total goodness is quite unbiblical. The discovery of the so-called inner life dates from the Renaissance, probably from Petrarch. The "heart" in the biblical sense is not the inner life, but the whole person in relation to God. But as people live just as much from "outwards" to "inwards" as from "inwards" to "outwards," the view that their essential nature can be understood only from their intimate spiritual background is wholly erroneous.

I therefore want to start from the premise that God shouldn't be smuggled into some last secret place, but that we should frankly recognize that the world, and people, have come of age, that we shouldn't run people down in their worldliness, but confront them with God at their strongest point, that we should give up all our clerical tricks, and not regard psychotherapy and existentialist philosophy as God's pioneers. The importunity of all these people is far too unaristocratic for the Word of God to ally itself with them. The Word of God is far removed from this revolt of mistrust, this revolt from below. On the contrary, it reigns.[16]

July 16, 1944

In politics Machiavelli detaches politics from morality in general and founds the doctrine of "reasons of state." Later, and very differently from Machiavelli, but tending like him towards the autonomy of human society, comes Grotius, setting up his natural law as international law, which is valid *etsi deus non daretur*, "even if there were no God..... "

And we cannot be honest unless we recognize that we have to live in the world *etsi deus non daretur.* And this is just what we do recognize—before God! God himself compels us to recognize it. So our coming of age leads us to a true recognition of our situation before God. God would have us know that we must live as humans who manage our lives without him. The God who is with us is the God who forsakes us (Mark 15.34). The God who lets us live in the world without the working hypothesis of God is the God before whom we stand continually. Before God and with God we live without God. God lets himself be pushed out of the world on to the cross. He is weak and powerless in the world, and that is precisely the way, the only way, in which he is with us and helps us. Matt. 8.17 makes it quite clear that Christ helps us, not by virtue of his omnipotence, but by virtue of his weakness and suffering.

Here is the decisive difference between Christianity and all religions. Humans' religiosity makes them look in their distress to the power of God in the world: God is the *deus ex machina.* The Bible directs people to God's powerlessness and suffering; only the suffering God can help. To that extent we may say that the development towards the world's coming of age outlined above, which has done away with a false conception of God, opens up a way of seeing the God of the Bible, who wins power and space in the world by his weakness. This will probably be the starting-point for our "secular interpretation."[17]

July 18, 1944

... Jesus asked in Gethsemane, "Could you not watch with me one hour?" That is a reversal of what the religious people expect from God. People are summoned to share in God's sufferings at the hands of a godless world.

They must therefore really live in the godless world, without attempting to gloss over or explain its ungodliness in some religious way or other. They must live a "secular" life, and thereby share in God's sufferings. They *may* live a "secular" life (as those one who have been freed from false religious obligations and inhibitions). To be a Christian does not mean to be religious in a particular way, to make something of oneself (a sinner, a penitent, or a saint) on the basis of some method or other, but to be a human— not a type of human, but the human that Christ creates in us. It is not the religious act that makes the Christian, but participation in the sufferings of God in the secular life. That is *metanoia:* not in the first place thinking about one's own needs, problems, sins, and fears, but allowing oneself to be caught up into the way of Jesus Christ, into the messianic event, thus fulfilling Isa. 53. Therefore "believe in the gospel," or, in the words of John the Baptist, "Behold, the Lamb of God, who takes away the sin of the world" (John 1.29). (By the way, Jeremias has recently asserted that the Aramaic word for "lamb" may also be translated "servant"; very appropriate in view of Isa. 53!)

This being caught up into the messianic sufferings of God in Jesus Christ takes a variety of forms in the New Testament. . . . The only thing that is common to all these is their sharing in the suffering of God in Christ. That is their "faith." There is nothing of religious method here. The "religious act" is always something partial; "faith" is something whole, involving the whole of one's life. Jesus calls people, not to a new religion, but to life.

But what does this life look like, this participation in the powerlessness of God in the world? I will write about that next time, I hope. Just one more point for today. When we speak of God in a "non-religious" way, we must speak of him in such a way that the godlessness of the world is not in some way concealed, but revealed, and thus exposed to an unexpected light. The world that has come of age is more godless, and perhaps for that very reason nearer to God, than the world before its coming of age. Forgive me for still putting it all so terribly clumsily and badly, as I really feel I am. But perhaps you will help me again to make things clearer and simpler, even if only by my being able to talk about them with you and to hear you, so to speak, keep asking and answering.[18]

July 21, 1944

During the last year or so I've come to know and understand more and more the profound this-worldliness of Christianity. The Christian is not a *homo religiosus,* but simply a human, as Jesus was a human—in contrast, shall we say, to John the Baptist. I don't mean the shallow and banal this-worldliness of the enlightened, the busy, the comfortable, or the lascivious, but the profound this-worldliness, characterized by discipline and the constant knowledge of death and resurrection. I think Luther lived a this-worldly life in this sense.

I remember a conversation that I had in America thirteen years ago with a young French pastor. We were asking ourselves quite simply what we wanted to do with our lives. He said he would like to become a saint (and I think it's quite likely that he did become one). At the time I was very impressed, but I disagreed with him, and said, in effect, that I should like to learn to have faith. For a long time I didn't realize the depth of the contrast. I thought I could acquire faith by trying to live a holy life, or something like it. I suppose I wrote *The Cost of Discipleship* as the end of that path. Today I can see the dangers of that book, though I still stand by what I wrote.

I discovered later, and I'm still discovering right up to this moment, that is it only by living completely in this world that one learns to have faith. One must completely abandon any attempt to make something of oneself, whether it be a saint, or a converted sinner, or a churchman (a so-called priestly type!), a righteous person or an unrighteous one, a sick person or a healthy one. By this-worldliness I mean living unreservedly in life's duties, problems, successes and failures, experiences and perplexities. In so doing so we throw ourselves completely into the arms of God, taking seriously not our own sufferings, but those of God in the world—watching with Christ in Gethsemane. That, I think, is faith; that is *metanoia;* and that is how one becomes a human and a Christian (cf. Jer. 45!) How can success make us arrogant, or failure lead us astray, when we share in God's sufferings through a life of this kind?

I think you see what I mean, even though I put it so briefly. I'm glad to have been able to learn this, and I know I've been able to do so only along the road that I've traveled. So I'm grateful for the past and present, and content with them. . . . [19]

ETHICS

The Love of God and the Decay of the World

The World of Conflicts The knowledge of good and evil seems to be the aim of all ethical reflection. The first task of Christian ethics is to invalidate this knowledge. In launching this attack on the underlying assumptions of all other ethics, Christian ethics stands so completely alone that it becomes questionable whether there is any purpose in speaking of Christian ethics at all. But if one does so notwithstanding, that can only mean that Christian ethics claims to discuss the origin of the whole problem of ethics, and thus professes to be a critique of all ethics simply as ethics.

Already in the possibility of the knowledge of good and evil Christian ethics discerns a falling away from the origin. Humans at their origin know only one thing: God. It is only in the unity of their knowledge of God that individuals know of other individuals, of things, and of themselves. They know all things only in God, and God in all things. The knowledge of good and evil shows that they are no longer at one with this origin. . . .

The overcoming of the knowledge of good and evil is accomplished in Jesus. . . .

Proving . . . The will of God is not a system of rules which is established from the outset; it is something new and different in each different situation in life, and for this reason a person must ever anew examine what the will of God may be. The heart, the understanding, observation and experience must all collaborate in this task. It is no longer a matter of a person's own knowledge of good and evil, but solely of the living will of God; our knowledge of God's will is not something over which we ourselves dispose, but it depends solely upon the grace of God, and this grace is and requires to be new every morning. . . .

Ethics as Formation

The Idolization of Death The person whom God has taken to Himself, sentenced and awakened to a new life, this is Jesus Christ. In Him it is all humankind. It is ourselves. Only the form of Jesus Christ confronts the world and defeats it. And it is from this form alone that there comes the formation of a new world, a world which is reconciled with God.

Conformation The word "formation" arouses our suspicion. We are sick and tired of Christian programmes and of the thoughtless and superficial slogan of what is called "practical" Christianity as distinct from "dogmatic" Christianity.... Whenever [the scriptures] speak of forming they are concerned only with the one form which has overcome the world, the form of Jesus Christ. Formation can come only from this form. But here again it is not a question of applying directly to the world the teaching of Christ or what are referred to as Christian principles, so that the world might be formed in accordance with these. On the contrary, formation comes only by being drawn in into the form of Jesus Christ. It comes only as formation in His likeness, as *conformation*, with the unique form of Him who was made a man, was crucified, and rose again.

This is not achieved by dint of efforts "to become like Jesus," which is the way in which we usually interpret it. It is achieved only when the form of Jesus Christ itself works upon us in such a manner that it molds our form in its own likeness (Gal. 4.19)....

... The longing of the Incarnate to take form in all humans is as yet still unsatisfied. He bore the form of humans as a whole, and yet He can take form only in a small band. These are His Church.

"Formation" consequently means in the first place Jesus' taking form in His Church. What takes form here is the form of Jesus Christ Himself. The New Testament states the case profoundly and clearly when it calls the Church the Body of Christ. The body is the form. So the Church is not a religious community of worshipers of Christ but is Christ Himself who has taken form among humans....

The form of Christ is one and the same at all times and in all places.... And yet Christ is not a principle in accordance with which the whole world must be shaped. Christ is not the proclaimer of a system of what would be good today, here and at all times. Christ teaches no abstract ethics such as must at all costs be put into practice. Christ was not essentially a teacher and legislator, but a person, a real person like ourselves. And it is not therefore His will that we should in our time be the adherents, exponents and advocates of a definite doctrine, but that we should be humans, real humans before God.

The Concrete Place This leads us away from any kind of abstract ethic and towards an ethic which is entirely concrete. What can and must be said is not what is good once and for all, but the way in which Christ takes form among us here and now. The attempt to define that which is good once and for all has, in the nature of the case, always ended in failure. Either the proposition was asserted in such general and formal terms that it retained no significance as regards its contents, or else one tried to include in it and elaborate the whole immense range of conceivable contents, and thus to say in advance what would be good in every single conceivable case; this led to a casuistic system so unmanageable that it could satisfy the demands neither of general validity nor of concreteness. The concretely Christian ethic is beyond formalism and casuistry. Formalism and casuistry set out from the conflict between the good and the real, but the Christian ethic can take for its point of departure the reconciliation, already accomplished, of the world with God and the human Jesus Christ and the acceptance of the real human by God.

The Last Things and the Things Before the Last

The Penultimate Justification by grace and faith alone remains in every respect the final word and for this reason, when we speak of the things before the last, we must not speak of them as having any value of their own, but we must bring to light their relation to the ultimate. It is for the sake of the ultimate that we must now speak of the penultimate. This must now be made clearly intelligible. . . . Radicalism always springs from a conscious or unconscious hatred of what is established. Christian radicalism, no matter whether it consists in withdrawing from the world or in improving the world, arises from the hatred of creation. The radical cannot forgive God His creation. . . .

Compromise always springs from hatred of the ultimate. The Christian spirit of compromise arises from hatred of the justification of the sinner by grace alone. . . .

To contrast the two attitudes in this way is to make it sufficiently clear that both alike are opposed to Christ. For in Jesus Christ those things which are here ranged in mutual hostility are one. The question of the Christian life will not, therefore, be decided and answered either by radicalism or by compromise, but only by reference to Jesus Christ Himself. In Him alone lies the solution for the problem of the relation between the ultimate and the penultimate.

The Preparing of the Way What is this penultimate? It is everything that precedes the ultimate, everything that precedes the justification of the sinner by grace alone, everything which is to be regarded as leading up to the last thing when the last thing has been found. It is the same time everything which follows the ultimate and yet again precedes it. There is, therefore, no penultimate in itself; as though a thing could justify itself in itself as being a thing before the last thing; a thing becomes penultimate only through the ultimate, that is to say, at the moment when it has already lost its own validity. The penultimate, then, does not determine the ultimate; it is the ultimate which determines the penultimate. . . .

... For the sake of the ultimate the penultimate must be preserved. Any arbitrary destruction of the penultimate will do serious injury to the ultimate. ...

Preparing the way for the word: this is the purpose of everything that has been said about the things before the last. ...

But all this does not exclude the task of preparing the way. This task is, on the contrary, a charge of immense responsibility for all those who know of the coming of Christ. The hungry person needs bread and the homeless person needs a roof; the dispossessed need justice and the lonely need fellowship; the undisciplined need order and the slave needs freedom. To allow the hungry to remain hungry would be blasphemy against God and one's neighbor, for what is the nearest to God is precisely the need of one's neighbor. To provide the neighbor with bread is to prepare the way for the coming of grace.

The Natural The concept of the natural has fallen into discredit in Protestant ethics. For some it was completely lost to sight in the darkness of general sinfulness, while for others, conversely, it was lighted up by the brilliance of absolute historicity. In both cases this was a disastrous mistake, for its consequence was that the concept of the natural no longer had a place in Protestant thought but was entirely abandoned to Catholic ethics. Now this meant a serious and substantial loss to Protestant thought, for it was now more or less deprived of the means of orientation in dealing with the practical questions of natural life. ...

The concept of the natural must, therefore, be recovered on the basis of the gospel. We speak of the natural, as distinct from the creaturely, in order to take into account the fact of the Fall; and we speak of the natural rather than of the sinful so that we may include in it the creaturely. The natural is that which, after the Fall, is directed towards the coming of Christ. The unnatural is that which, after the Fall, closes its doors against the coming of Christ. ...

Natural Life To idealistic thinkers it may seem out of place for a Christian ethic to speak first of rights and only later of duties. But our authority is not Kant; it is the Holy Scripture, and it is precisely for that reason that we must speak first of the rights of natural life, in other words of what is given to life, and only later of what is demanded of life. God gives before He demands. ... The rights of natural life are in the midst of the fallen world the reflected splendour of the glory of God's creation. They are not primarily something that a person can sue for his own interest, but they are something that is guaranteed by God Himself. The duties, on the other hand, derive from the rights themselves, as tasks are implied by gifts. They are implicit in the rights. Within the framework of the natural life, therefore, we in every case speak first of the rights and then of the duties, for by so doing, in the natural life too, we are allowing the gospel to have its way.

Christ, Reality, and Good

Thinking in Terms of Two Spheres ... Since the beginnings of Christian ethics after the times of the New Testament the main underlying conception in ethical thought, and the one which consciously or unconsciously has determined its whole course, has been the conception of a juxtaposition and conflict of two spheres, the one divine, holy, supernatural and Christian, and the other worldly, profane, natural and un-Christian. ...

It may be difficult to break the spell of this thinking in terms of two spheres, but it is nevertheless quite certain that it is in profound contradiction to the thought of the Bible and to the thought of the Reformation, and that consequently it aims wide of reality. There are not two realities, but only one reality, and this is the reality of God, which has become manifest in Christ in the reality of the world. ... Thus the theme of the two spheres, which has repeatedly become the dominant factor in the history of the Church, is foreign to the New Testament. The New Testament is concerned solely with the manner in which the reality of Christ assumes reality in the present world, which it has already encompassed, seized and possessed. ...

Ethical thinking in terms of spheres, then, is invalidated by faith in the revelation of the ultimate reality in Jesus Christ, and this means that there is no real possibility of being a Christian outside the reality of the world and that there is no real worldly existence outside the reality of Jesus Christ. There is no place to which the Christian can withdraw from the world, whether it be outwardly or in the sphere of the inner life. Any attempt to escape from the world must sooner or later be paid for with a sinful surrender to the world. ...

The Four Mandates The world, like all created things, is created through Christ and with Christ as its end, and consists in Christ alone (John 1.10; Col. 1.16). To speak of the world without speaking of Christ is empty and abstract. The world is relative to Christ, no matter whether it knows it or not. This relativeness of the world to Christ assumes concrete form in certain mandates of God in the world. The Scriptures name four such mandates: labour, marriage, government and the Church. We speak of divine mandates rather than of divine orders because the word "mandate" refers more clearly to a divinely imposed task rather than to a determination of being. It is God's will that there shall be labour, marriage, government and church in the world; and it is His will that all these, each in its own way, shall be through Christ, directed towards Christ, and in Christ. . . . It is not because labour, marriage, government and church *are* that they commanded by God, but it is because they are commanded by God that they *are*. And they are divine mandates only in so far as their being consciously or unconsciously subordinated to the divinely imposed task. If a concrete form of labour, marriage, government or church persistently and arbitrarily violates the assigned task, then the divine mandate lapses in this particular concrete instance.

The mandate of labour confronts us, according to the Bible, already with the first human. Adam is "to dress and to keep" the Garden of Eden (Gen. 2.15). Even after the Fall labour remains a mandate of divine discipline and grace (Gen. 3.17–19). In the sweat of their brow humans wrest their nourishment from the soil, and the range of human labour soon embraces everything from agriculture and economy to science and art (Gen. 4.17ff.). The labour which is instituted in Paradise is a participation by humans in the action of creation. . . .

Like the mandate of labour, the mandate of marriage also confronts us after the creation already with the first human. In marriage man and woman become one in the sight of God, just as Christ becomes one with His Church. "This is a great mystery" (Eph. 5.32f). God bestows on this union the blessing of fruitfulness, the generation of new life. Humans enter into the will of the Creator in sharing in the process of creation. . . .

The divine mandate of government presupposes the divine mandates of labour and marriage. In the world which it rules, the governing authority finds already present the two mandates through which God the Creator exercises his creative power, and is therefore dependent on these. Government cannot itself produce life or values. It is not creative. It preserves what has been created, maintaining it in the order which is assigned to it through the task which is imposed by God. It protects it by making law to consist in the acknowledgement of the divine mandates and by securing respect for this law by the force of the sword. . . . By the establishment of law and by the force of the sword the governing authority preserves the world for the reality of Jesus Christ. Everyone owes obedience to this governing authority—for Christ's sake.

The divine mandate of the Church is different from these three. This mandate is the task of enabling the reality of Jesus Christ to become real in the preaching and organization of the Church and the Christian life. It is concerned, therefore, with the eternal salvation of the whole world. The mandate of the Church extends to all humankind, and it does so within all the other mandates. The person is at the same time a labourer, a partner in marriage, and the subject of a government, so that there is an overlapping of the three mandates in the person and all three must be fulfilled simultaneously; and the mandate of the Church impinges on all these mandates, for now it is the Christian who is at once labourer, partner in marriage, and subject of a government. No division into separate spheres or spaces is permissible here. The whole person stands before the whole earthly and eternal reality, the reality which God has prepared for the person in Jesus Christ. . . .

History and Good

Correspondence with Reality   Action which is in accordance with Christ is in accordance with reality because it allows the world to be the world; it reckons with the world as the world; and yet it never forgets that in Jesus Christ the world is loved, condemned and reconciled by God. . . . It is the essence of Greek tragedy that a person's downfall is brought about by the conflict of incompatible laws. Creon and Antigone, Jason and Medea, Agamemnon and Clytemnestra, all are subject to the claim of these eternal laws which cannot be reconciled in one and the same life; obedience is rendered to the one law at the price of guilt in respect of the other law. The meaning of all genuine tragedies is not that one person is right and the other wrong, but that both incur guilt towards life itself; the structure of their life is an incurring of guilt in respect of the laws of the gods. This is the most profound experience of classical antiquity. Especially since the Renaissance it has exercised a decisive influence over western thought; . . . but in modern times it has only very rarely been perceived that this tragic experience has been overcome by the message of Christ. Even the modern Protestant ethic invokes the pathos of tragedy in its representation of the irreconcilable conflict of the Christian in the world, and claims that in this it is expressing an ultimate reality. All this unconsciously lies entirely under the spell of the heritage of antiquity; it is not Luther, but it is Aeschylus, Sophocles and Euripides who have invested human life with this tragic aspect. The seriousness of Luther is quite different from the seriousness of the classical tragedians. For the Bible and for Luther what ultimately requires to be considered in earnest is not the disunion of the gods in the form of their laws, but it is the unity of God and the reconciliation of the world with God in Jesus Christ; it is not the inescapability of guilt, but it is the simplicity of the life which follows from the reconciliation; it is not to fate, but the gospel as the ultimate reality of life; it is not the cruel triumph of the gods over falling humanity, but it is the election of the human to be human as the child of God in the world which is reconciled through grace. . . .

The Acceptance of Guilt From what has just been said it emerges that the structure of responsible action includes both readiness to accept guilt and freedom. . . .

When people take guilt upon themselves in responsibility, and no responsible person can avoid this, they impute this guilt to themselves and to no one else; they answer for it; they accept responsibility for it. They do not do this in the insolent presumptuousness of their own power, but they do it in the knowledge that this liberty is forced upon them and that in this liberty they are dependent on grace. Before other people the people of free responsibility are justified by necessity; before themselves they are acquitted by their conscience; but before God they hope only for mercy.

Freedom We must therefore conclude our analysis of the structure of responsible action by speaking of freedom.

Responsibility and freedom are corresponding concepts. Factually, though not chronologically, responsibility presupposes freedom and freedom can consist only in responsibility. Responsibility is the freedom of humans which is given only in the obligation to god and to our neighbor. . . .

. . . What is the place and what are the limits of my responsibility?

The Place of Responsibility

Vocation . . . It is not in the loyal discharge of the earthly obligations of their calling as citizens, workers and parents that a people fulfill the responsibility which is imposed on them, but is in hearing the call of Jesus Christ. This call does indeed summon them to earthly duties, but that is never the whole of the call, for it lies always beyond these duties, before them and behind them. The calling, in the New Testament sense, is never a sanctioning of worldly institutions as such; its "yes" to them always includes at the same time an extremely emphatic "no," an extremely sharp protest against the world.

The "Ethical" and the "Christian" as a Theme

The Commandment of God This brings us to the only possible object of a "Christian ethic," an object which lies beyond the "ethical," namely, the "commandment of God."

. . . God's commandment is the speech of God to humans. Both in its contents and in its form it is concrete speech to the concrete human. God's commandment leaves the human no room for application or interpretation. It leaves room only for obedience or disobedience. God's commandment cannot be found and known in detachment from time and place; it can only be heard in a local and temporal context. If God's commandment is not clear, definite and concrete to the last detail, then it is not God's commandment.

. . . Does this mean that at every moment of our lives we may be informed of the commandment of God by some special direct divine inspiration? . . . No, it does not mean that, for the concreteness of the divine commandment consists in its historicity; it confronts us in a historical form. Does this mean, then, that we are utterly lacking in certainty in the face of the extremely varying claims of the historical powers, and that, so far as the commandment of God is concerned, we are groping in the darkness? No, the reason why it does not mean this is that God makes His commandment heard in a definite historical form. We cannot now escape the question where and in what historical form God makes His commandment known. For the sake of simplicity and clarity, and even at the risk of a direct misunderstanding, we will begin by answering this question in the form of a thesis. God's commandment, which is manifested in Jesus Christ, comes to us in the Church, in the family, in labour and in government. . . .

. . . The commandment of God becomes the element in which one lives without always being conscious of it, and, thus it implies freedom of movement and of action, freedom from the fear of decision, freedom from fear to act, it implies certainty, quietude, confidence, balance and peace. I honour my parents, I am faithful in marriage, I respect the lives and property of others, not because at the frontiers of my life there is a threatening "thou shalt not," but because I accept as holy institutions of God these realities, parents, marriage, life and property, which confront me in the midst and in the fulness of life. It is only when the commandment no longer merely threatens me as a transgressor of the limits, it is only when it convinces and subdues me with its real contents, that it sets me free from the anxiety and the uncertainty of decision. If I love my wife, if I accept marriage as an institution of God, then there comes an inner freedom and certainty of life and action in marriage; I no longer watch with suspicion every step that I take; I no longer call into question every deed that I perform. The divine prohibition of adultery is then no longer the centre around which all my thought and action in marriage revolves. (As though the meaning and purpose of marriage consisted of nothing except the avoidance of adultery!) But it is the honouring and the free acceptance of marriage, the leaving behind of the prohibition of adultery, which is now the precondition for the fulfilment of the divine commission of marriage. The divine commandment has here become the permission to live in marriage in freedom and certainty.

The commandment of God is the permission to live as human before God.

The commandment of God is permission. It differs from all human laws in that it commands freedom. It is by overcoming this contradiction that it shows itself to be God's commandment; the impossible becomes possible, and that which lies beyond the range of what can be commanded, liberty, is the true object of this commandment. . . .

Before the commandment of God people do not permanently stand like Hercules at the crossroads. They are not everlastingly striving for the right decision. They are not always wearing themselves out in a conflict of duties. They are not continually failing and beginning again. Nor does the commandment of God itself make its appearance only in these great, agitated and intensely conscious moments of crisis in life. On the contrary, before the commandment of God humans may at last really move forward along the road and no longer stand endlessly at the crossroads. They can now have the right decision really behind them, and not always before them. Entirely without inner conflict they can do one thing and leave undone another thing which, according to theoretical ethics, is perhaps equally urgent. They can already have made a beginning and they can allow themselves to be guided, escorted and protected on their way by prayers as though by a good angel. And God's commandment itself can give life unity of direction and personal guidance only in the form of seemingly small and insignificant everyday words, sayings, hints and help.

The purpose of the commandment lies not in the avoidance of transgression, and not in the torment of ethical conflict and decision, but in freely accepted, self-evident life in the Church, in marriage, in the family, in work and in the state. . . .

State and Church

The Basis of Government

A. In the Nature of Humanity. The ancients, especially Aristotle, base the state on the character of humans. The state is the supreme consummation of the rational character of humans, and to serve it is the supreme purpose of human life. All ethics is political ethics. Virtues are political virtues. This theory of the state was taken over in principle by Catholic theology. The state is a product of human nature. Human's ability to live in society derives from the Creation, as does also the relation of rulers and ruled. . . .

B. In Sin. The Reformation, by taking up ideas of St. Augustine, broke away from the ancient Greek concept of the state. The Reformation does not represent the state as a community arising from the created nature of humanity, although traces of this idea, too, can be found in the writings of some of the Reformers; it places the origin of the state, as government, in the Fall. It was sin that made necessary the divine institution of government. The sword which God has given to government is to be used by it in order to protect humans against the chaos which is caused by sin. Government is to punish the criminal and to safeguard life. . . .

C. In Christ. It becomes clear from these last remarks, and indeed from everything that we have said so far on this subject, that the basing of the state on sin or on the nature of humanity leads to a conception of the state as a self-contained entity, a conception which fails to take account of the relation of the state to Jesus Christ. . . . It is through Jesus Christ and for Jesus Christ that all things are created (John 1.2; I Cor. 8.6; Heb. 1.2), and in particular "thrones, dominions, principalities and powers" (Col. 1.16). It is only in Jesus Christ that all these things "consist" (Col. 1.17). And it is He who is "the head of the church" (Col. 1.1). A theological proposition with regard to government, with regard, that is to say, to the government which is instituted by God and not to some general philosophical idea of government, is therefore in no circumstances possible without reference to Jesus Christ, and to Jesus Christ as the head of His Church; no such proposition is possible without reference to the Church of Jesus Christ. The true basis of government is therefore Jesus Christ Himself. . . .

The Divine Character of Government

A. In Its Being. Government is given to us not as an idea or a task to be fulfilled but as a reality and as something which "is" (. . . Rom. 13.1c). It is in its being that it is a divine office. . . . The being of government is independent of the manner of its coming into being. No matter if human's path to governmental office repeatedly passes through guilt (cf. Shakespeare's histories), the being of government lies beyond its earthly coming into being; for government is an institution of God, not in its coming into being but in its being. . . . This is that historical relationship of one actual entity to another which is found again in the relationship between father and child. . . . There can be no ethical isolation of the son from his father, and indeed, on the basis of actual being, there is a necessity of sharing in the assuming and carrying of the guilt of a father or a brother. There is no glory in standing amid the ruins of one's native town in the consciousness that at least one has not oneself incurred any guil. . . .

B. In Its Task. The being of government is linked with a divine commission. Its being is fulfilled only in the fulfilment of the commission. A total apostasy from its commission would jeopardize its being. But by God's providence this total apostasy is possible only as an eschatological event, and as such it leads amidst grievous torments to a total separation of the congregation from the government as the embodiment of Antichrist. The mission of government consists in serving the dominion of Christ on earth by the exercise of the worldly power of the sword and of justice. Government serves Christ by establishing and maintaining an outward justice by means of the sword which is given to it, and to it alone, in deputyship for God. And it has not only the negative task of punishing the wicked; but also the positive task of praising the good or "them that do well" (I Pet. 2.14). It is therefore endowed, on the one hand, with a judicial authority, and on the other hand, with a right to educate for goodness, i.e., for outward justice or righteousness. . . .

C. In Its Claim. . . . In the exercise of the mission of government the demand for obedience is unconditional and qualitatively total; it extends both to conscience and to bodily life. Belief, conscience and bodily life are subject to an obligation of obedience with respect to the divine commission of government. A doubt can arise only when the contents and the extent of the commission of government become questionable. Christians are neither obliged nor able to examine the rightfulness of the demand of government in each particular case. Their duty of obedience is binding on them until government directly compels them to offend against the divine commandment, that is to say, until government openly denies its divine commission and thereby forfeits it claim. . . . The refusal of obedience in the case of a particular historical and political decision of government must, therefore, like this decision itself, be a venture undertaken on one's own responsibility. A historical decision cannot be entirely resolved into ethical terms; there remains a residuum, the venture of action. That is true both of the government and of its subjects.[20]

NOTES

1. [Dietrich Bonhoeffer, "The Nature of the Church," in *A Testament to Freedom: The Essential Writings of Dietrich Bonhoeffer*, ed. Geffrey B. Kelly and F. Burton Nelson (San Francisco: HarperSanFrancisco, 1990), 91.]
2. [Dietrich Bonhoeffer, "Thy Kingdom Come: The Prayer of the Church for the Kingdom of God on Earth," in *A Testament to Freedom*, 94, 97.]
3. [Dietrich Bonhoeffer, "Creation and Fall: The Image of God on Earth," in *A Testament to Freedom*, 113–115.]
4. [Dietrich Bonhoeffer, *Discipleship*, trans. Martin Kaske and Ilse Tödt, in *Dietrich Bonhoeffer Works* (Minneapolis: Fortress Press, 1996–), 4:39, 43–45.]

5. [Dietrich Bonhoeffer, *Temptation*, ed. Eberhard Bethge, trans. Kathleen Down-ham (London: SCM Press Ltd, 1955), 9–11. The Confessing Church seminary held a reunion in 1937. Bonhoeffer began each day with a Bible study for the group. The manuscript for his presentations was found and was published as *Temptation*.]

6. [Dietrich Bonhoeffer, *Letters and Papers from Prison*, ed. Eberhard Bethge, trans. Reginald Fuller, enlarged edition (New York: Simon & Schuster, 1997), 3–7, 9–11, 16–17. Eberhard Bethge was able to save letters and papers that Bon-hoeffer had sent him from prison. In 1950 he overcame his reluctance to make them public and began making extracts of them into a small volume to share with friends and others who might be interested. He was surprised at the re-sponse that would ultimately make it a best seller and stimulate intense inter-est and debate. Bonhoeffer wrote this essay, 'Prologue: After Ten Years," as a 1943 Christmas gift for his fellow conspirators, friends, and family. The final, unfinished paragraph may have been intended for inclusion with this essay.]

7. [*Letters from Prison*, 156–158. Bethge had been Bonhoeffer's student, then col-league, then closest friend. And after Bonhoeffer's imprisonment he became the person with whom Bonhoeffer could frankly explore his new theological approaches. The correspondence—in spite of delays, interruptions and other difficulties—allowed Bethge to raise questions and make suggestions about the developments in Bonhoeffer's thinking. It must have been a great, influen-tial help to Bonhoeffer.]

8. [Ibid., 168.]

9. [Ibid., 279–282.]

10. [Ibid., 285–287.]

11. [Ibid., 300.]

12. [Ibid., 311–312.]

13. [Ibid., 325–328.]

14. [Ibid., 336–337.]

15. [Ibid., 341–342.]

16. [Ibid., 344–346.]

17. [Ibid., 359–361.]

18. [Ibid., 361–362.]

19. [Ibid., 369–370.]

20. [Dietrich Bonhoeffer, *Ethics*, trans. Neville Horton Smith (New York: Simon & Schuster, 1995), 21, 40, 41, 81–82, 84, 86, 87, 125, 128–130, 133–136, 142–143, 150, 193–198, 204–208, 227–228, 236, 244, 250, 251, 272–280, 328–332, 335, 334–339. Bonhoeffer regarded his *Ethics* as the great task of his life, and he deeply re-gretted not having the chance to complete it. He worked on a manuscript from 1940–43. During this period, his theology was changing, his life was sub-ject to ongoing disruption and the extraordinary demands of the conspiracy against Hitler, and he had no opportunity to develop his thoughts into a whole. Eberhard Bethge retrieved the existing pieces of the manuscript from their hiding places and published them in 1949. The various sections carried

no definitive proposal for their proper sequence. In writing earlier books, Bonhoeffer never followed a set plan. He allowed his work to grow organically, subject to constant change. Bethge had no easy task in settling on a fit ordering of the pages. He revised the 1949 sequence for a 1963 edition, and the *Dietrich Bonhoeffer Werke* edition of 1992 has established yet a third sequence. The following excerpts follow the 1949 ordering. What Bonhoeffer was able to set down is creatively and intriguingly challenging. "Ethics" did not mean for him establishing a system or set of principles but a way of describing specific, relational conformation to the living presence of Christ in the world. Because Christ is the person who exists for others, and because the Church is the body of Christ in the world, she, too, exists for others. The "others" are all those with whom Christ identifies, and in Bonhoeffer's circumstance this meant those, especially Jews, who were Nazi victims. In solidarity with them, members of the Church are in conscience free to take bold, responsible action and to accept guilt in the process.]

[CHAPTER 5]

Reinhold Niebuhr (1892–1971)

COMMENTARY

DAVISON M. DOUGLAS

Reinhold Niebuhr was the twentieth century's most influential American theologian and, after Martin Luther King Jr., the most prominent American preacher. Extraordinarily prolific—he wrote twenty-one books and more than 2,600 articles[1]—Niebuhr interpreted the theological significance of contemporary national and world events for a broad and diverse audience. Niebuhr was also a highly influential political theorist, particularly in the field of international relations. In 1962, the distinguished political theorist Hans Morgenthau called Niebuhr "the greatest living political philosopher of America, perhaps the only creative political philosopher since Calhoun."[2]

Niebuhr articulated a "Christian realist" perspective in which he challenged many of the secular and religious orthodoxies of his day by emphasizing the depths of human sinfulness. Possessed of a passion for social justice characteristic of the biblical prophets, Niebuhr urged the creation of political structures that might contribute to a more just society; at the same time, he realized the profound difficulty of achieving such a society in light of the realities of human nature. Niebuhr directed his incisive critiques at both the church and the secular world. He sought to bring "the judgment of Christ to bear as rigorously on the household of faith as upon the secular and pagan world, even as the prophets of Israel were as severe in mediating the divine judgment upon Israel as upon Babylon."[3] In the process, Niebuhr caused many modern secular thinkers to take more seriously the claims of Christianity. As one Niebuhr scholar puts it, Niebuhr "attempted to overcome, and to a remarkable degree has succeeded in overcoming, the estrangement of the modern mind from the insights and content of the Christian faith."[4]

BIOGRAPHY

Born in 1892, Niebuhr grew up in Missouri and Illinois, the son of a minister of the German Evangelical Synod of North America, a church in the tradition of the Union Church of Prussia with both Lutheran and Reformed roots. Niebuhr was educated for three years at Elmhurst College, near Chicago, and then at Eden Theological Seminary, near St. Louis, both institutions operated by the German Evangelical Synod. Upon graduation from Eden at the age of twenty, Niebuhr was ordained a minister in his denomination, but he promptly left for two years' additional training at Yale Divinity School. Upon receiving his B.D. and M.A. degrees from Yale, Niebuhr began a parish ministry in 1915 at Bethel Evangelical Church in Detroit, where he remained until 1928.

Niebuhr's years in the parish would be formative in his thinking. Niebuhr witnessed at close hand the racism that oppressed southern blacks who had migrated to Detroit during and after World War I, as well as the poor treatment of workers in the city's automobile industry. Niebuhr spoke publicly against the Ku Klux Klan and its influence in Detroit politics, and he chaired an interracial committee to investigate racial conflicts in the city. A sharp critic of Henry Ford, Niebuhr helped lead a campaign against the industrialist's labor policies and published a series of articles in which he documented the harsh conditions of the assembly line in Ford's automobile factories. Aspiring to build a labor party in the United States modeled on the British Labour party, Niebuhr would later comment that his experience with Ford made him a socialist.[5] While in Detroit, Niebuhr also embraced pacifism and served for a time as national chairman of the Fellowship of Reconciliation.

During these years in his Detroit parish, Niebuhr obtained a national reputation as a compelling speaker and thoughtful writer, a renown fueled in part by his service as a writer for the liberal Protestant publication *The Christian Century*. In 1928, Niebuhr accepted a position as associate professor of applied Christianity at Union Theological Seminary in New York City, where he would remain until his retirement in 1960. But Niebuhr's immersion into the academy did not stem his interest in the political struggles of the day. When Niebuhr moved to New York City, he became actively involved in politics, joining the Socialist Party, editing its journal *World Tomorrow*, and helping to found the Fellowship of Socialist Christians. Writing in 1930, Niebuhr claimed that the concentration of economic power in private industry in modern society had become the source of great injustice "because the private ownership of the productive processes and the increased centralization of the resultant power in the hands of a few, make inevitably for irresponsibility."[6] Niebuhr ran unsuccessfully for the New York state senate in 1930 and for the United States Congress in 1932 as a candidate of the Socialist Party.

Over the course of the 1930s, however, Niebuhr became disenchanted with both socialist politics and pacifism. In significant measure, Niebuhr's shift in viewpoint owed to the rise and abuses of authoritarian states in Europe—in particular, Stalinism in the Soviet Union and Nazism in Germany. In addition to leaving the Socialist Party, Niebuhr resigned in 1940 from the editorial board of *The Christian Century* because of its advocacy of a policy of neutrality in the face of Nazi Germany's aggressive expansionism. Niebuhr founded another journal instead, *Christianity and Crisis*, which articulated his "Christian realist" theology, grounded in the reality of human sinfulness and the need to develop political and legal institutions to corral the manifestations of that sinfulness.

Niebuhr actively urged American entry into World War II. As chair of the Union for Democratic Action, founded in 1941, Niebuhr vigorously supported the Lend-Lease program to assist Great Britain as well as American participation in the war. During the war, Niebuhr was one of the few prominent Americans who spoke publicly of the plight of European Jews and who urged a more generous immigration policy to relieve their suffering.

After World War II, Niebuhr joined a number of other former socialists to form the Americans for Democratic Action, committed to both the continuation of New Deal domestic programs and a strong anticommunist foreign policy. Before the war, Niebuhr, like many socialists, had viewed the New Deal as an ill-fated attempt to reform capitalism; in time, he embraced it as a pragmatic effort to deal with the devastating consequences of the Depression. Niebuhr became an important figure in the postwar democratic left; he served as advisor to Secretary of State George Marshall and helped to define what would be described as the "vital center" of American politics. Indeed, during the postwar era, Niebuhr exercised considerable influence over the development of American foreign and domestic policy. Niebuhr's "political realism" helped to justify America's postwar domestic and international commitments, even though Niebuhr ultimately found all "political and social constructs wanting when measured against the yardstick of divine justice."[7]

In addition to his political engagements, Niebuhr was a remarkably productive writer throughout his life. In several of his books, Niebuhr combined his theological reflections with his political insights. During the early 1930s, Niebuhr attempted to synthesize certain aspects of Marxism and Christianity. By the late 1930s, Niebuhr had concluded that such a synthesis was "neither possible nor desirable . . . and [instead] worked out the design for a Christian realism, grounded equally in the Augustinianism of the Reformation and his own hard-won political wisdom."[8] Although Niebuhr's early writings were more social criticism than theological reflection, many of his subsequent works were more explicitly theological. In this regard, Niebuhr was influenced by both Paul Tillich, the great German theologian who joined the Union Seminary faculty in 1933, and his brother, H. Richard Niebuhr, a Christian ethicist at Yale Divinity School.

During the late 1930s and early 1940s, Niebuhr wrote his most systematic theological compilation, the two-volume *The Nature and Destiny of Man*, which Niebuhr presented in 1939 as the Gifford Lectures in Edinburgh. The publication of these lectures established Niebuhr as a major Christian thinker and cultural critic. But throughout his life, Niebuhr resisted describing himself as a theologian: "I cannot and do not claim to be a theologian. I have taught Christian Social Ethics for a quarter of a century and have also dealt in the ancillary field of 'apologetics.' . . . I have never been very competent in the nice points of theology; and I must confess that I have not been sufficiently interested heretofore to acquire the competence."[9] Rather than consider the finer points of Christian theology, such as the doctrine of God or of Christ, Niebuhr addressed most of his attention to the meaning of contemporary events in light of his Christian understandings. As one Niebuhr scholar noted: "Probably more than any other U.S. theologian, Niebuhr moved with utter ease between the language of Zion and that of regnant secular culture."[10] Niebuhr's production was slowed by a series of strokes that beset him beginning in 1952, but he remained an active writer until his death in 1971.

Niebuhr, throughout his life, offered a "Christian realist" critique of twentieth-century utopian movements such as socialism, pacifism, communism, and statist liberalism. He powerfully influenced those interested in pursuing social justice, while at the same time urging recognition of the limits of such efforts. Niebuhr continually counseled reformers to have a healthy skepticism about their work, to retain "the firm resolve that inherited dogmas and generalizations will not be accepted, no matter how revered or venerable, if they do not contribute to the establishment of justice in a given situation."[11] One of the striking ironies of Niebuhr and his work is the broad array of later thinkers who claim him as their intellectual antecedent—from conservatives drawn to his emphasis on the depths of human sinfulness and the corruption of authoritarian government, to liberals drawn to his unbridled passion for social justice. Niebuhr's influence extended far beyond those with religious sensibilities. Arthur Schlesinger Jr. noted of Niebuhr that he articulated the great themes of Christianity "with such irresistible relevance to contemporary experience that even those who have no decisive faith in the supernatural find their own reading of experience and history given new and significant dimensions."[12]

THEOLOGICAL AND INTELLECTUAL CONTEXT OF NIEBUHR'S WRITINGS

Niebuhr, appropriate to his task of teaching applied Christianity at Union Theological Seminary, was deeply influenced by the contemporary intellectual and political currents of his day. His writings reflect an effort to articulate a Christian theology in the context of contemporary social realities. Hence, one cannot fully understand Niebuhr's writings without exploring the theological and intellectual context in which he wrote.

Niebuhr began his parish ministry during the Progressive Era, a time of great optimism among religious and secular liberals about the possibility of social reform. Religious liberals of the early twentieth century championed the ability of humanity to be "redeemed" and sought to establish a "kingdom of God" on earth, marked by justice for all groups. Writing from a variety of Protestant traditions, these religious liberals "were confident that a new age of social Christianity was about to begin, transforming the raw realities of life in industrial cities and ushering in an era of international peace by the application of Christian love."[13] For example, Walter Rauschenbusch, the leading proponent of the Christian Social Gospel movement, claimed that "for the first time in religious history we have the possibility of so directing religious energy by scientific knowledge that a comprehensive and continuous reconstruction of social life in the name of God is within the bounds of human possibility."[14] Other religious liberals extended this optimism to class and race relations. Presbyterian theologian William Adams Brown wrote in 1930, "In relations between races; in strife between capital and labor; in our attitude toward the weaker and more dependent members of society . . . we are developing a social conscience and situations which would have been accepted a generation ago as a matter of course are felt as an intolerable scandal."[15]

Secular liberals shared the optimism of their religious counterparts about the capacity for human progress and expressed confidence in the capacity of science and education to lead to greater progress and to mitigate human suffering. John Dewey, for example, believed that social injustice had "its main roots in ignorance—which must itself gradually yield before the extension of enlightenment through education and before the power of moral suasion."[16] These secular liberals, Dewey included, developed a theory of history that emphasized an upward trajectory of human moral development.

Niebuhr rejected this optimistic conception of the development of human history and held that liberal optimism toward moral progress was profoundly misplaced. "We have interpreted world history as a gradual ascent to the Kingdom of God which waits for final triumph only upon the willingness of Christians to 'take Christ seriously,'" Niebuhr wrote in 1940. "There is nothing in Christ's own teachings . . . to justify this interpretation of world history."[17] Influenced by the racial and labor strife he witnessed initially during his years in Detroit, Niebuhr expressed pessimism about the "moralistic utopianism of the liberal Church"[18] that in his view failed to grasp the dark realities of human nature. In particular, Niebuhr charged that liberal optimists located the cause of evil in certain social conditions that can be overcome, as opposed to certain inherent features of human nature that are much more difficult to control.[19] To Niebuhr, contrary to the religious and secular liberals of the 1920s and 1930s, the ultimate source of evil in human society is not lack of education or deficient social or economic arrangements, but is rather the self-interestedness of human nature. Niebuhr viewed self-interest, coercion, and the struggle for power as inevitable in human relations.

For the rest of his life, Niebuhr would challenge those political and social philosophies that lacked a due regard for the depths of human sinfulness. During the late 1930s and 1940s, he criticized the utopian enthusiasm of those who embraced Marxist solutions to economic problems, particularly when such solutions were accompanied by authoritarian government. Niebuhr was strongly influenced by the biblical tradition of the Hebrew prophets, who railed against injustice, and by the apostle Paul, who recognized the depths of human sinfulness. Moreover, both Augustine and the Protestant reformers who also emphasized the problem of human sin had a profound influence on the development of Niebuhr's thinking.

NIEBUHR'S THEOLOGY OF HUMAN NATURE

The starting point for Niebuhr's theology was clearly his understanding of human nature. Virtually all of his theological and political reflections were rooted in the problem of human self-interest and how it impedes the struggle to establish a society grounded in principles of love and justice. Niebuhr believed that the modern world did not fully grasp the realities of human nature and that many of the world's thorniest social and political problems were grounded in that failure.

Niebuhr's first major book, *Moral Man and Immoral Society*, published in 1932, "sent a series of shockwaves through America's liberal Protestant community."[20] Niebuhr targeted his book at "the moralists, both religious and secular, who imagine that the egoism of individuals is being progressively checked by the development of rationality or the growth of a religiously inspired goodwill and that nothing but the continuance of this process is necessary to establish social harmony between all the human societies and collectives."[21] Liberal reviewers suggested that Niebuhr's "emphasis on sin made him a traitor to progress."[22] Niebuhr, for his part, never retreated from his pessimistic assessment of human self-interest. Writing almost thirty years later, Niebuhr commented that he should have titled his book *The Not So Moral Man in His Less Moral Communities.*[23]

In *Moral Man and Immoral Society*, Niebuhr conceded that individuals, despite their sinful nature, may on occasion be capable of moral behavior in the sense that they are "capable, on occasion, of preferring the advantages of others to their own."[24] But this capacity for moral behavior is far less prevalent among social groups: "Human groups, classes, nations, and races are selfish, whatever may be the moral idealism of individual members within the groups."[25] Accusing liberalism of embracing a "romantic overestimate of human virtue and moral capacity," Niebuhr complained that "what is lacking among all these moralists, whether religious or rational, is an understanding of the brutal character of the behavior of all human collectives, and the power of self-interest and collective egoism in all inter-group relations."[26]

Niebuhr argued that although an individual may occasionally restrain his or her self-interested behavior, "every human group which benefits from a present order in society will use every ingenuity and artifice to maintain its privileges and to sanctify them in the name of public order; that political life is, in short, a thinly veiled barbarism."[27] Recognizing that Christianity articulates self-sacrifice as a central ethic, Niebuhr argued that this ideal "is achieved only rarely in individual life and is not achieved in group life at all. No nation, race, or class sacrifices itself. Human groups make a virtue of the assertion of self-interest and will probably do so until the end of history."[28]

Noting that secular and religious liberals believe that deep-seated self-interest can be controlled through either "the development of rationality or the growth of a religiously inspired goodwill,"[29] Niebuhr was emphatic that the tendency of groups toward self-interest is too great to overcome through education or moral instruction:

> Social intelligence and moral goodwill . . . may serve to mitigate the brutalities of social conflict, but they cannot abolish the conflict itself. That could be accomplished only if human groups, whether racial, national or economic, could achieve a degree of reason and sympathy which would permit them to see and to understand the interests of others as vividly as they understand their own, and a moral goodwill which would prompt them to affirm the rights of others as vigorously as they affirm their own. Given the inevitable limitations of human imagination and intelligence, this is an ideal which individuals may approximate but which is beyond the capacities of human societies . . . Thus, scientists "who dream of 'socializing' man and religious idealists who strive to increase the sense of moral responsibility . . . are not conscious of the limitations in human nature which finally frustrate their efforts."[30]

While *Moral Man and Immoral Society* was primarily a social and political critique of liberal optimism, in *The Nature and Destiny of Man* Niebuhr developed a theological basis for his earlier social and political theories. Surveying classical, biblical, and modern views of human nature, Niebuhr concluded that modern thinkers were too optimistic about the essence of human nature:

> Modern man has an essentially easy conscience; and nothing gives the diverse and discordant notes of modern culture so much harmony as the unanimous opposition of modern man to Christian conceptions of the sinfulness of man. The idea that man is sinful at the very center of his personality . . . is universally rejected . . . If modern culture conceives man primarily in terms of the uniqueness of his rational faculties, it finds the root of his evil in his involvement in the natural impulses and natural necessities from which it hopes to free him by the increase of his rational faculties.[31]

By contrast, Niebuhr articulated an Augustinian notion of human sin that manifests itself as pride. Niebuhr identified three types of pride that humans exhibit as a means of dealing with the anxieties and insecurities of life: pride of power, pride of knowledge, and pride of virtue. Expanding on certain ideas about group behavior that he had introduced in *Moral Man and Immoral Society*, Niebuhr argued that this tendency toward pride is particularly nefarious when exhibited in groups: "Collective pride is thus man's last, and in some respects most pathetic, effort to deny the determinate and contingent character of his existence. The very essence of human sin is in it . . . Collective egotism and group pride are a more pregnant source of injustice and conflict than purely individual pride."[32] Some feminist theologians would later criticize Niebuhr's emphasis on pride as the core human sin by arguing that pride "is a peculiarly male temptation" and is "an inadequate description of women."[33] Rather, argued one feminist critic of Niebuhr, the problem that a woman confronts is not the sin of pride but instead that "she insufficiently values herself."[34]

One manifestation of human pride is what Niebuhr termed the "will-to-power," a concept that he developed in his 1944 book, *The Children of Light and the Children of Darkness.* Niebuhr observed that humans, like animals, have a will-to-live, which is essentially a survival instinct. The problem for society, however, is that humans also have a will-to-power:

> The will-to-live is also spiritually transmuted into the will-to-power or into the desire for "power and glory." Man, being more than a natural creature, is not interested merely in physical survival but in prestige and social approval. Having the intelligence to anticipate the perils in which he stands in nature and history, he invariably seeks to gain security against these perils by enhancing his power, individually and collectively. Possessing a darkly unconscious sense of his insignificance in the total scheme of things, he seeks to compensate for his insignificance by pretensions of pride.[35]

Thus, conflicts between humans are not merely conflicts driven by the need to survive. The will-to-power places humans "fundamentally in conflict" with other humans:

> The conflicts between men are thus never simple conflicts between competing survival impulses. They are conflicts in which each man or group seeks to guard its power and prestige against the peril of competing expressions of power and pride. Since the very possession of power and prestige always involves some encroachment upon the prestige and power of others, this conflict is by its very nature a more stubborn and difficult one than the mere competition between various survival impulses in nature.[36]

Niebuhr identified the root of many of the problems that beset the twentieth century, particularly World War II, in this will-to-power: "If we survey any period of history, and not merely the present tragic era of world catastrophe, it becomes quite apparent that human ambitions, lusts and desires, are more inevitably inordinate ... [and] are of more tragic proportions" than previously understood.[37]

THE LAW OF LOVE

Against this will-to-power grounded in human self-interest is the "law of love," best articulated in the ethic "Thou shalt love thy neighbor as thyself."[38] Niebuhr wrote extensively about the "law of love," which he described as the ultimate norm for all human conduct.[39] "Love is really the law of life," Niebuhr wrote. "It is not some ultimate possibility which has nothing to do with human history."[40] Though difficult to obtain, the law of love must remain the normative goal for individuals and communities:

> What is significant about the Christian ethic is precisely this: that it does not regard the historic as normative. Man may be, as Thomas Hobbes observed, a wolf to his fellowman. But this is not his essential nature. Let Christianity beware, particularly radical Protestantism, that it does not accept the habits of a sinful world as the norms of a Christian collective life. For the Christian only the law of love is normative.[41]

Niebuhr believed that this law of love, or "original justice," is part of the essential nature of humans. But Niebuhr conceded that humans, in their sinfulness, reject this law of love: "The freedom of man creates the possibility of actions which are contrary to and in defiance of the requirements of this essential nature."[42] Nevertheless, this essential nature has not been completely obliterated, because "sin neither destroys the structure by virtue of which man is man nor yet eliminates the sense of obligation toward the essential nature of man, which is the remnant of his perfection."[43] Niebuhr reasoned from experience that the "universal testimony of human experience is the most persuasive refutation of any theory of human depravity which denies that man has any knowledge of the good."[44] In fact, argued Niebuhr, "faith in Christ could find no lodging place in the human soul, were [the human soul] not uneasy about the contrast between its true and present state."[45] Thus, for Niebuhr, "sin is a corruption of man's true essence *but not its destruction.*"[46] For Niebuhr, "against pessimistic theories of human nature which affirm the total depravity of man it is important to assert the continued presence in man of the *justitia originalis* [original justice], of the law of love."[47]

By the same token, Niebuhr emphasized the extraordinary difficulty of living the law of love and noted, "It is equally important, in refutation of modern secular and Christian forms of utopianism, to recognize that the fulfillment of the law of love is no simple possibility."[48] Reflecting the paradoxical style so typical of his writings, Niebuhr described the law of love as an "impossible possibility."[49] For Niebuhr, "the law of love stands on the edge of history and not in history . . . [and] it represents an ultimate and not an immediate possibility."[50] Simply teaching the law of love is insufficient: "If we believe that the only reason men do not love each other perfectly is because the law of love has not been preached persuasively enough, we believe something to which experience does not conform."[51]

So, then, is true love of neighbor ever attainable? This question took Niebuhr directly into the heart of the concept of grace and the meaning of Christ's atoning death. As Niebuhr put the question: is the grace of Christ "primarily a power of righteousness which so heals the sinful heart that henceforth it is able to fulfill the law of love," or is it "primarily the assurance of divine mercy for a persistent sinfulness which man never overcomes completely"?[52] Niebuhr claimed that "the general answer of pre-Reformation Christianity was that the *justitia originalis*, the law of love, was not a possibility for natural man but that it could be realized by the redeemed man in whom 'grace' had healed the hurt of sin."[53] Niebuhr disagreed. Though he does suggest that grace is "the power of God in man" and "represents an accession of resources, which man does not have of himself, enabling him to become what he truly ought to be,"[54] Niebuhr ultimately concluded that humans will not completely overcome their sinful inclinations, even as they find the religious peace "of being accepted by God despite the continued sinfulness of the heart."[55] For Niebuhr, "this is the truth which the Reformation emphasized and which modern Protestant Christianity has almost completely forgotten."[56] Niebuhr elaborated on the Reformation perspective: "The Reformation took the fact of sin as a perennial category of historic existence more seriously [than pre- Reformation thinkers] and . . . defined divine 'grace' not so much as a divine power in man which completes his incompletion but as a divine mercy toward man which brings his uneasy conscience to rest despite the continued self-contradiction of human effort."[57] In reaching this conclusion, Niebuhr turned, as he often did, to the teachings of human experience:

> The sorry annals of Christian fanaticism, of unholy religious hatreds, of sinful ambitions hiding behind the cloak of religious sanctity, of political power impulses compounded with pretensions of devotion to God, offer the most irrefutable proof of the error in every Christian doctrine and every interpretation of the Christian experience which claim that grace can remove the final contradiction between man and God.[58]

Niebuhr's consideration of the limits of the law of love in light of human nature led him directly into a reconsideration of pacifism, which he embraced in his early adulthood but jettisoned as his understanding of the depths of human sinfulness became more profound. By the late 1930s, Niebuhr concluded that pacifism is unrealistic in light of the need to resist evil in the world: "The [pacifist] ethic of Jesus [is] finally and ultimately normative, but [is] not immediately applicable to the task of securing justice in a sinful world. . . . In every political situation it is necessary to achieve justice by resisting pride and power."[59] The pacifists miss this point, argued Niebuhr, because they "do not know human nature well enough to be concerned about the contradictions between the law of love and the sin of man."[60] Rather, Niebuhr concluded, pacifists "assert that if only men loved one another, all the complex, and sometimes horrible, realities of the political order could be dispensed with. They do not see that their 'if' begs the most basic problem of human history. It is because men are sinners that justice can be achieved only by a certain degree of coercion on the one hand, and by resistance to coercion and tyranny on the other hand."[61]

Niebuhr also identified a certain naiveté in the church with respect to the possibility of living by the law of love: "The sum total of the liberal Church's effort to apply the law of love to politics without qualification is really a curious medley of hopes and regrets. The Church declares that men ought to live by the law of love and that nations as well as individuals ought to obey it. . . . These appeals to the moral will and this effort to support the moral will by desperate hopes are politically as unrealistic as they are religiously superficial."[62]

For Niebuhr, mere appeals to the "love thy neighbor" ethic of Jesus do not deal with the realities of human nature: "The ethic of Jesus does not deal at all with the immediate moral problem of every human life—the problem of arranging some kind of armistice between various contending factions and forces."[63] Or, put another way, "the gospel is something more than the law of love. The gospel deals with the fact that men violate the law of love."[64]

THE STATE: POSSIBILITIES FOR BOTH JUSTICE AND EVIL

Given the depths of human sinfulness that impede fulfillment of the law of love, how then should we organize our social and political institutions accordingly? As Niebuhr posed the issue, "The contradiction between the law of love and the sinfulness of man raises not only the ultimate religious problem how men are to have peace if they do not overcome the contradiction . . . it also raises the immediate problem how men are to achieve a tolerable harmony of life with life, if human pride and selfishness prevent the realization of the law of love."[65] In addressing this dilemma, Niebuhr displayed his fundamental "realist" perspective on human nature. For Niebuhr, given the realities of the will-to-power and human failure to fulfill the law of love, justice demands that society use the coercive power of the state to resist tyranny and evil.

The problem, of course, is that those who utilize the power of the state to resist evil are subject to the same will-to-power that inflicts all humans. Accordingly, Niebuhr devoted considerable attention to the question of how to structure the power of the state so that it might resist evil without becoming evil itself. "Governments must coerce," Niebuhr conceded, but he also recognized that "there is an element of evil in this coercion. It is always in danger of serving the purposes of the coercing power rather than the general weal. We cannot fully trust the motives of any ruling class or power. That is why it is important to maintain democratic checks upon the centers of power."[66] Niebuhr's distrust of the potential of those in power to abuse their authority extended to all governments, both the authoritarian states of Germany and the Soviet Union as well as democratic ones. "To look at human communities from the perspective of the Kingdom of God is to know that there is a sinful element in all the expedients which the political order uses to establish justice. That is why even the seemingly most stable justice degenerates periodically into either tyranny or anarchy."[67]

As authoritarian governments gained power in Europe during the 1930s, leading to extraordinary human suffering during the 1940s, Niebuhr emerged as an articulate apologist for democratic government. "Man's capacity for justice makes democracy possible," Niebuhr famously wrote in *The Children of Light and the Children of Darkness* in 1944, "but man's inclination to injustice makes democracy necessary."[68] Niebuhr elaborated: "Democracy is a perennial necessity because justice will always require that the power of government be checked as democracy checks it; and because peace requires that social conflict be arbitrated by the non-violent technique of the democratic process."[69]

Beginning with the presupposition that "it is not possible to eliminate the sinful element in the political expedients,"[70] Niebuhr urged that society create checks and balances in its political structures that might control the natural human impetus toward self-aggrandizement: "Justice is basically dependent upon a balance of power. Whenever an individual or a group or a nation possesses undue power, and whenever this power is not checked by the possibility of criticizing and resisting it, it grows inordinate."[71] In Niebuhr's view, diffusion of power is necessary to prevent oppression: "It may be taken as axiomatic that great disproportions of power lead to injustice, whatever may be the efforts to mitigate it. Thus the concentration of economic power in modern technical society has made for injustice, while the diffusion of political power has made for justice."[72] Niebuhr was an enthusiastic proponent of the checks and balances in the American constitutional system. As he often commented, the framers of the Constitution were individuals who embraced the notion of original sin.[73]

Niebuhr viewed the world cataclysm of the early 1940s as due in part to the lack of an international body capable of controlling the aggressive actions of individual nation states: "One reason why the balances of power, which prevent injustice in international relations, periodically degenerate into overt anarchy is because no way has yet been found to establish an adequate organizing center, a stable international judicatory, for this balance of power."[74]

Some of Niebuhr's contemporaries, sharing his pessimistic view of human nature, urged the necessity of authoritarian government. Niebuhr disagreed: "A consistent pessimism in regard to man's rational capacity for justice invariably leads to absolutistic political theories; for they prompt the conviction that only preponderant power can coerce the various vitalities of a community into a working harmony."[75] But Niebuhr viewed the unchecked power characteristic of authoritarian government as particularly nefarious: "But the pessimism which prompts and justifies this policy is not consistent; for it is not applied, as it should be, to the ruler. If men are inclined to deal unjustly with their fellows, the possession of power aggravates this inclination. That is why irresponsible and uncontrolled power is the greatest source of injustice."[76]

One Niebuhr scholar has aptly described Niebuhr as a "pessimistic optimist." Humans can use "power creatively in the service of justice, and that is our glory. But we can also abuse power destructively in the service of self . . . and that is our demonry."[77] Niebuhr urged that we become neither too pessimistic nor too optimistic about human nature. In his 1959 foreword to a new edition of *The Children of Light and the Children of Darkness*, Niebuhr wrote that a "free society prospers best in a cultural, religious and moral atmosphere which encourages neither a too pessimistic nor too optimistic view of human nature. Both moral sentimentality in politics and moral pessimism encourage totalitarian regimes, the one because it encourages the opinion that it is not necessary to check the power of government, and the second because it believes that only absolute political authority can restrain the anarchy, created by conflicting and competitive interests."[78]

In support of his embrace of democracy as the superior organizing imperative for human society, Niebuhr appealed to the prophetic tradition of Judaism and Christianity:

> Who can deny that the development of prophetic religion, which challenges rather than supports political majesty in the name of the majesty of God, helps to destroy priestly-military oligarchies and to create democratic societies? In this way, the prophetic elements in Christianity have contributed to the rise of modern democratic societies, just as conservative elements in the Christian tradition have strengthened the pretensions of oligarchies by their uncritical identification of political power with the divine authority.[79]

Niebuhr elaborated on the ways in which certain insights of the Christian faith support the dispersion of power in democratic government:

> The facts about human nature which make a monopoly of power dangerous and a balance of power desirable are best understood from the standpoint of the Christian faith. . . . It cannot be denied that Biblical faith is unique in offering three insights into the human situation which are indispensable to democracy.
>
> The first is that it assumes a source of authority from the standpoint of which the individual may defy the authorities of this world. ("We must obey God rather than man.") The second is an appreciation of the unique worth of the individual which makes it wrong to fit him into any political program as a mere instrument. . . .
>
> The third insight is the Biblical insistence that the same radical freedom which makes man creative also makes him potentially destructive and dangerous, that the dignity of man and the misery of man therefore have the same root.[80]

Niebuhr also commented about the relationship between the believer and the state. Niebuhr acknowledged that there are two biblical traditions that address this issue. According to one tradition, which draws from Paul's discussion in Romans 13 about the relationship of the Christian and the state, government "is an ordinance of God and its authority reflects the Divine Majesty," which suggests that the Christian must respect the state's authority. According to the other tradition, represented by the Old Testament prophets such as Amos (about whom Niebuhr said, "All theology really begins with Amos"[81]), "the 'rulers' and 'judges' of the nations are particularly subject to divine judgment and wrath because they oppress the poor and defy the divine majesty."[82] Niebuhr sought to reconcile the two traditions, recognizing the tension between them: Government "is a principle of order and its power prevents anarchy; but its power is not identical with divine power. . . . It cannot achieve the perfect union of goodness and power which characterizes divine power. The pretension that its power is perfectly virtuous represents its false claim of majesty."[83] Niebuhr noted that "St. Paul's very 'undialectical' appreciation of government in Romans 13 has had a fateful influence in Christian thought, particularly in the Reformation."[84] In fact, Niebuhr argued that Luther's undue emphasis on respect for civil authorities had contributed to the tradition of German authoritarianism.[85]

NATURAL LAW

Niebuhr's reflections about the state and its role in securing justice in human society inevitably brought him into a consideration of whether there are "general principles of justice," or natural law, against which all positive law norms must be assessed. He observed the broad embrace of notions of natural law across cultures:

> There are no living communities which do not do have some notions of justice, beyond their historic laws, by which they seek to gauge the justice of their legislative enactments. Such general principles are known as natural law in both Catholic and earlier liberal thought. . . . Every human society does have something like a natural-law concept; for it assumes that there are more immutable and purer principles of justice than those actually embodied in its obviously relative laws.[86]

Niebuhr, himself, identified the law of love as the "one fundamental principle"[87] against which all behavior is to be assessed and claims that the "ideal of love . . . transcends all law."[88] How did Niebuhr know that love is the fundamental norm for human life? Niebuhr claimed that "all human life is informed with an inchoate sense of responsibility toward the ultimate law of life—the law of love."[89] Furthermore, humans in a "moment of self-transcendence" gain understanding of the fundamental nature of love.[90] He also noted that the New Testament regards love "as the final norm of human life."[91] Along with his assertion that the law of love is *the* fundamental principle, however, Niebuhr remained deeply skeptical of articulations of the specific content of natural law or particular applications of the law of love, particularly the self-confident articulations of the parameters of natural law in Catholic moral theology.

For Niebuhr, one of the central questions concerning natural law was who possesses the ultimate authority to give definition to such fundamental principles. Should they be subject to redefinition through the democratic process? Niebuhr commented, "Should [natural law principles] not stand above criticism or amendment? If they are themselves subjected to the democratic process and if they are made dependent upon the moods and vagaries of various communities and epochs, have we not sacrificed the final criterion of justice and order?"[92] He argued that it "is on this question that Catholic Christianity has its final difficulties with the presuppositions of a democratic society in the modern, liberal sense. . . . For Catholicism believes that the principles of natural law are fixed and immutable. . . . It believes that the freedom of a democratic society must stop short of calling these principles of natural law in question."[93]

Given the difficulties of human self-interest, Niebuhr questioned whether humans can accurately define the contours of the natural law. To those who think natural law principles could be fully articulated, Niebuhr replied that such persons fail "to appreciate the perennial corruptions of interest and passion which are introduced into any historical definition of even the most ideal and abstract moral principles."[94]

Niebuhr criticized both the Catholic Church and eighteenth-century Enlightenment thinkers' articulations of how we come to know and define the parameters of the natural law. Niebuhr contended that the Catholic Church "wrongly sought to preserve some realm of institutional religious authority which would protect the uncorrupted truths of the natural law."[95] As for Enlightenment thinkers, with their notions of "inalienable rights" and other natural law concepts, Niebuhr argued that they "erroneously hoped for a general diffusion of intelligence which would make the truths of the natural law universally acceptable."[96]

Niebuhr rejected both Catholic and Enlightenment assumptions about the ability of institutions or individuals to identify an immutable natural law. Evoking the thinking of later postmodernists, Niebuhr argued that natural law claims are invariably contextual: "There is no historical reality, whether it be church or government, whether it be the reason of wise men or specialists, which is not involved in the flux and relativity of human existence; which is not subject to error and sin, and which is not tempted to exaggerate its errors and sins when they are made immune to criticism."[97] The problem, as Niebuhr saw it, is that humans who articulate natural law principles are inevitably influenced by their own biases: "The question which must be raised [concerning natural law] is whether the reason by which standards of justice are established is really so pure that the standard does not contain an echo and an accent of the claims of the class or the culture, the nation or the hierarchy which presumes to define the standard."[98] Indeed, Niebuhr contended that it is not possible "to arrive at completely valid principles, free of every taint of special interest and historical passion. . . . The interests of a class, the viewpoint of a nation, the prejudices of an age and the illusions of a culture are consciously and unconsciously insinuated into the norms by which men regulate their common life. They are intended to give one group an advantage over another. Or if that is not their intention, it is at least the unvarying consequence."[99]

In fact, Niebuhr worried, if natural law principles become "fixed," they "will destroy some of the potentialities of a higher justice, which the mind of one generation is unable to anticipate in the life of subsequent eras."[100] Niebuhr agreed with Karl Marx about the contingent character of articulations of natural law principles:

> The Marxist cynicism in regard to the pretended moral purity of all laws and rules of justice is justified. Marxism is right, furthermore, in regarding them as primarily rationalizations of the interests of the dominant elements of a society. The requirements of "natural law" in the medieval period were obviously conceived in a feudal society; just as the supposed absolute and "self-evident" demands of eighteenth-century natural law were bourgeois in origin.
>
> The relative and contingent character of these ideals and rules of justice refutes the claim of their unconditioned character, made alike by Catholic, liberal and even Marxist social theorists.[101]

Niebuhr's skepticism about natural law can be illustrated by his consideration of natural law claims in the area of gender relations. Niebuhr noted that "Catholic natural law . . . enjoins the supremacy of the husband over the wife."[102] Although Niebuhr conceded that both the Bible and the "natural fact that the woman bears the child" help create a differentiated role for women, he argued, "It is important to realize that no definition of the natural law between the sexes can be made without embodying something of the sin of male arrogance into the standard."[103] Niebuhr elaborated: "Any premature fixation of certain historical standards in regard to the family will inevitably tend to reinforce male arrogance. . . . The sinfulness of man . . . makes it inevitable that a dominant class, group, and sex should seek to define a relationship, which guarantees its dominance, as permanently normative."[104] Niebuhr also persistently criticized Catholic prohibition of birth control, justified on the theory that it is "intrinsically against nature,"[105] as an example of an improper use of natural law.[106]

Yet despite Niebuhr's deep skepticism about the articulation of natural law principles, he did hold that there are certain ethical norms that are "permanent" applications of the fundamental law of love. In *The Nature and Destiny of Man*, Niebuhr claimed that "there are of course certain permanent norms, such as monogamy, which. . . . are maintained not purely by Scriptural authority but by the cumulative experience of the race."[107] Niebuhr then wrote tantalizingly, "About these universalities, amidst the relativities of standards, a word must be spoken presently."[108] He did not elaborate as to why ethical norms such as monogamy are "permanent," while others are culturally contextual.

Although Niebuhr criticized the Catholic Church on a variety of issues, including its position on natural law and its "tendency to be too sure of its truth,"[109] he grew to have a profound respect for many aspects of Catholicism, particularly its embrace of racial and economic justice. Niebuhr, for example, admired the Catholic Church's opposition to racial segregation in the American South during the 1950s. In 1961, he commented that it "has always been one of the virtues of Catholicism that it. . . . never doubted that political authority should exercise dominance over the economic sphere in the interest of justice."[110] Niebuhr had particularly high regard for Pope Leo XIII's encyclical *Rerum novarum* and Pope John XXIII's encyclical *Pacem in terris*, both of which reflected a deep commitment to social justice.[111]

RACIAL JUSTICE

Although racism was by no means the primary focus of Niebuhr's social ethics, he wrote extensively about the treatment of African Americans, a choice of subject influenced in part by his exposure to southern blacks who had migrated to Detroit during and after World War I as part of the Great Migration. Niebuhr's reflections on the problem of race in America offer a useful application of his theories about individual and group self-interest. "It is a gentle conceit of northern people that race prejudice is a vice peculiar to the south," Niebuhr wrote from his Detroit parish in 1927. "The tremendous migration of southern Negroes into the industrial centers of the north is rapidly dispelling this illusion."[112] In that same 1927 essay, Niebuhr called racial discrimination "one of the greatest challenges to the spirit of real Christianity. The whole validity of the Christian faith is in the balance as men try to solve the race problem. Either there is in Christ neither white nor black or the whole Christian faith becomes absurd."[113]

Niebuhr conceived of racial discrimination as a manifestation of group pride. He explained in a 1942 essay: "Racial prejudice, as every other form of group prejudice, is a concomitant of the collective life of man. Group pride is the sinful corruption of group consciousness. Contempt of another group is the pathetic form that respect for our own group frequently takes."[114] During the late 1950s, for example, Niebuhr wrote that southern white resistance to school desegregation "was caused by the ineradicable tendency of men to build integral communities upon the sense of ethnic kinship and to exclude from that kinship any race which diverges too obviously from type. In the white South, the Negro's primary offense is that he is black."[115] In commenting on the difficulties of securing civil rights legislation in the United States during the early 1960s, Niebuhr noted: "The effort . . . to give Negroes the full and equal status of citizenship and of a common humanity was bound to prove more difficult than even the most realistic idealists imagined . . . [because] Western man—in common with all men—remains an unregenerate tribalist."[116]

Niebuhr also believed that efforts to combat racial discrimination by relying solely on moral appeals would be of limited utility. Commenting on ongoing efforts at "interracial cooperation," Niebuhr concluded that these efforts "accomplish little more than spin a thin veil of moral idealism under which the white man does not really hide his determination to maintain the Negro in a subordinate position in our civilization."[117] Moral idealism alone, Niebuhr wrote in 1932, will never be sufficient to overcome the deeply entrenched self-interest of majority groups:

> It is hopeless for the Negro to expect complete emancipation from the menial social and economic position into which the white man has forced him, merely by trusting in the moral sense of the white race. . . . However large the number of individual white men who do and who will identify themselves completely with the Negro cause, the white race in America will not admit the Negro to equal rights if it is not forced to do so. Upon that point one may speak with a dogmatism which all history justifies.[118]

Writing in 1942, Niebuhr concluded, "There are, in other words, no solutions for the race problem on any level if it is not realized that there is no absolute solution for this problem. There is no absolute solution in the sense that it is not possible to purge man completely of the sinful concomitant of group pride in his collective life."[119]

Throughout his life, Niebuhr retained his pessimism about the possibilities of meaningful racial reform. Writing in 1963 at the height of the civil rights movement, Niebuhr responded critically to the suggestion of Robert Kennedy that African Americans, like Irish Americans, would eventually overcome discrimination and enter the political mainstream: "But the analogy is not exact. The Irish merely affronted us by having a different religion and a different place of origin than the 'true' Americans. The Negroes affront us by diverging from the dominant type all too obviously. Their skin is black. And our celebrated reason is too errant to digest the difference."[120] While much of liberal America hailed the enactment of the Civil Rights Act of 1964 as a triumph of the American creed of equal treatment, Niebuhr remained decidedly pessimistic about the ability of law to corral human behavior. Writing four days after President Lyndon Johnson signed into law the 1964 civil rights legislation, Niebuhr dissented from the euphoria surrounding this landmark event. In an essay entitled "Man, the Unregenerate Tribalist," Niebuhr expressed pessimism that the new statute would transform race relations in the United States.[121] In another essay published the same day, Niebuhr commented: "It will be a crisis-filled decade and century before the nation has solved—or even taken the most rigorous steps toward the solution of—this 'American dilemma.' The dilemma is actually wider than our national life; it is the dilemma of validating the humanity of man despite the strong tribal impulses in his nature."[122]

Niebuhr's profound pessimism about human nature and the ability of white America to embrace African Americans earned him rebukes from many civil right proponents who accused him of being "too pessimistic about [the possibility of] radical social change."[123] Niebuhr, who had consistently urged racial reform in the United States since the 1920s, welcomed the civil rights legislation of the 1960s. His view of the profound human tendency toward self-interest, however, prevented him from sharing the enthusiasm of many racial liberals about the ultimate significance of those legislative gains.

What, then, in Niebuhr's view, should African Americans do in the face of persistent racial discrimination? Niebuhr argued, "The relations between groups must therefore always be predominantly political rather than ethical, that is, they will be determined by the proportion of power which each group possesses at least as much as by any rational and moral appraisal of the comparative needs and claims of each group."[124] As a result, "outsiders" such as blacks or workers must "develop both economic and political power to meet the combination of political and economic power which confronts him."[125] For example, Niebuhr recommended that African

Americans use various cooperative arrangements such as economic boycotts to confront majority power—"boycotts against banks which discriminate against Negroes in granting credit, against stores which refuse to
employ Negroes while serving Negro trade, and against public service corporations which practice racial discrimination."[126]

NIEBUHR'S IMPACT ON THE NEXT GENERATION

Niebuhr has had a significant impact on a broad range of thinkers—religious and secular—as well as political figures. Indeed, some of the most
influential individuals of the second half of the twentieth century were
profoundly shaped by Niebuhr. For example, Niebuhr's writings about
human nature had a significant influence on Martin Luther King's understanding of the nature of social change. Writing in 1958, King observed of Niebuhr:

> Niebuhr's greatest contribution to contemporary theology is that he has re-
> futed the false optimism characteristic of a great segment of Protestant liber
> alism.... [Niebuhr's] theology is a persistent reminder of the reality of sin
> on every level of man's existence. These elements in Niebuhr's thinking
> helped me to recognize the illusions of a superficial optimism concerning
> human nature and the dangers of a false idealism.[127]

Indeed, one King scholar has concluded that "the Christian realism of Reinhold Niebuhr . . . was probably . . . the greatest sobering influence upon
King's optimistic anthropological assumptions."[128] Moreover, although
King did not embrace Niebuhr's rejection of pacifism, Niebuhr's influence
caused King to conclude that "too many [pacifists] had an unwarranted
optimism concerning man." King also credited Niebuhr for "the fact that
in spite of [my] strong leaning toward pacifism, [I] never joined a pacifist
organization."[129]

Many national politicians of the second half of the twentieth century
also asserted Niebuhr's influence on the development of their thinking. In
1966, Vice President Hubert Humphrey addressed Niebuhr's influence on
the generation who "came out of the Great Depression":

> We knew there were urgent demands of social justice that required direct
> action and idealism. At the same time, we learned that politics was compli-
> cated and many-sided, that life just wasn't that simple. Dr. Niebuhr was the
> man more than any other who put these two things together, and showed

how they are both connected with religious faith. Yes, he helped us to see that politicians and theologians had a mutual interest in sin in the world.[130]

Other public figures for whom Niebuhr served as a primary intellectual mentor include McGeorge Bundy, George Kennan, and Arthur Schlesinger Jr.[131]

Niebuhr's influence on President Jimmy Carter was more personal. Early in his political career, Carter struggled with the question of whether a Christian could serve in politics. He read a collection of Niebuhr's writings, *Reinhold Niebuhr on Politics*, which became Carter's "political Bible."[132] Niebuhr's writings helped Carter to reconcile his Christian faith with his passion for politics and allowed Carter to see politics as a venue for bringing justice to the world. Carter's favorite quotation was one from Niebuhr: "The sad duty of politics is to establish justice in a sinful world."[133]

CONCLUSION

Niebuhr's "realist" perspective of human nature influenced all of his theological and political positions. Despite his apparent pessimism about the possibilities of fulfilling the "law of love," however, Niebuhr's passion for justice for the oppressed caused him to urge believers not to abandon hope:

> A Christian pessimism which becomes a temptation to irresponsibility toward all those social tasks which constantly confront the life of men and nations ... cannot speak redemptively to a world constantly threatened by anarchy and suffering from injustice. The Christian gospel which transcends all particular and contemporary social situations can be preached with power only by a Church which bears its share of the burdens of immediate situations in which men are involved, burdens of establishing peace, of achieving justice, and of perfecting justice in the spirit of love.[134]

By the same token, Niebuhr, always the realist, urged the church to recognize that "perfecting justice in the spirit of love" would never be fully achieved on this earth. Appropriately, Niebuhr's best-known single work is the "Serenity Prayer" made famous by Alcoholics Anonymous: "God give us the grace to accept with serenity the things that cannot be changed, courage to change the things that should be changed, and the wisdom to distinguish the one from the other."[135]

NOTES

1. Larry Rasmussen, introduction to *Reinhold Niebuhr: Theologian of Public Life*, ed. Larry Rasmussen (Minneapolis: Fortress Press, 1991), ix.
2. Hans J. Morgenthau, "The Influence of Reinhold Niebuhr in American Political Life and Thought," in *Reinhold Niebuhr: A Prophetic Voice in Our Time*, ed. Harold R. Landon (Greenwich, Conn.: Seabury, 1962), 109.
3. Quoted in Nathan A. Scott Jr., *Reinhold Niebuhr* (Minneapolis: University of Minnesota Press, 1963), 7.
4. Paul Lehmann, "The Christology of Reinhold Niebuhr," in *Reinhold Niebuhr: His Religious, Social, and Political Thought*, ed. Charles W. Kegley and Robert W. Bretall (New York: Macmillan, 1956), 2:253.
5. Dennis P. McCann, *Christian Realism and Liberation Theology: Practical Theologies in Creative Conflict* (Maryknoll, N.Y.: Orbis Books, 1981), 14.
6. Reinhold Niebuhr, *The Contribution of Religion to Social Work* (New York: Columbia University Press, 1932), 77.
7. Robert McAfee Brown, introduction to *The Essential Reinhold Niebuhr: Selected Essays and Addresses*, ed. Robert McAfee Brown (New Haven, Conn.: Yale University Press, 1986), xvi.
8. McCann, *Christian Realism*, 12.
9. Reinhold Niebuhr, "Intellectual Autobiography," in Kegley and Bretall, *Reinhold Niebuhr*, 2:3.
10. Rasmussen, "Introduction," 3.
11. Reinhold Niebuhr, "Theology and Political Thought in the Western World," in *Faith and Politics: A Commentary on Religious, Social and Political Thought in a Technological Age*, ed. Ronald H. Stone (New York: George Braziller, 1968), 55.
12. Quoted in Scott, *Reinhold Niebuhr*, 40–41.
13. Robin W. Lovin, *Reinhold Niebuhr and Christian Realism* (New York: Cambridge University Press, 1995), 5.
14. Walter Rauschenbusch, *Christianity and the Social Crisis* (Louisville, Ky.: Westminster John Knox Press, 1991), 209.
15. William Adams Brown, *Pathways to Certainty* (New York: Charles Scribner's Sons, 1930), 247.
16. Scott, *Reinhold Niebuhr*, 14.
17. Reinhold Niebuhr, *Christianity and Power Politics* (New York: Charles Scribner's Sons, 1940), 20.
18. Reinhold Niebuhr, *An Interpretation of Christian Ethics* (New York: Meridian Books, 1958), 155.
19. Lovin, *Reinhold Niebuhr and Christian Realism*, 6.
20. Daniel F. Rice, *Reinhold Niebuhr and John Dewey: An American Odyssey* (Albany: State University of New York Press, 1993), 17.
21. Reinhold Niebuhr, *Moral Man and Immoral Society* (New York: Charles Scribner's Sons, 1932), xii.

22. Taylor Branch, *Parting the Waters: America in the King Years, 1954–63* (New York: Simon & Schuster, 1989), 84.

23. Brown, "Introduction," xv.

24. Niebuhr, *Moral Man and Immoral Society*, xi.

25. Reinhold Niebuhr, "Moralists and Politics," *The Christian Century* 49 (July 6, 1932): 857.

26. Niebuhr, *Moral Man and Immoral Society*, xx.

27. Niebuhr, "Moralists and Politics," 857.

28. Ibid., 858.

29. Niebuhr, *Moral Man and Immoral Society*, xii.

30. Ibid., xxiii–xxiv.

31. Reinhold Niebuhr, *The Nature and Destiny of Man: A Christian Interpretation*, 2 vols. (New York: Charles Scribner's Sons, 1941–43), 1:23.

32. Ibid., 213.

33. Daphne Hampson, "Reinhold Niebuhr on Sin: A Critique," in *Reinhold Niebuhr and the Issues of Our Time*, ed. Richard Harries (London: Mowbray, 1986), 47. See also Judith Plaskow, *Sex, Sin, and Grace: Women's Experience and the Theologies of Reinhold Niebuhr and Paul Tillich* (Washington, D.C.: University Press of America, 1980).

34. Hampson, "Reinhold Niebuhr on Sin," 49.

35. Reinhold Niebuhr, *The Children of Light and the Children of Darkness: A Vindication of Democracy and a Critique of its Traditional Defense* (New York: Charles Scribner's Sons, 1960), 20.

36. Ibid.

37. Ibid., 22.

38. Niebuhr, *An Interpretation of Christian Ethics*, 101.

39. Brown, "Introduction," xvi.

40. Niebuhr, *Christianity and Power Politics*, 21–22.

41. Ibid., 215.

42. Niebuhr, *The Nature and Destiny of Man*, 1:269.

43. Ibid., 272.

44. Ibid., 266.

45. Ibid.

46. Ibid., 269 (emphasis added).

47. Ibid., 296.

48. Ibid.

49. Niebuhr, *An Interpretation of Christian Ethics*, 109.

50. Niebuhr, *The Nature and Destiny of Man*, 1:298.

51. Niebuhr, *Christianity and Power Politics*, 6.

52. Ibid., 18.

53. Niebuhr, *The Nature and Destiny of Man*, 1:299.

54. Ibid., 2:99.

55. Niebuhr, *Christianity and Power Politics*, 19.

56. Ibid.

57. Niebuhr, *The Nature and Destiny of Man*, 1:299.

58. Ibid., 2:122.

59. Niebuhr, *Christianity and Power Politics*, 9–10.

60. Ibid., 14.

61. Ibid.

62. Niebuhr, *An Interpretation of Christian Ethics*, 160–161.

63. Ibid., 45.

64. Niebuhr, *Christianity and Power Politics*, 18.

65. Ibid., 21.

66. Ibid., 14–15.

67. Ibid., 22.

68. Niebuhr, *The Children of Light and the Children of Darkness*, xiii.

69. Niebuhr, *Christianity and Power Politics*, 85.

70. Ibid., 22.

71. Ibid., 26.

72. Niebuhr, *The Nature and Destiny of Man*, 2:262.

73. Brown, "Introduction," xii.

74. Niebuhr, *Christianity and Power Politics*, 26.

75. Niebuhr, *The Children of Light and the Children of Darkness*, xii–xiii.

76. Ibid., xiii–xiv.

77. Brown, "Introduction," xi–xii.

78. Niebuhr, *The Children of Light and the Children of Darkness*, viii.

79. Niebuhr, *The Nature and Destiny of Man*, 2:264.

80. Reinhold Niebuhr, "Government and the Strategy of Democracy," in *Reinhold Niebuhr on Politics: His Political Philosophy and Its Application to Our Age as Expressed in His Writings*, ed. Harry R. Davis and Robert C. Good (New York: Charles Scribner's Sons, 1960), 187.

81. Quoted in Rasmussen, *Reinhold Niebuhr: Theologian of Public Life*, 269.

82. Niebuhr, *The Nature and Destiny of Man*, 2:269.

83. Ibid.

84. Ibid., 270.

85. Charles C. Brown, *Niebuhr and His Age: Reinhold Niebuhr's Prophetic Role in the Twentieth Century* (Philadelphia: Trinity Press International, 1992), 84–85.

86. Niebuhr, *The Children of Light and the Children of Darkness*, 67–68.

87. Paul Ramsey, "Love and Law," in Kegley and Breatall, *Reinhold Niebuhr*, 2:91.

88. Niebuhr, *An Interpretation of Christian Ethics*, 136.

89. Ibid., 105.

90. Niebuhr, *The Nature and Destiny of Man*, 1:277.

91. Reinhold Niebuhr, *Faith and History: A Comparison of Christian and Modern Views of History* (New York: Charles Scribner's Sons, 1949), 184.

92. Niebuhr, *The Children of Light and the Children of Darkness*, 68.

93. Ibid., 68–69.

94. Ibid., 70.

95. Ibid.

96. Ibid.

97. Ibid., 70–71.

98. Niebuhr, *Faith and History*, 186.

99. Niebuhr, *The Nature and Destiny of Man*, 2:256.

100. Niebuhr, *The Children of Light and the Children of Darkness*, 71.

101. Niebuhr, *The Nature and Destiny of Man*, 2:252–253.

102. Ibid., 1:281.

103. Ibid., 282.

104. Ibid.

105. Niebuhr, *Faith and History*, 181, quoting Pope Pius XI, *Encyclical on Christian Marriage in Our Day*, par. 55.

106. John C. Bennett, "Reinhold Niebuhr's Contribution to Christian Social Ethics," in *Reinhold Niebuhr: A Prophetic Voice in Our Time*, ed. Harold R. Landon (Greenwich, Conn.: Seabury, 1962), 74.

107. Niebuhr, *The Nature and Destiny of Man*, 1:282–283.

108. Ibid., 283.

109. Charles C. Brown, *Niebuhr and His Age*, 225.

110. Quoted in Richard Wightman Fox, *Reinhold Niebuhr: A Biography* (New York: Pantheon Books, 1985), 286.

111. Brown, *Niebuhr and His Age*, 225–226.

112. Reinhold Niebuhr, "Race Prejudice in the North," *The Christian Century* 44 (May 12, 1927): 583.

113. Ibid., 584.

114. Reinhold Niebuhr, "The Race Problem," *Christianity and Society* 7 (Summer 1942): 3.

115. Reinhold Niebuhr, "The States' Rights Crisis," *New Leader* 41 (September 29, 1958): 7.

116. Reinhold Niebuhr, "Man, the Unregenerate Tribalist," *Christianity and Crisis* 24 (July 6, 1964): 133.

117. Niebuhr, "Moralists and Politics," 857.

118. Niebuhr, *Moral Man and Immoral Society*, 252–253.

119. Niebuhr, "The Race Problem," 4.

120. Reinhold Niebuhr, "Revolution in an Open Society," *New Leader* 46 (May 27, 1963): 8.

121. Niebuhr, "Man, the Unregenerate Tribalist," 133.

122. Reinhold Niebuhr, "The Struggle for Justice," *New Leader* 47 (July 6, 1964): 11.

123. Ronald Preston, "Reinhold Niebuhr and the New Right," in Harries, *Reinhold Niebuhr and the Issues of Our Time*, 90.

124. Niebuhr, *Moral Man and Immoral Society*, xxiii.

125. Niebuhr, "Moralists and Politics," 858.

126. Niebuhr, *Moral Man and Immoral Society*, 254.

127. Martin Luther King Jr., *Stride Toward Freedom: The Montgomery Story* (New York: Harper & Brothers, 1958), 99.

128. Lewis V. Baldwin, *There is A Balm in Gilead: The Cultural Roots of Martin Luther King, Jr.* (Minneapolis: Fortress Press, 1991), 78.

129. King, *Stride Toward Freedom*, 99.

130. Quoted in Paul Merkley, *Reinhold Niebuhr: A Political Account* (Montreal: McGill-Queen's University Press, 1975), 205.

131. Merkley, *Reinhold Niebuhr*, vii.

132. William Lee Miller, *Yankee from Georgia: The Emergence of Jimmy Carter* (New York: Times Books, 1978), 214–215.

133. Leslie Griffin, "Jimmy Carter's Absolute Separation of Church and State," unpublished manuscript.

134. Niebuhr, "The Christian Church in a Secular Age," 216.

135. Quoted in Ronald H. Stone, *Professor Reinhold Niebuhr: A Mentor to the Twentieth Century* (Louisville, Ky.: Westminster John Knox Press, 1992), 140.

Pages 281–85 and 295–98 of this chapter were drawn in part from Davison M. Douglas, "Reinhold Niebuhr and Critical Race Theory," *Christian Perspectives on Legal Thought*, Michael W. McConnell, Robert F. Cochran, Jr., and Angela C. Carmella, eds. (New Haven: Yale University Press, 2001).

ORIGINAL SOURCE MATERIALS

THE NATURE AND DESTINY OF MAN:
A CHRISTIAN INTERPRETATION

Our present interest is to relate the Biblical and distinctively Christian conception of sin as pride and self-love to the observable behaviour of men. It will be convenient in this analysis to distinguish between three types of pride, which are, however, never completely distinct in actual life: pride of power, pride of knowledge and pride of virtue. The third type, the pride of self-righteousness, rises to a form of spiritual pride, which is at once a fourth type and yet not a specific form of pride at all but pride and self-glorification in its inclusive and quintessential form.

. . . "Of the infinite desires of man," declares Bertrand Russell, "the chief are the desires for power and glory. . . ."[1] Mr. Russell is not quite clear about the relation of the two to each other, and the relation is, as a matter of fact, rather complex. There is a pride of power in which the human ego assumes its self-sufficiency and self-mastery and imagines itself secure against all vicissitudes. It does not recognize the contingent and dependent character of its life and believes itself to be the author of its own existence, the judge of its own values and the master of its own destiny. This proud pretension is present in an inchoate form in all human life but it rises to greater heights among those individuals and classes who have a more than ordinary degree of social power. Closely related to the pride which seems to rest upon the possession of either the ordinary or some extraordinary measure of human freedom and self-mastery, is the lust for power which has pride as its end. The ego does not feel secure and therefore grasps for more power in order to make itself secure. It does not regard itself as sufficiently significant or respected or feared and therefore seeks to enhance its position in nature and in society. . . .

The second form of the pride of power is more obviously prompted by the sense of insecurity. It is the sin of those, who knowing themselves to be insecure, seek sufficient power to guarantee their security, inevitably of course at the expense of other life. . . .

Greed as a form of the will-to-power has been a particularly flagrant sin in the modern era because modern technology has tempted contemporary man to overestimate the possibility and the value of eliminating his insecurity in nature. Greed has thus become the besetting sin of a bourgeois culture. . . .

Since man's insecurity arises not merely from the vicissitudes of nature but from the uncertainties of society and history, it is natural that the ego should seek to overcome social as well as natural insecurity and should express the impulse of "power over men" as well as "power over matter." The peril of a competing human will is overcome by subordinating that will to the ego and by using the power of many subordinated wills to ward off the enmity which such subordination creates. The will-to-power is thus inevitably involved in the vicious circle of accentuating the insecurity which it intends to eliminate. . . . The will-to-power in short involves the ego in injustice. It seeks a security beyond the limits of human finiteness and this inordinate ambition arouses fears and enmities which the world of pure nature, with its competing impulses of survival, does not know. . . .

The truth is that man is tempted by the basic insecurity of human existence to make himself doubly secure and by the insignificance of his place in the total scheme of life to prove his significance. The will-to-power is in short both a direct form and an indirect instrument of the pride which Christianity regards as sin in its quintessential form. . . .

. . . The egotism of man has been defined and illustrated thus far without a careful discrimination between group pride and the pride and egotism of individuals. This lack of discrimination is provisionally justified by the fact that, strictly speaking, only individuals are moral agents, and group pride is therefore merely an aspect of the pride and arrogance of individuals. It is the fruit of the undue claims which they make for their various social groups. Nevertheless some distinctions must be made between the collective behaviour of men and their individual attitudes. This is necessary in part because group pride, though having its source in individual attitudes, actually achieves a certain authority over the individual and results in unconditioned demands by the group upon the individual. Whenever the group develops organs of will, as in the apparatus of the state, it seems to the individual to have become an independent centre of moral life. He will be inclined to bow to its pretensions and to acquiesce in its claims of authority, even when these do not coincide with his moral scruples or inclinations.

A distinction between group pride and the egotism of individuals is necessary, furthermore, because the pretensions and claims of a collective or social self exceed those of the individual ego. The group is more arrogant, hypocritical, self-centered and more ruthless in the pursuit of its ends than the individual. An inevitable moral tension between individual and group morality is therefore created. "If," said the great Italian statesman, Cavour, "we did for ourselves what we do for our country, what rascals we would be." This tension is naturally most apparent in the conscience of responsible statesmen, who are bound to feel the disparity between the canons of ordinary morality and the accepted habits of collective and political behaviour. Frederick the Great was not, as statesmen go, a man of unique moral sensitivity. His confession of a sense of this tension is therefore the more significant. "I hope," said he, "that posterity will distinguish the philosopher from the monarch in me and the decent man from the politician. I must admit that when drawn into the vortex of European politics it is difficult to preserve decency and integrity. One feels oneself in constant danger of being betrayed by one's allies and abandoned by one's friends, of being suffocated by envy and jealousy, and is thus finally driven to the terrible alternative of being false either to one's country or to one's word."[2]

The egotism of racial, national and socio-economic groups is most consistently expressed by the national state because the state gives the collective impulses of the nation such instruments of power and presents the imagination of individuals with such obvious symbols of its discrete collective identity that the national state is most able to make absolute claims for itself, to enforce those claims by power and to give them plausibility and credibility by the majesty and panoply of its apparatus. In the life of every political group, whether nation or empire, which articulates itself through the instrument of a state, obedience is prompted by the fear of power on the one hand and by reverence for majesty on the other. The temptation to idolatry is implicit in the state's majesty. Rationalists, with their simple ideas of government resting purely upon the consent of the governed, have never appreciated to what degree religious reverence for majesty is implicit in this consent. The political history of man begins with tribal polytheism, can be traced through the religious pretensions of empires with their inevitable concomitants of imperial religions and their priest-kings and god-kings, and ends with the immoderate and idolatrous claims of the modern fascist state. No politically crystallized social group has, therefore, ever existed without entertaining, or succumbing to, the temptation of making idolatrous claims for itself. Frequently the organs of this group pride, the state and the ruling oligarchy which bears the authority of the state, seek to detach themselves from the group pride of which their majesty is a symbol and to become independent sources of majesty. But this inversion is possible only because the original source of their majesty lies in something which transcends their individual power and prestige, namely the pride and greatness of the group itself.

Sinful pride and idolatrous pretension are thus an inevitable concomitant of the cohesion of large political groups. This is why it is impossible to regard the lower morality of groups, in comparison with individuals, as the consequence of the inertia of "nature" against the higher demands of individual reason. It is true of course that the group possesses only an inchoate "mind" and that its organs of self-transcendence and self-criticism are very unstable and ephemeral compared to its organs of will. A shifting and unstable "prophetic minority" is the instrument of this self-transcendence, while the state is the organ of the group's will. For this reason the immorality of nations is frequently regarded as in effect their unmorality, as the consequence of their existence in the realm of "nature" rather than the realm of reason. "I treat government not as a conscious contrivance," wrote Professor Seeley in a sentiment which expresses the conviction of many modern political scientists, "but as an half-instinctive product of the effort of human beings to ward off from themselves certain evils to which they are exposed."[3]

Such an interpretation has a measure of validity but it certainly does not do justice to the "spiritual" character of national pride, nor to the contribution which individuals, with all their rational and spiritual faculties, make to pride of groups and the self-deification of nations. The most conducive proof that the egotism of nations is a characteristic of the spiritual life, and not merely an expression of the natural impulse of survival, is the fact that its most typical expressions are the lust-for-power, pride (comprising considerations of prestige and "honour"), contempt toward the other (the reverse side of pride and its necessary concomitant in a world in which self-esteem is constantly challenged by the achievements of others); hypocrisy (the inevitable pretension of conforming to a higher norm than self-interest); and finally the claim of moral autonomy by which the self-deification of the social group is made explicit by its presentation of itself as the source and end of existence.

It cannot be denied that the instinct of survival is involved in all these spiritual manifestations of egotism; but that is equally true of individual life. We have previously noted that the fear of death is a basic motive of all human pretensions. Every human self-assertion, whether individual or collective, is therefore involved in the inconsistency of claiming, on the one hand, that it is justified by the primary right of survival and, on the other hand, that it is the bearer of interests and values larger than its own and that these more inclusive values are the justification of its conflict with competing social wills. No modern nation can ever quite make up its mind whether to insist that its struggle is a fight for survival or a selfless effort to maintain transcendent and universal values. In the World War both claims were constantly made; and it is significant that even modern

Germany, though it has constructed a primitive tribal religion which makes the power and pride of the nation a self-justifying end, nevertheless feels constrained to pretend that its expected victory in Europe is desired as a triumph of a high type of (Aryan) culture over an allegedly inferior and decadent form of (Jewish or liberal) culture. The nation claims (or the claim is made for it) that it is the instrument of a value more universal than its contingent self, because, like the individual, the determinateness of its life is too obvious to be denied, at least by modern man. But the claim that it is itself the final and ultimate value, the cause which gives human existence meaning, is one which no individual can plausibly make for himself. It is plausible, though hardly credible, only because the social unit, particularly the nation, to which the individual belongs, transcends the individual life to such a degree in power, majesty, and pseudo-immortality that the claim of unconditioned value can be made for it with a degree of plausibility.

The significance of this claim is that through it human pride and self-assertion reach their ultimate form and seek to break all bounds of finiteness. The nation pretends to be God. A certain ambiguity which envelops this claim has already been noted. It is on the one hand a demand of a collective will and mind upon the individual. The social group asks for the individual's unconditioned loyalty, asserting that its necessities are the ultimate law of the individual's existence. But on the other hand it is a pretension which the individual makes for himself, not as an individual but as a member of his group. Collective egotism does indeed offer the individual an opportunity to lose himself in a larger whole; but it also offers him possibilities of self-aggrandizement beside which mere individual pretensions are implausible and incredible. Individuals "join to set up a god whom each then severally and tacitly identifies with himself, to swell the chorus of praise which each then severally and tacitly arrogates to himself."[4] It may be that such group pride represents a particular temptation to individuals who suffer from specific forms of the sense of inferiority. The relation of modern fascist nationalism to the insecurity and sense of inferiority of the lower middle classes is therefore significant. But it hardly can be denied that extravagant forms of modern nationalism only accentuate a general character of group life and collective egotism; and that specific forms of inferiority feeling for which this pride compensates only accentuate the general sense of inferiority from which all men suffer. Collective pride is thus man's last, and in some respects most pathetic, effort to deny the determinate and contingent character of his existence. The very essence of human sin is in it. It can hardly be surprising that this form of human sin is also most fruitful of human guilt, that is of objective social and historical evil. In its whole range from pride of family to pride of nation, collective egotism and group pride are a more pregnant source of injustice and conflict than purely individual pride.

The pride of nations is, of course, not wholly spurious. Their claim to embody values which transcend their mere existence has foundations in fact. It is the very character of human life, whether individual or collective, that it incarnates values which transcend its immediate interests. A particular nation or group of nations may actually be the bearers of a "democratic civilization" or of a communist one. Men are not animals and never fight merely for existence, because they do not have a mere animal existence. Their physical life is always the base for a superstructure of values which transcends physical life.

The pride of nations consists in the tendency to make unconditioned claims for their conditioned values. The unconditioned character of these claims has two aspects. The nation claims a more absolute devotion to values which transcend its life than the facts warrant; and it regards the values to which it is loyal as more absolute than they really are. Nations, may fight for "liberty" and "democracy" but they do not do so until their vital interests are imperiled. They may refuse to fight and claim that their refusal is prompted by their desire to "preserve civilization." Neutral nations are not less sinful than belligerent ones in their effort to hide their partial interests behind their devotion to "civilization." Furthermore the civilization to which they claim loyalty does not deserve such absolute devotion as the nation asks for it. . . .

The pride of nations and the arrogance of self-deification of collective man are the more extravagant for being expressed in and against a Christian culture in which it must consciously negate and defy the highest insights of the faith which formed the culture of the western world.

The most daemonic form of nationalism today is expressed against rather than in a Christian culture. The German Nazis were quite right in regarding the Christian faith as incompatible with their boundless national egoism. While Christianity may itself be made the tool of nationalism, the Christian faith, if it retains any vitality, is bound to mediate some word of divine judgment upon the nation, which the Nazis find intolerable. No nation is free of the sin of pride, just as no individual is free of it. Nevertheless it is important to recognize that there are "Christian" nations, who prove themselves so because they are still receptive to prophetic words of judgment spoken against the nation. It may be that only a prophetic minority feels this judgment keenly. But there is a genuine difference between nations which do not officially destroy the religious-prophetic judgment against the nation and those which do. While all modern nations, and indeed all nations of history, have been involved in the sin of pride, one must realize, in this as in other estimates of human sinfulness, that it is just as important to recognize differences in the degree of pride and self-will expressed by men and nations, as it is to know that all men and nations are sinful in the sight of God. Here, as in individual life, the final sin is the unwillingness to hear the word of judgment spoken against our sin. By that criterion, the modern fascist nations have achieved a daemonic form of national self-assertion which is more dangerous even than that of the ancient religious empires because it is expressed within and against the insights of a Christian culture.[5]

CHRISTIANITY AND POWER POLITICS: WHY THE CHRISTIAN CHURCH IS NOT PACIFIST

The pacifists do not know human nature well enough to be concerned about the contradictions between the law of love and the sin of man, until sin has conceived and brought forth death. They do not see that sin introduces an element of conflict into the world and that even the most loving relations are not free of it. They are, consequently, unable to appreciate the complexity of the problem of justice. They merely assert that if only men loved one another, all the complex, and sometimes horrible, realities of the political order could be dispensed with. They do not see that their "if" begs the most basic problem of human history. It is because men are sinners that justice can be achieved only by a certain degree of coercion on the one hand, and by resistance to coercion and tyranny on the other hand. The political life of man must constantly steer between the Scylla of anarchy and the Charybdis of tyranny.

Human egotism makes large-scale co-operation upon a purely voluntary basis impossible. Governments must coerce. Yet there is an element of evil in this coercion. It is always in danger of serving the purposes of the coercing power rather than the general weal. We cannot fully trust the motives of any ruling class or power. That is why it is important to maintain democratic checks upon the centers of power. It may also be necessary to resist a ruling class, nation or race, if it violates the standards of relative justice which have been set up for it. Such resistance means war. It need not mean overt conflict or violence. But if those who resist tyranny publish their scruples against violence too publicly the tyrannical power need only threaten the use of violence against non-violent pressure to persuade the resisters to quiescence. (The relation of pacifism to the abortive effort to apply non-violent sanctions against Italy in the Ethiopian dispute is instructive at this point.) . . .

The gospel is something more than the law of love. The gospel deals with the fact that men violate the law of love. The gospel presents Christ as the pledge and revelation of God's mercy which finds man in his rebellion and overcomes his sin.

The question is whether the grace of Christ is primarily a power of righteousness which so heals the sinful heart that henceforth it is able to fulfil the law of love; or whether it is primarily the assurance of divine mercy for a persistent sinfulness which man never overcomes completely. When St. Paul declared: "I am crucified with Christ; nevertheless I live, yet it is no more I that live but Christ that dwelleth in me," did he mean that the new life in Christ was not his own by reason of the fact that grace, rather than his own power, enabled him to live on the new level of righteousness? Or did he mean that the new life was his only in intention and by reason of God's willingness to accept intention for achievement? Was the emphasis upon sanctification or justification?

This is the issue upon which the Protestant Reformation separated itself from classical Catholicism, believing that Thomistic interpretations of grace lent themselves to new forms of self-righteousness in place of the Judaistic-legalistic self-righteousness which St. Paul condemned. If one studies the whole thought of St. Paul, one is almost forced to the conclusion that he was not himself quite certain whether the peace which he had found in Christ was a moral peace, the peace of having become what man truly is; or whether it was primarily a religious peace, the peace of being "completely known and all forgiven," of being accepted by God despite the continued sinfulness of the heart. Perhaps St. Paul could not be quite sure about where the emphasis was to be placed, for the simple reason that no one can be quite certain about the character of this ultimate peace. There must be, and there is, moral content in it, a fact which Reformation theology tends to deny and which Catholic and sectarian theology emphasizes. But there is never such perfect moral content in it that any man could find perfect peace through his moral achievements, not even the achievements which he attributes to grace rather than the power of his own will. This is the truth which the Reformation emphasized and which modern Protestant Christianity has almost completely forgotten.

We are, therefore, living in a state of sorry moral and religious confusion. In the very moment of world history in which every contemporary historical event justifies the Reformation emphasis upon the persistence of sin on every level of moral achievement, we not only identify Protestant faith with a moralistic sentimentality which neglects and obscures truths in the Christian gospel (which it was the mission of the Reformation to rescue from obscurity), but we even neglect those reservations and qualifications upon the theory of sanctification upon which classical Catholicism wisely insisted.

We have, in other words, reinterpreted the Christian gospel in terms of the Renaissance faith in man. Modern pacifism is merely a final fruit of this Renaissance spirit, which has pervaded the whole of modern Protestantism. We have interpreted world history as a gradual ascent to the Kingdom of God which waits for final triumph only upon the willingness of Christians to "take Christ seriously." There is nothing in Christ's own teachings, except dubious interpretations of the parable of the leaven and the mustard seed, to justify this interpretation of world history. In the whole of the New Testament, Gospels and Epistles alike, there is only one interpretation of world history. That pictures history as moving toward a climax in which both Christ and anti-Christ are revealed.

The New Testament does not, in other words, envisage a simple triumph of good over evil in history. It sees human history involved in the contradictions of sin to the end. That is why it sees no simple resolution of the problem of history. It believes that the Kingdom of God will finally resolve the contradictions of history; but for it the Kingdom of God is no simple historical possibility. The grace of God for man and the Kingdom of God for history are both divine realities and not human possibilities.

The Christian faith believes that the Atonement reveals God's mercy as an ultimate resource by which God alone overcomes the judgment which sin deserves. If this final truth of the Christian religion has no meaning to modern men, including modern Christians, that is because even the tragic character of contemporary history has not yet persuaded them to take the fact of human sinfulness seriously.

The contradiction between the law of love and the sinfulness of man raises not only the ultimate religious problem how men are to have peace if they do not overcome the contradiction, and how history will culminate if the contradiction remains on every level of historic achievement; it also raises the immediate problem how men are to achieve a tolerable harmony of life with life, if human pride and selfishness prevent the realization of the law of love.

The pacifists are quite right in one emphasis. They are right in asserting that love is really the law of life. It is not some ultimate possibility which has nothing to do with human history. The freedom of man, his transcendence over the limitations of nature and over all historic and traditional social situations, makes any form of human community which falls short of the law of love less than the best. Only by a voluntary giving of life to life and a free interpenetration of personalities could man do justice both to the freedom of other personalities and the necessity of community between personalities. The law of love therefore remains a principle of criticism over all forms of community in which elements of coercion and conflict destroy the highest type of fellowship.

To look at human communities from the perspective of the Kingdom of God is to know that there is a sinful element in all the expedients which the political order uses to establish justice. That is why even the seemingly most stable justice degenerates periodically into either tyranny or anarchy. But it must also be recognized that it is not possible to eliminate the sinful element in the political expedients. They are, in the words of St. Augustine, both the consequence of, and the remedy for, sin. If they are the remedy for sin, the ideal of love is not merely a principle of indiscriminate criticism upon all approximations of justice. It is also a principle of discriminate criticism between forms of justice.

As a principle of indiscriminate criticism upon all forms of justice, the law of love reminds us that the injustice and tyranny against which we contend in the foe is partially the consequence of our own injustice, that the pathology of modern Germans is partially a consequence of the vindictiveness of the peace of Versailles, and that the ambition of a tyrannical imperialism is different only in degree and not in kind from the imperial impulse which characterizes all of human life.

The Christian faith ought to persuade us that political controversies are always conflicts between sinners and not between righteous men and sinners. It ought to mitigate the self-righteousness which is an inevitable concomitant of all human conflict. The spirit of contrition is an important ingredient in the sense of justice. If it is powerful enough it may be able to restrain the impulse of vengeance sufficiently to allow a decent justice to emerge. This is an important issue facing Europe in anticipation of the conclusion of the present war. It cannot be denied that the Christian conscience failed terribly in restraining vengeance after the last war. It is also quite obvious that the natural inclination to self-righteousness was the primary force of this vengeance (expressed particularly in the war guilt clause of the peace treaty). The pacifists draw the conclusion from the fact that justice is never free from vindictiveness, that we ought not for this reason ever to contend against a foe. This argument leaves out of account that capitulation to the foe might well subject us to a worse vindictiveness. It is as foolish to imagine that the foe is free of the sin which we deplore in ourselves as it is to regard ourselves as free of the sin which we deplore in the foe.

The fact that our own sin is always partly the cause of the sins against which we must contend is regarded by simple moral purists as proof that we have no right to contend against the foe. They regard the injunction

"Let him who is without sin cast the first stone" as a simple alternative to the schemes of justice which society has devised and whereby it prevents the worst forms of anti-social conduct. This injunction of Christ ought to remind every judge and every juridical tribunal that the crime of the criminal is partly the consequence of the sins of society. But if pacifists are to be consistent they ought to advocate the abolition of the whole judicial process in society. It is perfectly true that national societies have more impartial instruments of justice than international society possesses to date. Nevertheless, no impartial court is as impartial as it pretends to be, and there is no judicial process which is completely free of vindictiveness. Yet we cannot dispense with it; and we will have to continue to put criminals into jail. There is a point where the final cause of the criminal's anti-social conduct becomes a fairly irrelevant issue in comparison with the task of preventing his conduct from injuring innocent fellows.

The ultimate principles of the Kingdom of God are never irrelevant to any problem of justice, and they hover over every social situation as an ideal possibility; but that does not mean that they can be made into simple alternatives for the present schemes of relative justice. The thesis that the so-called democratic nations have no right to resist overt forms of tyranny, because their own history betrays imperialistic motives, would have meaning only if it were possible to achieve a perfect form of justice in any nation and to free national life completely of the imperialistic motive. This is impossible; for imperialism is the collective expression of the sinful will-to power which characterizes all human existence. The pacifist argument on this issue betrays how completely pacifism gives itself to illusions about the stuff with which it is dealing in human nature. These illusions deserve particular censure, because no one who knows his own heart very well ought to be given to such illusions.

The recognition of the law of love as an indiscriminate principle of criticism over all attempts at social and international justice is actually a resource of justice, for it prevents the pride, self-righteousness and vindictiveness of men from corrupting their efforts at justice. But it must be recognized that love is also a principle of discriminate criticism between various forms of community and various attempts at justice. The closest approximation to a love in which life supports life in voluntary community is a justice in which life is prevented from destroying life and the interests of the one are guarded against unjust claims by the other. Such justice is achieved when impartial tribunals of society prevent men "from being judges in their own cases," in the words of John Locke. But the tribunals of justice merely codify certain equilibria of power. Justice is basically dependent upon a balance of power. Whenever an individual or a group or a nation possesses undue power, and whenever this power is not checked by the possibility of criticizing and resisting it, it grows inordinate. The equilibrium of power upon which every structure of justice rests would degenerate into anarchy but for the organizing center which controls it. One reason why the balances of power, which prevent injustice in international relations, periodically degenerate into overt anarchy is because no way has yet been found to establish an adequate organizing center, a stable international judicatory, for this balance of power.[6]

THE CHILDREN OF LIGHT AND THE CHILDREN OF DARKNESS: A VINDICATION OF DEMOCRACY AND A CRITIQUE OF ITS TRADITIONAL DEFENCE

Democracy has a more compelling justification and requires a more realistic vindication than is given it by the liberal culture with which it has been associated in modern history. The excessively optimistic estimates of human nature and of human history with which the democratic credo has been historically associated are a source of peril to democratic society; for contemporary experience is refuting this optimism and there is danger that it will seem to refute the democratic ideal as well.

A free society requires some confidence in the ability of men to reach tentative and tolerable adjustments between their competing interests and to arrive at some common notions of justice which transcend all partial interests. A consistent pessimism in regard to man's rational capacity for justice invariably leads to absolutistic political theories; for they prompt the conviction that only preponderant power can coerce the various vitalities of a community into a working harmony. But a too consistent optimism in regard to man's ability and inclination to grant justice to his fellows obscures the perils of chaos which perennially confront every society, including a free society. In one sense a democratic society is particularly exposed to the dangers of confusion. If these perils are not appreciated they may overtake a free society and invite the alternative evil of tyranny.

But modern democracy requires a more realistic philosophical and religious basis, not only in order to anticipate and understand the perils to which it is exposed; but also to give it a more persuasive justification. Man's capacity for justice makes democracy possible; but man's inclination to injustice makes democracy necessary. In all nondemocratic political theories the state or the ruler is invested with uncontrolled power for the sake of achieving order and unity in the community. But the pessimism which prompts and justifies this policy is not consistent; for it is not applied, as it should be, to the ruler. If men are inclined to deal unjustly with their fellows, the possession of power aggravates this inclination. That is why irresponsible and uncontrolled power is the greatest source of injustice.

The democratic techniques of a free society place checks upon the power of the ruler and administrator and thus prevent it from becoming vexatious. The perils of uncontrolled power are perennial reminders of the virtues of a democratic society; particularly if a society should become inclined to impatience with the dangers of freedom and should be tempted to choose the advantages of coerced unity at the price of freedom.

The consistent optimism of our liberal culture has prevented modern democratic societies both from gauging the perils of freedom accurately and from appreciating democracy fully as the only alternative to injustice and oppression. When this optimism is not qualified to accord with the real and complex facts of human nature and history, there is always a danger that sentimentality will give way to despair and that a too consistent optimism will alternate with a too consistent pessimism.

I have not sought to elaborate the religious and theological convictions upon which the political philosophy of the following pages rests. It will be apparent, however, that they are informed by the belief that a Christian view of human nature is more adequate for the development of a democratic society than either the optimism with which democracy has become historically associated or the moral cynicism which inclines human communities to tyrannical political strategies. . . .

In illumining this important distinction more fully, we may well designate the moral cynics, who know no law beyond their will and interest, with a scriptural designation of "children of this world" or "children of darkness." Those who believe that self-interest should be brought under the discipline of a higher law could then be termed "the children of light." This is no mere arbitrary device; for evil is always the assertion of some self-interest without regard to the whole, whether the whole be conceived as the immediate community, or the total community of mankind, or the total order of the world. The good is, on the other hand, always the harmony of the whole on various levels. Devotion to a subordinate and premature "whole" such as the nation, may of course become evil, viewed from the perspective of a larger whole, such as the community of mankind. The "children of light" may thus be defined as those who seek to bring self-interest under the discipline of a more universal law and in harmony with a more universal good.

According to the scripture "the children of this world are in their generation wiser than the children of light." This observation fits the modern situation. Our democratic civilization has been built, not by children of darkness but by foolish children of light. It has been under attack by the children of darkness, by the moral cynics, who declare that a strong nation need acknowledge no law beyond its strength. It has come close to complete disaster under this attack, not because it accepted the same creed as the cynics; but because it underestimated the power of self-interest, both individual and collective, in modern society. The children of light have not been as wise as the children of darkness.

The children of darkness are evil because they know no law beyond the self. They are wise, though evil, because they understand the power of self-interest. The children of light are virtuous because they have some conception of a higher law than their own will. They are usually foolish because they do not know the power of self-will. They underestimate the peril of anarchy in both the national and the international community. Modern democratic civilization is, in short, sentimental rather than cynical. It has an easy solution for the problem of anarchy and chaos on both the national and international level of community, because of its fatuous and superficial view of man. It does not know that the same man who is ostensibly devoted to the "common good" may have desires and ambitions, hopes and fears, which set him at variance with his neighbor.

It must be understood that the children of light are foolish not merely because they underestimate the power of self-interest among the children of darkness. They underestimate this power among themselves. The democratic world came so close to disaster not merely because it never believed that Nazism possessed the demonic fury which it avowed. Civilization refused to recognize the power of class interest in its own communities. It also spoke glibly of an international conscience; but the children of darkness meanwhile skilfully set nation against nation. They were thereby enabled to despoil one nation after another, without every civilized nation coming to the defence of each. Moral cynicism had a provisional advantage over moral sentimentality. Its advantage lay not merely in its own lack of moral scruple but also in its shrewd assessment of the power of self-interest, individual and national, among the children of light, despite their moral protestations. . . .

The confidence of modern secular idealism in the possibility of an easy resolution of the tension between individual and community, or between classes, races and nations is derived from a too optimistic view of human nature. This too generous estimate of human virtue is intimately related to an erroneous estimate of the dimensions of the human stature. The conception of human nature which underlies the social and political attitudes of a liberal democratic culture is that of an essentially harmless individual. The survival impulse, which man shares with the animals, is regarded as the normative form of his egoistic drive. If this were a true picture of the human situation man might be, or might become, as harmless as seventeenth- and eighteenth-century thought assumed. Unfortunately for the validity of this picture of man, the most significant distinction between the human and the animal world is that the impulses of the former are "spiritualized" in the human world. Human capacities for evil as well as for good are derived from this spiritualization. There is of course always a natural survival impulse at the core of all human ambition. But this survival impulse cannot be neatly disentangled from two forms of its spiritualization. The one form is the desire to fulfill the potentialities of life and not merely to maintain its existence. Man is the kind of animal who cannot merely live. If he lives at all he is bound to seek the realization of his true nature; and to his true nature belongs his fulfillment in the lives of others. The will to live is thus transmuted into the will to self-realization; and self-realization involves self-giving in relations to others. When this desire for self-realization is fully explored it becomes apparent that it is subject to the paradox that the highest form of self-realization is the consequence of self-giving, but that it cannot be the intended consequence without being prematurely limited. Thus the will to live is finally transmuted into its opposite in the sense that only in self-giving can the self be fulfilled, for: "He that findeth his life shall lose it: and he that loseth his life for my sake shall find it" (Matthew 10:39).

On the other hand the will-to-live is also spiritually transmuted into the will-to-power or into the desire for "power and glory." Man, being more than a natural creature, is not interested merely in physical survival but in prestige and social approval. Having the intelligence to anticipate the perils in which he stands in nature and history, he invariably seeks to gain security against these perils by enhancing his power, individually and collectively. Possessing a darkly unconscious sense of his insignificance in the total scheme of things, he seeks to compensate for his insignificance by pretensions of pride. The conflicts between men are thus never simple conflicts between competing survival impulses. They are conflicts in which each man or group seeks to guard its power and prestige against the peril of competing expressions of power and pride. Since the very possession of power and prestige always involves some encroachment upon the prestige and power of others, this conflict is by its very nature a more stubborn and difficult one than the mere competition between various survival impulses in nature. It remains to be added that this conflict expresses itself even more cruelly in collective than in individual terms. Human behaviour being less individualistic than secular liberalism assumed, the struggle between classes, races and other groups in human society is not as easily resolved by the expedient of dissolving the groups as liberal democratic idealists assumed.

Since the survival impulse in nature is transmuted into two different and contradictory spiritualized forms, which we may briefly designate as the will-to-live-truly and the will-to-power, man is at variance with himself. The power of the second impulse places him more fundamentally in conflict with his fellowman than democratic liberalism realizes. The fact he cannot realize himself, except in organic relation with his fellows, makes the community more important than bourgeois individualism understands. The fact that the two impulses, though standing in contradiction to each other, are also mixed and compounded with each other on every level of human life, makes the simple distinctions between good and evil, between selfishness and altruism, with which liberal idealism has tried to estimate moral and political facts, invalid. The fact that the will-to-power inevitably justifies itself in terms of the morally more acceptable will to realize man's true nature means that the egoistic corruption of universal ideals is a much more persistent fact in human conduct than any moralistic creed is inclined to admit. . . .

But the question arises, how the strategies of coercion of the community are judged and prevented from becoming inordinate. If it is granted that both the rulers and the community as such are also centers of vitality and expansive impulse, would not their use of restrictive power be purely arbitrary if it were not informed by some general principles of justice, which define the right order of life in a community? The fact is that there are no living communities which do not have some notions of justice, beyond their historic laws, by which they seek to gauge the justice of their legislative enactments. Such general principles are known as natural law in both Catholic and earlier liberal thought. Even when, as in the present stage of liberal democratic thought, moral theory has become too relativistic to make appeal to natural law as plausible as in other centuries, every human society does have something like a natural-law concept; for it assumes that there are more immutable and purer principles of justice than those actually embodied in its obviously relative laws.

The final question to confront the proponent of a democratic and free society is whether the freedom of a society should extend to the point of allowing these principles to be called into question. Should they not stand above criticism or amendment? If they are themselves subjected to the democratic process and if they are made dependent upon the moods and vagaries of various communities and epochs, have we not sacrificed the final criterion of justice and order, by which we might set bounds to what is inordinate in both individual and collective impulses?

It is on this question that Catholic Christianity has its final difficulties with the presuppositions of a democratic society in the modern, liberal sense, fearing, in the words of a recent pronouncement of the American bishops, that questions of "right and wrong" may be subjected to the caprice of majority decisions. For Catholicism believes that the principles of natural law are fixed and immutable, a faith which the secular physiocrats of the eighteenth century shared.[7] It believes that the freedom of a democratic society must stop short of calling these principles of natural law into question.

The liberal democratic tradition of our era gave a different answer to this question. It did not have very plausible reasons for its answer; but history has provided better ones. The truth is that the bourgeois democratic theory held to the idea of absolute and unrestricted liberty, partly because it assumed the unlimited right of private judgment to be one of the "inalienable" rights which were guaranteed by the liberal version of the natural law.[8] Its adherence to the principle of complete liberty of private judgment was also partly derived from its simple confidence in human reason. It was certain that reason would, when properly enlightened, affirm the "self-evident" truths of the natural law. Both the Catholic and the liberal confidence in the dictates of the natural law, thus rest upon a "non-existential" description of human reason. Both fail to appreciate the perennial corruptions of interest and passion which are introduced into any historical definition of even the most ideal and abstract moral principles. The Catholic confidence in the reason of common men was rightly less complete than that of the Enlightenment. Yet it wrongly sought to preserve some realm of institutional religious authority which would protect the uncorrupted truths of the natural law. The Enlightenment erroneously hoped for a general diffusion of intelligence which would make the truths of the natural law universally acceptable. Yet it rightly refused to reserve any area of authority which would not be subject to democratic criticism.

The reason this final democratic freedom is right, though the reasons given for it in the modern period are wrong, is that there is no historical reality, whether it be church or government, whether it be the reason of wise men or specialists, which is not involved in the flux and relativity of human existence; which is not subject to error and sin, and which is not tempted to exaggerate its errors and sins when they are made immune to criticism.

Every society needs working principles of justice, as criteria for its positive law and system of restraints. The profoundest of these actually transcend reason and lie rooted in religious conceptions of the meaning of existence. But every historical statement of them is subject to amendment. If it becomes fixed it will destroy some of the potentialities of a higher justice, which the mind of one generation is unable to anticipate in the life of subsequent eras.

Alfred Whitehead has distinguished between the "speculative" reason which "Plato shared with God" and the "pragmatic" reason which "Ulysses shared with the foxes."[9] The distinction is valid, provided it is understood that no sharp line can be drawn between the two. For man's spirit is a unity; and the most perfect vantage point of impartiality and disinterestedness in human reason remains in organic relation to a particular center of life, individual or collective, seeking to maintain its precarious existence against competing forms of life and vitality. Even if a particular age should arrive at a "disinterested" vision of justice, in which individual interests and passions were completely transcended, it could not achieve a height of disinterestedness from which it could judge new emergents in history. It would use its apparatus of "self-evident truths" and "inalienable rights" as instruments of self-defence against the threat of the new vitality.

Because reason is something more than a weapon of self-interest it can be an instrument of justice; but since reason is never dissociated from the vitalities of life, individual and collective, it cannot be a pure instrument of the justice. Natural-law theories which derive absolutely valid principles of morals and politics from reason, invariably introduce contingent practical applications into the definition of the principle.[10]

LOVE AND LAW IN PROTESTANTISM AND CATHOLICISM

The whole question about the relation of love to law in Christian thought is really contained in the question how love is the fulfillment of the law. The analysis of this issue may well begin with a definition of the nature of law. Subjectively considered, law is distinguished by some form of restraint or coercion, or, as Aquinas puts it, it is the direction to "perform virtuous acts by reason of some outward cause." The compulsion may be the force and prestige of the mores and customs of a community, persuading or compelling an individual to act contrary to his inclinations. But there is also an inner compulsion of law. It is the compulsion of conscience, the force of the sense of obligation, operating against other impulses in the personality. If there is no friction or tension between duty and inclination law is, at least in one sense, dissolved into love.

Materially, law usually represents detailed prescriptions of duties and obligations which the self owes to itself, to God, and to its neighbors. There may of course be general principles of law which gather together the logic of detailed prescriptions, as for instance the proposition, defined in Catholic thought as the "preamble" of the natural law, "that we ought to do good and avoid evil"; or Jesus' own summary of the law and the prophets. But that summary is, significantly, the "law of love" and therefore no longer purely law, but a law transcending law. Some degree of detail is characteristic of pure law. The "positive law" of historic communities gains its force primarily from its specificity. Many a law has been annulled by our Supreme Court on the ground that "vagueness" invalidated it. Even if we do not accept the Catholic theory of a highly specific "natural law" we all do accept principles of justice which transcend the positive enactments of historic states and which are less specific and not so sharply defined as positive law, and yet more specific than the law of love. These are generated in the customs and mores of communities; and they may rise to universal norms which seem to have their source not in particular communities but in the common experience of mankind.

The question of how love is related to law must be considered in terms of both the subjective and the material dimensions of both love and law. Subjectively, the question is how the experience of love, in which the "ought" is transcended, nevertheless contains a "thou shalt." Materially, the question is how the indeterminate possibilities of love are related to the determinate and specified obligations defined by law. The dialectical relation of love to law as both its fulfillment and its end (*pleroma* and *telos*), as fulfilling all possibilities of law and yet as standing in contradiction to it ("The law was given by Moses, but grace and truth came by Jesus Christ," John 1:17), is the basis and the problem of all Catholic and Protestant speculations on the relation of love to law.

In this debate Catholic thought, both in its classical version and in such a modem treatise as D'Arcy's *Mind and Heart of Love*, is more inclined than the Reformation to interpret love as *pleroma* of everything intended in nature and in law. But it is also inclined to interpret love as yet a more rigorous law, thus obscuring the elements of ecstasy and spontaneity, which are the marks of "grace." Reformation thought (or at least Lutheran thought, for Calvin does not deviate essentially from the Catholic version), on the other hand, is much nearer in its apprehension of a dimension of love which transcends law and even contradicts it; but it usually fails to do justice to love as the fulfillment of law and therefore tends to obscure the intimate relation between love and justice. Modern liberal

Protestantism is inclined to equate law and love by its effort to comprehend all law within the love commandment. It does not deny the higher dimensions of love which express themselves in sacrifice, forgiveness, individual sympathy, and universal love, but it regards them as simple possibilities and thereby obscures the tensions between love and law, both on the subjective and the objective side. . . .

In terms of the subjective dimension of the problem of love and law is the problem of the "push" of duty and the "pull" of grace. If the law of love comes to us as a "thou shalt" it is obviously a law. We can have a sense of obligation toward the interests of others without a definition of specific obligations. In this case love is simply the summary of all our obligations. This is why Thomas Aquinas includes love in the "old law" though this inclusion is inconsistent with his definition of the "old law" as the "law of fear" and his confining it to the restraint of actions rather than attitudes, to "restraining the hand rather than the will." On the other hand, love means a perfect accord between duty and inclination in such a way that duty is not felt as duty and "we love the things that thou commandest." This second aspect of love is disregarded in Kant's interpretation of love, for instance. For him the sense of obligation in its most universal and least specific form is identical with the law of love.

In Luther's exposition of the life of grace, "law" and "conscience" are left behind with sin and self. This freedom from the sense of "ought" is described by him as an ecstatic experience in which the self calculates no advantages, rises above every form of prudence, and feels itself at one with Christ, being motivated purely by a sense of gratitude for the divine forgiveness. Brunner stands in the Lutheran tradition when he also emphasizes this transcendence over the "ought" and declares that "if we feel we ought it is a proof that we cannot." It is a question whether this point of "grace" is understood by Calvin at all. For his ethic is one of obedience to the divine law. Love is a summary of this law, but he is also careful to spell it out in specific detail. The detail is as specific as Catholic "natural law" except that he draws the details not from the intuitions of reason but from "various portions of Scripture." He is convinced that we need this law in specific form to guide our conscience, corrupted by sin; and there is no suggestion that law and conscience do not operate in the state of grace.

This contrast between the conception of an identity of love and the sense of obligation, on the one hand, and a contradiction between them, on the other, is the proof of a complicated relationship between love and law in both the subjective and the objective sphere. What is described by Luther as freedom from law may well conform to momentary heights of spiritual experience in which there is such a "pull" of grace (which may include everything from ecstatic religious experience to the "common grace" of family love) that we are not conscious of any "ought" or any sense of obligation. But it may be questioned whether it can describe anything more than such moments. It certainly does not describe the ongoing experience of even the most consecrated Christian, particularly not if it is true about him, as Luther asserts, that he is "*justus et peccator simul.*" For if he remains a sinner it must be true of him that he feels the tension between his self-interest, his anxieties and insecurities and the obligation to forget himself for the sake of his concern for others. It may well be that everything defined as the "sense of justice" is an expression of the law of love within the limits of law. There are some aspects of the law of love, objectively considered, which are more clearly in the realm of duty than in the realm of grace. The injunction "If ye love them that love you what thanks have ye?" for instance, points to the universalistic tendencies in the law of love. It expresses our obligations beyond the boundaries of the natural communities of family, tribe, and nation. But paradoxically the love within the family may be by "grace" rather than law, while the love of "mankind" must be by law. That is, there may be such conjugal or paternal or filial affection as disposes us to seek the good of wife, husband, or child without any sense of duty, "common grace" or "habitual grace" having drawn the self beyond itself and out of itself into the lives of others. But our concern for those beyond our circle, our obligation to the peoples of the world and the community of mankind, comes to us very much with the push of the "ought" against the force of our more parochial habits of grace.

Yet on the other hand, pure obligation, while not so impotent as Brunner suggests, is more impotent than generally recognized, which is why purely moralistic sermons, which always tell us what we ought to do, tend to be boring. The best modern psychiatry, when dealing with the problem of delinquency in children, significantly does not preach to them what they ought to do, not even that they "ought to accept themselves." It insists that they must be accepted, must find security in the love of others, out of which security they gain sufficient freedom from self to "let go" and love others. Common grace, in short, rather than law is offered as a cure for their ills. It might be added that a good deal of modern Christian teaching about Christian love may be by comparison very loveless. For the preacher chides his congregation endlessly for not meeting the most ultimate possibilities of the law of love, such as sacrifice, forgiveness, and uncalculated freedom from self, as if these were simple possibilities of the will. Thus the law of love becomes the occasion for loveless castigation because it is not recognized that, on the subjective side, love is a curious compound of willing through the strength of the sense of obligation and of willing not by the strength of our will but by the strength which enters the will through grace. This defect in the liberal Protestant attitude toward love is the subjective aspect of its lack of a doctrine of grace. The objective aspect, which must be considered subsequently, is revealed in its lack of distinction between love and justice. In both aspects the basis of the defect lies in the failure to appreciate the force of self-love in life. The consequence of this failure creates the belief that love is a law which can be easily fulfilled if only the preacher will establish its validity and present it persuasively. Grace, whether "common" or "saving," has meaning only when life is measured at the limits of human possibilities and it is recognized that there are things we ought to do which we cannot do merely by the strength of our willing but which may become possible because we are assisted by the help which others give us by their love, by the strength which accrues to our will in moments of crisis, and by the saving grace of the Spirit of God indwelling our spirit. . . .

This analysis of love as law and love as transcending law is incomplete without consideration of one further problem: the relation of love to law as such. Law as such is composed of norms of conduct prescribed by custom, legal enactment, scriptural injunction, or rational intuition, in which duties and obligations are prescribed without seeming reference to the ultimate spirit of law, namely, love. What is the standing of such law in a Christian scheme of ethics and how is love related to it? In Catholic thought this law is drawn from the intuitions or logical deductions of reason, so that even the Decalogue is regarded as normative by Aquinas only in so far as it corresponds to the natural law. In Reformation thought, systematically in Calvin and less systematically in Luther, this law is drawn from Scripture, either from explicit law, such as the Decalogue, or from moral admonitions in various portions of Scripture which are raised to the authority of explicit norms for the Christian life.

All such law will be found to have two characteristics: a) It states our obligations to our neighbor is minimal and usually in negative terms. "Thou shalt not kill." "Thou shalt not steal." b) It states our obligations to our neighbors in terms which presuppose the fact of sin and self-interest and the complexity of claims and counterclaims which are arbitrated by some "rule of reason" rather than by the ultimate scruples of the law of love.

Thus the law, however conceived, accepts and regulates self-interest and prohibits only the most excessive forms of it. It does not command that we love the neighbor but only that we do not take his life or property. It does not command that we seek our neighbor's good but that we respect his rights. Broadly speaking, the end of the law is justice. But we have already seen that justice is related to love. Thus there is a dialectical relation between love and law even as there is between love beyond law and love as law. It might be stated as follows: The law seeks for a tolerable harmony of life with life, sin presupposed. It is, therefore, an approximation of the law of love on the one hand and an instrument of love on the other hand. Consequently the distinction between law and love is less absolute and more dialectical than conceived in either Catholic or Reformation thought.

If this conclusion be correct, it follows that law, however conceived, whether drawn from Scripture (as in Reformation thought) or from rational intuitions (as in Catholicism) or from historical tradition, is less fixed and absolute than all these theories assume. The scriptural authority, below the level of love, is less valid in the realm of law than the Reformation assumes because there is always an element of historical contingency in the allegedly absolute norms of Scriptures which makes its authority questionable in a different historical context. (St. Paul's attitude toward women in the Church is a case in point.) The authority of rational "natural" law is less valid than Catholicism supposes. The whole concept of natural law rests upon a Stoic-Aristotelian rationalism which assumes fixed historical structures and norms which do not in fact exist. Furthermore, it assumes a human participation in a universal reason in which there is no ideological taint. The moral certainties of natural law in Catholic thought are all dubious. Sometimes they rest upon deductive reason. It is assumed that it is impossible to draw logical conclusions in the field of material ethics, from the formal ethical principle that good is to be done and evil avoided. But there is no guide in the formal principle of ethics about the norms of good and evil. Sometimes they rest upon the "intuitions" of reason. While there are some seemingly universal moral judgments such as the prohibition of murder, it must be noted that they are the most universal if they are the most minimal and most negative expressions of the law of love. The more specific they become the more they are suspect as "self-evident" propositions of the natural law.

Sometimes Catholic natural theory sinks to the level of eighteenth-century rationalism, which it ostensibly abhors. It regards the propositions of natural law as propositions of analytic reason. This reason analyzes the structures of nature, including human nature, and arrives at certain conclusions about what nature "intends," as, for instance, that nature intends procreation in sexual union. In this case it forgets that human nature is characterized not only by an indeterminate freedom but by an intimate and organic relation between the impulses of nature and human freedom which permits endless elaborations of human vital capacities for which it is not easy to find a simple descriptive norm.

In short, both Catholic and Reformation theory are too certain about the fixities of the norms of law. All law, whether historical, positive, scriptural, or rational, is more tentative and less independent in its authority than orthodox Christianity, whether Catholic or Protestant, supposes, even as it is more necessary than liberal Protestantism assumes. The final dyke against relativism is to be found, not in these alleged fixities, but in the law of love itself. This is the only final law, and every other law is an expression of the law of love in minimal or in proximate terms or in terms appropriate to given historical occasions.[11]

NOTES

1. Power, *A New Social Analysis*, p. 11.
2. Quoted by F. Meinecke, *Die Idee der Staatsraison*, p. 377.
3. *Political Science*, p. 129. . . .
4. Philip Leon, *The Ethics of Power*, p. 140.
5. [*Nature and Destiny of Man: A Christian Interpretation* (New York: Charles Scribner's Sons, 1941, 1943), 1:188–192, 208–213, 218–220. In 1939, Niebuhr delivered the prestigious Gifford Lectures at the University of Edinburgh. Niebuhr actually delivered two series of lectures in Edinburgh—one on human nature (published in 1941) and the second on human destiny (published in 1943). In his lectures on human nature, Niebuhr surveyed classical, biblical, and modern views on the issue. Niebuhr concluded that modern thinkers were too optimistic in their assessment of human nature, uncomfortable with Christian conceptions of human sinfulness. By contrast, Niebuhr articulated an Augustinian notion of human sin that manifests itself as pride. Niebuhr identified three types of pride that humans exhibit as a means of dealing with the anxieties and insecurities of life: pride of power, pride of knowledge, and pride of virtue. Expanding on certain ideas that he had first introduced in his 1932 book *Moral Man and Immoral Society*, Niebuhr argued that this tendency toward human pride is particularly nefarious when exhibited by social groups and nations. Niebuhr delivered the lectures against the backdrop of the rise of Nazism. As he notes in his preface to the two volumes, the "first of these lectures was given in April and May of 1939 when the clouds of war were already hovering ominously over Europe; dark forebodings had become a dreadful reality before the second series was given in October, 1939." As Niebuhr speaks of the perils of the "pride of nations," he clearly has Nazi Germany in mind. Ironically, during one of Niebuhr's lectures, his audience could literally hear the bombs of the German Luftwaffe exploding at a nearby naval base.]
6. ["Why the Christian Church Is Not Pacifist," in *Christianity and Power Politics* (Hamden, Conn.: Archon Books, 1940), 14–15, 18–26. During the 1920s and early 1930s, Niebuhr was a pacifist and served as national chair of the Fel-

lowship of Reconciliation. In time, however, influenced in part by the expansionism of Nazi Germany, Niebuhr rejected pacifism, believing that in a sinful world, evil must be resisted. On the eve of America's entry into World War II, many Christian groups in the United States opposed American participation in the war. Niebuhr did not. He believed that America should enter the war to restrain the expansionism of Nazi Germany. Niebuhr resigned in 1940 from the editorial board of the *Christian Century*, to which he had contributed for many years, because of the journal's advocacy of a policy of American neutrality. Niebuhr founded another journal instead, *Christianity and Crisis*, which he used to articulate his "Christian realist" theology—a theology grounded in the reality of human sinfulness and the need to develop political and legal institutions to corral the manifestations of that sinfulness. Niebuhr's Christian realism also encompassed a rejection of pacifism.

In 1940, Niebuhr published an essay "Why the Christian Church is Not Pacifist" in his book *Christianity and Power Politics*. This essay was one of Niebuhr's clearest expressions of his Christian realist theology and its implications for public life.]

7. Catholic theory regards natural law as prescriptive and as derived from "right reason," whereas modern naturalism frequently defines it as merely descriptive, that is, as the law, which men may observe by analyzing the facts of nature. Jacques Maritain defines the natural law as "an order or a disposition which human reason can discover and according to which the human will must act in order to attune itself to the necessary ends of the human being." *The Rights of Man and Natural Law*, p. 61.

8. The fact that the content of the natural law as Catholicism conceives it differs so widely from the content of the natural law as the eighteenth century conceived it, though the contents of both are supposed to represent "self-evident" truths of reason, must make the critical student skeptical.

9. *The Function of Reason*, pp. 23–30.

10. [*The Children of Light and the Children of Darkness: A Vindication of Democracy and a Critique of its Traditional Defense* (New York: Charles Scribner's Sons, 1944), xii–xv, 9–12, 18–22, 67–72. During the early 1940s, Niebuhr continued to engage the question of the political and social implications of his view of human nature that he had articulated in earlier works such as *The Nature and Destiny of Man*. At the height of the struggle between western democracies and totalitarian states, Niebuhr reconsidered the traditional justifications for democracy. Niebuhr presented the results of his reflections in a series of lectures at Stanford University in 1944 that he subsequently published as a book, *The Children of Light and the Children of Darkness*, which provided an intellectual blueprint for the postwar Americans for Democratic Action, founded in 1947.

In these lectures, Niebuhr argued that the "excessively optimistic estimates of human nature and of human history with which the democratic credo has been historically associated are a source of peril to democratic society" (xii) and sought to explain why. Niebuhr observed that some people, whom he labeled "children of light," do not understand the power of human self-interest while others, whom he labeled "children of darkness," understand all too well the power of self-interest and how both to pursue and to harness it for their own purposes. For Niebuhr, the children of light must come to appreciate the depths of human self-interest and then establish and retain political institutions designed to control this self-interest. In Niebuhr's view, the "democratic techniques of a free society place checks upon the power of the ruler and administrator and thus prevent it from becoming vexatious" (xiv).]

11. ["Love and Law in Protestantism and Catholicism," in *Christian Realism and Political Problems* (New York: Charles Scribner's Sons, 1953), 147–154, 170–173. Throughout his writings, Niebuhr addressed the relationship between the "law of love," which was Niebuhr's fundamental ethical principle, and ethical norms found in the natural law or the positive law of particular communities. In his 1952 essay, "Love and Law in Protestantism and Catholicism," Niebuhr revisited this question of the relationship between the law of love and natural law and positive law from the perspective of both the Catholic and Protestant traditions. For Niebuhr, all laws should be "an approximation of" or "an instrument of" the law of love. Every legal norm, whether derived from natural law, historical tradition, or even scripture, must ultimately be assessed against the law of love. Niebuhr concludes that "both Catholic and Reformation theory are too certain about the fixities of the norms of law" and have not sufficiently appreciated the preeminence of the law of love as the lodestone against which all law must be measured.]

[CHAPTER 6]

Martin Luther King Jr. (1929–1968)

COMMENTARY

TIMOTHY P. JACKSON

Any person . . . who shall be guilty of printing, publishing, or circulating printed, typewritten or written matter urging or presenting for public acceptance or general information, arguments or suggestions in favor of social equality or of intermarriage between whites and negroes, shall be guilty of a misdemeanor and subject to fine of [sic] not exceeding five hundred (500.00) dollars or imprisonment not exceeding six (6) months or both.

—MISSISSIPPI "JIM CROW" LAW

It seemed as though I could hear the quiet assurance of an inner voice, saying, "Stand up for righteousness, stand up for truth. God will be at your side forever."

—MARTIN LUTHER KING JR.

Martin Luther King Jr. was neither an influential legal theorist nor a major systematic theologian. Rather, he was something much more necessary to his time, and arguably all times: a person of righteousness and faith who stood up for his convictions in obedience to God and in service to his neighbors. He was schooled in sociology and divinity, as well as skilled in practical jurisprudence, and he wrote very insightfully of his creed and causes. Yet King is included in this volume chiefly because he brought about constructive social change, by both legal and extralegal means, and because he inspired others to do the same. He embodied, above all, the "uses" of the law and theology, rather than their innovation or scholarly analysis. In short, he was a prophet rather than a pedant.

King courageously cross-fertilized Christian doctrines and democratic principles in a way that is rare today. In an age in which preeminent theorists of both the Christian church and the liberal state often seem to lose their way—by retreating into a narrow sectarianism on one hand and an empty proceduralism on the other—King's example still has much to teach us about justice, law, and human nature. He refused to divorce the sacred (the God worshipped by Jews and Christians) and the secular (the legal realities of American democracy). As a Baptist clergyman, King considered it not merely permissible but actually obligatory to engage publicly controversial political and economic issues. He offered neither dogmatic self-congratulation to believers nor neutral self-interest to non-believers, and in the process, he lived out the meaning of the First Amendment. Indeed, it was precisely because he believed that the call to and capacity for justice is built into the nature of "all of God's children"[1] that King was the foremost American public intellectual of the second half of the twentieth century.

King's legacy turns, in large measure, on a concrete moral commitment and a more elusive personal talent: his lived dedication to the poor and oppressed, together with his capacity for holism and synthesis. In his life, work, and death we have a model of service to the marginalized and vulnerable—the scriptural "widow and orphan"—as well as a guide to balancing a range of human goods, public and private. We have, more specifically, a picture of how to relate American law and the Christian gospel. This prophet eventually averred that "we as a nation must undergo a radical revolution of values,"[2] and the dialectic he suggested between politics and scripture is necessarily incomplete. Indeed, he gave decisive priority to the gospel. But King knew that "all life is interrelated" and that "life at its best is a creative synthesis of opposites in fruitful harmony."[3] He knew that a good society could no more separate social justice from personal charity, for instance, than it could segregate its white and black citizens.[4] King's life and thought were not without flaws, of course,[5] and one may question, as I do, aspects of his optimism and personalism. His ongoing influence for the good is testified to, however, by the fact that both lawyers and theologians still read and discuss him in trying to comprehend civic virtue.

One more introductory point must be addressed before I turn to the body of my text. There is often a backlash today when Martin King is held up as a moral hero. The understandable fear is that King, since his assassination, has become the darling of white conservatives, that invoking King's name will call up images of patient suffering and a "color-blind" community that take the edge off radical calls for black pride, black self-defense, and black separatism. What of the countervailing messages of W. E. B. Du Bois and Marcus Garvey, of Elijah Muhammad and Malcolm

X, of Huey P. Newton and Stokely Carmichael, of Louis Farrakhan and Elaine Brown? In focusing so much on King, the thesis runs, the impression may be given that resistant African American identity is monolithic; it might even seem that the struggle for civil rights and racial justice is a thing of the past. I hope to illustrate in this chapter, in contrast, the depth of King's critique of American law and culture, together with the height of his faith in the biblical God. His critique and the faith are still relevant today; in fact, in King's case (if not our own), the latter is indispensable to the former.

BIOGRAPHY

In dealing with a prophet, an exemplary public voice, there can be little understanding without some biography. In the case of Martin Luther King Jr., law and human nature are writ large in the story of a particular life, leaving us to comprehend and respond.

Martin Luther King Jr. was born on January 15, 1929, into an upper-middle-class home on Auburn Avenue in Atlanta, Georgia. His father was a Baptist preacher and active in the NAACP, while his mother was a homemaker and church organist. Young Martin, called "M.L.," was shaped by three basic factors: his family's emphasis on spiritual and cultural values, such as biblical literacy and piety, secular education, and social service; his family's social and financial standing in a comparatively prosperous (though largely segregated) black neighborhood; and the racism of the South, including the Jim Crow laws that enforced white supremacy and racial separatism. Growing up on "Sweet Auburn," just a few hundred yards up the road from Ebenezer Baptist Church, where his father was pastor, allowed King to see three worlds at once: a vibrant black church, a thriving black community, and an unjust wider society. This vantage point clearly influenced how he would eventually understand justice, law, and human nature. He was given a moral education and sense of self that allowed him both to perceive social problems and to address them without despair, to see the importance and power of human laws and to appreciate their limit and fallibility.

This education took time. "In his preschool years," Stephen B. Oates informs us, "M.L.'s closest playmate was a white boy whose father owned a store across the street from the King home."[6] When the two boys eventually entered separate schools, his friend's parents declared that Martin could no longer play with their son. This was King's first real experience of the race problem. "I was determined to hate every white person," King later wrote,[7] and his ire was further aggravated when, as a high school student, he and a teacher were forced to give up their seats to whites on a crowded bus. "It was the angriest I have ever been in my life," he subsequently observed.[8]

How did King avoid growing into a bitter and lawless young man? The maturing prophet did not initially endorse Christianity. Though his father was a Protestant minister, the younger King grew up doubting that religion could ever be "emotionally satisfying" or "intellectually respectable." Fundamentalist belief in particular seemed to have little relevance to the modern world, Oates informs us, including interracial relations.[9]

When King entered Morehouse College at age fifteen, however, several teachers began to revolutionize his worldview. George D. Kelsey helped him to see that Daddy King's fundamentalism was not the only form of Christianity, and thus Martin started to rethink his religious opinions. Benjamin Mays, the college president, also deeply affected King with his attack on "socially irrelevant patterns of escape" for the black church and his accent on liberation through knowledge and social engagement.[10] By 1946, the once-skeptical King felt called to the ministry, and in 1947 he was licensed to preach and became assistant to his father at Ebenezer Baptist Church. On February 25, 1948, King was ordained to the Baptist clergy. While still at Morehouse, he read Thoreau's "Civil Disobedience" and for the first time was exposed to the idea of nonviolent resistance: the power "of refusing to cooperate with an evil system."[11] In June 1948, King graduated from Morehouse College with a B.A. in sociology, and in September he entered Crozer Theological Seminary in Chester, Pennsylvania.

At Crozer, King became a disciple of Walter Rauschenbusch and the Christian activism of the Social Gospel movement. In Rauschenbusch, King found what Oates calls "a theological foundation for the social concerns he'd had since he was a boy," "a socially relevant faith" that could "deal with the whole man—his body and soul, his material and spiritual well-being."[12] King also read Marx and Lenin at this time, but he came to have three major objections to their thought. As he later recalled in *Stride Toward Freedom*, "First I rejected their materialistic interpretation of history. . . . Second, I strongly disagreed with communism's ethical relativism. . . . Third, I opposed communism's political totalitarianism."[13] King concluded that both communism and capitalism are partial truths, and he forever after insisted that no just reform movement could separate means from ends.[14] We are so embedded in our actions, he recognized, that to do evil that good might come is to pervert our selves as well as our societies.[15]

About this time, King heard a lecture by Mordecai W. Johnson, president of Howard University, on the life and teachings of Mahatma Gandhi. Johnson argued that the moral power of nonviolence (*ahimsa*) could improve race relations in the United States. King was impressed by the fact that Gandhi was not out to harm or humiliate the British but to redeem them through love.[16] After reading Marx and Nietzsche, King had "about despaired of the power of love in solving social problems."[17] But Gandhi's notion of *Satyagraha* (literally "truth-power") reconciled love and force and convinced King that it was the only moral and practical means for an oppressed people to struggle against social injustice. As King later noted:

> Prior to reading Gandhi, I had about concluded that the ethics of Jesus were only effective in individual relationship. The "turn the other cheek" philosophy and the "love your enemies" philosophy were only valid, I felt, when individuals were in conflict with other individuals; when racial groups and nations were in conflict a more realistic approach seemed necessary. But after reading Gandhi, I saw how utterly mistaken I was.
>
> Gandhi was probably the first person in history to lift the love ethic of Jesus above mere interaction between individuals to a powerful and effective social force on a large scale. Love for Gandhi was a potent instrument for social and collective transformation. It was in this Gandhian emphasis on love and non-violence that I discovered the method for social reform that I had been seeking for so many months.[18]

King always insisted that Christ provided the "spirit and motivation," and Gandhi the practical "method," of the civil rights movement.[19]

In June 1951, King graduated from Crozer with a bachelor of divinity degree; in June 1953, he married Coretta Scott in Marion, Alabama; and in June 1955, he received his doctorate in systematic theology from Boston University. Shortly after he embraced Gandhi at Crozer, King had to come to grips with Reinhold Niebuhr and his critique of Protestant liberalism's optimism about human nature and tendency toward a vapid pacifism. This King did at Boston University. For all of Niebuhr's insight, King concluded,

> Many of his statements revealed that he interpreted pacifism as a sort of passive nonresistance to evil expressing naïve trust in the power of love. But this was a serious distortion. My study of Gandhi convinced me that true pacifism is not nonresistance to evil, but nonviolent resistance to evil.
>
> I came to see that Niebuhr had overemphasized the corruption of human nature. His pessimism concerning human nature was not balanced by an

optimism concerning divine nature. He was so involved in diagnosing man's sickness of sin that he overlooked the cure of grace.[20]

Part of what contributed to King's own optimism was his study at Boston University of personalist philosophy with Edgar S. Brightman and L. Harold DeWolf. "Personalism's insistence that only personality—finite and infinite—is ultimately real strengthened me in two convictions: it gave me metaphysical and philosophical grounding for the idea of a personal God, and it gave me a metaphysical basis for the dignity and worth of all human personality."[21]

In January 1954, King received an offer from Dexter Avenue Baptist Church in Montgomery, Alabama, to give a trial sermon. He preached on "The Three Dimensions of a Complete Life"—love of self, love of neighbor, and love of God—was offered the post, and began his full-time pastorate on September 1, 1954.[22] The Kings' first child, Yolanda Denise, was born in Montgomery on November 17, 1955. On December 1, Rosa Parks, a forty-two-year-old Montgomery seamstress, refused to relinquish her bus seat to a white man and was arrested. On December 5, local organizers (mostly black churchmen and churchwomen) began a boycott of city buses to coincide with the trial of Mrs. Parks. At a meeting of movement leaders that same day, King was unanimously elected president of what had come to be called the Montgomery Improvement Association (MIA). On December 10, the Montgomery Bus Company suspended service in black neighborhoods.

At biweekly meetings of the MIA, King related his philosophy of nonviolent love and redemptive suffering. Yet his call for Negro self-respect and his appreciation of the vagaries of law and violence were also evident from the beginning. In an early essay entitled "Our Struggle," written in 1956, King summarized several of his basic beliefs and objectives:

> The extreme tension in race relations in the South today is explained in part by the revolutionary change in the Negro's evaluation of himself and of his destiny and by his determination to struggle for justice. *We Negroes have replaced self-pity with self-respect and self-depreciation with dignity.*[23]

> Although law is an important factor in bringing about social change, there are certain conditions in which the very effort to adhere to new legal decisions creates tension and provokes violence. We had hoped to see demonstrated a method that would enable us to continue our struggle while coping with the violence it aroused. Now we see the answer: face violence if necessary, but refuse to return violence. If we respect those who oppose us, they may achieve a new understanding of the human relations involved.[24]

We do not wish to triumph over the white community. That would only result in transferring those now on the bottom to the top. But, if we can live up to nonviolence in thought and deed, there will emerge an interracial society based on freedom for all.[25]

The vision of an interracial society governed by the "liberal" values of freedom and equality continued, in part, to define the balance of King's career.

Even as King and others attempted to put a just vision into practice in Montgomery, hate mail and crank calls flowed in. On January 26, 1956, King was arrested on speeding charges—going 30 in a 25 mph zone—and feared for his life when he was taken out of town to the jailhouse. In the face of death threats and legal obstructionism, anxiety and frustration grew among members of the MIA and in King's own soul. The day after his short stay in jail, as King later recalled, things came to a head:

After a particularly strenuous day, I settled in bed at a late hour. My wife had already fallen asleep and I was about to doze off when the telephone rang. An angry voice said, "Listen, nigger, we've taken all we want from you. Before next week you'll be sorry you ever came to Montgomery." I hung up, but I could not sleep. It seemed that all of my fears had come on me at once. I had reached the saturation point.

I got out of bed and began to walk the floor. Finally, I went to the kitchen and heated a pot of coffee. I was ready to give up. I tried to think of a way to move out of the picture without appearing to be a coward. In this state of exhaustion, when my courage had almost gone, I determined to take my problem to God. My head in my hands, I bowed over the kitchen table and prayed aloud. The words I spoke to God that midnight are still vivid in my memory. "I am here taking a stand for what I believe is right. But now I am afraid. The people are looking to me for leadership, and if I stand before them without strength and courage, they too will falter. I am at the end of my powers. I have nothing left. I've come to the point where I can't face it alone."

At that moment I experienced the presence of the Divine as I had never before experienced him. It seemed as though I could hear the quiet assurance of an inner voice, saying, "Stand up for righteousness, stand up for truth. God will be at your side forever." Almost at once my fears began to pass from me. My uncertainty disappeared. I was ready to face anything. The outer situation remained the same, but God had given me inner calm.[26]

Thus unfolded the most memorable moment of King's life, one resonant with the legendary pronouncement of his sixteenth-century namesake[27] and one to which King returned again and again for inspiration.[28] Three nights later, an unknown assailant threw a bomb onto the porch of King's Montgomery home. Though Coretta, Yolanda, and a family friend were in the house, no one was injured. Three days after that, on February 2, a suit was filed in federal district court asking that Montgomery's travel segregation laws be declared unconstitutional. On June 4, the federal district court ruled that racial segregation on city bus lines was unconstitutional. On November 13, the Supreme Court affirmed the lower court, thus voiding Alabama's state and local segregation laws. And on December 21, 1956, a year and twenty days after Rosa Parks's protest, the Montgomery buses were integrated.

King's leadership of the MIA inaugurated a dozen years of crusading for social justice. Elected to the leadership of the Southern Christian Leadership Conference (SCLC) in Atlanta on January 10–11, 1957, he was assassinated on a balcony of the Lorraine Motel in Memphis on April 4, 1968. King and his associates were strikingly effective in bringing about legal reforms in America and often used federal courts to challenge state practices and regulations. But King also suffered many setbacks. It is notable that, in his 1956 "kitchen table epiphany," he was not promised legal successes or even personal safety. (He was murdered before reaching the age of forty, after all.) Instead, he was given a mandate to champion those things that undergird positive law—righteousness and truth—together with an assurance of the presence of God. The distinction between political efficacy and moral principles, between temporal goods and an eternal God, shaped much of King's subsequent thought and action.

LAW AND JUSTICE

Two of King's favorite biblical passages were "Be not conformed to this world, but be ye transformed by the renewing of your mind" (Rom. 12:2 KJV) and "Let judgment [justice] roll down as waters, and righteousness as a mighty stream" (Amos 5:24 KJV).[29] The ability to hold these two quotations together in a lived unity, faithful to both heaven and earth, defined King's genius. More concretely, he recognized and acted on both the limits to and the potency of human laws. On the side of law's limits, King was no moral constructivist or legal positivist, refusing to appeal to a higher authority than regnant social conventions.[30] In his famous "Letter from a Birmingham Jail" (1963), for example, he insisted that there are "two types of laws": just and unjust. With Augustine, he held that "an unjust law is no law at all," and with Thomas Aquinas, he affirmed that "an unjust law is a human law that is not rooted in eternal and natural law."[31] More politically, "an unjust law is a code inflicted upon a minority which that minority had no part in enacting or creating because they did not have the unhampered right to vote."[32] These distinctions permitted King to explain how he could advocate the breaking of certain legal statutes in the name of civil rights; civil disobedience is permitted, even required, in order to resist codified social wrongs, because there is "a higher moral law" with a prior claim on us.[33]

The logic of King's lawbreaking is notable. One might expect him to hold that, since an unjust law is not really a law, one might violate it at will and with impunity. There will be *practical* consequences, of course—one will likely be arrested and imprisoned, or worse—but *morally* one is unconstrained. One might even expect King to conclude that, in the face of a system of predominantly unjust laws, the entire system is null and void. These were not King's judgments, however. He argued that, rightly understood, civil disobedience must be properly motivated and should not be allowed to slip into anarchic disregard for law in general. As King wrote: "One who breaks an unjust law must do it *openly, lovingly* . . . and with a willingness to accept the penalty. I submit that an individual who breaks a law that conscience tells him is unjust, and willingly accepts the penalty by staying in jail to arouse the conscience of the community over its injustice, is in reality expressing the very highest respect for law."[34]

Why accept a penalty for violating an immoral (non-) law? One reason, of course, is pragmatic; in undergoing punishment without retaliation, one is more likely to engage the scruples of the wider society and thus to encourage legal reform. But political utility is not the whole story. Requiring that civil disobedience be practiced in a particular way and that a penalty be accepted was King's way, I believe, of granting that even an unjust law remains a "law" in some sense. It is a fundamental Protestant conviction that, after the Fall, all human efforts and institutions are tainted by sin and that even an unjust law is the fruit of temporal powers ordained by God to restrain evil. For King, this means that, especially within a society that aspires to be democratic, the social processes by which laws are passed, as well as the political actors who interpret and enforce these laws, are due a measure of respect. This is the case even when the processes are in fact undemocratic, the actors personally corrupt, and the laws themselves horribly unfair. In spite of statements suggesting the contrary, even unjust laws retain some moral force for King. What he objected to was these laws' being given *undue* force or authority, their "lawness" alone being taken as a compelling reason for obedience.[35]

Especially troubling to King in the 1950s and 1960s was the appeal by "the white moderate" to "law and order," well-meaning but paternalistic advice to the American Negro to be "patient" and to "wait" for a more opportune moment for social protest. King saw this advice as "more devoted to 'order' than to justice," and he insisted that "law and order exist for the purpose of establishing justice, and . . . when they fail to do this they become dangerously structured dams that block the flow of social progress."[36] As *Why We Can't Wait* makes clear, it was precisely because King had a sense of the patience of a personal God that he could be "impatient" with human injustice without becoming either cynical or despairing.[37] In learning over a cup of coffee how to wait for the righteous Lord, he also learned how *not* to wait for an unjust or indifferent humanity.

On the side of law's potency, King recognized the power of constitutional ideals and jurisprudential traditions. In "Letter from a Birmingham Jail," he called the nation back to "those great wells of democracy which were dug deep by the Founding Fathers in the formulation of the Constitution and the Declaration of Independence."[38] And in his "I Have a Dream" speech, he again makes a point of referring to "the architects of *our* republic" and "the promise that all men, yes, black men as well as white men, would be guaranteed the unalienable rights of life, liberty, and the pursuit of happiness."[39] He was well aware that the Constitution itself had left slavery intact—even as had the Bible. But he typically countered American history with more American history, in citing the Emancipation Proclamation and the Thirteenth, Fourteenth, and Fifteenth Amendments, for example.[40] That said, King was not an historicist; he had no interest in merely codifying the practices of a distant past. Rather, he availed himself of both natural law arguments and a version of what Ronald Dworkin has recently called "the moral reading of the Constitution."[41] In interpreting and appealing to the Constitution, that is, King sought to honor American ideals and principles, not simply to follow American practices and precedents.[42]

In 1957, King had vigorously condemned the Supreme Court's 1896 *Plessy v. Ferguson* decision, which endorsed a "separate but equal" understanding of race relations. "Through this decision," he wrote, "segregation gained legal and moral sanction. The end result of the Plessy doctrine was that it led to a strict enforcement of the 'separate,' with hardly the slightest attempt to abide by the 'equal.' So the Plessy doctrine ended up making for tragic inequalities and ungodly exploitation."[43] On the hundredth anniversary of the Emancipation Proclamation, which was issued in 1863, King lamented how little progress had been made in the true liberation of African-Americans over the past century.[44] But his critique of Plessy and his refusal to be satisfied with the paper equality promised by *Brown v. Board of Education* (1954) avoided the snare of looking *only* to legal remedies from Washington. Law was important, but so was education. As King, presumably thinking of the debates between Booker T. Washington and W. E. B. Du Bois over a generation earlier, put it, "We must continue to struggle through legalism and legislation. There are those who contend that integration can come only through education, for no other reason than that morals cannot be legislated. I choose, however, to be dialectical at this point. It is neither education nor legislation; it is both legislation and education. . . . The law cannot make a man love—religion and education must do that—but it can control his efforts to lynch."[45] In addition to pushing for legal redress and reform (for example, a voting rights act), then, King's discontent with the status quo took the form of petitions to individual conscience (in the Negro and in the nation at large) as well as calls for community resistance (direct but nonviolent protest). King's strength was always to wed theory and praxis, but he was emphatic that "nonviolence is no longer an option for intellectual analysis, it is an imperative for action."[46]

King knew how important state legislatures, Congress, federal courts, the Supreme Court, and finally the public could be in insuring civil rights for African Americans. He knew the power of laws and lawmakers to resist or reform other laws and lawmakers. He also knew the power of the executive branch to rein in or augment the other two branches of government, especially at the local level. King had a sound understanding of American political theory—majority rule subject to judicial review, constitutional checks and balances, and so forth. And he explicitly acknowledged that in demonstrating for the rights to adequate housing, adequate income, and adequate education, "we have left the realm of constitutional rights and we are entering the area of human rights."[47] But his signal contribution was to galvanize all these legal, political, and cultural mechanisms into proper practice, at least for a time and to some significant degree. Put most briefly, King helped induce the American system (morally and materially) to recognize and act on its highest principles, even as he inspired individuals (black and white) to be their best selves. His success was not complete, of course, but it was remarkable even so.

Again, King was not merely interested in conserving past historical practices or even in realizing stated yet unattained legal and ethical goals. King's Christian faith in an eternal and righteous God allowed him to relativize *all* temporal human systems and to question *each* temptable human heart. Like Socrates having glimpsed the Good above Athenian "democracy," King was able to challenge even the (erstwhile) highest principles of his country and the (putative) best selves of his interlocutors. Especially in the mid- to late 1960s, King vigorously denounced "the giant triplets of racism, materialism, and militarism."[48] He proclaimed the need for "a radical restructuring of the architecture of American society" and asserted that "a new set of values must be born."[49] He brought capitalism under particularly sharp criticism and called for an economy that is "more person-centered than property- and profit-centered."[50] This meant, among other things, "a guaranteed income," "a revitalized labor movement," and "a broader distribution of wealth."[51] King's prophetic gift to the American state was to challenge it to become what it was not and perhaps never wanted to be: a democracy without "compromise."[52] Similarly, King's prophetic gift to the American church was to call it to become much more than it had ever been: "the true Body of Christ."[53] Neither the democratic state nor the integrated church, as such, is the realized kingdom of Heaven,[54] but both can plausibly aspire to be part of what King, following Josiah Royce, called "the beloved community."[55]

Always the Baptist minister, King focused on spiritual ends as well as political means, and he was far from alone in his efforts.[56] Andrew Young and a cadre of lawyers were often King's point people in court, and King himself emphasized his dispensability in the context of the mass movement for racial justice; as David Garrow has observed, as early as Montgomery, King and other leaders came to realize that "the people, and not simply their lawyers, could win their own freedom."[57] Yet the record, starting with the MIA bus boycott, is impressive. King and the SCLC had a significant hand in President Eisenhower's setting up the Civil Rights Commission and sending in the National Guard to integrate Arkansas public schools; in President Kennedy's federalizing the Alabama National Guard to integrate that state's schools and then delivering a televised speech to the nation in which he spoke out against segregation and racism; in Congress's passing and President Johnson's signing the Civil Rights Act of 1964, "to enforce the constitutional right to vote" and "to provide injunctive relief against discrimination in public accommodations"[58] and more.

King did not hesitate to use the language of "freedom and equality" and "citizenship rights," so dear to liberal democrats—indeed, he boldly declared that "the goal of America is freedom."[59] But neither did he flinch from a trumping emphasis on spiritual values such as faith, nonviolence, "soul force," and "the glory of the Lord."[60] To those who were tempted to accommodate Christianity too completely to temporal politics, King insisted that "the calling to be a son of the living God" is "beyond the calling of race or nation or creed."[61] "I just want to do God's will," he often

declared.[62] Even his identity as civil rights activist or Vietnam War pro-
tester was second to "my commitment to the ministry of Jesus Christ."[63]
To those who were tempted to withdraw from political and economic
struggles as too messy or worldly, in contrast, he emphasized that faith
without works is sterile. He advocated "nonviolent direct action" and "a
practical pacifism" as obligations in the quest for social justice. Only in
this way could one be true to both "the sacred heritage of our nation and
the eternal will of God."[64]

LAW AND GOSPEL

In both Martin Luther and John Calvin, as well as in Thomas Aquinas, the
word "law" can denote one or more of four things: (1) eternal law, which is
the very Being of God, God's heart/mind as it is in itself; (2) divine law,
which is the special revelation of God's requirements for humanity, as recorded, for example, in the Old Testament Decalogue; (3) natural law, the
principles of moral order built by God into creation itself, including human reason and will; and (4) human law, the civil statutes of a particular
political regime aimed at applying the natural law to concrete times,
places, actions, and individuals.

Beyond the denotation of "law," there is the question of its connotation,
its purpose or meaning.[65] According to Calvin, the three meanings or
"uses" of the law are: (1) theological: "by exhibiting the righteousness of
God—in other words, the righteousness which alone is acceptable to God—
it admonishes every one of his own unrighteousness, certiorates, convicts,
and finally condemns him;"[66] (2) civil: "by means of its fearful denunciations and the consequent dread of punishment, to curb those who, unless
forced, have no regard for rectitude and justice;"[67] and (3) didactic: "enabling [believers] daily to learn with greater truth and certainty what that
will of the Lord is which they aspire to follow, and to confirm them in this
knowledge."[68] For his part, Luther spoke of only two "uses" of the law: (1)
the civil use (*usus civilis*), in which political norms and mechanisms both
restrain evil behaviors and encourage good ones; and (2) the theological use
(*usus theologicus*), in which God employs the law as a hammer or fire to indict the conscience of the sinner.[69] All of these senses of the "law" were evident, more or less explicitly, in the life and work of Martin Luther King Jr.

As we have seen, King also distinguished between the positive statutes of a specific political body and the eternal law and natural law that
the statutes are ideally to express or apply. He, too, thought that one of
the functions of human law is to restrain evil actions, and he, too, held

that divine law aims to prick the consciences of persons and thereby goad them to repentance and reform. Foundational to all these points about the law, however, was an additional commitment that he shared with Aquinas, Luther, Calvin, and ultimately Augustine: the priority of the Gospel of Jesus Christ. Because King believed that Christ embodies the very person of God, Immanuel here with us, King had confidence that God's mercy and forgiveness are even more basic or powerful than God's condemnation and punishment. In the cross of Christ, God gratuitously restored right relationship to a fallen world by taking its guilt and suffering onto Himself. Christ named personal sins and resisted social evils, but he did so without indulging in hatred or violence. Faith in Christ, in turn, allowed King to identify human injustices and to struggle against them, but also to trust in divine providence (not just in human law or power) to carry the day.

LAW AND POWER

Confidence in the gospel (good news) of God's love did not render King naive about social realities. He saw the importance of power in human relations, including those between the races. He frequently noted that oppressors do not give up their privileges voluntarily but must be forced to do so by "determined legal and nonviolent pressure" from the oppressed.[70] Moreover, he never confused legal statutes alone with real power. "Laws only declare rights," he observed; "they do not deliver them."[71] King never tired of highlighting the "tragic gulf between civil rights laws passed and civil rights laws implemented,"[72] a gulf that required African Americans in the North and South alike to continue to agitate for social equality. If the *goal* of America is freedom, its *history* was that of "the inexpressible cruelties of slavery."[73]

Eventually defining power as "the ability to achieve purpose ... the strength required to bring about social, political or economic changes,"[74] King emphasized that "power is not only desirable but necessary."[75] Even so, he insisted that law is not merely a matter of power but also of right. It is remarkable that in spite of centuries of slavery, lynchings, and Jim Crow,[76] King did not give up on law as one means of human advancement. It is even more remarkable that he insisted that law is wedded to a "new kind of power"—"power infused with love and justice."[77]

To the end of his life, King continued to believe in the project of marrying American law with biblical morality. Put less pointedly, he steadfastly refused to segregate positive law (acts actually on the books) from natural law (timeless dictates of a good conscience) and eternal law (the will of

God). The latter two must ground and judge the first, and without this moral foundation, no one in the struggle for racial justice could hope for true victory. This cognizance of something beyond time and chance, something transcending skin color and factional interest, allowed King to be critical of both whites and blacks. He could indict white racists for their overt hatred and aggression, as well as white moderates for valuing peace and mere (positive) legality over justice. But he could also fault black leaders who were tempted to lapse into a hatred or irresponsibility of their own. King was able to appreciate "the marvelous new militancy"[78] that surged up among young black activists in the 1960s, and he saw a "broad and positive meaning" in Black Power as "a call to black people to amass the political and economic strength to achieve their legitimate goals."[79] He did not refrain, nevertheless, from also identifying "Black Power" as a slogan fraught with peril. To the extent that it suggested violent intimidation or cynical lawlessness, he believed it to be both counterproductive and wrong. "Power and morality must go together, implementing, fulfilling and ennobling each other."[80]

LAW AND NONVIOLENT RESISTANCE

Yet why, specifically, should nonviolence have been so key to King's social activism? Once one rejects passivity, complete nonresistance, and accepts the moral obligation to stand athwart injustice, and once one maintains that some positive laws are unjust and thus that civil disobedience may be legitimate, why insist on *nonviolent* resistance? Why not work against evil "by any means necessary," to echo Malcolm X's notorious phrase?[81] King's answer was that actions and intentions matter, as well as consequences.[82]

In addition to maintaining that some laws are improper ends, King held that violence is an improper means for several reasons. In *Stride Toward Freedom*, King's first book, he listed six basic points to help explain and justify the nonviolent resistance under way in Montgomery:

1. "Nonviolent resistance is not a method for cowards; it does resist."
2. "Nonviolence . . . does not seek to defeat or humiliate the opponent, but to win his friendship and understanding."
3. "It is evil that the nonviolent resister seeks to defeat, not the persons victimized by evil."
4. "Nonviolent resistance is [characterized by] a willingness to accept suffering without retaliation, to accept blows from the opponent without striking back."

5. "Nonviolent resistance . . . avoids not only external physical violence but also internal violence of spirit. The nonviolent resister not only refuses to shoot his opponent but he also refuses to hate him."

6. "Nonviolent resistance . . . is based on the conviction that the universe is on the side of justice. Consequently, the believer in nonviolence has deep faith in the future. This faith is another reason why the nonviolent resister can accept suffering without retaliation. For he knows that in his struggle for justice he has cosmic companionship."[83]

Across the years, King's briefs for nonviolence appealed to traits of character, principles of justice, social utility, as well as theological convictions. The moral eclecticism of his views is quite clear in this oft-quoted passage: "[Violence] is impractical because it is a descending spiral ending in destruction for all. The old law of an eye for an eye leaves everybody blind [a consequentialist argument]. It is immoral because it seeks to humiliate the opponent rather than win his understanding; it seeks to annihilate rather than to convert [a deontological argument]. Violence is immoral because it thrives on hatred rather than love [an aretological argument]. It destroys community and makes brotherhood impossible."[84] As King summarized in his final book, *Where Do We Go from Here?*: "Beyond the pragmatic invalidity of violence is its inability to appeal to conscience."[85]

HUMAN NATURE/PERSONALITY AND AGAPIC LOVE

Having a conscience was, for King, central to being made in the image of God. And being made in God's image was, in turn, foundational to what he intermittently called "the nonviolent affirmation of the sacredness of all human life" and "respect [for] the dignity and worth of human personality."[86] In a powerful Christian universalism, King affirmed that "every man is somebody because he is a child of God. . . . Man is more than a tiny vagary of whirling electrons or a wisp of smoke from a limitless smoldering. Man is a child of God, made in His image, and therefore must be respected as such. . . . We are all one in Christ Jesus. And when we truly believe in the sacredness of human personality, we won't exploit people, we won't trample over people with the iron feet of oppression, we won't kill anybody."[87] The common integrity of the human personality is the lynchpin in much of King's comments on law. Or, rather, the creative kindness of the *divine* Personality is the *anti*-lynching pin. "Human worth lies in relatedness to God."[88] If all finite persons are equal before God, how then can they be treated as unequal before the state or the wider society? Because all human persons are loved by God, they have value and are capable of loving themselves and one another. Injustice is quite often due to willful blindness to the image of God in others, a point King could put in either Kantian or biblical terms. "The immorality of segregation," for instance, "is that it treats men as means rather than ends, and thereby reduces them to things rather than persons."[89] Conversely, "the highest good is love."[90] One of the most sublime lines that King ever wrote, in my estimation, is this: "Since the white man's personality is greatly distorted by segregation, and his soul is greatly scarred, he needs the love of the Negro."[91]

The New Testament Greek name for the love in question is *agape*, "the love of God operating in the human heart."[92] This graced capacity allows individuals to hold in balance justice and power by transcending yet comprehending both. *Agape* transcends justice in that it does not limit itself to economies of exchange, calculations of merit and demerit, or even the natural sympathies of friendship. (Think of the parable of the generous vineyard owner in Matthew 20:1–16.) Rather, *agape* entails "an all-embracing and unconditional love for all men."[93] *Agape* comprehends power in that it is active and bold rather than passive and timid. "Structures of evil do not crumble by passive waiting."[94] As King put it, "When I speak of love I am not speaking of some sentimental and weak response. I am speaking of that force which all of the great religions have seen as the supreme unifying principle of life."[95]

King unabashedly placed agapic love at the core of his political thought and social action and offered four defining theses about such love:

1. "*Agape* is disinterested love. It is a love in which the individual seeks not his own good, but the good of his neighbor (I Cor. 10:24). *Agape* does not begin by discriminating between worthy and unworthy people, or any qualities people possess. It begins by loving others *for their sakes.*"

2. "[*Agape*] springs from the *need* of the other person—his need for belonging to the best in the human family. The Samaritan who helped the Jew on the Jericho Road was 'good' because he responded to the human need that he was presented with. God's love is eternal and fails not because man needs his love."

3. "*Agape* is a willingness to sacrifice in the interest of mutuality. *Agape* is a willingness to go to any length to restore community. . . . The cross is the eternal expression of the length to which God will go in order to restore broken community. The resurrection is a symbol of God's triumph over all the forces that seek to block community."

4. "*Agape* means a recognition of the fact that all life is interrelated. All humanity is involved in a single process, and all men are brothers... Whether we call it an unconscious process, an impersonal Brahman, or a Personal Being of matchless power and infinite love, there is a creative force in this universe that works to bring the disconnected aspects of reality into a harmonious whole."[96]

If *agape* comprehends yet transcends justice and power, it also embodies both law and Gospel. King suggested more than thirty-five years ago that, as a matter of *justice*, the United States government owes African Americans reparations for slavery.[97] And he was clear that *agape* never intentionally falls below the just requirements of the law, in all four senses. But King also knew that, in expanding sympathy and inspiring forgiveness, love rises above legalism to the prophetic. It is divine love, King would "re-mind" the world, that transforms and renews us (cf. Romans 12:2), by breaking us out of grasping self-interest (me vs. you) and invidious group elitism (us vs. them).

As understandable, historically, as was Marcus Garvey's call for black nationalism; as inspiring, intellectually, as was W.E.B. Du Bois's insistence that "the talented tenth" pursue a liberal education; as indispensable, legally, as was Thurgood Marshall's victory in *Brown v. Board*; as galvanizing, psychologically, as were Malcolm X's and Angela Davis's commitments to black manhood and womanhood; the most effective remedy, both politically and morally, for American racism and Jim Crow laws has been Martin King and Christlike love.

KING'S PROPHETIC OPTIMISM AND PERSONALISM

King's realism, what might be called his "holistic pessimism," enabled him to see that "injustice anywhere is a threat to justice everywhere."[98] As the preceding four quotes make clear, however, King's holistic optimism triumphed in his account of the harmonizing power of love. King was well aware that practitioners of *agape* would suffer at the hands of their unjust fellows, but he continued across the years to affirm "the faith that unearned suffering is redemptive."[99] He was not indiscriminate or masochistic in his call for suffering, any more than he was Machiavellian or cynical in his call for resistance. As he allowed in "Letter from a Birmingham Jail": "it is wrong to use immoral means to attain moral ends ... [but] it is just as wrong, or even more so, to use moral means to preserve immoral ends."[100] Yet even when moral means and ends seem to fail, he held that "right defeated is stronger than evil triumphant."[101]

Unquestionably, Jesus Christ was "an extremist for love,"[102] but does love always employ exclusively nonviolent means? I am not as sure as King that *agape* must eschew the use of lethal or injurious force under all circumstances. King consistently affirmed "the reality of evil" and "man's capacity for sin," and, at his best, he avoided both "superficial optimism" and "crippling pessimism."[103] Still, I am not as confident as he that "evil carries the seed of its own destruction."[104] In a fallen world, at any rate, I believe that protecting the innocent may move some Christians, properly, to take up the sword against evil, as in the American Civil War. Regrettably, the law sometimes needs the support of police forces, national guards, and armies, and love itself may enlist in these services.[105] One may doubt the consistency of King's protesting to President Eisenhower that Montgomery blacks were "without protection of law,"[106] when King himself was unwilling to endorse the necessary (moral) means to enforce the law.

Unquestionably, American blacks have for centuries been "drained of self-respect and a sense of 'somebodiness.' "[107] But is personality the highest good? I sometimes worry that King neglected the value of the *im*personal: the natural or animal world and those shared human needs and potentials that have nothing to do with freedom or self-conscious dignity.[108] Human nature is more than autonomous personality, as fetuses, babies, the retarded, and the senile demonstrate. Still, it is important to emphasize that, for King, the person is not some disembodied mind or self-sufficient will. King consistently took care to avoid "a completely otherworldly religion which makes a strange, unbiblical distinction between body and soul, between the sacred and the secular."[109] Moreover, for him, "other-preservation is the first law of life . . . precisely because we cannot preserve self without being concerned about preserving other selves."[110]

I have suggested that part of what made Martin Luther King Jr. prophetic was his commitment to the will of God and the full range of human existence: bodies and souls, self and others, thought and action, church and state, the private and the public, means and ends, love and justice, time and eternity.[111] I have also suggested that his upbringing at the intersection of societies in tension—black and white, rich and poor—prepared him for his prophetic vocation of recognizing the marginalized and empathizing with the weak. Indeed, as an embodiment of the theological, civil, and didactic "uses" of the law, King himself indicted our consciences, helped restrain social evils, and educated the church concerning the will of God.

Secular liberals typically fear that admitting the prophet's "Thus saith the Lord" into public discourse will lead to intolerance: Christian optimism and personalism run amok into theocratic dogmatism and oppression.[112] This was a reasonable worry in the West during the six-teenth and seventeenth centuries, even as the dangers of fundamental-ism remain a concern in the Near East today. But our chief domestic threat is currently from social fragmentation and the hegemony of pos-sessive individualism, rather than from religious tyranny and the hege-mony of the Protestant church. In King's case, Christian convictions led him to affirm freedom of conscience and the ubiquity of sin and er-ror, as well as to champion racial equality, the right to vote, and so on. His righteous indignation at injustice was paired with a self-limiting humility. Rather than denying liberal values, then, he clarified and dis-ciplined them.

Christian traditionalists often fear, in turn, that prophetic defenses of liberal democracy and human rights will erode true virtue and amount to a sellout of the ancient church to the modern state. They suspect, in Robert Kraynak's words, "that democracy is tyrannical in its ruthless leveling of higher and lower goods and of the hierarchies of the soul that are absolutely necessary for spiritual life."[113] Ever since Constantine, the argument goes, secular laws and loyalties have per-verted the Christian gospel. On King's behalf, nevertheless, I must en-ter a plea of "not guilty." The epiphany at the kitchen table in Montgomery—hearing God over a cup of coffee and in the midst of a bus boycott—provides a graphic image of how the sacred and the pro-fane, Christian faith and democratic politics, converged in King's life. By placing all of human existence under the governance of *agape*, he taught Christians to be in the world but not of it. King was under no il-lusions about the sins of U.S. culture—its history of slavery, its ongoing racial and economic exploitation—but he was still able to trust God and serve his neighbors in situ.

King's legacy partly consists in the civil rights acts he helped to pass into law, and a legal holiday now honors his memory. But perhaps his main contribution was to stir in Christians in America (and around the world) a political conscience. His example may still move us to ask: Even though religious fanaticism is dangerous, did not democracy itself spring, in part, from Christian teachings about God and humanity? Are we to forget the Puritans and the religious rationales behind so many of the state constitutions of the newly liberated colonies? If commitments to freedom, equality, and the rule of law seem to undermine biblical faith, hope, and love, are the latter virtues really being practiced?

There is more than one version of liberal democracy and its relation to law, society, and human nature, just as there is more than one version of Christian faith. Yet Martin Luther King Jr. was a peculiarly American prophet in being able to speak the broad languages of democracy and Christianity, simultaneously, without confusing the two. For all the preceding observations, even so, it is ultimately a mystery what makes someone prophetic.[114] Jurisprudes, religion professors, and the general population can only be grateful, both to God and to the individual, for the prophet's life and work. It is appropriate, therefore, that I give our American Amos the last word:

> Man-made laws assure justice, but a higher law produces love. . . . A vigorous enforcement of civil rights will bring an end to segregated public facilities, but it cannot bring an end to fears, prejudice, pride and irrationality, which are the barriers to a truly integrated society. These dark and demonic responses will be removed only as men are possessed by the invisible inner law which etches on their hearts the conviction that all men are brothers and that love is mankind's most potent weapon for personal and social transformation. True integration will be achieved by men who are willingly obedient to unenforceable obligations.[115]

NOTES

1. Martin Luther King Jr., "I Have a Dream" (1963), in *I Have a Dream: Writings and Speeches That Changed the World*, ed. James M. Washington (San Francisco: HarperCollins, 1992), 105.
2. Martin Luther King Jr., *The Trumpet of Conscience* (San Francisco: Harper & Row, 1967), 32.
3. Ibid., 69; Martin Luther King Jr., *Strength to Love* (Philadelphia: Fortress Press, 1963), 9.
4. Compare the appraisals of King by Stanley Hauerwas in *Wilderness Wanderings: Probing Twentieth-Century Theology and Philosophy* (Boulder, Colo.: Westview Press, 1997), 225–237, and by John Rawls in *Political Liberalism* (New York: Columbia University Press, 1993), 247 n. and 250.
5. With respect to the charges of plagiarism and marital infidelity, I can only say that in Dr. King, "we have this treasure in earthen vessels" (2 Cor. 4:7 KJV). For more, see the work of Clayborne Carson, senior editor of the King Papers Project and professor of history at Stanford University, including the introductions to *The Papers of Martin Luther King, Jr.*, 4 vols. (Berkeley: University of California Press, 1992–2000). See also Scott McCormack, "Carson: King Borrowed Ideas for Famous Speech," *The Stanford Daily*, March 6, 1991.
6. Stephen B. Oates, *Let the Trumpet Sound: The Life of Martin Luther King, Jr.* (New York: New American Library, 1982), 10. I am dependent on Oates for a good deal of the biographical material that follows. I have also relied on the chronology provided in King, *I Have a Dream*, xxiii–xxx; and on David J. Garrow,

Bearing the Cross: Martin Luther King, Jr., and the Southern Christian Leadership Conference (New York: Vintage Books, 1988).

7. Oates, *Let the Trumpet Sound*, 10.

8. Ibid., 16.

9. Ibid., 14; the phrases in quotations in this paragraph are King's, as quoted by Oates.

10. Ibid., 19; the phrase in quotations in this sentence is Mays's, as quoted by Oates.

11. Martin Luther King Jr., *Stride Toward Freedom* (New York: Harper & Row, 1958), 91.

12. Oates, *Let the Trumpet Sound*, 26.

13. King, *Stride Toward Freedom*, 92.

14. Ibid., 94–95.

15. See, e.g., King, *Strength to Love*, 98.

16. See Oates, *Let the Trumpet Sound*, 32.

17. King, *Stride Toward Freedom*, 95.

18. Ibid., 96–97.

19. Ibid., 85. For an engaging study of "the prior basis for Gandhi's appeal in the African-American community," one that explores the "pre-1950s traditions upon which King and others built," see Sudarshan Kapur, *Raising Up a Prophet: The African-American Encounter with Gandhi* (Boston: Beacon Press, 1992); quoted phrases from ibid., 3–4.

20. King, *Stride Toward Freedom*, 98, 100.

21. Ibid., 100.

22. Ibid., 16–23; see also Martin Luther King Jr., *The Words of Martin Luther King, Jr.*, ed. Coretta Scott King (New York: Newmarket Press, 1983), 64.

23. Martin Luther King Jr., "Our Struggle" (1956), in *I Have a Dream*, 5.

24. Ibid., 7.

25. Ibid., 13.

26. King, *Strength to Love*, 113.

27. Martin Luther is often quoted as concluding his remarks before the Imperial Diet of Worms with the words, "Here I stand, I can do no other. God help me. Amen." This may be an early redacted press report, however. Many scholars believe he actually said, "I cannot and I will not recant anything, for to go against conscience is neither right nor safe. God help me. Amen." See "Luther at the Imperial Diet of Worms (1521)," http://www.luther.de/en/worms.html.

28. For more on the historical context and aftermath of this night, see Garrow, *Bearing the Cross*, 56–60.

29. He quoted both of these lines often; see, e.g., King, *Strength to Love*, chaps. 2 and 10.

30. How precisely to define "legal positivism" is much disputed, as is its cogency as a theory of law. At one extreme, some construe positivism as making only the descriptive, conceptual claim that, given a certain historical pedigree, something may be both a law and immoral. Having the status of law says little

or nothing about whether the law should be obeyed, on this account. At the other extreme, some see positivism as defending the normative thesis that something's being a law is, in and of itself, a compelling (perhaps even the only) ground for obeying it. My use above of the phrase "legal positivist" presumes the latter, stronger definition. For careful discussions of positivism, especially its relation to competing views (such as natural law theory), see Robert P. George, ed., *The Autonomy of Law: Essays on Legal Positivism* (Oxford: Oxford University Press, 1996).

31. Martin Luther King Jr., "Letter from a Birmingham Jail" (1963), in *I Have a Dream*, 89.

32. Ibid., 90.

33. Ibid. As King puts it in *Stride Toward Freedom*, 212: "Noncooperation with evil is as much a moral obligation as is cooperation with good."

34. King, "Letter from a Birmingham Jail," 90.

35. Kent Greenawalt has offered an interesting critique of the view that an unjust law is not truly a law, as well as a sympathetic reading of chastened forms of legal positivism; see his "Too Thin and Too Rich: Distinguishing Features of Legal Positivism," in George, ed., *The Autonomy of Law*, 1–29. For Greenawalt, positivism involves both descriptive and normative theses. Nonetheless, its descriptive emphasis on the social origins of law makes it more plausible to an "outsider-observer" of the legal system than to an "insider-participant," who looks more tellingly to law's content and moral validity (20). King, for his part, often straddled these two perspectives. In giving more weight to moral validity, however, his accent is on the participant who must decide whether to obey an unjust law or to go to jail. King's personalism dictates that, in cases of conflict, individual conscience and decision must supersede group structures and traditions.

36. King, "Letter from a Birmingham Jail," 91.

37. Martin Luther King Jr., *Why We Can't Wait* (New York: Mentor Books, 1963).

38. King, "Letter from a Birmingham Jail," 100.

39. King, "I Have a Dream," 102 (italics mine).

40. King, *Why We Can't Wait*, 25.

41. Ronald Dworkin, *Freedom's Law: The Moral Reading of the American Constitution* (Cambridge, Mass.: Harvard University Press, 1996).

42. James E. Fleming discussed the distinction between "aspirational principles" and "historical practices" in constitutional interpretation in "Are We All Originalists Now? I Hope Not!" Lecture given at Princeton University, September 19, 2002.

43. Martin Luther King Jr., "Facing the Challenge of a New Age" (1957), in *I Have a Dream*, 17.

44. King, *Why We Can't Wait*, 23–25.

45. King, "Facing the Challenge of a New Age," 25.

46. King, *The Trumpet of Conscience*, 64. For a detailed examination of how King combined the "theoretical and experiential deconstruction/reconstruction" of

law and society, see Anthony E. Cook, "Beyond Critical Legal Studies: The Reconstructive Theology of Dr. Martin Luther King, Jr.," *Harvard Law Review* 103 (March 1990): 985–1044.

47. Martin Luther King Jr., "Nonviolence: The Only Road to Freedom" (1966), in *I Have a Dream*, 131.
48. Martin Luther King Jr., "A Time to Break Silence" (1967), in *I Have a Dream*, 148.
49. Martin Luther King Jr., *Where Do We Go from Here: Chaos or Community?* (Boston: Beacon Press, 1968), 133.
50. Ibid.
51. Ibid., 162, 142, and Martin Luther King Jr., "Where Do We Go from Here?" (1967), in *I Have a Dream*, 176.
52. King, *Why We Can't Wait*, 131.
53. King, *Strength to Love*, 141.
54. King warned against this mistaken identification in *Stride Toward Freedom*, 91.
55. Ibid., 220.
56. For a compelling narration of the larger context of King's activism, including his dependence on and disagreements with other civil rights leaders (among them Ralph Abernathy, Septima Clark, W. E. B. Du Bois, and Medgar Evers), see Taylor Branch, *Parting the Waters: America in the King Years, 1954–1963* (New York: Simon & Schuster, 1988).
57. Garrow, *Bearing the Cross*, 86.
58. *Civil Rights Act of 1964*, *U.S. Code*, vol. 42, title VII, beginning at section 2000e.
59. King, "Letter from a Birmingham Jail," 98.
60. See King, "I Have a Dream," 102–105.
61. King, "A Time to Break Silence," 140.
62. See, for instance, Martin Luther King Jr., "I See the Promised Land" (1968), in *I Have a Dream*, 203.
63. King, "A Time to Break Silence, 139.
64. King, "Letter from a Birmingham Jail," 98.
65. See Edward A. Dowey, "Law in Luther and Calvin," *Theology Today* 41, no. 2 (July 1984): 148.
66. John Calvin, *Institutes of the Christian Religion* (1536/1539), book 2, chap. 7, trans. Henry Beveridge, 2 vols. (Edinburgh: Calvin Translation Society, 1845), 1:304.
67. Ibid., 1:307.
68. Ibid., 1:309.
69. Martin Luther, "A Commentary on Saint Paul's Epistle to the Galatians" (1531), in *Martin Luther: Selections from His Writings*, ed. John Dillenberger (Garden City, N.Y.: Anchor Books, 1961), 139–145.
70. King, "Letter from a Birmingham Jail," 87.
71. King, *Where Do We Go From Here?* 158.
72. Ibid., 82.

73. King, "Letter from a Birmingham Jail," 98.

74. King, *Where Do We Go From Here?* 37.

75. Ibid.

76. Visitors entering the display area of the Martin Luther King, Jr., Center for Nonviolent Social Change in Atlanta are confronted by a range of Jim Crow laws displayed on a large glass wall. The laws, from several southern states, date from the 1880s to the 1960s; for examples (such as this one from Mississippi: "The marriage of a white person with a negro or mulatto or person who shall have one-eighth or more of negro blood, shall be unlawful and void"), see http://www.nps.gov/malu/documents/jim_crow_laws.htm.

77. King, *Where Do We Go from Here?* 66.

78. King, "I Have a Dream," 103.

79. King, *Where Do We Go from Here?* 36.

80. Ibid., 59.

81. John Kelsay has noted in conversation that in some Islamic texts, the Arabic phrase commonly translated into English as "by any means necessary" is better read as "by the necessary (i.e., appropriate) means." I am not sure whether Malcolm X had this latter sense in mind, but, given his other early views, I doubt it.

82. At one point, Malcolm X considered "an integrationist like King" to be akin to a "house Negro" of pre–Civil War days, a slave who identified with "the master" and ultimately sold out to him. Minister Malcolm clearly had Reverend King in mind when he said in a 1963 interview, "I think that any black man who goes among so-called Negroes today who are being brutalized, spit upon in the worst fashion imaginable, and teaches those Negroes to turn the other cheek, to suffer peacefully, or love their enemy is a traitor to the Negro." Malcolm X, "The Old Negro and the New Negro," in *The End of White World Supremacy*, ed. Imam Benjamin Karim (New York: Arcade, 1971), 116. Malcolm met King face to face only once, in March 1964. After Malcolm's transforming trip to Mecca the following month, he tempered his remarks on the SCLC and its leadership.

83. King, *Stride Toward Freedom*, 102–103, 106. In his "Letter from a Birmingham Jail," written five years after the publication of *Stride*, King responded to various white clergy's deploring of the civil rights "demonstrations" underway in Birmingham by noting that "in any nonviolent campaign there are four basic steps: (1) collection of the facts to determine whether injustices are alive, (2) negotiation, (3) self-purification, and (4) direct action." He went on to assert, "We have gone through all of these steps in Birmingham," adding that the protests were thus appropriate (85).

84. King, *The Words of Martin Luther King, Jr.*, 73; see also King, *Stride Toward Freedom*, 213.

85. King, *Where Do We Go from Here?* 59.

86. King, *The Trumpet of Conscience*, 72, 77; see also King, *Where Do We Go from Here?* 180.

87. King, *The Trumpet of Conscience*, 72.

88. King, *Where Do We Go from Here?* 97.
89. Ibid.
90. King, *Strength to Love*, 145.
91. King, *Stride Toward Freedom*, 105.
92. Ibid., 104.
93. King, "A Time to Break Silence," 150; see also his *Where Do We Go from Here?* 190.
94. King, *Where Do We Go from Here?* 128.
95. King, "A Time to Break Silence," 150.
96. King, *Stride Toward Freedom*, 104–107. King's lines on Christian love are highly indebted to the writings of Anders Nygren and Paul Ramsey; see Garrow, *Bearing the Cross*, 112. Nicholas Wolterstorff has maintained, in discussion, that King's comments on *agape*, its appreciation of mutuality and of the worth and dignity of the individual, are actually more applicable to *eros*. To the extent that *eros* looks to the merit of the other and to what that merit can do for one's own interests, however, I believe that King is correct in distinguishing it from *agape*. As King defines *eros*, it is concerned with justice and giving admirable persons their due rather than with charity and service to needy strangers. *Agape* and *eros* are not necessarily opposed, but they are not identical either.
97. King, *Where Do We Go from Here?* 79, 109; see also King, *Why We Can't Wait*, 134–139.
98. King, "Letter from a Birmingham Jail," 85.
99. King, "I Have a Dream," 104; see also *Stride Toward Freedom*, 103.
100. King, "Letter from a Birmingham Jail," 99.
101. Ibid., 98.
102. Ibid., 94.
103. King, *Strength to Love*, 109, 130, and 83, respectively.
104. Ibid., 82.
105. See Timothy P. Jackson, *The Priority of Love: Christian Charity and Social Justice* (Princeton, N.J.: Princeton University Press, 2003), esp. chap. 3.
106. See Branch, *Parting the Waters*, 191.
107. King, "Letter from a Birmingham Jail," 93.
108. See Jackson, *The Priority of Love*, esp. chap. 5.
109. King, *Why We Can't Wait*, 90. This phrase from "Letter from a Birmingham Jail" is printed somewhat differently in the version of the letter in *I Have a Dream*, 96. I use the quoted version because its employment of the present tense better suits my purposes.
110. King, *Where Do We Go from Here?* 180.
111. For more on these themes, see King, *Stride Toward Freedom*, 36, 91.
112. Jeffrey Stout has pressed this point, in conversation; see also Richard Rorty, *Philosophy and Social Hope* (London: Penguin, 1999), chap. 11.
113. Robert Kraynak, "Statement of Author Prepared for Background for Discussion at American Maritain Association Meeting," October 2002, Princeton

University. On Christianity and democracy, see also Stanley Hauerwas, *Wilderness Wanderings*; *Against the Nations: War and Survival in a Liberal Society* (Minneapolis: Winston Press, 1985); *In Good Company: The Church as Polis* (Notre Dame, Ind.: University of Notre Dame Press, 1995); and *With the Grain of the Universe: The Church's Witness and Natural Theology* (Grand Rapids, Mich.: Brazos Press, 2001).

114. King himself observed: "Not every minister can be a prophet, but some must be prepared for the ordeals of this high calling and be willing to suffer courageously for righteousness." King, *Stride Toward Freedom*, 210.

115. King, *Where Do We Go from Here?* 100–101.

ORIGINAL SOURCE MATERIAL

LETTER FROM A BIRMINGHAM JAIL

April 16, 1963

MY DEAR FELLOW CLERGYMEN:

While confined here in the Birmingham city jail,[1] I came across your recent statement calling my present activities "unwise and untimely." Seldom do I pause to answer criticism of my work and ideas. If I sought to answer all the criticisms that cross my desk, my secretaries would have little time for anything other than such correspondence in the course of the day, and I would have no time for constructive work. But since I feel that you are men of genuine good will and that your criticisms are sincerely set forth, I want to try to answer your statement in what I hope will be patient and reasonable terms.

I think I should indicate why I am here in Birmingham, since you have been influenced by the view which argues against "outsiders coming in." I have the honor of serving as president of the Southern Christian Leadership Conference, an organization operating in every southern state, with headquarters in Atlanta, Georgia. We have some eighty-five affiliated organizations across the South, and one of them is the Alabama Christian Movement for Human Rights. Frequently we share staff, educational and financial resources with our affiliates. Several months ago the affiliate here in Birmingham asked us to be on call to engage in a nonviolent direct-action program if such were deemed necessary. We readily consented, and when the hour came we lived up to our promise. So I, along with several members of my staff, am here because I was invited here; I am here because I have organizational ties here.

But more basically, I am in Birmingham because injustice is here. Just as the prophets of the eighth century B.C. left their villages and carried their "thus saith the Lord" far beyond the boundaries of their home towns, and just as the Apostle Paul left his village of Tarsus and carried the gospel of Jesus Christ to the far corners of the Greco-Roman world, so am I compelled to carry the gospel of freedom beyond my own home town. Like Paul, I must constantly respond to the Macedonian call for aid.

Moreover, I am cognizant of the interrelatedness of all communities and states. I cannot sit idly by in Atlanta and not be concerned about what happens in Birmingham. Injustice anywhere is a threat to justice every-where. We are caught in an inescapable network of mutuality, tied in a single garment of destiny. Whatever affects one directly, affects all indi-rectly. Never again can we afford to live with the narrow, provincial "out-side agitator" idea. Anyone who lives inside the United States can never be considered an outsider anywhere within its bounds.

You deplore the demonstrations taking place in Birmingham. But your statement, I am sorry to say, fails to express a similar concern for the conditions that brought about the demonstrations. I am sure that none of you would want to rest content with the superficial kind of social analysis that deals merely with effects and does not grapple with underlying causes. It is unfortunate that demonstrations are taking place in Birmingham, but it is even more unfortunate that the city's white power structure left the Negro community with no alternative.

In any nonviolent campaign there are four basic steps: collection of the facts to determine whether injustices exist; negotiation; self-purifi-cation; and direct action. We have gone through all these steps in Bir-mingham. There can be no gainsaying the fact that racial injustice engulfs this community. Birmingham is probably the most thoroughly segregated city in the United States. Its ugly record of brutality is widely known. Negroes have experienced grossly unjust treatment in the courts. There have been more unsolved bombings of Negro homes and churches in Birmingham than in any other city in the nation. These are the hard, brutal facts of the case. On the basis of these conditions, Negro leaders sought to negotiate with the city fathers. But the latter consistently re-fused to engage in good-faith negotiation.

Then, last September, came the opportunity to talk with leaders of Birmingham's economic community. In the course of the negotiations, certain promises were made by the merchants—for example, to remove the stores' humiliating racial signs. On the basis of these promises, the Reverend Fred Shuttlesworth and the leaders of the Alabama Christian Movement for Human Rights agreed to a moratorium on all demonstra-tions. As the weeks and months went by, we realized that we were the victims of a broken promise. A few signs, briefly removed, returned; the others remained.

As in so many past experiences, our hopes bad been blasted, and the shadow of deep disappointment settled upon us. We had no alternative except to prepare for direct action, whereby we would present our very bodies as a means of laying our case before the conscience of the local and the national community. Mindful of the difficulties involved, we decided to undertake a process of self-purification. We began a series of workshops on nonviolence, and we repeatedly asked ourselves: "Are you able to accept blows without retaliating?" "Are you able to endure the ordeal of jail?" We decided to schedule our direct-action program for the Easter season, realizing that except for Christmas, this is the main shopping period of the year. Knowing that a strong economic-withdrawal program would be the by-product of direct action, we felt that this would be the best time to bring pressure to bear on the merchants for the needed change.

Then it occurred to us that Birmingham's mayoral election was coming up in March, and we speedily decided to postpone action until after election day. When we discovered that the Commissioner of Public Safety, Eugene "Bull" Connor, had piled up enough votes to be in the run-off we decided again to postpone action until the day after the run-off so that the demonstrations could not be used to cloud the issues. Like many others, we waited to see Mr. Connor defeated, and to this end we endured postponement after postponement. Having aided in this community need, we felt that our direct-action program could be delayed no longer.

You may well ask: "Why direct action? Why sit-ins, marches and so forth? Isn't negotiation a better path?" You are quite right in calling for negotiation. Indeed, this is the very purpose of direct action. Nonviolent direct action seeks to create such a crisis and foster such a tension that a community which has constantly refused to negotiate is forced to confront the issue. It seeks so to dramatize the issue that it can no longer be ignored. My citing the creation of tension as part of the work of the non-violent-resister may sound rather shocking. But I must confess that I am not afraid of the word "tension." I have earnestly opposed violent tension, but there is a type of constructive, nonviolent tension which is necessary for growth. Just as Socrates felt that it was necessary to create a tension in the mind so that individuals could rise from the bondage of myths and half-truths to the unfettered realm of creative analysis and objective appraisal, so must we see the need for nonviolent gadflies to create the kind of tension in society that will help men rise from the dark depths of prejudice and racism to the majestic heights of understanding and brotherhood.

The purpose of our direct-action program is to create a situation so crisis-packed that it will inevitably open the door to negotiation. I therefore concur with you in your call for negotiation. Too long has our beloved Southland been bogged down in a tragic effort to live in monologue rather than dialogue.

One of the basic points in your statement is that the action that I and my associates have taken in Birmingham is untimely. Some have asked: "Why didn't you give the new city administration time to act?" The only answer that I can give to this query is that the new Birmingham administration must be prodded about as much as the outgoing one, before it will act. We are sadly mistaken if we feel that the election of Albert Boutwell as mayor will bring the millennium to Birmingham. While Mr. Boutwell is a much more gentle person than Mr. Connor, they are both segregationists, dedicated to maintenance of the status quo. I have hope that Mr. Boutwell will be reasonable enough to see the futility of massive resistance to desegregation. But he will not see this without pressure from devotees of civil rights. My friends, I must say to you that we have not made a single gain in civil rights without determined legal and nonviolent pressure. Lamentably, it is an historical fact that privileged groups seldom give up their privileges voluntarily. Individuals may see the moral light and voluntarily give up their unjust posture; but, as Reinhold Niebuhr has reminded us, groups tend to be more immoral than individuals.

We know through painful experience that freedom is never voluntarily given by the oppressor; it must be demanded by the oppressed. Frankly, I have yet to engage in a direct-action campaign that was "well timed" in the view of those who have not suffered unduly from the disease of segregation. For years now I have heard the word "Wait!" It rings in the ear of every Negro with piercing familiarity. This "Wait" has almost always meant "Never." We must come to see, with one of our distinguished jurists, that "justice too long delayed is justice denied."

We have waited for more than 340 years for our constitutional and God-given rights. The nations of Asia and Africa are moving with jetlike speed toward gaining political independence, but we still creep at horse-and-buggy pace toward gaining a cup of coffee at a lunch counter. Perhaps it is easy for those who have never felt the stinging darts of segregation to say, "Wait." But when you have seen vicious mobs lynch your mothers and fathers at will and drown your sisters and brothers at whim; when you have seen hate-filled policemen curse, kick and even kill your black brothers and sisters; when you see the vast majority of your twenty million Negro brothers smothering in an airtight cage of poverty in the midst of an affluent society; when you suddenly find your tongue twisted and your speech stammering as you seek to explain to your six-year-old daughter why she can't go to the public amusement park that has just been advertised on television, and see tears welling up in her eyes when she is told that Funtown is closed to colored children, and see ominous clouds of inferiority beginning to form in her little mental sky, and see her beginning to distort her personality by developing an unconscious bitterness toward white people; when you have to concoct an answer for a five-year-old son who is asking: "Daddy, why do white people treat colored people so mean?"; when you take a cross-county drive and find it necessary to sleep night after night in the uncomfortable corners of your automobile because no motel will accept you; when you are humiliated day in and day out by nagging signs reading "white" and "colored"; when your first name becomes "nigger," your middle name becomes "boy" (however old you are) and your last name becomes "John," and your wife and mother are never given the respected title "Mrs."; when you are harried by day and haunted by night by the fact that you are a Negro, living constantly at tiptoe stance, never quite knowing what to expect next, and are plagued with inner fears and outer resentments; when you are forever fighting a degenerating sense of "nobodiness"—then you will understand why we find it difficult to wait. There comes a time when the cup of endurance runs over, and men are no longer willing to be plunged into the abyss of despair. I hope, sirs, you can understand our legitimate and unavoidable impatience.

You express a great deal of anxiety over our willingness to break laws. This is certainly a legitimate concern. Since we so diligently urge people to obey the Supreme Court's decision of 1954 outlawing segregation in the public schools, at first glance it may seem rather paradoxical for us consciously to break laws. One may well ask: "How can you advocate breaking some laws and obeying others?" The answer lies in the fact that there are two types of laws: just and unjust. I would be the first to advocate obeying just laws. One has not only a legal but a moral responsibility to obey just laws. Conversely, one has a moral responsibility to disobey unjust laws. I would agree with St. Augustine that "an unjust law is no law at all."

Now, what is the difference between the two? How does one determine whether a law is just or unjust? A just law is a man-made code that squares with the moral law or the law of God. An unjust law is a code that is out of harmony with the moral law. To put it in the terms of St. Thomas Aquinas: An unjust law is a human law that is not rooted in eternal law and natural law. Any law that uplifts human personality is just. Any law that degrades human personality is unjust. All segregation statutes are unjust because segregation distorts the soul and damages the personality. It gives the segregator a false sense of superiority and the segregated a false sense of inferiority. Segregation, to use the terminology of the

Jewish philosopher Martin Buber, substitutes an "I-it" relationship for an "I-thou" relationship and ends up relegating persons to the status of things. Hence segregation is not only politically, economically and sociologically unsound, it is morally wrong and sinful. Paul Tillich has said that sin is separation. Is not segregation an existential expression of man's tragic separation, his awful estrangement, his terrible sinfulness? Thus it is that I can urge men to obey the 1954 decision of the Supreme Court, for it is morally right; and I can urge them to disobey segregation ordinances, for they are morally wrong.

Let us consider a more concrete example of just and unjust laws. An unjust law is a code that a numerical or power majority group compels a minority group to obey but does not make binding on itself. This is *difference* made legal. By the same token, a just law is a code that a majority compels a minority to follow and that it is willing to follow itself. This is *sameness* made legal.

Let me give another explanation. A law is unjust if it is inflicted on a minority that, as a result of being denied the right to vote, had no part in enacting or devising the law. Who can say that the legislature of Alabama which set up that state's segregation laws was democratically elected? Throughout Alabama all sorts of devious methods are used to prevent Negroes from becoming registered voters, and there are some counties in which, even though Negroes constitute a majority of the population, not a single Negro is registered. Can any law enacted under such circumstances be considered democratically structured?

Sometimes a law is just on its face and unjust in its application. For instance, I have been arrested on a charge of parading without a permit. Now, there is nothing wrong in having an ordinance which requires a permit for a parade. But such an ordinance becomes unjust when it is used to maintain segregation and to deny citizens the First-Amendment privilege of peaceful assembly and protest.

I hope you are able to see the distinction I am trying to point out. In no sense do I advocate evading or defying the law, as would the rabid segregationist. That would lead to anarchy. One who breaks an unjust law must do so openly, lovingly, and with a willingness to accept the penalty. I submit that an individual who breaks a law that conscience tells him is unjust, and who willingly accepts the penalty of imprisonment in order to arouse the conscience of the community over its injustice, is in reality expressing the highest respect for law.

Of course, there is nothing new about this kind of civil disobedience. It was evidenced sublimely in the refusal of Shadrach, Meshach and Abednego to obey the laws of Nebuchadnezzar, on the ground that a higher moral law was at stake. It was practiced superbly by the early Christians, who were willing to face hungry lions and the excruciating pain of chopping blocks rather than submit to certain unjust laws of the Roman Empire. To a degree, academic freedom is a reality today because Socrates practiced civil disobedience. In our own nation, the Boston Tea Party represented a massive act of civil disobedience.

We should never forget that everything Adolf Hitler did in Germany was "legal" and everything the Hungarian freedom fighters did in Hungary was "illegal." It was "illegal" to aid and comfort a Jew in Hitler's Germany. Even so, I am sure that, had I lived in Germany at the time, I would have aided and comforted my Jewish brothers. If today I lived in a Communist country where certain principles dear to the Christian faith are suppressed, I would openly advocate disobeying that country's antireligious laws.

I must make two honest confessions to you, my Christian and Jewish brothers. First, I must confess that over the past few years I have been gravely disappointed with the white moderate. I have almost reached the regrettable conclusion that the Negro's great stumbling block in his stride toward freedom is not the White Citizen's Counciler or the Ku Klux Klanner, but the white moderate, who is more devoted to "order" than to justice; who prefers a negative peace which is the absence of tension to a positive peace which is the presence of justice; who constantly says: "I agree with you in the goal you seek, but I cannot agree with your methods of direct action"; who paternalistically believes he can set the timetable for another man's freedom; who lives by a mythical concept of time and who constantly advises the Negro to wait for a "more convenient season." Shallow understanding from people of good will is more frustrating than absolute misunderstanding from people of ill will. Lukewarm acceptance is much more bewildering than outright rejection.

I had hoped that the white moderate would understand that law and order exist for the purpose of establishing justice and that when they fail in this purpose they become the dangerously structured dams that block the flow of social progress. I had hoped that the white moderate would understand that the present tension in the South is a necessary phase of the transition from an obnoxious negative peace, in which the Negro passively accepted his unjust plight, to a substantive and positive peace, in which all men will respect the dignity and worth of human personality. Actually, we who engage in nonviolent direct action are not the creators of tension. We merely bring to the surface the hidden tension that is already alive. We bring it out in the open, where it can be seen and dealt with. Like a boil that can never be cured so long as it is covered up but must be opened with all its ugliness to the natural medicines of air and light, injustice must be exposed, with all the tension its exposure creates, to the light of human conscience and the air of national opinion before it can be cured.

In your statement you assert that our actions, even though peaceful, must be condemned because they precipitate violence. But is this a logical assertion? Isn't this like condemning a robbed man because his possession of money precipitated the evil act of robbery? Isn't this like condemning Socrates because his unswerving commitment to truth and his philosophical inquiries precipitated the act by the misguided populace in which they made him drink hemlock? Isn't this like condemning Jesus because his unique God-consciousness and never-ceasing devotion to God's will precipitated the evil act of crucifixion? We must come to see that, as the federal courts have consistently affirmed, it is wrong to urge an individual to cease his efforts to gain his basic constitutional rights because the quest may precipitate violence. Society must protect the robbed and punish the robber.

I had also hoped that the white moderate would reject the myth concerning time in relation to the struggle for freedom. I have just received a letter from a white brother in Texas. He writes: "All Christians know that the colored people will receive equal rights eventually, but it is possible that you are in too great a religious hurry. It has taken Christianity almost two thousand years to accomplish what it has. The teachings of Christ take time to come to earth." Such an attitude stems from a tragic misconception of time, from the strangely irrational notion that there is something in the very flow of time that will inevitably cure all ills. Actually, time itself is neutral; it can be used either destructively or constructively. More and more I feel that the people of ill will have used time much more effectively than have the people of good will. We will have to repent in this generation not merely for the hateful words and actions of the bad people but for the appalling silence of the good people. Human progress never rolls in on wheels of inevitability; it comes through the tireless efforts of men willing to be co-workers with God, and without this hard work, time itself becomes an ally of the forces of social stagnation. We must use time creatively, in the knowledge that the time is always ripe to do right. Now is the time to make real the promise of democracy and transform our pending national elegy into a creative psalm of brotherhood. Now is the time to lift our national policy from the quicksand of racial injustice to the solid rock of human dignity.

You speak of our activity in Birmingham as extreme. At fist I was rather disappointed that fellow clergymen would see my nonviolent efforts as those of an extremist. I began thinking about the fact that I stand in the middle of two opposing forces in the Negro community. One is a force of complacency, made up in part of Negroes who, as a result of long years of oppression, are so drained of self-respect and a sense of "somebodiness" that they have adjusted to segregation; and in part of a few middle-class Negroes who, because of a degree of academic and economic security and because in some ways they profit by segregation, have become insensitive to the problems of the masses. The other force is one of bitterness and hatred, and it comes perilously close to advocating violence. It is expressed in the various black nationalist groups that are springing up across the nation, the largest and best-known being Elijah Muhammad's Muslim movement. Nourished by the Negro's frustration over the continued existence of racial discrimination, this movement is made up of people who have lost faith in America, who have absolutely repudiated Christianity, and who have concluded that the white man is an incorrigible "devil."

I have tried to stand between these two forces, saying that we need emulate neither the "do-nothingism" of the complacent nor the hatred and despair of the black nationalist. For there is the more excellent way of love and nonviolent protest. I am grateful to God that, through the influence of the Negro church, the way of nonviolence became an integral part of our struggle.

If this philosophy had not emerged, by now many streets of the South would, I am convinced, be flowing with blood. And I am further convinced that if our white brothers dismiss as "rabble-rousers" and "outside agitators" those of us who employ nonviolent direct action, and if they refuse to support our nonviolent efforts, millions of Negroes will, out of frustration and despair, seek solace and security in black-nationalist ideologies—a development that would inevitably lead to a frightening racial nightmare.

Oppressed people cannot remain oppressed forever. The yearning for freedom eventually manifests itself, and that is what has happened to the American Negro. Something within has reminded him of his birthright of freedom, and something without has reminded him that it can be gained. Consciously or unconsciously, he has been caught up by the *Zeitgeist*, and with his black brothers of Africa and his brown and yellow brothers of Asia, South America and the Caribbean, the United States Negro is moving with a sense of great urgency toward the promised land of racial justice. If one recognizes this vital urge that has engulfed the

Negro community, one should readily understand why public demonstrations are taking place. The Negro has many pent-up resentments and latent frustrations, and he must release them. So let him march; let him make prayer pilgrimages to the city hall; let him go on freedom rides— and try to understand why he must do so. If his repressed emotions are not released in nonviolent ways, they will seek expression through violence; this is not a threat but a fact of history. So I have not said to my people: "Get rid of your discontent." Rather, I have tried to say that this normal and healthy discontent can be channeled into the creative outlet of nonviolent direct action. And now this approach is being termed extremist.

But though I was initially disappointed at being categorized as an extremist, as I continued to think about the matter I gradually gained a measure of satisfaction from the label. Was not Jesus an extremist for love: "Love your enemies, bless them that curse you, do good to them that hate you, and pray for them which despitefully use you, and persecute you." Was not Amos an extremist for justice: "Let justice roll down like waters and righteousness like an ever-flowing stream." Was not Paul an extremist for the Christian gospel: "I bear in my body the marks of the Lord Jesus." Was not Martin Luther an extremist: "Here I stand; I cannot do otherwise, so help me God." And John Bunyan: "I will stay in jail to the end of my days before I make a butchery of my conscience." And Abraham Lincoln: "This nation cannot survive half slave and half free." And Thomas Jefferson: "We hold these truths to be self-evident, that all men are created equal . . . " So the question is not whether we will be extremists, but what kind of extremists we will be. Will we be extremists for hate or for love? Will we be extremists for the preservation of injustice or for the extension of justice? In that dramatic scene on Calvary's hill three men were crucified. We must never forget that all three were crucified for the same crime—the crime of extremism. Two were extremists for immorality, and thus fell below their environment. The other, Jesus Christ, was an extremist for love, truth and goodness, and thereby rose above his environment. Perhaps the South, the nation and the world are in dire need of creative extremists.

I had hoped that the white moderate would see this need. Perhaps I was too optimistic; perhaps I expected too much. I suppose I should have realized that few members of the oppressor race can understand the deep groans and passionate yearnings of the oppressed race, and still fewer have the vision to see that injustice must be rooted out by strong, persistent and determined action. I am thankful, however, that some of our white brothers in the South have grasped the meaning of this social revolution and committed themselves to it. They are still all too few in quantity, but they are big in quality. Some—such as Ralph McGill, Lillian Smith, Harry Golden, James McBride Dabbs, Ann Braden and Sarah Patton Boyle—have written about our struggle in eloquent and prophetic terms. Others have marched with us down nameless streets of the South. They have languished in filthy, roach-infested jails, suffering the abuse and brutality of policemen who view them as "dirty nigger-lovers." Unlike so many of their moderate brothers and sisters, they have recognized the urgency of the moment and sensed the need for powerful "action" antidotes to combat the disease of segregation.

Let me take note of my other major disappointment. I have been so greatly disappointed with the white church and its leadership. Of course, there are some notable exceptions. I am not unmindful of the fact that each of you has taken some significant stands on this issue. I commend you, Reverend Stallings, for your Christian stand on this past Sunday, in welcoming Negroes to your worship service on a non-segregated basis. I commend the Catholic leaders of this state for integrating Spring Hill College several years ago.

But despite these notable exceptions, I must honestly reiterate that I have been disappointed with the church. I do not say this as one of those negative critics who can always find something wrong with the church. I say this as a minister of the gospel, who loves the church; who was nurtured in its bosom; who has been sustained by its spiritual blessings and who will remain true to it as long as the cord of life shall lengthen.

When I was suddenly catapulted into the leadership of the bus protest in Montgomery, Alabama, a few years ago, I felt we would be supported by the white church. I felt that the white ministers, priests and rabbis of the South would be among our strongest allies. Instead, some have been outright opponents, refusing to understand the freedom movement and misrepresenting its leaders; all too many others have been more cautious than courageous and have remained silent behind the anesthetizing security of stained-glass windows.

In spite of my shattered dreams, I came to Birmingham with the hope that the white religious leadership of this community would see the justice of our cause and, with deep moral concern, would serve as the channel through which our just grievances could reach the power structure. I had hoped that each of you would understand. But again I have been disappointed.

I have heard numerous southern religious leaders admonish their worshipers to comply with a desegregation decision because it is the law, but I have longed to hear white ministers declare: "Follow this decree because integration is morally right and because the Negro is your brother." In the midst of blatant injustices inflicted upon the Negro, I have watched white churchmen stand on the sideline and mouth pious irrelevancies and sanctimonious trivialities. In the midst of a mighty struggle to rid our nation of racial and economic injustice, I have heard many ministers say: "Those are social issues, with which the gospel has no real concern." And I have watched many churches commit themselves to a completely otherworldly religion which makes a strange, un-Biblical distinction between body and soul, between the sacred and the secular.

I have traveled the length and breadth of Alabama, Mississippi and all the other southern states. On sweltering summer days and crisp autumn mornings I have looked at the South's beautiful churches with their lofty spires pointing heavenward. I have beheld the impressive outlines of her massive religious-education buildings. Over and over I have found myself asking: "What kind of people worship here? Who is their God? Where were their voices when the lips of Governor Barnett dripped with words of interposition and nullification? Where were they when Governor Wallace gave a clarion call for defiance and hatred? Where were their voices of support when bruised and weary Negro men and women decided to rise from the dark dungeons of complacency to the bright hills of creative protest?"

Yes, these questions are still in my mind. In deep disappointment I have wept over the laxity of the church. But be assured that my tears have been tears of love. There can be no deep disappointment where there is not deep love. Yes, I love the church. How could I do otherwise? I am in the rather unique position of being the son, the grandson and the great-grandson of preachers. Yes, I see the church as the body of Christ. But, oh! How we have blemished and scarred that body through social neglect and through fear of being nonconformists.

There was a time when the church was very powerful—in the time when the early Christians rejoiced at being deemed worthy to suffer for what they believed. In those days the church was not merely a thermometer that recorded the ideas and principles of popular opinion; it was a thermostat that transformed the mores of society. Whenever the early Christians entered a town, the people in power became disturbed and immediately sought to convict the Christians for being "disturbers of the peace" and "outside agitators." But the Christians pressed on, in the conviction that they were "a colony of heaven," called to obey God rather than man. Small in number, they were big in commitment. They were too God-intoxicated to be "astronomically intimidated." By their effort and example they brought an end to such ancient evils as infanticide and gladiatorial contests.

Things are different now. So often the contemporary church is a weak, ineffectual voice with an uncertain sound. So often it is an archdefender of the status quo. Far from being disturbed by the presence of the church, the power structure of the average community is consoled by the church's silent—and often even vocal—sanction of things as they are.

But the judgment of God is upon the church as never before. If today's church does not recapture the sacrificial spirit of the early church, it will lose its authenticity, forfeit the loyalty of millions, and be dismissed as an irrelevant social club with no meaning for the twentieth century. Every day I meet young people whose disappointment with the church has turned into outright disgust.

Perhaps I have once again been too optimistic. Is organized religion too inextricably bound to the status quo to save our nation and the world? Perhaps I must turn my faith to the inner spiritual church, the church within the church, as the true *ekklesia* and the hope of the world. But again I am thankful to God that some noble souls from the ranks of organized religion have broken loose from the paralyzing chains of conformity and joined us as active partners in the struggle for freedom. They have left their secure congregations and walked the streets of Albany, Georgia, with us. They have gone down the highways of the South on tortuous rides for freedom. Yes, they have gone to jail with us. Some have been dismissed from their churches, have lost the support of their bishops and fellow ministers. But they have acted in the faith that right defeated is stronger than evil triumphant. Their witness has been the spiritual salt that has preserved the true meaning of the gospel in these troubled times. They have carved a tunnel of hope through the dark mountain of disappointment.

I hope the church as a whole will meet the challenge of this decisive hour. But even if the church does not come to the aid of justice, I have no despair about the future. I have no fear about the outcome of our struggle in Birmingham, even if our motives are at present misunderstood. We will reach the goal of freedom in Birmingham and all over the nation, because the goal of America is freedom. Abused and scorned though we may be, our destiny is tied up with America's destiny. Before the pilgrims landed at Plymouth, we were here. Before the pen of Jefferson etched the majestic words of the Declaration of Independence across the pages of history, we were here. For more than two centuries our forebears labored in this country without wages; they made cotton king; they built the homes of their masters while suffering gross injustice and shameful humiliation—and yet out of a bottomless vitality they continued to thrive and develop. If the inexpressible cruelties of slavery could not stop us, the opposition we now face will surely fail. We will win our freedom because the sacred heritage of our nation and the eternal will of God are embodied in our echoing demands.

Before closing I feel impelled to mention one other point in your statement that has troubled me profoundly. You warmly commended the Birmingham police force for keeping "order" and "preventing violence." I doubt that you would have so warmly commended the police force if you had seen its dogs sinking their teeth into unarmed, nonviolent Negroes. I doubt that you would so quickly commend the policemen if you were to observe their ugly and inhumane treatment of Negroes here in the city jail; if you were to watch them push and curse old Negro women and young Negro girls; if you were to see them slap and kick old Negro men and young boys; if you were to observe them, as they did on two occasions, refuse to give us food because we wanted to sing our grace together. I cannot join you in your praise of the Birmingham police department.

It is true that the police have exercised a degree of discipline in handling the demonstrators. In this sense they have conducted themselves rather "nonviolently" in public. But for what purpose? To preserve the evil system of segregation. Over the past few years I have consistently preached that nonviolence demands that the means we use must be as pure as the ends we seek. I have tried to make clear that it is wrong to use immoral means to attain moral ends. But now I must affirm that it is just as wrong, or perhaps even more so, to use moral means to preserve immoral ends. Perhaps Mr. Connor and his policemen have been rather nonviolent in public, as was Chief Pritchett in Albany, Georgia, but they have used the moral means of nonviolence to maintain the immoral end of racial injustice. As T.S. Eliot has said: "The last temptation is the greatest treason: To do the right deed for the wrong reason."

I wish you had commended the Negro sit-inners and demonstrators of Birmingham for their sublime courage, their willingness to suffer and their amazing discipline in the midst of great provocation. One day the South will recognize its real heroes. They will be the James Merediths, with the noble sense of purpose that enables them to face jeering and hostile mobs, and with the agonizing loneliness that characterizes the life of the pioneer. They will be old, oppressed, battered Negro women, symbolized in a seventy-two-year-old woman in Montgomery, Alabama, who rose up with a sense of dignity and with her people decided not to ride segregated buses, and who responded with ungrammatical profundity to one who inquired about her weariness: "My feets is tired, but my soul is at rest." They will be the young high school and college students, the young ministers of the gospel and a host of their elders, courageously and nonviolently sitting in at lunch counters and willingly going to jail for conscience' sake. One day the South will know that when these disinherited children of God sat down at lunch counters, they were in reality standing up for what is best in the American dream and for the most sacred values in our Judaeo-Christian heritage, thereby bringing our nation back to those great wells of democracy which were dug deep by the founding fathers in their formulation of the Constitution and the Declaration of Independence.

Never before have I written so long a letter. I'm afraid it is much too long to take your precious time. I can assure you that it would have been much shorter if I had been writing from a comfortable desk, but what else can one do when he is alone in a narrow jail cell, other than write long letters, think long thoughts and pray long prayers?

If I have said anything in this letter that overstates the truth and indicates an unreasonable impatience, I beg you to forgive me. If I have said anything that understates the truth and indicates my having a patience that allows me to settle for anything less than brotherhood, I beg God to forgive me.

I hope this letter finds you strong in the faith. I also hope that circumstances will soon make it possible for me to meet each of you, not as an integrationist or a civil-rights leader but as a fellow clergyman and a Christian brother. Let us all hope that the dark clouds of racial prejudice will soon pass away and the deep fog of misunderstanding will be lifted from our fear-drenched communities, and in some not too distant tomorrow the radiant stars of love and brotherhood will shine over our great nation with all their scintillating beauty.

Yours for the cause of Peace and Brotherhood,

Martin Luther King, Jr.[2]

NOTES

1. This response to a published statement by eight fellow clergymen from Alabama (Bishop C.C.J. Carpenter, Bishop Joseph A. Durick, Rabbi Hilton L. Grafman, Bishop Paul Hardin, Bishop Holan B. Harmon, the Reverend George M. Murray, the Reverend Edward V. Ramage and the Reverend Earl Stallings)

was composed under somewhat constricting circumstances. Begun on the margins of the newspaper in which the statement appeared while I was in jail, the letter was continued on scraps of writing paper supplied by a friendly Negro trusty, and concluded on a pad my attorneys were eventually permitted to leave me. Although the text remains in substance unaltered, I have indulged in the author's prerogative of polishing it for publication.

2. [Martin Luther King Jr., "Letter from Birmingham Jail," in *Why We Can't Wait* (New York: Harper & Row, 1964), 77–100.]

[CHAPTER 7]

William Stringfellow (1928–1985)

COMMENTARY

FRANK S. ALEXANDER

William Stringfellow spoke to the world in which he lived. His actions and his words were set in a context of community and conflict, of power and pretension, of advocacy and authority, of opportunity and oppression. His words and his deeds, however, were not designed to confront or to condemn, but simply to understand that context biblically. In his own words, he sought "to understand America biblically . . . *not* to construe the Bible Americanly."[1] With his intentionally awkward grammar, this graduate of Harvard Law School made poignant his passion for understanding not the gospel in light of our lives, but our lives in light of the gospel.

In a world coming of age in the aftermath of World War II and Hiroshima, Stringfellow himself came of age as he completed law school and went to work for an East Harlem Protestant parish in 1956. For the next three decades until his death in 1985, he sought to interpret the American experiences of the 1950s, the 1960s, and the 1970s in light of the incarnation, the crucifixion, and the resurrection. He was present in the poverty and racism of Harlem. His voice was raised in criticism of the McCarthy hearings. He was active in the civil rights movement. He was charged with harboring Daniel Berrigan, a fugitive during the antiwar movement. He represented the Episcopal priests charged with the illegal ordination of women. He served as a warden in the local government of his community. Though he happened to be a lawyer, an active Episcopalian, and certainly an advocate, he recoiled from the common label given to him of a prophet. Stringfellow's response to scripture was a sense of calling to his vocation as a Christian, no more and no less.

The author of sixteen books and more than one hundred essays,[2] Stringfellow wrote as one more concerned with communicating his message than with proving his sources. With the exception of his first extensive law review article,[3] Stringfellow rarely included footnotes, bibliographies, or references to other scholars. Quite self-consciously, his writings were polemic in nature, relying solely on scriptural references; they were never designed to be treatises or systematic treatments of theology and jurisprudence. Though he described himself as "theologically illiterate,"[4] he was quite familiar with a broad range of Roman Catholic, Orthodox, and Protestant theologians writing in the middle of the twentieth century. He simply chose, in his writings and in his speaking, to call upon the biblical story. The absence of formal scholarship is, however, anything but an indictment of the depth or purity of his message. Karl Barth, participating in a panel discussion with Stringfellow in 1962, exhorted the audience, "Listen to this man!"[5]

The theological foundations of Stringfellow's views, and the implications for his views of law and human nature, can be traced conceptually to the intellectual and philosophical context of the 1950s. In the aftermath of World War II, simultaneous and parallel struggles emerged in both theology and jurisprudence. In theology the struggle primarily took the form of articulating a common Christian message to a world community that now knew the horrors of Auschwitz and Hiroshima, of state-imposed terror and state-sponsored triumphs. In jurisprudence the struggle took the form of articulating not only a theory of law adequate to define law with precision both across cultures and within cultures, but also a conception of law that could condemn as lawless those statutes and decrees that violate fundamental norms. In theology the focus became that of the relationship of law and gospel; in jurisprudence it became the debates between positivism and natural law. Stringfellow was present in both of these struggles and proclaimed a clear position that left most theologians and most legal scholars uncomfortable. The biblical witness, from his perspective, leaves little room for doctrines of natural law, for theologies based upon a social gospel, or for a Christian jurisprudence. "Instead of proposition or principle, the biblical witness offers precedent and parable. The Bible does not propound guidelines but relates events; the biblical ethic does not construct syllogisms but tells stories; the gospel is not confined in verities but confesses the viability of the Word of God."[6]

Within a year of his graduation from law school and the beginning of his legal practice in East Harlem, Stringfellow became a key voice in conferences on law and Christianity. In two such conferences, in 1957 and in 1958, a wide range of theologians, practicing attorneys, judges, and professors gathered to explore the relationship of law and gospel, of theology and jurisprudence, of the religious and ethical obligations of attorneys.[7]

In these conferences and in the published essays of the conferences, Stringfellow's voice rose against the dominant attempts to find common grounds for theology and law, as well as for recognition of a Christian ethic about law, if not a Christian jurisprudence. The great danger of all such attempts, according to Stringfellow, is the failure to acknowledge the radical tension between law and gospel and between law and grace as reflected in Romans 13:1–8. "When the Gospel is taken seriously, the decisive issue between theology and jurisprudence and the central vocational problem of a lawyer who is a Christian is the tension between grace and law."[8] For Stringfellow, any conflation of gospel and law diminishes the crucifixion, and thereby also the resurrection.

The struggle in legal theory and jurisprudence differed from the theological debates only (and crucially!) in being devoid of the gospel. The debates in the halls of the legal academy were those of H. L. A. Hart and Lon Fuller, of positivism and the connections between law and morality. Such debates arise from the same need—to see the connections between the normative and the descriptive, between law and those things that are the limits of the law. Such debates, according to Stringfellow, suffer from the same dangers of reduction to either radical relativism or of self-righteous authority. "The Gospel is opposed to the imagination of both positivists and natural lawyers. The tension between grace and law is absolute."[9]

As a Christian who happened to be a lawyer, Stringfellow's expression of the biblical witness included the institutions that sought to define the identity of the Christian and of the lawyer. Within his own Episcopal denomination he was initially appointed a representative of the church on formal commissions, though he was later removed because of his criticism of the ecclesiastical structure. He defended Bishop James Pike of California, whom, in 1966, the Episcopal House of Bishops charged with heresy for having questioned doctrine on original sin, the Trinity, and the infallibility of scripture, among other things.[10] Similarly, he defended the Episcopal priests who participated in the first ordination of women to the priesthood.[11] In both cases he challenged the church to recall its own vocation of life in worship and in advocacy. As a member of the legal profession, Stringfellow found that at times his advocacy as a Christian coincided with his advocacy as a lawyer; yet at other times he felt that the legal profession itself was a restraining and constraining principality. He was, as he put it, "haunted with the ironic impression that I may have to renounce being a lawyer the better to be an advocate."[12]

Three themes permeate Stringfellow's writings in a manner that allows his calling on the word of God for us today to blossom in a uniquely

"Stringfellow" manner: the centrality of worship, the experience of vocation, and the presence of death.

WORSHIP, VOCATION, DEATH

At its core, Stringfellow's theology was confessional. The experience of worship is not just the purest but also the only acceptable form of our expression of the incarnation, the crucifixion, and the resurrection.[13] His reluctance to proceed down the paths toward philosophical ethics or systematic theology stemmed from his deep conviction that any humanly created formula is a broken distortion of the word of God. His view of worship thus was one far more expansive than ecclesiastical, far more demonstrative than doctrinaire, far more creative than conforming. Liturgy is a participatory event that is at once confessional, communal, and political.[14]

Worship is not some peculiar cultural practice, some esoteric folk activity, to which Christians resort out of sentiment or superstition, or even for inspiration or self-motivation. On the contrary,

> worship is the celebration of God's presence and action in the ordinary and everyday life of the world. Worship is not separated or essentially distinguishable from the rest of the Christian life. It is the normative form and expression of the Christian life; it is the integration of the whole of the Christian life into history.[15]

As worship is the experience of the word of God, the understanding of role and identity in response to the word of God is the concept of vocation. Vocation, as developed by Stringfellow, bears little correlation to work, career, or socially defined roles and expectations. It is simply the response to the antecedent grace of God. "Vocation has to do with recognizing life as a gift and honoring the gift in living."[16] For individuals, vocation is a sense of one's own story as revealed through the gospel,[17] and the gospel is what permits us not to become gods but indeed to become human. "In the Gospel, vocation means being a human being, now, and being neither more, nor less than a human being, now."[18] The concept of vocation, however, is not limited to the human; it applies to all of creation. All institutions, most particularly the church and the political authorities, are called to a vocation, and the ethical is understood as faithfulness to vocation.[19]

The third theme that permeates Stringfellow's writings is the theme of death. Stringfellow wrote of death in its conventional physical sense because he became aware of it wherever he lived and worked. He encountered death in his legal ministry in Harlem and saw death in the civil rights movement, in the Vietnam War, and in political assassinations. Stringfellow was only in his late thirties when he was told he was dying of a terminal illness,[20] and he later wrestled with his deep loss in the death of his companion, Anthony Towne.[21] Though he wrote of death personally and interpersonally in his later works, he had identified death as a powerful concept in his early writings.[22] Death is a characteristic of all of creation, a consequence of the Fall, and the experience of isolation from God. The primacy of death in his writings was not a sense of despair or of melancholy; rather, it was a description of the power of the gospel and its proclamation of life in the midst of death. A depiction of death, for William Stringfellow, is an affirmation of the triumph of the resurrection over the crucifixion. The "essential and consistent task of Christians is to expose the transience of death's power in the world."[23] With his wonderful dry wit, Stringfellow explained that he had a passion for the circus precisely because the circus performer excels in mocking the power of death in our lives.[24]

DEATH UNTO THE LAW: LAW AND SIN

Though he said he read little theology, Stringfellow once admitted to his desire to read all of Augustine, Luther, Bonhoeffer, and Barth.[25] His own writings bore deep resemblance to the points of emphasis of each of these scholars, but nowhere was the connection stronger than on the nature of sin and death.

The story of the Fall into sin in Genesis 1–3 is the story of the alienation of all of creation from God. The incarnation stands as God's affirming presence, but the crucifixion stands as our rejection of the incarnation. The resurrection is God's gift to us despite our rejection. What happens in the Fall, and what is relived in the crucifixion, is our refusal to acknowledge and accept our own frailty, the hopelessness of our own insistence on being in control. Stringfellow had no patience for Pelagian or semi-Pelagian assertions of limited goodness or limited free will. He insisted, as did each of the scholars he sought to read, on our complete and total inability, in the absence of grace, to know or to do that which God asks of us. As was true of these earlier scholars, Stringfellow insisted on naming this nature *sin*: "It is the essence of human sin for man to boast of the power to discern what is good and what is evil, and thus to be like God."[26] Convinced that "most Americans are grossly naïve or remarkably misinformed about the Fall,"[27] he designed his writings to educate about the Fall in order that the gospel could become manifest:

> Sin is not essentially the mistaken, inadvertent, or deliberate choice of evil by men but the pride into which men fall in associating their own self-interest with the will of God. Sin is the denunciation of the freedom of God to judge men as it pleases Him to judge them. Sin is the displacement of God's will with one's own will. Sin is the radical confusion in men's lives as to whether God or man is morally sovereign in history.[28]

The Fall is pervasive; it is not limited to the nature of individuals or even social groups. "The Fall implicates the whole of creation, not human life alone and not human beings uniquely, and further, that each and every creature or created thing suffers fallenness in its own right."[29] The state, the government, and the church are all equally characterized by their fallen reality. Principalities and powers are simply institutions, and we tend to forget that they, too, possess a fallen nature.

With this heavy emphasis on the nature of the Fall, the nature and function of law could have become critical in the development of Stringfellow's writings. Perhaps because he was a practicing attorney, or more likely because of his own self-identification as a Christian who happened to be a lawyer, he chose to reject the possibility that law exists as more than the indicative declaration of reality. Law, as God's proclamation, is the word that all have sinned and fall short of the glory of God (Rom. 3:23): "For law, the proclamation of the Gospel means, in the first instance, the comprehension that law, though sometimes it can name sin, originates itself in sin and cannot overcome the power of sin."[30]

The moral reality of death follows from the doctrine of the Fall. "Death is not only the terminal experience; it is the imminent truth about every and any event in this world."[31] Death is not to be equated with evil, though the evil that lies within death is the refusal to acknowledge that death is not the only reality.

Stringfellow's strong emphasis on the Fall and the radical and pervasive nature of all of moral reality as sinful was precisely what enabled him to point to the resurrection as the complete word, and story, of God's sovereignty. His emphasis on death was overwhelmed by his emphasis on the completeness of the grace of God. "The grace of Jesus Christ in this life is that death fails."[32] Understanding the fallen nature of all of creation simply makes possible an understanding of the sovereignty of Jesus Christ over all of creation.

THE HEARING OF THE WORD: GOSPEL AND LAW

With his view of the Fall, Stringfellow was most uncomfortable with any interpretation, theory, or approach that would tend to blur the distinction between gospel and law. Three dangers flow from the failure to adhere to this difference: the impoverishment of the critique of law and of the state; the arrogance of the righteousness of the church; and the loss of justification by faith. To the extent that the gospel becomes merged with or even subordinate to law, the gospel no longer stands as a declaration of the fallen nature of law itself. Legal institutions and legal theories then become sources of their own lawless authority.[33] Correspondingly, a blurring of the distinction between law and gospel allows the institutions that proclaim the gospel to become righteous in their proclamations not just of the gospel but also of the law. In both the first and second dangers we forget that the crucifixion followed the incarnation. The third danger in the blurring of distinctions between law and gospel is the failure to recall that justification is by faith through grace. Fulfillment of the law can become a means to grace. This third danger is the failure to know that the resurrection followed the crucifixion. Such is simply not the gospel as Stringfellow understood it. "Faith is the success of God's quest for men, not the outcome of men's search for God."[34]

In preserving the tension between gospel and law, Stringfellow's theology bears close affinity to the theology not only of Augustine and Luther, but also of Karl Barth,[35] Jacques Ellul,[36] and Dietrich Bonhoeffer. Accused of being "Barthian" in his theology, Stringfellow responded that, in the most important sense, not even Karl Barth was "Barthian," for Barth refused to create a systematic theology or structure for the relationship of gospel and law.[37] Stringfellow insisted, as did Barth, that the work of theology is at its core a confessional act, "the marvel of the Word of God addressing men in ordinary history."[38] He was also clearly influenced in this context by Nicholas Berdyaev: "Christian faith is the revelation of grace, and Christian ethics is the ethics of redemption and not of law."[39]

The centrality of the gospel in Stringfellow's writings, as well as his views on the tension between gospel and law, also bear close relationship with the writings of Dietrich Bonhoeffer. The extent to which Stringfellow had access to Bonhoeffer's work is unknown, since Bonhoeffer's work was still being translated into and published in English early in Stringfellow's career. But it is clear that Stringfellow relied on Bonhoeffer. Stringfellow made explicit reference to what he termed "The Bonhoeffer Dilemma" in describing Bonhoeffer's struggle with the necessity of violence against a violent lawless authority,[40] and many points in Bonhoeffer's own writings are echoed in Stringfellow's works. Both Bonhoeffer and Stringfellow cautioned the church, in finding its role in the world, against the pitfalls of "cheap grace,"[41] and both followed Barth in speaking of the need to distinguish religion from the message of Jesus Christ.[42] As Stringfellow expressed it: "I am reminded, if sometimes ruefully, that the Gospel is no mere religion in *any* essential respect."[43]

If a tension between gospel and law is to be maintained, it is in order that we might hear the gospel unconstrained by our own attempts to judge it worthy. If the crucifixion is our response to the incarnation, the resurrection is God's response to the crucifixion. "The power to discern the presence of the Word of God in the world is the knowledge of the Resurrection."[44] The presence of the word of God, not a system of laws or set of principles, is what ultimately conquers the power of death in this world and makes life possible. "His power over death is effective, not just at the terminal point of a man's life, but throughout his life, during *this* life in *this* world right now . . . His resurrection means the possibility of living in this life, in the very midst of death's works, safe and free from death."[45]

CONFIDENCE PLACED AND MISPLACED:
LAW, GRACE, KNOWLEDGE

When Christian theology is grounded in the Fall, in sin and death, and thus leaves the starkness of the resurrection as the proclamation of God's gift to us, the hearer of the word of God must come to a new understanding of knowledge itself. If the Fall is the story of the existential futility of the search for the knowledge of good and evil, and the crucifixion is the declaration of the utter impoverishment of our knowledge, the puzzle then becomes the nature of knowledge itself. The emphasis is on sin in order that the clarity of the gospel be known, and this emphasis is combined with an insistence on the tension between gospel and law in order that the fullness of the gospel not be undermined. This perspective forces the epistemological question of how we know the contents of law, of that which is asked of us. Well aware of the importance of this issue, both in theology and in jurisprudence, Stringfellow's response was that knowledge can flow, if at all, only from first understanding who and what we are. The epistemological question can be asked only after the ontological question is answered.

The starting point is the gift of faith, and the prayer in faith for faith.[46] The "double-minded" person (James 1:6–8) is one who insists on holding on to a claim of knowledge and of wisdom while being aware that the knowledge may not be perfect—resulting in instability and uncertainty. It is not possible to grasp the completeness of sin and at the same time claim knowledge of law. The attempt to create or to discern a theology of law will be inherently unsuccessful. "To contort the word of grace into the law of nature is to make the Gospel unintelligible, however neatly it resolves the query about the relations of theology and law."[47] The ontological premise is the confessional presence of faith, and the response is action, not ideology. "I look for style, not stereotype, for precedent, not model, for parable, not proposition, for analogue, not aphorism, for paradox, not syllogism, for signs, not statutes. The encounter with the biblical witness is empirical, as distinguished from scholastic, and it is confessional, rather than literalistic."[48]

As a consequence, Stringfellow was deeply suspicious of any attempt to develop a theory or system of theology and jurisprudence. Indeed, the very concept of Christian jurisprudence is not a viable endeavor. "The tension between law and grace is such that there is no Christian Jurisprudence. . . . To have no special Christian jurisprudence does not mean that Christians are indifferent, or wholly negativist, toward law. Rather their concern is primarily an issue of vocation, not of jurisprudence."[49] The natural law tradition, Stringfellow felt, runs the risk of a Pelagian comfort with the human capacity to know and to do what is good, tempered (but not vitiated) by the existence of sin.[50]

The biblical witness that Stringfellow understood as the vocation of a Christian was to resist creating a jurisprudence of daily life. He did not seek, nor did he offer, prescriptions for ethical actions, nor "some rules, some norms, some guidelines, some rubrics for a sacred discipline that, if pursued diligently, would establish the holiness of a person. I do not discern that such is the biblical style, as admirable as that may happen to be in the worldly sense."[51] In this approach Stringfellow again echoed the words of Dietrich Bonhoeffer: "Christ did not, like a moralist, love a theory of good, but He loved the real man. He was not, like a philosopher, interested in the 'universally valid' but rather in that which is of help to the real and concrete human being. . . . For indeed, it is not written that God became an idea, a principle, a program, a universally valid proposition or a law, but that God became man."[52]

The gospel story and the biblical style Stringfellow embraced was the response in one's actions to the gift of the word of God. We are more likely to be more faithful in our actions than in our theories. The word of God is present in all aspects of life, and there is no part of life in which the presence of Jesus Christ is not felt. The vocation of the Christian is the discernment of, the reliance upon, and the celebration of this presence.[53] "What the ordinary Christian is called to do is to open the Bible and listen to the Word."[54]

PRINCIPALITIES AND POWERS: LAW AND THE STATE

Principalities and powers are those aspects of fallen reality that demand attention, loyalty, service, commitment, and obedience all in contradiction to the word of God. The biblical witness is a call to resist the principalities and powers[55] or to seek to impart wisdom to them.[56] Principalities and powers are the state and the church, but are also "the institutions, systems, ideologies, and other political and social powers."[57] They are "legion in species, number, variety, and name (e.g., Luke 8:29–33; Galatians 4:3; Ephesians 1:21, 6:10–13; Colossians 1:15–16, 2:10–23)."[58] The existence of principalities and powers reveals each of the aspects of the gospel story emphasized repeatedly by Stringfellow. These principalities and powers are themselves part of fallen reality and cannot be the source of either truth or salvation. They lay claim to obedience in asserting righteousness and assert authority in searching for righteousness. They become a source of their own justification and are intolerant of those who seek to unmask their pretentiousness. "The fallenness of the nations and powers is conjunctive with the fallenness of humanity, but it is not dependent or derivative."[59] The difficulty lies not just with these principalities and powers, but also with our failure to realize how we have become subservient to them. "Human beings do not readily recognize their victim status in relation to the principalities."[60]

The most common principality, but certainly not the sole or even primary one, is the state. Charged with harboring Daniel Berrigan, a fugitive due to his protests against the war in Vietnam,[61] Stringfellow relished the opportunity to respond to the federal government agent's admonition that he should "obey the emperor" and be subject to the governing authorities (1 Pet. 2:17; Rom. 13:1). Having just completed the manuscript for *An Ethics for Christians and Other Aliens in a Strange Land*, Stringfellow responded to the agent's admonition by writing *Conscience and Obedience: The Politics of Romans 13 and Revelation 13 in Light of the Second Coming*. In this text, he addressed directly the dual words that are spoken to political authority. Political authority is instituted by God and is part of fallen reality. It is not one without the other. It is both.

Stringfellow offered two keys to a biblical view of the state as a principality. The first is that Romans 13 and Revelation 13 portray, respectively, conceptions of legitimate political authority and conceptions of illegitimate political authority, which Stringfellow further explained do not resolve the simultaneous characteristic of lawful or lawless political authority.[62] The second key is that these essential elements of legitimacy (or illegitimacy) and lawfulness (or unlawfulness) are to be understood as honoring the sovereign and calling the "emperor" to its own vocation.[63] To honor the sovereign means holding the sovereign accountable to its faithfulness to the word of God. "The relationship between the Christian and the state is never one of uncritical allegiance or obedience. . . . This means that the Christian is not only concerned with what the content and policy of the law is, but with how it is enacted and promulgated as law, how it achieves the status of law, how it is administered, when it is invoked, and against whom it is enforced, how it is adjudicated, and how it is changed and modified."[64]

The institution of the church is just as much a principality and power as is the state, and both exist as part of fallen reality. Stringfellow viewed the "Constantinian Arrangement" as a reversal of the apostolic relationship between the church and the political authority, and an arrangement that has cast a heavy burden on the church ever since. By virtue of accommodating privileges such as tax exemption, the church loses its vocation. "Thus the church becomes confined, for the most part, to the sanctuary, and is assigned to either political silence or to banal acquiescence."[65]

Just as vocation and witness are keys to understanding the state as a principality, the vocation of the church as a witness is central to its faithfulness to the word of God. The vocation of the church is to be an advocate and witness for all victims, and all victims of victims.

> Advocacy is how the church puts into practice its own experience of the victory of the word of God over the power of death, how the church lives in the efficacy of the resurrection amid the reign of death in this world, how the church expends its life in freedom from both intimidation and enthrallment of death or of any agencies of death, how the church honors the sovereignty of the word of God in history against the counterclaims of the ruling principalities. This advocacy, in its ecumenical scope as well as its actual specificity, constitutes the church's political task, but, simultaneously, exemplifies the church's worship of God, as intercession for anyone in need, and for the need of the whole of creation, which exposes and confounds the blasphemy of predatory political authority.[66]

THE POSSIBILITY OF HOPE: LAW AND JUSTICE

The pervasiveness of death and the fallen nature of all of creation is not a cause for despair. To the contrary, William Stringfellow claimed celebration in the midst of death because the gospel is the word of triumph over death. He wrote in order to share the word of the possibility of hope.[67] He was never disillusioned by human beings, because he was never enchanted by them. He was never let down by political institutions, because he never believed in their ultimate power. To the question of whether there is any American hope, he simply stated, "The categorical answer is no."[68] What he believed in was the simple power of the risen Lord. "In the face of death, live humanly. In the middle of chaos, celebrate the Word. Amidst babel, I repeat, speak the truth. Confront the noise and verbiage and false-hood of death with the truth and potency and efficacy of the Word of God."[69]

The possibility of hope lies in the gospel and is expressed in several forms. One form of expression of hope is the certainty of the gospel itself. The faith that is given by God "is the assurance of things hoped for, the conviction of things not seen" (Heb. 11:1 NASV). A witness of advocacy is possible and is powerful; Stringfellow offered the life and work of Dorothy Day as an example of the biblical witness in the life of the church.[70] A bib-lical witness of advocacy, however, will never bring triumph in and of it-self. While sharing a common political agenda with proponents of the "social gospel," Stringfellow distanced himself from their theology out of concern that it assumed too much on the part of human nature and social institutions. We cannot be assured that our actions will achieve justice in this world, in this time; we are assured that nothing in this world can in-terfere with the presence of the word of God. The biblical experience of hope is quite distinct from optimism about the world, for "optimism re-fers to the capabilities of principalities and human beings, while hope be-speaks the effort of the Word of God in common history."[71] The absence of optimism in human nature allows the presence of the fullness of the word of God.

From a biblical point of view, there is nothing whatever that the Su-preme Court or any school board or any principalities or any persons—including the president of the United States—can say or do that can determine the character or action of the word of God in common his-tory—and nothing, issuing from any such source, that can obviate, di-minish, alter, modify, prejudice, detract from, or otherwise change the pervasive presence of the word of God in this world.[72]

A second expression of hope lies in the constant experience of worship. Worship is not an optional activity to be expressed on certain occasions; neither is it solely a collective activity. Worship is the primary mode of re-sponding to the word of God. In the context of law, whether one under-stands law in terms of gospel or of advocacy as legal counsel for victims, worship can and does take place. "Worship is not peripheral, but decisive in the relationships of Christian faith and secular law."[73]

The hope made possible by the gospel is that we can become human. The vocation of the Christian, and the central ethical issue confronting every Christian, "concerns how to live, what to decide, how to act humanly in the midst of the Fall."[74] When we forget, or ignore, or diminish the gospel, we denigrate the very persons we are called to be, and called to be with. "Deception is more humiliating than rejection. Exploitation is more inhuman than exclusion. Indifference is more embittering than open hostility. Condescension is more provocative than hate."[75] By stark contrast, the gospel allows us not to become god, but to become human. "In the face of death, live humanly."[76] Dietrich Bonhoeffer articulated this same christological foundation of hope: "Man becomes man because God became man. But man does not become God. It is not he, therefore, who was or is able to accomplish his own transformation, but it is God who changes his form into the form of man, so that man may become, not indeed God, but, in the eyes of God, man."[77]

Hope is possible because death is not the final word. In its repudiation of death, the gospel makes life possible. "To be ethical is to live sacramentally. To discern apocalyptic signs heightens the expectation of the eschatological events. In resistance persons live more humanly. *No* to death means *yes* to life."[78]

In a culture struggling to hold together and to hold up for all to see a vision of law that coincides with a vision of the gospel, William Stringfellow's life and work and voice stand as a proclamation of the futility of such a gesture. His life was one of service to those on the margins of power, indeed to the powerless in the face of oppression. His work was a vocation of responding to the word of God. His voice was a call to hear that word. Rare among theologians, scholars, and advocates of the late twentieth century is the centrality of the gospel in understanding the law. The legacy that Stringfellow has given is a constantly renewed understanding that law cannot be conflated with gospel, that death is not the final word, and that human nature can never be the source of its own justification.

NOTES

1. William Stringfellow, *An Ethic for Christians and Other Aliens in a Strange Land* (Waco, Tex.: Word Books, 1973), 13.
2. The most comprehensive bibliography of Stringfellow's writings has been prepared by Paul West; it is found in Bill Wylie Kellermann, ed., *A Keeper of the Word: Selected Writings of William Stringfellow* (Grand Rapids, Mich.: Eerdmans, 1994), 416–426.

3. William Stringfellow, "The Christian Lawyer as a Churchman," *Vanderbilt Law Review* 10 (1956–57): 939.

4. "People assume that I have read prodigiously in theology, whereas the truth is that I am practically a theological illiterate, so far as the works of the theologians are concerned. In my whole life I have, maybe, read two dozen theological books, Aquinas or Calvin or Tillich or the like.... The truth is I have, practically, just read the Bible." William Stringfellow, *A Second Birthday* (Garden City, N.Y.: Doubleday, 1970), 151.

5. Kellermann, *A Keeper of the Word*, 1.

6. William Stringfellow, *Conscience and Obedience: The Politics of Romans 13 and Revelation 13 in Light of the Second Coming* (Waco, Tex.: Word Books, 1977), 24.

7. The 1957 conference was sponsored by the Faculty Christian Fellowship and the United Student Christian Council, with essays prepared by Wilber Katz, Samuel Enoch Stumpf, William Ellis, and William Stringfellow. These essays were published as "A Symposium on Law and Christianity," *Vanderbilt Law Review* 10 (1957): 879–968. The second conference was held at the University of Chicago with papers prepared by James A. Pike, Albert Mollegen, Markus Barth, Harold J. Berman, Paul Lehmann, and Jacques Ellul. The essays from the second conference were published as "A Symposium on Law and Christianity," *Oklahoma Law Review* 12 (1959): 45–146.

8. Stringfellow, "The Christian Lawyer as a Churchman," 956.

9. Ibid., 962.

10. See William Stringfellow and Anthony Towne, *The Death and Life of Bishop Pike* (Garden City, N.Y.: Doubleday, 1976).

11. See William Stringfellow, "A Matter of Conscience," *The Witness* 62 (May 1979): 4–6.

12. William Stringfellow, *A Simplicity of Faith: My Experience in Mourning* (Nashville, Tenn.: Abingdon, 1982), 133.

13. "The approach to Romans 13 and Revelation 13 here is confessional, that is to say, a living contact betwixt the Word of God exposed in the biblical texts and the same Word of God active now in the situation of the common reader so that the encounter in Bible study becomes, in itself, an event characteristically biblical." Stringfellow, *Conscience and Obedience*, 13. See also William Stringfellow, *My People Is the Enemy: An Autobiographical Polemic* (New York: Holt, Rinehart and Winston, 1964), 96: "The characteristic approach to the Bible of the Christian is confessional."

14. William Stringfellow, *Dissenter in a Great Society: A Christian View of America in Crisis* (New York: Holt, Rinehart and Winston, 1966), 150–154.

15. William Stringfellow, *Instead of Death*, 2d ed. (New York: Seabury, 1976), 48.

16. Stringfellow, *A Second Birthday*, 95.

17. Stringfellow, *A Simplicity of Faith*, 21.

18. Stringfellow, *A Second Birthday*, 95.

19. See Stringfellow, *Conscience and Obedience*, chaps. 1 and 5. In one of the rare instances in which Stringfellow offered a citation to another scholar, he cited

Dietrich Bonhoeffer's *Creation and Fall* (New York: Macmillan, 1959), as a text for the interpretation of vocation in light of the Fall. Stringfellow, *Conscience and Obedience*, 27.

20. See Stringfellow, *A Second Birthday*.

21. Stringfellow, *A Simplicity of Faith*, 15–23.

22. See Stringfellow, *Instead of Death*.

23. William Stringfellow, *Free in Obedience* (New York: Seabury, 1964), 44.

24. "The circus performer is the image of the eschatological person—emancipated from frailty and inhibition, exhilarant, militant, transcendent over death—neither confined nor conformed by the fear of death any more." Stringfellow, *A Simplicity of Faith*, 90.

25. Stringfellow, *A Second Birthday*, 151.

26. William Stringfellow, *A Private and Public Faith* (Grand Rapids, Mich.: Eerdmans, 1962), 25.

27. Stringfellow, *An Ethic for Christians*, 19.

28. Stringfellow, *Instead of Death*, 10.

29. Stringfellow, *Conscience and Obedience*, 64. "Biblically, all men and all principalities are guiltily implicated in the violence which pervades all relationships in the Fall." Stringfellow, *An Ethic for Christians*, 130.

30. Stringfellow, "The Christian Lawyer as a Churchman," 964.

31. Stringfellow, *Free in Obedience*, 68–69.

32. Stringfellow, *A Second Birthday*, 133.

33. Stringfellow, *Conscience and Obedience*, 37–48.

34. William Stringfellow, *Count It All Joy: Reflections on Faith, Doubt, and Temptation Seen Through the Letter of James* (Grand Rapids, Mich.: Eerdmans, 1967), 47.

35. Stringfellow had occasion to meet with Karl Barth during a conference at the University of Chicago in 1962. He described their close affinity in theology as more than "an intuitive thing," to which Barth replied, "How could it be otherwise? We read the same Bible, don't we?" Quoted in Stringfellow, *A Second Birthday*, 151–152. See also chapter 3, this volume.

36. Stringfellow spent time with Ellul shortly after the end of World War II. See Stringfellow, *An Ethic for Christians*, 117. Among the few works cited by Stringfellow is Jacques Ellul, *The Theological Foundation of the Law* (Garden City, N.Y.: Doubleday, 1960), which first appeared in English in 1960. On Stringfellow's view of the importance of Ellul's thinking, see William Stringfellow, "The American Importance of Jacques Ellul," *Katallagete* 2 (Spring 1970): 47–48, and William Stringfellow, "Kindred Mind and Brother," *Sojourners* (June 1977): 12.

37. Stringfellow, *Count It All Joy*, 58–59.

38. Ibid., 58.

39. Nicholas Berdyaev, *The Destiny of Man*, trans. Natalie Duddington (New York: Charles Scribner's Sons, 1937), 85–86, quoted in Stringfellow, "The Christian Lawyer as a Churchman," 957 n. 70. In this same note Stringfellow describes

Karl Barth and Jacques Ellul as the only other scholars "who take seriously the extremity of the tension between grace and law."

40. Stringfellow, *An Ethic for Christians*, 131–133.

41. See Dietrich Bonhoeffer, *The Cost of Discipleship*, trans. R. H. Fuller (New York: Macmillan, 1963), 45–60, and Stringfellow, *Free in Obedience*, 107–116.

42. See Stringfellow, *A Private and Public Faith*, 14 ("The crisis is the real possibility that Protestantism has become mere religion"); Dietrich Bonhoeffer, *Letters and Papers from Prison*, ed. Eberhard Bethge (New York: Macmillan, 1972), 328. See also chapter 4, this volume.

43. Stringfellow, *A Private and Public Faith*, 14.

44. Ibid., 63.

45. Stringfellow, *Free in Obedience*, 72.

46. Stringfellow, *Count It All Joy*, 47–61.

47. William Stringfellow, "Christian Faith and the American Lawyer," *Federation News* (January–February 1957): 81.

48. Stringfellow, *Conscience and Obedience*, 11.

49. Stringfellow, "The Christian Lawyer as a Churchman," 964.

50. "Indeed, the natural lawyers invert the Biblical conception of sin in order to accommodate the intrinsic necessities of the natural law hypothesis. The natural lawyers treat too lightly the Gospel, for if sin is just moral deficiency then grace and natural law amount to the same thing, that is, the final corrective of moral deficiency, and men need not look for their salvation to Jesus Christ our Lord but may as well look to Sophocles." Stringfellow, "The Christian Lawyer as a Churchman," 958.

51. William Stringfellow, *The Politics of Spirituality* (Philadelphia: Westminster, 1984), 89.

52. Dietrich Bonhoeffer, *Ethics*, trans. Neville Horton Smith (New York: Macmillan, 1965), 85.

53. Colossians 3:17. See Stringfellow, *A Private and Public Faith*, 56.

54. Stringfellow, *Count It All Joy*, 16.

55. Romans 8:38; Ephesians 6:12; Colossians 2:15.

56. Ephesians 3:10; Colossians 1:16.

57. Stringfellow, *An Ethic for Christians*, 17. See also Stringfellow, *Free in Obedience*, 52: "What the Bible calls 'principalities and powers' are called in contemporary language 'ideologies,' 'institutions,' and 'images.'"

58. Stringfellow, *An Ethic for Christians*, 77.

59. Stringfellow, *Conscience and Obedience*, 30.

60. Stringfellow, *An Ethic for Christians*, 84.

61. See William Stringfellow and Anthony Towne, *Suspect Tenderness: The Ethics of the Berrigan Witness* (New York: Holt, Rinehart and Winston, 1971).

62. Stringfellow, *Conscience and Obedience*, 39, 43.

63. Ibid., 32, 46.

64. William Stringfellow, "Race, The Church, and the Law," *The Episcopalian* 127 (November 1962): 34.

65. Stringfellow, *Conscience and Obedience*, 103.

66. Ibid., 94–95.

67. "My sole intention in this book is to affirm a biblical hope which comprehends politics and which transcends politics." Stringfellow, *Conscience and Obedience*, 9.

68. Stringfellow, *An Ethic for Christians*, 155.

69. Ibid., 142–143.

70. Stringfellow, *Conscience and Obedience*, 96.

71. Stringfellow, *A Simplicity of Faith*, 95.

72. Stringfellow, *The Politics of Spirituality*, 59.

73. Stringfellow, "The Christian Lawyer as a Churchman," 939.

74. Stringfellow, *An Ethic for Christians*, 62–63.

75. Stringfellow, *My People Is the Enemy*, 105.

76. Stringfellow, *An Ethic for Christians*, 142.

77. Bonhoeffer, *Ethics*, 82.

78. Stringfellow, *An Ethic for Christians*, 156.

ORIGINAL SOURCE MATERIALS

A SIMPLICITY OF FAITH: MY EXPERIENCE IN MOURNING

A Lawyer's Work

If politics, from time to time, has spawned for me prosaic temptation to mistake career for vocation, being a lawyer has not bothered me in any comparable way. I was spared that before I even entered Harvard Law School because of my disposition of the substantive issue of career versus vocation while I was a graduate fellow at the London School of Economics and Political Science. As I have remarked heretofore, I had elected then to pursue *no* career. To put it theologically, I died to the idea of career and to the whole typical array of mundane calculations, grandiose goals and appropriate schemes to reach them. I renounced, simultaneously, the embellishments—like money, power, success—associated with careers in American culture, along with the ethics requisite to obtaining such condiments. I do not say this haughtily; this was an aspect of my conversion to the gospel, so, in fact, I say it humbly.

. . . I believed then, as I do now, that I am called in the Word of God—as is *everyone* else—to the vocation of being human, nothing more and nothing less. I confessed then, as I do now, that to be a Christian means to be called to be an exemplary human being. And, to be a Christian *categorically* does not mean being religious. Indeed, all religious versions of the gospel are profanities. Within the scope of the calling to be merely, but truly, human, any work, including that of any profession, can be rendered a sacrament of that vocation. On the other hand, no profession, discipline or employment, as such, is a vocation.

Law students, along with those in medicine, engineering, architecture, the military, among others, are subjected to indoctrinations, the effort of such being to make the students conform quickly and thoroughly to that prevailing stereotype deemed most beneficial to the profession and to its survival as an institution, its influence in society, and its general prosperity. At the Harvard Law School, this process is heavy, intensive, and unrelenting, though I imagine that such indoctrinations are all the more so in pseudo-professional institutions, like those training insurance agents, stockbrokers, or realtors. Over and over again, while I was in the law school, I was astonished at how eagerly many of my peers surrendered to this regimen of professionalistic conditioning, often squelching their own most intelligent opinions or creative impulses in order to conform or to appear to be conforming.

... I understand in hindsight that the vocational attitude I had formed in London, and later, the experience I had as law student, apprehended the legal profession specifically, and the professions, disciplines and occupations in general, in their status among the fallen principalities and powers engaged (regardless of apparently benign guises and pretenses) in coercing, stifling, captivating, intimidating, and otherwise victimizing human beings. The demand for conformity in a profession commonly signifies a threat of death.

In that connection, my commitment to vocation instead of career began, while I was still in law school, to sponsor far-reaching implications for how I could spend the rest of my life. Anyway, I suffered the overkill ethos of the Harvard Law School—I think—with enough poise as a human being to quietly, patiently, vigilantly resist being conformed to this world.

The upshot of that resistance was that I emerged from the law school as someone virtually opposite of what a Harvard Law School graduate is projected by the prevailing system to be. I do say *that* proudly, and gladly.

Do not misunderstand me: I enjoyed the law school, but I did not take it with the literally dead earnestness of those of my peers who had great careers at stake. I respected the intellectual vigor of its environment, but I was appalled by the overwhelming subservience of legal education to the commercial powers and the principalities of property. I thought that a law school should devote at least as much attention in its curriculum to the rights and causes of people as it does to vested property interests of one kind or another. I also thought, while I was in law school, that *justice* is a suitable topic for consideration in practically every course or specialization. Alas, it was seldom mentioned, and the term itself evoked ridicule, as if justice were a subject beneath the sophistication of lawyers.

Advocacy as a Pastoral Gift

When I first arrived in 1956 in East Harlem, I supposed that the rudimentary problem respecting the law was a failure to fully implement the existing American legal system among citizens who were economically dispossessed and who were victimized by racism. My supposition was, I soon enough discovered, mistaken. The issue, so far as the law was concerned, in the ghetto was the existence of another ruling system, distinct and apart from the constitutional and legal system pertaining elsewhere in the nation, based on coercion and the threat of coercion by those institutions and people who had commandeered the capabilities of coercion. It was a system of lawless authority, of official violence, a primitive substitution for the law. I wrote then that if such an extraordinary condition were allowed to continue and to fester, it would, sooner or later, infect and afflict the whole of this society. It has. There is a connection—direct and terrible and coherent—between the kind of regime to be found in the ghettoes in the Fifties and the way lawless authority and official violence dominate the life of most of this society today. . . .

. . . A critical dimension of this tension occasioned by being a biblical person who works as a lawyer is that the role of legal advocate at once coincides with and interferes with the pastoral calling to which I am disposed charismatically. In that calling, advocacy expresses the freedom in Christ to undertake the cause of another—including causes deemed "hopeless," to intercede for the need of another—without evaluating it, but just because the need is apparent, to become vulnerable—even unto death—in the place of another. By contrast, advocacy in the law is contained within the bounds of the adversary system, with all its implications of competitiveness, aggression, facetious games, debater's craft, and winning *per se*. There have been circumstances in my experience when the advocacy of the Christian in the world coincides with the advocacy of the lawyer (as in cases concerning the ordination of women), but there seem to be far more instances when the one interferes with the other (as in war resister cases). In part, here, of course, I am pleading within the legal profession for a more holistic approach to clients and cases than that afforded by the adversary system. Yet, more than that, I continue to be haunted with the ironic impression that I may have to renounce being a lawyer the better to be an advocate.[1]

THE CHRISTIAN LAWYER AS A CHURCHMAN

The Proclamation of the Gospel

The Church as the congregation is the event in which reconciliation between God and men accomplished in Jesus Christ is already known and celebrated and thereby the message of reconciliation is entrusted for proclamation in all the world and to the whole world. . . .

The most lucid and cogent witness of God's love for men is that through Jesus Christ He gives men a new life now, in the very midst of the old life, that the new life begins in history in His Church and in the faith of His Church, that men are born anew in His Church, that in His Church the new life is celebrated. The message of reconciliation for the world is entrusted to the Church by the event of reconciliation which constitutes the Church and which the Church celebrates. The Gospel is entrusted to the Church, the Church possesses the Gospel, but the Church is not possessive about the Gospel, for the Gospel does not mean that God loves the Church, the Gospel means that God loves the world and therefore elects the Church. Hence nothing is more demonstrative of the Gospel in the world and to the world than the concrete life of the Church in history. That is why it is always a very great tragedy for the world when the actual life of the Church is not a celebration of the Gospel but a conformation to the world. Where apostasy or heresy or sorcery are celebrated, the Gospel is not proclaimed. But where the celebration has integrity in the Gospel, it is integral to the Gospel, and celebration is proclamation.

The Obviation of a Christian Jurisprudence

What is before implicit, must now be put directly. The tension between law and grace is such that there is no Christian jurisprudence. There is not a particular philosophy of law which has special integrity in the Gospel. Nor is that a way really to make the positive law or the ethics of law, the purposes of law which men offer as a measure for positive legislation, compatible with the Gospel.

This does not at all mean that Christians disregard the law, rather they regard it for exactly and only what it is: law and justice are the manner in which men maintain themselves in history. Law is a condition of historical existence, a circumstance of the fall. Christians, both in congregation and in dispersion, are in the world, living in history, under the sanctions of secular law, and this is the locus of their proclamation of the Gospel for the world. For law, the proclamation of the Gospel means, in the first instance, the comprehension that law, though sometimes it can name sin, originates itself in sin and cannot overcome the power of sin.

This obviates, of course, a Christian jurisprudence, but poses—for Christians and for the world—just what any jurisprudence does not—the tension between grace and law. The Christian sees that the striving of law is for justice, but knows that the justice men achieve has no saving power; it does not justify them, for justification of man is alone in Jesus Christ. The grace of God is the only true justice any man may ever receive.

To have no special Christian jurisprudence does not mean that Christians are indifferent, or wholly negativist, toward law. Rather their concern is primarily an issue of vocation, not of jurisprudence.[2]

FREE IN OBEDIENCE

A Radical Life

The style of life, this ethics of witness, means that the essential and con-sistent task of Christians is to expose the transience of death's power in the world. That is a task which will not be exhausted until God's mercy brings this history to an end and fulfillment on the Last Day. Thus, the Christian in secular society is always in the position of a radical—not in the conventional political sense of that word, but in the sense that noth-ing which is achieved in secular life can ever satisfy the insight which the Christian is given as to what the true consummation of life in soci-ety is. The Christian always complains of *status quo*, whatever that hap-pens to be; he always seeks more than that which satisfies even the best ideals of other men. Or, to put it differently, the Christian knows that no change, reform, or accomplishment of secular society can modify, threaten, or diminish the active reign of death in the world. Only Christ can do that, and now his reign is acknowledged and enjoyed in the soci-ety which bears his name and has the task of proclamation in all the world for the sake of that part of the world still consigned to the power of death.

At the same time the witness of Christians in the world is always both repentant and penitential. It is repentant in that Christians acknowledge the fallenness of life and the reality of sin and then confess—as much in and through their action in the world as in their worship—their own sins: shortcomings, omissions, failings, infidelities, profanities, weaknesses, vanities, angers, indulgences, errors, and corruptions. By intercession (as representatives before God, in behalf of and in the place of other men) they also confess the sins of the world, in which they share, and which they call upon other men to confess for themselves. This confession and intercession is repentance. But it is also penitential: recognition and real-ization of sorrow, regret, remorse, grief, mourning, and contrition for the offense of their own sins and the sins of others against God's own person and to his creation.

The penitential act, the authentication of true repentance, which in-variably follows repentance and is the sacramental expression of repen-tance, is not an act of recrimination by which a man indulges in judging and punishing himself. Nor is it some form of restitution as if what has been done could be undone or as if there could be a return to the situa-tion prior to the sin. Both recrimination and restitution are ways in which men attempt, even after acknowledging their sins specifically, to justify themselves by allaying God's judgment or earning his forgiveness. Such tactics may work between a child and a parent, between a criminal and society, or in the moralistic and legalistic religions, but they have nothing to do with the event of repentance and the penitential act characteristic of Christian witness in action and worship in the world. . . .

That *this* is the accusation should, by the way, dispose of the legend, so popular in modern treatments of the trial of Christ both in Good Friday sermons and popular secular versions of the event, that Christ is innocent of any offense and tried and condemned because of some corruption or failure or miscarriage of justice. Of the charge against him, Christ is guilty beyond any doubt.

In any case, the significant aspect of the trial is that it is not just an encounter between Christ and some men who were his enemies. The most decisive clash in all history is this one between Christ and the principalities and powers of this world, represented by and symbolized in Israel and Rome.

. . . It appears, in other words, to be widely believed in the churches in the United States that the history of redemption is encompassed merely in the saga of relationships between God and men. What there is of contemporary Protestant moral theology typically ignores any attempt to account for, identify, explicate, and relate the self to the principalities, although empirically the principalities seem to have an aggressive, in fact possessive, ascendancy in American life. Because of the biblical references to principalities and angelic powers are so prominent, and because the powers themselves enjoy such dominance in everyday life, their meaning and significance cannot be left unexamined.

What are the principalities and powers? What is their significance in the creation and in the fall? What is their relationship to human sin? How are these powers related to the presence and power of death in history? What is the meaning of the confrontation between Christ and the principalities? Does a Christian have any freedom from their dominion? There can be no serious, realistic, or biblical comprehension of the witness of the Church in the world unless such questions as they are raised and pondered.

What are Principalities?

There is nothing particularly mysterious, superstitious, or imaginary about principalities, despite the contemporary failure to discuss them theologically. The realities to which the biblical terms "principalities and powers" refer are quite familiar to modern society, though they may be called by different names. What the Bible calls "principalities and powers" are called in contemporary language "ideologies," "institutions," and "images."

A principality, whatever its particular form and variety, is a living reality, distinguishable from human and other organic life. It is not made or instituted by men, but, as with men and all creation, made by God for his own pleasure.

In the biblical understanding of creation, the principalities or angelic powers, together with all other forms of life, are given by God into the dominion of men and are means through which men rejoice in the gift of life by acknowledging and honoring God, who gives life to all men and to the whole of creation. The dominion of men over the rest of creation, including the angelic powers, means the engagement of men in the worship of God as the true, realized, and fulfilled human life and, at the same time and as part of the same event, the commitment by men of all things within their dominion to the very same worship of God, to the very same actualization of true life for all things. All men, all angels, and all things in creation have origination, integrity, and wholeness of life in the worship of God. . . .

The Meaning of Demonic

Like all men and all things, the angelic powers and principalities are fallen and are become demonic powers. "Demonic" does not mean evil; the word refers to death, to fallenness. An angelic power in its fallen estate is called a demonic power, because it is a principality existing in the present age in a state of alienation from God, cut off from the life originating in his life, separated from its own true life and, thus, being in a state of death. In the fall, every man, every principality, every thing exists in a condition of estrangement from his or its own life, as well as from the lives of all other men, powers, and things. In the fall, the whole of creation is consigned to death.

The separation from life, the bondage to death, the alienation from God which the fall designates is not simply to be accounted for by human sin. The fall is not just the estate in which men reject God and exalt themselves, as if men were like God. The term does not merely mean the pretensions of human pride. It is all that and something more. The fall is also the awareness of men of their estrangement from God, themselves, each other, and all things, and their pathetic search for God or some substitute for God within and outside themselves and each other in the principalities and in the rest of creation. So men, in their fallenness, are found sometimes idolizing themselves, sometimes idolizing snakes, bugs, other creatures, or natural phenomena, or sometimes idolizing nation, ideology, race, or one of the other principalities. It is to such as these that men look to justify their existence, to find and define the lost meaning of their lives, and to fill the place of God himself. . . .

. . . All this is not for the sake of the Christians, not for their justification either individually or as the Church, but for the sake of the world, for other men. A Christian is free in his knowledge and experience of the love of God for the world to love the world himself. A Christian does not love another man for himself—else how would one love his own enemy?—but for his sake, that is, because of what God has done for him. A Christian loves another man in a way that affirms his true humanity, vouchsafed for him and for all men in the resurrection.

The life of the Christian both within and outside the gathered congregation is sacramental. But of what practical significance is that for a Christian in his daily decisions and actions? The witness which is obedience to God's freedom is one which celebrates the gospel, but of what guidance is that in choosing a job, casting a ballot, raising a child, facing illness, spending money, or any of the other ordinary issues of daily existence?

The short answer to such questions is that the witness which is truly obedience to the freedom of God means freedom without measure for men. That means that the Christian is free to take the world and every aspect of its existence, every person and every principality, seriously. Out of respect, as it were, for God's creation and for both the incarnation and the Holy Spirit, the Christian deals with history in this world just as it is and makes decisions in terms of the actual events in which he is involved as they happen. In doing so he knows that there is no place in which his presence is forbidden, no person whom he may not welcome, no work in which he may not engage, no situation into which he may not enter, without first of all finding that he has been preceded, so to speak, by the Word of God.

The Christian does not need to construct any hypothetical presuppositions, any theoretics of decision, after the manner of the Greeks, the Hebrews in the early Church, or the later pietists of one sort or another. To do that denigrates the freedom of God in judging the world and all the decisions and actions of men and nations in the way that it pleases him to do, by enthroning some principles of decision in the place of God. Such ethics, in any of their varieties, are no armor against the realities of the world, the temptations of the flesh, or the power of death; they are only means of hiding from all of these.

There are, to be sure, certain marks of the ministry and witness of the Church and of Christians in the world: radicality, penitence, intercession for the outcast, and the like; but that is not the same thing as some legalistic ethics. Such ethics have no saving power for the world for they invariably

are the expression of the self-interest of the very persons and principalities which adhere to them and attempt to implement and enforce them.
Nor do they have any efficacy in justifying those beholden to them.

Nor will any such scheme of ethics save any man from God's judgment.
All men and nations are judged in all their ethics, motives, decisions, and
actions by God himself. No one aids him in this office, and no one can
take another's place, nor can one be spared God's judgment by any other
means, though that be the intention of all ethics. That being so, the freedom of the Christian consists of his acceptance of the fact that his own
justification by the working of God's freedom relieves him even of the
anxiety over how he is judged by God.

The Christian goes about—wherever he be, which may be anywhere,
whomever he is with, which may be anyone—edified and upheld by the
sacramental community which is the church in the congregation. He is
ready to face whatever is to be faced knowing that the only enemy is the
power of death, whatever form or appearance death may take. He is confident that the Word of God has already gone before him. Therefore he can
live and act, whatever the circumstances, without fear of or bondage to either his own death or the works of death in the world. He is enabled and
authorized by the gift of the Holy Spirit to the Church and to himself in
baptism to expose all that death has done and can do, rejoicing in the freedom of God which liberates all men, all principalities, all things from
bondage to death.

That being so, the Christian is free to give his own life to the world, to
anybody at all, even to one who does not know about or acknowledge the
gift, even to one whom the world would regard as unworthy of the gift.
He does so without reserve, compromise, hesitation, or prudence, but
with modesty, assurance, truth, and serenity. That being so, the Christian is free, within the freedom of God, to be obedient unto his own
death.[3]

*AN ETHIC FOR CHRISTIANS AND
OTHER ALIENS IN A STRANGE LAND*

Revelation as Ethics

It is a pity that Americans have been so recalcitrant toward the Bible, for all
the contrary pretenses in the country's public rituals and despite the grandiose religiosity in America concerning the familiar fictions about the nation's
destiny. It is specifically a misfortune, it seems to me, that most Americans,
whether or not they keep a church connection, are either ignorant or obtuse

about Revelation and the issues which the Book raises in its Babylon passages. Had the American inheritance been different, had Americans been far less religious and much more biblical, had the American experience as a nation not been so Babylonian, we might have been edified—in a fearful and marvelous and timely way—by this biblical witness, and Americans might be in more hopeful and more happy circumstances today.

Instead, Americans for the most part have dismissed the Bible as apolitical—a private witness shrouded in holy neutrality so far as politics is concerned, having nothing beyond vague and innocuous exhortation to do with the nation as such, relegated to the peripheries of social conflict. Thereby Americans have actually suppressed the Bible, since the Bible is *essentially* political, having to do with the fulfillment of humanity in society or, in traditional words, with the saga of salvation.

The treatment of the particular book of the Bible which I cite here, the Revelation to John, is the striking illustration at point. We have deemed it esoteric poetry, to be put aside as inherently obscure and impractical by definition; or we have regarded it, somewhat apprehensively, as a diary of psychedelic visions inappropriately appended to the rest of Scripture; or else we have suffered the arrogant pietism of itinerant evangelists preaching a quaint damnation from fragments of the book and acquiesced to their boast that *that* is what Revelation is about. Some have demeaned the whole of the Bible by distorting this book as a predestinarian chronicle. Seldom is the specific political use to which the book was put in its original context in the first century even mentioned in church or known to contemporary church folk. Most often, I observe, Americans, including the professed Christians and the habituated churchgoers, have just been wholly indifferent to Revelation.

Whatever reasons can be assigned for it, Americans fail to comprehend Revelation as an ethical literature concerning the character and timeliness of God's judgment, not only of persons, but over nations and, in truth, over all principalities and powers—which is to say, all authorities, corporations, institutions, traditions, processes, structures, bureaucracies, ideologies, systems, sciences, and the like. As such—except for the accounts of the Crucifixion of Jesus Christ in the Gospels—Revelation is manifestly the most political part of the New Testament. . . .

. . . The ethics of biblical politics offer no basis for divining specific, unambiguous, narrow, or ordained solutions for any social issue. Biblical theology does not deduce "the will of God" for political involvement or social action. The Bible—if it is esteemed for it own genius—does not yield "right" or "good" or "true" or "ultimate" answers. The Bible does not do that in seemingly private or personal matters; even less can it be said to do so in politics or institutional life. . . .

Yet human wickedness in this sense is so peripheral in the biblical version of the Fall that the pietistic interpretation that it represents the heart of the matter must be accounted gravely misleading. The biblical description of *the Fall concerns the alienation of the whole of Creation from God*, and, thus, the rupture and profound disorientation of all relationships within the whole of Creation. Human beings are fallen, indeed! But all other creatures suffer fallenness, too. And the other creatures include, as it were, not only cows, but corporations; the other creatures are, among others, the nations, the institutions, the principalities and powers. The biblical doctrine of the Fall means the brokenness of relationships among human beings and the other creatures, and the rest of Creation, and the spoiled or confused identity of each human being within herself or himself and each principality within itself. . . .

Biblical living honors the life-style of the people of God set out for us in the Bible. A spontaneous, intimate, and incessant involvement in the biblical Word as such—that is, Bible study—is the most essential nurture of contemporary biblical people while they are involved, patiently and resiliently, in the common affairs of the world. Biblical living means, concretely, practicing the powers of discernment, variously perceiving and exposing the moral presence of death incarnate in the principalities and powers and otherwise. And biblical living means, moreover, utilizing the diverse and particular charismatic gifts as the ethics and tactics of resistance to the power of death in the assurance that these gifts are in their use profoundly, radically, triumphantly humanizing.

Biblical living discloses that the ethical is sacramental, not moralistic or pietistic or religious. The identify of the ethical in the sacramental is, perhaps, most obvious in liturgy, where liturgy retains biblical style and scope and content, where liturgy has Eucharistic integrity and is not an absurd theatrical charade disguising the idolatry of death. But the sacramental reality of the ethics is, also, enacted empirically, day by day, transfiguring mundane politics by appealing to the presence of the Word of God in all events.[4]

THE POLITICS OF SPIRITUALITY

. . . The problem of America as a nation, in biblical perspective, remains this elementary issue of repentance. The United States is, as all nations are, called in the Word of God to repentance. That, in truth, is what the church calls for, whether knowingly or not, every time the church prays *Thy Kingdom Come.*

America needs to repent. Every episode in the common experience of America as a nation betells that need. If such be manifest in times of trauma and trouble—such as now—it is as much the need in triumphal or grandiose circumstances.

The nation needs to repent. If I put the matter so baldly, I hope no one will mistake my meaning for the rhetoric of those electronic celebrity preachers who sometimes use similar language to deplore the mundane lusts of the streets or the ordinary vices of people or to berate the Constitutional bar to prayer, so-called, in public schools while practicing quietism about the genocidal implications of the Pentagon's war commerce or extolling indifference toward the plight of the swelling urban underclasses.

Topically, repentance is *not* about forswearing wickedness as such; repentance concerns the confession of vanity. For America—for any nation at any time—*repentance means confessing blasphemy.*

Blasphemy occurs in the existence and conduct of a nation whenever there is such profound and sustained confusion as to the nation's character, place, capabilities, and destiny that the vocation of the Word of God is preempted or usurped. Thus the very presumption of the righteousness of the American cause as a nation *is* blasphemy.

Americans, for some time now, have been assured, again and again, that the United States will prevail in history because the American cause is righteous. Anyone who believes that has, to say the very least, learned noting from the American adventurism in Vietnam. Then, a succession of presidents made similar pronouncements, but America suffered ignominious defeat nonetheless. And if in the last few years some sense of guilt about Vietnam has begun to surface, this has been, for the most part, a strange and perverted sentiment because it has attached not to the crimes of American intervention in Southeast Asia—to massacre, despoilment, and genocide—but to the event of American defeat. To feel guilty because America lost, rather than because of what America did, is another, if macabre, instance of false righteousness. That is only the more underscored when the unlawful invasion of Grenada is examined as an attempt to fantasize the victory for American superpower which was missed in Vietnam.

Furthermore, the confusion of a nation's destiny, and of a nation's capabilities, with the vocation of the Word of God in history—which is the *esse* of blasphemy—sponsors the delusion that America exercises domination over creation as well as history and that it can and should control events in the life of creation. Other nations, ancient and modern, as has been mentioned, suffered similar delusions, but if there ever been a nation which should know better (that is, which should repent), it is America, if only because of the American experience as a nation and a society in these past few decades.

After all, it is only in the period since, say, Hiroshima, in which American power, rampant most conspicuously in the immense, redundant, overkill nuclear-weapons arsenal, has been proven impotent, because if it is deployed, it portends self-destruction, and if it is not, it amounts to profligate, grotesque waste. In either instance, American nuclear arms are rendered practically ineffectual in dominating events, but they still mock the sovereignty of the Word of God in history.

Much of the same must, of course, be said of the nation's society and culture, which has become, as I have earlier remarked, overdependent upon the consumption ethic, with its doctrines of indiscriminate growth, gross development, greedy exploitation of basic resources, uncritical and often stupid reliance upon technological capabilities and incredible naiveté about technological competence, and crude, relentless manipulation of human beings as consumers. Increasingly, now, people can glimpse that this is no progress, no enhancement of human life, but wanton plunder of creation itself. People begin to apprehend that the penultimate implementation of the American consumption ethic is, bluntly, self-consumption. In the process, it has become evident as well that the commerce engendered by the American consumption ethic, together with the commerce of weapons proliferation, relates consequentially to virtually every injustice of which human beings are victims in this nation and in much of the rest of the world.

And so I say the United States needs to repent; the nation needs to be freed of blasphemy. There are, admittedly, theological statements. Yet I think they are also truly practical statements. America will remain frustrated, literally demoralized, incapable of coping with its concrete problems as a nation and society until it knows that realism concerning the nation's vocation which only repentance can bring.

One hopes repentance will be forthcoming. If not, it *will* happen: in the good time of the Judgment of the Word of God.

Meanwhile, in this same context, persons repent and all persons are called to repentance. The confession and repentance of an individual does not take place, as some preachers and the like aver, in a great void, abstracted from the everyday existence of this world. The experience of each penitent is peculiar to that person, but that does not mean it is separated from the rest of created life.

This is the reason why the foisting of any stereotype of the experience upon people is coercive and false and, indeed, self-contradictory. It must be recognized, however, that this is quite what is involved where, for an example, a so-called born-again Christian stereotype is asserted. I can testify personally that I have been "born again"—my account constitutes the book aptly titled *A Second Birthday*—but that appears to mean something substantively different from sudden, momentary trauma. I do not thus imply that the latter is invalid or necessarily incomplete or otherwise questionable, but I do question the composition of *any* stereotype of the experience and the insinuation that it is normative, much less mandatory.

What is implicated in confession and repentance, which inaugurates the practice of a biblical spirituality whatever the style or detail of what happens to a particular person, is the establishment or restoral by the Word of God of that person's identity in the Word of God in a which in which the query *Who am I?* merges with the question *Where is God?* The transaction comprehends, as has been said, the risk that there is no one or nothing to affirm a person's existence and identity. As I have put it before, the confession of utter helplessness, the repentance which is requisite and efficacious, always involves the empirical risk of death. At the very same time, this repentance foreshadows and anticipates the perfection of each person's and each principality's vocation in the Kingdom of God.

Justification and Hope

Since the disillusionment and defection of Judas, a recurrent issue for people of biblical faith has been the confusion between justification and justice. It is, in fact, out of contemporary manifestations of that very confusion, especially during the decade of the sixties, that many Christian activists (as the media style them) have become more curious about spirituality and have begun to explore the significance of biblical spirituality for political decisions and actions. The widespread posthumous interest in the witness and ministry of Thomas Merton is one significant sign of that, as I have said.

I do not venture to unravel the confusion regarding justification and justice in terms of its prolonged and agitated annals in Christendom. I speak of the matter only theologically, not historically and analytically. As I understand it, justice is the accomplishment of the Judgment of the Word of God in the consummation of this age and embodies all the specifications, all the particular details of the Judgment with respect to all things whatsoever. Justice, as it is articulate in the Judgment, is essentially an expression of the faithfulness of the Word of God to the creation of the Word of God.

There is no capability in human effort or in the enterprise of nations or other principalities to approximate the justice of the Judgment. The decisions and actions of persons and powers may, in a sense, aspire to or render tribute to the justice of the Judgment, but they cannot fabricate it or duplicate it or preempt it. And, as has been mentioned, when they suppose that they have in given circumstances imitated or second-guessed the Judgment and its justice, they are most in jeopardy so far as the integrity of their respective vocations is concerned. Persons and principalities can neither play God nor displace God without risking self-destruction. This does not denigrate at all the struggle for justice in merely human and institutional terms; in fact, it upholds that struggle even in recognizing how fragile, transient, and ambiguous it is—and dynamic—how open it is to amendment, how vulnerable to change.

Within the scene of this world, now, where the struggle for justice in merely human and institutional translations is happening, and in the midst of the turmoil that stirs, the Word of God, as a matter of God's own prerogative, freedom, and grace, offers the assurance of redemption, the promise of wholeness and integrity and communication, the message of hope in the Kingdom which is to come together with the Judgment of the Word of God and the justice which that Judgment works.

This justification is both credible and accessible, not because any person, or any society, is worthy but because the Word of God is extravagant or, if you will, because the *Word of God is godly.* So the grace of the Word of God transcends the injustice of the present age, agitates the resilience of those who struggle now to expose and rebuke injustice, informs those who resist the rulers of the prevailing darkness, and overflows in eagerness for the coming of One who is the Judge of this world and whose justice reigns forevermore. By virtue of justification, we are freed now to live in hope.[5]

NOTES

1. [William Stringfellow, *Simplicity of Faith: My Experience in Mourning* (Nashville, Tenn.: Abingdon, 1982), 125–128, 131–133.]
2. [William Stringfellow, "The Christian Lawyer as Churchman," *Vanderbilt Law Review* 10 (August 1957): 953, 964.]
3. [William Stringfellow, *Free in Obedience* (New York: Seabury, 1964), 44–45, 50–53, 62–63, 126–128.]
4. [William Stringfellow, *An Ethic for Christians and Other Aliens in a Strange Land* (Waco, Tex: Word Books, 1973), 26–27, 54, 76, 151–152.]
5. [William Stringfellow, *The Politics of Spirituality* (Philadelphia: Westminster, 1984), 62–68.]

[CHAPTER 8]

John Howard Yoder (1927–1997)

COMMENTARY

DUNCAN B. FORRESTER

John Howard Yoder was born in 1927 and raised in an Amish Mennonite family, living in Wayne County, Ohio. He was nurtured as a Christian in Oak Grove Mennonite Church, where his father, a prominent leader, was declared to be "one of the most powerful, influential, and widely known bishops in the Amish Mennonite church during the last four decades of the nineteenth century."[1] Yoder was educated largely in Mennonite schools, but his education was in no way narrow or sectarian. After World War II, with other young American Mennonites, he helped with postwar reconstruction in Europe, played a part in the revival of the Mennonite cause in France, was active in ecumenical discussions, particularly of pacifism, and took a doctorate after studying with Karl Barth and others in Basel, Switzerland.

When Yoder returned from Europe to the United States, he was at the height of his powers, but he held down a variety of jobs, some administrative, some educational, many of them part-time. He taught at the Mennonite Biblical Seminary in Elkhart from 1960 to 1965, and from 1965 to 1973 he was at Goshen Biblical Seminary. All the while he was producing essays, articles, and lectures, although he published mainly with small Mennonite publishing houses and was not yet widely known outside Mennonite circles. The publication of *The Politics of Jesus* in 1972, however, caused something of a theological sensation and gave him a high profile as a constructive and critical theological thinker of the highest rank, one whose work had to be taken seriously by Christian theologians of all varieties. In 1977 Yoder became a full-time professor at the University of Notre Dame, an interesting sign of recognition, which provided him with a platform from which to address a wider audience and an opportunity for dialogue with Roman Catholic theological traditions. He became a respected dialogue partner with a number of legal scholars, perhaps most notably Thomas L. Shaffer, whose work he deeply influenced.[2] Yoder was now quickly and widely recognized as a fresh and distinctive theological voice, and he became well known partly through the work of his disciples, of whom Stanley Hauerwas (not always a totally reliable interpreter of Yoder) is the best known, and, of course, through his own teaching, publishing, and lecturing.[3]

Yoder's particular Christian heritage, which he embraced with great but not uncritical conviction throughout his life, was Mennonite. In brief, this meant that his thought had from the beginning four distinctive emphases. First, his theology was always biblical. He was not a fundamentalist, but he accepted the Bible as the ultimate authority in Christian discipleship and Christian theology, and his exegesis was often fresh, imaginative, and penetrating. Second, he believed in the gathered church, with the local worshipping congregation of believers as the primary manifestation of what it is to be a "church." This church has a structure of "discipline"—a way of dealing with offenses and failures that is directed toward reconciliation. Third, the church and individual Christians alike are expected to express, in their relations both within the community and outside of it, loving service or "servanthood." Finally, the peace witness is central for Yoder. Not only are believers expected to be peaceable themselves, but they should also seek peace in the wider society as a necessary expression of their faith.

From the beginning, the Mennonite Church offered Yoder no pietistic escape from the problems of the world or from rigorous academic debate. He was early regarded primarily as a Mennonite Church theologian, but, like Karl Barth, he was always a theologian who swam "against the stream" and maintained his own critical judgment. Yoder was in Europe at a crucial and challenging moment. Barthian theology and the broader movement much influenced by Barth and labeled "biblical theology" or "biblical realism" was at its peak. Yoder found much that was congenial in this new theological mood—and much to question. In particular, he was attracted by the distinctive blending of theological orthodoxy with social and political radicalism—and disturbed that Western theology was still so deeply "infected" with what he believed were Constantinian assumptions. He saw these assumptions as distorting the theological understanding and giving the church a false view of its nature and mandate.

KARL BARTH AND BIBLICAL THEOLOGY

Partly as a result of his involvements in Europe, Yoder quickly found himself deeply immersed in a new and vigorous theological movement in

Europe and the United States. As a critical disciple, he saw Barth's theology, although deeply rooted in the tradition of the magisterial Reformation, as converging with the radical Reformation tradition as represented by the Mennonites. This makes Barth's thought a useful point of comparison and contrast with Yoder's own. Both Barth and Yoder were deeply suspicious of liberal theology and uneasy about the heritage of the Enlightenment. Both took the Bible with profound seriousness, but they resisted fundamentalism as an attempt to reduce scripture to a system of absolute and infallible propositions. Both Barth and Yoder saw theology as necessarily *ecclesial*, rooted in the life of the church and the church's proclamation. And Barth, from the Reformed tradition, became increasingly suspicious of the intertwining of church and state, the Christianity and culture characteristic of the Constantinian settlement, of "Christendom." Indeed, in some ways, Barth's mature understanding of the church is congenial to the Mennonite belief in a "gathered church" that represents a sort of counterculture. Yoder agreed that, in a broad sense, Barth's early socialism was the harbinger of his "radical ecclesiology."[4] Both Barth and Yoder combined a fairly conservative theological orthodoxy with social and political radicalism. And although Barth was never a pacifist, his position on war and peace issues in the aftermath of World War II moved remarkably close to the traditional peace witness of the Mennonites.[5]

The initial impact of Yoder's theology was certainly helped by the fact that from the beginning of his career as a theologian he engaged constructively and sympathetically not only with Barth, whom he recognized as probably the most important Reformed theologian since the Reformation, but also with the debates in and about the post–World War II movement loosely labeled "biblical theology." Here Yoder recognized themes with which he had a great deal of sympathy. But he also represented a distinctive theological voice that was heard at an opportune moment, as many churches around the world reconciled themselves to minority status and as the foundations of Christendom (or what Yoder preferred to call Constantinianism) were rapidly eroded, particularly in Europe.

Barth and Yoder both sought to root their theology in the Bible, but they were innovative in their approach to biblical interpretation. Both believed that fundamentalism and most Protestant readings of scripture "subordinated the actual reading of scriptural texts to an *a priori* discussion of how the texts were so written and preserved as to be infallibly revelatory and how they should be so read as to coincide with an all-inclusive system of propositions."[6] The Bible must rather be seen as in tension with the cultural assumptions of this, and every, age. For both Barth and Yoder, the Bible is not primarily a law book or a collection of rules. Barth saw it as the indispensable aid or stimulus to hearing and responding to the specific commands of God to us here and now. Yoder tended to regard scripture, responsibly interpreted within the church, as a chosen vehicle through which God speaks to us today.

Much of Yoder's writing on ethics was unabashedly exegetical. He was himself a well-regarded biblical scholar. Richard B. Hays speaks of Yoder's *The Politics of Jesus* as "a path-breaking attempt to do Christian ethics in vigorous dialogue with biblical scholarship" and "an impressive foray by a theological ethicist into exegetical territory."[7] Yoder, according to Hays, argued for three central theses: that the Jesus of the New Testament eschews violence and coercion; that the example of Jesus is binding on the Christian community; and that discipleship is a political choice that necessarily has implications for the public realm. The church appears as the conscience, critic, and servant of human society, and the role of the state is presented in terms of the New Testament teaching on the "principalities and powers," which are intended to be servants of God that enable human beings to flourish in peaceableness. In fact, however, these principalities and powers often rebel and deny their divine mandate.[8] Long before liberation theology became fashionable, Yoder saw the Bible as a handbook of liberation, a liberating narrative.

Hays suggests that Yoder, like Barth, "eschews the hermeneutical strategy of extracting moral *principles* from Scripture . . . [because] the exercise of applying principles to situations leaves too much room for straying away from the truth revealed in Jesus."[9] Jesus, for Yoder, "reveals the true nature and vocation of human beings" in all times and places.[10] He was too responsible an exegete to attempt to derive moral rules directly from the Bible. But he did give the Bible, and in particular the picture of Jesus and his teaching that emerges from the Gospels, an absolute normative status, and he was reluctant to see scripture as reflecting the assumptions of a very different age.

NATURE AND NATURAL LAW

Like Barth, but with his own emphases, Yoder was critical of the use of nature and natural law in ethical discourse.[11] But, unlike Barth, Yoder saw the discourse of natural law, or something very like it, as having a necessary place in the search for a common morality in pluralistic societies, as people strive together to resolve complex ethical issues in, say, the area of bioethics. Frequently, however, in his judgment, too much is claimed for natural law and "common morality." Yoder tended to see natural insights as reflecting the assumptions of the age and the culture rather than any universal reality. The Thomist and classical visions of nature, Yoder suggested, privilege things as they are. Such ways of understanding nature thus easily become oppressive, and they make virtually impossible a subversive ethics such as, Yoder believed, the gospel teaches. Furthermore, natural law thinking has an overly optimistic understanding of the ability of human reason to discern moral truth. Yoder, on the other hand, spoke freely of the fallenness and finiteness of human reason, limitations that make it often a confusing guide to moral truth.

There are, Yoder suggested, two broad approaches to the understanding of nature. In the first:

> Nature is the way things obviously are. The epistemology is simple, descriptive. Socially it is positivistic; the institutions of slavery, of patriarchy, of monarchy are obviously the way it is. Biologically it is also positivistic: contraception and artificial insemination interfere with the "natural" functioning of the body. Its first ethical impact is usually conservative, since the nation, the class structure, the marketplace, the repertory of roles or vocations is the way it is. The system will seem convincing as long as all parties have been educated under the same customs, so that they really think "everyone knows . . ." whatever they know, and as long as no skeptic draws attention to the is/ought equation.[12]

The second family of understandings of nature was more congenial to Yoder. It speaks of "things as they ought to be":

> The essence of things is different from the appearance, the "true nature"' as contrast with the empirical one, the "real me" as better than the me you see. This normative, non-empirical or 'ideal' nature can be rooted in an ideal past (Eden, the Founding Fathers) or in the command of God, or perhaps in the future toward which one holds that we are moving or should move.[13]

This second family is not rooted in the way things are, and therefore it is capable of being more critical, or even subversive, of existing realities. But the way ethical guidance is derived from such an understanding of nature is still complex and confusing. It is certainly not a simple deduction from examination of the world around us and its potentialities. Yet even after all necessary cautions and qualifications have been made, Yoder still believed that arguments from nature have a necessary place in moral discernment. Nonetheless, *Christian* ethics must never sacrifice the priority of the call and demand of Jesus, or forget that what Jesus demanded was and is *unreasonable* behavior.

"There is the need in public life [not only in politics] for a common de-
nominator language in order to collaborate with relative strangers in
running the world despite our abiding differences," Yoder acknowledged.
But he was rather reluctant to spell out how this shared language is related to the gospel, whether it is separate and independent, and how, if at
all, it relates to the call to discipleship. Yoder recognized the need for
some common language of morals, but he argued that this common morality is limited and needs constantly to be challenged and enriched by
insights from Christian discipleship. Christians need in discussion with
non-Christians to decide what the right thing to do is. "In ethics," he
wrote, "we have to act, and sometimes act together, by the nature of the
issue. Scarce resources cannot be spent everywhere. Life will be taken or
spared; we can't have it both ways."[14] In such situations we cannot simply
appeal to the Bible, to Christian doctrine, or to a command of God without giving reasons. Yoder was deeply suspicious of claims that natural
law on its own can provide an adequate "neutral" structure for such decision-making discussions.

Yoder then pushed the argument further:

> The function of the notion of "nature" in medieval Catholic thought was
> *not* the modern one of knowing how to talk with outsiders. . . . The appeal
> to "nature" was an instrument of *less* rather than *more* commonality with
> non-Christians. . . . The concern with "nature" then bespoke not a grow-
> ing readiness to converse with others in non-Christian language, but
> rather a growing conviction that the way Christians see reality is the way it
> really is. But the way to affirm our respect for others is to respect their
> particularity and learn their languages, not to project in their absence a
> claim that we see the truth of things with an authority unvitiated by our
> particularity.[15]

Yoder was thus uneasy also about an ethical method that starts from
the universal and expects the particular to conform. "The Biblical story
and the Biblical world view," he argued, "widen out from the particular
to take in the general, not the other way 'round."[16] And so it should be
with moral reasoning. It should start not from principles with a claim to
universality, nor from moral laws, but from specific cases, issues, and
commands of God. Yoder would have found himself siding with Mahatma Gandhi against Immanuel Kant in that Gandhi implied a rejection of the Kantian stress on "universalizing one's maxim"; instead,
Gandhi asserted that when one is facing an awkward moral choice, the
thing to do is to recall the face of the poorest and weakest person one

may have seen and ask if the step one contemplates is going to be of any use to that person.

"The reason I do not trust claims to 'natural insight,'" Yoder wrote, "is that the dominant moral views of any *known* world are oppressive, provincial, or (to say it theologically) 'fallen.'"[17] Yoder was less likely than Barth to argue that natural law introduces a different lord, at odds with the lordship of Christ. But both agreed that ethics for Christians, and in principle for all, is ultimately a matter of obedience to the command and call of the living God as made known in Jesus Christ, rather than the falling back on a set of rules, principles, or laws that claim universal validity.

Ethics, for Yoder, was thus primarily a matter of obedience to the command and example of Jesus in concrete situations in relation to specific issues and challenges. Nature and natural law too easily lend a spurious universality and absoluteness to the assumptions of the age. When Yoder spoke of nature and human nature, he usually stressed the need to transform nature, to challenge nature with grace, rather than speaking about some sort of complementarity between nature and grace or of "nature" as having some kind of inherent normative status.

GOSPEL AND LAW

Yoder was suspicious of the traditional distinction and relationship between law and gospel, particularly as Martin Luther and nineteenth-century Lutherans expounded it. In the Lutheran tradition, law and gospel operate on different, usually opposed, principles in separate spheres largely independent of one another. Yoder's position can be expounded as giving priority to the gospel over the law. In some ways echoing Barth's affirmation that dogmatics is ethics,[18] Yoder spoke of social ethics as gospel, or "The Kingdom as Social Ethics." The inner or true nature of law, he claimed, is the gospel. The law is essentially the command and call of the gracious God, which are themselves expressions of grace. The law is not independent of the gospel, or opposed to the gospel, or merely a preliminary to the gospel. Both law and gospel have at their heart the same gracious reality. And that means that grace, forgiveness, encouragement, and hope rather than limitation, threat, and despair are the core of the law. "Normal Christian moral discourse," he wrote, "should be about enablement more than prohibition; about law as a form of grace, not a polar alternative to it; about pardon more than duty."[19] Forgiveness and reconciliation are in fact an integral part of a Christian understanding of justice. Both criminal and social justice are directed toward the restoration of fellowship and the healing of relationships. Obedience to God's law is, Yoder suggested, a way of proclaiming the gospel.

For Yoder, the law is enriched and clarified by the gospel. Apart from the gospel, the law becomes destructive. A system of criminal law, for instance, that is not open to the possibility of forgiveness and reconciliation makes situations and people worse rather than better. Law and gospel do not operate in separate, insulated spheres. When Christians discuss legal matters or apply the law, they must not leave the gospel behind, for that would be to deny what is indeed the heart of the law.

CHURCH AND ETHICS

Disciples are never alone, Yoder insisted; they are always part of the church, which is the body of Christ. Most theology in the aftermath of World War II was ecclesial and deeply rooted in the life of the church. But Yoder brought to the fore a rather different emphasis in his understanding of the church. The true church for him was the *free* gathered church, which regards minority status as a challenge and an opportunity rather than a disaster. Since Constantine, Yoder argued, the church and the world had been fused; now it was again possible to distinguish them and spell out the responsibilities of the church toward the world, which are essentially to proclaim and to exemplify the gospel rather than attempting to impose a law. As an evangelical theologian, Yoder saw scripture as it is interpreted within the community of faith—rather than the academy—as at the heart of discipleship and proclamation. What Barth called "the strange new world of the Bible" is always, Yoder believed, in tension with the cultural and political assumptions of every age. The church's language must always be culture-critical and politically constructive. Yoder presented his mature work as "a late ripening, in the field of ethics, of the same biblical realist revolution, in which precisely ecclesiology and eschatology come to have a new import for the substance of ethics."[20]

The church, according to Yoder, is an alternative community in which disciples and people of virtue—or rather of holiness—are formed. In Nancey Murphy's words, it is "a laboratory for imagining and practicing new forms of social life."[21] Yoder called the church "a hermeneutic community."[22] It is a creative minority in diaspora, rather than sheltering in a ghetto, and witnessing to and exemplifying the loving community that is to come. Yoder asserted very strongly "the paradigmatic role of the people of God in offering the world a vision of God's restoration of humanity, in Christ, in the faith community, and beyond."[23] This goal is accomplished through the various distinctive practices of the community—baptism, eucharist, discipline, and the like—that sustain the life of the community and are exemplary for the broader society.[24] Worship is, Yoder suggested, "the communal cultivation of an alternative construction of society and of history."[25]

Yoder emphatically did not regard the church as a fellowship of moral giants, or of those whose behavior and virtues are exemplary. Nor did he understand the church as being beyond error and sin. Christians, members of the church, are not Pharisees, trusting in their own righteousness, but rather forgiven sinners, people who know themselves to be offenders and rely on God's grace and the experience of forgiveness. For this reason, like most Reformed Christians, he regarded a structure of "discipline" as essential to the faithful being of the church, as a "mark" of the true church. Yoder used the typical Mennonite term for ecclesiastical discipline—"binding and loosing"—as a power and a task given to the Mennonite Church whereby members who fall into sin may be brought back to the true path and find reconciliation and forgiveness. Yoder himself in his last years was disciplined in this way, and after showing penitence he was forgiven by the community and restored to fellowship.

To grasp the implications of Yoder's ecclesiology, it is useful to bring him into conversation with his disciple and colleague, Stanley Hauerwas. Yoder sometimes came close to reiterating Stanley Hauerwas's rather triumphalistic slogan, "The Church does not have, but is, a social ethic."[26] For neither in works nor in grace are we alone, rather in fellowship. Yoder was more cautious than Hauerwas, and more sensitive to the dangers of ecclesiastical triumphalism, however. In Yoder's words, "The new peoplehood constituted by the grace to which the readers of these [apostolic] texts had responded is *by its very essence* a message to the surrounding world."[27] The message is grace, and the church is a testimony to the triumph of grace. This position is to be welcomed for its rejection of the false individualism of the pietist tradition and the Enlightenment. But there are problems when we ask what message in fact is being communicated to the world by the empirical, fallible, and often bitterly divided churches of this or any age.

"The church does not have, but is, a social ethic," an epigram worthy of Yoder himself, appears in many places in Hauerwas's writings.[28] It is a very attractive notion, suggesting that Christian ethics must be embodied in the life of a community, that ethics is not a possession of the church but the gift to the church that constitutes it. The church, for Hauerwas and for

Yoder, is a social ethic insofar as it is a "faithful manifestation of the peaceable Kingdom in the world."[29] Its first task is to *be* the church, a community that "can clearly be distinguished from the world."[30] It is shaped by a story that is sharply different from the world's story. "Its most important social function is *to be itself*."[31] It is called to be a community of the cross, and an alternative to the hostilities and divisions to be found elsewhere.

This is all heady stuff, to which one is tempted to say that the church that we know provides an empirical refutation: *that* church is not very much like the church of which Hauerwas and Yoder speak. Paradoxically, the virtues that they see as central to the Christian community are often exemplified in costly ways far from the orbit of the church. And is it not true that the actual visible church to which we belong falls far short of living up to its calling? This truth simply underlines the fact that the church must be a community of forgiven sinners who have learned to live by grace rather than a fellowship of moral heroes and virtuous achievers.

In itself, the existence of the body is a moral statement, a demonstration and exemplification of the ethic that is integral to the gospel. The behavior of the community confirms or questions the truth of the gospel that its members proclaim. The congregation, the body, the church is thus a kind of hermeneutic of the gospel. The message and the ethics are inseparable from the life of the church.

Within the body, divisions of hostility, suspicion, and competition are pathological and can destroy its vitality and integrity. Yet the unity and harmony of the body does not remove particularity, plurality, and difference; indeed, the former enhances and enriches the latter and blends them into a common purpose. In Christ, the old animosities and separations, as exemplified in the classic division between Jew and Gentile, are overcome. God's purpose is to create a single new humanity—the unity of the church is simply a sign and foretaste of the broader unity of humankind, which is God's goal. The unity of the church is therefore not simply for its own sake, a matter, perhaps, of streamlining church structures. The New Testament teaches that the way the church is structured and operates is to be at the service of the gospel and to confirm that gospel. Eucharist, baptism, and discipline mean that "the church can be a foretaste of the peace for which the world was made."[32] The church points to and already expresses in a partial way the coming unity of humankind. For Yoder, the being of the church is therefore a vital expression of the gospel and of the law, as well as a demonstration of the truth of the gospel and the validity of the law.

CHRISTOLOGY AND DISCIPLESHIP

Yoder said little about human nature, but much about Jesus Christ and much about discipleship. His anthropology, like Barth's, is christological: *Ecce Homo*, in Christ, and only in Christ, is true humanity to be found. The moral character of God and true humanity are revealed in Jesus. "God," Yoder wrote, "broke through the borders of man's definition of what is human, and gave a new, formative definition in Jesus."[33] In principle, the call to discipleship is universal, available for all, and at its heart is a challenge of obedience to Jesus Christ rather than to some universal law or set of principles. Humans are sinners, called to be disciples, and the real test is whether we follow and whether we obey. But in Yoder's understanding, the sin of human beings does not have the central place that it possesses in the Augustinian tradition and in modern times, especially perhaps in the theology of Reinhold Niebuhr. Sin is a problem, a defect, an issue that has to be faced and responded to with repentance and forgiveness. But it is not part of the essence of humanity.

According to Yoder, discipleship involves deep engagement with the life of the world and grappling with the issues and challenges of the world; it is not withdrawal to a ghetto or an isolated church. Yoder was thus moved to engage with the traditional theology of vocation, whereby God is understood as calling people to salvation and discipleship, and to a "secular" vocation or vocations in which discipleship is manifested in a particular sphere of life. Yoder was, however, unhappy about the classical understanding of vocation as presented, for instance, by Martin Luther. This understanding of vocation seems to offer a source of ethical challenge and opportunity alternative to the gospel, another source of moral authority not dissimilar to natural law, two spheres in which we find different, and sometimes contradictory, moral guidance.

Yoder's caution here is well taken. Luther's understanding of vocation has often been understood as effectively relegating rigorous discipleship to the private realm. In public affairs, the disciple is expected to follow the accepted standards and responsibilities of the office, which are the same for disciples and for nonbelievers. We have here an autonomous and independent ethics that is in fact secular, although it is capable of receiving a theological interpretation. And the standard theological account both affirms the God-givenness of the worldly structure of vocations and provides a ready-made justification for disciples doing things in their vocations that appear to be in stark contrast to the ethic of Jesus. Luther did not hesitate to affirm that the politician, Christian or not, is obliged in seeming contradiction to both law and gospel to resort to force, coercion, and violence. He, characteristically, took the argument to the extreme: "For the hand that wields this sword and slays with it is then no more man's hand, but God's, and it is not man, but God, who hangs, tortures, beheads, slays and fights. All these are His works and His judgments."[34]

In reaction to this extreme line of reasoning, Yoder seemed reluctant to engage fully with the fact that disciples are judges, and physicians, and police officers, and stockbrokers, and fulfill their discipleship in large part through their various "worldly" vocations. It is not enough to suggest that Christians should express "servanthood" in their various spheres of responsibility. A viable and convincing Christian ethic must address head-on the dilemmas and problems such people face day by day.

"To affirm the normativeness of discipleship is simply classical," Yoder wrote.[35] The way of discipleship, following Jesus, not any theory of human nature, exemplifies the truly human. Such an affirmation means that Jesus' vulnerable love of the enemy and renunciation of dominion comes to the center of the picture, as against the classical virtues of prudence, temperance, justice, and so on. People are defined by their relationships to God and to their neighbors, near and far.

MORAL DISCERNMENT

In discipleship within the community of faith, something of the true humanity that was fully manifested in Christ may be glimpsed. The household of faith needs a structure of discipline for shaping and reshaping disciples and for guiding believers in a life of servanthood. Within the community of faith, gathered around the table and the scriptures, a process of communal ethical discernment takes place, which is inseparable from the striving for faithful discipleship. Discipleship is understood as more radical, free, and distinctive involvement in public life than the "responsible involvement" advocated by the "Christian realists" and indeed by the World Council of Churches at its Amsterdam Assembly.

Reflection on issues of identity, character, and virtue leads directly to a recognition that these concepts are socially shaped. We do not choose or fashion afresh for ourselves accounts of virtue, character, and identity; we have to draw on resources that have not been devised by us as we develop our characters, learn how to seek virtue, and refashion our identity. These things arise in communities that are stewards of a tradition, that constantly tell and retell a story, that nurture new generations. We situate ourselves, we decide who we are, and we establish guidelines for moral behavior by reference to the communities to which we belong and to the tradition we have inherited.

Any great community of shared faith, such as the Christian Church, has at its heart a canonical story that is constantly examined and reinterpreted, and that presents a rich mosaic of models of virtue and vice. Out of this process of retelling, of criticism, and of debate comes a tradition of disciplined reflection on the kinds of behavior which are praiseworthy or to be deplored. The community nurtures new generations by inducting them into the story and thus into the community. All communities of shared faith and commitment are concerned with the moral formation of their members. Most are also concerned with reformation, because human lives are so easily distorted.

When we speak about the church as a moral community, we do not mean simply that it is a forum for serious moral discourse—although the church ought to be that, contributing insights from its heritage to public debate and deciding how to witness to the truth of the gospel in the way it organizes its life. The church is also concerned with the moral formation and reformation of believers, so that they may live lives of virtue: "Let your light so shine before others that they may see your good works and give glory to your Father in heaven."[36] The church must attend to Christian values and how these may be best expressed in acts and in social structures, as well as to commands and principles that take a concrete form. And in many ways most important of all, the church offers a moral vision that enables discernment and a distinctive way of seeing. All of these elements are necessary if the church is to be a lively moral community.

The church that is holy is a communion of saints, of holy people. Saints are not people who have arrived at some plateau of moral achievement, but people on a journey together who have learned and are still learning to live by grace. Characteristically, Christian saints are regarded by others as good people but know themselves to be sinners constantly in need of forgiveness. The community shapes and sustains the individuals in their discipleship, and they in their turn are the agents and representatives of the church. The way a church is structured and operates expresses an ethic and is morally formative.

Yoder rarely spoke in terms of virtue ethics, but he agreed that ethics is not at its heart simply a matter of dealing with quandaries and ethical choices. It is about character, *habitus*, a way of life, an orientation of the whole person. He saw the ethical life as the life of discipleship, as responding to the call and command and example of Jesus Christ. Moral formation takes place in community through education, the discipline of binding and loosing, and the ongoing worship of the congregation.

Yoder was uncomfortable with the commonly affirmed position that there is an ugly ditch between the ethics of Jesus and that of the early church. It was important for Yoder to challenge this ethical duality, partly because it has been used to suggest that, since the early church found the "absolutist ethics" of Jesus impossible to apply, modern Christians are also permitted to compromise or even abandon the ethics of Jesus as a challenging possibility. As Søren Kierkegaard suggested, "Most people really believe that the Christian commandments (e.g., to love one's neighbor as oneself) are intentionally a little too severe—like putting the clock on half an hour to make sure of not being late in the morning."[37]

Yoder responded with a vigorous, but not fully convincing, counterattack to this view of Christian ethics as an impossible standard. The ugly ditch between the ethical thinking of Jesus and the compromises of the early church does not exist. In fact, the household tables (*Haustafeln*) of the epistles, which are often cited as ethical compromises with the standards of the contemporary context, express rather "the revolutionary innovation in the early Christian style of ethical thinking for which there is no explanation in borrowing from other contemporary cultural sources."[38] These household tables do not simply confirm the hierarchical structures of the broader society by instructing slaves to be obedient, wives to obey their husbands, and so on; rather, according to Yoder, "The *subordinate* person in the social order is *addressed as a moral agent.* He is called upon to take responsibility for the acceptance of his position in society as meaningful before God."[39] In other words, people who have no independent moral status in the culture and society are declared to have personal moral responsibility before God in a manner that is subtly corrosive of the hierarchical moral order in which they find themselves. Their position in society is not a matter of fate, to be passively accepted, but a destiny, and even a vocation, a context in which they may witness to the freedom of the gospel and the liberation they have received in Christ.[40]

ESCHATOLOGY AND ETHICS

Yoder resisted the liberal assumption that the language of eschatology and the apocalypse has had its day and is no longer relevant. He would have suggested, I feel, that in the world after September 11, 2001, we must perforce fall back on apocalyptic language, so laden with calls to action and to doxology, if we are to understand and engage as Christians with today's realities.[41] The language with which the Bible, particularly the New Testament, is peppered about principalities and powers, angels and demons, thrones and dominions, seemed, to many liberal exegetes, to be "obscure mythology" that should and must now be dispensed with. But when Christians had to struggle with the manifest evil of Nazism and the language of nature seemed inadequate, they turned to these themes in the Bible and found in them clues and guidance as to how to respond faithfully and well to Hitler's evil tyranny. This particular symbolic structure sprang back to life.[42] It seemed to provide meaning and guidance. It was a symbolic structure in which many people found they could live.

The apocalyptic, as it were, comes to life, is reborn, in times of crisis.[43] Characteristically, it arises among groups that despair about the conditions of the present world order and believe in its imminent destruction or overthrow.[44] The apocalyptic has three functions that are particularly relevant to our present discussion. First, the apocalyptic claims to reveal, unveil, make manifest the inner reality of what is actually happening in the world today. It is concerned to understand things as they are now, not simply to predict the future.[45] It seeks to discern what is happening in history, and what God is calling God's people to do. The powers of evil that have presented themselves as angels of light are unmasked, and believers are enabled to discern what is really happening. Second, the apocalyptic denies the finality and acceptability of the existing order of things. The pretensions of rulers and dominant authorities are cut down to size and relativized. The apocalyptic declares that the existing powers that be are not the final manifestation of God's purposes; their days are numbered. An alternative order in which the weak and the excluded will have an honored place is not only possible but is also promised, and it will break in and disrupt the existing order. And, third, the apocalyptic nourishes a confident hope not only that things *can* be different, but that they *will* be different, for if believers are faithful God will bring out of the present disorder a new era that will be characterized by peace and justice and the vindication of the oppressed.

In much apocalyptic literature, as in the book of Revelation, alongside a radical political critique there is much imagery of a holy war. In this war, martyrs are the real victors, despite appearances. The holy war may be a spiritual or a real conflict; God may take the initiative, or call on the saints to wage war on God's behalf. And "waging war" may simply be a metaphor for keeping the faith in times of persecution. But the Christian nature of an authentically Christian apocalyptic is represented, according to Yoder, by the centrality in the book of Revelation of the triumphant Lamb that has been slain and is praised by the faithful, singing a new song.[46]

There are, of course, specific problems associated with a lively apocalyptic worldview. In the first place, the dualism of Jerusalem and Babylon (or their equivalents in other systems of apocalyptic thought) presents as central to its radical political critique a polarization between absolute evil and absolute good, which is at the least a colossal simplification of any actual situation in the world. It can breed a very dangerous and unqualified self-righteousness. And these distortions can have a malign effect on political judgments—as can a relativism that hesitates to make a clear distinction between good and evil. A second major problem is that, although much apocalyptic thought encourages the saints to be patient until God brings their deliverance, other forms encourage the faithful to take things into their own hands, so that they understand themselves as saints combating and destroying unqualified evil in the name of God and at the direct command of God. This is not a conception that I find in the book of Revelation or as a significant element in Jewish and Christian apocalyptic generally.

More positively, apocalyptic thought holds out an open future and offers hope to the poor, the powerless, and the excluded. Its message to the powerful, the prosperous, and the complacent is one of judgment and a challenge to hear the uncomfortable word that the Spirit is saying to the churches. Apocalyptic language is language of people who feel themselves weak, marginalized, oppressed, and forgotten.[47] It is a language of hope for change, and it is language of judgment. It is language that motivates powerfully, for good or ill, and it is language that polarizes between Jerusalem and Babylon, the good and the evil, the saints and the wicked, in a quite Manichaean way. This kind of polarization is always, of course, a huge simplification at the very least. In the real world we have always to deal in subtle shades of gray rather than a contrast between black and white. But sometimes we need to highlight the awfulness of evil or the wonder of goodness. The temptation simply to dismiss it all as irrational and pathological should be resisted, as should the temptation of simply reversing the polarization of radical evil and radical good. We have to deal with it discerningly and sensitively, if we are to respond wisely.

Yoder's vindication of a Christian apocalyptic goes right to the heart of his theological/ethical project:

> To see history doxologically meant for John's addressees that their primordial role within the geopolitics of the *Pax Romana* was neither to usurp the throne of Nero or Vespasian, Domitian or Trajan, nor to pastor Caesar prophetically, but to persevere in celebrating the Lamb's lordship and in building the community shaped by that celebration. They were participating in God's rule over the cosmos, whatever else they were or were not allowed by the civil powers to do. That it was not given them to exercise

those other more blatantly "powerful" roles—whether assassinating Trajan or becoming his chaplain—was not for them either a renunciation or a deprivation. They considered themselves to be participating in ruling the world primordially in the human practices of doxological celebration—perhaps in Ephesus?—of which John's vision of the Heavenly Throne Hall is the projection. Some would take John's vision to mean "if we keep the faith through these tough times, in a century or two the tides will turn and we can dominate the Empire then the way Domitian does today." Others would think it meant: "If we keep the faith, the world as we know it will very soon be brought to a catastrophic end, and a new nonhistorical state of things will be set up, with us on top." Some would favor this latter interpretation because they are themselves enthusiasts, believing themselves to be on the brink of the final saving catastrophe, as its beneficiaries. Others would ascribe that meaning to John's vision in order to discredit it, since, after all, that catastrophic victory did not happen.

What then did the vision mean? "Neither of the above," we must respond. Each of those restatements is incompatible with the hymnic text.... Our strophe, the "new song" elicited by the work of the Lamb, describes the seer's present, the same age in which people of every tribe and tongue are being called into a new community. It is not about a future, either organic and therefore distant, or imminent and therefore catastrophic. It has to be taken as a statement about their own time, the late first or early second century, and about what they were then involved in doing.[48]

Or, again: "The point that apocalyptic makes is not only that people who wear crowns and who claim to foster justice by the sword are not as strong as they think.... It is that people who wear crosses are working with the grain of the universe ... by sharing the life of those who sing about the Resurrection of the slain Lamb."[49]

PEACE

The central, and nonnegotiable, ethical issue for Yoder and the peace churches, of course, was peace and nonviolence. This matter was for him an absolute beyond question. And in creating and sustaining peace the church has a central role. "The Church," he writes, "can be a foretaste of the peace for which the world was made. It is the function of minority communities to remember and to create utopian visions."[50]

There is at this point a problem that Yoder did not fully resolve. Accepting, as one must if one takes the New Testament seriously, that the ruling authorities receive their power from God and are "God's servants for your good,"[51] including in the use of the sword, it would appear clear that there is a place in God's ordering for the use of coercion and state-sanctioned violence in police action, in criminal law, and—in extreme cases—in war. One may accept that violence has no place in the life of disciples or in the church. But what happens when disciples are the rulers? Is it then legitimate for them to use the sword? And, following this line of argument, does Yoder not explicitly have to acknowledge a distinction between the sphere of the gospel, where violence has no place, and the sphere of law, where violence and coercion persist in a fallen world as the ultimate sanctions?

Barth combined a rejection of "principled pacifism" with a thoroughgoing critique of war and political violence and was a stout nuclear pacifist after World War II. But through his understanding of the *Grenzfall,* or "boundary situations," he left open a chink allowing Christians to take up arms in extreme situations, such as a threat to the independence of Switzerland! In relation to Nazism, Barth in 1940 issued a resounding, unambiguous call to arms. In his *Letter to Great Britain from Switzerland* he declared, "The obedience of the Christian to the clear will of God compels him to support this war."[52] During the Cold War period, Barth disagreed with those who saw close parallels between Nazism and Bolshevism and argued strongly in favor of nuclear disarmament.

Yoder was, in a way, far more consistent in his commitment to peaceableness in all circumstances than was Barth. Perhaps this unswerving commitment makes Yoder an ethical absolutist rather than a situationalist or one who believes that the specific command of the living God is not the same in every context and cannot be confidently predicted.

Yoder engaged with great penetration and cogency with traditional just war thinking and with the thought on war and peace of Karl Barth, Reinhold Niebuhr, and Paul Ramsey in particular.[53] Yoder was sympathetic with Barth's move to the very fringe of a pacifist commitment in the Cold War period, and even with his reluctance to adopt "principled pacifism" of a sort that might limit the freedom of the God who commands. Yoder saw Niebuhr as failing to allow his "Christian realism" to be controlled entirely by the gospel. Like much just war thinking, Christian realism, Yoder felt, is too prudential and unwilling to give absolute priority to the challenge of Jesus' nonviolence.

For Yoder, our attitude to the enemy is the test of whether we really love our neighbor, and a willingness to refrain absolutely from violence seemed to be for him the central test of discipleship. His arguments are challenging and must be taken seriously. But once more it needs to be said that he did not really engage with the fact that in the post-Constantinian era disciples are still often responsible for others and must sometimes make decisions that are necessary rather than good, and that force them to fall back on the divine grace. Nor did Yoder totally convincingly show that nonviolence and peace must have the centrality in Christian ethics in a fallen world that he claimed. Yet he was, and looks set to continue to be, one of the most significant, radical, socially committed, and creative theologians of our time.

NOTES

1. Mark Thiessen Nation, "John H. Yoder, Ecumenical Neo-Anabaptist: A Biographical Sketch," in *The Wisdom of the Cross: Essays in Honor of John Howard Yoder*, ed. Stanley M. Hauerwas, Mark Thiessen Nation, Chris K. Huebner, and Harry J. Huebner (Grand Rapids, Mich.: Eerdmans, 1999), 3. Nation's essay provides a good brief biography of Yoder.

2. See the following works by Thomas L. Shaffer: "The Radical Reformation and the Jurisprudence of Forgiveness," in *Christian Perspectives on Legal Thought*, ed. Michael W. McConnell, Robert F. Cochran Jr., and Angela C. Carmella (New Haven, Conn.: Yale University Press, 2001), 321–339; *On Being a Christian and a Lawyer: Law for the Innocent* (Provo, Utah: Brigham Young University Press, 1981); "Maybe a Lawyer Can Be A Servant; If Not . . . ," *Texas Tech Law Review* 27 (1996): 1345–1357; "Faith Tends to Subvert Legal Order," *Fordham Law Review* 66 (1998): 1089–1099; and "Legal Ethics and Jurisprudence from Within Religious Congregations," *Notre Dame Law Review* 76 (2001): 961–992.

3. On Yoder's relation to Hauerwas and his other "disciples," see especially Arne Rasmusson, "Historicizing the Historicist: Ernst Troeltsch and Recent Mennonite Theology," in Hauerwas et al., *The Wisdom of the Cross*, 213–248, and Stanley Hauerwas, "Remembering John Howard Yoder," *First Things* 82 (April 1998): 15–16.

4. John Howard Yoder, "Karl Barth, Post Christendom Theologian," http://www. nd.edu/~theo/jhy/writings/philsystheo/barth.htm.

5. See John Howard Yoder, *The Pacifism of Karl Barth* (Scottsdale, Pa.: Herald Press, 1968), and *Karl Barth and the Problem of War* (Nashville, Tenn.: Abingdon, 1970).

6. Yoder, "Karl Barth, Post Christendom Theologian."

7. Richard B. Hays, *The Moral Vision of the New Testament: A Contemporary Introduction to New Testament Ethics* (Edinburgh: T & T Clark, 1997), 239, 246.

8. Yoder translated Hendrik Berkhof's seminal *Christ and the Powers* (Scottsdale, Pa.: Herald Press, 1962) and anticipated Walter Wink's work on "the Powers" by some thirty years. I discuss this matter in *Beliefs, Values, and*

Policies: Conviction Politics in a Secular Age (Oxford: Clarendon Press, 1989), chap. 5.

9. Hays, *Moral Vision*, 249.

10. Ibid., 243.

11. See especially Yoder's unpublished paper, "Regarding Nature," http://www.nd.edu/~theo/jhy/writings/philsystheo/nature.htm. See also John Howard Yoder, *Christian Attitudes to War, Peace and Revolution: A Companion to Bainton* (Elkhart, Ind.: Peace Resource Center, 1983).

12. Yoder, "Regarding Nature."

13. Ibid.

14. Ibid.

15. John Howard Yoder, *The Priestly Kingdom: Social Ethics as Gospel* (Notre Dame, Ind.: University of Notre Dame Press, 1984), 42.

16. Yoder, "Regarding Nature."

17. Yoder, *The Priestly Kingdom*, 40.

18. Karl Barth, *Church Dogmatics*, 4 vols. (Edinburgh: T & T Clark, 1956–1975), 1:782ff.

19. John Howard Yoder, "'Patience' as Method in Moral Reasoning: Is an Ethic of Discipleship 'Absolute'?" in Hauerwas et al., *The Wisdom of the Cross*, 42.

20. John Howard Yoder, *The Politics of Jesus: Vicit Agnus Nostra* (Grand Rapids, Mich.: Eerdmans, 1972), 5–6.

21. Nancey Murphy, "John Howard Yoder's Systematic Defense of Christian Pacifism," in Hauerwas et al., *The Wisdom of the Cross*, 60.

22. Yoder, *The Priestly Kingdom*, 117.

23. Yoder, "Karl Barth, Post Christendom Theologian."

24. John Howard Yoder, "Sacrament as Social Process: Christ the Transformer of Culture," *Theology Today* 48 (1991): 33–44.

25. Yoder, *The Priestly Kingdom*, 43.

26. See, for example, Hauerwas, *The Peaceable Kingdom: A Primer in Christian Ethics* (London: SCM Press, 1983), 99.

27. John Howard Yoder, *For the Nations: Essays Public and Evangelical* (Grand Rapids, Mich.: Eerdmans, 1997), 41.

28. For a fuller discussion, see Duncan B. Forrester, "The Church and the Concentration Camp: Some Reflections on Moral Community," in *Faithfulness and Fortitude: In Conversation with the Theological Ethics of Stanley Hauerwas*, ed. Mark Thiessen Nation and Samuel Wells (Edinburgh: T & T Clark, 2000), 189–207.

29. Hauerwas, *The Peaceable Kingdom*, 99, quoted in Forrester, "The Church and the Concentration Camp," 205.

30. Stanley Hauerwas, *Christian Existence Today: Essays on Church, World, and Living in Between* (Durham, N.C.: Labyrinth Press, 1988), 101.

31. Stanley Hauerwas, *Vision and Virtue: Essays in Christian Ethical Reflection* (Notre Dame, Ind.: University of Notre Dame Press, 1981), 240.

32. Yoder, *The Priestly Kingdom*, 93–94.

33. Yoder, *Politics of Jesus*, 101.
34. Martin Luther, "Whether Soldiers, Too, Can Be Saved," trans. C. M. Jacobs, in *Works of Martin Luther*, 6 vols. (Philadelphia: Holman, 1915–1932), 5:36.
35. Yoder, *The Priestly Kingdom*, 8 (emphasis added).
36. Matthew 5:16 (NRSV).
37. Søren Kierkegaard, *The Journals of Søren Kierkegaard*, ed. and trans. Alexander Dru (London: Fontana, 1958), 142.
38. Yoder, *Politics of Jesus*, 174.
39. Ibid.
40. Ibid., 174–190.
41. See especially Yoder, *The Politics of Jesus*, chap. 12 ("The War of the Lamb") and "To Serve Our God and to Rule the World," *Annual of the Society for Christian Ethics* (1988): 3–14.
42. For a fuller discussion, see Forrester, *Beliefs, Values, and Policies*, 70–74.
43. H. H. Rowley, *The Relevance of Apocalyptic: A Study of Jewish and Christian Apocalypses from Daniel to the Revelation*, 2d ed. (London: Butterworth, 1947), 8.
44. Christopher Rowland, *The Open Heaven: A Study of Apocalyptic in Judaism and Early Christianity* (London: SPCK, 1982), 1–2.
45. Ibid., 2.
46. See Yoder, "To Serve Our God."
47. On this see especially the sociological literature on millenarianism, such as Norman Cohn, *The Pursuit of the Millennium: Revolutionary Millenarians and Mystical Anarchists of the Middle Ages* (London: Paladin, 1970).
48. Yoder, "To Serve Our God."
49. John Howard Yoder, "Armaments and Eschatology," quoted in Stanley Hauerwas, *With the Grain of the Universe* (London: SCM Press, 2002), 6.
50. Yoder, *The Priestly Kingdom*, 94.
51. Romans 13:4 (NRSV).
52. Karl Barth, *A Letter to Great Britain from Switzerland* (London: Sheldon, 1941), 9. On Barth on war, see especially Rowan Williams, "Barth, War and the State," in *Reckoning with Barth: Essays in Commemoration of the Centenary of Karl Barth's Birth*, ed. Nigel Biggar, 170–190 (London: Mowbray, 1988).
53. See Michael G. Cartwright, "Sorting the Wheat from the Tares: Reinterpreting Reinhold Niebuhr's *Interpretation of Christian Ethics*," in Hauerwas et al., *The Wisdom of the Cross*, 349–372; John Howard Yoder, *When War Is Unjust: Being Honest in Just-War Thinking*, 2d ed. (Maryknoll, N.Y.: Orbis Books, 1996); and Hauerwas, *Vision and Virtue*, 197–221.

ORIGINAL SOURCE MATERIALS

REGARDING NATURE

Why is the Particular No Longer Respectable?

We call "modernity" the notion that there has been a normative historical development which has left its origins behind and become self-authenticating. We call "secularity" the world view which claims to make sense of present meaning without reference to the transcendent dimensions of cultural origins. We may call "cosmopolitan" or "pluralistic" a culture in which you may only participate if you outgrow the "provincial" or "ghetto" qualities of your cultural background. This is partly because there are people out there who do not respect your scriptures or your rabbis; it is even more so because the liberal political settlement forbids the shared polity to deal with religion. We are further embarrassed by the memories of empire, whereby one particular culture, namely that of a European elite, was imposed by force of arms and commerce on other peoples.

How This Formulation Makes Reasonable Dialogue More Difficult

The distinction between truths which are particular and truths which are for all assumes that the line between them is clear. Yet when Roman Catholics are told by "pro-choice" advocates that they should not impose their denominational convictions on the whole society, they respond that "the sacredness of the life of the fetus is not a Catholic truth but a natural one." To say that to kill a fetus is homicide is not a religious statement. It is true for everyone. But how do you get the others to accept your vision of truth as true for them? To call that truth claim "natural" identifies the kind of claim you are making but it does not help to convince.

The matter becomes not only complex but paradoxical when we add the claim, which is historically credible . . . that the appeal to nature is itself a Catholic doctrine. A second dimension of paradox is that the very notion of "natural law" posits the access of all people of good will to these truths, yet in fact most people do not see them, so that after all they need to be told them by the Catholic magisterium.

Sorting Out the Varieties of "Nature" Claims

A much fuller catalog of the varieties of usage of the appeal to "nature" would be imperative, but to begin with we can say that they fall into two families. For the first large family, "nature" is the way things obviously are. The epistemology is simple, descriptive. Socially it is positivistic; the institutions of slavery, of patriarchy, of monarchy are obviously the way it is. Biologically it is also positivistic: contraception and artificial insemination interfere with the "natural" functioning of the body. Its first ethical impact is usually conservative, since the nation, the class structure, the marketplace, the repertory of roles or vocations is the way it is. The system will seem convincing as long as all parties have been educated under the same customs, so that they really think "everyone knows . . . " whatever they know, and as long as no skeptic draws attention to the is/ought equation. The appeal to nature in this sense works when there is no context.

This kind of argument can however be turned around and used against the consensus, when one chunk of the historical consensus can be read differently. The claim that homosexuality is "counter to nature" can be turned around by claiming that one's sexual capacities or inclinations are inborn.

The other large family of notions of "nature" is things as they ought to be, the essence of things as different from appearance, the "true nature" as contrast with the empirical one, the "real me" as better than the me you see. This normative non-empirical or "ideal" nature can be rooted in an ideal past (Eden, the Founding Fathers) or in the command of God, or perhaps in the future toward which one holds that we are moving or should move. Obviously the epistemology here is more complex than with the other family. This view is capable of being ethically critical, since its criteria are not drawn from the way things are. It is congenial with claiming that "an unjust law is no law," which enables civil disobedience (Martin Luther King Jr.) or the rejection of extant positive law. . . . Yet where does it get the knowledge by which it judges the present?

Other examples: social critics from the Czech Brethren of the 15th century to the English Diggers and Levellers of the 17th rejected social class distinctions on the basis of the equality of Eden:

When Adam delved
and Eve span
where was then the gentleman?

Thus both the ideal and the real, both the given and the critical, can and do claim to be "nature," the appeals are intrinsically contradictory, and can only be held together if a particular magisterium rules on which form fits where, and/or if the society is homogeneous so that awareness of the intrinsic logical contradictions does not arise.

The appeal to nature is mostly apt when it does not need to adjudicate in a setting of debate, and when it provides leverage or a safeguard over against some specific pitfall:

- against provincialism or the reproach of being in a ghetto
- against "heteronomous" or "alien" expectations
- against asking the impossible
- against exporting particular standards to another culture
- against hasty readings of "what everyone thinks"
- against interpreting Christian loyalty so as not to include everyone.

Trial Balance: What the "Nature" Appeal Cannot Do

- It cannot resolve the tension between the given and the critical;
- It cannot adjudicate debates between different definitions of the given.
- It cannot resolve the paradox of someone with a particular position telling others what they are supposed already naturally to know but in fact do not.
- It cannot ultimately keep the promise of offering security or validation through ontology i.e., resolving "ought" conflicts by an "is" claim.

The formal description of why "nature" arguments are needed does not deliver the specific ethical substance claims which we need for the purposes of social ethics:

- slavery is a given institution;
- the nation is a morally binding identity definition, which determines whom I may/should kill.
- a national enemy is to be killed;
- the role of a prince is to dominate and to kill.

All of these elements are traditionally at stake. Thus the "Just War Tradition" is one of the primary instances of "natural argument." Yet the people who today argue for "nature" language do not support them all.

Yet the fact that it cannot ultimately convince does not make it useless. The territory which the "nature" debate names, and the kinds of arguments it uses, still are usable, as long as one does not attempt:

- to give this wisdom normative weight over against Jesus;
- to use it to resolve a debate between incompatible worlds.

There are arguments appealing to general lessons of experience; e.g.:

A. Revolutionary tyranny cannot last, even though the US establishment and the CIA from Dulles to Reagan made "the evil empire" larger than life. Central dictatorship abandons via coercion and centralization its capacity to build a healthy society. A tyranny which lasts more than a few years becomes less able to terrorize and coerce, thanks to some honest human values, the corruption and selfishness of cadres, the post-ideological skepticism of the next generation of youth, the survival of ethnicity. . . .

B. *Noblesse oblige*; if you claim to be of superior moral stature, that entitles us to hold you to a higher standard.

C. Turn about is fair play; I can check whether you should have done (x) to me by asking whether you want me to do (x) to you; trading places is a moral epistemology. This is one naive lay form of what Kant escalates into the "categorical imperative."

Each of these modes of argument is in some sense "natural"; yet they do not fall into the pitfalls identified above. They cannot be used to adjudicate deep debates, and they do not claim to set Jesus aside.[1]

THE PRIESTLY KINGDOM

The Kingdom as Social Ethic

The alternative community discharges a modeling mission. The church is called to be now what the world is called to be ultimately. To describe their own community Jews and Christians have classically used terms like those claimed by the structures of the wider world: "people," "nation," "kingdom," even "army." These are not simply poetic figures of speech. They imply the calling to see oneself as doing already on behalf of the wider world what the world is destined for in God's creative purpose. The church is thus not chaplain or priest to the powers running the world: she is called to be a microcosm of the wider society, not only as an idea, but also in her function. Let us look at some examples:

1. The church undertakes pilot programs to meet previously unmet needs or to restore ministries which have collapsed. The church is more able to experiment because not all ministries need to pay off. She can take the risk of losing or failing, more than can those who are in charge of the state. Popular education, institutionalized medicine, and the very concept of dialogical democracy in the Anglo-Saxon world generalize patterns which were first of all experimented with and made sense of in free-church Christianity.

2. The church represents a pedestal or a subculture in which some truths are more evidently meaningful and some lines of logic can be more clearly spelled out than in society as a whole. The credibility and the comprehensibility of an alternative vision which does not always convince on the part of an individual original or "prophetic" person, is enormously more credible and comprehensible if it is tested, confirmed, and practiced by a community. This theme will be treated under another heading later.

3. The church exemplifies what has come to be called "sacramentality," which means that meanings which make sense on an ordinary level make more of the same kind of sense when they are embedded in the particular history of the witness of faith. Catholics now talk about the existence of the church as itself a "sacrament," in the sense that the church represents the kind of society that all of society ought to be. The church is able to be that because of the presence in her midst of witness and empowerment which are not in the same way accessible to the wider society. Sometimes this sacramental quality is read in the direction of saying about the church what one says about the rest of society. For instance, if in society we believe in the rights of employees, then the church should be the first employer to deal with workers fairly. If in the wider society we call for the overcoming of racism or sexism or materialism, then the church should be the place where that possibility first becomes real.

More striking and more concrete cases of "sacramentality" can be developed if we look at those specific activities which the church has more traditionally called "sacraments." Here the logic flows the other way; from what the sacrament means to what the world should be.

a. The Eucharist originally was and could again become an expression not only of the death of Christ for our sins but also of the sharing of bread between those who have and those who have not.

b. Baptism could again come to be, as it was in the New Testament, the basis of Christian egalitarianism, in the face of which male and female, barbarian and cultured, slave and free, etc., are all ascribed the same dignity.

c. The process of binding and loosing—i.e., deliberative morally accountable dialogue, dealing with offense and forgiveness (and thereby dealing with moral discernment)-may recover the connection with forgiveness and with decision-making which "church discipline" lost when it came to be tied with formal excommunication and the sanctions of hierarchical authority.

4. The church can be a foretaste of the peace for which the world was made. It is the function of minority communities to remember and to

create utopian visions. There is no hope for society without an awareness of transcendence. Transcendence [is] kept alive not on the grounds of logical proof to the effect that there is a cosmos with a hereafter, but by the vitality of communities in which a different way of being keeps breaking in here and now. That we can really be led on a different way is the real proof of the transcendent power which offers hope of peace to the world as well. Nonconformity is the warrant for the promise of another world. Although immersed in this world, the church by her way of being represents the promise of an- other world, which is not somewhere else but which is to come here. That promissory quality of the church's present distinctiveness is the making of peace, as the refusal to make war is her indispensable negative transcendence.[2]

The Forms of Ethical Discourse

What are the axioms of radical reformation ethics? Which of these matters the most will depend on the perspective of the interlocutor. The primary substantial criterion of Christian ethical decisions for the radical reformers is the humanity of Jesus of Nazareth. What he did is the primordial definition of the human obedience which God desires. There are issues concerning which his example gives us no guidance and for which other kinds of wisdom will be indispensable, but at those points where his example is relevant it is also revelatory and is not to be set aside in favor of other criteria.

Jesus was not only a model actor, but he was also a foundational teacher. He thereby incorporated into the body of guidance of which his disciples dispose an accumulation of wisdom which not only is predominantly Jewish in idiom and origin, but also no less Jewish at the points where he differed from some other Jewish traditions. That body of moral wisdom includes notions about nature and human nature, God and God's law, which can of course be classified in several types. General rules such as the love commandment, specific rules such as the prohibition of the oath or adultery, and parabolic examples combine to provide a rich repertory of tools for illuminating moral decision. This excludes any single-issue system whereby once one key theme is struck (law and gospel, or nature and grace, or love and justice, or providence, or creation, or vocation) the rest of ethics will unfold simply, almost deductively.

There would be no memory of Jesus if it had not been for the early communities' recording and interpreting his words in the ongoing process of defining the meaning of obedience in the first-century Mediterranean world. We have in the New Testament canon the ground floor of a few decades' experience. Stretching from then to the present we possess an additional nearly infinite accumulation of applications and interpretation. The extent to which various strata of these traditions can be fruitful for our guidance is a question too complex to unfold here. The radical reformation was with Protestantism in general in claiming that the canonical witness remains the baseline for judging subsequent evolution. Yet it would be a misinterpretation to be led at this point into a simple repetition of the naive sixteenth-century debate about Scripture versus the church.

The knowledge of the meaning for today of participation in the work of Christ is mediated ecclesiastically. The bridge between the words of Jesus or of the apostolic writings and obedience in the present is not a strictly conceptual operation, which could be carried out by a single scholar at his desk, needing only an adequate dictionary and an adequate description of the available action options. The promise of the presence of Christ to actualize a definition of his will in a given future circumstance (i.e., future to Jesus or to the apostolic writers) was given not to professional exegetes but to the community which would be gathered in his name (Matt. 18:19) with the specific purpose of "binding and loosing" (Matt. 18:18). Classical Protestantism tended to deny the place of this conversational process in favor of its insistence on the perspicuity and objectivity of the words of Scripture. Catholicism before that had provoked that extreme Protestant answer by making of this hermeneutical mandate a blank check which the holders of ecclesiastical office could use with relative independence. The free-church alternative to both recognizes the inadequacies of the text of Scripture standing alone uninterpreted, and appropriates the promise of the guidance of the Spirit throughout the ages, but locates the fulfillment of that promise in the assembly of those who gather around Scripture in the face of a given real moral challenge. Any description of the substance of ethical decision-making criteria is incomplete if this aspect of its communitarian and contemporary form is omitted.

A popular slogan which has become operative in the contemporary search to recapture the validity of the radical reformation tradition is the notion of the "hermeneutic community" . . . The Spirit, the gathering, and the Scripture are indispensable elements of the process. A technical exegete alone in his office could not replace the actual conversational process in empirical communities where the working of the Spirit is discerned in the fact that believers are brought to unity around this Scripture. This "hermeneutic" process of conversation will often not be done with much explicit self-awareness in terms of the styles of ethical discourse or meta-ethical self-criticism. It is thus not possible, as it is in some of the other traditions, to distill out of the body of ethical teachings a few very broad axioms from which the total system is derived. One could as an ethicist try to formulate such a distillate, but it would be the observer's own concoction and would not be recognized as representative of what really happens when two or three gather and find Christ speaking in their midst.

This gathering process is in one sense a situational ethic. It does not seek advance wisdom on problems not being faced. It takes off immediately from a problem or an offense.[3]

The Constantinian Sources of Western Social Ethics

From Genesis to Apocalypse, the meaning of history had been carried by the people of God as people, as community. Leadership *within* the people was dispersed (Moses, prophets, priests, judges). When kingship was introduced in order to be "like the other nations" it did not work long or well, and the king was not elevated above common humanity. Other rulers (Nebuchadnezzar, Cyrus, Caesar) were historically significant only as they have an incidental part in the history of the people of God. But the fact that with Constantine the civil sovereign becomes God's privileged agent is thus not merely a shift of accent but a change of direction.

A New Universality

After Constantine not only is the ruler the bearer of history; the nonsovereign ethical agent has changed as well. The "Christian" used to be a minority figure, with numerous resources not generally available to all people: personal commitment, regeneration, the guidance of the Holy Spirit, the consolation and encouragement of the brotherhood, training in a discipleship life-style. But now that Christianity is dominant, the bearer of history is Everyman—baptized but not necessarily thereby possessed of the resources of faith. Ethical discourse must now meet two more tests:

1. Can you ask such behavior of everyone? Are not servanthood and the love of enemy, or even contentment and monogamy, more than we have the right to expect of everyone? Is not the love ethic of the New Testament unrealistic, too heroic? The pressure builds rapidly for a duality in ethics. The "evangelical counsels" will be commended to the religious and the highly motivated. The "precepts," less demanding, will suffice for catechesis and the confessional. Two levels, two kinds of motivations and sanctions will be discerned, entailing different specific duties (contradictory ones, in fact, at points such as power, property, marriage, bloodshed, which were morally proper for the laity but not for the religious). Then the Reformation polemic against works righteousness and monasticism removed the upper, more demanding, level.

2. What would happen if everyone did it? If everyone gave their wealth away what would we do for capital? If everyone loved their enemies who would ward off the Communists? This argument could be met on other levels, but here our only point is to observe that such reasoning would have been preposterous in the early church and remains ludicrous wherever committed Christians accept realistically their minority status. For more fitting than "What if everybody did it" would be its inverse, "What if nobody else acted like a Christian, but we did?"

A New Value for Effectiveness A third dimension of the great reversal is the transformation of moral deliberation into utilitarianism. Minorities and the weak have numerous languages for moral discourse:

- conscience, intention, inspiration, and other similar "subjective" measures of right action;
- revelation, "nature," "wisdom," and other "received" standards;
- covenant, tradition, "style," reputation, training, and other "community-maintenance" criteria.

Each of these ways of moral reasoning has its logical and psychological strengths and limits. We cannot evaluate them here. Yet it is important that each can, in given circumstances, lead persons to act sacrificially, for the sake of others, or for the sake of a "cause" more important than the individual. Each can lift decision and action above immediate cost/benefit calculation. But once the evident course of history is held to be empirically discernible, and the prosperity of our regime is the measure of good, all morality boils down to efficacy. Right action is what works; what does not promise results can hardly be right.

Perhaps the most evident example of the dominion of this axiom is today's debate about revolution, liberation, and violence. Any ethic, any tactic, is, in the minds of many, self-evidently to be tested by its promised results. To them, the rejection of violence is morally sustainable only if nonviolent techniques are available which are able to promise an equally rapid "revolution." Again it would be petitionary to argue that the utilitarian world view is "wrong" or that an ethic of "principles" would be "right." For the present our concern is only to report that the dominance of the engineering approach to ethics, reducing all values to the calculation of pressures promising to bring about imperative results, is itself a long-range echo of the Constantinian wedding of piety with power; it is an approach foreign to the biblical thought world and makes no sense in a missionary situation where believers are few and powerless.

A New Metaphysic A fourth, more doctrinal implication of the Constantinian reversal must be named: it is the victory of metaphysical dualism. Historically the source of this view is predominantly Neoplatonism. But naming its source does not explain its success. Certainly one reason it took over was the usefulness of dualism to justify the new social arrangement and resolve the problems it raised. The church we see is not the believing community; the visible/invisible duality names, and thereby justifies, the tension. The dominant ethic is different from the New Testament in content (Lordship is glorified rather than servanthood) as in source (reason and the "orders of creation" are normative, rather than the particularity of Jesus' and the apostles' guidance). What could be easier than to reserve the ethics of love for the inward or for the personal, while the ethics of power are for the outward world of structures? Interiorization and individualization, like the developments of the special worlds of cult and meditation, were not purely philosophical invasions which took over because they were intellectually convincing. They did so also because they were functional. They explained and justified the growing distance from Jesus and his replacement by other authorities and another political vision than that of the Kingdom of God.[4]

WHEN WAR IS UNJUST

Making the Tradition Credible

Are there people who affirm that their own uncoerced allegiance as believers gives them strength and motivation to honor the restraints of the just-war tradition and to help one another to do so? This might be the only angle from which the development of the needed institutions could be fostered. Would believers commit themselves, and commit themselves to press each other, to be willing to enter the political opposition, or to resign public office, or to espouse selective objection? Does any church teach future soldiers and citizens in such a way that they will know beyond what point they cannot support an unjust war or use an unjust weapon?

Since the capacity to reach an independent judgment concerning the legality and morality of what is being done by one's rulers depends on information, which by the nature of the case must be contested, does the religious community provide alternative resources for gathering and evaluating information concerning the political causes for which their governments demand their violent support? What are the preparations being made to obtain and verify an adequately independent and reliable source of facts and of analytical expertise, enabling honest dissent to be so solidly founded as to be morally convincing? Is every independent thinker on his or her own, or will the churches support agencies to foster dissent when called for?

Neither the pacifist nor the crusader needs to study in depth the facts of politics in order to make a coherent decision. The person claiming to respect just-war rationality must do so, however, and therefore must have a reliable independent source of information. I have stated this as a question about the church, but it also applies to the society. Is there free debate? Are the information media free? Is opposition legitimate? Does the right of conscientious objection have legal recognition?

Are soldiers when assigned a mission given sufficient information to determine whether this is an order they should obey? If a person under orders is convinced he or she must disobey, will the command structure, the society, and the church honor that dissent? It is reported that in the case of the obliteration bombing of Dresden the pilots were not informed that it could hardly be considered a military target. For most of the rest of the just-war criteria factual knowledge is similarly indispensable.

Until today church agencies on any level have invested little effort in literature or other educational means to teach the just-war limitations. The few such efforts one sees are in no way comparable to the way in which the churches teach their young people about other matters concerning which they believe morality is important, such as sexuality. The understanding of the just-war logic that led American young men to refuse to serve in Vietnam came to them not primarily from the ecclesiastical or academic interpreters of the tradition but rather from the notions of fair play presupposed in our popular culture.

A Fair Test

Those who conclude, either deliberately or rapidly, that in a given situation of injustice there are no nonviolent options available, often do so in a way that avoids responsibility for any intensive search for such options. The military option for which they so quickly reach has involved a long lead time in training and equipping the forces. It demands the preparation of a special class of leadership, for which most societies have special schools and learning experiences. It demands costly special resources dependent on abundant government funding, and it demands broad alliances. It includes the willingness to lose lives and to take lives, to sacrifice other cultural values for a generation or more, and the willingness of families to be divided.

Yet the decision that nonviolent means will not work for comparable ends is made without any comparable investment of time or creativity, without comparable readiness to sacrifice, and without serious projection of comparable costs. The American military forces would not "work" if we did not invest billions of dollars in equipping, planning, and training. Why should it be fair to measure the moral claims of an alternative strategy by setting up the debate in such a way that that other strategy should have to promise equivalent results with far less financial investment and less planning on every level? The epigram of the 1960s—People give nonviolence two weeks to solve their problems and then say it has failed; they've gone on with violence for centuries, and it seems never to have failed-is not a pacifist argument. It is a sober self-corrective within just-war reasoning.

In sum, the challenge should be clear. If the tradition which claims that war may be justified does not also admit that in particular cases it may *not* be justified, the affirmation is not morally serious. A Christian who prepares the case for a justifiable war without being equally prepared for the negative case has not soberly weighed the *prima facie* presumption that any violence is wrong until the case for the exception has been made. We honor the moral seriousness of the nonpacifist Christian when we spell out the criteria by which the credibility of that commitment, shaped in the form of the just-war system, must be judged.[5]

THE POLITICS OF JESUS: VICIT AGNUS NOSTER

Trial Balance

... Relevance must be redefined. If it is not enough to say with the Reformation traditions that Jesus purges our will and dampens our pride, sending us back to follow the dictates of our "office" or "station" with greater modesty and thoroughness; if it is not enough to say with the Puritan traditions that we derive from Josiah and Theodosius the vision of a holy commonwealth constantly being reformed to approach increasingly the theocratic ideal; if it is not enough with the "natural law" to find our instructions in the givenness of the fallen world; if it is not enough with the quietist and sectarian traditions to let someone else take care of the world out there what can then be the shape of a reformulated social responsibility illuminated by the confession that it is Jesus who is Messiah who is Lord? Where are we called to an ethicist's repentance, i.e. to a reformulation of the thought patterns that underlie moral choice? I suggest that this reformulation must take five lines:

1. Recent systematic tradition tells us that we must *choose between the Jesus of history and the Jesus of dogma.*

If Jesus is the divine Word incarnate, then what we will be concerned about is the metaphysical transactions by means of which he saved humanity by entering into it. We will then leap like the creed from the birth of Jesus to the cross. His teachings and his social and political involvement will be of little interest and not binding for us.

If, on the other hand, we seek to understand the "Jesus of history" in his human context, as this is reconstructed by the historical disciplines, this will be in order to find a man like any other, a reforming rabbi fully within the limits attainable by our human explanations, who is sometimes mistaken, especially about the future, and whose authority over us will depend on what we ourselves can consent to grant to his teachings.

The nineteenth century chose the Jesus of history, until Albert Schweitzer showed us that Jesus "as he really was" really did take himself to be an apocalyptic figure and his age to be the one just before the New Order begins. Then the systematic tradition veered back to metaphysics, using literary criticism to demonstrate how the Gospel documents project onto Jesus the existential self-awareness of the young church-an awareness closely tied to the name of Jesus but not to his historical reality, so that if he hadn't really been who he was it wouldn't jeopardize anything of his "meaning for us."

If we confess Jesus as Messiah we must refuse this choice.

The Jesus of history is the Christ of faith. It is in hearing the revolutionary rabbi that we understand the existential freedom which is asked of the church. As we look closer at the Jesus whom Albert Schweitzer rediscovered, in all his eschatological realism, we find an utterly precise and practicable ethical instruction, practicable because in him the kingdom has actually come within reach. In him the sovereignty of Yahweh has become human history.

2. The systematic tradition tells us that we are obligated to *choose between the prophet and the institution.*

The prophet condemns and crushes us under his demand for perfection. He is right, ultimately, both in convincing us of our sinfulness and in pointing us toward the ideal which, although unattainable, must remain our goal. But as far as that social order is concerned which it is up to us to administer today and tomorrow, his demands are without immediate relevance. Love, self-sacrifice, and nonviolence provide no basis for taking responsibility in this world. Dependent upon the grace of God alone, one cannot act in history. Those who are called to assure the survival and the administration of institutions will therefore accept violence in order, one day, to diminish or eliminate it. They will accept inequality and exploitation with the goal of progressively combating them. This is a very modest task and one in which one dirties oneself, but an indispensable task if something worse is to be prevented. While respecting the prophet, the rest of us will choose the institution.

The new regime instituted by Jesus as Messiah forbids us to make this choice.

The jubilee which Jesus proclaims is not the end of time, pure event without duration, unconnected to either yesterday or tomorrow. The jubilee is precisely an *institution* whose functioning within history will have a precise practicable, limited impact. It is not a perpetual social earthquake rendering impossible any continuity of temporal effort, but a periodic revision permitting new beginnings.

3. The systematic tradition tells us to *choose between the catastrophic kingdom and the inner kingdom.*

Jesus announced the imminent certain end of history as an event which could happen tomorrow or which was, at the latest, sure to come soon after his death. The apostles maintained this intensity of expectation for a few decades but finally it had to be admitted that there had been a mistake about the date, or perhaps about what they were looking for so soon.

The other option begins by assuming that Jesus could not have been wrong. It must then be concluded that he was speaking of the kingdom of God and its coming only in order to teach, by means of the mythical language which was current in his time, about an inner, spiritual, existential kingdom, whose reality properly will always remain hidden to the eyes of the unbeliever and of the historian.

Once again if Jesus is the Christ we must refuse this choice.

The kingdom of God is a social order and not a hidden one. It is not a universal catastrophe independent of the will of men; it is that concrete jubilary obedience, in pardon and repentance, the possibility of which is proclaimed beginning right now, opening up the real accessibility of a new order in which grace and justice are linked, which men have only to accept. It does not assume time will end tomorrow; it reveals why it is meaningful that history should go on at all.

That men would refuse this offer and promise, pushing away the kingdom that had come close to them, this Jesus had also predicted. He was not mistaken.

4. The systematic tradition tells us we must *choose between the political and the sectarian.*

In the tradition of Ernst Troeltsch, Western theological ethics assumes that the choice of options is fixed in logic and for all times and places by the way the Constantinian heritage dealt with the question. Ei-

ther one accepts, without serious qualification, the responsibility of politics, i.e. of governing, with whatever means that takes, or one chooses a
withdrawn position of either personal-monastic, vocational or sectarian
character, which is "apolitical." If you choose to share fully in the duties
and the guilt of government, you are exercising responsibility and are
politically relevant; if you choose not to, it is because you think politics
is either unimportant or impure, and are more concerned for other matters, such as your salvation. In so doing you would have Jesus on your
side, but having Jesus on your side is not enough, for there are issues to
which Jesus does not speak. . . . We must therefore supplement and in effect correct what we learn from him, by adding information on the nature and the goodness of the specifically "political" which we gain from
other sources.

If Jesus is confessed as Messiah this disjunction is illegitimate. To say
that any position is "apolitical" is to deny the powerful (sometimes conservative, sometimes revolutionary) impact on society of the creation of
an alternative social group, and to overrate both the power and the manageability of those particular social structures identified as "political." To
assume that "being politically relevant" is itself a univocal option, so that
in saying "yes" to it one knows where one is going, is to overestimate the
capacity of "the nature of politics" to dictate its own direction.

Because Jesus' particular way of rejecting the sword and at the same
time condemning those who wielded it *was* politically relevant, both the
Sanhedrin and the Procurator had to deny him the right to live, in the
name of both their forms of political responsibility. His alternative was so
relevant, so much a threat, that Pilate could afford to free, in exchange for
Jesus, the ordinary Guevara-type insurrectionist Barabbas. Jesus' way is
not less but more relevant to the question of how society moves than is the
struggle for possession of the levers of command; to this Pilate and Caiaphas testify by their judgment on him. . . .

5. The tradition tells us we must *choose between the individual and the
social.*

The "ethics of the Sermon on the Mount" is for face-to-face personal encounters; for social structures an ethic of the "secular vocation" is needed.
Faith will restore the individual's soul, and Jesus' strong language about
love for neighbor will help with this; but then how a restored man should
act will be decided on grounds to which the radical personalism of Jesus
does not speak.

But Jesus doesn't know anything about radical personalism. The personhood which he proclaims as a healing, forgiving call to all is integrated
into the social novelty of the healing community. . . .

We could extend the list of traditional antinomies of which we must repent if we are to understand. Tradition tells us to choose between respect for persons and participation in the movement of history; Jesus refuses because the movement of history is personal. Between the absolute *agape* which lets itself be crucified, and effectiveness (which it is assumed will usually need to be violent), the resurrection forbids us to choose, for in the light of resurrection crucified agape is not folly (as it seems to the Hellenizers to be) and weakness (as the Judaizers believe) but the wisdom and power of God (I Cor. 1:22–25).[6]

"PATIENCE" AS A METHOD IN MORAL REASONING: IS AN ETHIC OF DISCIPLESHIP ABSOLUTE?

What I do deny is (1) that such hard cases should be made, as they tend to be, the *center* of ethical deliberation, as if the fundamental moral question were ever simply either (a) whether in an imperfect world we can't have everything we want or (b) in case of collision which values take priority.

What I do deny is (2) that such crunch decisions are prototypical: i.e., that they represent the essential nature of ethical deliberation, so that it is by lining up crunch cases that one can prove a point, with regard, for instance, to the morality of war or abortion or lying, or that it is by listing hard cases that one can best teach and learn ethics. As has been said more fully by a roster of colleagues (Stanley Hauerwas, James McClendon, Alasdair MacIntyre . . .) in the fields of philosophical and Christian ethics recently, such "quandarism," or "decisionism," or "punctualism" sets aside precisely those elements of moral discourse which are the most fundamental, those where the specificity of a Christian perspective counts the most, and those where there is the most room for improvement.

What I do deny is (3) that such casuistic crunch decisions are typical: i.e., that most people most of the time are making decisions of that kind, which test at their outer edges the applicability of basic rules. Most of the time the basic rules do suffice, once one has identified an issue honestly. To concentrate only on where the basic rules do not quite reach, or on hard cases where two basic rules are in inevitable collision, is precisely to concentrate on the atypical. "Hard cases make bad law." Preoccupation with looking for loopholes is one of the most insidious ways to undermine the claims of ordinary moral obligation, and the viability of ordinary community relationships.

What I do deny is (4) that powerful people have more crunch decisions than weak people or victimized people or middle-level people do. It is usually such questions as "what would you do if you were the president?" which people use to test how far general rules about love of the enemy can reach. Making the ruler the prototypic moral decider in that way is part of the Constantinian legacy to which our culture is heir. But the person in a position of much power is less torn between conflicting pressures and obligations than is the subordinate: the middle-level bureaucrat, the lieutenant or noncommissioned officer, the member of a team who shares equally in discussion but not in decision, the member of a minority whose priority wishes are never heard. Such middle-level people, who know enough to dissent but have less authority, are in the worse moral bind.

What I do deny is (5) that such casuistic crunch decisions are the definition of tragedy. Since Reinhold Niebuhr, the notion of "tragedy" has been cheapened by appealing to it as a way of self-justification when a person in political responsibility decides he must hurt someone (regularly an adversary; not himself) in order to serve someone else or some cause. Those are hard choices, although it is because of his desire to be able to make them his way (this usually is a masculine stance), rather than letting someone else make them otherwise, that the person in political responsibility got himself into that difficult position: to call them "tragedy" (or sometimes "courage") domesticates and exploits the concept. Its basic assumption, that moral obligation usually takes the form of a prohibition, in such a way that moral courage most of the time is a question of justifying exceptions, is itself anti-Judaic and unevangelical. To claim the label of "tragedy" for regularized and justified arrangements, whereby the defense of one's own interests is favored over the dignity or life of others, and further to claim, tacitly or overtly, that being "tragic" is itself a mark of being true, is a self-righteous abuse of language. It adds blasphemy to injury. It too is part of what has given "casuistry" a bad name. . . .

What I do deny is (6) that my critics are any more temperate or moderate, any less "absolute" than I, in what they consider decisive for obedience. They challenge my values because they prefer other values; but those other values are no less determining for them. After all, what they want to convince me of is that in the crunch case their values should overrule mine. They are willing to kill for their other values, as I am not. In the light of this fact about the lay of the land in the debate, the very popular use of terms like "ambiguity" or "ambivalence" to describe their view is misleading. Such terms seem to suggest fine differences of shading, debatable readings in complicated situations—but in fact the real choices usually being talked about are something very decisive and simple like bombing or not bombing a city.

What I do deny is (7) that these borderline cases are so probable, so frequent, and so predictable that we ought institutionally to honor them by planning ahead of time to be ready to respond to a worst-case projection of how bad it might be. To institutionalize readiness for war is already to deny that it is, as the theorists claim, an extreme last resort. One does not prepare ahead of time to be able to inflict overkill in a situation of last resort. Especially one does not delegate the decision about the cases which meet the logical requirements for the extreme case to professional Pentagon people running through the provisions of their briefing books.

Thus the very fact of institutionalizing the readiness to do something extreme means that it is no longer truly being considered extreme. It has been brought into the realm of the thinkable and therefore of the likely. Not only has it been built into a hypothetical scenario; it has been written up as an authorized "standard operating procedure" in the officers' manuals. This can be demonstrated by the fact that the real historical cases in which cities and populations have been destroyed in war have not been like the extreme imaginable borderline crunch cases with which the speculative debate of ethicists seeks to demonstrate that not all killing can be avoided. They are worse, less justifiable, and could have been more avoidable, but they were not avoided, because readiness for them was institutionalized, as the restraints were not.

What I do deny is (8) that an ethic responding to the Gospel of Jesus Christ is any more open to be strained, tested, challenged, or called into doubt, by facing "hard cases," than is an ethic claiming to possess as a warrant a nondialogical knowledge derived from "nature" or "reason" or even realistic self-interest. In fact, an ethic claiming to be founded in "nature" or "reason" is by definition less able to be "patient" in the sense I am talking about. It must *by the nature of its argument* claim that those values are defined self-evidently i.e., nondialogically.

What I do deny is (9) . . . that the question "can there be an exception?" ought to be one of the primary ways to test and exposit a rule. This is the methodological error of "quandarism." To look for exceptions, especially to be driven, before the hard case and as a general exercise in method, by the concern that there must be an exception to every rule, is the mirror image of the legalism it rejects. To use the general formal statement that "there may be exceptions" as a basis to institutionalize the infractions . . . is ultimately dishonest, since it clothes as an exception to one rule what is in fact a commitment to the greater authority of a different rule.

What I do deny is (10) . . . the appropriateness of the special tilt toward permissiveness which once gave to the adjective "jesuitical" (not to Ignatius of Loyola himself) a bad name. Casuistry is not wrong, but essential. The same is true for exception making, an indispensable part of casuistry. But when the analysis, either in the actual practice of the sacrament of absolution or in the intellectual ground laid in manuals of moral theology for the exercise of that ministry, is tilted toward the individual convenience of the penitent and away from the values borne by (or in modern parlance the "rights of") the other parties to the case, with the result that one invests more ingenuity in authorizing exceptions than in helping to keep the rules, then the discipline has gone wrong.

What I do deny is (11) that, in holding to the priority of the prima facie duty more strongly than others do, I am thereby either in thought or in action more "pure" than others. . . . It is the Catholic casuistry which by cleanly distinguishing between physical and moral evils fosters the notion that moral purity is possible. The Niebuhrian or the Sartrian has no corner on dirty hands. The question is not whether one can have clean hands but which kind of complicity in which kind of inevitable evil is preferable.[7]

NOTES

1. [John Howard Yoder, unpublished text, 1994. Drafted and circulated, January 1994, in connection with a Notre Dame course on the tradition of just war (http://www.nd.edu/-theo/jhy/writings/philsystheo/nature.htm).]

2. [John Howard Yoder, "The Kingdom as Social Ethic," in *The Priestly Kingdom: Social Ethics as Gospel* (South Bend, Ind.: University of Notre Dame Press, 1984), 92–94.]

3. [John Howard Yoder, "The Forms of Ethical Discourse," in *The Priestly Kingdom*, 116–118.]

4. [John Howard Yoder, "The Constantinian Sources of Western Social Ethics," in *The Priestly Kingdom*, 138–141.]

5. [John Howard Yoder, "Making the Tradition Credible," in *When War Is Unjust*, rev. ed. (Maryknoll, N.Y.: Orbis Books, 1996), 77–80.]

6. [John Howard Yoder, "Trial Balance," in *The Politics of Jesus: Vicit Agnus Noster* (Grand Rapids, Mich.: Eerdmans, 1972), 105–114.]

7. [John Howard Yoder, "'Patience' as a Method in Moral Reasoning: Is an Ethic of Discipleship Absolute," in *The Wisdom of the Cross: Essays in Honour of John Howard Yoder*, ed. Stanley Hauerwas et al. (Grand Rapids, Mich.: Eerdmans, 1999), 37–40.]

Copyright Information

Index to Biblical Citations

Index